ORIGINALITY OF THE PIONEERS OF THE RAMAKRISHNA ORDER

Panchugopal Baksi

ALLIED PUBLISHERS PVT. LTD.

New Delhi • Mumbai • Kolkata • Chennai • Bangalore • Hyderabad

ALLIED PUBLISHERS PRIVATE LIMITED

D-5, Sector-2, **Noida**–201 301
Ph. Nos.: 0120-4320295/2542557/4352866
E-mail: delhi.books@alliedpublishers.com

17 Chittaranjan Avenue, **Kolkata**–700072
Ph.: 033-22129618 • E-mail: cal.books@alliedpublishers.com

15 J.N. Heredia Marg, Ballard Estate, **Mumbai**–400001
Ph.: 022-42126969 • E-mail: mumbai.books@alliedpublishers.com

No. 25/10, Commander-in-Chief Road, Ethiraj Lane (Next to Post Office)
Egmore, **Chennai**–600008
Ph.: 044-28223938 • E-mail: chennai.books@alliedpublishers.com

P.B. No. 9932, No. 15, 3rd Floor (Next to Vijaya Bank), 5th Cross, Gandhinagar,
Karnataka, **Bangalore**–560009. Ph.: 080-41530285 / 22386239
• E-mail: bngl.journals@alliedpublishers.com / apsabng@airtelmail.in

Sri Jayalakshmi Nilayam, No. 3-4-510, 3rd Floor (Above More Super Market)
Barkatpura, **Hyderabad**–500027
Ph.: 040-27551811, 040-27551812 • E-mail: hyd.books@alliedpublishers.com

Website: www.alliedpublishers.com

ISBN: 978-93-90951-22-2

Published by Sunil Sachdev and printed by Ravi Sachdev
at Allied Publishers Pvt. Ltd., D-5, Sector-2, Noida–201 301

SYNOPSIS

Importance of Bringing out this Book

Swami Vivekananda the matchless personality of the second millennium emphasized the word 'Original' while describing the unfathomable uniqueness and greatness of his master Sri Ramakrishna the greatest incarnation and embodiment of renunciation, austerity, and love. Swamiji wished that his brother-disciples should also possess originality of their own.

An extensive research has been carried out to find out the testimonies of originality of not only the Master but of Holy Mother and their sixteen monastic disciples also. A painstaking attempt has been made to focus on the contribution of the illuminated souls to the history of genesis of the Ramakrishna order along with its multifaceted non-political, global philanthropic movement in this magnum opus.

Once Swami Vivekananda said to his disciple Sharat Chandra Chakraborty: "Do you think these Sannyasin Children of Sri Ramakrishna are born simply to sit for meditation under trees lighting dhuni-fires? Whenever any of them will take up some work, people will be astonished to see their energy. Learn from them how to work."

Sri Ramakrishna's teachings are very useful and relevant to people of all ages. The world heard the short but significant utterances—'As many faiths so many paths.', 'To serve jiva as Shiva'; first from his lips. Swamiji a leading exponent of fearlessness and positive thinking, introduced 'man-making religion'—a universal religion. He said," The first of all worship is the worship of the Virat—of those all around us....These are all our gods—men and animals, and the first gods we have to worship are our countrymen."

In this age of the 'the fret and the fever' these historic proclamations are the antidote to fanaticism, intolerance towards different religions and pessimism.

The author has meticulously discussed how the direct monastic disciples of Sri Ramakrishna had made Vedanta an organized religion that does not stress rituals, a rigid set of practices, theory, dogma or doctrine and the living being and its reason is the centre of the religion and how they had shown quite apart from their scrupulous honesty and unfailing dedication—a degree of organizational, managerial and administrative ability that could be the envy of professional specialists in different spheres of activity. This glorious history deserves wide circulation for the promotion of religious tolerance, catholic outlook and the ideals of equality and fraternity.

Target Readers: People interested in spirituality, researchers, people fond of thought-provoking repository articles and curious book-lovers.

CONTENTS

INTRODUCTION

The Sun owes to none. It has enormous heat and light of its own. The animate world and the plant kingdom can not do without the incessant grace of this great star. The solar energy that helps this planet sustain life is obviously original and absolutely unique; indispensable and primordial. It is only by the grace of the Sun-God that we survive.

The word 'Original' denotes new and interesting in a way that is different from anything that has existed before. It implies natural ability to produce new and significant ideas. It is fundamental or pertaining to the root and not a copy or imitation or artificial. The quality of originality is common to all geniuses or great personalities. It is a signature of a person's inner self that makes him distinguished and different from other people.

To elaborate on originality it is the quality or state of being original. Some of the remarkable characteristics of originality are : firstly, freshness of aspect, design or style—originality is the aspect of created or invented works as being new or novel, and thus distinguishable from reproductions, clones, forgeries, or derivative work. Secondly, an original work is one not received from others, nor one copied from or based upon the work of others. Thirdly, it is a work created with a unique style and substance. Fourthly, originality is a precious treasure of its possessor. It is an innate quality that enables an individual to think, imagine, act or create somewhat different from those of common run of people. It is an ability to produce new and interesting ideas in a way that is different from anything that has existed before. Fifthly, originality is essential for effective leadership because it is a necessary stepping stone for innovation, efficiency, growth, augmentation and most importantly, success. It is the main element of a complex recipe ensuring business flourish and without it no innovation is possible. Sixthly, the concept of originality is culturally constituent. At the beginning of the 18th century the concept of originality evolved into an ideal in Western culture. Lastly, some characteristic qualities provide impetus to arresting originality for innovating new things or ideas or bringing about radical change in the nature of activities of an organization.

While referring to his great Master Sri Ramakrishna Swamiji emphasized the word 'original' at least four times if not more; twice in two different epistles and in two lectures.

It was one of the longest epistles written from High View, Caversham Reading, England on 27th April, 1896 and addressed to the members of the Alambazar Math. Swamiji reminded his brother disciples, "...He (the Lord Sri Ramakrishna) gave me the charge of you all and you shall contribute to the great well-being of the world—though most of you are not yet aware of it—this is the special reason of my writing to you..."

As a farsighted leader and compassionate friend Swamiji made wise suggestions about the management of the Math, the governing body, departments, some dos and don'ts, the office bearers and commented in the letter :

"About doctrines and so forth I have to say only this, that if anyone accepts Paramahamsa Deva as Avatâra etc. it is all right; if he doesn't do so, it is just the same. The truth about it is that in point of character, Paramahamsa Deva beats all previous records; and as regards teaching, he was more liberal, more original, and more progressive than all his predecessors..."[1]

Again in an epistle Swamiji wrote from Dehra Dun on 24th November, 1897 to M (Mahendra Nath Gupta, chiefly known as 'Master' a 'marked' disciple of Paramahamsa Deva and author of The Gospel of Sri Ramakrishna) :

"Many many thanks for your second leaflet (leaves from the *Gospel*). It is indeed wonderful. The move is quite original, and never was the life of a great Teacher brought before the public untarnished by the writer's mind, as you are presenting this one. The language also is beyond all praise, so fresh, so pointed, and withal so plain and easy.

"I can not express in adequate terms how I have enjoyed the leaflets. I am really in a transport when I read them. Strange, isn't it? Our Teacher and Lord was so original, and each one of us will have to be original or nothing..."[2]

Friedrich Max Muller wrote in an article headed 'A Real Mahatman' in August 1896 issue of *'The Nineteenth century'* : "The late Ramakrishna Paramahamsa was a far more interesting specimen of a *Sannyāsin.* He seems to have been, not only a high-souled man, a real Mahātman, but a man of original thought."

In two lectures delivered in New York and England in 1896 and combined subsequently under the title 'My Master', Swamiji quoted the reflections of Max Muller on Sri Remakrishna :

"...Well has Prof. Max Muller said in the article I have just referred to that this was a clean, original man; and the secret of that originality was that he was not brought up within the precincts of a university..."[3]

Swamiji, with his unyielding pertinacity and blazing virility strove to make his Master's dream a true. He was always in high spirits and optimistic about the prospects of their noble organization and expected originality from each of his co-disciples. He laid such stress on his conviction as to remind us of Hamlet :

> To be, or not to be–that is the question;
> whether 'tis nobler in the mind to suffer
> The slings and arrows of outrageous fortune,
> Or to take arms against a sea of troubles,
> And by opposing end them?
>
> [Act three, Sc. I][4]

In this book a painstaking attempt has been made to trace originality of the core of the Ramakrishna Order consisting of the Master, Holy Mother and their sixteen monastic disciples.

Chapter – 1

SRI RAMAKRISHNA

There was something strange about the birth of Sri Ramakrishna. During his stay at Gaya as a pilgrim in 1835, Khudiram Chattopadhyaya of Kāmārpukur in the Hooghly District dreamt of Lord Vishnu who promised to be born as his son. On the other hand, his wife Chandra Devi one day felt that a huge flood of marvellous light coming from the holy image of Lord Shiva of the Yogi Shiva Temple next to their house entered into her body and she had conceived. On February 18, 1836 the divine child i.e. the third son of the couple was born and was named 'Gadadhar', the 'Bearer of the Mace' and was known as Ramakrishna afterwards.

Romain Rolland in his popular book 'The Life of Ramakrishna' has sketched the uncommon physical and mental features of Sri Ramakrishna with mathematical precision.

"He was a little boy full of fun and life, mischievous and charming with a feminine grace he preserved to the end of his life. Nobody imagined—himself least of all–what infinite spaces, what tremendous depths lay hidden in the little body of this laughing child...

"Ramakrishna was a small brown man with a short beard and beautiful eyes, 'long dark eyes, full of light, obliquely set and slightly veiled', never very wide open, but seeing half-closed a great distance both outwardly and inwarldly. His mouth was half open over his white teeth in a bewitching smile, at once affectionate and mischievous. Of medium height, he was thin to emaciation and extremely delicate. His temperament was exceptionally highly strung, for he was supersensitive to all the winds of joy and sorrow, both moral and physical. He was indeed a living reflection of all that happened before the mirror of his eyes, a two-sided mirror turned both out and in. His unique plastic power allowed his spirit instantaneously to shape itself according to that of others, without, however, losing its own *feste Burg*, the immutable and infinite centre of endless mobility." (p.p. 6, 33 - 34)

Sri Ramakrishna spoke of his parents :

> My mother was the personification of rectitude and gentleness. She did not know much about the ways of the world; innocent of the art of concealment, she would say what was in her mind. People loved her for her open-heartedness. My father, an orthodox brahmin, never accepted gifts from the sudras. He spent much of his time in worship and meditation, and in repeating God's name and chanting His glories. Whenever in his daily prayers he invoked the Goddess Gayatri, his chest flushed and tears rolled down his cheeks. He spent his leisure hours making garlands for the family deity, Raghuvir.

Sri Ramakrishna in his childhood was strongly influenced by some genetic qualities of his parents such as simplicity and open-heartedness of his mother and honesty and profound devotion of his father to God. Of course, he was singled out for some of his characteristics uncommon for small boys. He had his first experience of transcendental ecstasy when he was only six or seven. One day in June or July while walking along a narrow path between paddy-fields, he chanced to see a flight of snow-white cranes on the canvas of the sky overcast with dark thunder-cloud. The beauty of the sight overwhelmed him by great joy and he fell to the ground.

At the age of seven Gadadhar lost his father and realized the mortality of life. He became more introspective and used to spend hours absorbed in thoughts in the mango orchard or in a cremation ground of the village.

Gadadhar took great delight in listening to the stories from Hindu mythology and the epics and recounting those from his marvellous memory to the villagers.

In those days pious pilgrims and wandering monks used to stay at the guest house of Dharmadas Laha of Kāmārpukur on their way to Puri. The monks, the janitors of India's spiritual heritage and the very embodiment of renunciation, self-control and devotion to God, cast a strong impression on Gadadhar who served them in numerous ways (e.g. fetching fuel and water) and heard stories from them and observed their meditation and prayer. From those monks and from his own intuition he had learned that the ideal of life was the realization of God.

Gadadhar took a revolutionary step at the age of only nine by accepting a meal prepared by his nurse Dhani, daughter of a Sudra (blacksmith) the lowest of the four Hindu castes ignoring objection and interdiction of relatives during his sacred-thread ceremony. Dhani's affection and sentiment and his promise to take her food were more important to the boy than the prevailing prejudices and conventions of society.

Gadadhar, a bonafide brahmin with his sacred thread, was allowed to worship Raghuvir and other family deities. He devoted himself so deeply to the worship that the inert stone images appeared to him as the living Lord of the Universe. Thus his tendency to sink in meditation was strengthening. About this time on the occasion of *Shivarātri* (a spring festival of Lord Shiva) a dramatic performance was arranged. The main actor, who was supposed to play the role of Shiva, suddenly fell ill and friends persuaded Gadadhar to act the part. They smearing his body with ashes, matting his locks, placing a trident in his hand and string of rudrāksha beads around his neck, dressed him for the role of Shiva. He looked absent-minded. As he had approached the stage with the help of his friends with bright face and teary eyes, he lost outer consciousness.

Gadadhar was very interested in moulding clay images of the god and goddesses, acting particularly the role of Radha or Krishna, singing devotional songs, mimicry and drawing and painting.

On March 9, 1883, the Master looking at a picture of Yaśodā, on the wall of his room remarked 'It is not well done. She looks like a garland-seller.'

On 9 April 1886 at dusk Shashi (afterwards Swami Ramakrishnananda) came to Narendranath (afterwards Swami Vivekananda), Taraknath (afterwards Swami Shivananda), Kali Prasad (afterwards Swami Abhedananda) and M with a piece of paper on one side of which there was written : 'May the Mother bestow wisdom upon Narendra;' followed by a drawing of a tiger and a horse and on the reverse side a drawing of a woman with her hair dressed in bun. The artistry of the Master made them charmed.

Swamiji said to Priyanath Sinha, a friend of his childhood days and disciple : 'How great an artist was Shri Ramakrishna himself!'

On the threshold of youth, this healthy and intelligent boy of clear skin, smiling countenance, beaming eyes, flowing hair, purity of soul, natural feminine grace and spontaneous fun had become great favourite of the women who considered him Gopāla, the Baby Krishna. He appeared to be the youthful Krishna of Vrindāvan to the younger ones.

Ramkumar, elder brother of Gadadhar, went to Kolkata (then Calcutta) to support his poverty-stricken family in 1849. Three years later he asked his younger brother to come to the city for two reasons. Firstly, he sought for his assistance in his priestly duties and secondly, to turn his mind to formal education. Gadadhar's worship, as family-priest, was very different from that of the professional priests. He took pleasure in decorating the images and singing hymns and devotional songs. His devotion and passion impressed all.

Ramkumar thought that his brother in the near future, as a householder, must earn his livelihood through priestcraft and other brāhminical activities those required fair knowledge of Hindu scriptures, astrology, law and related subjects. Naturally brother's strong aversion to studies and his indifference to the world made him anxious. He advised his brother to pay more attention to his lessons. The anguished cries of the inner soul of India found an echo in the spirited words of the young Gadadhar : "Brother, what shall I do with a mere bread-winning education? I would rather acquire that wisdom which will illumine my heart and give me satisfaction for ever." In this passionate utterance one may hear the first call of India's spiritual awakening.

Ramchandra Dutta one of the chief patrons and devotees and author of the first and authentic biography of Sri Ramakrishna, observed that his activities were strange and his actual mood could be known by no means.[1] A learned atheist like him became a theist and staunch adherent of Sri Ramakrishna coming in contact with him perhaps in 1879.

Rare purity of mind and power of concentration :

Principal William Hastie of General Assembly's Institution (now Scottish Church College) in course of explaining the term 'trance' as used in Wordsworth's *Excursion* told the students,

> Such an experience is the result of purity of mind and concentration on some particular object and it is rare indeed, particularly in these days. I have seen only one person who has experienced that blessed state of mind, and he is Ramakrishna Paramahamsa of Dakshineswar. You can understand if you go there and see for yourself.

These two precious possessions helped Sri Ramakrishna attain Nirvikalpa samādhi within a very short time and remain completely absorbed in that state for three days. The transcendental incident made his Gurudeva Totapuri cry out in utter astonishment, "Is it possible that he has attained in a single day what it took me forty years of strenuous practice to achieve? Great God! It is nothing short of a miracle!"

The Master never allowed to compromise with the fundamental principles of purity. He used to say that an aspirant had to keep his body, mind, senses and soul immaculate, had to have deep love for God and an ever increasing spirit of yearning. The rest would be done by the Mother. On January 2, 1884 he said to Jaygopal Sen one of the Brahmo devotees of the Master,

> ...You will feel restless for God when your heart becomes pure and your mind free from attachment to the things of the world. Then alone will your prayer reach God. A telegraph wire can not carry messages if it has a break or some other defect...
>
> The thing is that one must love God. Through intense love one attains the vision of Him. The attraction of the husband for the chaste wife, (in the 'Sri Ramarkrinana Kathamrita' by M. 'the chaste wife's attraction for her husband'), the attraction of the child for its mother, the attraction of worldly possessions for the worldly man– when a man can blend these into one, and direct it all to God, then he gets the vision of God." (The Gospel of Sri Ramakrishna, P. 375) The next year on March 11 the Master said to Girish Chandra Ghosh, "...He (God) is, no doubt, unknowable by this ordinary mind, but He can indeed be known by the pure mind. The mind and intellect become pure the moment they are free from attachment to 'woman and gold'. The pure mind and pure intellect are one and the same. God is known by the pure mind. Didn't the sages and seers of olden times see God? They realized the All-pervading Consciousness by means of their inner consciousness." (The Gospel, P. 726)

Spiritual ecstasy :

One of the most significant manifestations of Sri Ramakrishna's originality was his frequent spiritual ecstasy that required no strong inciting every time.

Sri Ramakrishna, like Sri Gouranga, lost all consciousness of the World while uttering the name of God.

Narendranath while undergoing spiritual struggle heard the name of Ramakrishna from Prof. Hastie for the first time in that class only to be his most beloved disciple afterwards. Swami Vivekananda quoted his master, "Do you think then that a man, firmly persuaded that there is a Reality behind all these appearances, that there is a God, that there is One who never dies, One who is infinite bliss, a bliss compared with which these pleasures of the senses are simply playthings, can rest contented without struggling to attain It? Can he cease his efforts for a moment? No. He will become mad with longing." Swamiji added, "This divine madness seized the boy. At that time he had no teacher, nobody to tell him anything, and everyone thought that he was out of his mind. This is the ordinary condition of things. If a man throws aside the vanities of the world, we hear him called mad. But such men are the salt of the earth. Out of such madness have come the powers that have moved this world of ours, and out of such madness alone will come the powers of the future that are going to move the world."[2]

During Sri Ramakrishna's samadhi (ecstasy) his nephew Hriday or his disciples had to support him so that he would not fall. Referring to his Master's visit to the Star Theatre Kolkata to see the play *Chaitanya Lila* (The Divine Play of Sri Chaitanya) on 21 September 1884. Swami Premananda reminisced :

> Before we left Dakshineswar, he said to me : "Look, if I go into samadhi there, people will turn towards me and there will be a commotion. If you see me on the verge of samadhi, talk to me about various other things.' But when he went to the theatre he could not stop going into samadhi, even though he tried. I began to repeat the name of God, and slowly he came round. Such experiences of *bhava* [ecstasy], *mahavhava* [great ecstasy] and samadhi were natural with him. He had to struggle hard in order to hold his mind down to the normal plane."[3]

With reference to divine inebriation and Samadhi of the God-intoxicated Master, his disciple Swami Saradananda wrote in his treasure-book 'Sri Ramakrishna the Great Master', "...And immediately afterwards we happened to meet this extraodinary Master. Not only did we meet him, but observed him at all times; day and night, and with the eyes of sceptics. We saw his unrestrained dance and constant loss of normal consciousness in the bliss of Kirtan (singing aloud the song of the Lord's name and divine sports); his losing consciousness of the outside world in pain at the touch of a coin or any metal; his deep inebriation at the mention of intoxicants by their association with the inebriation of divine bliss. And what did we see of him at the mention of the Lord's name or those of His incarnations? Why? The utterance of the word that rouses the basest animal passion in ordinary men, by its association with the female organ of generation, sent him into divine immaculate supersensuous ecstasy, bringing before his mind the womb of the blissful Mother of the universe from which worlds are created every moment. Are we still to tell you, reader, what qualities of this extra-ordinary god-man dazzled our eyes for ever in a way that led us to adore him in our hearts as a divine incarnation?" (P. 757)

A synthesis of wonderful head and beautiful heart :

A synthesis of sharp intellect of Shankaracharya and broad heart of Sri Chaitanya in Sri Ramakrishna made him an ideal and most reverend personality. M (Mahendranath Gupta) once told Subodh (Swami Subodhananda) about the profound wisdom of the Master, "I am nobody, but I live beside the ocean of knowledge and bliss, and I keep a few pitchers of that water with me. When a guest comes, I offer that to him. What else am I to talk about?

"You see, after I met the Master, all my university education became insignificant. When I got my degrees, I felt I had learned everything in this world. But after I talked to the Master, I realized that all my academic knowledge was nothing but ignorance. 'That knowledge is true knowledge which removes ignorance and helps one to attain Brahman.' : This one sentence of the Master's removed my pride of learning."[4]

Prof. Max Muller in the August 1896 issue of 'The Nineteenth Century' wrote in an article headed 'A Real Mahatman', "The late *Ramakrishna Paramahamsa* was a far more interesting specimen of *Sannyasin*. He seems to have been, not only a high-souled man, a real *Mahatman*, but a man of original thought. Indian literature is full of wise saws and sayings, and by merely quoting them a man may easily gain a reputation for profound wisdom. But it was not so with *Ramakrishna*. He seems to have deeply meditated on the world from his solitary retreat. Whether he was a man of extensive reading is difficult to say, but he was certainly thoroughly imbued with the spirit of the vedanta philosophy...

"His mind seems like a Kaleidoscope of pearls, diamonds and sapphires shaken together at random but always producing precious thoughts in regular, beautiful outlines.... Everything seems to become purified in his mind."

To answer in a word about his Guru (Master) Swamiji said to one of his American disciples Miss Josephine MacLeod (Joe), 'Not that he was holy, but he was Holiness!'

Sri Ramakrishna loved his disciples and gave them freedom so that they could grow in their own way. Swamiji often used to say, "Ever since our first meeting, it was the Master alone who always had faith in me– no one else, not even my own mother and brothers. That faith and that love of his have bound me to him for ever. The Master was the only one who knew how to love and who really loved. Worldly people only feign love to gratify their own self-interest."

Once Swamiji said to his brother-disciple Swami Turiyananda, "What do I say more about the Master? He is LOVE personified."

Keshab Chandra Sen wrote about Shri Ramakrishna in the 'Indian Mirror' on 28th March, 1875 : ' We met not long ago Paramahamsa of Dakshineswar, and were charmed by the depth, penetration and simplicity of his spirit... The characteristics of his mind are the very opposite to those of Pandit Dayananda Saraswati, the former being so gentle, tender and contemplative, as the latter is sturdy, masculine and polemical.'

In 1894 Swamiji wrote to his brother-disciple Swami Shivananda:

> Without studying Ramakrishna Paramahamsa first, one can never understand the real import of the Vedas, the Vedanta, of the Bhâgavata and the other Puranas. His life is a searchlight of infinite power thrown upon the whole mass of Indian religious thought. He was the living commentary to the Vedas and to their aim. He had lived in one life the whole cycle of the national religious existence in India." (Works, Vol. 7, P. 483)

He was his own book :

Referring to his Master's astonishing uniqueness Swamiji said, "The man at whose feet I sat all my life – and it was only a few ideas of his that I try to teach - could [hardly] write his name at all. All my life I have not seen another man like that, and I have travelled all over the world. When I think of that man, I feel like a fool, because I wanted to read books and never did. He never wanted to lick the plates after other people had eaten. That is why he was his own book."[5]

Sri Ramakrishans's manuscript headed 'Ramkrishnayan' and a few books testify to the fact that he was not illiterate. As he had not bothered to fetch some degrees, he did not attend college, even high school. It benefitted him by giving plenty of scope to nurture his originality and potentiality. To quote Swami Vivekananda, "... a poor man, who scarcely can speak the language of his own motherland, yet half the nation worships him in his own lifetime as God. When in India the idea somehow or other gets abroad that a man has raised himself to that state of realization, that religion is no more a matter of conjecture to him, that he is no more groping in the dark in such momentous questions as religion, the immortality of the soul, and God, people come from all quarters to see him and gradually they begin to worship him...

"...We have seen that of books, of education in our sense of the word, he had none, and so much the more natural, so much the more healthy, was his mind, so much the purer his thoughts, undiluted by drinking in the thoughts of others. Because he did not go to the university, therefore he thought for himself. Because we have spent half our lives in the university we are filled with a collection of other people's thoughts."[6]

As a priest Sri Ramakrishna differed from other professional priests. Mathuranath (Mathuramohan) Biswas, son-in-law of Rāni Rasmani was much impressed by the religious fervour and rustic simplicity of young Gadadhar, brother of Ramkumar, priest of the Kāli temple at Dakshineswar. He insisted him on taking part in the worship in the Kāli temple. After much hesitation he agreed to discharge his duties with the help of his distant nephew Hriday. His first duty was to dress and decorate the image of Kali, the Divine Mother, also known as Bhavatarini (the Saviour of the Universe). Since then this holy place experienced frequent variation of his mood and activities.

Rational and straight forward :

One day the priest of the Rādhākānta temple (also known as Vishnu temple) adjacent to the Kali temple, by chance dropped the image of Krishna on the floor, breaking one of its legs. The pundits opined that the worship of an image with a broken limb was unscriptural and advised the Rani to replace the defective image with a new one. The idol was so dear to the Rani who sought for junior priest's suggestion. Sri Ramakrishna, in an abstracted mood, said, "This solution is ridiculous. If a son-in-law of the Rani broke his leg, would she discard him and put another in his place? Wouldn't she rather arrange for his treatment? Why should she not do the same thing in this case too? Let the image be repaired and worshipped as before." The Rani gladly accepted the easy and wise solution. Sri Ramakrishna himself mended the break and at the earnest request of Mathur Babu he accepted the office of priest in the Radhakanta temple in the event of dismissal of the old priest for his carelessness. This incident acts as another example of Sri Ramakrishna's originality – originality of power of straight forward and rational thinking.

Novelty of *Sādhanā* and unconventional method of worship of Sri Ramakrishna :

The world has never seen such a strange process of sādhanā as Paramahamsa Deva practised in varied states of inertia or madness or nefariousness—sometimes laughing, sometimes weeping, sometimes starving, sometimes feeding of left-overs with dogs, spending sleepless day and nights yearning for God only.

With reference to the novelty and originality of Sri Ramakrishna's *sādhanā*, Joseph Campbell commented in an essay, 'Sri Ramakrishna' published in the 'Prabuddha Bhārata' in November, 1941 :

The Europeans who protested against the empire of mediocrity, themselves failed to attain to the springs of power. So their world of ideas went down before the steamroller. But in Dakhineswar, only a few miles outside the Victorian metropolis of Calcutta, practising his *sādhanā* not according to enlightened, modern methods, but after the most ancient, most superstitious, most idolatrous traditions of timeless India : now hanging to a tree, like a monkey; now posturing and dressing as a girl; now weeping before an image : now sitting, night and day, like a stump; six years unable to close his eyes, himself terrified at what was happening to him, swooning in the ocean of the Mother's love; stunned by the experience of Brahman – Sri Ramakrishna cut the hinges of the heavens and released the fountains of divine bliss. (p. 499)

Sri Ramakrishna is perhaps the only votary in the world who worshipped the Mother of the Universe and himself simultaneously.

After the death of Ramkumar Rani Rasmani appointed his brother Gadadhar the priest of Kali. Born in an orthodox brāhmin family, he was well acquainted with the formalities and rituals of worship and at the same time knew the ludicrousness of worshipping God–the All-pervading Consciousness with material articles and rites though deemed helpful for a devotee initially.

The awesome image of Kali appears the Goddess of death and destruction to the devotees in general. Sri Ramakrishna discovered in

Her the all-loving Mother. Sitting before the image–the embodiment of the supreme spirit throbbing with Life and Consciousness, as priest he did not follow the conventional and intricate rituals and used to spend hours decorating her with garlands and flowers, singing devotional songs of the great *sakta* (worshiper of the Goddess of creation) votaries namely Rāmprasād, Kamalākānta and Nareshchandra. The more intensified was his longing for direct vision of God, the more he became restless. Sometimes he would rub his face against the floor and weep bitterly. Sometimes he, goaded by scepticism, would cry, "Art thou true, Mother, or is it all fiction—mere poetry without any reality? If thou dost exist, why do I not see thee? Is religion a mere fantasy and art Thou only a figment of man's imagination?" Under a spell of divine meditation he almost gave up food and sleep. At last he succeeded to have the first vision of the Mother. Regarding this thrilling and pleasant experience Sri Ramakrishna said,

> I felt as if my heart were being squeezed like a wet towel. I was over powered with a great restlessness and a fear that it might not be my lot to realize Her in this life. I could not bear the separation from Her any longer. Life seemed to be not worth living. Suddenly my glance fell on the sword that was kept in the Mother's temple. I determined to put an end to my life. When I jumped up like a madman and seized it, suddenly the blessed Mother revealed Herself. The buildings with their different parts, the temple and everything else vanished from my sight, leaving no trace whatsoever and in their stead I saw a limitless, infinite, effulgent Ocean of Consciousness. As far as the eye could see, the shining billows were madly rushing at me from all sides with a terrific noise, to swallow me up! I was panting for breath. I was caught in the rush and collapsed, unconscious. What was happening in the outside world I did not know; but within me there was a steady flow of undiluted bliss, altogether new, and I felt the presence of the Divine Mother.

Since then Sri Ramakrishna had become more eager for continuous vision of the Mother and wept bitterly during the hours of separation from Her. During worship in the temple emotion overpowered him and sometimes he would look high-spirited and joyous, sometimes he would remain inert and sometimes he would almost pass into trance. Some of his activities as a priest appeared unconventional and sacrilegious to the people. As for example, taking a flower he would touch it to his head body and feet and then offer it to the Mother. He would stagger like a drunkard to the throne of Kāli, touch Her chin affectionately and taking a morsel of food hold it to Her mouth, beg Her to eat so long he was not sure that She had really eaten. He would talk, joke, laugh, sing and dance in the temple. One day he fed a cat with the food that was to be offered to Kāli. He would say to the Divine Mother, "I am ignorant of mantras and the scriptures. Teach me, Mother, how to realize Thee. Who else can help me? Art Thou not my only refuge and guide?"

The manager of the temple garden had taken the young priest for an insane and lodged a complaint with Mathur Babu against his whimsical activities in the name of,worship. Mathur Babu had secretly watched the worship and was deeply impressed with his sincerity guilelessness and devotion. He felt that the discriminating priest had converted the stone image into the living Goddess. To quote Sri Ramakrishna, "But Mathur Babu had insight into the state of my mind. He wrote back to the manager : 'Let him do whatever he likes. You must not say anything to him."

It was in fact a significant break through in the method of worship. Though appointed a Hindu priest of the Kali temple at Dakshineswar, Sri Ramakrishna had no urge to follow strictly scriptural hard and fast rules or strictures during worship of the divine Mother. He entered into a relation between the Goddess and him as mother and child. He was an aspirant of Mahaprabhu Sri Chaitanya and followed Bhairabi Brahmani in the disciplines of Vaishnavism which is exclusively a religion of intense love of God,

Bhakti. He was fond of Sahaj sadhana a form of worship in which a Vaishnava or a Buddhist or a Sufi or a devotee acts according to the dictates of his or her instincts. Thus through his devotion to Kali he had worshipped God as his Mother i.e. had humanized God.

Sri Ramakrishna selected a solitary spot known as the Panchavati in the northern wooded part of the temple garden to spend in meditation the time not engaged in the temple service.

Sri Ramakrishna would imagine the presence of the 'sinner' in himself and the destruction of this 'sinner' during worship following the scriptural directives and suffer from a strange burning sensation in his body. One day while meditating in the Panchavati, he saw a red-eyed man of black complexion come out of him and soon a man of calm face wearing the ochre cloth of a sannyāsi and carrying a trident in his hand. The second man killed the 'sinner' with his trident. He was relieved of pain.

Hanumān, the monkey chieftain was the ideal servant of Rāma and living ideal of dispassionate work and devotion. Sri Ramakrishna began to worship God by assuming the attitude of a servant like Hānuman. He tried to imitate the mood and mode of living of Hanumān. Mathur Babu saw him jumping about with a tail made of a portion of his cloth, like a monkey. One day Rāni Rasmani was apparently listening to the song of Sri Ramakrishna in the temple though she had actually been thinking of a law-suit. Sensing absent-mindedness of the Rani he suddenly turned and slapped her. She did not mind for she considered that the Mother Herself had inflicted the punishment on her. To think of a destitute priest beating a queen is unimaginable though it happened!

Mathur Babu begged to Sri Ramakrishna to control his emotion and feelings and to follow the conventional norms of worship but in vain. He and his mother-in-law guessed that perhaps their young priest, due to his strict observance of continence, had become mentally ill. Considering that a natural life would quieten his excitement, they hit upon a plan. Accordingly two fallen women were sent to his room. Sri Ramakrishna saw in them the manifestation of the Mother of the Universe and uttering Her name passed into a trance.

Owing to the failing health of the young priest, Mathur Babu appointed Haladhari (Ramatarak Chattopadhyay) a cousin of Sri Ramakrishna, priest in the Kali temple. He was an orthodox erudite but almost unaware of the spirit of the scriptures. He was a staunch critic of Sri Ramakrishna's spiritual realization. He sowed the seeds of doubt in the mind of his cousin by saying that God is incomprehensible to the human mind. Referring to his constantly wavering state of mind Sri Ramakrishna said, "With sobs I prayed to the Mother, 'Canst Thou have the heart to deceive me like this because I am a fool?' A stream of tears flowed from my eyes. Shortly afterwards I saw a volume of mist rising from the floor and filling the space before me. In the midst of it there appeared a face with flowing beard, calm, highly expressive and fair. Fixing its gaze steadily upon me, it said solemnly, 'Remain in bhāvamukha on the threshold of relative consciousness.' This it repeated three times and then it gently disappeared in the mist, which itself dissolved. This vision reassured me."

Thus some uncommon entities of Sri Ramakrishna's originality– his firm faith in and total submission to God, his child like simplicity and purity of heart above all his unquenchable thirst for realization enabled him to forge an incessant bond between God and His unyielding son.

Severe divine fever :

Sri Ramakrishna returned alone to Dakshineswar in 1860. A divine fever was consuming him. He described his experiences during that period of spiritual storm and stress :

> No sooner had I passed through one spiritual crisis than another took its place. I was like being in the midst of a whirlwind– even my sacred thread was blown away, and I could seldom keep hold of my *dhoti* [cloth]. Sometimes I'd open my mouth, and it would be as if my jaws reached from

heaven to the underworld. "Mother!" I'd cry desperately. I felt I had to pull Her in, as a fisherman pulls in fish with his dragnet. A prostitute walking the street would appear to me to be Sita going to meet her victorious husband. An English boy standing cross-legged against a tree reminded me of the boy Krishna, and I lost consciousness. Sometimes I would share my food with a dog. My hair became matted. Birds would perch on my head and peck at the grains of rice that had lodged there during the worship. Snakes would crawl over my motionless body.

"An ordinary man couldn't have borne a quarter of that tremendous fervour; it would have burnt him up. I had no sleep at all for six long years. My eyes lost the power of winking. I stood in front of a mirror and tried to close my eyelids with my finger—but then, suddenly, I'd be filled with ecstasy. I saw that my body didn't matter–it was of no importance, a mere trifle. Mother appeared to me and comforted me and freed me from my fear."[8]

The quoted words of Sri Ramakrishna reveal that he indirectly identified himself as an extraordinary man possessing such original power of undergoing spiritual torment till attainment of divine grace.

Renunciation personified :

Sri Ramakrishna had realized that the ideas of money and lust or sex were two enemies (*maya*) those prevented him from seeing the Mother of the Universe. So he gave up all the little property he had and saw Mother in every woman literally. He was renunciation personified. To quote Swami Vivekananda, "He was a triumphant example, a living realization of the complete conquest of lust and of desire for money. He was beyond all ideas of either, and such men are necessary for this century. Such renunciation is necessary in these days when men have begun to think that they can not live a month without what they call their 'necessities', and which they are increasing out of all proportion. It is necessary in a time like this that a man should arise to demonstrate to the sceptics of the world that there yet breathes a man who does not care a straw for all the gold or all the fame that is in the universe. Yet there are such men."[9]

It is worth noting that the physiology of Sri Ramakrishna was perfectly in tune with his psychology. In the earlier part of his life he used his golden amulet. Afterwards his renunciation was so absolute that he could not touch money or anything metallic. One day Narendranath visited Dakshineswar to find that his Master had gone to Kolkata. In order to test his Master he hid a rupee under the mattress of the Master's couch and waited for him. Entering his room no sooner did he touch the bed than he moved away in pain. He asked a temple attendant to examine the bed, and the rupee was discovered. Narendra admitted that he had made the mischief. Learning this the Master gladly said to Narendra : "You must test me as the money-changers test their coins. You must not accept me until you've tested me thoroughly."[10]

One day the Mother said to Swami Keshavananda, '...He (the Master) was always in his mood of divine ecstasy. ...Days and nights passed by him without any notice. But what you should note, my dear, is that renunciation is his special message in this age. Did anyone see such natural renunciation any time before?' On another day she said to a devotee, 'Men are ever forgetful of God. And hence, whenever the occasion demands, He comes down now and then to show the way to the worldly by following it Himself. This time He showed renunciation.'

Besides, the Master had strong apathy towards things used by only rajasic people. In the house of Nandalal Bose (Bagbazar, Calcutta) he did not use a brass bowl to wash his hands and did not accept betel-leaf from a tray for other guests had already taken some from the same tray.

Uniqueness of the Master's spititual realization :

One of the remarkable evidences of the Master's originality of spiritual realization was the reconciliation of Non-Dualism,

Qualified Non-Dualism and Dualism. On August 5, 1882 he said to Vidyasagar : "...The Vijnāni sees that the Reality which is nirguna, without attributes, is also saguna, with attributes....

"The vijnāni further sees that what is Brahman is the Bhagavān, the personal God. He who is beyond the three gunas is the Bhagavān, with His six supernatural powers...." [The Gospel of Sri Ramakrishna, by M. P.-104.]

Synthesis of religions :

A tremendous thirst for knowing the truth, a divine madness for seeing the Mother of the Universe seized Sri Ramakrishna. Regarding this madness Swami Vivekananda said, "If a man throws aside the vanities of the world, we hear him called mad. But such men are the salt of the earth. Out of such madness have come the powers that have moved this world of ours, and out of such madness alone will come the powers of the future that are going to move the world."[11]

At this time (1861) there arrived at Dakshineswar a beautiful nun commonly known as Bhairavi Brāhmani (real name Yogeswari) aged about 40 whom Sri Ramakrishna described as 'the embodiment of learning.' This sannyâsini was the first to recognize the nature of his mental unrest and help him. She said to him, "My son, blessed is the man upon whom such madness comes. ...Blessed is the man who is mad after God. Such men are very few."[12]

She discovered two aspects of his rare originality–his great ecstatic delight of divine love described in the scriptures as *mahābhāva* and a power to transmit spirituality to others. Experience of *bhava* (ecstasy), *mahabhava* (great ecstasy) and samadhi were natural with him and he had to strive hard in order to hold his mind down to the relative plane. It was his striking originality.

She taught him the forms of the religions of India and initiated him into tantric disciplines. He practiced sixty-four methods of Tantra under her guidance and attained perfection through each of them.

Then Sri Ramakrishna practised various methods such as *Vatsalya bhava* (the affectionate attitude towards God), *madhura bhava* (the lover's attitude towards the beloved) of the Vaishnava tradition.

The Brāhmani declared on the basis of Sri Ramakrishna's spiritual experiences and physical symptoms that he, like Sri Chaitanya, was an Avātar (Incarnation of God) and two reputed pundits of the time Vaishnavcharan and Gauri agreed with the view of the Brāhmani.

In 1864 Sri Ramakrishna was initiated into sannyasa and was given the famous name of Ramakrishna by Totapuri belonging to the Naga sect whom Sri Ramakrishna affectionately called 'Nangta' or the naked one because of his total renunciation of all temporal objects including even a piece of wearing-cloth. He was a famous expounder of the non-dualistic Vedānta philosophy. Under his guidance Sri Ramakrishna sat to meditate and attained the *Nirvikalpa Samadhi.*

Only those who are born with a special mission for the mankind and endowed with a supreme spiritual power, can descend from the dizzy height to the relative plane for the welfare of the world as Sri Ramakrishna did. On advice of the Divine Mother he remained in the Bhāvamukha on the border line between the Absolute and the Relative. "He gently oscillated back and forth across the dividing line. Ecstatic devotion to the Divine Mother alternated with serene absorption in the Ocean of Absolute Unity. He thus bridged the gulf between the Personal and the Impersonal, the immanent and the transcendent aspects of Reality. This is a unique experience in the recorded spiritual history of the world."[13]

Totapuri, a born non-dualistic monk of the most orthodox type who never stayed at a place more than three days, had remained at Dakshineswar eleven months to learn some valuable lessons from his trainee and to modify his faith. To him Maya was a lie and he did not understand that love could be one of the ways leading to God. This scorner of cults, loud prayers, devotional songs, hymns and religious dances; unconsciously had the weakness to adore a symbol in the shape of fire that he kept alighted near him always. One day when Guru Totapuri and his disciple Sri Ramakrishna were engaged in conversation on Vedanta, a servant of the temple garden picked up a coal from the sacred fire to light his tobacco. Totapuri raged against such disrespect. Rocking with childish laughter, Sri Ramakrishna said, "What a shame! You are explaining to me the reality of Brahman and the illusoriness of the world, yet now you have so far forgotten yourself as to be about to beat a man in a fit of passion. The power of māyā is indeed inscrutable!" Totapuri was deeply ashamed of his behaviour.

While suffering from chronic dysentery one night Totapuri decided to drown his pain-stricken body in the Ganga. When he entered the river, an invisible hand restrained him. He had neither the will nor the power to commit suicide anymore. He had experienced the power of Maya. He acknowledged before his disciple Sri Ramakrishna who had become his master that Brahman and Shakti (Maya or Prakriti i.e. Divine Energy) are one and the same Being. A changed man Totapuri identified the Divine Mother Kali with the Brahman and went to the Kali temple with Sri Ramakrishna and prostrated himself before the image of *Bhavatarini*.

Coming in contact with Sri Ramakrishna Totapuri had to realize that the Supreme Being when inactive (neither creating nor preserving nor destroying) is called Brahaman or Purusha–the Impersonal God and as active (creating, preserving and destroying) it is called Shakti or Maya or Prakriti, the Personal God. But despite this distinction both are identical.

Towards the end of 1866 Sri Ramakrishna practised the disciplines of Islam under the guidance of a Sufi named Gobinda Roy. Staying outside the temple precincts he dressed as a Mussalmān and repeated the name of Āllah and said their prayers (namaj) five times daily. He had forgotten all of the Hindu gods and goddesses, even the Mother Kali and remained three days in that mood. He had the full realization of Islam as he had seen the vision of a radiant figure, perhaps Muhammad.

In 1868 while visiting Vrindavan and Mathura with his chief patron (rasaddār) Mathur Babu and his party of some one hundred and twenty-five persons, Sri Ramakrishna yearned for the grace of Krishna. Overwhelmed by divine emotion he, like Sri Chaitanya, supposing himself Radha offered *ragatmika* devotion to the Lord and had numerous visions. He called on Gangāmāyi, a great woman saint and regarded as the reincarnation of Lalita an intimate attendant of Rādhā by Vaishnava devotees. She identified Sri Ramakrishna as an incarnation of Rādhā and affectionately called him 'Dulali' (darling).

In 1874 Sri Ramakrishna fell under a spell of Christianity. Shambhu Charan Mallick, one of his devotees, used to read the Bible to him and speak of Jesus. He became very interested in the life and teachings of Christ. One day he visited Jadu Mallick's garden house adjacent to the Dakshineswar temple while gazing at a painting of the Madonna with the child Jesus sitting on her lap in the parlour, he was overwhelmed with divine emotion. The figures in the picture appeared animate and he saw that the rays of light were coming out of them and entering his soul. For three days he did not enter the Kali temple and entered a new realm of ecstasy. On the fourth day, while walking in the Panchavati in the afternoon, he had a vision of a person with calm face, brilliant large eyes and fair skin coming towards him. As he wondered who this stranger could be, a voice from within rang out, "Behold the Christ, who shed His heart's blood for the redemption of the world, who suffered a sea of anguish for love of men. It is He, the Master Yogi, who is in eternal union with God. It is Jesus, Love Incarnate," Then Jesus embraced Sri Ramakrishna and merged in him. He believed that Christ, like Buddha and Krishna, was an Incarnation of God and realized his identity with Christ, as he had already realized his identity with Kāli, Rāma, Hanumān, Rādhā, Krishna, Brahman and Mohammad.

Sri Ramakrishna had great respect for Buddhism and Jainism and Sikhism. There were a small statue of Tirthankara Mahāvira and a picture of Jesus in his room at Dakshineswar. He thus realized the ideals of religions other than Hinduism and discovered the truth that each faith was a path leading to God-Consciousness. He spoke with authority, "I have practised, all religions–Hinduism, Islām, Christianity–and I have also followed the paths of the different Hindu sects. I have found that it is the same God toward whom all are directing their steps, though along different paths. You must try all beliefs and traverse all the different ways once. Wherever I look, I see men quarrelling in the name of religion–Hindus, Mohammedans, Brāhmos, Vaishnavas, and the rest. But they never reflect that He who is called Krishna is also called Siva, and bears the name of the Primal Energy, Jesus and Allāh as well–the same Rāma with a thousand names. A lake has several ghāts. At one the Hindus take water in pitchers and call it 'Jal', at another the Mussalmāns take water in leather bags and call it 'pani'. At a third the Christians call it 'water'. Can we imagine that it is not 'jal', but only 'pani' or 'water'? How ridiculous ! The substance is One under different names, and everyone is seeking the same substance; only climate, temperament and name create differences. Let each man follow his own path. If he sincerely and ardently wishes to know God, peace be unto him ! He will surely realize him."[14]

This practising the spiritual ways of different religious traditions in one lifetime indeed unprecedented. And attainment of perfection in the paths he practised in an incredibly short time is also amazing. Among the great prophets of the world, it was Sri Ramakrishna who first made a synthesis of all religions and uttered a unique and unprecedented message : "As many faiths, so many paths.' This realization marks one of the outstanding and significant specimen of his originality and acts as an antidote to fanaticism, dogmatism, narrow outlook and intolerance towards different religions prevailing in this age of terror and tension.

Dr Mahendralal Sarkar an eminent physician, founder of The Indian Association for the cultivation of Science (1876) and who spoke of Sri Ramakrishna, 'As a man I have the greatest regard for him'; said on October 24, 1885 :

> ...Similarly, the study of comparative religion is highly beneficial.
>
> Why do his [meaning the Master's] words go straight to our hearts? He has experienced the truths of different religions. He himself has practised the disciplines of the Hindu, Christian, Mussalmān, Sākta and Vaishnava religions. The bees can make good honey only if they gather nectar from different flowers.

The spiritual consciousness of the Master was based on liberalism and rationalism. Naturally he and his disciples preached a positive, scientific and universal philanthropic religion—the oneness of God, the divinity of soul and harmony of religions.

As Sri Ramakrishna had followed all the main paths only to reach the same goal, similarly he practised the three systems of thought —Dvaita (Dualism), Visishtadvaita (Qualified Non-dualism) and Advaita (Absolute Non-dualism) and realized that they were not contradictory but complementary and suited to different categories of people. A dualistic form of religion associated with symbols, songs and other material supports is helpful for the ordinary men with strong attachment to the senses. Qualified Non-dualism is appreciable to one having a bent for spiritualism. And one free from sensuous attachment and eager to submit oneself to the Lord may opt for Absolute Non-dualism.

The Master was original and as a scientist, used to see that different people required different treatment. He, as taught by Narada, used to preach devotion to the ordinary people who were incapable of any higher training. To quote Swami Vivekananda, "He used generally to teach dualism. As a rule, he never taught Advaitism. But he taught it to me. I had been a dualist before." (Works Vol. 7, P. 414)

Shri Ramakrishna was a syncretist. In an interview with a journalist of the Sunday Times, London in 1896 Swamiji said of his Master, 'This great Sannyasin never assumed the negative or critical attitude towards other religions, but showed their positive side –

how they could be carried into life and practised. To fight, to assume the antagonistic attitude, is the exact contrary of his teaching, which dwells on the truth that the world is moved by love.' (Works Vol. 5, P. 190)

When the Aryans broke up the grand synthesis of all the aspects of the spiritual ideal of the Eternal Religion of the Vedas (Sanatana Dharma) into conflicting sects; Shri Ramakrishna appeared before them as a living embodiment of the Eternal Religion to demonstrate what the true religion of the Aryans is and where the true unity of their religion lies. He infused in his wonderful life the universal spirit and character of this religion, so long consigned to oblivion.

In reference to Swamiji's love for the Muhammedans, sister Nivedita asked her Master where that habit of seeing every people from their strongest aspect had come from. The Swami replied, "It must have been the training under Ramakrishna Paramahamsa. We all went by his path to some extent. Of course it was not so difficult for us as he made it for himself. He would eat and dress like the people he wanted to understand, take their initiation, and use their language. 'One must learn', he said, 'to put oneself into another man's very soul.' And this method was his own! No one ever before in India became Christian and Mohammedan and Vaishnava by turns!" (The Master As I Saw Him, P. 195)

Regarding religious outlook Sri Ramakrishna Paramahamsa Deva an expounder of the Perennial Philosophy was rational and liberal. A harmonious combination of monotheism and polytheism is seen in his spiritual life and teaching. He realized the wonderful truth that the religions of the world are not antagonistic or contradictory rather they are all part and parcel of the one infinite religion. So he respected the faith of any man and saw nothing but good.

As a true vedantist Sri Ramakrishna believed in the sacred mantras of the Upanishads, and at the same time implemented in the practical field of his spiritual life the message of synthesis of all religions as has been said by Lord Sri Krishna in the Bhagavad Gita :

> However men approach me, in the same manner do I favour them; men follow my path in all ways, O Arjuna, (Chapter IV, couplet 11)

To quote from the back-side blurb of 'The Gospel of Sri Ramakrishna', "Sri Ramakrishna stands as the verification not only of the Sanatana Dharma, the Eternal Religion of the Hindus, but of all religious faiths and creeds. His life is a living laboratory of religious experiment."

Though a householder, an ideal monk :

The life of Sri Ramakrishna was an amazing synthesis of the ways of life of a householder and a monk. He approved of utility of marriage in man's spiritual development; simultaneously he demonstrated the vital importance of continence, purity and self-control in the realization of God. He instructed Sarada Devi everything from housekeeping to the Knowledge of Brahman. The first lesson he taught her was : "God is everybody's beloved, just as the moon is dear to every child. Everyone has the same right to pray to Him. Out of His grace He reveals Himself to all who call upon him. You too will see Him if you but pray to Him."

One day at Dakshineswar, while stroking her husband's feet, Sarada Devi asked him, "What do you think of me?" Sri Ramakrishna quipped, "The Mother who is worshipped in the temple is the mother who has given birth to my body and is now living in the nahabat, and it is She again who is stroking my feet at this moment. Indeed, I always look on you as the personification of the Blissful Mother Kāli." Regarding her experience in the company of her husband Sarada Devi said, "I have no words to describe my wonderful exaltation of spirit as I watched him in his different moods. Under the influence of divine emotion he would sometimes talk on abstruse subjects, sometimes laugh, sometimes weep, and sometimes become perfectly motionless in samadhi. This would continue throughout the night. There was such an extraordinary divine presence in him that now and then I would shake with fear and wonder how the night would pass. Months went by in this way. Then one day he discovered that I had to keep awake the whole night lest, during my sleep, he should go into samadhi – for it might happen at any moment—, and so he asked me to sleep in the nahabat." Though lived together, their minds rose above the relative plane.

Learning about Sri Ramakrishna's marriage, Totapuri commented, "What does it matter? He alone is firmly established in the Knowledge of Brahman who can adhere to his spirit of discrimination and renunciation even while living with his wife. He alone has attained the supreme illumination who can look on man and woman alike as Brahman. A man with the idea of sex may be a good aspirant, but is still far from the goal."

Wife-worship :

Sri Ramakrishna had great respect for women even for the fallen ones whom he looked upon as his mother. Certain Brahmo Samajists namely Shivnath Shastri and Pratap Chandra Mazumdar very coarsely blamed Sri Ramakrishna for his dispassionate attitude toward Sarada Devi his wife. In fact, Sri Ramakrishna did not sacrifice her. Swamiji, in his lecture entitled 'My Master' said, "...When at last she stood in her husband's presence, he at once admitted her right to his life, although in India any person, man or woman, who embraces a religious life, is thereby freed from all other obligations. The young man fell at the feet of his wife and said, 'As for me, the Mother has shown me that She resides in every woman, and so I have learnt to look upon every woman as Mother. That is the one idea I can have about you; but if you wish to drag me into the world, as I have been married to you, I am at your service.'"

Sarada Devi of pure and noble heart, honoured her husband's aspirations and assured him that she had no wish to drag him down to a life of mere worldliness; but that all she wished was to stay near him, to serve him, and to learn of him. She turned one of his most devoted disciples.

As has earlier been mentioned, one day Sarada Devi asked her husband what he thought of her. Sri Ramakrishna replied that he always looked on her as the personification of the Mother Kali.

Sarada Devi never showed the least grievance or grudge against her husband. On the contrary she said, "I have no words to describe my wonderful exaltation of spirit as I watched him in his different moods."

A few months after Sarada Devi's first visit to her husband at Dakshineswar, Sri Ramakrishna arranged, on an auspicious day of 5th June 1872 (Phalaharini-Kalika Puja), a special worship Shodashi Puja (Adoration of woman) in his room secretly. Instead of an image of the Divine-Mother Shodashi (Srividya or Tripursundari) he placed his wife on that holy seat and worshipped her following the tantra-formalities, reciting mystic and esoteric words and chanting a hymn to the Goddess and surrendered at the feet of the living idol, himself, his rosary and even the fruit of his life-long sadhana. Thus he was the first perhaps the only religious prophet recorded in history to worship his wife as the Great Goddess.

Innovator of a new age :

In 1861 there came to Dakshineswar Bhairavi Brahmani whom Sri Ramakrishna made his Guru and practised all the disciplines of the sixty-four principal Tantra books and who declared Sri Ramakrishna an avatar.

Totapuri initiated Sri Ramakrishna into monastic life and made him practise the disciplines of the non-dualistic Vedanta in 1865. The most orthodox monk taught his disciple : "When I think of the Supreme being as inactive–neither creating nor preserving nor destroying, —I call Him Brahman or Purusha, the Impersonal God. When I think of Him as active–creating, preserving, and destroying–I call him Shakti or Mayā or Prakriti, the Personal God. But the distinction between them does not mean a difference. The Personal and the Impersonal are the same thing, like milk and its whiteness, the diamond and its lustre, the snake and its wriggling motion. It is impossible to conceive of the one without the other. The Divine Mother and Brahman are one."

As already mentioned, at the new-moon night of 5th June, 1872, the auspicious time for the worship of Phalaharini Kali (destroyer of the effects of past deeds), Sri Ramakrishna worshipped his wife Sri Sarada Devi as Shodashi, the veritable Mother of the Universe or his own Shakti ceremonially in his room at Dakshineswar.

Thus the Master propelled the age of the Motherhood of God.

Exceptional spiritual power :

In order to cite another example of originality of the Master, the remarks of Totapuri may be repeated. Learning about Sri Ramakrishna's marriage he once said, "What does it matter? He alone is firmly established in the Knowledge of Brahman who can adhere to his spirit of discrimination and renunciation even while living with his wife. He alone has attained the supreme illumination who can look on man and woman alike as Brahman. A man with the idea of sex may be a good aspirant, but he is still far from the goal."

The events that minds of the Master and the Mother while living together at Dakshineswar always soared above the worldly plane and that the Master worshipped his wife and she calmly accepted that worship or submission; testify to the statement of Totapuri.

'I see Him...'

No prophet but Sri Ramakrishna, by virtue of his originality, was able to say that he had seen God. His beloved disciple Swami Vivekananda reminisced his experience : "I heard of this man, and I went to hear him. He looked just like an ordinary man, with nothing remarkable about him. He used the most simple language, and I thought "Can this man be a great teacher?" —crept near to him and asked him the question which I had been asking others all my life : "Do you believe in God, Sir?" "Yes", he replied. "Can you prove it, Sir?" "Yes." "How?" "Because I see Him just as I see you here, only in a much intenser sense." That impressed me at once. For the first time I found a man who dared say that he saw God, that religion was reality to be felt, to be sensed in an infinitely more intense way than we can sense the world,"[15]

Swami Subodhananda, one of the monastic disciples of Sri Ramakrishna said to the devotees : "One day I asked the Master : "I have read about gods and goddesses in books and heard about them from various people. Can one really see them? Sri Ramakrishna replied : 'One can see God as one sees two persons talking together or walking. But one should call on God from the bottom of one's heart. Pray and cry for Him. Demand His vision from Him as children demand toys from their parents with loud cries. Remove all worldly desires from the mind. Always remember : I have a Mother and I am Her son."[16]

Sri Ramakrishna said to all, 'I have seen God. You can also see Him through spiritual disciplines and longing.'

Faith in Physiognomy and power of infallible observation and prescience :

Another remarkable instance of Sri Ramakrishna's originality lies in his faith in physiognomy and skill in the study of human nature. He could judge a man by his physical traits or by weighing his hand and could read his mind and awaken spirituality by a mere touch. He could even transmit his power to other. There are innumerable instances of his incredible power : Sri Ramakrishna used to examine the breast of his disciples, their breathing capacity and the soundness of their circulation before allowing or forbidding them to undertake exercises of great concentration. In 1865 he examined the colour of the skin of the chest of Devendranath Tagore and discovered that he, like King Janaka at the same time enjoyed the world and attained the highest realizations. Examining Dayananda Saraswati in 1873 he found in him 'a little power' i.e. 'real contact with the Divine'. Though his egoism could not escape Sri Ramakrishna's eyes.

On June 4, 1883 Sri Ramakrishna said to Manilal Mallick "Bony people, the hollow-eyed, the cross-eyed–people with physical traits like those can not easily acquire faith. What can a man do if there are evil omens on all sides?"

On October 5, 1884 Sri Ramakrishna reading the palm of Hari's hand pointed out a mark as a good sign and feeling the weight of his hand he commented that he was still childlike as till then there was no blemish in him. He told the devotees that from the hand he could tell whether a person was deceitful or guileless. He said to M. and others : "Whether a person will make spiritual progress or not can be known to a great extent by his physical marks. The hand of a deceitful person is heavy. A snub nose is not a good sign. Sambhu had that kind of nose; hence he was not quite sincere in spite of all his wisdom. Pigeon-breast is not a good sign either. Hard bones and heavy elbow-joints are bad signs too; and yellow eyes, like a cat's.

"A man becomes very mean if he has lips that are thick, like a dome's. A brāhmin was here for a few months acting as priest of the Vishnu temple. I couldn't eat the food he touched. One day I suddenly exclaimed, 'He is a dome!' Afterwards he said to me : 'Yes, sir. We live in the dome quarters. I know how to make wicker baskets and such things, just like a dome.'

"There are other bad physical signs : One eye and squint eyes. It is rather better to have one eye, but never squint eyes. Squint-eyed people are wicked and deceitful.

"A student of Mahesh Nyayaratna's came here. He described himself as an atheist. He said to Hriday : "I am an atheist. You may take up the position of a believer in God and argue with me." Thereupon I watched him closely and noticed that his eyes were yellow, like a cat's.

"Whether a person is good or bad can also be known from the way he walks."

On December 27, 1884, Sri Ramakrishna said to a devotee, "You see, as Hazra says, I can read people's thoughts..."

On March 7, 1885 the Master took a hand of Tarak (Taraknath Ghoshal, afterwards known as Swami Shivananda) into his own and seemed to feel its weight. A few moments later he said : "There is a little crookedness in your mind; but that will go. Pray to God a little and come here now and then. Yes, that twist will go..."

Though Tarak, like Rakhal (Swami Brahmananda) Jogin (Swami Yogananda) or Gopalchandra (Swami Advaitananda) was married, dedicated himself to monastic life and thus fulfilled the expectation of the Master. On March 11, 1885 he said to Girishchandra, "There is a common adage that tells people to beware of the following : a man with a loose tongue, a man whose mind can not be fathomed even by an expert diver, a man who sticks the sacred tulsi-leaf in his ears as a sign of holiness, a woman wearing a long veil to proclaim her chastity, and the cold water of a reservoir covered with green scum, by bathing in which one gets typhoid fever. These are all dangerous things."[17]

On April 24, 1885 Sri Ramakrishna, with reference to Hazra, said to Narendra : "...You see, physical traits to a great extent influence character. Short stature and a body with dents here and there are not good traits. People with such traits take a long time to acquire spiritual knowledge."

On October 25 the same year the Master, referring to a change coming over Bijoy Krishna Goswami's mind, said to Narendra, "... You see, I can recognize a Paramahamsa by his neck and forehead. Yes, I can recognize a Paramahamsa."[18] He examined the physical features of Vishweshwari wife of Rakhal Chandra Ghosh minutely and learnt that she represented an auspicious aspect of the Divine Shakti and would not stand in the way of his spiritual son Rakhal. He taught Rakhal various signs by which one can recognize the character of a person. At the time of their first meeting the Master catching hold of the hand of Baburam (later known as Swami Premananda) said, "Come closer to the light. Let me see your face." He examined the newcomer's face, hands and feet thoroughly and then he weighed his forearm by placing it on his palm to judge his spirituality. Observing the auspicious signs the Master expressed great satisfaction. He possessed Yogic vision that enabled him to recognize the inner self of a person. He spoke of Baburam, "In a vision I saw Baburam as a goddess with a necklace around Her neck and with women companions about Her." Swami Vivekananda said, "He knew one's character by sight, and never changed his opinion. He could perceive, as it were, super-sensual things, while we try to know one's character by reason, with the result that our judgments are often fallacious."[19]

There are numerous instances of the amazing super-human power of Sri Ramakrishna. When M. (Mahendranath Gupta the recorder of 'Sri Sri Ramakrishana Kathamrita' that was translated into English by Swami Nikhilananda under the title 'The Gospel of Sri Ramakrishna') met the Master the first time on a Sunday (February 1882) at dusk, the latter said to him affectionately, "you see, you have certain good signs. I know them by looking at a person's forehead, his eyes, and so on. Tell me, now, what kind of person is your wife? Has she spiritual attributes, or is she under the power of avidya?"

The master was a great seer who could see distinctly what was going to happen in the future. Once he said to his monastic disciple Taraknath Ghosal (Swami Shivananda), "In the future many white-complexioned devotees will come here"[20] Again once he told his another disciple Harinath Chottopadhyay (Swami Turiyananda) that he had other disciples who spoke a different language, who had different customs, somewhere far away in the West. They also would worship him. He passed away on the auspicious day on 16 August 1886 that he had selected eight or nine days before his passing away. Swami Vivekananda said, "For he saw through the future life of those boys that he collected from the streets of Calcutta, so to say. People used to laugh at him when he said, "You will see– this boy, that boy, what he becomes.' His faith was unalterable : "Mother showed it to me. I may be weak, but when She says this is so–She can never make mistakes–it must be so."[21]

Sri Ramakrishna could read somebody's mind or thoughts. The Master himself said (as recorded in the Gospel P. 119) "One day, in that state of divine intoxication, I went to the bathing-ghat on the Ganges at Barānagore, There I saw Jay Mukherji repeating the name of God; but his mind was on something else. I went up and slapped him twice on the cheeks.

"At one time Rāni Rasmani was staying in the temple garden. She came to the shrine of the Divine Mother, as she frequently did when I worshipped Kāli, and asked me to sing a song or two. On this occasion, while I was singing, I noticed she was sorting the flowers for worship absent-mindedly. At once I slapped her on the cheeks. She became quite embarrassed and sat there with folded hands."

One day Harinath arriving at Dakshineswar saw the Master having his dinner with a number of bowls of curry and thought that to relish such delicious dishes was inappropriate for a monk. The Master at once read his mind and said, "Well the tendency of my mind is always towards the Infinite. It is by such rajasic devices that I hold it down to the lower planes. Otherwise I could not talk with you." Harinath was surprised at this.

It was the last outing of Sri Ramakrishna. He, with his companions Kali Prasad Chandra (Swami Abhedananda), Latu (Swami Adbhutananda) and Golap-ma (Annapurna Devi) was coming back from Dr. Durgacharan's Chamber (Kolkata) to Dakshineswar by boat at about 1:30 p.m. The Master and his companions were hungry. He asked the boatman to anchor the boat at the Baranagore ghat and then asked Kali to buy some sweets. Taking four paisa from Golap-ma he bought some *chanar murki* (small sweet cheese balls). The Master without sharing any sweets ate them all and drank some water from the Ganga. Swami Abhedananda recollected the incident :

> It was amazing! As soon as his hunger was relieved, our own stomachs felt full. We looked at each other silently. Then the Master smiled and like a boy began to make jokes–which he continued all the way to Dakshineswar. We all got out of the boat, and later the three of us discussed what had happened and realized that it was a miracle.

The incident reminds us of almost a similar miracle performed by Krishna who had eaten a few particles of rice and a little spinach left-over in the pot and drunk a glass of water and by doing so, filled the stomachs of the sage Durvasa and his twelve hundred disciples and saved helpless Draupadi in exile in an embarrassing situation.

The first time when Subodhchandra Ghosh (Swami Subodhananda) went to Sri Ramakrishna at Dakshineswar, Paramahamsadeva said to him, "Do you not belong to the family of Shankar Ghosh?" Subodh, to his utter amazement said, "Yes, Sir, but how did you know it?" The Master replied, "When I was staying at Jhamapukur, I often visited your home as well as your Kali Temple at Thanthania. That was before you were born. I knew you would come. Well, the Divine Mother sends here those who will attain spirituality. You belong to this place." Subodh quipped, "Sir, if I belong to this place, why did you not call me earlier?" The Master answered, "Look, everything happens at the right time." Holding Subodh's hand he closed his eyes for a few minutes and said, "You will attain the goal. Mother says so."

One day Subodh told the Master about his fear of ghosts. He at once pressed his thumbnail between Subodh's eyebrows. From then on he would see a soft light over his forehead and fear of ghosts was removed permanently.

One day the Master said to Hariprasanna Chattopadhyay (Swami Vijnanananda), "You know, I can see the inside of a man's mind just as I can see the objects inside a glass case." By seeing even one corner of a man's toe, he could understand what sort of man he was.

A very poor boy used to come almost daily to Sri Ramakrishna with some food. But the Master would not take any of the food. One day he said, "This poor fellow comes here because he has a great desire to be rich. Very well. Let me taste a little of what he has brought." He took a small quantity of food and the boy began to prosper immediately.

When the Master heard that his dear nephew Akshay fell ill in his father-in-law's house shortly after his marriage, he said, "Hridu, the omens are extremely bad; he has been married to a bride of Rakshasagana; the lad will die, I see."

Hriday forbade his uncle to utter such words. Sri Ramakrishna said to him, "Do I say so of my own accord? I say things involuntarily under the divine influence; I say what Mother makes me know and say. Do I wish that Akshay should die?"

Akshay suffered from a complicated remittent fever for about a month. When his last moment arrived the Master going to his bedside said, "Akshay, say 'Ganga, Narayana, Aum Rama." Repeating the Mantra thrice Akshay died.

Attainment of Nirvikalpa Samadhi in a day :

Nirvikalpa Samadhi is the highest non-dualistic experience very difficult to gain. When a seeker, completely detached from all sorts of temporal consciousness, dives deep in search of the Self, realizes It i.e. realizes his identity with Brahman through meditation. Totapuri helped Sri Ramakrishna attain the Infinite Bliss through the great knowledge beyond duality.

Describing the event Sri Ramakrishna said, "After the initiation Nangta began to teach me the various conclusions of the Advaita Vedanta and asked me to withdraw the mind completely from all objects and dive deep into the Ātman. But in spite of all my attempts I could not altogether cross the realm of name and form and bring my mind to the unconditioned state. I had not difficulty in taking the mind from all the objects of the world. But the radiant and too familiar figure of the Blissful Mother, the Embodiment of the essence of Pure Consciousness, appeared before me as a living reality. Her bewitching smile prevented me from passing into the Great Beyond. Again and again I tried, but She stood in my way every time. In despair I said to Nangta : 'It is hopeless. I can not raise my mind to the unconditioned state and come face to face with Ātman.' He grew excited and sharply said : 'What? You can't do it? But you have to.' He cast his eyes around. Finding a piece of glass he took it up and stuck it between my eyebrows. 'Concentrate the mind on this point!' he thundered. Then with stern determination I again sat to mediate. As soon as the gracious form of the Divine Mother appeared before me, I used my discrimination as a sword and with it clove Her in two. The last barrier fell. My spirit at once soared beyond the relative plane and I lost myself in samadhi."

Sri Ramakrishna remained absolutely absorbed in samadhi for three consecutive days. To his utter amazement Totapuri cried out, "Is it really true? Is it possible that he has attained in a single day what it took me forty years of strenuous practice to achieve? Great God! It is nothing short of a miracle!'

Thus Sri Ramakrishna showed his originality–his strong will-force, stern determination and deep concentration by attaining nirvikalpa samadhi within such a short time.

Swami Saradananda, one of the disciples of Sri Ramakrishna and well-versed in Hindu metaphysics and the spiritual fits of his Master; described how this demi-God after the departure of Totapuri towards the end of 1865, remained for more than six months in the great ecstasy of Nirvikalpa Samadhi in a state where the consciousness of the ego disappeared completely, coming back now and again very gently, just veiling the perfect 'realisation'. In those moments of semi consciousness the Master perceived the orders of the cosmic spirit 'which forced him to remain in the Bhavamukha'.

Romain Rolland who has described Ramakrishna as 'the younger brother of our Christ,' or 'the consummation of two thousand years of the spiritual life of three hundred million people'; has in connection with the aforesaid event, commented in his book, 'The Life of Ramakrishna' '...if such a statement is credible ...;' perhaps to hint at the depth of the wonder made by the Master.

Amazing inference and perception :

Sri Ramakrishna possessed a miraculous power of insight and vision. Sister Nivedita wrote, "He was so responsive that he would meet them (his disciples) at the door on their arrival, and began at once to answer, without being told of them, the questions that the boys carried written in their pockets. His perceptions were so fine that he could tell by touch the character of anyone who might already have come in contact with his food, his clothes, or his mat. It "burnt" him, he said, of an impress from which he shrank; or, on another occasion, "Look! I can eat this. The sender must have been some good soul!" His nervous system, again, had been so charged with certain ideas that even in sleep he shrank from the touch of metal, and his hand would, apparently of its own accord, restore a book or a fruit, whose return to its owner the conscious mind had failed to prompt."[23]

The Master was a sooth-sayer. On June 4, 1883 he said to M., "At that time everything happen that way. I would repeat the name of God and believe that a certain thing would happen, and it would invariably come to pass."

On June 20, 1884 Sri Ramakrishna said to M. : "I noticed the other day that Baburam, Bhavanath and Harish have a feminine nature. In a vision I saw Baburam as a goddess with a necklace around her neck and with women companions about her. He has received something in a dream. His body is pure. Only a very little effort will awaken his spiritual consciousness...

"Bhavanath, Baburam and a few others have a feminine nature. Harish sleeps in a woman's cloth. Baburam says that he too likes the womanly attitude. So I am right. Bhavanath also is like that. But Narendra, Rakhal and Niranjan have a masculine nature."

The Master told M too that it is not good to have occult powers and a man can not realise God if he possesses even one of the eight occult powers. Only the small-minded seek them.

On July 3, 1884 Sri Ramakrishna said to M. : "... The moment I saw Keshab, I said : 'Of all the people I see here, he alone has dropped his tail. He can now live on land as well as in water, like a frog.'

Here is an excerpt from the Master's conversation with Narendra and Hazra on September 6, 1884 :

Narendra : "That is why you didn't drink the water he (Pundit Shashadhar's host) touched. It happened the first day you met Shashadhar at his house. How did you come to know he was immoral?"

Master (smiling) : "Hazra knows of another instance. It happened at Sihore in Hriday's house."

Hazra : "The man was a Vaishanava. He came with me to see you [meaning Sri Ramakrishna], as soon as he sat in front of you, you turned your back on him."

Master : "We learnt later that he led an immoral life. (To Narendra) You used to say, at first, that these were all hallucinations."

Narendra : "How was I to know? Now I see that you are always right."

On April 9, 1887 Swamiji said to M. about the accuracy of his Master's conjectures : He loved me so much! But whenever an impure idea crept into my mind he at once knew about it. While going around with Ananda, sometimes I found myself in the company of evil people. On those occasions the Master could not eat any food from my hands. He could raise his hand only a little, and could not bring it to his mouth. On one such occasion, while he was ill, he brought his hand very close to his mouth, but it did not go in. He said to me, 'You are not yet ready.'

Astonishing divine power :

The Master appeared to be omnipresent. Frequent visits of Sarada Prasanna Mittra (Swami Trigunatitananda) to Dakshineswar worried his parents and they made arrangements for his marriage. Sarada wrote a short letter "My respected parents, I will not marry. I have no desire to be trapped in the meshes of maya. In whatever direction my eyes go, I am going." He put the letter on his desk and went to Cossipore to receive the Master's blessings. Then he left for Puri on foot where he met his parents. He narrated his journey to them :

After writing (the second note from Panshkura, Midnapore) to you I began to walk and did not get any food for two days. I was hungry and exhausted. I expected to find a village before evening, but unfortunately I reached a dense forest. I followed a zigzag path for some time and then I was lost in darkness. I began to chant Sri Ramakrishna's name and prayed to God for help. Without finding any way out, I climbed up a big tree and fell asleep on its branch. Suddenly I heard a man's voice, saying : "Hello, holy man. Here are some sweets. Please come down and appease your hunger." After a short while he brought a jug of water and disappeared in the darkness. I was impressed with his sympathy and received that food and drink as the grace of the compassionate God. At daybreak I searched for that man in the forest, but I couldn't find any human being or any village nearby."

During his second and third visits to Sri Ramakrishna Narendranath underwent mental change and wonderful experiences. He realized that it was through the inscrutable divine power of his Master that he had those strange experiences.

The Master himself spoke about his astounding divine power to M. (on July 13, 1885) "... If a man gathers his whole mind and fixes it on me, then, indeed, he achieves everything.

"But what am I? It is all He. I am the machine and He is its Operator. It is God alone who exists in this [meaning his body]. That is why so many people are feeling more and more attracted to it. A mere touch is enough to awaken their spirituality. This attraction, this pull, is the attraction of God and of none else.

"Tarak of Belgharia was going home from Dakshineswar. I clearly noticed that a flame-like thing came out of this [meaning his body] and followed him. A few days later Tarak came back to Dakshineswar. In a state of samādhi He who dwells in this body placed his foot on Tarak's chest...."

Perfect mind-reader :

Sri Ramakrishna Paramahamsa Deva knew well what somebody else was thinking without being told.

M. has recorded an instance of July 13, 1885 : "A man dressed in an ochre robe entered the room and greeted the Master. Privately he was in the habit of criticizing Sri Ramakrishna; so at the sight of him Balaram laughed. Sri Ramakrishna could read a man's mind. He said to Balaram : "Never mind. Let him say I am a cheat."

To cite another example of the Master's capability of thought-reading : One or two days before the passing away of the Master, Narendra being alone with the Master, said to himself, "If in the midst of this racking physical pain he declares his Godhead, then only shall I accept him as an Incarnation of God." Though it was a passing thought, Sri Ramakrishna smiled and said, "He who was Rāma and Krishna is now, in this body Ramakrishna–but not in your Vedantic sense." Narendra felt ashamed.

Transmission of power :

At Cossipore garden on January 1, 1886 Sri Ramakrishna, falling into a spiritual mood gave historic utterances, "What more shall I say? I bless you all. Be illumined!" He touched each of the devotees who experienced ineffable bliss–some laughed, some wept, some began to meditate or pray, some saw light, some had visions of their respective Ideals while some felt the flow of spiritual power within their bodies.

The Master, three or four days before his passing away, stared at his most beloved disciple Narendra and went into samādhi. Narendra gradually felt the incoming of a delicate power and lost outer consciousness. When he regained normal state of mind, Sri Ramakrishna, with tears in his eyes said to him, "Today I have given you my all and I am now only a poor fakir, possessing nothing. By this power you will do immense good in the world, and not until it is accomplished will you return."

Unfailing benediction and pledge of safety :

Even after the passing away of the Master his grace and protection were still with his disciples and devotees.

Hari Prasanna Chattopadhyay (Swami Vijnanananda) recalled : "The day the Master passed away [16 August 1886] I saw him standing in front of me. I wondered : 'How did the Master come here? What is the cause of this vision?' The next day I read of the Master's passing away in the *Basumati* newspaper."

In Detroit in the U.S.A. One day when Swami Vivekananda was going to sip his drink, the apparition of his Master forbade him to take the poisoned drink and thus saved his life.

Swami Abhedananda reminisced : In 1915 I was in London. On 6 May I went to the booking office to purchase a ticket from London to New York on the *S. S. Lusitania*. While I was in that office, a mysterious thing happened. I was about to buy the ticket, but immediately heard a clear voice forbidding me to buy it. I was dumbfounded. I thought it might be a freak of my mind. I looked around but couldn't find anybody. So again I went to the counter and the same thing happened. Then I decided to return to the apartment without buying any ticket. However, I planned to buy the ticket the following day. The next morning I saw in the newspaper in big letters "*S. S. Lusitania* Is No More." I was overwhelmed. Tears rolled down my cheeks. I realized that the Master had saved my life.[24]

[The British ship *S. S. Lusitania* was destroyed by a German submarine in the Atlantic Ocean, near the Cork coast of Ireland on 7 May 1915, during world War 1. One thousand one hundred ninety-eight passengers died.]

Swami Trigunatitananda was sceptical about the existence of ghosts. Some one told him that he could see a ghost in an old haunted house near Baranagore Monastery at midnight. Going there secretly at night he waited for the ghost. All of a sudden he saw a faint light in the corner of the room. There appeared an eye in the midst of the light which was growing brighter. He was horrified by the malicious light approaching him. He was about to faint. Suddenly the Master appeared and said, "My child, why are you so foolishly taking chances with certain death? It is sufficient for you to keep your mind fixed on me."

During their intense spiritual practices at the Baranagore Monastery, Swami Trigunatitananda was eager to perform some tantric rituals at midnight in the cremation ground. He knew that their leader Swami Vivekananda would not allow him to do that. So one night when his brother-disciples slept, Trigunatita (the name shortened by Swamiji) silently prepared to go to the cremation ground. All of a sudden to his utter amazement he heard Swami Vivekananda calling out, "Where are you going? Sri Ramakrishna appeared to me in my sleep and told me where you were going. He said that you should not go, that he has done all these things for us, and that it is quite sufficient for us to keep our minds fixed on him."

It was June or July 1895. One evening on his way to Mount Kailas and Manas Sarovar in Tibet Trigunatita reached the bank of a river and found a dilapidated dam the only way to cross. He decided to cross the river by jumping from one rock to another in the moonlight. As he reached the middle, a dark cloudlet covered the moon. Losing his vision he was in a fix. One false step meant that he would be carried away by the strong current of the river. He began to chant the name of Sri Ramakrishna. Suddenly he heard a voice say, "Follow me," and he stepped forward and reached the other bank. The moon shone again but he found none around.

Magical touch or glance :

One touch or one glance of a godly man can change a whole life. In one of his Inspired Talks on June 24, 1895 Swamiji said, 'Prophets preach, but the Incarnations like Jesus, Buddha, Ramakrishna, can give religion; one glance, one touch is enough. That is the power of the Holy Ghost, the "laying on of hands"; the power was actually transmitted to the disciples by the Master–the "chain of Guru-power". (Works, Vol. 7, p. 8)

Sri Ramakrishna testified to his originality by casting a miraculous spell over the mind of any person by his slight touch. An old monk named Swami Purnananda from the north-western region initiated Sarada Devi and Lakshmi Devi (niece of Sri

Ramakrishna) into Shakti mantra. Later on the Master wrote mystic words on the tongue of the Mother. The first time when Narendra (afterwards Swami Vivekananda) came to Sri Ramakrishna at Dakshineswar the Master took him alone by the hand and leading him to the screened verandah north of his room said with sobs, "Ah! You have come very late. Why have you been so unkind as to make me wait all these days? My ears are tired of hearing the futile words of worldly men. Oh, how I have longed to pour my spirit into the heart of someone fitted to receive my message!" Then with folded hands, he addressed Narendra as Narayana, born on earth to remove the distress of humanity and grasping his hand asked him to come again, very soon and alone. The words and gesture of Sri Ramakrishna hurt the ego of Narendra who said to himself "What is this I have come to see? He must be stark mad. Why, I am the son of Viswanath Dutta. How dare he speak this way to me?"

Naraendra was startled when he heard Sri Ramakrishna say that he had seen God and talked to him. Though he thought that Sri Ramakrishna was a monomaniac, he could not avoid the magnetic personality and went to him about a month later. During this second visit, at the touch of the Master, Narendra had a strong irresistible emotional feeling and saw everything around him including the walls of the room whirling and disappearing suddenly. He was terrified and said, "What are you doing to me? I have my father and mother at home." He saw the whole universe along with his own ego faded away. Swamiji said to one of his disciples, 'One day in the temple-garden at Dakshineswar Sri Ramakrishna touched me over the heart, and first of all I began to see that the houses–rooms, doors, windows, verandahs–the trees, the sun, the moon–all were flying off, shattering to pieces as it were–reduced to atoms and molecules–and ultimately became merged in the Âkâsha. Gardually again, the Âkâsha also vanished, and after that, my consciousness of the ego with it; what happened next I do not recollect. I was at first frightened. Coming back from that state, again I began to see the houses, doors, windows, verandahs, and other things. (Works, Vol. 5, P. 392) During his third visit Narendra lost his consciousness at the touch of Sri Ramakrishna and answered in that state to all the questions regarding his previous birth, whereabouts and his mission in the world. He was confirmed that Sri Ramakrishna was not at all a cunning hypnotist or monomaniac and bore a great love and respect for him.

On March 25 (Monday) 1887 Narendra said to M., "... In Jadu Mallick's garden house the master one day touched me and muttered something to himself. I became unconscious. The effect of the touch lingered with me a month, like an intoxication."[25]

Taraknath Ghosal (Swami Shivananda, chiefly known as '*Mahapurush*') another monastic disciple of Sri Ramakrishna, recollected :

> During my second or third visit I was serving him when he suddenly touched my chest while in an ecstatic mood. That touch made me lose outer consciousness and sent me into a deep meditative state. I do not know how long I remained in that state. As a result, everything became revealed to me. I realized that I was the Atman, eternal and free. I realized that the Master was the Lord born as man for the good of humanity, and that I was on earth to serve him. He gave me a similar blessing another day under the banyan tree in the Panchavati.[26]

Taraknath reminisced his wonderful experiences during his early meetings with Sri Ramakrishna :

> Another day when I was meditating in the Panchavati grove, my concentration became very deep. The Master came towards me from the pine grove, and as soon as he looked at me, I burst into tears. The Master stood still. I felt something creeping up inside my chest, and I was overcome by a fit of shaking. The Master said that my crying was not insignificant. It was a type of ecstasy. I then followed him to his room where he gave me something to eat. The awakening of the Kundalini [the spiritual energy] was an easy matter for him. He could do this even without a touch, but by a mere look.[27]

Kumudbandhu Sen, a reputed writer and very close to the companions of the Master and the Mother, reminisced, one day Vijay Krishna Goswami, to his utter amazement told Swami Vivekananda that when he told Sri Ramakrishna at Dakshineswar that he could not subdue lust, the Master touched him saying 'Plunge into the eternal and omniscient and ever blissful ocean' and was absorbed in trance. He at once felt some sort of electric energy in him. (Smritir Aloy Swamiji, Ed. Swami Purnatmananda, Udbodhan office, P. 196)

Swami Saradananda one of the monastic disciples of the Master wrote :

> Shortly after the arrival of such a devotee [who had been born to carry his message] the Master would call him aside, ask him to meditate, and then under the influence of divine inspiration he would touch certain parts of his body like the chest or the tongue. By that potent touch the devotee's mind would become indrawn and sense objects would vanish from its perception. His accumulated impressions of the past would be activated and produce spiritual realization in him.[28]

As a cowboy knows each of the cows of his hard, so Sri Ramakrishna could recognize the true disciples who were destined to cater his message. He had the strange power to see inside a person as one sees an object inside a glass case. Swami Adbhutananda, a disciple of Sri Ramakrishna, gave an interesting and convincing eye witness account related to this power :

> One day the Master touched brother Niranjan, and for three days and three nights Niranjan did not get one wink of sleep. He had the continuous vision of a mysterious light and kept repeating the Lord's name. His tongue could not stop saying Japam for three days. Prior to meeting the Master, Niranjan was employed by spiritualists as a medium for contacting spirits. So one day the Master humorously said : 'Now, my boy, another ghost–the Holy Ghost–is upon you. However much you try, you will not be able to dismiss him.'[29]

Swami Abhedananda recalled :

> ...Then he (Sri Ramakrishna) took me to the northern verandah. He asked me to sit on a cot. When I was seated in the lotus posture, the Master asked me to stick out my tongue. As soon as I did that, he wrote a mantram on it with the middle finger of his right hand and advised me to meditate on Kali, the Divine Mother. I did what he said. Gradually I lost outer consciousness and sat in deep meditation. I felt an unspeakable joy within. I don't know how long I stayed in that condition. After some time the Master touched my chest and brought me back to outer consciousness. He then asked me what had happened, and I told him about my blissful experience during meditation. He was very pleased.[30]

During the second visit of Subodh Chandra Ghosh (Afterwards known as Swami Subodhananda) to Dakshineswar temple garden with his friend Kshirod Chandra Mitra, Sri Ramakrishna asked them to sit down before the Shiva temples. Then he bade them unbutton their shirts and stick out their tongues. Writing something with his finger on their tongue, the Master stroked their bodies from the navel to the throat saying, 'Awake, Mother, awake!' No sooner did Subodh start to meditate than his whole body shivered and he felt a current rushing along his spinal cord to his brain. He saw the forms of numerous gods and goddesses in a strange light within him and was overwhelmed by joy. He sank into deep meditation and lost sense-perception. He regained consciousness as the Master stroked his body in the reverse direction from the head downwards. Thus the magic touch of the Master awakened the dormant spirituality of Subodh gradually.

With reference to the originality of Sri Ramakrishna sister Nivedita observed :

"There were still other remarkable traits in Sri Ramakrishna. He had his own nervous force so entirely under control that he could remove all consciousness from his throat, for instance, during his last illness, and allow it to be operated on, as if under a local anaesthetic. His faculties of observation, again, were quite unique. The smallest detail of the physical constitution had a meaning for him, as casting light on the personality within. He would throw the disciple who had just come to him into an hypnotic sleep, and learn from his subconscious mind, in a few minutes, all that was lodged there, concerning the far past. Each little act and word, insignificant to others, was to him like a straw, borne on the great current of character, and showing the direction of its flow. There were times, he said, when men and women seemed to him like glass, and he could look them through and through.

"Above all, he could by his touch give flashes of supreme insight, which exercised a formative and compelling power over whole lives. In the matter of Samâdhi this is well-known, especially in reference to women-visitors at Dakshineswar....

"By such stimulating of each man to his own highest and best, or by such communication of experience as one and another could bear at the time, Ramakrishna Paramahamsa built up the rigorous integrity and strong discrimination that one sees in all who were made by his hand..."[31]

In her book in reference to Limits of Consciousness, Sister Nivedita has quoted comments of her spiritual father Swamiji, "Consciousness", he said on one occasion, "is a mere film between two oceans, the sub-conscious and the super-conscious." Again he exclaimed "I could not believe my own ears, when I heard Western people talking so much of *consciousness*! consciousness? What does consciousness matter! Why, it is NOTHING, as compared with the unfathomable depths of the sub-conscious, and the heights of the super-conscious! In this I could never be misled, for had I not seen Ramakrishna Paramahamsa gather in ten minutes, from a man's sub-conscious mind, the whole of his past, and determine from that his future and his powers!"[32]

A true expounder of the Vedas :

Sri Ramakrishna did not indiscriminately accept the comments of Shankaracharya and his school on the Vedas. The latter considered that the whole of the Vedas spoke the same truth and thus tortured those of the apparently conflicting vedic texts which go against their own doctrines, into the meaning of their particular schools. Sri Ramakrishna was the first to realize and exemplify in his life and teach that the apparently contradictory vedic statements are meant for different grades of aspirants and are arranged in the order of evolution. Swamiji said, "But the life of Sri Ramakrishna upsets all records of history. It is a remarkable phenomenon that in Sri Ramakrishna there has been an assemblage of ideas deeper than the sea and vaster than the skies.

"We must interpret the Vedas in the light of the experience of Sri Ramakrishna. ...As, in the olden times, it was the Lord alone, the deliverer of the *Gita*, who partially harmonized these apparently conflicting statements, so with a view to completely settling this dispute, immensely magnified in the process of time, He Himself has come as Sri Ramakrishna. Therefore no one can truly understand the Vedas and Vedanta, unless one studies them in the light of the utterances of Sri Ramakrishna..."[33]

On November 30, 1894 Swamiji wrote to one of his Madras friends and well wishers Alasinga Perumal, "The life of Sri Ramakrishna was an extraordinary searchlight under whose illumination one is able to really understand the whole scope of Hindu religion. He was the object-lesson of all the theoretical knowledge given in the Shâstras (scriptures). He showed by his life what the rishis and Avatâras really wanted to teach. The books were theories, he was the realization. This man had in fifty-one years lived the five thousand years of national spiritual life and so raised himself to be an object-lesson for future generations. The Vedas can only be explained and the Shastras reconciled by his theory of Avastha or stages–that we must not only tolerate others, but positively embrace them, and that truth is the basis of all religions." (works, Vol. 5, P. 53)

The same year the Swami wrote his brother-disciple Swami Shivananda almost the same words as he told Alasinga : "Without studying Ramakrishna Paramahamsa first, one can never understand the real import of the Vedas, the Vedanta, of the *Bhâgavata* and the other Purânas. His life is a searchlight of infinite power thrown upon the whole mass of Indian religious thought. He was the living commentary to the Vedas and to their aim. He had lived in one life the whole cycle of the national religious existence in India." (Works, Vol. 7, P. 483)

The magnitude of the Master's unprecedented utterances :

Sri Ramakrishna was a wonderful treasure of profound gifted wisdom and deep realization both temporal and spiritual. Those enabled him to say epigrammatic or proverbial words to his disciples or devotees or some other in his own inimitable style of articulation.

During his visit to Vidyasagar, a great scholar, social-reformer, educator, writer and one of the architects of modern Bengali prose Sri Ramakrishna, with reference to the knowledge of Brahman said, "Brahman is beyond vidyā, and avidya, knowledge and ignorance. It is beyond māyā, the illusion of duality.

"The world consists of the illusory duality of knowledge and ignorance. It contains knowledge and devotion, and also attachment to 'woman and gold'; righteousness and unrighteousness; good and evil. But Brahman is unattached to these. Good and evil apply to the jīva, the individual soul, as do righteousness and unrighteousness; but Brahman is not at all affected by them.

"One man may read the Bhāgavata by the light of a lamp, and another may commit a forgery by that very light; but the lamp is unaffected. The sun sheds its light on the wicked as well as on the virtuous.

"You may ask, 'How, then, can one explain misery and sin and unhappiness?' The answer is that these apply only to the jīva. Brahman is unaffected by them. There is poison in a snake; but though others may die if bitten by it, the snake itself is not affected by the poison.

"What Brahman is cannot be described. All things in the world–the Vedas, the Purānas, the Tantras, the six systems of philosophy–

have been defiled, like food that has been touched by the tongue, for they have been read or uttered by the tongue. Only one thing has not been defiled in this way, and that is Brahman. No one has ever been able to say what Brahman is."[34]

Listening to these words Vidyasagar exclaimed, "Oh! That is a remarkable statement. I have learnt something new today."

Sri Ramakrishna was the first among the prophets who repeatedly advocated the synthesis of all religions, tolerance for other faith :

"God can be realized through all paths. All religions are true. The important thing is to reach the roof. You can reach it by stone stairs or by wooden stairs or by bamboo steps or by a rope. You can also climb up by a bamboo pole.

"You may say that there are many errors and superstitions in another religion. I should reply : Suppose there are. Every religion has errors. Everyone thinks that his watch alone gives the correct time. It is enough to have yearning for God. It is enough to love Him and feel attracted to Him. Don't you know that God is the Inner Guide? He sees the longing of our heart and the yearning of our soul. Suppose a man has several sons. The older boys address him distinctly as 'Bābā or 'Pāpā', but the babies can at best call him 'Bā' or 'Pā'. Now, will the father be angry with those who address him in this indistinct way? The father knows that they too are calling him, only they can not pronounce his name well. All children are the same to the father. Likewise, the devotees call on God alone, though by different names. They call on one Person only. God is one, but His names are many."[35]

The Master said to M. "...One should follow various paths. One should practise each creed for a time. In a game of satrancha a piece can't reach the centre square until it completes the circle; but once in the square it can't be overtaken by any other piece....

"I had to practise each religion for a time–Hinduism, Islām, Christianity. Furthermore, I followed the paths of the Saktas, Vaishnavas, and Vedāntists. I realized that there is only one God toward whom all are travelling; but the paths are different."[36]

During a boat-trip on the Ganga with Keshab Chandra Sen, a scholar and Brāhmo leader and his followers and M. Vijay Krishna Goswami on October 27, 1882, Sri Ramakrishna said :

"But you should remember that the heart of the devotee is the abode of God. He dwells, no doubt, in all beings, but He especially manifests Himself in the heart of the devotees. A landlord may at one time or another visit all parts of his estate, but people say he is generally to be found in a particular drawing-room. The heart of the devotee is the drawing-room of God."

"He who is called Brahman by the jnānis is known as Ātman by the yogis and as Bhagavān by the bhaktas. The same brāhmin is called priest, when worshiping in the temple, and cook, when preparing a meal in the kitchen.

"...The devotee of God wants to eat sugar, not to become sugar."

"... Thus Brahaman and Sakti are identical. If you accept the one, you must accept the other. It is like fire and its power to burn. If you see the fire, you must recognize its power to burn also. You can not think of fire without its power to burn, nor can you think of the power to burn without fire. You can not conceive of the sun's rays without the sun, nor can you conceive of the sun without its rays....

"The Primordial Power is ever at play. She is creating, preserving, and destroying in play, as it were. This power is called Kāli. Kāli is verily Brahman, and Brahman is verily Kāli. It is one and the same Reality. When we think of It as inactive, that is to say, not engaged in the acts of creation, preservation and destruction, then we call It Brahman. But when It engages in these activities, then we call It Kali or Sakti. The Reality is one and the same; the difference is in name and form.

"It is like water, called in different languages by different names, such as 'jal', 'pāni', and so forth. There are three or four ghats on a lake. The Hindus, who drink water at one place, call it 'jal'. The Mussalmāns at another place, call it 'pāni'. And the English at a third place call it 'water'. All three denote one and the same thing, the difference being in the name only. In the same way, some address the Reality as 'Āllāh', some as 'God', some as 'Brahman', some as 'Kali', and others by such names as 'Rāma', 'Jesus', 'Durga', 'Hari'. ...

"I tell you the truth : there is nothing wrong in your being in the world. But you must direct your mind toward God; otherwise you will not succeed. Do your duty with one hand and with the other hold to God. After the duty is over, you will hold to God with both hands.

"It is all a question of the mind. Bondage and liberation are of the mind alone. The mind will take the colour you dye it with...."[37]

Sri Ramakrishna did not approve of Calvinism. The French Protestant and leader of the Reformation Movement, John Calvin (1509–64) taught that man is born a sinner and the few of them selected previously may be absolved from sins by the grace of God.

With reference to this doctrine the Master said, "Once someone gave me a book of the Christians. I asked him to read it to me. It talked about nothing but sin. (To Keshab) Sin is the only thing one hears of at your Brāhmo Samāj, too. The wretch who constantly says, 'I am bound, I am bound' only succeeds in being bound. He who says day and night, 'I am a sinner, I am a sinner' verily becomes a sinner.

"One should have such burning faith in God that one can say : What? I have repeated the name of God, and can sin still cling to me? How can I be a sinner any more? How can I be in bondage any more?

"If a man repeats the name of God, his body, mind, and everything become pure. Why should one talk only about sin and hell, and such things? Say but once, 'O Lord, I have undoubtedly done wicked things, but I won't repeat them'. And have faith in His name."[38]

During that eventful journey Sri Ramakrishna said to Keshab Chandra and the other Brāhmo devotees, "Whether you accept Radha and Krishna, or not please do accept their attraction for each other. Try to create that same yearning in your heart for God. Yearning is all you need in order to realize Him."

On Wednesday, November 15, 1882 Sri Ramakrishna accompanied by Rakhal (later known as Swami Brahmananda), M. and several other devotees saw the Wilson circus show in the Calcutta (Kolkata) Maidan with great delight and then visited the house of Balaram Bose one of the most beloved of his disciples. Having been engaged in spiritual talk, there he said :

"The caste-system can be removed by one means only, and that is the love of God. Lovers of God do not belong to any caste. The mind, body and soul of a man become purified through divine love. Chaitanya and Nityananda scattered the name of Hari to everyone, including the pariah, and embraced them all. A brāhmin without this love is no longer a brāhmin. And a pariah with the love of God is no longer a pariah. Through bhakti an untouchable becomes pure and elevated."[39]

On the auspicious occasion of the Jagaddhātri Puja (the festival of the Divine Mother) on Sunday, November 19, 1882 Sri Ramakrishna went to the house of Surendranath Mitra, a beloved householder devotee whom the Master designated as one of those commissioned by the Divine Mother to defray a great part of his expenses. There in reference to the freedom of women and the abolition of the caste-system preached by the Brāhmo Samaj, he said : "Men feel that way when they are just beginning to develop spiritual yearning. A storm raises clouds of dust, and one cannot distinguish between the different trees– the mango, the hog plum, and the tamarind. But after the storm blows over, one sees clearly. After the first storm of divine passion is quelled, one gradually understands that God alone is the Highest Good, the Eternal Substance, and that all else is transitory. One cannot grasp this without tapasyā and the company of holy men. What is the use of merely reciting the written parts for the drum? It is very difficult to put them into practice on the instrument. What can be accomplished by a mere lecture? It is austerity that is necessary. By that alone can one comprehend.

(To Surendra's brother) "You asked about caste distinctions. There is only one way to remove them and that is by love of God. Lovers of God have no caste. Through this divine love the untouchable becomes pure, the pariah no longer remains a pariah. Chaitanya embraced all, including the pariahs.

"The members of the Brāhmo Samāj sing the name of Hari. That is very good. Through earnest prayer one receives the grace of God and realizes Him. God can be realized by means of all paths. The same God is invoked by different names."[40]

On March 11, 1883 Sri Ramakrishna told a Vaishnava Goswami, "With sincerity and earnestness one can realize God through all religions. The Vaishnavas will realize God, and so will the Sāktas, the Vedāntists, and the Brāhmos. The Mussalmāns and Christians will realize Him too. All will certainly realize God if they are earnest and sincere.

"Some people indulge in quarrels, saying, 'One cannot attain anything unless one worships our Krishna', or, 'Nothing can be gained without the worship of Kāli, our Divine Mother', or, 'One cannot be saved without accepting the Christian religion'. This is pure dogmatism. The dogmatist says, 'My religion alone is true, and the religions of others are false.' This is a bad attitude. God can be reached by different paths.

"Further some say that God has form and is not formless. Thus they start quarrelling. A Vaisnava quarrels with a Vedāntist.

"One can rightly speak of God only after one has seen Him. He who has seen God knows really and truly that God has form and that He is formless as well. He has many other aspects that cannot be described...."[41]

On June 4, 1883 Manilal Mallick asked Sri Ramakrishna, "Sir where shall I meditate on God when I perform my daily worship?"

The Master replied, "Why, the heart is a splendid place. Meditate on God there."

On Friday, June 15, 1883 Rakhal's father's father-in-law asked the Master, "Sir, can one realize God while leading the life of a householder?" Sri Ramakrishna replied with a smile, "Why not? Live in the world like a mudfish. The mudfish lives in the mud but itself remains unstained. Or live in the world like a loose woman. She attends to her household duties, but her mind is always on her sweetheart. Do your duties in the world, fixing your mind on God. But this is extremely difficult. I said to the members of the Brāhmo Samāj : "Suppose a typhoid patient is kept in a room where there are jars of pickles and pitchers of water. How can you expect the patient to recover? The very thought of spiced pickles brings water to one's mouth." To a man, woman is like that pickle. The craving for worldly things, which is chronic in man, is like the patient's craving for water. There is no end to this craving. The typhoid patient says, 'I shall drink a whole pitcher of water.' The situation is very difficult. There is so much confusion in the world. If you go this way, you are threatened with a shovel; if you go that way, you are threatened with a broomstick; again, in another direction, you are threatened with a shoe-beating. Besides, one cannot think of God unless one lives in solitude. The goldsmith melts gold to make ornaments. But how can he do his work well if he is disturbed again and again? Suppose you are separating rice from bits of husk. You must do it all by yourself. Every now and then you have to take the rice in your hand to see how clean it is. But how can you do your work well if you are called away again and again?"

A devotee asked the Master, 'What then is the way, sir?' Sri Ramakrishna answered, "There is a way. One succeeds if one develops a strong spirit of renunciation. Give up at once, with determination, what you know to be unreal. Once, when I was seriously ill, I was taken to the physician Gangaprasad Sen. He said to me : 'I shall give you a medicine, but you mustn't drink any water. You may take pomegranate juice.' Everyone wondered how I could live without water; but I was determined not to drink it. I said to myself : 'I am a Paramahamsa and not a goose. I shall drink only milk."[42]

On July 21, 1883 the Master while going to Adhar's (Adharlal Sen, one of Sri Ramakrishna's householder devotees) house, said to M :

"Dwell in the truth and you will certainly realize God."

In the house of Khelat Ghosh the same day the Master repeated almost the same words related to liberal religious outlook :

It is not good to feel that one's own religion alone is true and all others are false. God is one only, and not two. Different people call on Him by different names : some as Allāh, some as God, and others as Krishna, Siva, and Brahman. It is like the water in a lake. Some drink it at one place and call it 'Jal', others at another place and call it 'pani', and still others at a third place and call it 'water'. The Hindus call it 'Jal', the Christians 'water', and the Mussalmāns 'Pani'. But it is one and the same thing. Opinions are but paths. Each religion is only a path leading to God; as rivers come from different directions and ultimately become one in the one ocean.

The truth established in the Vedas, the Purānas, and the Tantras is but one Satchidānanda. In the Vedas It is called Brahman, in the Purānas It is called Krishna, Rama, and so on, and in the Tantras It is called Siva. The one Satchidānanda is called Brahman, Krishna and Siva."[43]

On Sunday, February 24, 1884 Sri Ramakrishna advised Mani Mallick, "What will a man gain by knowing many scriptures? The one thing needful is to know how to cross the river of the world. God alone is real, and all else illusory."

The Master said to Manilal, M and other devotees, "Why do people worship virgins? All women are so many forms of the Divine Mother. But her manifestation is greatest in pure-souled virgins.

"...In the Kali temple I found that the Mother herself had become everything–even the wicked, even the brother of Bhagavat Pundit.

"...I worship virgins because I see in them the Divine Mother. My wife strokes my feet, but I salute her afterwards.

"You see, one cannot exclude even a wicked person. A tulsi leaf, however dry or small, can be used for worship in the temple."[44]

On Saturday, May 24, 1884 Sri Ramakrishna said to an actor who had taken part of Vidya in a theatrical performance of the *Vidyāsundar* :

"You asked me about self-realization. Longing is the means of realizing Ātman. A man must strive to attain God with all his body, with all his mind, and with all his speech. Because of an excess of bile one gets jaundice. Then one sees everything as yellow; one perceives no colour but yellow. Among you actors, those who take only the roles of woman acquire the nature of woman; by thinking of woman your ways and thoughts become womanly. Just so, by thinking day and night of God one acquires the nature of God.

"The mind is like white linen just returned from the laundry. It takes on the colour you dip it in."[45]

On Sunday, June 15, 1884 Sri Ramakrishna with reference to Radha's one hundred and twenty-five per cent of divine love and Sri Chaitanya's intense yearning for God said to M. :

This is what it means to be intoxicated with ecstatic love of God. The sum and substance of the whole matter is that a man must love God, must be restless for Him. It doesn't matter whether you believe in God with form or in God without form. You may or may not believe that God incarnates Himself as man. But you will realize Him if you have that yearning. Then He Himself will let you know what He is like. If you must be mad, why should you be mad for the things of the world? If you must be mad, be mad for God alone."[46]

Sri Ramakrishna said to Bhavanath a householder devotee on September 7, 1884 :

"You see how many opinions there are about God. Each opinion is a path. There are innumerable opinions and innumerable paths leading to God.

"You must stick to one path with all your strength. A man can reach the roof of a house by stone stair or a ladder or a rope-ladder or a rope or even by a bamboo pole. But he cannot reach the roof if he sets foot now on one and now on another. He should firmly follow one path. Likewise, in order to realize God a man must follow one path with all his strength.

"But you must regard other views as so many paths leading to God. You should not feel your path is the only right path and that other paths are wrong. You mustn't bear malice toward others."[47]

On September 21, 1884 Sri Ramakrishna said to the devotees, "An egotistic person cannot realize God. Do you know what egotism is like? It is like a high mound, where rain-water cannot collect : the water runs off. Water collects in low land. There seeds sprout and grow into trees. Then the trees bear fruit.

"Therefore I say to Hazra, 'Never think that you alone have true understanding and that others are fools.' One must love all. No one is a stranger. It is Hari alone who dwells in all beings. Nothing exists without Him....

(To M.) "You see, mere study of books avails nothing. One may recite the written part for the drum glibly from memory, but to play the drum is exceedingly difficult."[48]

On October 26, 1884 the Master said to Mahima Charan Chakravorty, "In the world a man must fight against passions like lust and anger, against many desires, against attachment. It is convenient to fight from inside a fort– from his own home. At home he gets his food and other help from his wife. In the Kaliyuga the life of a man depends entirely on food. It is better to get food at one place than to knock at seven doors for it. Living at home is like facing the battle from a fort."

Sri Ramakrishna advised M on December 27, 1884 : "... One cannot succeed in religious life if one has shame, hatred or fear. These are fetters. Haven't you heard of the eight fetters?"[49]

The Master said to Girish Chandra Ghosh one of his beloved householder devotees and reputed dramatist, actor and director on February 22, 1885 :

"By being guileless one can speedily realize God. There are several kinds of people who do not attain divine knowledge. First, a man with a perverse mind; he is not guileless. Second, one who is very fastidious about outer purity. Third, a doubting person."[50]

Sri Ramakrishna advised Girish and other devotees on February 25, 1885 :

"One must worship the Ādyāsakti. She must be propitiated. She alone has assumed all female forms. Therefore I look on all women as mother. The attitude of looking on woman as mother is very pure. The Tantra mentions the Vāmāchāra method also. But that is not a good method; it causes the aspirant's downfall. A devotee keeping an object of enjoyment near him has reason to be afraid.

"Looking on woman as mother is like fasting on the ekādaśi day without touching even a drop of water; in this attitude there is not the slightest trace of sensual enjoyment. Another way of observing the ekādaśi allows the taking of fruit and the like. One can also observe the day by eating luchi and curries! But my attitude is not to touch even a drop of water while I observe the fast. I worshipped the Shodaśhi as my mother, I looked on all parts of her body as those of my mother. This attitude of regarding God as Mother is the last word in sādhanā. 'O God, Thou art my Mother and I am Thy child'–this is the last word in spirituality."[51]

On March 7, 1885 the Master spoke to a young brāhmin :

"Have faith. Depend on God. Then you will not have to do anything yourself. Mother kāli will do everything for you.

"Jnāna goes as far as the outer court, but bhakti can enter the inner court. The Pure Self is unattached. Both vidyā and avidyā are in it, but It is unattached. Sometimes there is a good and sometimes a bad smell in the air, but the air itself is unaffected."[52]

The same day during their discourse a devotee said to Sri Ramakrishna, "Suppose someone's mother says to him, 'Don't go to Dakshineswar.' Suppose she curses him, saying, 'If you go there you will be drinking my blood!'"

The Master replied, "A mother who says that is no mother; she is the embodiment of avidyā. There is no sin in disobeying such a mother. She obstructs her son's path to God. There is no harm in disobeying your elders for the sake of God. For Rāma's sake Bharat did not obey his mother Kaikeyi. The gopis did not obey their husbands when they were forbidden to visit Krishna. Prahlāda disobeyed his father for God. Vali disregarded the words of Sukrāchārya, his teacher in order to please God. Bibhishana went against the wishes of Rāvana, his elder brother, to please Rāma. But you must obey your elders in all other things...."[53]

On March 11, 1885 Sri Ramakrishna said to Girish, "In the scriptures you will find the way to realize God. But after getting all the information about the path, you must begin to work. Only then can you attain your goal.

"What will it avail a man to have mere scholarship? A pundit may have studied many scriptures, he may recite many sacred texts, but if, he is still attached to the world and if inwardly he loves 'woman and gold;' then he has not assimilated the contents of the scriptures. For such a man the study of scriptures is futile.

"The almanac forecasts the rainfall for the year. You may squeeze the book, but you won't get a drop of water–not even a single drop."

In the evening the Master, perhaps to teach the devotees how to pray, addressing the Divine Mother said, "O Mother, I throw myself on Thy mercy. I take shelter at Thy Hallowed Feet. I do not want bodily comforts; I do not crave name and fame; I do not seek the eight occult powers. Be gracious and grant that I may have pure love for Thee, a love unsmitten by desire, untainted by any selfish ends–a love craved by the devotee for the sake of love alone. And grant me the favour, O Mother, that I may not be deluded by Thy world-bewitching māyā, that I may never be attached to the world, to 'woman and gold', conjured up by Thy inscrutable māyā! O Mother, there is no one but Thee whom I may call my own. Mother, I do not know how to worship, I am without austerity. I have neither devotion nor knowledge. Be gracious, Mother, and out of Thy infinite mercy grant me love for Thy Lotus Feet."

M. commented, "Every word of this prayer, uttered from the depths of his soul, stirred the minds of the devotees. The melody of his voice and the childlike simplicity of his face touched their hearts very deeply."[54]

On May 9, 1885 in the drawing-room of Balaram Bose the Master said to Ramchandra Datta a medical practitioner, chemist and one of his foremost lay disciples : "You are a physician. You know that medicine works only when it mixes with the patient's blood and becomes one with it. Likewise, in the state of Brahmajnāna one sees God both within and without. One sees that it is God Himself who has become the body, mind, life and soul."

After some interaction between the teacher and the taughts, Sri Ramakrishna said in the ecstatic mood, "There is no one else here; so I am telling you this. He who from the depth of his soul seeks to know God will certainly realize Him. He must. He alone who is restless for God and seeks nothing but Him will certainly realize Him.[55]

On July 28, 1885 in the house of Nanda Bose the host said to the guest Sri Ramakrishna, 'But how can we obtain God's grace? Has he really the power to bestow grace?'

The Master answered, smiling, "I see. You think as the intellectuals do : one reaps the results of one's actions. Give up these ideas. The effect of Karma wears away if one takes refuge in God. I prayed to the Divine Mother with flowers in my hand : 'Here Mother take Thy sin; here, take Thy virtue. I don't want either of these; give me only real bhakti. Here, Mother, take Thy good; here, take Thy bad. I don't want any of Thy good or bad; give me only real bhakti. Here, Mother, take Thy dharma; here, take Thy adharma. I don't want any of Thy dharma or adharma; give me only real bhakti. Here, Mother, take Thy knowledge; here, take Thy ignorance. I don't want any of Thy knowledge or ignorance; give me only real bhakti. Here, Mother, take Thy purity; here, take Thy impurity. Give me only real bhakti."[56]

On September 1, 1885 during his conversation with the Vaishnava from Kātwa, Sri Ramakrishna said to him, "Man should possess dignity and alertness. Only he whose spiritual consciousness is awakened possesses this dignity and alertness and can be called a man. Futile is the human birth without the awakening of spiritual consciousness."[57]

The next day (Sept. 2, 1885) the Master said to Dr. Bhagavan Rudra, "I say that God can be realized if one feels drawn to Him by the intensity of these three attractions : the child's attraction for the mother, the husband's attraction for the chaste wife, (In Sri Sri Ramakrishna Kathamrita by M. : the chaste wife's attraction for her husband) and the attraction of worldly possessions for the worldly man."[58]

On October 22, 1885 Sri Ramakrishna said to Mahendralal Sarkar :

> ...A lover of God does not burn himself to death, like a moth. The light to which he rushes is like the light of a gem. That light is brilliant, no doubt, but it is also cooling and soothing. That light does not scorch his body; it gives him joy and peace.

When Dr. Sarkar told the Master that his son Amrita was a disciple of the latter, Sri Ramakrishna said, with a smile, "There is not a fellow under the sun who is my disciple. On the contrary, I am everybody's disciple. All are the children of God. All are His servants. I too am a child of God. I too am his servant. 'Uncle Moon' is every child's uncle!"[59]

On October 23, 1885 Sri Ramakrishna said to Dr. Sarkar and Dr. Dukari : "Total renunciation is for sannyāsis. They must not look even at the picture of a woman. To them a woman is poison. They must keep themselves at least ten cubits away from her; and if that is not possible, at least one cubit. And they must not talk much with a woman, no matter how devout she may be. Further, they should choose their dwelling at a place where they will never, or scarcely ever, see the face of a woman.

"Money, too, is like poison to a sannyāsi. If he keeps money with him, he has worries, pride, anger, and the desire for physical comforts. Money inflames his rajas, which brings tamas in its train. Therefore a sannyāsi must not touch 'gold'. 'Woman and gold' makes him forget God.

"For householders moncy is a means of getting food, clothes and a dwelling place, worshipping the Deity, and serving holy men and devotees.

"It is useless to try to hoard money. With great labour the bees build a hive; but a man breaks it and takes the honey away."[60]

On October 27, 1885 addressing Dr. Sarkar, the Master said, "Go beyond knowledge and ignorance; only then can you realize God. To know many things is ignorance. Pride of scholarship is also ignorance. The unwavering conviction that God alone dwells in all beings is Jnāna, knowledge. To know Him intimately is vijnāna, a richer knowledge. If a thorn gets into your foot, a second thorn is needed to take it out. When it is out both thorns are thrown away. You have to procure the thorn of knowledge to remove the thorn of ignorance, then you must set aside both knowledge and ignorance. God is beyond both knowledge and ignorance..."[61]

On October 30, 1885 Sri Ramakrishna said to Dr. Sarkar :

> Shall I tell you the truth? What will you gain by mere scholarship? The pundits hear many things and know many things– the Vedas, the Purānas, the Tantras. But of what avail is mere scholarship? Discrimination and renunciation are necessary. If a man has discrimination and renunciation, then one can listen to him. But of what use are the words of a man who looks on the world as the essential thing?
>
> What is the lesson of the Gita? It is what you get by repeating the word ten times. As you repeat 'Gitā', 'Gitā', the word becomes reversed into 'tāgi', 'tāgi' – which implies renunciation. He alone has understood the secret of the Gitā who has renounced his attachment to 'woman and gold' and has directed his entire love to God. It isn't necessary to read the whole of the Gitā. The

purpose of reading the book is served if one practises renunciation.[62]

On April 16, 1886 Girish asked Sri Ramakrishna, "Sir, my mind is now on a very lofty plane. Why does it come down again?"

The Master replied, "That always happens when one leads a worldly life. Sometimes the householder's mind goes up; sometimes it goes down. Sometimes he feels a great deal of devotion; sometimes he feels less. This happens because he lives in the midst of 'woman and gold'. Sometimes a householder contemplates God or chants His name, and sometimes he diverts his mind to 'woman and gold'. He is like an ordinary fly, which now sits on a sweetmeat and now on filth or rotting sores.

"But it is quite different with sannyāsis. They are able to fix their minds on God alone, completely withdrawing them from 'woman and gold'. They can enjoy the Bliss of God alone. A man of true renunciation cannot enjoy anything but God. He leaves any place where people talk of worldly things; he listens only to spiritual talk. A man of true renunciation never speaks about anything but God. The bees light only on flowers, in order to sip honey; they do not enjoy anything else."[63]

Here are some more examples of Ramakrishna's unforgetable teachings :

1. As many faiths so many paths.
2. God dwells in all beings, but all beings do not identify themselves with God, so they suffer.
3. The Sun may shine equally everywhere, but it reflects more clearly in clean water, mirrors, and other transparent objects. Similarly, God may dwell in every heart, but He manifests more completely in the hearts of holy people.
4. When shall I be free? When 'I' ceases to be. If 'I' wants to remain, let it stay as a servant - I of God.
5. Let the boat be in the water, but not water in the boat. Let a spiritual aspirant live in the world, but not let worldliness enter inside him.

6. One who eats radish belches radish; one who eats cucumber belches cucumber. What is inside of a person comes out through his or her speech.
7. As long as I live so long do I learn.
8. An empty stomach is not good for religion.

The Master occasionally repeated almost the same words for two reasons firstly, in order to emphasize the importance of the matter concerned e.g. synthesis of religions, caste-distinction, consistent austerity, discrimination and renunciation, true devotion, earnest eagerness to know God etc. Secondly, there was a constant flow of new comers who were eager to hear Sri Ramakrishna. His valuable teachings are still relevant today and will be so in the days to come.

The Master seldom quoted the scriptures rather he taught from his profound spiritual realization and personal experience. He included anecdotes from everyday life, scientific reasoning, examples from nature as well as the behaviour of humans and animals. As a result, his teachings are practical and universal and of course free from doctrines and dogmas.

Use of simplest language, dialect, example, simile, fable, folk-tale, myth, parable and blend of convincing explanation and emotion, song and dance in ecstasy made his lessons impressive, lucid and acceptable. His teachings suit any temperament.

Leo Tolstoy an eminent Russian novelist and social reformer, on reading the book '*Shri Ramakrishna, Paramahamsa's* Sayings' in English, with interest, exclaimed : "Wonderful saying! ... A remarkable sage." (Great Thinkers on Ramakrishna-Vivekananda, R.M.I.C. Kol. P. 33)

Swamiji said to his brother-monk Swami Ramakrishnananda, 'Not one word of his proves untrue.' (Works, Vol. 6, P. 284)

An exceptional teacher :

Swamiji wrote in Bhakti-yoga : "Higher and nobler than all ordinary ones, is another set of teachers, the Avataras of Ishvara, in the world. They can transmit spirituality with a touch, even with a mere wish. The lowest and the most degraded characters become in one second saints at their command. They are the teachers of all teachers, *the highest manifestations* of God through man..."

Sri Ramakrishna was one of the great teachers of all teachers. As a guru he was in a class of his own. Swami Chetanananda rightly pointed out, "We can read in the scriptures or in the lives of the mystics about the aspirants' longing for God but never about God's longing for the aspirants." (God lived with them, P. 16) Sri Ramakrishna reminisced, "There was no limit to the longing I felt at that time. During the day-time I somehow managed to control it. The secular talk of the worldly-minded was galling to me, and I would look wistfully to the day when my own beloved companions would come. I hoped to find solace in conversing with them and relating to them my own realizations. Every little incident would remind me of them, and thoughts of them wholly engrossed me. I was already arranging in my mind what I should say to one and give to another, and so on. But when the day would come to a close I would not be able to curb my feelings. The thought that another day had gone by, and they had not come, oppressed me. When during the evening service, the temples rang with the sounds of bells and conch-shells, I would climb to the roof of the Kuthi in the garden and, writhing in anguish of heart, cry at the top of my voice : 'Come, my children! Oh, where are you? I cannot bear to live without you.' A mother never longed so intensely for the sight of her child, nor a friend for his companions, nor a lover for his sweet heart, as I longed for them. Oh, it was indescribable! Shortly after this period of yearning the devotees began to come."

There were two categories of disciples–young men, some of whom became monks afterwards and male and female householder devotees. Naturally he had two types of teaching. One was for his would-be monastic disciples or 'Antarangas' and the other was for the householder devotees or 'Bahirangas'. Before accepting his disciples into his inner-circle he tested their genuineness using diverse methods.

Swami Premananda recollected, "His teachings to the monastic disciples were given in private. As soon as the householder devotees would leave the room, he would get up and lock the door and then speak to us living words of renunciation. He would try to impress upon our young minds the emptiness and vanity of worldly enjoyments."[64]

We should note the very phrase "living words' those would come out not of the lips of the master but from the core of his heart with cordial affection and touching earnestness.

His method of imparting lessons to them was also original. He did not conform to the usual stereotype of teaching. He did not teach through books or through any set curriculum. He had the superhuman power of reading the thoughts of the devotees and knowing their inmost souls, their past trend and future possibilities. He understood short-coming and limitations of them, group-dynamics and realized that what is good for one may be bad for another. He guided the eating and sleeping habits and manners of his intimate disciples. Because self-control and perseverance are essential to spiritual life and only a good student can be a good teacher. He did not allow Niranjan to take so much ghee (clarified butter), Baburam to eat more than four pieces of chapati and Latu to sleep in the evening. He told the Holy Mother how many pieces of bread should be given to each disciple.

He would select a particular yoga most suitable to the temperament of an individual monastic disciple and send them to different temples or spots in the temple-garden of Dakshineswar to practise meditation in order to awaken their spiritual power. Again his instructions varied according to the temperaments of the aspirants. He taught men and women of tender nature to be stern and those of opposite nature to be tender, Swami Saradananda in his magnum-opus 'Sri Ramakrishna the great Master' narrated in details (pp 1103 – 1106) how the Master had scolded soft-hearted would-be monk Yogin for setting a cockroach free instead of killing it and thus violating the order of the Master and another day for listening to a vicious slander on his Master by a boat-passenger silently without any protest. On the other hand, once the Master came to know that his disciple Niranjan of a harsh temperament, hearing some boat-passengers speak ill of the Master, was ready to retaliate by sinking the boat and the passengers saved their life by begging his pardon. The Master rebuked him, saying, "Anger is a most dangerous and reprehensible sin. Should one be under its spell? The anger of a good man is like a mark on water, which vanishes as soon as it is made. Mean-minded men speak many improper things. If one is to quarrel over them, one has to spend one's whole life that way. Consider such men as no better than insects and be indifferent to their words. Just think what a great wrong you were going to commit under the influence of anger. What offence did the helmsman and oarsmen give you for which you were ready to cause harm even to those poor people?"

The Master demonstrated to them how to meditate and how to practise jnana, karma, bhakti and raja yogas. Besides being an affectionate father he was a friend, philosopher and guide to them and sang, danced, played, made jokes and had fun with them. Sometimes he was strong like a thunder bolt and crushed their egos by rebuking them and other times he was soft as a flower and gladdened and invigorated them with his unselfish love and care. He was never boring or dry.

On July 15, 1885 the Master told M., Balaram Bose and a few other devotees, "Why do I love boys like Purna and Narendra so much? Once, in a spiritual mood, I felt intense love for Jagannāth, love such a woman feels for her sweetheart. In that mood I was about to embrace him, when I broke my arm. It was then revealed to me : 'You have assumed this human body. Therefore establish with human beings the relationship of friend, father, mother, or son.'

"I now feel for Purna and the other young boys as I once felt for Rāmlālā. I used to bathe Rāmlālā, feed Him, put Him to bed, and take Him wherever I went. I used to weep for Rāmlālā. Now I have the same feeling for these young boys..."

Sri Ramakrishna took great pleasure of feeding his would-be monastic disciples and sleeping with them.

The words of Sri Ramakrishna were so impressive and convincing that Tarak (later Swami Shivananda) felt tempted to take notes of his conversations. One day at Dakshineswar he was listening to him and looking at his face intently. The Master suddenly said to him, "Look here! Why are you listening so attentively? You don't have to do that. Your life is different."

Tarak was the first among the disciples of Sri Ramakrishna to renounce worldly attachments in quest of God. So the Master did not approve of taking notes.

Swami Premananda recalled,

> ...Sometimes the Master would entertain us by imitating a dancing girl, placing one hand on his waist and moving his other hand about. Again, through humour, tales and parables, he would explain to us the most intricate philosophies, which were confusing even to scholars. His wonderful skill in teaching left a deep impression on our hearts forever. The Master was adept in explaining the supreme spiritual truths in simple, sweet language.[65]

Sri Ramakrishna believed in the proverb, 'Example is better than precept'. He never inflicted his ideas on anybody, rather made himself an embodiment of renunciation and purity. He did not allow the aspirants to compromise with the fundamental principles of purity and truth. He set forth the monastic ideal for his would-be monastic disciples. On May 25, 1884, he said to Vijaykrishna Goswami, "...The sannyāsi must renounce 'woman and gold' for his own welfare. Even if he is unattached, and consequently not in danger, still, in order to set an example to others, he must not keep 'woman and gold' near him. The sannyāsi, the man of renunciation, is a world teacher. It is his example that awakens the spiritual consciousness of men."

In reference to his Master, Swamiji said, "The only true teacher is he who can convert himself, as it were, into a thousand persons at a moment's notice. The only true teacher is he who can immediately come down to the level of the student, and transfer his soul to the student's soul and see through the student's eyes and hear through his ears and understand through his mind. Such a teacher can really teach and none else. All these negative, breaking-down, destructive teachers that are in the world can never do any good."[66]

Sri Ramakrishna encouraged his disciples to question him and forbade them to follow him blindly. "Test me as the money-changers test coins,' said he. 'Before you decide to accept a guru watch him by day and by night." He was perhaps the only teacher in the world who would talk twenty hours in the twenty-four, and that not for one day, but for months and months till the end of his life. Ignoring unbearable pain and physical weakness the Master went on teaching and would say, "While I can speak, I must teach them."

The Master taught his disciples through his life, not merely through knowledge acquired from scriptures. So living with him was a great teaching. He used to keep a watchful eye over his would-be monastic disciples and protect them from harmful influences. He used to say about Baburam's purity, "He is pure, pure to the very marrow of his bones." One day at Dakshineswar he said to Baburam, "I can't touch you today. Did you do anything wrong?" Baburam replied, "No, Sir." "Then why can't I touch you?" –retorted the Master. Later on Baburam recalled that while chatting with his friends in the morning he told a lie and confessed it to the Master.

The Master gave his would-be monastic disciples spiritual instructions and would send them to different areas in the temple garden to practise meditation at night. One day Rakhal (Swami Brahmananda) saw the Master singing the same for more than an hour before Latu (Swami Adbhutananda). Another day he saw him fanning Latu bathed in perspiration during deep mediation in one of the Shiva temples. Swami Brahmananda remarked, "Thus even through songs he would transmit spiritual power to us."[67]

Swamiji wrote to his brother-disciple Swami Shivananda from the U.S.A. in 1894 : "... You must let people find out for themselves what he used to teach—"

In his famous lecture on his Master Swamiji summed up the message of Shri Ramakrishna to the modern world :

> Do not care for doctrines, do not care for dogmas, or sects, or churches, or temples ; they count for little compared with the essence of existence in each man, which is spirituality; and the more this is developed in a man, the more powerful is he for good. Earn that first, acquire that, and criticise no one, for all doctrines and creeds have some good in them. Show by your lives that religion does not mean words, or names or sects, but that it means spiritual realization. Only those can understand who have felt. Only those who have attained to spirituality can communicate it to others, can be great teachers of mankind. They alone are the powers of light...
>
> Therefore my Master's message to mankind is : "Be spiritual and realize truth for yourself."

The Master pointed out the inaccessible path of both external and internal renunciation to the would-be monastic disciples and told them that those who would be teachers would have to study scriptures too.

To emphasize the harmony of various paths to God, Sri Ramakrishna said to his young disciples, "Don't be one-sided. Our attitude towards the Lord must by symphonic in nature, made up of many instruments. It is a feast of many dishes."

While teaching the young men destined to be monks the Master did not allow householder devotees to stay there.

There were a good number of householder devotees of Sri Ramakrishna. They followed his teachings. The householders are obliged to take care of their families and practise spiritual discipline simultaneously. The Master prescribed no hard and fast rule of renunciation for them. He wanted them to discharge their responsibilities and duties for their family. He advised them to perform their worldly obligations with one hand, and hold to God with the other, and pray to God to make their duties fewer and fewer so that in the long run they might cling to Him with both hands.

On October 22, 1885 Sri Ramakrishna said to Ishan (Ishan Chandra Mukhopadhyay), a householder devotee : "Blessed indeed is the householder who performs his duties in the world, at the same time cherishing love for the Lotus Feet of God. He is indeed a hero. He is like a man who carries a heavy load of two mounds on his head and at the same time watches a bridal procession. One can not lead such a life without great spiritual power. Again, such a man is like the mudfish, which lives in the mud but is not stained by it. Further, such a householder may be compared to a waterfowl. It is constantly diving under water ; yet, by fluttering its wings only once, it shakes off all trace of wet.

"But a man must practise some spiritual discipline in order to be able to lead a detached life in the world. It is necessary for him to spend some time in solitude – be it a year, six months, three months, or even one month. In that solitude he should fix his mind on God and pray with a longing heart for love of God. He should also say to himself : There is nobody in this world who is my own. Those whom I call my own are here only for two days. God alone is my own. He alone is my all in all. Alas, how shall I realize Him?

> One can live in the world after acquiring love of God. It is like breaking the jack-fruit after rubbing your hands with oil; the sticky juice of the fruit will not smear them.

The Master taught that renunciation of the householders was to be mental. They could not attain spiritual life by escaping responsibilities. He said (on October 26, 1884) to Mahimacharan Chakraborty, "In the world a man must fight against passions like lust and anger, against many desires, against attachment. It is convenient to fight from inside a fort– from his own home. At home he gets his food and other help from his wife. In the Kaliyuga the life of a man depends entirely on food. It is better to get food at one place than to knock at seven doors for it. Living at home is like facing the battle from a fort."

Sri Ramakrishna reminded the householder devotees constantly, "First God and then the world." Though married but a life-long celibate and God-man like Sri Ramakrishna cannot be called a devoted bonafide family-man yet his teachings to the householder devotees had a pragmatic approach to the complications and problems in family life.

The words of the Master manifest not only his profound wisdom but his keen observation of the daily life around him also and those are beneficial to all– a mystic, a materialist, an agnostic or a sceptic for those came out of the depth of Truth he realized. Describing the essence of Sri Ramakrishna's instructions as 'intensely mystical and therefore universal', Aldous Huxley in the foreword of the Gospel opined,

> To read through these conversations in which mystical doctrine alternates with an unfamiliar kind of humour, and where discussions of the oddest aspects of Hindu mythology give place to the most profound and subtle utterances about the nature of Ultimate Reality, is in itself a liberal education in humility, tolerance and suspense of judgment.
>
> With reference to the significance of the teachings of his Master, Swamiji said, "The whole world will undoubtedly forget its fights and disputes and be united in a fraternal tie in religious and other matters as a consequence of these teachings."

To note again, the monastic disciples could not prevent their ailing Master form continuous teaching the people. Without the least regard for his health and gnawing pain he said, "I do not care. I will give up twenty thousand such bodies to help even one man. It is glorious to help even one man."[68]

To differentiate between his Master and other teacher Swamiji said,

> To proclaim and make clear the fundamental unity underlying all religions was the mission of my Master. Other teachers have taught special religions which bear their names, but this great teacher of the nineteenth century made no claim for himself. He left every religion undisturbed because he had realised that in reality they are all part and parcel of the one eternal religion.[69]

Rightly has been said in the Gospel, "His very presence was a great teaching; words were superfluous."[70]

On December 14, 1882 Sri Ramakrishna said to Vijay (Vijay Krishna Goswami) "The task of a religious teacher is indeed difficult. One can not teach men without a direct command from God. People won't listen to you if you teach without such authority. Such teaching has no force behind it. One must first of all attain God through spiritual discipline or some other means. Thus armed with authority from God, one can deliver lectures."

Telling a story about a bullfrog and a water-snake the Master added, "A man's ego is destroyed after three croaks, as it were, if he gets into the clutches of a real teacher. But if the teacher is an 'unripe' one, then both the teacher and the disciple undergo endless suffering. The disciple cannot get rid either of his ego or of the shackles of the world. If a disciple falls into the clutches of an incompetent teacher, he doesn't attain liberation." A real teacher the Master as 'a cobra' (of the story) seized the croaks of egotism of his monastic disciples and even most of his household disciples as well.

Swami Saradananda, one of his direct disciples, wrote in his magnum opus 'Sri Ramakrishna The Great Master', "The Master's teaching did not end with merely giving instructions to the disciple. He would keep the disciple with him, make him in all respects his own through love and affection and then give him instructions. Even at that, the Master would not stop. He would keep a keen eye on how far the disciple carried them into practice; and if the disciple acted by mistake contrary to his instructions, he would correct him by pointing it out to him."

Describing Sri Ramakrishna as 'the Great Master among all Masters' and referring to his method of teaching and ambrosial words Swami Saradananda said, "... we find now how unique the method of his teaching was. In it there was no parade of scholarship, logic-chopping, nor festooning of fine phrases, neither was there in it any attempt to cause a small idea look big with turgid words; nor, as with the writers of philosophical aphorisms, an effort to express the deepest thoughts in the fewest possible words making them unintelligible. We cannot say whether the Master, who was the living embodiment of the ideas he expressed, paid any attention at all to the language he used. But, whoever have heard him speak even once have noticed how he held before them picture after picture drawn from the materials of daily occurrence, from the things and events and audience were familiar with, in order to imprint these ideas on their minds. The listeners also became fully freed from doubts and perfectly satisfied with the truth of his words, as if they saw them enacted before their very eyes. Going on to inquire how those pictures came immediately to his mind, we consider as the cause of his extraordinary memory, his wonderful comprehension, his keen power of observation or his uncommon presence of mind. But the Master always said that the divine Mother's grace was the only cause of it....

"Another peculiar characteristic that was observed in the Master's method of teaching was that he never confused the mind of his hearer by speaking unnecessary words. He discerned aright the subject and the aim of the inquirer's question and answered it in a few homely sentences giving the conclusion and by way of illustrations drawing pictures before him in the aforesaid manner. We call this the especial characteristic of his method of teaching "the statement of the conclusion"; for he used to state as answer only that which he knew as true in his heart of hearts. ...If, on account of past education and impressions, any hearer brought forward contrary reasons and arguments and would not accept his conclusions, which he knew by Sadhana as true, he would wind up the topic saying, "I have said whatever came to mind; take as much or as little of it as you like (or, literally translated, accept it minus the head and tail)" (p. 996–999).

Girish Chandra Ghosh pointed out a unique method of teaching of the Master. Girish Chandra's nature from his boyhood was to do that what was supposed to be prohibited. Sri Ramakrishna did not forbid him to do any work for a single day and this absence of prohibition acted as strictures on him. He admitted. The Master said to Jogin (later Swami Jogananda), "You saw his bad side, how he scolded me. Did you not also see his good side– how much love and devotion he had for me and how he bowed down to me? Girish is in a special class of devotee– a very high class– but his path is different from yours." He criticised or condemned no one, but saw the good in all.

Sri Ramakrishna did not like to interfere in other's freedom or emotion or to thrust his ideas upon anyone. If anybody owing to his acquired education or prejudice would argue with him instead of accepting his wise solution, he was not offended rather suggested to consider his words leaving head and tail.

Sri Ramakrishna never imposed constraints on his would-be monastic disciples. Rather he tried to help them develop their true religious senses and their own true and highest individuality. He never said to them, 'You ought to give yourselves to me.' Herein lies one of the fundamental differences between his teaching and that of Jesus Christ.

In March 1905 during his short stay in Rangoon (Yangon) Swami Ramakrishananananda one day met an Irish Buddhist monk who asked him about the specialty of Sri Ramakrishna's teaching. The Swami replied : "He realized and preached the harmony of religions. Buddha, Christ, Muhammad and other world teachers— each proclaimed that the religion taught by him is the only way to salvation. The difference between Sri Ramakrishna and other prophets is that he himself preached no new religion, but practised all religions in his life and experienced the universal truth underlying them all. His message can be summed up in the sentence : 'As many faiths so many paths.'"

Arnold Joseph Toynbee said, "Sri Ramakrishna's message was unique in being expressed in action....

"In the Atomic Age the whole human race has a utilitarian motive for following this Indian way. No utilitarian motive could be stronger or more respectable in itself. The survival of the human race is at stake. Yet even the strongest and most respectable utilitarian motive is only a secondary reason for taking Ramakrishna's and Gandhi's and Ashoka's teaching to heart and acting on it. The primary reason is that this teaching is right– and is right because it flows from a true vision of spriritual reality." [Swami Gahanananda, Sri Ramakrishna and his Unique Message (Ramakrishna Vedanta Centre, London, 1970) Foreword, vii–ix]

Swami Chetanananda observed, "To me, Sri Ramakrishna is like a chandelier and his disciples and devotees are like bulbs of different wattages radiating the light, or wisdom, of their Master...

"Among the sixteen monastic disciples, five went to college (two graduated), ten did not finish their formal education, and one was completely unlettered– but all of them learned from their guru true spirituality, which no educational institution could provide. Sri Ramakrishna was an extraordinary teacher and his methods were unique. Through his subtle spiritual influence, he enflamed his disciples' hearts, thereby creating hunger and passion for God. As a result, they became so inebriated with divine bliss that almost forgot the world. Recognizing each disciple's uniqueness, Sri Ramakrishna made each one a role model and an ideal spiritual teacher in his own right."[71]

The holy life of Sri Ramakrishna was a living illustration of the ideas that he preached. Swamiji wrote to the members of the Alambazar Math,

> The truth about it is that in point of character, Paramahamsa Deva beats all previous records; and as regards teaching, he was more liberal, more original, and more progressive than all his predecessors. In other words, the older Teachers were rather one-sided, while the teaching of this

> new incarnation or teacher is that the best point of Yoga, devotion, knowledge, and work must be combined now so as to form a new society.... The older ones were no doubt good, but this is the new religion of this age– the synthesis of Yoga, knowledge, devotion, and work– the propagation of knowledge and devotion to all, down to the very lowest, without distinction of age or sex. The previous Incarnations were all right, but they have been synthesised in the person of Ramakrishna. (Works, Vol. 7, p. 496)

Sister Nivedita commented in her introduction to the *complete works of Swami Vivekananda* (Vol. 1, p. X) : Never may we allow it to be forgotten that on Indian soil first was heard the command from a Teacher to His disciples. "Go ye out into all the world and preach the Gospel to every creature!"

Impressive articulation :

The reputed French actor, Coquelin has said, "Articulation is the courtesy of the actor as punctuality is the courtesy of kings." (Articulation, A.M. Henderson)

The Master's art of speaking virtually was of his own. While advising the devotees he used to tell myths, parables, folk tales and fables in simple language with a flavour of dialect and his village accent. He would cite examples to support his arguments. Thus those what he said were lucid, interesting and convincing. The listeners felt an urge to hear him again. Not only the laymen but reputed personalities nurtured by western education and ideas namely M. (Mahendranath Gupta) Dr. Ramchandra Datta, Dr. Mahendralal Sarkar and his son Dr. Amritalal Sarkar, Ishan Chandra Mukhopadhyay, Surendranath Mitra, Dr. Rajendralal Gupta, Jadu Mallick, Bhabanath Chattopadhyay and spititual luminaries for example, Keshab Chandra Sen, Vijay Krishna Goswami, Shibnath Shastri, Pratapchandra Majumdar also were captivated by his talks. On October 25, 1885 Dr. Sarkar told M. that he had waked at three in the morning and had been thinking of the Paramahamsa ever since and added, "You don't know how much money I am losing every day. Everyday I miss two or three calls." Dr. Sarkar said to the Master, "Nobody can beat you in talk!"

In his teachings aforesaid the charm of lucidity and sharpness is evident. Here is another example of the same. Regarding observance of caste system the Master said to Aswini Kumar Dutta, "How can I say yes? I ate curry at Keshab Sen's house. Let me tell you what once heppened to me. A man with a long beard brought some ice here, but I didn't feel like eating it. A little later some one brought me a piece of ice from the same man, and I ate it with great relish. You see, caste restrictions fall away of themselves. As coconut and palm trees grow up, the branches drop off of themselves. Caste conventions drop off like that. But don't tear them off as those fools do."

Aswini Kumar asked the Master, "What is the difference between a Hindu and a Brahmo?" The Master replied, "There is not much difference. In the serenade we have here, one flutist plays a single note right along, while another plays various melodies. The Brahmos play one note, as it were; they hold to the formless aspect of God. But the Hindus bring out different melodies; that is to say, they enjoy God in his various aspects."[72]

Definitions or explanations given by Sri Ramakrishna were short but sound. On January 1, 1883 a Marwari devotee asked him, "Sir, what is the way?" The Master replied, "There are two ways. One is the path of discrimination, the other is that of love...."

On May 24, 1884 the Actor who played the part of vidya well in the *Vidyāsundar* play staged in the Natmandir at Dakshineswar, asked the Master, "Sir, what is the difference between lust and desire?" The Master replied, "Lust is like the root of the tree and desires are branches and twigs."

The Master told the Actor, "Live in the world but keep the pitcher steady on your head; that is to say, keep the mind firmly on God...

In Kamarpukur I have seen the women of carpenter families making flattened rice with a husking-machine. One woman kicks the end of the wooden beam, and another woman, while nursing her baby, turns the paddy in the mortar dug in the earth. The second woman is always alert lest the pestle of the machine should fall on her hand. With the other hand she fries the soaked paddy in a pan. Besides, she is talking with customers; she says : 'You owe us so much money. Please pay it before you go.' Likewise, do your different duties in the world, fixing your mind on God. But practice is necessary, and one should also be alert. Only in this way can one safeguard both– God and the world....

"For this reason a man cannot comprehend spiritual things with his ordinary intelligence. To understand them he must live in the company of holy persons. You learn to feel the pulse by living with a physician."

The Actor admitted that he had understood. The Master persuaded :

> You must practise tapasya. Only then can you attain the goal. It will avail you nothing even if you learn the texts of the scriptures by heart. You cannot become intoxicated by merely saying 'siddhi' over and over. You must swallow some.
>
> One cannot explain the vision of God to others. One cannot explain conjugal happiness to a child five years old.

On June 30, 1884 the Master said to the Pundit (Shashadhar) : "What is samadhi? It is the complete merging of the mind in God-Consciousness...."

On October 29, 1885 the Master said to Shyam Basu, a devotee, "... To know many things is ignorance. To know that God dwells in all beings is knowledge. And what is Vijnāna? It is to know God in a special manner, to converse with Him and feel Him to be one's own relative.

"To know that there is fire in wood is knowledge. But to make a fire with that wood, cook food with that fire, and become healthy and strong from that food is Vijnāna."

Owing to non-attachment to enjoyment and pleasure the Master's senses, mind and intellect were keener than those of ordinary people. He tried to make the hearers understand intricate spiritual truths with the help of suitable illustrations, metaphors and examples. According to the Sankhya philosophy Purusha is a non-doer and Prakriti does everything though not independently. Purusha looks on all the doings of Prakriti as a witness. Sensing the inability of the audience to grasp the truth, he compared Purusha with the master in a marriage house smoking and giving orders and Prakriti with the mistress running to and fro and supervising everything, welcoming the lady guests and reporting to her husband. All could understand the exposition of the Sankhya philosophy and laughed to hear the Master's words.

To explain the identity of Brahman and Maya the Master said, "Take for example a snake, now in motion, now at rest. When it is lying motionless, it is compared to Purusha. Prakriti is then united with Purusha and has become one with it. And when the snake is in motion, Prakriti is, as it were, separated from Purusha and is working." The listeners said to themselves, "Ah! Why could we not understand this simple thing?"

In answer to the question, 'Is Isvara bound by Maya like ourselves, inasmuch as Maya is His Power and exists in Him?' Sri Ramakrishna said, " No, my children, though Maya belongs to Isvara and always exists in Him, He is never bound by it. Consider, whoever is bitten by snake dies; poison is always there in the mouth of the snake; the snake always takes its food, gulps in saliva with that food but does not itself die. It is just like that."

It may be noted that Jesus used to explain something with the help of parable.

In a short article entitled, 'A Real Mahâtman' in the leading monthly English journal, *'The Nineteenth Century'* Prof. Max Muller a great well-wisher of India "expressed himself to the effect that this new sage (Sri Ramakrishna) easily won his heart by the originality of his thoughts, couched in novel language and impregnate with fresh spiritual power which he infused into India when she was merely echoing the thoughts of her ancient sages for several centuries past, or, as in recent times, those of Western scholars." (Works, Vol. 4 p. 411)

Prof. Max Muller realized that the fervent love of God has nowhere found a stronger and more eloquent expression than in the utterances of Ramakrishna and could not but quoted a few of those wise sayings in his book, *Ramakrishna : His life and Sayings* (Advaita Ashrama Mayavati) such as—

'Why does the God-lover find such pleasure in addressing the Deity as Mother? Because the child is more free with its mother, and consequently she is dearer to the child than anyone else.'

'Knowledge and love of God are ultimately one and the same. There is no difference between pure knowledge and pure love.'

'Verily, verily, I say unto you, that he who yearns for God, find Him.'

'He who has faith has all, and he who wants faith wants all.'

'As a lamp does not burn without oil, so a man cannot live without God.'

'God is in all men, but all men are not in God : that is the reason why they suffer.'

Romain Rolland has quoted in his book 'The Life of Ramakrishna' the words of an eye-witness Nagendranath Gupta : "His speech was Bengali of a homely kind.... with a slight though delightful stammer; but his words held men enthralled by the wealth of spiritual experience, the inexhaustible store of simile and metaphor, the unequalled powers of observation, the bright and subtle humour, the wonderful catholicity of sympathy and the ceaseless flow of wisdom."

Keshab Chandra Sen commented in the 'Indian Mirror' on March 28, 1875 : 'The never-ceasing metaphors and analogies in which he indulged, are most of them as apt as they are beautiful.'

Swami Nikhilananda made a wise comment in the preface of 'The Gospel of Sri Ramakrishna' :

"Human language is an altogether inadequate vehicle to express supersensuous perception. Sri Ramakrishna was almost illiterate. He never clothed his thoughts in formal language. His words sought to convey his direct realization of Truth. His conversation was in a village patois. Therein lies its charm. In order to explain to his listeners an abstruse philosophy, he, like Christ before him, used with telling effect homely parables and illustrations, culled from his observation of the daily life around him.

...The words of Sri Ramakrishna have already exerted a tremendous influence in the land of his birth. Savants of Europe have found in his words the ring of universal truth."

Swamiji said to his disciple Sharat Chandra Chakravarty : 'The universal teachings that he offered, if spread all over the world, will do good to humanity and the world. Not for many a century past has India produced so great, so wonderful, a teacher of religious synthesis.' (Works, Vol. 6 p. 465)

A magnetic personality :

There goes a proverb, 'Morning shows the day.' At the age of six or seven Gadadhar, while walking along a narrow path between paddy-fields at Kamarpukur, saw a flight of snow-white cranes passing in front of a beautiful dark thunder-cloud and overwhelmed by the beauty of the contrast he fell to the ground, unconscious. It was his first experience of spiritual ecstasy. The boy who was so soft hearted and thoughtful, turned to be a hard nut to crack at the age of nine by accepting a meal prepared by his nurse Dhani, daughter of a sudra (blacksmith) the lowest of the four Hindu castes to keep his promise in the teeth of strong opposition during the ceremony of investiture. A boy with such a fire within, when grew old did not compromise with the basic principles of purity or truth.

It mattered nothing whether the Master was clothed or not. Seated on the cot naked he once asked the visitor Aswini Kumar Dutta if he considered him ungentlemanly. Aswini Kumar replied, "Of course not. You are a perfect gentleman...."

The Master convinced sceptics, materialists, agnostics and atheists by his rational words, spiritual power and magnanimous personality.

Distinguished American journalist Louis Fischer in his book 'Gandhi– His Life and Message for the World', said,

> Close informal proximity at talks, walks, and meals with this man four-fifths naked was least conducive to awe or veneration, yet for that very reason it brought out the miracle of his personality with a mighty impact. All the props of the big man's impressiveness –the palace or historic mansion, the guards, the wait in the antechamber, the closed door about to open, the power of the office– were lacking. Gandhi's on-the-earth simplicity, devoid of the appearances or reality of power, emphasized his authority. ...Living with him one could see why he was loved : he loved. Not merely in isolated incidents, but day in, and day out, morning, noon and night, for decades, in every act and word, he had manifested his love of individuals and of mankind.

These words are applicable to Sri Ramakrishna too.

Most of the people who came into contact with him, fell under his spell.

The Master apparently looked a mixture of opposites. He could give away a singer his wearing cloth but did not forgo his share of prasad. He once rebuked Jogin (Later Swami Yogananda) for digesting reprehension of his guru. But one day when he heard that Niranjan (Later Swami Niranjanananda) furiously had threatened to capsize a boat for some of its passengers spoke ill of his guru and his monastic brothers; he scolded him saying, "Anger is a deadly sin. You ought never to let it carry you away. The seeming anger of a good man is something different. It's no more than a mark made on water. It vanishes as soon as it's made. As for those mean-minded people who talked against me, they weren't worth getting into a quarrel with–you could waste your whole life in such quarreling.

Think of them as being no more than insects. Be indifferent to what they say. See what a great crime you were about to commit, under the influence of this anger! Think of the poor helmsman and the oarsmen in that boat–you were ready to drown them too, and they had done nothing!"

Sri Ramakrishna was a man of child like nature. He would go to the theatre with his disciples, join them in picnics, play with them or watch their amusing games, as M. recorded in The Gospel of Sri Ramakrishna :

The devotees were engaged in a game of golokdham. Hazra joined them. The Master stood by, watching them play. M. and Kishori reached "heaven". Sri Ramakrishna bowed before them and said, "Blessed are you two brothers." He said to M. aside, "Don't play any more." Hazra fell into "hell". The Master said : "What's the matter with Hazra? Again!" No sooner had Hazra got out of "hell" than he fell into it again. All burst into laughter. Latu at the first throw of the dice went to "heaven" from "earth". He began to cut capers of joy. "See Latu's joy!" said the Master. "He would have been terribly sad if he hadn't achieved this. (Aside to the devotees) This too has a meaning. Hazra is so vain that he thinks he will triumph over all even in this game. This is the law of God, that He never humiliates a righteous person. Such a man is victorious everywhere." (Page 571)

One day he said to Vijay Krishna Goswami and an official of the temple, "Look, Keshab has offered flowers at my feet and requested me not to tell anyone. Please don't tell it to others." Even while suffering from terminal cancer, he one day said to Niranjan, "You are my father, I shall sit on your lap." But at the same time he was uncompromising and strict about spiritual activities and discipline of his disciples.

Humour breaks the barrier of age and removes monotony and sorrow from life. Sri Ramakrishna had natural feminine grace and a keen sense of humour. The women of Kamarpukur enjoyed not only the songs, acting or recitation of boy Gadadhar but his knack of imitating voices also. In Dakshineswar while looking at the moon, his feet tripped over a railing and his arm was broken. Dr. Madhusudan set it with a splint and put a bandage around it. When the devotees came to see him, he jokingly said to them, 'Hello, Ram says that I am a avatar. What do you say? Have you ever heard that an avatar's arm had been broken?"

When Tarak (later Swami Shivananda) told the Master that by his mere wish he could be cured; the addressee replied, "No. Suffering from this affliction is good, for those who come here with desires will see the condition I am in and will go away. They won't bother me." Then he said, "Mother, you played a clever trick."

Like St. Francis who started a religious organization in Italy in 1209, Sri Ramakrishna believed that everybody should turn a smiling face to God and to humanity. He taught his monastic disciples that humour too has its role in religion. He did not care for "dry monks".

On December 14, 1884 Sri Ramakrishna accompanied by M., Baburam, Narayan and other devotees saw a play about the life of Prahlāda at the Star Theatre in Calcutta. When he was seated in the Manager's room, a man entered and said, "Will you see the farce, 'The confusion of Marriage'? It is being played now."

The Master said to Girish Chandra, "What have you done? This farce after the life of Prahlāda! First sweets and rice pudding and then a dish of bitter herbs!"

On February 22, 1885 Girish Chandra said to Sri Ramakrishna, "I am not your equal even in joking." Then the Master said to him, "I once went to Jaygopal Sen's garden house wearing a red-bordered cloth. Keshab was there. Looking at the red borders Keshab said : 'What's this? Such a flash of colour today! Such a display of red borders!' I said, 'I have to cast a spell on Keshab; hence this display."

On a Summer's day in 1880 Ramachandra Dutta and his cousin Manomohan Mitra visited Keshab Chandra Sen at his house Kamal Kutir and asked him about his impression of Sri Ramakrishna. Keshab Chandra told them that Paramahamsa of Dakshineswar was not an ordinary man; there was no such a great man as he in the world then. He was such a beautiful and extraordinary person who deserved to be kept carefully and very cautiously such as a pretty and precious object was to preserve in a glass case. In the event of lack of care his body would not last.

His disciples reminisced about how they would enjoy fun and frolic with the Master and regard him as their friend and playmate, but afterwards would quiver to think of their frivolities in the presence of such a great personality.

The Master's dealing with drunkard Girishchandra Ghosh and Kalipada Ghosh (Danakali) testifies to his sweetness of temper, his forbearance and paternal love. He tackled the malicious or peevish persons or men like the dry pundit of Bhadrakali with irrefutable words and presence of mind.

He made a number of unparalleled proverbial or witty remarks e.g. : "As many faiths so many paths." With reference to ego the Master said to Keshab Chandra Sen, "...You may wash seven times a cup that onions have been kept in, but the wretched smell never leaves it."

Swami Vivekananda said, "People came by thousands to see and hear this wonderful man who spoke in a *patois* every word of which was forceful and instinct with light. For it is not what is spoken, but it is the personality of the speaker which dwells in everything he says that carries weight. Every one of us feels this at times. ...The words of a man who can put his personality into them take effect, but he must have tremendous personality."[73]

Even Pratap Chandra Mazumdar, one of the most outspoken critics of Sri Ramakrishna could not but extolled the Master's personality in an article published in the 'Theistic Quarterly Review' :

> What is there in common between him and me? I, a Europeanized, civilized, self-centred, semi-sceptical, so-called educated reasoner, and he, a poor, illiterate, unpolished, half-idolatrous, friendless Hindu devotee? Why should I sit long hours to attend to him, I, who have listened to Disraeli

> and Fawcett, Stanley and Max Muller, and a whole host of European scholars and divines? ...And it is not I only, but dozens like me, who do the same.... He worships Siva, he worships Kāli, he worships Rāma, he worships Krishna, and is a confirmed advocate of Vedāntic doctrines. ...He is an idolater, yet is a faithful and most devoted meditator on the perfections of the One Formless, Absolute, Infinite Deity... His religion is ecstasy, his worship means transcendental insight, his whole nature burns day and night with a permanent fire and fever of a strange faith and feeling... So long as he is spared to us, gladly shall we sit at his feet to learn from him the sublime precepts of purity, unworldliness, spirituality and inebriation in the love of God. ...He, by his child-like bhakti, by his strong conceptions of an ever-ready Motherhood, helped to unfold it [God as our Mother] in our minds wonderfully. ...By associating with him we learnt to realize better the divine attributes as scattered over the three hundred and thirty millions of deities of mythological India, the gods of the Purānas.

From the Rani and dignitaries to lay-men of the society–all and sundry could not but bowed down before this magnanimous and towering personality. Describing Sri Ramakrishna as 'Child of Nature', Dr. Mahendralal Sarkar said, 'As a man I have the greatest regard for him.' In one of his famous lectures on his Master Swamiji said, "The life of Sri Ramakrishna is interesting, as it was a living illustration of the ideas that he preached.,"

An architect of a spiritual movement :

On April 5, 1884 Girindranath Mitra, one of the householder devotees said to Sri Ramakrishna, "The Brahmos say that the Paramahamsadeva has no faculty for organization."

Master : 'What does that mean?"

M : "That you don't know how to lead a sect; that your intellect is rather dull. They say things like that." (All laugh)

History also laughed that day for the pitiable Brahmos did not know that an international organization would be set up and named after Paramahamsadeva in the near future and that he himself would be the pioneer of that highly esteemed organization.

When Narendra (later known as Swami Vivekananda) first visited Dakshineswar, the Master, with tearful eyes, said to him, "You've come so late! Was that proper? Couldn't you have guessed how I've been waiting for you? My ears are nearly burned off, listening to the talk of these worldly people. I thought I should burst, not having anyone to tell how I really felt." Then he with folded hands, said, "I know who you are, my Lord. You are Nara, the ancient sage, the incarnation of Narayana. You have come to earth to take away the sufferings and sorrows of mankind."[74]

He was not hesitant to show his favour to Narendra and was eager to make people near and far acquainted with his ideas and messages for their welfare with the help of a band of his monastic disciples led by this most beloved youth of marvellous potentiality. He intended to make him his spiritual heir who would continue the work after his passing.

Two days before passing away Sri Ramakrishna said to Narendra, "I leave these young men in your charge. See that they develop their spirituality and do not return home."

In India it is the custom of monks to beg their food from house holders. In preparation for a monastic life, one day the Master asked the boys to beg their food from door to door irrespective of caste and creed. They left with begging-bowls to carry out the significant order. A few days later Gopal Chandra Ghosh, a disciple of Sri Ramakrishna who called him 'the elder Gopal' or 'Overseer' (later Swami Advaitananda) in order to acquire virtue bought twelve pieces of cloth those he himself dyed in the ochre colour and twelve rosaries of rudraksha beads to distribute among the monks going to Gangasagar (the confluence of the Ganga and the Bay of Bengal) for a holy bath on the auspicious day of *makar sankranti* (in the middle of January). Learning about it the Master said to Gopal, "You will attain a thousand times more virtue if you present those ochre cloths and rosaries to my children rather than giving them to the monks of Jagannath ghat. Where else will you find such all-renouncing monks? Each of them is equal to a thousand monks."

Accordingly on 12 January 1886 Gopal gave the ochre cloths and rosaries to Sri Ramakrishna. Sanctifying them with a mantram the Master himself offered them to his eleven disciples–Narendra, Rakhal, Jogindra, Baburam, Niranjan, Tarak, Sharat, Shashi, Gopal, Kali and Latu. They put on the ochre cloths, and fell prostrate before the Master who was happy to see them in monastic attire and blessed them. The twelfth cloth and rosary, according to his instruction, were set aside for Girish Chandra who late touched them to his head and felt the Master's blessing. By virtue of renunciation, celibacy and spiritual activities the Master's children had been inwardly sannyasin and henceforth they got its glow outwardly.

It may be noted that once Christ chose twelve apostles to tell people about him and his teachings.

Realizing that the Master's days were numbered, Narendra begged him for the experience of nirvikalpa samadhi, the highest realization of Advaita Vedanta. But he got a scolding from him, "Shame on You! You are asking for such an insignificant thing. I thought that you would be like a big banyan tree, and that thousands of people would rest in your shade. But now I see that you are seeking your own liberation. There is a state higher than that. It is you who sing, 'O Lord, Thou art all that exists.' Actually Sri Ramakrishna advised his disciples to see God in all beings and to serve them in a spirit of worship. However, one evening on the ground floor of the garden house at Cossipore Narendra during deep meditation felt as if a lamp were burning behind his head and he lost consciousness and reached the coveted state of nirvikalpa samadhi, while the embodied soul realizes its unity with the Absolute. After a long time regaining partial consciousness he cried, 'Where is my body?' His frightened brother-disciple Gopal (later Swami Advaitananda) rushed upstairs to the Master to report the incident. He only said, "Let him stay that way for a time. He has worried me long enough."

Regaining full consciousness when Narendra went to the Master, he said, "Now the Mother has shown you everything. But this revelation will remain under lock and key, and I shall keep the key. When you have accomplished the Mother's work you will find the treasure again."

Narendranath's pedigree, training and outlook were the opposite of the Master's. Romain Rolland wrote (in his book 'The Life of Vivekananda and the Universal Gospel' Prelude) : "The great disciple whose task it was to take up the spiritual heritage of Ramakrishna and disseminate the grain of his thought throughout the world, was both physically and morally his direct antithesis." Yet considering the potentiality of his foremost disciple Sri Ramakrishna selected him as his effective conduit and transmitted his tremendous divine energy to him.

The prudent Master's transmission of spiritual power into Narendra was the next step of a well thought-out plan. Narendra once in 1901 said to one of his disciples Sharat Chandra Chakravarty, "...two or three days before his leaving the body he called me to his side one day and asking me to sit before him looked steadfastly at me and fell into samadhi. Then I really felt that a subtle force like an electric shock was entering my body! In a little while, I also lost outward consciousness and sat motionless. How long I stayed in that condition I do not remember; when consciousness returned I found Sri Ramakrishna shedding tears. On questioning him, he answered me affectionately : 'Today, giving you my all, I have become a beggar. With this power you are to do many works for the world's good before you will return.' I feel that power is constantly directing me to this or that work. This body has not been made for remaining idle."[75]

In this way Sri Ramakrishna himself laid the foundation of the future Ramakrishna Order of monks informally or indirectly.

When Swami Vivekananda was in America, he felt the need of a monastic Order that would carry the message of Vedanta and spread the ideas and teachings of his Master as well all over the world. Accordingly coming back to India (January 1897) he called a meeting of the monastic and lay devotees of his Master at the Kolkata residence of Balaram Basu on 1 May 1897. He discussed the importance of the establishment of an organization to continue their Vedanta work systematically and properly. He proposed that the organization should 'bear the name of him in whose name we have become sannyasins, taking whom as your ideal you are leading the life of householders, and whose holy name, influence, and teachings have within twelve years of his passing away, spread in such unthought-of ways both in the East and in the West." All the members present accepted the proposal cordially. To sum up the main resolutions passed were :

1. An association is to be founded under the name of the Ramakrishna Mission.
2. Its aim is to preach the truths which Ramakrishna, for the good of humanity, preached and taught by the practice of his own life, and to help others to put them into practice in their lives for their temporal, mental, and spiritual progress.
3. Its duty is to direct in a fitting spirit the activities of this movement, inaugurated by Ramakrishna 'for the establishment of fellowship among the followers of different religions, knowing them all to be only so many forms of one undying Eternal Religion."
4. Its methods of action are : (i) 'to train men so as to make them competent to teach such knowledge or science as are conducive to the material and spiritual welfare of the masses; (ii) to promote and encourage arts and industries'; (iii) to introduce and spread among the people in general Vedantic and other religious ideas as elucidated in the life of Ramakrishna.
5. It was to have two branches of action : The first to be Indian : Maths (monasteries) and Ashramas (convents for retreat) were to be established in different parts of India for the education of Sannyasins and lay brethren (house holders)

'as may be willing to devote their lives to the teaching of others.' The second foreign : it was to send members of the Order into countries outside India for the foundation of spiritual centres, and 'for creating a close relationship and spirit of mutual help and sympathy between the foreign and the Indian centres.'

6. 'The Aims and Ideals of the Mission being purely spiritual and humanitarian, it would have no connection with politics.'

With reference to these resolutions Romain Rolland commented,

> The definitely social, humanitarian, and 'pan human' apostolic nature of the Order founded by Vivekananda is obvious. Instead of opposing, as do most religions, faith to reason and the stress and necessity of modern life, it was to take its place with science in the front rank; it was to co-operate with progress; material as well as spiritual, and to encourage arts and industries. But its real object was the good of masses. It laid down that the essence of its faith was the establishment of brotherhood among the different religions, since their harmony constituted the Eternal Religion. The whole was under the aegis of Ramakrishna, whose great heart had embraced all mankind within its love.[76]

The Ramakrishna Monastery had been shifted from Baranagore to Alambazar in 1892 but in the event of the earthquake on 12 June 1897 causing several damage to the building, it was again moved to the garden house of Nilambar Mukherjee in Belur village in February 1898. A donation of a lump sum of rupees 39,000 by Miss Muller and Mrs. Ole Bull helped Swamiji much to purchase a plot of land on the western bank of the Ganga in Belur and to start construction of the building of the central Math in April, 1898. The dedication took place on 9 December of the same year when Swamiji carrying the urn of relics and photo of his Master on his own shoulder installed those in the shrine. On his way he said to a disciple, "The Master once told me, 'I will go and live wherever you take me, carrying me on your shoulder, be it under a tree or in the humblest cottage.' With faith in that gracious promise I myself am now carrying him to the site of our future Math. Know for certain my boy, that so long as his name inspires his followers with the ideal of purity, holiness, and charity for all men, even so long shall he, the Master sanctify this place with his presence."[77]

It appeared as the headquarters of the Association on January 2, 1899. The Association is divided into two twin institutions, with considerable differences between them : the Ramakrishna Math– a purely monastic body with its Maths and Ashramas dedicated to the maintenance and propagation of the Universal Religion; and the Ramakrishna Mission–governed by the trustees and President of the Math, open to all aspirants and dedicated to all activities of public utility, both charitable and philanthropic.

Thus Sri Ramakrishna's dream has come true under the able leadership of Swamiji. With numerous centres and ceaseless spiritual and multipurpose social-welfare activities the Ramakrishna Math and Mission has become an international organization held in high esteem. To quote Swamiji, 'his Math, which represents the physical body of Ramakrishna'.

Swami Shivananda said to Lady Minto who was under the impression that Swami Vivekananda had founded the Ramakrishna Order, "Neither Vivekananda nor the disciples founded the Order. It was Sri Ramakrishna himself who initiated the Order during his last illness at Cossipore. At that time the Master took Swamiji aside and taught him how to organize and conduct the work, telling him the secrets of the monastic organization to be." (The Life of Swami Vivekananda, His Eastern and Western Disciples, Advaita Ashrama : Calcutta, 1979, 1 : 418)

Progressive out-look :

Sri Ramakrishna taught that one must first experiment with the truth, then verify it, and at last accept it. His disciples learnt a scientific religion from him.

Narendra realized that as long as prejudices persist, Brahman has not been fully realized. So in order to break prejudices of his brother disciples Kali (later Swami Abhedananda), Jogin (later Swami Yogananda) and Tarak (later Swami Shivananda) who had never eaten Muslim food, he took them to a Muslim restaurant on Beadon Street and ordered Chicken curry. After dinner they returned to the garden house at Cossipore. Later that night when Kali told the Master the whole story, he heartily laughed and said, "It is all right. You are now free from all prejudices."

Sri Ramakrishna came to fulfill and not to destroy. So he observed his brahminical caste rules and could not ordinarily eat any food cooked by a nonbrahmin or touched by an impure person. But one day he asked Baburam Ghosh (a nonbrahmin, later Swami Premananda) to cook food for him and he ate from his hand. A day or two before his passing away, he asked all of his monastic disciples to feed him pudding, and thus he withdrew all his restrictions.

Sri Ramakrishna believed in the proverb : 'Example is better than precept.' He was able to carry theory into practice. One day in Dakshineswar the Master saw a woman sweeper carrying on her head a tub of excrement from a privy. He prostrated before her, stretching fully on the ground, saying, "Mother, who can do this work except you?" Another day he requested a Pariah an untouchable to allow him to clean his house. But the Pariah did not allow him because he believed that to permit a Brahmin to do such menial work was an awful sin. The Master entered the house of the Pariah in the dead of night, when all were sleeping and wiped the place with his long hair, saying, "Oh, my Mother, make me the servant of the Pariah, make me feel that I am even lower than the Pariah." In this way the great prophet taught his devotees to love all and not to look down upon anybody.

Sri Ramakrishna had liberal and humanitarian outlook. Regarding the abolition of the caste-system he said (on November 19, 1882) to Surendra's brother, "There is only one way to remove them, and that is by love of God. Lovers of God have no Caste. Through this divine love the untouchable becomes pure, the pariah no longer remains a pariah. Chaitanya embraced all, including the pariahs."

The Master who cleaned the house of his beloved Rasik a sweeper of the Kāli temple of Dakshineswar, had unhesitatingly eaten at the house of non-Brahimin Keshab Chandra Sen or low-caste Hindu Adharlal Sen. Besides, he touched his head and lips with the leaf-plates from which the beggars had eaten their food in the guest-house of the Kāli temple.

The Master was worried not only about the poor citizens of Kolkata or the thirsty villagers of Sikra Kulingram but all the suffering multitudes of the world also.

Sri Ramakrishna considered that we have no right to show mercy to anybody. He discovered vanity, hankering after fame or an attempt to alleviate a guilty conscience in most acts of philanthropy or charity. It was he who first uttered the revolutionary words, perhaps the last words of humanity : Serve Jivas as Siva. He taught, "True charity is the result of love of God–service to man in a spirit of worship."

The Master was eager to have new information or spiritual knowledge from any appropriate source. On June 15, 1884 he said to Pratap Chandra Majumdar, "You have been to England. Tell us what you saw there." On October 5, 1884 he advised Baburam to go to Narayan with one of his English text-books. He was interested in photography, zoo, Asiatic Society's Museum, drama etc.

The teachings of Sri Ramakrishna played a significant role in liberalizing the minds of orthodox hermits and scholars. His manners and opinions were progressive, humane, and not trite.

An unfathomable sublime life :

Sri Ramakrishna was truth and purity personified. As regards character he beat all previous records. All the previous Incarnations had been synthesized in the person of Paramahamsa Deva. In a letter addressed to the members of the Alambazar Math,

Swamiji wrote (from England on April 27, 1896 Works, Vol. 7, pp. 496–497) :

> For the ordinary man and the beginner, steady devotion (Nishthâ) to an ideal is of paramount importance. That is to say, teach them that all great Personalities should be duly honoured, but homage should be paid now to Ramakrishna.... Now we have a new India, with its new God, new religion, and new Vedas.... Well, a little bigotry also is a necessity. But we must harbour no antagonistic feelings towards others.
>
> ...My friends, many have no doubt served the Master, but whenever anyone would be disposed to consider himself an extraordinary personage; he should think that although he has associated with Sri Ramakrishna, has seen only the trash that was uppermost in his mind! Were it not so, he would manifest the results. The Master himself used to quote, "They would sing and dance in the name of the Lord but come to grief in the end." The root of that degeneration is egotism–to think that one is just as great as any other, indeed! ...Bear in mind that through His grace lots of men will be turned out with the nobility of gods —ay, wherever His mercy would drop!

Swami Saradananda said to Swami Shuddhananda (in 1925) : "When I began to write the *Lilaprasanga*, I thought I understood the Master. But now I clearly see that the life of the Master is very deep. I was merely hovering over the top branches; the root is far beneath the ground." (God lived with them, Swami Chetanananda, Advaita Ashrama, Kol. p. 338)

Nothing trifling to the Master :

There go maxims : 'For want of a nail', 'A stich in time saves nine', 'An ounce of prevention is worth a pound of cure' etc. Sri Ramakrishna quite often fell into trance and was unaware of the happenings around him but when his spirit came down the relative plane, he was careful even of so-called trivials.

As he did not forget the balance of the money, he got his dear Jogin (later Swami Yogananda) back. Having been compelled to marry Jogin suffered utter despair and repentance and avoided Sri Ramakrishna who repeatedly summoned him. At last he hit upon a plan. He sent a message to Jogin, "What sort of man are you? A man gave you money to buy certain articles, and you have neither returned the balance nor even sent word when you will return it!" It offended Jogin who in the afternoon went to the Master to pay the dues and then detach all relation with him. The Master said to him, "What if you are married? Haven't I too been married? What is there to be afraid of in that? If you have the grace of this place; even a hundred thousand marriages will be powerless to affect you. If you want to live a family life and realize God at the same time, bring your wife here once. I will make both of you fit for that. And if you want to renounce worldly life and attain God, I'll make that also possible for you." Hearing these words the cloud of grievance and depression hovering in the mind of Jogin dispersed. When Jogin referred to the payment of the balance of the money, Sri Ramakrishna did not bother about it. The spiritual bond between them was reestablished.

While going to Balaram's house from Dakshineswar by carriage the Master learnt that Jogin had forgotten to carry his Master's cloth, he ordered to stop the carriage and bring the cloth lest the host be put to trouble or embarrassment.

One morning Sri Ramakrishna discovered that his share of prasad (food offered to the deities) had not been sent to his room. He was displeased at the irregularity and went to the temple office to inquire about it. The temple Manager immediately sent the Master's portion to his room. Jogin was surprised to see his Master so interested in trifle and misunderstood that he, despite his great spirituality, could not control the petty tendency of his priestly class.

Sri Ramakrishna said to Jogin, "Look here, Rani Rashmani has bequeathed her large estate to the service of this temple so that the offerings may be distributed among devotees and sadhus. That part of the offerings which comes to this room is taken only by devotees who come here with yearning for God, so the gift of Rani Rasmani is turned to good account. But what use is made of the other portion that goes to the priests of this temple? They sell it in the market, and some even feed their mistresses with it! I fight with the temple officials for the share that comes here so that Rasmani's objective may at least be partially fulfilled."[79] Jogin's wrong impression of the Master vanished.

One day the Master heard that Jogin bought an iron pan and returning home he found that the pan had a crack. He said to him "Because you are a devotee of God, does that mean that you should be a fool? Do you think any shopkeeper opens a shop to practise religion? Why did you not examine the pan before you purchased it? Never act so foolishly again. When you go out shopping, first determine the usual price of the item by going around to several shops and then thoroughly examine the thing you want to buy. And do not fail to demand the little extras where allowed."[80] The Master forbade his disciples to believe others blindly and advised them to discriminate both in the spiritual as well as in worldly matters.

Sri Ramakrishna did not indulge in carelessness of any body. According to him if a person is forgetful in minor matters, he will be forgetful in the essential aspects of life. On 25 May 1884 he went to the Panchavati to listen to devotional songs Kirtan. The elder Gopal (later Swami Advaitananda) carried an umbrella for the Master. Owing to torrential rain the Master came back to his room and said to Gopal, "Have you brought the umbrella?" "No Sir, I forgot all about it while listening to the music." —saying this Gopal hurried to the Panchavati and brought back the umbrella. The Master said, "I am generally unmindful about the world, but not to that extent. Rakhal also is very careless. Referring to the date of an invitation, he says, 'the eleventh' instead of 'the thirteenth'. And Gopal–he belongs in a herd of cows!"[81] The Master was careful even about trivial details such as to keep something in a particular place, to form a small conical cup of betel-leaf after putting betel-nut, catechu, lime etc. within this cup. With him, 'cleanliness is next to Godliness'. He used to sweep the floor or act as a gardener.

There are numerous evidences of this kind to show the Master's attention to small things when he was on the sense plane.

No formal initiation :

Sri Ramakrishna did not give any formal initiation to his disciples. He would transmit spiritual power to them in other ways such as whispering a mantram in the ear, or writing a mantram on the tongue, or touching them, or singing an appropriate song, or just through a glance.

Subodh Chandra Ghosh (later Swami Subodhananda) and his friend Kshirod Chandra Mittra fleeing from school rushed to Sri Ramakrishna. Washing his hands with Ganga water, the Master took them to the Shiva temples at the south of his room. He asked them to sit down and himself sat cross-legged on the floor. Then he ordered them to unbutton their shirts and stick out their tongues. He first wrote something with his finger on Kshirod's tongue and stroked his body from the navel to the throat saying, "Awake, Mother, awake!" He did the same to Subodh. Then he bade them meditate.

No sooner did Subodh begin to meditate than his whole body trembled and he felt a current rushing along his spinal column to his brain. He was overwhelmed by joy as he saw forms of numerous gods and goddesses flashed in a strange light within him. Gradually he lost all sense of personal identity. The Master stroked his body in the reverse direction, from the head downwards and Subodh regained consciousness. The Master came to learn that Subodh was able to concentrate so easily because hearing of gods and goddesses from his mother, he used to think a little of them. When Kshirod replied that he neither saw nor felt anything, the Master said, "All right, you will do so later on."

Another incident of initiation was described by Swami Adbhutananda, "Once, before the noon meal, the Master was walking alone in the temple garden of Dakshineswar. Gopal-da took the opportunity to express his desire for initiation to the Master. I saw from a distance that Gopal-da knelt down on the ground and, holding the feet of the Master, began to cry. The Master lifted him up from the ground holding his arms. Gopal-da was still crying profusely. What the Master said to him, I did not hear. Since that time I have noticed Gopal-da chanting God's name every evening in front of the Krishna Temple."[82]

Learning that Hariprasanna (later Swami Vijnanananda) could not concentrate on meditation, the Master wrote something on his tongue. At once the youngman felt a strange sensation and delight.

Metonymy : Self identification in third person instead of first person :

Sometimes in the evening in Dakshineswar Sri Ramakrishna used to repeat "Hari is my guru, my guru is Hari. O Krishna, O Krishna. O Govinda, you are my life and soul. Not I, not I– but Thou, Thou. I am an instrument, you are the operator."

Sri Ramakrishna was able to overcome ego sense completely. As a true nondualist Vedantist he was imbued with collective consciousness. His own ego being virtually eradicated, the ego of Kali, the Mother of the universe would reveal through him in various ways. He could not utter a few self-denoting words namely 'I', 'My' 'Mine' or 'Me'. In that case where people generally say 'my'; the Master placing his palm on the chest would say, 'of this place' to denote the possessive form of I. For example, one day he said to Jogin, "What if you are married? Haven't I too been married? What is there to be afraid of in that? If you have the grace of this place, even a hundred thousand marriages will be powerless to affect you..." One day the Master said to Subodh with a smile, "Some people donate money for this place. You will not have to worry about that. Please take some money and go by carriage." On July 1885 the Master said to M. "Yes Yes! One! One! It is indeed one. Don't you see that it is He alone who dwells here in this way." M. has noted in the Gospel (P. 825), "As he said this, Sri Ramakrishna pointed with his finger to his own body." The Master used to say so because he did not indulge in the slightest 'I' consciousness in him. In fact, after the experience of nirvikalpa sāmadhi, when Sri Ramakrishna's mind finally came down to the relative plane, he was devoid of ideas of 'I' and 'mine' as he realized that it is the one Brahman that manifests Itself through everything. In the event of devastation of the body and mind, he, piercing the spell of narrow egotism attained wider collective consciousness for he was invested with a supreme spiritual power and destined to live for the welfare of mankind.

Incarnation of God : the Master's self-proclamation

Various people, impressed by Sri Ramakrishna's strange personality and divinity, formed different opinions about him. Some Dashanami sadhus regarded him as a Paramahamsa, some Vaishnavas as a Gosain, a group of Kartabhajas as Alekh, Bauls as a Sain and some Sikhs saw in him the image of Guru Nanak and some Christian devotees saw Jesus in him while the Brahmos held that he was a knower of Brahman. A Navarasik group believed that he was an embodiment of the nine sentiments while some thought that he was a great tantric. Some Muslim devotees considered him to be one of them. Totapuri a veteran Vedantist recognised him to be a knower of pure Brahman. According to some others Shri Chaitanya had descended in the form of Shri Ramakrishna.

While explaining the term 'incarnation of God' to a Christian preacher of Bhowanipore, Kolkata and a friend of Sivnath Sastri as well, Sri Ramakrishna said, "Just take the case of the ocean. It is a wide and almost infinite expanse of water. But owing to special causes, in special parts of this wide sea, the water becomes congealed into ice. When reduced to ice it can be easily manipulated and applied to special uses. An incarnation is something like that. Like that infinite expanse of water, there is the Infinite Power, immanent in matter and mind, but for some special purposes in special regions, a portion of that Infinite Power, as it were, assumes a tangible shape in history, that is what you call a great man; but he is properly speaking a local manifestation of the all-pervading

Divine Power, in other words, an incarnation of God. The greatness of great men is essentially the manifestation of divine Energy..."[83]

In the Gita Lord Krishna said :

Whenever there is decline of Dharma, O Arjuna, and uprising of Adharma, then I incarnate myself.

To deliver the good and to destroy the wicked and to establish Dharma, I am born from age to age. [Chapter IV, Verse 7–8] There are references of incarnation of God in the Taittiriya Samhita and Satpatha Brahmana. In the Mahabharata, Buddha was not mentioned among ten incarnations of God. Later in the Puranas his name was also included. There are twenty two incarnations of God in the Bhagavatam and Sri Krishna has been described as God or the Supreme Being Himself and all incarnations are parts of Him.

In 1861 Yogeshwari (popularly known as Bhairabi Brahmani) in orange robe of a nun came to Dakshineswar. She was versed in the Tantrik and Vaishnava methods of worship. Watching Sri Ramakrishna's various physical symptoms, ecstasy during the kirtan and meditation, mahābhāva (the most exalted rapture of divine love), his samādhi, mad yearning for God, a power to transmit spirituality to others etc Yogeshwari declared openly that Sri Ramakrishna, like Sri Chaitanya, was an Incarnation of God. Not only that she asked Mathur to convene a conference of scholars who should discuss the matter with her. Vaishnavcharan Goswami the leader of the Vaishnava society proclaimed in a meeting that Sri Ramakrishna had evidently experienced mahābhāva and that this was the certain sign of the rare manifestation of God in a man. In another meeting (in 1870) Pundit Gauri (Gaurikanta Bhattacharya) agreed with Brāhmani and Vaishnavcharan about their views on Sri Ramakrishna. When Sri Ramakrishna told the Pundit that Vaishnavcharan had declared him to be an Avatār, Gauri replied,

> Is that all he has to say about you? Then he has said very little. I am fully convinced that you are that Mine of Spiritual Power, only a small fraction of which descends on earth, from time to time, in the form of an Incarnation."

> When Sri Ramakrishna asked the Pundit what he had found in him (the speaker) that made him (the addressee) form such an idea; Gauri replied : "I feel it in my heart and I have the scriptures on my side. I am ready to prove it to anyone who challenges me.

The Master accepted those proclamation stoically and said, "Do they think they will enhance my glory that way? ...But that did not make any change in my mind." He was a specially commissioned person whose spiritual realization was for the welfare of humanity.

Pundit Padmalochan, the court pundit of the Maharaja of Burdwan, famous for his scholarship in both the Vedanta and the Nyaya systems of philosophy, proclaimed Sri Ramakrishna an Incarnation of God.

On June 25, 1883 the Master said to M., "...God has different forms, and he sports in different ways. He sports as Iśvara, deva, man, and the universe. In every age He descends to earth in human form, as an Incarnation, to teach people love and devotion. There is the instance of Chaitanya. One can taste devotion and love of God only through His Incarnations. Infinite are the ways of God's play, but what I need is love and devotion. I want only the milk. The milk comes through the udder of the cow. The Incarnation is the udder."

Listening to these words of Sri Ramakrishna M. soliloquized, "Was Sri Ramakrishna hinting that he was an Incarnation of God? Did he suggest that those who saw him saw God? Did he thus speak about himself when speaking of Chaitanya?"

The first two householder devotees to visit Sri Ramakrishna at Dakshineswar were Dr. Ramchandra Dutta and Manomohan Mitra who acknowledged, the Master to be an Incarnation of God. In the biography of Sri Ramakrishna (in Bengali) Ramchandra Dutta wrote '...so he was an Avatar' (P. 205). Baikunthanath Sanyal a householder devotee and author of 'Sri Sri Ramakrishna Lilamrita' told the Master that he regarded him as Lord Siva appearing in person and not an incarnation or part of God.

On September 1, 1885 at Dakshineswar Girish Chandra Ghosh, a versatile genius described the Master as the Absolute Being. In the Cossipore garden in the afternoon of January 1, 1886 Sri Ramakrishna said : "Well, Girish, what have you seen in me, that you proclaim me before everybody as an Incarnation of God?" Girish, Kneeling, before the Master, said with folded hands, "What can an insignificant person like myself say about the One whose glory even sages like Vyasa and Valmiki could not adequately measure?'

On July 28, 1885 M. said to Sri Ramakrishna :

"I feel that Christ, Chaitanyadeva, and yourself–all three are one and the same. It is the same Person that has become all these three." The Master replied, "Yes, yes! One! One! It is indeed one. Don't you see that it is He alone who dwells here in this way."

M. has to this context added in the Gospel (P. 825) : As he said this, Sri Ramakrishna pointed with his finger to his own body. Once the Master had said, "I shall make the whole thing public before I go."

Swami Chetanananda has reproduced an anecdote in the book, 'Sri Ramakrishner Sannidhye'. One day Ramchandra Dutta one of the noted house holder devotees and the first biographer of Sri Ramakrishna, spoke about the greatness of his gurudeva and requested the eminent physician of Kolkata Kailaschandra Basu to examine him. Kailaschandra said, 'Look Ram, you people make a mountain out of a molehill. On seeing someone's goodness, you do not rest till you proclaim that person a "Paramahamsa" or an "incarnation". Also, you want to prove that you are great devotees and reputed people. On the one hand you say "Paramahamsadeva", "incarnation", and on the other you say that there is a deadly wound in his throat which needs to be examined. Indeed, the Paramahamsa has to be an incarnation and be afflicted with cancer too! Had it been me, I would have twisted the ears of such a Paramahamsa or incarnation.'

Shocked to hear this, Ramchandra said to Dr. Basu, 'Brother, one should not talk caustically about such a great soul. If one does so, it brings ill-fortune to both the speaker and the listener.' Dr. Basu begged Ramchandra's pardon and they left for Kashipur garden-house in a horse-carriage. When both Ramchandra and Dr. Basu entered his room, Sri Ramakrishna saluted Kailaschandra and said, 'Hello doctor, will you first treat me or twist my ears? Which will you do first?' To his utter amazement Dr. Basu understood that this Paramahamsa was definitely the omniscient Bhagavan otherwise he could not know what he had told Ramchandra elsewhere. He said to Sri Ramakrishna, 'Kindly pardon my mistake. Please do not make me feel further ashamed of the offence I committed unknowingly.' He examined Sri Ramakrishna with great care and became his devotee.

One day just before the Master's passing away, Narendranath said to himself, "If in the midst of this racking physical pain he declares his Godhead, then only shall I accept him as an Incarnation of God." He was alone by the bedside of the Master. Though it was a passing thought, Sri Ramakrishna suffering from the characteristic difficulty in breathing and throat-pain, smiled and distinctly said, "He who was Rama and Krishna is now, in this body, Ramakrishna–but not in your Vedantic sense."[84]

On March 25, 1887 Narendranath said to M at the Baranagore Math, "But times without number the Master said to me. 'In me alone are embodied Advaita, Chaitanya, and Nityananda. I am all these three.'[85]

In an epistile from The U.S.A. in 1894 Swamiji wrote to one of his brother-disciples Swami Shivananda, "My dear brother, that Ramakrishna Paramahamsa was God incarnate, I have not the least doubt..."

On the head of an epistle written in 1894 and addressed to Swami Brahmananda Swamiji wrote *'Salutation to Bhagavan Ramakrishna!'*

In 1897 at the garden of the late Gopal Lal Seal at Cossipore, Swamiji said to his disciple Sharatchandra Chakravarty : If the Brahman is manifested in one man, thousands of men advance, finding their way out in that light. Only the knowers of Brahman are the spiritual teachers of mankind.... To remove all this corruption in religion, the Lord has incarnated Himself on earth in the present age in the person of Sri Ramakrishna. (Works, Vol. 6, p.p. 464 – 465)

In a well-known hymn composed in 1898 in the house of Nabagopal Ghosh one of the Master's blessed disciples, Swamiji described Sri Ramakrishna as the greatest of the Avataras of God. Each of the monastic disciples regarded him as God as has been written by Swami Abhedananda, in his autobiography, *'Amar Jivan Katha'* in Bengali. "Then he would go into ecstasy. In that state he would importune Mother Kali, but his words would not be audible to us. Watching his God-intoxicated state we were amazed. We felt that the Master was in communion with the Divine Mother, that he was talking to Her, and that the Mother was answering his questions. We realized that Sri Ramakrishna was not a human being. He was God."

Sister Nivedita regarded Sri Ramakrishna as a 'great Incarnation of the spirit of the Mother towards Her children' (The Complete Works of Sister Nivedita, Sister Nivedita Girls' School, Kolkata, 1967, Vol. 1, p. 488)

Sri Aurobindo said, 'Of all these souls Sri Ramakrishna was the last and greatest, for while others felt God in a single or limited aspect, he felt Him in His illimitable unity as the sum of an illimitable variety. In him the spiritual experiences of the millions of saints who had gone before were renewed and united. Sri Ramakrishna gave to India the final message of Hinduism to the world.' (Sri Aurobindo and the New Thought in Indian Politics by Haridas Mukherjee & Uma Mukherjee, 2nd Ed. p. 279)

Truth–the only refuge :

सत्यमेव जयते नानृतं...[Mundaka Upanishad, 3rd Mundaka, Canto–1, Mantra–6] Truth alone wins, and not untruth.

Sri Ramakrishna was the living embodiment of renunciation. He was ready to offer all of his entities to the Divine Mother. But only one thing he did not forgo and that was Truth. He had legendary adherence to it. The following incidents show how much strict he was about the principle of Truth :

On March 29, 1883 Sri Ramakrishna said to the devotees :

"No lie of any sort is good. A false garb, even though a holy one, is not good. If the outer garb does not correspond to the inner thought, it gradually brings ruin. Uttering false words or doing false deeds, one gradually loses all fear. Far better is the white cloth of a householder. Attachment to worldliness, occasional lapses from the ideal, and an outer garb of gerrua— how dreadful!

"It is not proper for a righteous person to tell a lie or do something false even in a dramatic performance. Once I went to Keshab's house to see the performance of a play called *Nava-Vrindavan*. They brought something on the stage which they called the 'Cross'. Another actor sprinkled water, which they said was the 'Water of Peace'. I saw a third actor staggering and reeling in the role of a drunkard."

A Brahmo devotee said, "It was K—"

The Master continued, "It is not good for a devotee to play such parts. It is bad for the mind to dwell on such subjects for a long while. The mind is like white linen fresh from the laundry, it takes the colour in which you dip it. If it is associated with falsehood for a long time, it will be stained with falsehood."[86]

On November 26, 1883 in the house of Manilal Mallick Sri Ramakrishna, while praising Shivanath's absorption in the bliss of bhakti, commented, "But he has one great defect : he doesn't keep his word. Once he said to me that he would come to Dakshineswar, but he neither came not sent me word. That is not good. It is said that truthfulness alone constitutes the spiritual discipline of the Kaliyuga. If a man clings tenaciously to truth he ultimately realizes God. Without this regard for truth; one gradually loses every thing. If by chance I say that I will go to the pine-grove, I must go there even if there is no further need of it, lest I lose my attachment to truth. After my vision of the Divine Mother, I prayed to Her, taking a flower in my hands : 'Mother, here is Thy knowledge and here is Thy ignorance. Take them both, and give me only pure love. Here is Thy holiness and here is Thy unholiness. Take them both,

Mother, and give me pure love. Here is Thy good and here is Thy evil. Take them both, Mother, and give me pure love. Here is Thy righteousness and here is Thy unrighteousness. Take them both, Mother, and give me pure love.' I mentioned all these, but I could not say : 'Mother, here is Thy truth and here is Thy falsehood. Take them both.' I gave up everything at Her feet but could not bring myself to give up truth."87

On February 3, 1884 Sri Ramakrishna said to the devotees :

"The Mother has put me in such a state of mind that I can not hide anything from anyone. Mine is the condition of a child. Rakhal doesn't understand it. He covers my injured arm, wrapping my body with a cloth lest others should see my injury and criticize me. He took Dr. Madhu aside and reported my illness. But I shouted and said : 'Hello! Where are you, Madhusudan? Come and see. My arm is broken.

"I used to sleep in the same room with Mathur and his wife. They took care of me as if I were their own child. I was then passing through a state of divine madness. Mathur would ask me, 'Father, do you hear our conversation 'Yes', I would reply.

"Once Mathur's wife became suspicious of his movements and said to him, 'If you go anywhere, he must accompany you'. One day Mathur went to a certain place and asked me to wait downstairs. He returned after half an hour and said to me : 'Come; father, let us go now. The carriage is waiting.' When Mathur's wife asked me about it, I reported the thing correctly. I said to her, 'We went to a certain house. He told me to stay down stairs and himself went upstairs. He came down after half an hour and we left the place.' Of course she understood the thing in her own way.

"A partner of Mathur's estate used to take fruits and vegetables stealthily from the temple garden. When the other partners asked me about it, I told them the exact truth,"[88]

On April 5, 1884 Sri Ramakrishna said to Prankrishna Mukherji and the others : "If a man leads a householder's life he must have unflagging devotion to truth. God can be realized through truth alone. Formerly, I was very particular about telling, the truth, though now my zeal has abated a little. If I said, 'I shall bathe, then I would get into the water of the Ganga, recite the mantra, and sprinkle a little water over my head. But still there would remain some doubt in me as to whether my bath was complete. Once I went to Ram's house in Calcutta. I happened to say, 'I shall not take any luchi.' When I sat down for the meal I felt hungry. But I had said I would not eat the luchi; so I had to fill my stomach with sweets. (All laugh).

But my zeal for truthfulness has abated a little now. Once I said I would go to the pine-grove, but then I felt I had no particular urge to go. What was to be done? I asked Ram about it. He said I didn't have to go. Then I reasoned to myself : "Well, everyone is Narayana. So Ram, too, is Narayana. Why shouldn't I listen to him? The elephant is Narayana no doubt, but the mahut is Narayana too. Since the mahut asked me not to go near the elephant, then why shouldn't I obey him? Through reasoning like this my zeal for truthfulness is slightly less strong now than before."[89]

One day Sri Ramakrishna promised Jadu Mallick that he would visit his garden house at noon. But later he had forgotten all about it as he was engaged in talks with his devotees. While to bed at 11 P.M. he suddenly remembered the appointment and in order to keep his promise he at once accompanied by Rakhal with a lantern in his hand, went to the house. Then the house remained closed. Pushing back the door of the living room a little, and placing his foot inside the room he cried out, 'Hello! Here I am.' Then he left.

To quote Robert Frost :

> The woods are lovely, dark and deep,
> But I have promises to keep,
> And miles to go before I sleep,
> And miles to go before I sleep.
>
> [Stopping by woods on a Snowy Evening]

One day the Master handed a book in English over to

Hariprasanna, one of his monastic disciples and asked him to read and explain. The advice e.g. to speak the truth, to control self, not to become greedy of other's possessions etc. written in the book made him frolic like a child.

One day Sri Ramakrishna said to his spiritual-son Rakhal "Why can't I look at you? Have you done anything wrong?" Rakhal thought that wrong action meant stealing, robbery or adultery. So he replied, "No." The Master said, "Did you tell any lies?" Rakhal recollected that the previous day while chatting and joking with two friends, he had told a lie. The Master said to him, "Never do it again. Truthfulness alone is the spiritual discipline in the Kaliyuga."

Once a doctor prescribed the juice of three lemons for Sri Ramakrishna's upset stomach and Gopal was asked to fetch them. In lieu of only three he brought several extra lemons. The Master accepted three and asked him to return the additional lemons. "Gopal realized that the Master was an embodiment of truth and his speech and action were always congruous."[90]

Outwardly unconventional :

A mass of matted hair on head, a water-pot in one hand and a stick or tongs in another, ochre-cloth–these, in general, are the identity marks of Hindu ascetics. Sri Ramakrishna had no such conventional mark. He was not an itinerant ascetic like flowing water instead he lived a spiritual life in a particular place. In this respect he, as a saint, was exceptional. Yet he became the Master of his wonderful monastic disciples and is regarded as a compeer of Krishna, Buddha and Christ. Mahatma Gandhi said, "The story of Ramakrishna Paramahamsa's life is a story of religion in practice. His life enables us to see God face to face... Ramakrishna was a living embodiment of godliness."[91]

As an ascetic Sri Ramakrishna forsook social relations with all in the world. But he could not forget his devotion and duty to his aged mother Chandra Devi. Referring to the amazing and unprecedented harmony in him of apparently contradictory qualities, Swami Saradananda one of his direct disciples said, "Do you not see that, although he offered everything, body, mind, etc. at the lotus feet of the universal Mother he could not offer truthfulness to Her. Although he gave up worldly relation with all persons, he could not forget his affection and duty to his mother. And although he never retained the slightest tinge of carnal relationship with his wife, he never forgot always to maintain, in the mood of the Guru, a loving relationship with her. Ah, how many are the examples that can be given of his extraordinary actions! Who are the teachers, or incarnations of God, of past ages, in whose lives so many contradictions meet in such sweet harmony? Who will not say that such a harmony was never seen anywhere else?"[92]

The Master himself told his disciples many a time about how his aged mother lived the last twelve years of her life at Dakshineswar under his care when he used to perform daily with his own hand all kinds of service to her and considered himself blessed. He said to them, "I forgot everything when I went to Vraja. I thought I would no more return here. But, a few days later, I remembered my mother. I thought she would be in difficulty– who would look after her and serve her in that old age? That thought arose in the mind and made it impossible for me to live there."[93]

Sri Ramakrishna once said about his mother, "My mother was the personification of rectitude and gentleness. She did not know much about the ways of the world; innocent of the art of concealment, she would say what was in her mind. People loved her for her open-heartedness."[94]

When Mathur's intention of transferring an estate to Sri Ramakrishna failed (as the Master angrily roared, "Ah, you wretch, you want to make a worldly man of me!"), he repeatedly requested Chandra Devi saying, "Granny, you have never taken any service from me. If you really consider me to be your own, please ask for anything you want." She replied, "My child, God bless you; through your affectionate care, I lack nothing at present. When I require anything, I'll ask you for it." But Mathur did not spare her. Ultimately she agreed to accept only an anna (four paisa) worth of tobacco leaf to make ashes for her teeth. Mathur, with moist eyes saluted her saying, "Can any mother other than you give birth to such a self-denying son?"

Although a Sannyasin, the Master not only served his mother but shed profuse tears in sorrow also when she passed away. Being a Sannyasin, he was precluded by the scriptural injunctions from performing the obsequies and funeral ceremonies of his mother and those were performed by his nephew Ramlal. The Master said to his disciples, "In the world, O children, the parents are worthy of supreme veneration they should be served, according to one's power, as long as they live, and after their death their funeral ceremonies should be performed according to one's means..."[95]

Androgynous traits : Physical changes during Sadhana :

The Master undertook the Vaishnava disciplines after he had completed the Tantric ones. Brahman or Isvara is attainable through each of the 'five moods' (Rasa) namely, Santa, Dasya, Sakhya, Vatsalya and Madhura. During the first four years of the Vaishnava Sadhanas the Master attained success in three modes of santa, Dasya and Sakhya without accepting any external help. During the period when he inspired by the devout Bhairavi Brahmani devoted himself to the Sadhana of the two principal modes of Vatsalya and Madhura, he looked upon himself as a woman. His movements speech, gestures, glance, smile and other actions of body and mind would become womanly.

It is said in the Mundaka Upanishad (3.2.4) that self-realization is not possible by knowledge only without putting on the signs of Sannyasa. e.g. ochre cloth etc. Desirous of having the vision of Krishna and of getting Him as his spiritual husband, the Master was engaged in the practices of the Madhura Bhava which is considered the aggregate of the essences of the other four moods and something more. This time he was anxious to use suitable clothes and ornaments. Giving up food and sleep he yearned for the complete union for all times with the Lord. He told his disciples that during the early stage he had felt pangs of yearning, unbearable burning pain and intense heat all over his body and drops of blood oozed out at times from every pore of his body under the powerful sense of the separation from Krishna. He told also that during his Sadhana of the Madhura Bhava all the joints of the body seemed slackened, the senses became inactive and the body sometimes lay unconscious– all owing to his true transcendental love like that of Sri Radha or Sri Chaitanya.

The Bhairavi Brahmani, Vaishnavacharan and other Sadhakas were astonished to see the physical signs manifested during the Mahabhava of Sri Ramakrishna and paid their deep homage to him.

The Bhairavi Brahmani said, 'I mistook him very often for Sri Radharani when I saw him plucking flowers in that manner.'

With reference to the Master's practices of Vatsalya Bhava, M. wrote in the Gospel, "During these days Sri Ramakrishna's heart overflowed with motherly love like the love Yaśodā felt for Krishna. So he kept Rakhal with him. Rakhal felt toward the Master as a child feels toward its mother. He would sit leaning on the Master's lap as a young child leans on its mother while sucking her breast." (p. 185)

Swami Saradananda said, "Speaking of the Mahabhava, the Master told us on many occasions "It is written in the devotional scriptures that nineteen kinds of emotions manifested in one receptacle are together called the Mahabhava. The whole life of a man is required for the practice of one such emotion before he can attain perfection in it. Nineteen such moods were fully manifested all together here (showing his own body) in one receptacle."

An embodiment of Compassion :

The spirit of the Master frequently soared beyond the relative plane. Yet he, as a man of flesh and blood, could not turn a deaf ear to the cry of the ailing humanity as he would come down to the sense-plane.

While going through a village near Vaidyanath during his pilgrimage to Banaras, Vrindavan and other holy places with Mathur, Sri Ramakrishna was deeply moved by the poverty and plight of the people and said to his first and the foremost rasaddār (supplier of stores), "You are but a manager of Mother's estate. Give these people sufficient oil to cool their heads and a piece of cloth to each and feed them to their fill once." At first Mathur considering the requirement of money for the pilgrimage and the number of the villagers hesitated to spend money for them. The Master said, "You wretch, I will not go to your Kasi. I will remain here with them; they have none to call their own; I will not leave them behind and go." Saying so he sat down among the poor villagers. At the sight of the Master's compassion for the helpless people, Mathur could not but obeyed the order of him. Mathur had to do likewise once again when he visited a village near Ranaghat (Nadia) in his estate with the Master.

Sri Ramakrishna realized that an empty stomach is no good for religion. Owing to his deep concern for others he would explore the Divine Mother to put an end to the miseries of people. Kishori, one of the devotees of the Master had several children but his salary was too small to support his family. On September 7, 1884 at Dakshineswar the Master said to M. : "Naran said he would get a job for Kishori. Please remind him of it." (p. 515)

Once Sri Ramakrishna started telling a visitor about the means to improve the condition of one's family and about one's temporal responsibilities. The addressee commented, 'This I get to hear everywhere, please speak a few word about God.' The Master, with his fascinating yogic insight, saw that the man who has no job but had a daughter of marriageable age and starving family, needed advice about work and duty for his family and spiritual instruction to such a person would be of no use. So he said, 'My boy! Now I am telling this, you may go away if you do not like it.'

Akshay Kumar Sen has given in his book 'A Portrait of Sri Ramakrishna' a graphic account of the Master's unconditional love for a man who disliked and maligned him. The vilifier's son fell ill and he entreated the reputed physician Mahendralal Sarkar to see his son. Paying no attention to the man's request Dr. Sarkar got into a carriage to visit the Master at Shyampukur. The man had followed the doctor and both of them reached there. The father, stricken with fear and shame, found himself standing in front of the Master who asked him the reason for his visit and heard about his son's critical condition. Shedding tears, the Master said 'I am old and have an ordinary pain in my throat... I can imagine how painful is the suffering of your child.' Then he requested Dr. Sarkar to treat the child first. The Master's all-embracing compassion and love won the heart of the man who, with tears in his eyes, begged his pardon.

Once at Cossipore the Master in a tone of complaint said to the Mother, "Well, my dear, won't you do anything? Should this (pointing to his own body) do everything single-handed?" When the Mother expressed her helplessness as a woman, he reprimanded, "No, no, you'll have to do a lot." About three days later he said to the Mother, "See, the people of Calcutta appear to be crawling about like worms in the dark. Do look after them." The Mother said, "I am a woman. How can that be?" Pointing to his body, the Master replied, "What after all has this one done? You'll have to do much more."

Previously the Master used to say to the Mother, "Is this my trouble alone? It's yours too."

To the Master, the miserable plight of the people was a great 'trouble' to solve.

It was the first day of January 1886. Sri Ramakrishna who had been suffering from terminal throat cancer since 1885, feeling rather well that day came downstairs of the Cossipore garden house in order to have a stroll in the garden for sometime at three in the afternoon. There were more than thirty householder devotees in the garden. When the Master came to the middle of the path leading to the gate, he saw Girish Chandra Ghosh, his brother Atul, Ramchandra Datta and a few others sitting under trees to the West of the path. Seeing the Master they saluted him and came joyfully to him. He said, "Girish, you, I find, say to one and all everywhere so many things about me (that I am an incarnation of God), what have you seen and understood (about me) that you do so?" Girish, kneeling down before the Master replied in a choked voice with his hands folded, "What can an insignificant person like myself say about the One whose glory even sages like Vyasa and Valmiki could not adequately measure?' The Master, charmed by this ardent utterance of his beloved 'Bhairav' said, "What more shall I say to you? May you all be blessed with the spiritual awakening." At once he went into Bhavasamadhi. Thus the great Master appeared as 'Kalpataru' or the Wish-fulfilling Tree (God) and blessed all the devotees assembled there. To quote Swami Saradananda :

Those words of profound blessing, untouched by the slightest tinge of selfishness, directly entered the devotees' hearts where they raised high billows of bliss. They forgot time and space, forgot the disease of the Master and forgot their previous determination not to touch him till he recovered, and were aware only that out of sympathy for them in their plight, an extraordinary divine Being, feeling excruciating pain at their misery and his heart overflowing with compassion, had come down to them from heaven and called them affectionately to Him for giving protection, like a mother sheltering her children against all ills by covering them lovingly with the upper part of her sari. Then they became eager to bow down to him and take the dust of his feet and, filling the quarters with cries of "Victory to Ramakrishna," began saluting him one after another. As they were thus bowing down to him the sea of the Master's compassion transcended all bounds and brought about a wonderful phenomenon. (Sri Ramakrishna the great Master, p. 1268)

Mahatma Gandhi, in his introduction to the 'Life of Sri Ramakrishna' (Advaita Ashrama, Kol.) Commented : 'Ramakrishna's life was an object-lesson in *ahimsā*. His love knew no limits, geographical or otherwise. May his divine love be an inspiration to all.'

A striking phenomenon of assimilation :

Such a unique personality as Sri Ramakrishna, such a synthesis of the utmost of Jnana, Yoga, Bhakti and Karma, a combination of idolatry and formlessness, of supernal ecstasy and sense of reality, of renunciation and domestic duties, an assemblage of ideas deeper than the ocean and vaster than the space has never before appeared on the earth. Swamiji observed, "But the life of Sri Ramakrishna upsets all records of history.... The life of Sri Ramakrishna proves that the greatest breadth, the highest catholicity and the utmost intensity can exist side by side in the same individual, and that society also can be constructed like that, for society is nothing but an aggregate of individuals."[97]

Romain Rolland introduced Sri Ramakrishna to the Western world as 'the Messiah of Bengal' 'the symphony of India,' 'the younger brother of our Christ' and added, 'The man whose image I here evoke was the consummation of two thousand years of the spiritual life of three hundred million people. Although he has been dead forty years, his soul animates modern India.... But his inner life embraced the whole multiplicity of men and Gods.'[98]

His extraordinary and mysterious words and deeds eventually gave rise to the 'Ramakrishna phenomenon', a term coined by Christopher Isherwood, an anglo-American novelist and playwright in 'Ramakrishna and His disciples' (Advaita Ashrama, 1980, p. 1).

Swami Vivekananda summarized the originality and uniqueness of his master, "His life was a thousandfold more than his teaching, a living commentary on the texts of the Upanishads, nay, he was the spirit of the Upanishads living in human form. Nowhere else in this world exists that unique perfection, that wonderful kindness for all that does not stop to justify itself, that intense sympathy for man in bondage. He lived to root out all distinction between man and woman, the rich and the poor, the literate and the illiterate, the Brahmanas and the Chandalas. He came to bring about the synthesis of the Eastern and Western Civilization. Indeed, not for many a century past India produced so great, so wonderful a teacher of religious synthesis. ...The new dispensation of the age is the source of great good to the whole world, specially to India; and the inspirer of this dispensation, Bhagavan Sri Ramakrishna, is the reformed and remodelled manifestation of all the past great epoch-makers in religion."[99]

Chapter – 2

THE HOLY MOTHER

"Do you mean to say that God married the daughter of a woman who maintained herself by gathering cow dung?"[1] –Swami Saradananda once said this to a devotee who had told him that he could easily believe in the divinity of Sri Ramakrishna; at least he cherished that faith but he could not comprehend the Holy Mother as the Divine Mother.

Distinctive physical appearance and personality :

Referring to the distinctive traits of the Holy Mother's physical appearance, and personality Swami Nikhilananda, a disciple of her wrote in his book 'Holy Mother' :

Holy Mother was well built for a Hindu woman of Bengal. She had a fair complexion and was of medium height, though in several of her photographs she gives the impression of being rather tall. The soles of her feet were ruddy. Her thick black hair, which Yogin-ma used to braid, almost reached her knees. Before Sri Ramakrishna's death she usually wore a white sari with a wide red border. She also wore some gold jewellery that the Master had given her : two bracelets for her upper arms, bangles for her wrists, a necklace, earrings, and a nose ring. When the Master gave her these ornaments he said to Hriday, Jokingly : "I suppose that's all there is to my relationship with her." As already mentioned, after wearing them a short while, she discarded most of them. After the Master's death she wore a single gold bracelet on each wrist. Speaking of her own appearance, she once remarked : "I was rather pretty in my youth. Later I became a little stout." Women often were struck by her physical beauty. As Golap-ma said, she looked like a goddess. While meditating, she appeared radiant. Swami Premananda's mother once asked her : "Mother where did you get such celestial beauty and charm?"

The Holy Mother's immaculate purity, her unceasing meditation and prayer, her all-embracing compassion and utter selflessness, endowed her with the delicacy and tenderness of a maiden, a subtle grace and quiet dignity, and withal guilelessness and simplicity. Her innate motherliness put visitors at ease. To a person coming to her for the first time, she conveyed the feeling that she had been eagerly waiting for him. The Holy Mother always inspired reverence but never gave a feeling of remoteness....

The Holy Mother, unlike any other orthodox Hindu widow, wore, after the Master's death, a sari with a narrow red border, using it as skirt, blouse, and veil. Before strangers she covered herself practically from head to foot with an additional white cotton chadar. Once, during the cold season, she was given a thin woolen undershirt. She expressed pleasure at this gift and used it for three days. On the fourth day she took it off and said to the devotees : "Is it proper for a woman to wear a shirt? I put it on for three days just to please you." ...The Holy Mother observed some of the caste rules. Like a Hindu widow, she was vegetarian, but again unlike a Hindu widow she did not cut her hair, she wore gold bracelets, she wore a sari with a narrow red border, and ate a light supper at night. (pp. 287–88, 292)

Significant Name :

In Bengali 'Sarada' means a woman who is the embodiment of some divine qualities such as austerity, serving, impartiality, tolerance, simplicity, virtuous practice, holiness etc. and bestows knowledge devotion conscience, spirit of renunciation and bliss and provides with food and clothing and shelter and protects beings.

Goddess Durga said to Shumbha, king of the demons :

एकैवाहं जगत्यत्र द्वितीया का ममापरा ।
पश्यैता दुष्ट मय्येव विशन्त्यो मद्विभूतयः ॥

Caṇḍī, X - 4

I am all alone in the world here. Who else is there besides me? See, O vile one, these Goddesses, who are but my own powers, entering into my own self![2]

Like Goddess Durga Sarada Devi too has innumerable names such as Durga, Bhagabati, Saraswati, Kali, Jagaddhatri, Lakshmi, Jagadamba, Mahamaya, Sati, Sita, Radha etc.

Lord Sri Krishna said :

हन्त ते कथयिष्यामि दिव्या ह्यात्मविभूतयः ।
प्राधान्यतः कुरुश्रेष्ठ नास्त्यन्तो विस्तरस्य मे ॥

Indeed I will tell you (Arjuna) my divine pervasive powers — those that are prominent of these : for there is no lend to my extent.

[Gita X : 19]

Like Sri Krishna the Holy Mother was simultaneously Immanent and Transcendent. Sarada Devi's various names after Goddesses and mythical characters and their nature are the effulgent manifestation of her distinction.

Innate divinity :

The birth and activities of the Mother also were divine. On various occasions Sri Ramakrishna made significant remarks about Sri Sarada Devi.

Before declaration of divinity of Sri Sarada Devi at Dakshineswar, Sri Ramakrishna hinted at it at Kamarpukur. When he talked to the village women of higher matters, the Mother then a mere girl of fourteen often fell asleep. They said, 'What a pity; she misses these fine things! She has fallen asleep!' The Master said, 'No, my dear, no; don't awaken her. Don't think she is asleep without reason. If she hears these things, she will fly headlong away.' The uncultured and uneducated village women did not probably understand the inner meaning of those words or the latent greatness of that girl.

The Master one day spoke to Golap-Ma about the Mother,

> 'She is Sarada, Saraswati; she has come to impart knowledge. She has descended by covering up her beauty this time, lest unregenerate people should come to grief by looking at her with impure eyes.' Once he said, 'She is the communicator of knowledge, she is full of the rarest wisdom. Is she of the common run? She is my Sakti (power)' On another occasion he said to his nephew Hriday, 'My dear, her name is Sarada, She is Saraswati. That's why she likes to put on ornaments.'

In the early days during the period of austerity Sri Ramakrishna had a vision of Sita at Panchavati. He noticed that her bracelets had diamonds cut on their surface. So he had made similar bracelets for the Mother about whom Yogin-Ma said, 'At that time the Mother lived at the Nahabat like the most revered Sita. She wore a piece of cloth with broad red borders and vermilion at the parting of her hair. Her thick black tresses almost touched her knee. She wore a gold necklace, a big nose-ring, ear-rings, and bracelets those which Mathur Babu gave the Master when he took to spiritual practice by assuming the role of a handmaid to the Divine Mother.'

Sri Ramakrishna's nephew Hriday showed his disrespect to the Holy Mother off and on. On one occasion noticing such rudeness to her the Master reprimanded him saying, 'My dear Hride, you may be talking to this (pointing to his own body) slightingly, but don't you do so to her. If the one that is in this (body) raises its hood, you may still be saved; but if the one that is in her raises its hood even Brahma, Vishnu and Maheswara can not save you.'[3]

Sister Nivedita, in her book, 'The Master as I saw Him' quoted, "can't you see," said Sri Ramakrishna, to one who had erred in some such way, "can't you see that *the woman* in her is wounded? And that is dangerous!" (p. 123)

In the shrines priests awaken the idol of Durga by investing it with life and worship. On 5th June 1872 an auspicious day for the worship of Phalaharini Kali Sri Ramakrishna arranged a special worship of the Mother of the Universe as Shodashi in his room at night at Dakshineswar secretly. Instead of an image of the Divine Mother Shodashi (Srividya or one of the ten manifestations of Goddess Durga) he placed his wife Sarada Devi on the holy seat and worshipped her after Tantra formalities. Reciting mystic and esoteric words and chanting a hymn to the Goddess he surrendered at the feet of the living idol, himself, his rosary and even the fruits of his life-long sadhana. Thus he recognized and glorified her innate divinity and made her aware of it. She was left by him to complete his sport in a men-dominated society where women folk were victims of miserable plight. Indeed entrusting the responsibility to the Mother, the Master indicated the unprecedented awakening of womankind in this country.

Besides, Sarada Devi personally at times disclosed her real form or nature and described herself as goddess directly or indirectly. Once during conversation Swami Keshabananda told the Mother that hence forth none would adore goddesses namely Sasthi Shitala. 'Why will not adore? They too are the parts of me,' replied the Mother.

During her stay in Udbodhan once in response to the curse of her insane sister-in-law Surobala the Mother told her that despite practising ascetical meditation a great number of sages and saints missed her whereas they got her but lost. One day in Banaras Surabala cursed her sister-in-law Sarada Devi desiring her death. Later on the Mother told the devotees that the youngest brother's wife did not know that she was immortal. Once in reference to Radhu's torture the mother told her that she should know that her body was holy and none but god only could bear with so much.

One day the Mother expressed her resentment when Radhu addicted to opium, pestered her for increasing the dose. At this the whiny niece hit her on the back with a brinjal. Rubbing the dust of her own feet over Radhu's head she said, 'Radhi, the Master never uttered a harsh word against this body, and you inflict such pain on it! How can you evaluate my worth? How lightly do you mean to deal with me just because I have chosen to live amidst you all? Radhi, if I become offended, then you can find no shelter anywhere in the three worlds. Master, don't be offended with her.'

The Mother appeared in various forms of goddesses before her curious aspirants and others for example, Swami Haripremananda, in his autobiography[4] narrated how while massaging the Mother's legs with oil one evening in Bankura he doubted her divinity and discovered the dazzling image of Jagaddhatri in her lean and thin body. Before looking her clearly he fainted saying 'Mother, Mother!'

One day when the Mother asked her Bagdi parents (the robber couple), 'Why, my dears, are you so attached to me?' They replied, 'You are not, in fact, an ordinary mortal, for we saw you as Kali.' When the Mother tried to suppress the incident, they emphasized. 'No, Mother, there was no mistake about what we saw. You want to hide this from us since we are sinners.' Referring to this incident once a devotee asked the Mother if she had revealed Herself to the robber-couple as Kali, the Mother said with a smile, 'You may take it that way if you like it so.'[5]

One day Chandramohan Dutta one of her devotees was travelling with the Mother by a bullock-cart via Koyalpada to Vishnupur. When the Mother was having a rest under a shady tree, he earnestly and repeatedly prayed that to see her real form was his last desire. He was fortunate to see the Mother's image of Jagaddhatri.

Sita Devi, Sri Radha and Sarada Devi identical :

It is she who was Janaki in Treta Yuga and Sri Radhika in Dwapara is Sarada in this Kali Yuga. It is suggestive that she was pleased when a devotee would adore her feet with white or yellow flowers.

One day a woman devotee said, 'Mother, why can't we comprehend that you are the Divine Mother?' The Holy Mother answered, 'How can everyone recognize divinity, my child? There was a big diamond lying at a bathing ghat. Considering it to be an ordinary stone people rubbed their feet against it to smooth their soles. One day a jeweller came there and immediately recognized it as a large and precious diamond.... In fact, the Master was God. He assumed a human form to mitigate the sufferings of humanity. He came to this world incognito, like a king who visits the city in disguise. I am Bhagavati [the goddess]' (Mayer Katha, Abhaya Dasgupta, Udbodhan office, Kol.).

Sri Ramakrishna uttered the salutation : 'O Thou, the most auspicious goodness among all auspicious things, the fulfiller of all aims, the refuge of all, Thou the three-eyed, golden hued consort of Siva, Thou the power of Narayana, I salute thee.' In this way the Mother inherited the most precious spiritual wealth and learnt how to look on all beings as manifestations of the Universal Mother. The Master thus roused the innate divinity of the Mother.

One day (February 1, 1907) at Jayrambati a devotee, in order to dispel his doubt about the divinity of the Mother, said to her, 'Then why do I see you as though making *chapāti* like any ordinary woman? What are all these? Are these māyā?' The Mother replied, 'What else but māyā? Why should I be in such a state if not because of māyā? I should have been sitting by Narayana as His Lakshmi in Vaikuntha. It's just because the Lord likes to disport as a man.' The devotee again said, "Doesn't your true nature flash in your mind?' The Mother answered, 'Yes, it does at times and then, I think, "What's this that I am doing? What's this I am engaged in?" Again all thesse things (pointing in front), —houses, children, etc., –come to the mind and I forget my essential nature.'

Swamiji, in a letter to his brother-disciple Swami Shivananda described the Mother as 'the living Durga' (elaborately mentioned later).

First to proclaim divinity of Sri Ramakrishna :

Sri Chaitanya was first worshipped by his second wife Vishnupriya. It was Sri Sarada Devi who first acknowledged the divinity of her husband Sri Ramakrishna by worshipping him.

The Holy Mother possessed at that tender age the ability to realize that her husband was not at all an insane as she had heard in her neighbourhood but in fact, he was a God-intoxicated great saint.

An embodiment of universal motherliness– 'stranger than fiction' :

There is no dearth of ideal women in the history of India. But the complete manifestation of motherliness in them is rare. Sri Sarada Devi appeared to fulfill the need in the history of the Indian women. She is the ideal of universal motherliness. All were equal to her.

In fact, the Mother, as an avatar or an illumined soul does; broke all barriers between human beings and religions with her universal out look and made not only the Hindus but Muslims and Christians also her own through her unparalleled maternal love and selfless affection.

She did not differentiate between Sharat (Swami Saradananda) and Amzad a dacoit and received sister Nivedita and other Western women devotees cordially. In March 1898 Swamiji wrote to his brother disciple Shashi (Swami Ramakrishnananda) '... The thing is working nicely. Shri (Holy) Mother is here, and the European and American ladies went the other day to see her, and what do you think, *Mother ate with them even there!* Is not that grand?'

The Master kept an eagle eye over his would-be monastic disciples. He even told the Holy Mother how many pieces of *Chapati* (unleavened bread) should be given to each disciple. When he came to know that the Mother gave Baburam (Swami Premananda) six instead of four, he immediately went to her and complained that her indiscriminate affection might blur Baburam's future life. The Holy Mother firmly answered, 'Why are you so much worried because he had a couple more chapatis? I shall look after his future.

Please don't make an issue about his food.' Narrating the incident Swami Chetanananda remarked 'The Master understood that Holy Mother's action was justified as she exercised her motherly prerogative towards her children.'[6]

> It was her historic utterances as she said to Girish Chandra Ghosh, 'I am your true mother, a mother not by virtue of being your guru's wife, nor because of any assumed relationship, nor by way of empty talk, but truly the mother.'[7]

One day Yogin-Ma inquired why the Mother appeared to be wilful even against the Master's advice in certain matters. The Mother replied with smile, 'Well my dear, whatever you may say, I shan't be able to turn away anybody if he addresses me as Mother.'

The Mother's life was an exceptional combination of maternal tenderness with strictness, earthly awareness with non-attachment. She always prayed for the good of each of her children. Once at Jayrambati during the worship of Durga when all had left after adoring her with flowers at the most sacred moment of the juncture of the eighth and the ninth lunar day, the Mother told a Brahmachari to bring more flowers and to offer them in the names of Rakhal, Tarak, Sarat, Khoka, Yogen (Yogin-Ma) and Golap (Golap-Ma) and of all her known and unknown children. Then she sat silently with folded hands before the Master and prayed to him for the prosperity of all. Again during her birthday celebration at the 'Udbodhan' in 1918 the Mother ordered Varada, a Brahmachari to offer flowers on behalf of all at Jayrambati and Koalpara. When that was done, she prayed to the Master for the well-being of all.

Once a doctor's wife, after saluting the Mother prayed to her to bless her so that her husband might have a good practice. She at once said sternly 'My dear daughter-in-law, to think that I should pronounce such a benediction, that people should fall sick, that they should suffer! Well, dear, I can never do that. Let all be well, let the world prosper.'

One of her children jnan (Swami Jnanananda) was unable to eat with his hand owing to pervasive and painful itches. Mixing rice and curry the Mother put them morsel by morsel into his mouth. Returning a few hours before sunset in winter from a distant village to Jayrambati Brahmachari Rashbihari came to know that the Mother waited for his return and would not lunch. He said, 'Mother, your health is bad, yet why have you kept fasting till this hour?' She answered, 'My son, how can I eat so long as you have not done so?' How deep, rare and unconditional affection it was!

One day Swami Vrajeshwarananda with an intention to leave the Belur Math for outside to undertake austerity, went to the Mother to obtain her permission. Learning that he would walk up to Banaras and was penniless, she said tenderly, This is Kartika (October – November) when people say that all the four doors of Yama (Death) are open. I am a mother; how can I say, "My son, you go?" Moreover, you say, you have nothing with you; who will feed you, my boy, when you are hungry?' Swami Vrajeshwarananda abstained from going elsewhere.

On the eve of a celebration in May 1914, a devotee came to take Swami Premananda to Malda. When the Swami sought for the Mother's consent, she disagreed owing to his bad health and considerable distance of Malda from Calcutta (Kolkata). The devotee importunated and the Mother realized that it was hard for the organizers to unsettle a settled fact. She told Swami Premananda to go for a while and forbade him to stay there for long time.

Brahmachari Nagen (Junior) was frightened when he heard from his friends that Swami Shivananda, the then Manager of the Belur Math would drive him out of the Math for his unbecoming activities. He at once left for Jayrambati without any notice. He reached the Mother's house with dirty clothes and haggard looks. Learning all from the terrified Brahmachari, the Mother gave him two pieces of cloth and a wrapper and had a letter written to Swami Shivananda to the effect : 'My dear son Tarak, the Junior Nagen has offended you in some way. Being afraid that you will turn him out of the Math, he has come to me covering the whole way on foot. As to that, my boy, can a mother mind her son's offence? Don't, my boy, take any action against him.' In reply Swami Shivananda requested the mother to send younger Nagen to him. When he reached the Math, the Swami embraced him warmly and said, 'How now, my boy! You went to the High Court to complain against me?'

Rightly has said Swami Gambhirananda in 'Holy Mother Sri Sarada Devi,' 'Though she was divine, the world has seen in her an all-loving Mother. This is very important phenomenon in human history. (p. 117)

The Mother's all-pervading affection knew no distinction between brahmin and non-brahmin, high and low, rich and poor. Cleaning the orts of the disciples and devotees was a part of her daily routine. She could not call her sons by their monastic names for it hurt her to call their Sannyasa names. As the Mother she could not dream of the idea of their separation (Sannyasa) from her. The Mother considered her sons 'rare jewels to be sought for by gods.' One day she said to a devotee who along with some other devotees walked from Koalpara Ashrama to Jayrambati in a dark wet night risking his life; 'My son, if a thorn pricks your foot, it hurts me like a spear entering my heart.'

Once the Mother said to Swami Vishweshwarananda, 'I look upon you as Narayana, and as sons also.' With reference to this remark Swami Gambhirananda wrote in his resourceful book, 'As in this synthesis, the Mother's conception of sonship consists in a fusion of the human and the divine, so also in another case we get a harmonization of the finite and the infinite in her conception of motherhood.' (p. 361)

One day a baby while sleeping by the Mother's side at the 'Udbodhan' soiled her blanket. She snatching the blanket from the child's mother washed it. When the baby's mother objected to it she answered, 'Why should I not? Is she (the baby) a stranger to me?'

Once the Mother seated Amzad one of the thatchers engaged in building her new house on the verandah for his meal. Nalini Devi caste-ridden as she was, standing at a distance on the courtyard tossed the food on his leaf-plate. The Mother dissatisfied with this, said, 'Can you have any relish for food if it is served in such a fashion? If yo can't serve him properly, I shall do it.' Finding the Mother engaged in cleaning the place herself, Nalini Devi denouncing the act cried out in horror, 'O dear aunt, you lose your caste thereby!' The Mother replied, 'Amzad is as truly my son as my Sarat (Swami Saradananda) himself is,' Another day she gladly accepted some bananas from one of the 'mulberry-robbers' for the Master. A woman devotee surprised at this told the Mother that she should not offer the things of a robber to the Master. The Mother put down the fruits in the store and ordered some fried-rice and sweets for the man. After his departure the Mother scolded her, 'I know who is good and who is not.'

In Jayrambati besides meeting the devotees or visitors, giving them *mantra* or Sannyasa the Mother had to discharge various household duties e.g. making provision for their food, accommodation, necessities and comforts.

The Mother realized that her life was to be a solace to thousands of sinners and spiritual wanderers. So she could not drive away any body even knowing of his or her dark past. At the same time she did not give Sannyasa to an unfit person. As her mission was to uplift the spiritually depraved, she used to say, 'To err is human; but few know how to lead an erring man?' For this reason she pardoned a servant who having been driven out by Swami Vivekananda for stealing, rushed to the Mother for shelter. Considering his poverty and plight she ordered Swami Premananda to take him back to the Math.

The Mother's love and sympathy extended to creatures of lower order also. As she patted a calf it stopped continuous bleating. Her love for cat and bird (Gangaram) was remarkable.

The Mother provided Radhu's pet cat half a pound of milk everyday. But Brahmachari Jnan disliked her for innate nature of stealing and used to beat her. One day the Mother looked pale and pained as he flung the cat away. While leaving for Kolkata she said, 'Jnan, you should cook rice for the cats, so that they may not have to go to other house; for then people will abuse us, my boy. Look here, Jnan, don't beat the cats; for even in them am I.' This was enough to awaken love and sympathy for the cats in the heart of the Brahmachari who, a strict vegetarian, went so far as to arrange for a regular supply of fish for them.

On several occasions the Holy Mother said, 'I shan't be able to turn away anybody if he addresses me as Mother'. 'I can't contain myself when one draws near me and calls me Mother.' If my son wallows in the dust or mud, it is I who have to wipe all the dirt off his body and take him to my lap.' These are nothing but the genuine expression of a true mother who though gave birth to no child yet became the most beloved and revered mother of large community of people cutting across sect and sex, colour and creed, race and language. On 22 May 1898 Sister Nivedita wrote to Mrs. Eric Hammond, "She is the very soul of sweetness — so gentle and loving and as merry as a girl." [Letter of Sister Nivedita, Ed. Sankari Prasad Basu, Vol. 1. p. 11]

To quote Swami Gambhirananda,

> This service of the devotees became something of a second nature with her. It might not have appeared as anything extraordinary; but we wonder how unassuming and diligent is the life of that unique personage who was none other than the Universal Mother, who was adored as such by thousands of devout people, and through whose mind and body was enkindled in the beginning of the twentieth century a mighty force which has addressed itself to the task of human regeneration and is calculated to be so occupied for ages. And how charming does that life become through a unique mixture of rural simplicity with unquestioning love! In the field of spirituality this is altogether a rare phenomenon. Facts are indeed stranger than fiction. (Holy Mother Sri Sarada Devi pp. 387 – 88)

A bridge between the ancient and the modern age :

In her words and activities, simplicity and hospitality in her everyday life the Mother built a bridge between the past and the present. She was respectful to our national tradition, old values and social ethos. At the same time she was open-minded and judicious uncommon for the contemporary Indian women. She vehemently criticized the barbarism of the British rulers in India but did not boycott the British goods. One day she asked one of the Brahmacharis to return indigenous coarse saris (an Indian woman's loincloth) to the shop and fetch fine saris made in England those were preferable to the women devotees. She encouraged the celebates to learn English so that they could communicate with the Westerners and first engaged Swami Dharmananda and then Krishnabhusan Babu for that purpose. She cordially accepted and loved the European and American devotees as her daughters ignoring the criticism of the headmen of the community.

Once in Dakshineswar, Sri Ramakrishna has a vision that he described to Sarada Devi, 'I was in the land of the white people. Their skin is white, hearts are white and they are simple and sincere. It is a very beautiful country. I think I shall go there.' The vision came true when his most beloved disciple Swami Vivekananda brought him– his life and teachings along with those of his wife to the West.

Western devotees and initiated disciples too visited India and the Mother. The Holy Mother used an endearing term 'Khooki' (literally a little girl) for sister Nivedita (Margaret Elizabeth Noble) and called Miss Josephine MacLeod 'Jaya' and her sister Mrs. Betty Leggett, 'Vijaya'. One day during their conversation Sister Nivedita and Sister Christine (Christine Green stidel) told Sarada Devi that she was their Kali. The Mother said with a laugh, 'No, my children, I can't be Kali or any such thing– I would have to stick out my tongue!' They said, 'No, you won't have to take that trouble. We shall regard you as our Mother Kali; Sri Ramakrishna is our Shiva.' The Holy Mother was fond of many other Western women namely, Mrs. Sara Bull, and sister Devamata (Miss Laura F. Glenn).

It is utterly amazing how the Mother a shy, orthodox, barefooted village woman wearing only one white cloth and ignorant of formal education, Western language or Western culture and etiquette, impressed the Western women deeply with her altruistic love and affection, spiritual power and compassion.

In her book 'The Master as I saw him' Sister Nivedita wrote about the Mother,

> To me it has always appeared that she is Sri Ramakrishna's final word, as to the ideal of Indian womanhood. But is she the last of an old order, or the beginning of a new? In her, one sees realised that wisdom and sweetness to which the simplest of women may attain. And yet, to myself the stateliness of her courtesy and her great open mind are almost as wonderful as her sainthood. (p. 122)

Josephine MacLeod was charmed by the Holy Mother's affection. She used to say : 'Sarada Devi is endowed with divine insight' and 'Sarada Devi is the Madonna, Mother Mary, of this new religious community.'

Sri Sarada Devi was the embodiment of Universal Motherhood. The ideal of universal motherhood was established for the first time by Sri Sarada Devi in the history of mankind.

Sharp intelligence, prudence and frugality :

The Holy Mother refused to accompany her husband on a trip to attend the festival at Panihati. Referring to this incident the Master said, "so great was the crowd; besides, all were observing me on account of my ecstasy. She (the Holy Mother) did well in not accompanying us. Had people seen her with me, they would have said, 'A pair of swans has come!' She is very intelligent." In the context of Panihati festival the Mother said, "I could understand from the very way in which he sent me word in the morning regarding my going to Panihati, that he did not heartily approve of it. He would have otherwise said, 'Yes certainly she may go.' When he placed on me the responsibility of making the decision on the matter, and said, 'Let her come, if she likes.' I decided it was advisable to give up the idea of going."

One day Lakshmi Narayan, a Marwari devotee proposed to offer the Master a fat amount of rupees ten thousand. He could not accept the sum and in order to test his wife he asked her if she would take the money. The Mother replied immediately, 'How can that be? The money can't be accepted. If I receive it, it will be as good as your receiving it; for if I take it, I shall spend it on you; and hence it will amount to your own acceptance. People respect you for your renunciation; therefore the money can never be accepted.'[8] The reasonable decision made the Master pleased.

At that time the Master's colour was as fair and bright as gold. One day a discussion just for fun cropped up whether the Master or a certain votary had a fairer skin. The Master appointed the Mother as the judge and told her that she would have to watch them as they walked by the Nahabat and pronoune her judgment. The Mother as an impartial umpire, declared his rival winner.

One night a woman devotee suddenly snatching away the plate of food from the Mother's hand placed it before the Master. The Master could not touch the food defiled by that immoral woman and insisted on the Mother promising that she would not hand it over to anybody else thereafter. The Mother, with folded hands said, 'That I can not, Master! I shall certainly bring your food myself but if any one begs me by calling me "Mother", I shan't be able to contain myself. Besides, you are not my Master alone, you are for all.' This made him contended and he started eating.

To quotc Swami Gambhirananda (Holy Mother Sri Sarada Devi) : One day the Master wanted to test the Mother's capacity to appreciate his deep spiritual moods. That day he asked Mother to prepare betel rolls, tidy up his bed and sweep the floor; and then he proceeded to the Kali temple to prostrate himself before the goddess. The Holy Mother had nearly finished her work when the Master entered the room unnoticed, with red eyes, staggering gait, and fuddled speech like those of a man in a state of intoxication.

The Mother was so engrossed in her work that she did not notice him even though he came within reach. Then he suddenly pushed her from behind and said, 'Hullo, my dear, have I drunk wine!' Though the Mother was taken aback by this unexpected sight, she promptly replied, 'No, no, why should you be under wine?' 'Why do I then wobble?' argued the Master. 'Why am I fuddled in speech? Am I tipsy?' In haste the Mother replied, 'No, no, why should you have drunk wine? You have drunk of the nectar of Mother Kali's love.' Highly delighted, the Master said, 'You have spoken rightly indeed!' (p. 105 - 106)

Once the Master said to Narendra and other young devotees, 'I have a desire to eat the food you get by begging.' They decided to approach the Holy Mother first. When they begged her, she dropped full sixteen annas (one rupee) and thus she signified her bestowing on them all that they could wish for.

The Mother's affection won the heart of Amzad one of the 'mulberry robbers' and thus she protected her village Jayrambati from the attention of those robbers.

Sister Nivedita remarked, 'I have never known her (the Mother) hesitate, in giving utterance to large and generous judgement, however new or complex might be the question put before her. Her life is one long stillness of prayer. Her whole experience is of theocratic civilisation. Yet she rises to the height of every situation... with unerring intuition she goes straight to the heart of the matter, and sets the questioner in the true attitude to the difficulty. Or is there need for severity? No foolish sentimentality causes her to waver.' ('The Master as I saw him'. pp. 122 - 123)

The Mother said, 'One should not trifle with a thing, though it may be very insignificant. If you respect a thing, the thing also respects you. Even a broomstick should be treated with respect. One should perform even an insignificant work with respect.'

Born of poor parents and wife of a poorer husband Sarada Devi had to struggle against poverty and adversity since her childhood. Naturally she learnt how to take proper care of things and did not like misuse or wastage of things. She said, 'We should give everyone his due. What is not edible for a man, give to a cow; what is not edible for a cow, give to a dog; what is not edible for a dog, throw into a lake for fishes to eat. But never waste.'

An unerring mind-reader :

Sri Sarada Devi was a diamond-mine of rare qualities mentioned already. Like her husband she could read anybody's mind and nature accurately and swiftly. Once a clerk in the Bihar Secretariat having been disgusted with carnal appetites, prayed to the Mother for the ochre robe. The Mother granted him his appeal and he left for the Himalayas for austerity. When some monks there advised him to perform the Virajā-homa, he sought for the consent of the Mother who replied, 'I did not permit you to perform the Virajā-homa as it is a difficult matter.' The Mother probably knew the mind of this devotee for he came home after many years.

In 1911 one day Swami Ramakrishnananda bringing a young man named Surendra Vijay to the 'Udbodhan' said, 'Mother, this boy is accompanying me to Madras. Will you kindly initiate him into Sannyasa?' 'Let Sarat do it,' replied the Mother. Swami Saradananda answered, 'I can't know anybody's mind; and as for Sannyasa and such things, it is for Maharaj (Swami Brahmananda) to grant it or not.' 'Then let him have it at Puri from Rakhal.' —said the Mother. In this case too perhaps the Mother saw the heart of the young man; for he returned home soon after.

One day Kumudbandhu Sen heard the Mother speak at the Sarkarbari Lane house : 'Sometimes people of little faith and of unsteady mind come for initiation. I mentally read their past history from their very appearance and behaviour and ask them whether they were previously initiated by someone else. When they reply in the affirmative, I tell them, "Strange you have come again for initiation! You have no faith in the *Mantra* already given by your guru. What is a *mantra* but the holy name of God? Why have you come for initiation again?" Then they beg to be forgiven and again implore me with tears in their eyes. I can't bear anybody's tears.

I pray to the Master for strengthening their faith and through his direction I give them initiation in addition to the *mantra* already received by them. This additional *mantra* is given for fresh stimulus and strength in order to increase their faith in the name of God.' (Prabuddha Bharat, June 1952, p. 261

Unequalled revolutionary :

Revolution is brought about not by arms alone and it is not confined to political change only. Real revolution means total transformation of the way of working and thinking. Sarada Devi was an ideal revolutionary during the renaissance of Bengal. With her liberal and humanitarian outlook and rational thinking she did not tolerate blind superstition, casteism, untouchability, baseless rituals and illogical customs. She courageously freed herself from prejudices and conventions when occasion or duty demanded it. Though a Brahmin widow she did not hesitate to clean the orts of a multitude of castes or to take food either cooked or served by a non-Brahmin. She asked her niece Radhu to touch the feet of certain vaidya Shyamadas Kabiraj and other non-Brahmin devotees namely Kshirodebala, Bhanu aunt in obeisance. An aspirant Pitamber Nath belonging to a so-called low caste (Yugi) hesitated to come to the Mother because of his caste. The Mother called him her son and cordially invited him to enter her room and sit. She gave away some offerings to be placed on the altar at the time of worship to a boy. Once again she gave an attendant a bowl of milk meant for the deity before worship. On the auspicious day of Mahastami she accpted offering of a devotee belonging to a low caste Bagdi of Tajpur who was standing hesitatingly outside her house. She fed all of her votaries fried-rice and jilapi together irrespective of caste and social stratum and enjoyed the scene with great pleasure. One of the bearers of the corpse of Nilmadhab Mukherjee uncle of the Mother was a Shudra. When Golap-Ma drew her attention to that unscriptural and unconventional incident, the Mother uttered revolutionary words : 'Who is a Shudra Golap? Has a devotee caste?' In fact, the Mother translated in her own life the highest ideal of humanity as has been said by saintly vaishnava poet Chandidas : The supreme truth is man, there is nothing more important than he is.

The Mother was eager to hear something of the meaning of the Christian festival Easter-Day and of a European wedding from sister Nivedita.

Before leaving for the U.S.A. to attend the World's Parliament of Religions in Chicago in 1893 Swami Vivekananda in order to be absolutely free from doubt wrote to the Mother seeking for her consent and blessing. After the passing away of the Master once she had a vision at Kamarpukur about the effulgent career of Narendranath still she found herself in conflict between affection and permission. As a mother she could not allow her son to cross the mighty ocean under the then prevailing uncertain conditions. One night she dreamt that the Master was walking over the waves and beckoning Narendranath to follow him. She readily consented to his endeavour and blessed him. On receiving her letter Swamiji enthusiastically said, 'Hey-day, now is everything fixed up; the Mother, too, wished me to go.'

Before going to the U.S.A. in 1896 Swami Saradananda whom the Mother called her 'burden-bearer', went to Jayrambati to seek for the Mother's blessing. As she had the vision of the vast field of the Master's activities, she blessed her son with tears in her eyes.

Humanity and rationalism– these two main characteristics of Renaissance were illuminated in the attitude of the Mother.

In January 1901 Swami Vivekananda visited Mayavati in order to console his bereaved disciple Mrs. Sevier and to see how his dream of setting up an Advaita Ashrama had come true. He chanced to discover a few monks worship a picture of Sri Ramakrishna at the headquarters of non-dualism and harboured deep resentment at such unethical activities. Accordingly idolatry was stopped there on and from March 18, 1902. A few disciples of Swamiji were hurt and Swami Vimalananda, with a view to know whether the authority of the Ramakrishna Mission particularly the

Mother consented to the opinion of Swamiji regarding the worship of the Master at Mayavati, wrote a letter to her. In a letter from Jayrambati on September 1, 1902, She replied that he who was their Guru was evidently a nondualist and as they were the disciples of that very Guru, so they too were nondualist. She firmly said that they were of course nondualist. Indeed, this short but significant letter of the Holy Mother is an evidential document in the history of the Ramakrishna Mission. Putting an end to the controversy over the identity of the devout devotees of Sri Ramakrishna, the Mother pronounced the judgment that ultimately they are all nondualist.

During freedom movement daring revolutionaries who were inspired by the ideals and message of Sri Ramakrishna, the Holy Mother and Swamiji and who were the terror of the British rulers, used to go to the Mother to lie prostrate in obeisance before her. The Mother had the guts to love and bless the great patriots and revolutionaries namely Aurobindo Ghosh, Jatindranath Mukherjee, Devabrata Bose, Shachindranath Sen, Ramchandra Majumdar, Bijoy Kumar Nag, Brahmabandhab Upadhyay and so on. The Mother affectionately called Aurobindo 'My brave son' and Aurobindo described her as 'so great a spiritual refuge' (Udbodhan, 47 yr. p. 55). Astonishingly some activists of the Anushilan Samiti, a secret society, most of whom were either imprisoned or interned, were initiated by the Mother and took to asceticism such as : Devabrata Basu (Swami Prajnananda), Sachindranath Sen (Swami Chinmayananda), Nagendranath Sarkar (Swami Sahajananda), Priyanath Dasgupta (Swami Atmaprakashananda), Radhika Goswami (Swami Sundarananda), Satish Dasgupta (Swami Satyananda), Dhiren Dasgupta (Swami Sambuddhananda), Atul Guha (Swami Abhayananda - 'Bharat Maharaj'), Nitai Das (Swami Baldevananda) and Ishwar Maharaj (Swami Mukteshwarananda). Besides, there were some notable freedom-fighters and revolutionaries namely, Sudhira Bose, Bibhutibhusan Ghosh, Bijoykrishna Basu, Satyendranath Majumdar, Rajanikanta Pramanik, Girija Gupta, Makhanlal Sen and his wife Mrinmoyee Devi and so forth who took initiation from the Holy Mother. In 1917 hearing about the gruesome tortures of the police on two women of same name Sindhubala (one of Yuthabehari village and the other of Sabajpur village in the district of Bankura), the Mother grew furious and asked if there was not a manly man who could slap the wickeds twice and rescue the women. Once in 1919, the Mother, learning from Probodh Kumar Chatterjee, the Head Master of Badanganj school about the brutal assault of the police on the male and female picketers, burst with anger and commented that the day of the fall of the English was not so far. Within fifty years all would be burnt down and reduced to ashes of course, she hated the British imperialism and atrocity but not the English. In Kolkata (according to another view in Delhi or Dhaka) on 11 December 1916 Lord Carmichael, the-then Governor of Bengal, in his durbar (court) address made some offensive and baseless remarks those hovered as threat to the existence of the Ramakrishna Mission. Learning about the comments from her 'doorkeeper' Swami Saradananda the Mother was aggrieved and she asked Swami Saradananda 'the jewel' of her head to meet with the Governor and to make him acquainted with the ideals and activities of the Ramakrishna Mission. Accordingly Swami Saradananda wrote a memorandum to the Governor on 23 January 1917. On 2 March Mr. Gourlay, the Governor's secretary, and Mr. Denham, the police chief visited Belur Math to discuss with Swami Saradananda. On 10 March the great Karma Yogi was invited by the Governor who talked with him for an hour and all doubt and misunderstanding were removed. Lord Carmichael in a letter to Swami Saradananda on 26 March expressed his regret ('... I regret very much to hear that words used by me at the Durbar in December last regarding the Mission should have led in any way to curtailment of the good religious, social, and educational work the Mission has done and is doing ...') Thus the withdrawal of the Governor's statement marked the victory of the Mother's sense of reality and stamina and bold step and the efficiency of the general secretary of the Ramakrishna Order.

The Mother was rational, social conscious and progressive and liberal in outlook and ideas. She was interested in spreading female education and making women self-supporting. Though she, like her husband regarded popular practices sometimes did such things those were contrary to prevailing customs as to cleanse orts of the devotees and visitors belonging to any caste and creed, to permit Swamiji to make a sea-voyage etc. It may be noted in this connection that even an eminent personality like Sir Gurudas Banerjee the first native justice in India, considered that being a monk one should not travel to the land of the Mlechchhas. Though a rustic Brahmin widow she discarded caste-system and as an affectionate mother loved all. She did not hesitate to overlook customs to satisfy a more basic need. One day she tasting a little of a mixture of mango, milk and sweets left it as *prasāda* for her 'son'. To her utter astonishment she found a woman devotee eating the whole stuff and saying, 'Her sons will eat everything, while we shall starve.' Instead of rebuking her, the Mother ordered some rice, soup of lentils and vegetable curry and then mixing all those together, tasted a little of it and left it as *prasāda* for her 'son'. Seeing this a woman devotee said to her, 'Well, Mother how is it that, though you are a brahmin's daughter, you have eaten rice twice and you have polluted your lips? The Mother calmly replied, 'I can do everything for the good of my children. No guilt is incurred thereby. And if it is *prasāda* there's no fault in taking it even five times; for *prasāda* is not to be classed as ordinary food. Don't you disturb your mind with such petty questions; these things make you forget the Master. In the name of the Master, do whatever you think right, not withstanding what others may say.'

The Mother denounced child-marriage. Referring to two unmarried girls from Madras of about twenty or twenty one years of age in the Nivedita School, she said, 'Ah! How they have learnt arts and crafts. And as for our girls! The people of these wretched parts go on clamouring when a girl is hardly eight years old. "Send her to a new family! Have her married!" Alas! If Radhu had not been married, she wouldn't have come to grief so early.'

The Mother educated her nieces Maku and Radhu. When Golap-Ma suggested that Radhu's attendance at school should be terminated as she had become grown-up; the Mother said, 'She's not quite grown up. Let her go to school. She can do immense good to other if she gets education and learn some useful arts from the school. She has been married in a backward village. Through education she will not only improve herself, but will be able to help others.' Once she said to a worried devotee, mother of five unmarried daughters, 'If you can't marry them, why should you worry so much? Put them in the Nivedita School where they will learn and live well.'

The Mother inaugurated the girls' school organized by Nivedita at Bagbazar on 13 November 1898. She affectionately called Nivedita 'Khuki' (a daughter) and loved Joe (Miss Josephine MacLeod), Sara Bull, christine, Lawra Franklin Glenn (Devamata) of the West and eagerly heard about the rituals related to nuptials in their society. While narrating how the Mother enjoyed the Easter music and magnificat, songs and how she expressed her delight on hearing the European marriage vow ("For better for worse, for richer for poorer, in sickness and in health–till death do us part.") Sister Nivedita remarked : 'And in the swiftness of her comprehension and the depth of her sympathy with these resurrection hymns, unimpeded by any foreignness or unfamiliarity in them, we saw revealed for the first time, one of the most impressive aspects of the great religious culture of Sarada Devi.' Swamiji wrote to swami Ramakrishnananda (March, 1898) from Belur Math, 'Shri (Holy) Mother is here, and the European and American ladies went the other day to see her, and what do you think, *Mother ate with them even there!* Is not that grand?' (Works, Vol. 8, P. 448)

During her stay in Banaras the Mother visited the Ramakrishna Mission Home of Service on 9 November 1912 and was much satisfied with what she had seen there – every department, houses, gardens and good administration. When she had reached her residence ('Lakshmi nivasa') a devotee asked her how she had found the Sevashrama. She replied, 'I saw the Master himself present there, and that is why this work goes on here. These are all his work.' This view of the Mother refuted the notion of Mahendranath Gupta and others who believed that it was opposite of the Master's teachings to engage in that kind of social service without first realizing God through spiritual disciplines like meditation, japa and austerity. Once the Mother said to Kshirodebala Roy, a widow from childhood, '...Your body is now lean like a log of wood. If the body is destroyed with what will you undertake spititual discipline, my dear?' She said to her maniac niece Nalini, '...All is in the mind– purity, as also impurity, is in the mind.'

The Mother, without distorting the method of catholic ascetic practice, made it befitting the age, simple and interesting and added a new dimension to it by infusing new life into it.

With reference to the Mother, Hemchandra Ghosh a famous revolutionary once told Shankar Maharaj (Swami Apurba Chaitanya) of Ramakrishna Mission that :

> The seeds of great revolution were lying hidden in that calm and engrossed and silent life. Ramakrishana-Sarada-Vivekananda this trio were the symbol of great revolution. They had brought about a great revolution in the arena of thoughts and consciousness of the whole world.

In a patriarchal society where women in general were victims of illiteracy, malnutrition, negligence, fradulence, early-marriage, early-widowhood, male-chauvinism and torture; the appearance of such a spirited woman personality as the Holy Mother is undoubtedly exceptional and historic event.

Unconsummated marriage–a unique model of transcendental conjugal life :

Learning about Sri Ramakrishna's indifferent health, stoical attitude towards temporal life and various abnormal activities Chandra Devi had been worried sick and asked her son to come home. In 1859 he returned to his village to live with his mother and for a change of air for a year and seven months. Within a few months his health improved and he regained to some extent his natural cheerfulness and freshness of spirit. His mother hoped that a wife would bring him back to earth. Accordingly he, at the age of twenty three married Sarada Mukhopadhyay, a little girl of five living in the neighbouring village of Jayrāmbati. Their nuptial life revealed certain originality and marvellous exception. They were married couple but the ceremonious marriage remained unconsummated for ever. The Holy Mother like goddess Durga or Kaushambi was married yet had unbroken chastity.

The Master helped the Mother have a clear conception of the aim and objectives of human life. He taught her everything ranging from such temporal affairs as good manners, domestic duties and responsibilities, dealing with relatives and capability of adjustment to varying situations, to spiritual practices namely meditation, self abnegation and service. He told his wife, 'Just as the moon is equally lovable to all, so also is God the nearest one to all. Everyone has an equal right to call on Him. If you invoke Him, you too will see Him.'

After his marriage the Master prayed earnestly to the Mother of the Universe to wipe out all passion from his wife completely. The Master admitted that living with her he had realized that the goddess had granted him his prayer. In order to test her one night the Master said to her, 'Well, my dear, have you come to drag me down to the worldly level?' The Mother at once answered, 'No. Why should I drag you to worldly ways? I have come to help you in your chosen path.' One night the Mother while massaging his feet said, 'How do you regard me?' Her husband replied, 'The same Mother that is in the (Kali) temple, gave birth to this body and now reside at the Nahabat, and she, again, is now massaging my feet. Truly do I see you as a veritable form of the Blissful Mother!'

The Mother in the prime of her youth slept with her husband continuously for eight months. But they were free from all sense of body-consciousness as their mind soared high. The husband spent the whole night in a state of divine trance while his wife was also lost in musing on eternal truth. To examine himself one night he looking at the youthful and attractive body of the Mother lying asleep by his side, said to himself, 'O mind, this is what is called a female form. People think of this as a thing of supreme enjoyment and wistfully run after it. But if this is accepted, one becomes enmeshed in body-consciousness and can not attain God who is Existence-Knowledge-Bliss Absolute. Don't be insincere to yourself : don't have a hidden hankering and yet make false profession. Tell me truly, do you want this or God? If you want this, then here it is before you; take it.' –saying these words no sooner had he stretched his hand to touch her than his mind shrank and rose to the higher plane of ecstasy.

The Master was deeply impressed by the spotless purity of the Mother's character and commented, 'If she had not been as pure as she really was; if she had lost self-control and seduced me, then who can say if I too might not have lost self-control and come down to the physical plane?'

With reference to the unearthly matrimonial love of the Master and the Mother, Swami Gambhirananda describing them as 'super normal characters' said,

> The fiery ordeal that they now undertook, or rather the drama that they were now to enact for the edification of the world, throws into the shade the hardest trial recorded in history.[9]

The unique couple Sri Ramakrishna and Sri Sarada Devi did not live as husband and wife but each saw in the other the Divine Mother.

Strong influence on the Master :

The Master regarded all women as the veritable manifestation of the Mother of the Universe. The Mother was held in high esteem by him. He used to salute her after she had rubbed his feet with her hands.

The Mother followed the Master's advice (e.g. one has to work; women should not sit idle, for if one sits idle, many vain thoughts, nay evil ideas, may crop up. Adapt yourself to time, space and person etc.) so sincerely that once the Master said to Hridaya, 'O

Hridu, I had great apprehension, lest she, a village girl, should, by her rustic behaviour incur public criticism and put us to shame. But as to that she is so cautious that nobody knows her movements; even I never saw her going out.' The Mother's prayer to the Mother of the Universe to protect her modesty was granted so completely that though she lived at Dakshineswar (as a wild bird living in a cage) for a long period, she escaped public eye so fully that the cashier of the temple, the chief resident officer, when asked about the Mother said, 'I have heard that she is here; but I have never seen her.'

The Mother by virtue of her intrinsic qualities exerted a strong influence on the Master. Once he said, 'I wanted to go to a certain place. When Ramlal's aunt (the Mother) was consulted she forbade me; so I gave up the idea.' The Mother could not see any devotee or visitor off without giving him or her some fruit or sweet. One day Gopal's Mother pointed out to her that she had not reserved anything for her Gopal. Just then wife of Nabagopal Ghosh arrived and handed over to her some sweets and saved the awkward situation. One day in his room the Master said to her, 'How can it be managed if there is such extravagance?' The Mother perhaps with her aggrieved mother's heart silently left for the Nahabat. The Master, at this, was in a dilemma and said to Ramlal, 'Hullo Ramlal, go and pacify your aunt. If she gets angry, everything will be undone with this (pointing to his body).'

Sister Nivedita wrote about the Holy Mother to her friend Mrs. Eric Hammond in London on 22 May 1898 :

> ... Yet this woman, when you know her well, is said to be the very soul of practicality and common sense, as she certainly gives every token of being, to those who know her slightly. Sri Ramakrishna always consulted her before undertaking anything and her advice is always acted upon by his disciples. She is the very soul of sweetness –so gentle and loving and as merry as a girl.... She really is, under the simplest, most unassuming guise, one of the strongest and greatest of women.

'A cat under ashes' :

All the props of the big person's impressiveness– blue blood, palace, pedigree, power and pelf, high education, modern polished culture etc. were lacking in the Holy Mother. Her character was formed by on-the-earth simplicity, modesty, purity and some other uncommon virtues. Her unique personality attained deep reverence of all.

> The Master spoke about the Mother in fun, 'She is a cat under ashes. He spoke about her divinity to Golap-Ma, his nephew Hriday and Latu.

A village-woman with the body almost covered with a narrow red bordered white sari from head to feet, hardly literate who pronounced 'N' for 'L' such as 'Natu' in place of 'Latu'; 'Nalit' for 'Lalit'; 'Kanjinal' in place of 'Kanjilal'; 'Kishtanal' for Krishnalal; who hearing a hissing sound coming through the water tap feared that a snake had entered the pipe of the running water in Kolkata and who was surprised by the simple mechanism of a hurricane lantern (as mathematics puzzled the Master); was in fact, the Mother of the Universe who, with a mere, glance behind her veil could transform the subtlest mechanism like the human heart.

In appreciation of the Mother's role and importance Swami Vivekananda wrote in 1894 from the U.S.A. to his brother-disciple Shivananda,

> ...You have not yet understood the wonderful significance of Mother's life– none of you. But gradually you will know. Without Shakti (Power) there is no regeneration for the world. Why is it that our country is the weakest and the most backward of all countries? —Because Shakti is held in dishonour there. Mother has been born to revive that wonderful Shakti in India; and making her the nucleus, once more will Gârgis and Maitreyis be born into the world. ...Hence we must first build a Math for Mother. First Mother and Mother's daughters then Father and Father's sons –can you understand this? ...To me, Mother's grace

> is a hundred thousand times more valuable than Father's. Mother's grace, Mother's blessings are all paramount to me. ...Brother, I shall show how to worship the living Durga and then only shall I be worthy of my name. I shall be relieved when you will have purchased a plot of land and established there the living Durga, the Mother. ...Brother, that is where my fanaticism lies, I tell you. Of Ramakrishna, you may aver, my brother, that he was an Incarnation or whatever else you may like but fie on him who has no devotion for the Mother.[10]

Almost similar warmth of profound devotion and emotion is felt in a letter written by Swami Premananda to Surendranath Mitra about the Mother :

> Who has understood the Holy Mother ? ....There's not a trace of grandeur. The Master had at least his power of *vidyā* (knowledge) manifested, but the Mother's? —her perfection of knowledge is hidden. What a mighty power is this! Glory to the Mother! Glory to the powerful Mother! ...A poison that we can't assimilate we pass on to the Mother. She draws everyone to her lap. An infinite power– an incomparable grace! Glory to the Mother! Not to speak of us; we haven't seen the Master himself doing this. With how much caution and what testing he accepted any one! ...And here– what do you see here at the Mother's place? Wonderful! Wonderful! She grants shelter to everyone, eats food from the hands of almost anyone, and all is digested! Mother, Mother, victory unto the Mother!'

Swami Premananda once said to Swami Keshavananda and other devotees,

> You have seen with your eyes, how the Mother, who is in reality the Great Goddess ruling over those who wield the destinies of kings and emperors, has yet elected to become a poor woman plastering the house with cow-dung, scouring utensils, winnowing rice and clearing the leavings of the devotees after their meals. She undertakes

all these tasks to teach the householders their domestic duties. What infinite endurance, limitless mercy and absolute absence of egotism are there!

Enormous capacity to shoulder great responsibility :

After suffering from dysentery for a year at Dakshineswar the ailing Mother left for Jayrambati probably in September - October, 1875 as she was a little better. But after a short while her illness aggravated and life was at stake. When the Master got that evil news, he, with a heavy heart said to Hriday, 'What is it all coming to, O Hride! Is she destined only to come and go, and not do anything worthy of a human birth?' In fact, he expected dynamic and altruistic role from her.

Once at Cossipore garden house the Master said to the Mother, 'Well, my dear, won't you do anything? Should this (pointing to his own body) do everything single-handed?' The Mother replied, 'I am a woman. What can I do?' The Master answered, 'No, no, you'll have to do a lot.'

A few days later the Master said to the Mother, 'See, the people of Caluctta appear to be crawling about like worms in the dark. Do look after them.' The Mother again pleaded, 'I am a woman. How can that be?' The Master pointing towards his body said to her, 'What after all has this one done? You'll have to do much more.'

In order to divert the topic the Mother told him that that would take its own time and insisted him on taking his food then. The Master retorted, 'Is this my trouble alone? It's yours too.'

At Cossipore garden house the Mother and the young devotees (i.e. the would-be monastic disciples of Sri Ramakrishna) were constitutive of constant service to the ailing Master. 'Thus the malady of the Master became an occasion for the crystallization of the future Ramakrishna Order, at the centre of which naturally sat the Holy Mother as the presiding deity.'[11]

The Master not only reminded the Mother of her real identity but invited her directly to take on the responsibility also. He indirectly authorized her to act in some cases for him. One day he sent Sarada, (later Swami Trigunatitananda) a young devotee, to the Mother for initiation and quoted a Bengali couplet to mention her infinite power :

> Radha's infinite power of maya is beyond description,
> Millions of Krishnas and Ramas evolve, abide, and dissolve in it.[12]

Jogin (later Swami Yogananda) and Sarada were the only two monastic disciples of Sri Ramakrishna who were initiated by Holy Mother.

A barren woman is generally condemned as unfortunate and inauspicious. The mother of Sri Sarada Devi (Shyamasundari Devi) lamented that she had married her daughter to a stark mad son-in-law and she had no family life, no child and did not hear anybody calling her 'mother'. Hearing this the Master one day said, 'Dear mother-in-law, you need have no disappointment on that score. Your daughter will have so many children, you will see in the long run, that the distressing call of 'mother' will make her bewildered.'

Like all other women Sri Sarada Devi, while very young, yearned for children even at Dakshineswar. Once the Master said spontaneously, 'Why do you worry? I shall leave you such jewels of children as one can hardly get even if one performs the severest of austerity, to the extent of cutting off one's head. You will find in the end so many children calling you 'mother', that you will be unable to manage them all.' The Mother herself has exposed her sadness : 'When the Master departed, I thought in solitude–I was then at Kamarpukur – " I have no son and nothing else; what will be my lot?" One day the Master appeared and said, "Why do you worry? You want one son– I have left for you all these jewels of sons. In time many will call you mother." History shows how the Mother's yearning for children and the Master's assurance bore fruit.

After the passing away of the Master on Sunday, 16 August, 1886 his monastic disciples drowned in sorrow, were at a loss what to do and thanks to Surendranath Mittra's financial help they managed to rent a dilapidated house at Baranagore where they established the Ramakrishna Monastery. They suffered from extreme poverty and hunger and dearth of the basic needs in everyday life. In the third week of January 1887 they took formal monastic vows by performing the traditional *virajā homa* (fire ceremony) in front of the Master's picture and took new monastic names. Most of them went on roaming about here and there.

At the end of March the Mother visited Bodh Gaya and compared the well-off monastery with the poverty-stricken monastery of her sons and was deeply moved by their plight. Then she prayed to the Master, "Master, you came, played and disported with these few and then went away; and should everything end with that? If so, where was the need for coming down in the midst of so much sorrow? I have seen in Banaras and Vrindaban Many holy men who get their food by begging and shifting their 'residence' from the shadow of one tree to that of another. There's no dearth of holy men of that type. I shan't be able to bear the sight of my sons, who come out in your name, going about begging for food. My prayer is that those who leave the world in your name may never be in need of bare subsistence. They will all live together holding to your ideas and ideals; and the people afflicted with the worries of the world will resort to them and be solaced by hearing about you. That's why you came. My heart is pained to see them wandering about."

The Mother earnestly wanted a permanent residence for her children and tried her best to see the Order well established and smoothly managed.

During her stay at Jayrambati or Kamarpukur she had to provide her disciples, devotees and other visitors despite dearth of daily necessaries there, with food and shelter. Besides, she had to deal with her relatives— her brothers, sister-in law, nieces and nephews and had to face troubles. Her brothers expected her help.

The Ramakrishna Monastery had been moved form Baranagore to Alambazar (1892) and then it was shifted to Nilambar Mukherjee's garden house in Belur village (1898). A plot of land was purchased on the western bank of the Ganga. Under the direction of Swami Vivekananda and supervision of his brother monks the levelling of the grounds and the construction of the shrine and living quarters were done. Several young men inspired by the personality and renunciation and message of Swamiji joined the monastery.

In March 1898 plague broke out in Calcutta. Swamiji returning form Darjeeling decided to launch relief service in the teeth of financial crisis and said to his brother disciples, "We shall sell, if necessary, the land which has just been purchased for the monastery. We are sannyasins, we must be ready to sleep under the trees and live on alms as we did before. Must we care for the monastery and possessions when by disposing of them we could relieve thousands of helpless people suffering before our own eyes?"

The Mother opposed to the sale of the land and Swamiji realized his mistake.

On 9 December 1898 Swamiji carried the urn of the Master's relics on his own shoulder and installed the holy relics in the shrine and thus Belur Math was formally consecrated. On 2 January 1899 it became the permanent headquarters of the Ramakrishna Order. Though there were Board of Trustees and Governing Body for the execution of activities of the Ramakrishna Math and Mission respectively; the Mother was all in all– the Mother of the Ramakrishna Order– 'the High Court' as has been described by Swami Shivananda.

Sagacious guidance :

The Mother was not directly associated with the management of the Ramakrishna Order. She guided it from a distance through spiritual influence and advice. In an incredible meticulous way she adjusted herself to the needs of various types of members of the organisation who were all junior to her, being disciples of the Master, of her own, or of the disciples of the Master and strengthened the bonds of love and understanding.

The Holy Mother was love personified and love was the life-force of the Ramakrishna Order. She wanted each of the members and each of the units of the Order to be tied to others by the bond of love and fraternity.

The following examples will suffice to illustrate her amazing skill as an administrator. The Mother scolded the head of the Koalpara Ashrama for his harsh treatment of the Brahmacharins and at the same time advised the inmates to be patient and disciplined. One day one of her sons told the Mother that some disciples considered that a monk should be engaged in worship, *japa*, meditation and singing devotional songs while other works such as to run hospitals, sell books, keep accounts etc. were unbecoming to him. The Master had not done such things. The Mother replied, 'If you don't work with what will you occupy yourself day and night? Is it possible to meditate and make *japa* all the twenty-four hours? They refer to the Master! He is an exception, and Mathur supplied him his dainty dishes. You get your food just because you have engaged yourself in some work here. Otherwise would you not be moving from door to door for a morsel of rice? Everything shall go on as the Master ordains. The Math will run as it is doing now. Those who can't put up with this will clear out.'[13]

Once a certain head of a monastery regretted before the Mother that their countrymen knew only how to destroy and not how to build and for that reason due to the lack of practical public sympathy the activities were not progressing satisfactorily. In reply the Mother quoted the Master, 'When the southern breeze blows, all trees that have developed hard-wood get transformed into sandal.'[14] Then she added, 'The southern breeze has blown; now all will be turned into sandal– except bamboos and bananas.' These words reflect the firm conviction and optimism of the Mother.

The Mother strongly believed that one who renounced for God was really blessed. Before granting a young man Sannyasa, she used to inquire of him about his family affairs, whether the members of the family had sufficient provision for their maintenance etc. Once she had granted Sannyasa, she did not deflect from her decision for criticism or tears.

Soon after an aspirant whom the Mother gave Sannyasa, left Jayrambalti, his mother and wife reached there crying bitterly and prayed to the Mother for cancellation of his Sannyasa and complained that such indiscretion would ruin a family. The Mother said to them, 'He has not done any wrong, he has chosen the right path; and I have been told that he has provided for your maintenance. The Mother's persuasion and affection made them calm and convinced.

On the contrary, on several occasions the Mother refused undeserving persons Sannyasa. Once a woman disciple of hers wrote that her husband wished to become a monk and had been insisting her on going away with her children and living with her parents. Hearing the letter read, the Mother retorted, 'Just see the impropriety of the thing. He will be a monk, for sooth! Why did you marry? If you really want to give up, first make suitable arrangement for the subsistence of your dependents.'[16]

Once on the first day of the worship of Durga two devout young men came there and offering lotuses at the Mother's feet prayed for Sannyasa-Sensing an unnatural sentimentalism in their talks and manners, the Mother dissuaded them saying, 'That will come in due course, my boys,'[17]

There are numerous examples of such use of meticulous discretion of the Mother.

Once a monk who was supposed to be adhered to and meditative on God, wrote from Rishikesh where he had gone for practising austerity, 'Mother you said, "You will see the Master in time." But I have not been granted this up till now." On hearing about the content of the letter the Mother said annoyingly, 'Do write to him, "The Lord is not under any obligation to come forward to meet you just because you have gone to Rishikesh." He has become a monk. What will he do now expect to call on God? God will reveal Himself when it pleases Him.'[18]

One day when the Mother heard that one of her disciples had changed his ochre clothes for the white dress of a householder she reacted with dismay, 'An earthen vessel can't hold a lioness's milk. By continuously eating food at the houses of worldly men his mind had become polluted.'[19]

The Mother did not give Sannyasa to her boy attendants Brahmachari Varada and Hari. While asking Varada to do certain things, she used to tell him, 'If you wore the ochre garment, my son, could I order you to do these? I would feel hesitant even if you touched my feet with your hands. You need have no anxiety at all. Afterwards whenever you feel the hankering you have merely to approach Sarat (Swami Saradananda), and he will arrange for it.'[20] Thus she herself by showing respect towards monks and monasticism, made people respect them.

As the supreme head of the Order the Mother was attentive to the spiritual needs of the monks and kept all round the strictest vigilance for their good. One day at Koalpara Ashram while she was dictating a list for the market to Brahmachari Varada, the end of a woman devotee's cloth by chance touched his back. Noticing it the Mother rebuked her for her careless walking about and asked her to bow down before the Brahmachari. On another occasion while living at the 'Udbodhan' she ordered Radhu to take off her anklets and advised her to maintain privacy of combing and arranging her locks in order to keep up spiritual ambience there.

According to the Mother the monks and the householders could not be same. Because the householders were victims of desires and craving for earthly pleasures while the monks left all for the Lord. She respected the monks but warned them against conceit. When Brahmachari Sadhan taking the ochre cloth from her wanted to know about the formalities to be followed for becoming a monk, the Mother replied that if he had the basic things namely faith and firmness, then he would have it all. Being not satisfied with the answer he kept repeating the same question of ceremonies. The Mother was compelled to say to the Brahmachari, 'Get those things done by my sons at the (Belur) Math.' In fact, she laid stress on inner detachment more than outer formalities. To quote Swami Gambhirananda, 'Her attitude to Brahmacharya (the vow of celibacy) was unique.'[21] One day at Jayrambati she said to Swami Vishweshwarananda, '...You are rare jewels to be sought for by gods.'

The Mother could see the inmost heart of the devotees. She gave a clerk in the Bihar Secretariat the ochre robe and he went to the Himalayas for austerity. When other monks advised him to perform the *Virajā-homa,* he asked the Mother for her opinion. She did not permit him to perform the *Virajā-homa* describing it 'a difficult matter'. The man returned home soon after. In 1911 Swami Ramakrishnananda brought a young man named Surendra Vijay to the Mother and told that the boy was accompanying him to Madras and requested her to initiate him into Sannyasa. The Mother referred the case to Swami Saradananda who forwarded it to Swami Brahmananda. Then the Mother said, 'Then let him have it at Puri from Rakhal.' The boy went back home soon after.

In the Order led by the Mother strict regulation was the condition of liberty. Once it was decided to sack the cook at the 'Udbodhan'; but the monk-manager hesitated to fire him considering that it would put the Mother to trouble. Hearing of this she said, 'You are monks whose one aim is renunciation; can't you get rid of a servant?' Again, when the Mother heard that a monk at the Belur Math had slapped a servant for disloyalty, she remarked 'They are (homeless) monks who should live under trees. And to think that they have their Math, their house, their servant and the beating of that servant to boost!'[22]

In 1919 about fortnight before the worship of Durga four Brahmacharis walked from Belur Math to Jayrambati to take the monastic vow from the Mother and then undertake austerity at Banaras for sometime by living on alms. When the Mother came to know that they had left the math without the permission of Swami Saradananda or Swami Shivananda, she in a pensive mood, directed them to return to the Math right then and reminded them that their absence before the festival might put the management to considerable inconvenience and it was the season of malaria. She told also that to live at the Math was not any less austerity and they had joined the Math recently and they should live with them for some time. She assured them that everything would happen slowly in due course. But they instead of obeying her instruction insisted her on initiating them into Sannyasa. Though their doggedness deeply hurt the Mother, she could not be unkind. She granted the ochre robe to only one Brahmachari Bholanath, the youngest of the group, whom she introduced to the Belur Math. But falling a prey to emotional group-psychology he too left for Banaras.

Swami Shivananda and the Mother exchanged informations regarding the disobedient absconding four. Swami Shivananda forbade Chandra Maharaj (Swami Nirbharananda), head of the Advaita Ashrama of Banaras to shelter those unruly Brahmacharis who defied all even the Mother. Bholanath, finding himself helpless and haggard, prayed for the Mother's indulgence to permit him to stay at the Advaita Ashrama. The Mother, deeply moved by his letter, pardoned him and wrote to him, 'I have written to Chandra about you; and to you I say, now that you are at Banaras, if you can live in the Master's Ashrama serving Chandra and the other monks for life, it will be to your own good.' She sent a note to Swami Shivananda to the effect. Bholanath abode by the Mother's instruction and spent the rest of his life at the Advaita Ashrama, Banaras under the name of Swami Amareshananda.

The Mother played a major role in taking possession of the Master's birth-place at Kamarpukur, Hooghly and arranging for the construction of a temple there. She suggested that the monks of the Belur Math should take charge of the birth-place and of the temple to be built and that they should build houses for Ramlal and others and a brick temple for the family deities, Raghuvir and Sitala who should be worshipped by the members of the family. Her proposals were heartily seconded by all. Accordingly a small piece of land adjacent to the birth-place was acquired by the trustees on December 14, 1917 and the birth-place was handed over to the trustees of the Belur Math, by a document signed by the Mother and others on July 27, 1918.

At Jayrambati a plot of land for a new home of the Mother along with the Punya-pukur was purchased. The home was ceremonially opened on May 15, 1916. She bought some paddy fields also for Jagad-dhatri. She made the trustees of the Belur Math the legal owners and absolute managers of all these properties.

The Holy Mother, with her profound affection, strong personality, prudence, simplicity and generosity made herself an imposing and untiring guiding force of the Ramakrishna Order. Swami Vivekananda's words are convincing evidence of the Mother's influence and authority over the organization :

> If but Mother orders, her demons can work anything. Brother, before proceeding to America I wrote to Mother to bless me. Her blessings came, and at once bound I cleared the ocean. There, you see. In this terrible winter I am lecturing from place to place and fighting against odds, so that funds may be collected for Mother's Math.[23]

The Mother's success as preserver, protector and propagator attested to the originality and uniqueness of her leadership skills.

An ideal woman :

Sri Sarada Devi with her divine love, service to all including her husband, holiness, tolerance, modesty, tenderness, renunciation and suffering and above all spirituality made herself an ideal woman.

In this land of the oldest civilization in the world exalted ladies namely Sita, Savitri, Damayanti, Bāk illuminated the glory of womanhood. In Bṛhadāraṇyaka Upanishad in the fourth Brahmana of the second chapter and in the fifth Brahmana of he fourth chapter Moitreyi wife of Yāg̃nabalkya said to her husband :

येनाहं नामृता स्यां किमहं तेन कुर्याम? यदेव भगवान्वेद तदेव मे ब्रूहोति ॥

'What shall I do with that which will not make me immortal?

Tell me, Sir, of that alone which you know (to be the only means of immortality).'

Similarly, the Holy Mother forsaking worldly pleasures and passion dedicated herself to be a worthy partner of her husband's mission in life, a devout disciple of him and an heir to his spiritual power; above all a propagator of the grace of motherhood in the world. To the shrewd question of Sri Ramakrishna ('Well, my dear, have you come to drag me down to the worldly level?'), she at once unhesitatingly replied, 'No. Why should I drag you to worldly ways? I have come to help you in your chosen path.' The blazing fire of their pure heart burnt away carnal desires.

Swami Vireswarananda, one of the direct disciples of the Mother said, 'Normally she gave diksha only after Thakur puja but she had no hard and fast rules about it. She gave diksha under any condition. It may be remembered that she gave diksha to a porter on the Vishnupur railway station platform itself. When she was very seriously ill at Udbodhan House, one day a Parsi young man came there to see her and get initiation. At that time nobody was allowed to see the Mother as she was seriously ill. This young man was sitting downstairs and was not allowed to go upstairs to see the Mother but she somehow got scent of this boy's arrival and asked someone to bring him to her. He was initiated by the Mother and sent downstairs. When Swami Saradananda came to know of this, he said, 'If Mother desires to have a Parsi disciple, what can I say?' This young man was none other than the well-known film actor and producer in Bombay, Sri Sohrab Modi. In this way she was never hesitant to initiate anybody at any moment, unto the last.'[24]

After the passing away of Sri Ramakrishna (on 16 August 1886) the Mother, inspired people, both her monastic sons and laymen with the ideals that the Master himself had preached and practised. Thus she dedicated herself to the cause of mankind.

In his famous lecture 'My life and Mission' Swamiji recollected the role of the Mother as a saviour during the days of agony after the passing away of the Master and her uniqueness : ...'Who would sympathise with the imaginations of a boy— imaginations that caused so much suffering to others? Who would sympathise with me? None – except one.

'That one's sympathy brought blessing and hope. She was a woman. Our teacher, this great monk, was married when he was a boy and she a mere child. When he became a young man, and all his religious zeal was upon him, she came to see him. Although they had been married for long, they had not seen very much of each other until they were grown up. Then he said to his wife, "Behold, I am your husband; you have a right to this body. But I can not live the sex life, although I have married you. I leave it to your judgment." And she wept and said, "God speed you! The Lord bless you! Am I the woman to degrade you? If I can, I will help you. Go on in your work."

'That was the woman. The husband went on and became a monk in his own way; and from a distance the wife went on helping as much as she could. And later, when the man had become a great spiritual giant, she came–really, she the first disciple–and she spent the rest of her life taking care of the body of this man. He never knew whether he was living or dying or anything...

'Well, that lady his wife, was the only one who sympathised with idea of those boys.' But she was powerless. She was poorer than we were...'

Swamiji concluded the speech with the words :

'...I told you of the lady who was my Master's wife. We have all great respect for her. She never dictates to us. So it is quite safe. That part has to be accomplished.' (Works. Vol. 8, pp. 73–91).

Sister Nivedita, in a letter to Mrs. Ratchiff on 2 September 1903 said about Sarada Devi that apparently she was a very ordinary Hindu woman yet she (Nivedita) considered her the greatest woman of the modern world. Sister in her book, 'The Master as I saw him' wrote, 'To me it has always appeared that she is Sri Ramakrishna's final word as to the ideal of Indian womanhood.' (P. 122)

Swami Nikhilananda, in his book, 'Holy Mother' wrote,

> "Holy Mother, in a unique way, fulfilled the duties of wife, mother, and nun. There have been before in the world the ideal wife, the ideal mother, and the ideal nun, but a combination of the three in one person is rare indeed. Holy Mother was wedded to Sri Ramakrishna at the age of five, lived with him as long as he lived, and ministered to his physical needs in the best tradition of a Hindu wife. She was his companion in spiritual life. She demonstrated that wifely devotion and love are possible without demanding physical satisfaction from one's mate. In spite of her marriage, she remained a nun, pure in body and mind, and in uninterrupted communion with God. Though she had no children of the flesh, she had many of the spirit. Like an earthly mother, she looked after her disciples' physical comfort. But unlike an earthly mother, she was totally unattached in her love and expected no return from it. Truly sister Nivedita declared that Holy Mother was Sri Ramakrishna's last word on the ideal of Indian womanhood. But why of Indian womanhood alone? She can very well represent the universal ideal of womanhood." (P. 297)

Injunction against widowhood :

Sarada Devi was the only woman in the world who was never a widow though her husband had passed away (August 16, 1886) about thirty four years before her mahasamadhi (July 21, 1920).

Having the obsequies of Sri Ramakrishna been completed at the cremation ground at Cossipore, a copper urn with the sacred ashes was carried to the garden house and placed on the Master's bed.

In the evening the Holy Mother was weeping in her room not for the bereavement of her husband but because she felt that Mother Kali left her. She sat to put the marks of a Hindu widow by removing ornaments. When she was about to take off her gold bracelets, the Master suddenly appeared in his body and taking hold of her hands said, 'Have I died that you are removing the signs of a married woman from your wrists?'[25] '...in a moment of revelation she heard the words of faith, "I have only passed from one room to another."[26] From that day the Mother kept wearing her bracelets and did not cut her tresses of hair and wore clothes with thin red borders and not the absolutely white ones without any coloured border meant for the widows. This context may be concluded with the eulogy of Swami Gambhirananda. "...There is really no end to the everlasting play of the Master; and there is really no separation of the Mother from him."

Like an inscrutable providence :

In those days (in the second half of the nineteenth century) the hamlets like Jayrambati (the sacred birth place of the Holy Mother) and Kamarpukur (the holy native land of Sri Ramakrishna) were far from town and shut out from modern civilization. The inhabitants suffered a dearth of daily necessaries there. Naturally, it was very difficult for the Mother to provide her disciples and devotees with food and lodging with scanty means particularly when there was a constant stream of visitors. She used to collect things namely milk, vegetables if needed from the village folks unhesitatingly only to reach the zenith of cordial hospitality. In that unfriendly situation she tried to provide the best possible care and comfort that reminds us of Supriya, daughter of Anathpindat a disciple of Lord Buddha, who, despite her utter misery, agreed to take on responsibility to feed the starving town of Shravastipur during famine while the big shots kept mum before the Lord.

The Mother was familiar with the taste of each of her devotees and attended him or her accordingly. Everybody thought that the Mother was most attentive to his needs and loved him the best for she had the same motherly affection and tender concern for each of her sons and daughters. One day she said to her sister-in-law confidently 'Hullo, my dear, I have no trouble on account of my children. Even though a hundred of my children come, I can tackle them all single-handed.'

Striking non-attachment :

Sarada Devi like her husband was an embodiment of renunciation. Sri Ramakrishna took care of his mother Chandra Devi, accepted his wife and moulded her to be his messenger and cried bitterly at the death of his nephew Akshay. But as an ideal monk he was detached from the cross-currents of a family life. Swami Vivekananda dedicated himself to the service of his motherland and the God in men but could not forget his own widow mother Bhuvaneshwari Devi. Similarly the Mother had to discharge duties towards her family but her inborn serenity and stoicism protected her inner self from the flames of temporal sorrows or personal pain.

As the mistress of the home, the Mother had to pacify her contending brothers Kali and Varada or to stand between them to stop them. She was evidently angry and anxious but within a very short time her excitement and resentment disappeared. The realization of futility of conflict of interests in the drama of mortal life on the stage of the world and the existence of the eternal peace at the end made her laugh and she said, 'What a maya (magic) is this of the Mahamaya (Conjuror)! There stretches the infinite earth, and these possessions, too, will be left behind. Can't man understand this simple fact?'[28]

A little while before the time for offering food to the Master at Koalpara, the Mother learnt of the death of Neda, the first son of her niece Maku from diphtheria on April 20, 1919 and shed profuse tears as an ordinary woman would. But when a devotee reminded her of the Master's worship, she at once quietened herself down as if nothing had occurred. She offered food and prayer calmly.

Once Yogin-Ma soliloquized, 'I have seen the Master as a man of extreme renunciation; but I find the Mother so worldly-minded! Day and night she is occupied with her brothers, nephews, and nieces.' Then one day when the pious widow sat in Japa (silent prayer) by the Ganga, she had a vision in which the Master appeared and said to her, 'See, see, what is flowing down the Ganga.' She saw a newly born baby red with blood and wound round in its navel string, floating on the river. Sri Ramakrishna added, 'Can the Ganga be polluted at any time? Think of her (Sri Sarada Devi) also in that way. Don't entertain these doubts. Know her and this (pointing to his own body) as identical.' In fact, both of the Master and the Mother were renunciation incarnate.

Thus a study of the Mother's domestic life reveals her incredible non-attachment. Indeed, she stressed inner detachment more than outer possessions.

Once a woman devotee requested the Holy Mother to advise her daughter to marry. The Mother answered, 'Is it not misery to remain in lifelong slavery to another and always dance to his tune? Though there is some risk in being a celibate, still, if one is not inclined to lead a married life, one should not be forced into it and subjected to lifelong wordliness. Those girls who are drawn to the ideal of complete renunciation should be encouraged to lead a celibate life.' (*Teachings of Sri Sarada Devi The Holy Mother* : A Compilation, Ramakrishna Math, Madras, P. 75)

In fact, the Mother wearing a red-bordered white cloth as her husband had, was 'a nun in white clothing' and her doings and sayings are permeated with renunciation.

Wonderful mistress of the home :

Sri Ramakrishna as the conventional monks, kept himself aloof from the whirlpool of a family life while the Mother was at the very heart of it. While living at Dakshineswar, she looked after her old widow mother-in-law and wavering husband with great care and devotion. Apart from that her dynamic role as the mistress was seen at Shyampukur, Cossipore Garden house, Kamarpukur and Jayrambati too.

In her father's house the Mother had to deal with her relatives on three levels–the first the brothers the second the sisters-in-law and the nieces, and the third the nephews and the sons of her nieces. She behaved towards them according to their age and nature.

To live with the members of her paternal family was to tread on a rope between two poles to the Mother. She was the head of a large and poor family comprising men and women of different nature. Some of them were docile and great souls while some were greedy, wicked and mean. Moreover, most of them were not even distantly related to her.

Two of the Mother's five brothers Umes Chandra and Abhaycharan died in youth. Abhay left behind him his widow Surabala and a daughter Radharani affectionately called Radhu or Radhi. Her first brother Prasanna was very frugal and improved his condition with the moderate income from his priestly services in Kolkata. Kalikumar her third brother was bad-tempered. The Mother herself said to Brahmachari Varada, 'Kali is mad after money. "Food is a problem that makes fool of a wise man." He seems to consider his sister a money-yielding tree. But he has a little love and regard for me; in stress and strain it is Kali who stands by his sister. As for the others, the more you give, the merrier they are.'[29]

Before the ceremony when Radhu's son would eat rice for the first time, the Mother told Varada that she had not got much money in cash that time and to ask Kali to do the marketing meant great expense. She advised the Brahmachari to purchase the more costly things after proper inquiry from Anur and Kotulpur. She added also that she would get some of the smaller items bought by Kali; otherwise he would be furious.

On the eve of the birthday (22nd December) celebration of the Mother, Kali was vested by her with the responsibility for purchasing and entire management so that she might be free from anxiety. But Kali who wanted an absolutely free hand in that auspicious day's matter, was some how bumped up and wanted to teach his elder sister a lesson. In the afternoon the Mother said sadly to Brahmachari Gopesh (later on Swami Saradeshananda) 'My son, this wretch Kali is a constant source of trouble; he worries me without rhyme or reason. See, for instance all have eaten, but

I am waiting here with his food. He is delaying on one excuse or another; and I, too, can't take rest.' The Brahmachari intelligently managed the situation by helping Kali in heaping up hay on his farm-yard and thus soothed him. The Mother gladly fed him as if nothing had happened.

The Mother was the centre of her birthday celebration and was being adored by innumerable monks and devotees. But she considered it her first duty to take care of her ailing sister-in-law (wife of Varadaprasad) Indumati. She herself arranged for some light diet, dressed and washed them in the pond, cooked them and carried to the patient's house quietly.

Kali Kumar proposed to the Mother that they should celebrate the birthday (18th February) of Paramahamsa Mahashaya (Sri Ramakrishna) on a befitting manner as she was there and many relatives and visitors would come to attend the celebration and to bid her farewell before her leaving for Kolkata. The Mother said, 'Brother, where have I the kind of devotion that you have, and where's that capacity to celebrate the Master's birthday on a grand scale after my heart? Manage it somehow with potatoes, pumpkins and such things as are available in this village. You can well see the state of my health; I am getting weaker day by day.' It was enough to set Kali in active role to celebrate the auspicious day properly and to feed people to his heart's content.

The brothers of the Mother looked to her for help. One day when Prasanna and Kali were quarreling, the Mother said, with a smile, 'My brothers are jewels indeed. It's because they had in their previous lives made penances to the extent of beheading themselves that I have been staying in their family.'

Surabala, widow of Abhay Charan, the youngest brother of the Mother, was known as mad aunt for her insanity. The covetous father of Surabala managed to snatch her box of ornaments when she went to her father's house in the beginning of February 1907. But the mad sister-in-law charged the Mother with occupying her ornaments. The Mother answered, 'If I had them I should throw away the trash.' She recovered the ornaments with the help of Lalit Chatterjee and Mahendranath Gupta (Master Mahashaya, known as 'M'). In February 1913 while the Mother was at the 'Udbodhan' in Kolkata, Surabala, under a detestable notion that the Mother kept her daughter Radhu under her control by administering drugs, abused the Mother that she was spending all she had without making provision for Radhu. Having been disgusted at such offensive words the Mother said, 'Don't you consider me an ordinary mortal. I don't take any offence though you revile me so much, casting slur on my father and mother, just because I think that these are mere words. Do you think you can have any escape if I am really offended? It's all to your advantage so long as I live. Your daughter will be yours only. I shall be there so long only as she is not properly brought up. Otherwise what attachment have I? I can rend all ties asunder this very moment. You won't so much as have an inkling of my disappearing some day like camphor.'

Surabala was a chronic problem to the Mother. She was not only insane but cross-grained and cantankerous also. It was the Mother's last stay at Jayrambati. One day Surabala fancied Manmatha, her son-in-law had been drowned and that was the work of her sister-in-law. She stopped abusing the Mother when Manmatha called for by the Mother, reached home from a grocer's shop where he was playing cards.

On the evening of that very day when the Holy Mother was dressing vegetables for the night, the quarrelsome and sceptic Surabala complained, 'It is you who have been administering opium to Radhu with a view to crippling her and keeping her under your thumb.' The Mother calmly said, 'Why don't you take away your daughter? There she lies. Have I kept her concealed?' Turning a deaf ear to the facts or reason Surabala taking in hand a piece of log, furiously tried to hit the Mother on the head. Hearing the shriek of the Mother, Brahmachari Varada rushed to the spot and snatching the fuel away drove the cranky lady out of the main gate. The Mother was in a flustered mood when some words slipped out of her lips, 'Mad woman, what were you about to do? That hand of yours will fall off from your body.' No sooner did she utter those unkind words out of anger than her inborn composure made her repent before the Master's picture, 'Master, what's this that I have done? What's the remedy now? Hitherto curse against anybody had ever escaped my lips; and yet that, too, comes to pass at last! Why tarry longer then?' The manifestation of compassion and self-reproach of the Mother kept Varada spell-bound.

Nalini, daughter of Prasanna and his first wife Rampriya Devi, was a victim of poverty and ill treatment in her husband's house. So she lived with the Mother. Naturally the Mother had a soft spot for her. Nalini was crazy about purity and irritated others. The Mother had to suffer and tackle her abnormal manners tenderly and skill fully.

Nalini and Surabala were always at daggers drawn. The Mother, regarding her art of adjustment to such members of her family said, 'Whatever you may do, you have, as a matter of fact, to give everybody due attention and consult his opinion. You have to grant a little freedom and watch from a distance so that nothing may go very wrong. ...When dealing with these conceited persons, I have to study their moods and move very cautiously and yet they fall out now and then– as though it's their nature! How can I help that? I think to myself, "It's His world, He is taking care of it."

Radhu (Radharani) daughter of Abhaycharan and Surabala inherited insanity from her mother. Once the Master indicated to the Mother in a vision that Radhu actually was Yoga-maya born to pull the mind of the Master to the normal plane from the lofty spiritual flight.

The Mother described Radhu as 'unfathomable sea' though she left no stone unturned for the restoration of her mental health. Radhu's nerves had become too sensitive to bear any sound. So the Mother tried to live with her in some comparatively quieter place e.g. the boarding house of the Nivedita Girls' School, the Jagadamba Ashrama at Koalpara. Besides, the Mother made Radhu wear the bangle of the 'Mad Kali' of Tirol, called for a Chandal *tāntrika* of

Sushnegede and performed rituals to invoke the help of a fierce spirit 'chanda' for the solace of all but in vain. Radhu had become addicted to opium and badgered the Mother into increasing the dose. The Mother, then in poor health, said to Radhu, 'Radhi, why do you continue this? Stand up straight now; I am fed up with you. I am going to lose my religious practices, duties, money, and all for your sake. Can you tell me from where to meet all these expenses?' At this Radhu furiously struck at the Mother's back with a brinjal. The Mother bending her red and swollen back in pain said, 'Master, don't be offended at her; she is ignorant.' Then rubbing the holy dust of her own feet over Radhu's head she said, 'Radhu, the Master never uttered a harsh word against this body, and you inflict such pain on it! How can you evaluate my worth? How lightly do you mean to deal with me just because I have chosen to live amidst you all? Radhi, if I become offended, then you can find no shelter anywhere in the three worlds. Master, don't be offended with her.'

Radhu's disease worsened day by day and the Mother's affection instead of softening her made her more adamant and aggressive. She abused kicked and cursed the Mother.

Referring to these and likewise self imposed bonds and burden, the Mother once said to a devotee at the Udbodhan, 'Do you notice, my daughter, how strange is this play of the Master? What a fine lot he has made of my mother's family. See what kind of company I have to keep. As for this one (Radhu's mother) she is rank mad; another (Nalini) is verging on insanity. And see there's another still (Radhu)! My daughter, what a strange being I brought up! She has not an iota of intelligence. ...'

Rightly has observed Swami Gambhirananda, 'Radhu really served two purposes in the Mother's life– on the one hand she acted like a bond binding her heart to this world, and on the other she supplied a background for the expression of her motherly qualities. The greatness that manifested itself in the midst of the currents and cross-currents of this world could not otherwise have been easily comprehended. ...The Holy Mother's life is full of meaning for either kind of critics. For she accepted the world *in toto* and played her game in it faultlessly. Her words are all soaked in life's experience; and yet every move she makes, sends forth bright rays of a light beyond.' (Holy Mother Sri Sarada Devi, P.P. 291–292)

Amazing diligence and forbearance :

Sarada Devi, the first child of her deserving parents used to help her mother in plucking the cotton pods, in spinning sacred thread with cotton and looking after her brothers in her childhood. She herself said, 'As a girl I would plunge into neck-deep water to cut grass for the cattle, and walk to the fields with fried-rice for the labourers. During one year when locusts had nearly destroyed the crop, I went round the fields gathering paddy.' Old people, contemporary with her said, 'From the young days, Sarada was as diligent in her work as she was intelligent, quiet, and well-behaved. She had never to be asked to work. Of her own accord and with her own resourcefulness she would meticulously perform her duties.'

In 1875 the Holy Mother, hardly recovering from dysentery, suffered from malaria accompanied by enlargement of the spleen. She went to Kayapat Badanganj with her mother Shyamasundari Devi for treatment of the spleen-trouble. The process of treatment was horrible and the suffering of the patient was indescribable. After bath, the patient had to lie on the ground and was held down by some persons, so that he might not get away. Then the medicine man would rub a burning piece of jujube wood on a plantain leaf laid over the region of the spleen. The skin would get singed and the patient would shriek in pain.

The Mother heard the scream and saw the plight of the patients undergoing the primitive treatment. After ablution, when she moved forward to the spot, some able-bodied men advanced to hold her firmly. But she pronounced, 'Nobody need hold me; I myself shall lie down quiet. And she went through the terrible ordeal calmly. Once the Mother said, 'I have done much more than is necessary for setting an ideal.'[30] The horripilant anecdote concerned testifies to the significance of the Mother's words– probably ideal of manifestation of self glory amidst adverse forces. It may be noted that the Master, also, had his spleen treated thus at the same place.

Hundreds of devotees with their burdens of sins and miseries used to come to the Mother. Their touch during salutation caused pain in her feet. But she bore the burning sensation as she endured the trails and tribulations of life willingly and calmly.

In certain cases the Mother was very strict. She did not allow him who transgressed her code of honour and delicacy, to enter her presence again. At the same time she was the embodiment of compassion and forgiveness. One day as the Mother refused to increase the dose of opium, Radhu grew angry and struck at the Mother's back with a big brinjal with all her might. It inflicted such pain that she bent her back and the place turned red and swollen. Yet she forgave her niece and prayed with folded hands, 'Master, don't be offended at her; she is ignorant.' There are innumerable examples of such forgiveness of the Mother.

The Mother said, 'Everyone has to be accommodating. Forbear everything. God is there to judge.' On another occasion she remarked, 'It is idle to expect that dangers and difficulties will not come. They are bound to come. But for a devotee they will pass away from under the feet like water.'

No acid-testing :

Sri Ramakrishna was very cautious about accepting a person as his disciple. He believed in physiognomy and examined the aspirant's physical features and put him to vairous tests to study his mental strength, sincerity, perseverence and nature. But the Mother had no hard and fast fascination for such selection. Like the Ganga she accepted all and everything yet remained holy. The Mother imparted *mantras* to a candidate if he was a desirable person and if she felt the inspiration without taking time and circumstances much into consideration. She initiated a Brahmachari at the age of thirteen, a devotee from Shillong just on the eve of his departure and an up-country porter on the railway platform at Vishnupur on her way to Kolkata. Of course, in some cases (e.g. a clerk in the Bihar Secretariat and Surendra Vijay etc.) the Mother did not permit Sannyasa perhaps knowing the mind of the candidate.

One day a disciple said to the Mother, 'What an abundance of spiritual trances and ecstasies had those who went to the Master! But nothing of that is being done by you to us.' The Mother answered. 'As to that, to how many indeed did he do such things, and how selectively at that? Even so his body fell down quite early. To me he has pushed on a line of ants. If I do just as he did, how long will my body last? What a number of children I have to tend!'

Swami Premananda wrote about her in a letter,

> ... who has understood the Holy Mother? There's not a trace of grandeur. ...A poison that we can't assimilate we pass on to the Mother. She draws everyone to her lap. An infinite power– an incomparable grace! Glory to the Mother! Not to speak of us; we haven't seen the Master himself doing this. With how much caution and what testing he accepted any one! And here– what do you see here at the Mother's place? Wonderful! Wonderful! She grants shelter to everyone, eats food from the hands of almost anyone and all is digested! Mother, Mother, victory unto the Mother.[31]

'The most wonderful thing of God'

Sri Ramakrishna, Sarada Devi and Swami Vivekananda cherished the same movement and dedicated themselves to the identical spiritual revolution. But each of them had original characteristics. The new movement of love and synthesis with its various traits was projected by their individual entity and capacity. Sri Ramakrishna, by dint of asceticism and meditation highlighted certain ideals and ideas. Swamiji carried those to everywhere in the world and told people in his inimitable style about how to manifest those ideals in every walk of their lives while the Holy Mother demonstrated the practical application of those ideals and messages.

The Mother was a perfectly chaste wife and intently devoted to her husband but she did not forgo her freedom of thought and action and expression.

The Master kept his would-be monastic disciples under constant surveillance. He was careful of their physical and mental health and told the Holy Mother how many pieces of *chapati* (unleavened bread) should be given to each disciple. One day he came to know that the Mother had given Baburam Ghosh (Swami Premananda) six chapatis instead of four. Hurrying to the Mother he complained that her indiscreet affection might spoil Baburam's future life. The Mother firmly replied : "Why are you so much worried because he had a couple more chapatis? I shall look after his future. Please don't make an issue about his food."[32]

The Mother did not hate the sinners rather felt compassion for them. One day at Daskhineswar she sent the meal of the Master through a depraved lady. She used to chat with an old woman who was corrupted in her early life. Once a fallen woman of a respectable family hesitated to enter the Mother's room at the Udbodhan. The Mother, stretching her holy arms round her neck, said 'come, my daughter, come in. You have realized what sin is, and you are repentant. Come, I shall initiate you. Lay everything at the Master's feet; and cast away all fear.'

Describing the Master and the Mother as 'like the two sides of one and the same coin', Swami Premananda once in the course of a talk at Belur Math, said to the devotees, "We have seen that she had a much greater capacity than the Master. She was the embodiment of Power, and how well she controlled it! Sri Ramakrishna could not do so though he tried. His power became manifest through his frequent ecstasies, which were seen by all. The Mother repeatedly experienced samadhi, but others did not know of it. What wonderful self-control she exercised! She covered herself with veil like a young bride in her husband's home."[33]

Swami Yogananda, the first initiated disciple of the Holy Mother, said, 'We saw how Holy Mother, even in the midst of her intense grief at the passing away of the Master, fully realized his divine grace and presence at all times. We thought of ourselves as helpless orphans, but the Mother's love became our sheet anchor.

'...During such periods of ecstasy, her manner of speech, her voice, her way of taking food, her way of walking, and her general behaviour were exactly like those of the Master. We have heard that in deep meditation the worshipper and the worshipped become one. The scriptures mention a spiritual state known as *tadatma-bhava* – being at one with God. We have read in the Bhagavata how the gopis [shepherd girls of Vrindaban], unable to bear separation from Krishna became so deeply absorbed in the thought of him that for the moment they forgot their own individualities and behaved as though they were Krishna. In the same manner the Mother, too, forgot her own separate existence and acted just like the Master, feeling her oneness with him. When I asked her some complex question about spiritual matters shortly after her states of samadhi, she replied in a God-intoxicated mood, very much like Sri Ramakrishna; that is, in the same manner characteristic of the Master, even using his same easy style of expression with metaphors and parables.

'We all were surprised to see the spirit of Sri Ramakrishna united with hers. It was unique. We then realized that the Master and the Mother were one in essence, though appearing in separate forms. Is not said in the scriptures : "Lord, thou art man, thou art woman?" The Master told me many times that there was no difference between him and the Mother.'[34]

The epigrammatic words of the Mother testify to her amazing depth of spiritual realization and vast experience. She said to brahmachari (celibate) Sadhan, 'Faith and firmness are the basic things; if faith and firmness are there, then you have it all.'

One day when the Mother heard that one of her disciples had changed his ochre robe for the white dress of a householder, she remarked with disgust, 'An earthen vessel can't hold a lioness's milk. By continuously eating food at the houses of worldly men his mind has become polluted.' Once a monk wrote from Rishikesh, 'Mother, you said, "You will see the master in time." But I have not been granted this up till now.' On hearing the letter read, the Mother said with resentment, 'Do write to him, "The Lord is not under any obligation to come forward to meet you just because you have gone to Rishikesh." He has become a monk. What will he do now except to call on God? God will reveal Himself when it pleases Him.' One day she said to Swami Keshavananda, '... But what you should note, my dear, is that *renunciation* is his special message in this age.' She said to a devotee, 'Through *Japa* and austerity the bondage of *Karma* is cut asunder, but God can not be realized unless through love and devotion. Did the cowherds get Krishna by *Japa* and meditation or by talking to him Chummily as "Come here, dear" "Take this, dear," "Eat this, dear"?' Once she said to a monk at the 'Udbodhan', 'Good gracious! Can the monk and the householder be equal? The householders are a prey of passions and desires, while the monks have come away leaving everything behind. Whom else have these besides the Lord? Can they be compared with monks?'

The Mother implemented the proverb, 'Example is better than precept' in her everyday life. The devotees and visitors were of varied nature and character. She knew well how to rectify an erring child by setting an example before him. She was confident that her sympathy, affection and proper guidance would help him overcome all his short-coming.

The Mother had not considerable formal education yet it is not to be supposed that she was an uneducated woman for as the wife of Sri Ramakrishna she has had the highest opportunity of personal development and learning from him (1872–1886). She was engaged in imparting mass-education and acting as the supremo of the monastic disciples and then of the Ramakrishna Math and Mission (1894–1920) after the completion of her arduous endeavour (1887–1893) and thus she revealed her amazing wisdom.

An exceptional magnetic personality Sarada Devi attracted all sorts of people such as an educated European of liberal out look

Sister Nivedita, Lady Abala Bose daughter and daughter-in-law of orthodox Brahmo family and wife of Sri Jagadish Chandra Bose a famous scientist, Girish Chandra Ghosh a great play-wright, actor and director and producer, the fearless revolutionaries patriots and the down-trodden people.

Rightly has said Swami Lokeswarananda,

> She was human, yet divine. Her divinity shone through everything she did, even if it was something entirely mundane. She was a simple woman, but in thought, speech, and action she was attuned to God. She was a true saint, but she never claimed she was. She passed as an ordinary woman, but everything about her was extraordinary.' (The Ramakrishna Movement, Ramakrishna Mission Institute of Culture, Kol. P. 13)

Sarada Devi is the only woman in the world who is regarded as Goddess in flesh and blood; a formless in form, a phenomenon in the form of a rustic village woman. In the history of religions and social service there was perhaps no woman but the Holy Mother Sarada Devi who was the supremo of a great philanthropic organization with absolute authority.

In 1896 while saluting the Mother, Girish Chandra Ghosh said to Swami Yogananda and others,

> It is difficult for human beings to believe that God can incarnate in a human form like our own. Can you realize that you are standing before the Mother of the Universe in the form of a village woman? Yet she is the Mother of the Universe– Maha-maya. Maha-Sakti– appearing on the earth for the salvation of all creatures and at the same time exemplifying the ideal of true motherhood.

One day, towards the end Swamiji, bowing down to the Mother said :

> Mother, I know for certain that with your blessing in the future many Narens will be born and hundreds of

> Vivekanandas will evolve. And I also know for certain that in this world there is only one Mother like you; there is no other.[35]

On 11 December, 1910 Sister Nivedita wrote to Holy Mother from Cambridge : Surely you are the most wonderful thing of God—

Charms of the Mother's language :

The Mother, like the Master, used to speak in a simple and sweet language and in a lucid style. She spoke to the Kolkata devotees in formal Bengali mixed with colloquial language and used the patois of the Bankura district while talking with her relatives and people of the locality. Swami Chetananda wrote about Holy Mother's articulation :

Her words were clear and charming; her examples were apt and beautiful; her descriptions were poetic and graphic; her ideas were profound and meaningful; her style of conversation was original and captivating.[36]

Originality of the Mother's sayings :

The Mother's teachings are precise and concise; well-thought-out born of her own experiences and relevant still today for she spoke only the truth. Her method of teaching was effective and original. She often quoted sayings of the Master instead of scriptures, stories or parables. Manada Shankar Dasgupta, a disciple and biographer of the Mother, categorized her teachings into three types; : First, short and clear; second, the gospel of hope and fearlessness; third, simple and classic.

Here we cite some examples from each group of teaching :[37]

(i) Short and clear :

Questioner : Mother, how shall I mediate?

Mother : Just think of the Master.

Questioner : How shall I practise spiritual disciplines?

Mother : My son, at the end, the mind becomes the guru,

Sadhana means to keep the mind on God and to be absorbed in Him. Repeat His name.

Questioner : Is it of any use merely to repeat His name without intense devotion?

Mother : Whether you jump into the water or are pushed into it, your cloth will get drenched. Meditate every day. Constant meditation will make the mind one-pointed.

Questioner : What is the goal of human life?

Mother : The goal of human life is to realize God and to be absorbed in Him.

(ii) Gospel of hope and fearlessness :

Questioner : Mother, I cannot concentrate my mind in meditation at all.

Mother : It does not matter much. Look at the picture of the Master and that will be enough. One should cultivate constant recollectedness.

Questioner : I cannot calm my mind and concentrate.

Mother : The mind will be steadied of itself if aspirants repeat God's name 15,000 or 20,000 times a day. I myself have experienced it.

Questioner : My mind becomes restless now and then. It craves enjoyment. That frightens me.

Mother : Don't be afraid. I tell you that in this Kali Yuga mental sin is no sin. Free your mind from all worries on this account.

Questioner : However I may try to remove evil thoughts, I do not succeed.

Mother : This is the result of what you have done in your past life. Can anyone altogether destroy lust? A little of it remains as long as one has a body. But it can be subdued, as a snake can be subdued by charmed dust.

The Mother once said to a disciple : Do not fear, my child. Always remember that the Master is behind you. I am also with you. As long as you remember me, your mother, why should you be frightened? The Master said to me, 'At the end of their life, I shall certainly liberate those who come to you.'

(iii) Simple and Classic :

Questioner : Mother, the mind is very restless. In no way can I steady it?

Mother : As the wind removes the cloud, so the name of God destroys the cloud of worldliness.

Questioner : Mother, I have practised austerities and japa so much, but I have not achieved anything.

Mother : God is not like fish or vegetables that you can buy for a price.

Questioner : How can one realize God– through worship, japa, or meditation"

Mother : God is realized only through His grace. Nonetheless, one must perform japa and meditation, for they remove the impurities of one's mind. As one gets the fragrance of a flower by handling it, or the scent of sandal wood by rubbing it against a stone, similarly, one becomes spiritually awakened by continuously contemplating the Divine. But you can become illumined right now if you become desireless.

Questioner : Does the Master really live in the picture?

Mother : Of course he does. The body and the shadow are the same. And what is his picture but a shadow? If you pray to him constantly before his picture, then he manifests himself through that picture.

On various occasions the Mother uttered significant and memorable words; as for example :

One must be patient like the earth. What iniquities are being perpetuated on her! Yet she quietly endures them all.

Forbearance is a great virtue; there is no other like it.

Everyone can break down something, but how many can build it up?

Whatever you yearn for, that you will get.

The purpose of one's life is fulfilled only when one is able to give joy to another.

Don't be afraid. Human birth is full of suffering and one has to endure everything patiently, taking the name of God. None, not even God in human form, can escape the sufferings of body and mind.

God is one's very own. It is the eternal relationship. He is everyone's own. One realizes Him in proportion to the intensity of one's feelings for Him.

To err is human. One must not take that into account. It is harmful for oneself. One gets into the habit of finding fault.

Only through work can one remove the bondage of work. Total detachment comes after. One should not be without work even for a moment. Work helps one to fend off idle thoughts.

Many think of God only after receiving blows from the world. But blessed indeed is he who can offer his mind, like a fresh flower, at the feet of the Lord from his very childhood. One should practise renunciation in youth.

One should not hurt others ever by words. One must not speak even an unpleasant truth unnecessarily. By indulging in rude words one's nature becomes rude. One's sensibility is lost if one has no control over one's speech.

Many are known to do great works under the stress of some strong emotion. But a man's true nature is known from the manner in which he does his insignificant daily task.

Misery is truly a gift of God. I believe it is a symbol of His compassion.

In the fullness of spiritual realization, a person finds that the God who resides in his heart, resides in the hearts of all – the oppressed, the persecuted, the lowly and the untouchable. This realization makes one truly humble.

Everything, no doubt, happens by God's will, yet man must work because God expresses His will through man's action. Do not relax your spiritual practices.

Love is our forte. It is through love that the Master's family has taken shape.

I am the mother of the wicked, as I am the mother of the virtuous. Never fear. Whenever you are in distress, say to yourself, "I have a mother."

In reply to a question of Girish Chandra Ghosh, 'What kind of a mother are you?' the Mother unhesitatingly said, 'I am your true mother, a mother not by virtue of being your guru's wife, nor because of any assumed relationship, nor by way of empty talk, but truly the mother.'

Five days before her valediction the Holy Mother said to a woman devotee known as Annapurna's mother, 'What fear is there? You have seen the Master. What fear can there be for you? But one thing I tell you– if you want peace, my daughter, don't find fault with others, but find fault rather with yourself. Learn to make the world your own. Nobody is a stranger, my dear; the world is yours.' This was her last message.

Thus the Mother's teachings are inspiring, pragmatic and feasible and of course original.

Chapter – 3

'JEWELS OF CHILDREN'

Pure soul— Narayana Himself

Shymasundari Devi, mother of Sarada Devi lamented at times thus : 'To what a mad son-in-law have I married my daughter! Alas, she has no family life, no child and does not hear any one calling her "mother". The Master one day heard this and said, 'Dear mother-in-law, you need have no disappointment on that score. Your daughter will have so many children, you will see in the long run, that the distressing call of "mother" will make her bewildered.'

Once the Master said to the Mother spontaneously, "Why do you worry? I shall leave you such jewels of children as one can hardly get even if one performs the severest of austerity, to the extent of cutting off one's head. You will find in the end so many children calling you 'mother', that you will be unable to manage them all."[1]

The prophecy of the Master came true. Their ideal, 'original' and exceptional monastic children loved and served them most and dedicated themselves to propagate their message and launch an international movement for the spiritual and social welfare of all mankind.

On June 4, 1883 Sri Ramakrishna said to Rakhal (afterwards Swami Brahmananda), M. (Mahendranath Gupta) and a few other devotees :

"Now and then Hazra comes forward to teach me. He says to me, 'Why do you think so much about the youngsters?' One day, as I was going to Balaram's house in a carriage, I felt greatly troubled about it. I said to the Divine Mother : 'Mother, Hazra admonishes me for worrying about Narendra and the other young boys. He asks me why I forget God and think about these youngsters.' No sooner did this thought arise in my mind than the Divine Mother revealed to me in a flash that it is She Herself who has become man. But she manifests Herself most clearly through a pure soul...

"I know these youngsters to be Narayana Himself..."[2]

Swami Vivekananda the jewel at the centre of the crown, reminisced about the monastic-disciples of Sri Ramakrishna in his lectures on 'My Master' : "His (Sri Ramakrishna's) thoughts and his message were known to very few capable of giving them out. Among others, he left a few young boys who had renounced the world, and were ready to carry on his work. Attempts were made to crush them. But they stood firm, having the inspiration of that great life before them. Having had the contact of that blessed life for years, they stood their ground. These young men, living as Sannyasins, begged through the streets of the city where were born, although some of them came from high families. At first they met with great antagonism but they persevered and went on from day to day spreading all over India the message of that great man, until the whole country was filled with the ideas he had preached. This man from a remote village of Bengal, without education, by the sheer force of his own determination, realised the truth and gave it to others, leaving only a few boys to keep it alive."[3]

In another address entitled 'My Life and Mission' Swamiji said: "The monk in India is the friend of the prince today, dines with him and tomorrow he is with the beggar, sleeps under a tree. He must come into contact with everyone, must always move about, As the saying is, "The rolling stone gathers no moss." The last fourteen years of my life, I have never been for three months at a time in any one place—continually rolling. So do we all.

"Now this handful of boys got hold of these ideas, and all the practical results that sprang out of these ideas. Universal religion, great sympathy for the poor, and all that are very good in theory, but one must practise.

"Then came the sad day when our old teacher died. We nursed him the best we could. We had no friends, who would listen to a few boys, with their crank notions? Nobody. At least in India boys are nobodies. Just think of it– a dozen boys telling people vast, big ideas saying they are determined to work these ideas out in life. Why, everybody laughed. From laughter it became serious, it became persecution. Why, the parents of the boys came to feel like spanking every one of us. And the more we were derided, the more determined we became."

"...It must crumble before your power of the Lord Himself in you if you are sincere and really unselfish. And those boys were that. They came as children, pure and fresh from the hands of nature. Said our Master : I want to offer at the alter of the Lord only those flowers that have not even been smelled, fruits that have not even been touched with the fingers. The words of the great man sustained us all. For he saw through the future life of those boys that he collected from the streets of Calcutta, so to say. People used to laugh at him when he said, "You will see— this boy, that boy, what he becomes." His faith was unalterable : "Mother showed it to me. I may be weak, but when She says this is so– She can never make mistakes– it must be so."[4] Thus the Swami extolled the originality and extra-ordinary qualities of his brother-disciples in general.

After Sri Ramakrishṇa's passing away, fourteen of the Master's young disciples (two more joined later), under the leadership of Swami Vivekananda formed a monastic brotherhood familiar as the Ramakrishna Math (Order) originally housed in a dilapidaed building of Baranagar, Kolkata. The names of these sixteen monastic disciples are :

Swamis Vivekananda, Brahamananda, Shivananda, Premananda, Yogananda, Niranjanananda, Ramakrishnananda, Saradananda,

Turiyananda, Adbhutananda, Abhedananda, Trigunatitananda, Advaitananda, Subodhananda, Akhandananda and Vijnanananda.

The Master, recognising each disciple's originality made him through his constant personal care and love and subtle spiritual influence, a role model and an ideal spiritual teacher in his own right. He described six of his disciples as *ishwarakotis* (Godlike souls or souls born with special spiritual qualities) : Narendra, Rakhal, Baburam, Yogin, Niranjan and Purna (a householder devotee).

Within a short period the Master's prediction came true as the band of his monastic disciples by dint of renunciation, profound spiritual realization, love for man, originality of their thoughts and plans, above all, philanthropic activities and dynamic personality were appreciated to be extraordinary and 'jewels of children'.

Chapter – 4

SWAMI VIVEKANANDA

One of the great seven sages :

It is said that a mighty vision of a prophet can create and produce that which it has seen. Sri Ramakrishna had a beautiful vision before he met his most favourite disciple Narendranath Datta—Swami Vivekananda. Regarding his wonderful vision he said, 'One day I found that my mind was soaring high in Samadhi along a luminous path. It soon transcended the stellar universe and entered the subtler region of ideas. As it ascended higher and higher, I found on both sides of the way ideal forms of gods and goddesses. The mind then reached the outer limits of that region, where a luminous barrier separated the sphere of relative existence from that of the Absolute. Crossing that barrier, the mind entered the transcendental realm, where no corporeal being was visible. Even the gods dared not peep into that sublime realm and were content to keep their seats far below. But the next moment I saw seven venerable sages seated there in Samadhi. It occurred to me that these sages must have surpassed not only men but even the gods in knowledge and holiness, in renunciation and love. Lost in admiration, I was reflecting on their greatness, when I saw a portion of that undifferentiated luminous region condense into the form of a divine child. The child came to one of the sages, tenderly clasped his neck with his lovely arms. and addressing him in a sweet voice, tried to drag his mind down from the state of Samadhi. That magic touch roused the sage from the superconscious state, and he fixed his half-open eyes upon the wonderful child. His beaming countenance showed that the child must have been the treasure of his heart. In great joy the strange child spoke to him, "I am going down. You too must go with me." The sage remained mute but his tender look expressed his assent. As he kept gazing at the child, he was again immersed in Samadhi. I was surprised to find that a fragment of his body and mind was descending to earth in the form of a bright light. No sooner had I seen Narendra than I recognised him to be that sage.'[1]

The child was the visionary—Sri Ramakrishna himself as he avowed to his disciples.

One night while Ramdayal Chakrabarty and Baburam Ghosh were sleeping on the southeast verandah of the Master's room at Dakshineswar, Sri Ramakrishna in an ecstatic mood said to Ramdayal,

> Look, I have not seen Narendra for a long time, and I feel as if my whole soul were being forcibly wrung like a wet towel. Please ask him to come once and see me. He is a person of pure sattva qualities. He is Narayana himself. I can not have peace of mind if I don't see him now and then.

Distinctive physical features :

Everybody could not but fell in love and respect for Swami Vivekananda at the very first sight. Really no one could look upon him unmoved.

Swami Saradananda in his magnum opus 'Sri Ramkrishna the great Master' wrote,

'On thus examining Narendra, he (Sri Ramakrishna) was pleased and said to him oneday 'All the parts of your body have good characteristics. The only defect is that you breathe a little heavily when asleep. Yogis say that one breathing so heavily is short-lived.' (p. 1099)

Devendranath Tagore the leader of the Brahmo Samaj said to Narendranath, 'My boy, you have the eyes of a yogi. You should practise meditation.' (God lived with them—Swami Chetenanda, p. 22)

Famous poetess and Editor of 'Poetry, a Magazine of Verse' Miss Harriet Monro who was present at the world's Parliament of Religions, Chicago, recorded her immpression of Swami Vivekananda in her autobiography, 'A poet's Life' :

"... the handsome monk in the orange robe gave us in perfect English a masterpiece. His personality, dominant, magnetic; his voice, rich as a bronze bell. the controlled fervour of his feeling; the beauty of his message to the Western World he was facing for the first time—these combined to give us a rare and perfect moment of supreme emotion. It was human eloquence at its highest pitch.'

Romain Rolland, the Nobel laureate great French savant pointed out the distinguishing physical traits of Swamiji :

'His athletic form was the opposite of the fragile and tender yet wiry body of Ramakrishna. He was tall (five feet, eight and a half inches) square-shouldered, broad-chested, stout, rather heavily built, his arms were muscular and trained to all kinds of sports. He had an olive complexion, a full face, vast forehead, strong jaw, a pair of magnificent eyes, large, dark and rather prominent, with heavy lids, whose shape recalled the classic comparison to a lotus petal. Nothing escaped the magic of his glance, capable equally of embracing in its irresistible charm, or of sparkling with wit, irony, or kindness, of losing itself in ecstasy, or of plunging imperiously to the very depths of consciousness and of withering with its fury. But his pre-eminent characteristic was kingliness. He was a born king and nobody ever came near him either in India or America without paying homage to his majesty.'[2]

Swamiji had pronounced wrists, muscular legs, arched feet suitable for bearing body-weight (170 pounds). He had a leonine beauty, sprightliness of a fawn and 'an admirable baritone, having the vibrations of a Chinese gong, as described by his devotee a famous singer Emma Calvé (while one of his devotees Miss

Josephine MacLeod said to Romain Rolland that her Master had a beautiful voice like a violoncello, grave without violent contrasts, but with deep vibrations that filled both hall and hearts.)

Romain Rolland added: 'When this quite unknown young man of thirty appeared in Chicago at the inaugural meeting of the Parliament of Religions, opened in Spetember 1893, by Cardinal Gibbons, all his fellow-members were forgotten in his commanding presence. His strength and beauty, the grace and dignity of his bearing, the dark light of his eyes, his imposing appearance and from the moment he began to speak, the splendid music of his rich deep voice enthralled the vast audience of American Anglo-Saxons previously prejudiced against him on account of his colour. The thought of this warrior prophet of India left a deep mark upon the United States.

'It was impossible to imagine him in the second place. Whereever he went he was the first..."[3]

With reference to the days at Baranagore monastery M. wrote in 'The Gospel of Sri Ramakrishna': "Narendra was clad in a new ochre cloth. The bright orange colour of his apparel blended with the celestial lustre of his face and body, every pore of which radiated a divine light. His countenance was filled with fiery brilliance and yet touched with the tenderness of love. He appeared to all as a bubble that had risen up in the Ocean of Absolute Existence and Bliss and assumed a human body to help in the propagation of his Master's message. All eyes were fixed on him. Narendra was then just twenty four years old..."(p. 979)

Regarding an irresistible attractiveness of Swami Vivekananda's appearance and personality Prema Nandakumar, in an article styled 'Swami Vivekananda: A presence and a Power' published in the 'Prabuddha Bharata' (January 2014) quoted his interview with Swami Sriranganananda :

> Once I asked the swami : 'How did you enter the Mission?' He laughed happily and pointed to a portrait of Swami Vivekananda. 'He inveigled me into all this by his photo.' As a school boy, he had seen in a friend's house the photo

> of Swami Vivekananda, in which Swamiji was seated on a chair, holding his chin in his hand, a little leaning to the front, the high-necked coat and curls pointing to an unusual personality. 'Who is this *rajakumaran* (prince), uncle?' he had asked his friend's father. The reply was enigmatic. 'No boy, it is not the *rajakumaran* of any state, he is the *rajakumaran*, of the world.' Swami Srirangananda told me: 'From that day onwards the face would not leave me alone and when I was seventeen, I entered the Ramakrishna Vivekananda world.'

At Belur Math once at two O'clock in the morning Swami Vijnanananda who lived in a room close to Swamiji's room saw Swamiji walking on the eastern verandah. He asked Swamiji why he could not sleep. The Swami answered, 'Peshan, I was sleeping nicely; but suddenly I felt a jolt, and my sleep broke. It seems to me that there must be a disaster somewhere and many people are suffering.'' Swami Vijnanananda wrote, "The next morning I saw in the newspaper that at the same time Swamiji awakened, there had been a terrible volcanic eruption near the Fiji Islands, and many people were killed. I was surprised to read this news, and then I realized that Swami's nervous system was more responsive to human misery than a seismograph." [Pratyakshadarshir Smritipate Swami Vijnanananda, General Printers and Publishers, Kol. 1977, p.p. 305-306.]

An Exceptional Child :

Bhuvaneshwari Devi said, "Narendra had a great foible even from his childhood. If he was angry at anytime for any reason, he lost himself altogether and would shatter furniture etc. to pieces and scatter them in all directions. I prayed to Visvanatha at Kasi for a son and vowed Him offerings if one should be born, and He perhaps sent me one of His demons. Otherwise why should he behave like a demon when angry?"[4] She adopted a strange method to pacify her child's anger. When Bileh (Narendra's nick name) grew angry she remembered Lord Visvanatha and poured one or two jarfuls of water over his head and his anger would at once vanish.

Narendra's method of learning lessons was peculiar. When his tutor would come to their house, he would bring his Bengali and English books and show to him the lessons to be learnt that day. He would lie or sit freely while the tutor would read aloud and repeat twice or thrice the spelling, pronunciation meaning etc. of the words of the lesson concerned as if the teacher himself was learning the protions of the books and would go away. That was sufficient for him to learn them.

Unlike other children Narendranath did not fear ghosts and one of his favourite games was meditation. One day when he was meditating with his friends a cobra appeared. The other boys got scared and shouting a warning to him ran away. But Narendra sat still. Afterwards he told his parents that he knew nothing of the venomous snake or anything else, rather he was feeling indescribable joy. He was adept at all physical exercises, fighting with sticks, fencing, boxing, exercising with clubs, swimming, rowing and driving horses.

Swamiji differed from other children in many respects. He said to one of his English disciples Mr. E. T. Sturdy :

"Well, Sturdy, in my childhood I used to observe an inexhaustible force arising in me, overflowing in my body, as it were. I used to become restless and could not keep quiet. This was why I used to fidget all the time... My insides would vibrate, as it were, and make me restless to do something."

This wonder-boy experienced spiritual ecstasy at the age of fifteen only when catching sight of a large beehive in the cleft in the rock, his mind was filled with awe and reverence for the inscrutable Providence on his way to Raipur (Madhya Pradesh).

Swamiji himself said : "While at school one night I was meditating behind closed doors and had a fairly deep concentration of mind. How long I meditated in that way I can not say. After the meditation was over I remained seated. Then from the southern wall of that room a lumious figure stepped out and stood in front of me. It was the figure of a *sannyasin* [monk], absolutely calm, with shaven head, and staff and *kamandalu* [water pot] in either hand. He gazed at me for sometime, and seemed as if he would address me. I too gazed at him in speechless wonder. Suddenly a kind of fright seized me. I opened the door and hurried out of the room. Then it struck me that it was foolish of me to run like that, perhaps he might say something to me. But I have never seen that figure since. I think it was the Lord Buddha whom I saw.'[5]

Referring to one of the originalities of Narendranath, the Master said : "At my first meeting with Narendra I found him completely indifferent to his body. When I touched his chest with my hand, he lost consciousness of the outer world. Regaining consciousness, Narendra said, 'Oh, what have you done to me? I have my father and mother at home!' The same thing happened at Jadu Mallick's house. As the days passed I longed more and more to see him. My heart yearned for him...." [Gospel p. 231]

Narendranath was a sāttvic man. Bholanath Mukhopadhyay, a clerk (later treasurer) of Kali temple, Dakshineswar, hinted at that.

A versatile genius :

Swamiji inherited some rare qualities from his parents and grandparents. His grandfather Durgadas Datta abandoned wife and children, fame and fortune during the ceremony of his only son's tasting rice for the first time at the age of twenty-five to become a monk and live in the forest for good. Shyamasundari Devi his grandmother had a bent for literature and composed 'Gangabhakti Tarangini'. His father, Vishwanath Datta, an attorney of the Kolkata High Court was progressive, generous and sceptic and fond of music and the poetry of Hafiz and the Bible. He was well versed in seven languages and wrote two books entitled 'Sulochana' and 'Shistachar'. His mother Bhuvaneshwari Devi was pious intelligent and educated and respectful of the spiritual traditions of India. One day Narendranath complained to her in tears that the Geography-teacher had caned him though he gave correct answer. His mother consoled her, 'Well, my son, what does it matter if you make no mistake? Whatever the result may be you will go on doing what you consider true always.' On another occasion she taught him, 'Remain pure all your life, guard your own honour and never transgress the honour of others. Be very tranquil, but when necessary, harden your heart.'

Evidently Narendranath owed the spirit of renunciation to his grandfather; his love of literature to his grandmother, his intelligence, compassion, passion for music and artistic sense to his father and his royal bearing, extraordinary memory and moral purity to his mother : He said, 'It is my mother who has been the constant inspiration of my life and work.'

At school and college Narendranath was distinguished for his marvellous intellect and equal interest in philosophy, Indian and Western languages, Sanskrit, Bengali and English literature, Sciences, astronomy, history and Mathematics. He spent his time in reading other books of his choice—the important books in Bengali and English literature and books on history. As a result, he had to master the text books only two or three months before the examination. One day he said to his friends namely Sharat Chandra Chakrobarty (later his brother-disciple Swami Saradananda), "I found just two or three days before the Entrance Examination that the pages of Euclid had not been turned over at all. I then sat up the whole night to study it; I mastered all the four books on the subject in twenty-four hours and appeared at the examination."[6]

In his student life he studied the Vedanta and 'The Imitation of Jusus Christ' (by Thomas a Kempis?) and 'Essays on Religion' by Stuart Mill. Besides, he read Descartes, Hume, Kant, Fichte, Spinoza, Hegel, Schopenhauer, Auguste Comte and Darwin. He corresponded with Herbert Spencer who was astonished by his daring criticisms and admired his philosophic intellect.

Narendra, during the turmoil period (1880-1884) of gnawing doubts about the existence of God and religious certainty, was deeply impressed by the message of the French Revolution : Liberty, Equality, Fraternity and the indomitable heroism of Napoleon Bonaparte and the pantheism and humanity of the poet Shelley 'child of the French Revolution'.

Owing to his profound knowledge, rational outlook and deep thinking Narendra was fond of argument, criticism, discrimination and philosophic discussion. Swami Saradananda wrote :

"But he never indulged in sophistry. He always used to support only that which he knew to be true in his heart of hearts. But if any one expressed before him an idea or opinion contrary to what he knew as true, he could never listen to it passively. He would bring to bear upon the topic a formidable array of arguments and silence the opponent in no time. Rare were the persons who did not bend their heads before his reasoning."[7]

Since his studentlife Narendra had an amazing power of rapid reading and extraordinary memory. He could commit from memory scriptures and literature e.g. the Chandi and Gita, the Pickwick Papers by Charles Dickens etc.

During their wanderings Swamiji and some of his brother disciples namely Swamis Akhandananda, Brahmananda, Saradananda, Turiyananda, Advaitananda and Kripananda stayed at a Shethji's garden-house in Meerut in 1890 for someweeks. Once Swamiji asked Swami Akhandananda to bring the works of Sir John Lubbock from the local library. Accordingly Swami Akhandananda borrowed them one volume each day. Swamiji would finish a volume in a day and return it the next day. The librarian argued with Swami Akhandananda that Swami Vivekananda had surely returned the volume without reading it and he was only making a show of reading. Hearing such caustic comments Swamiji himself went to the librarian and said, "Sir, I have mastered all those volumes : if you have any doubt, you may put any question to me about them.' Then the librarian examined the monk and was astonished to hear correct reply to each question. Swami Akhandananda asked Swamiji how he could do it. Swamiji answered : "I never read a book word by word. I read sentence by sentence, sometimes even paragraph by paragraph, in a sort of Kaleidoscopic form."

His disciple Sharat Chandra Chakravarty once (1901) discovered to his utter astonishment that his Gurudeva bore in his mind each of the volumes of the Encyclopaedia Britannica which he considered unlikely to happen to study in single lifetime. Swamiji told his disciple that one can master all learning and be capable of remembering whatever one hears or reads only by practising celibacy properly. He said :

> Since then (the time of his appearing for the Entrance examination) when I took up a book, I did not find it necessary to plod through it line by line in order to understand the author. I could grasp the point by reading the first and the last lines of a paragraph. Gradually that power became developed and it was not necessary to read the paragraphs also in the aforesaid way. Sometimes I read the first and the last lines of each page and the content was known. Again, when the author was explaining a particular point of view with arguments in any part of his book, I could understand his whole chain of reasoning by merely reading the beginning of his arguments.[8]

Swami Vijnanananda who was a civil engineer in his service-life was spellbound to hear about the basic method and theory of systems of architecture of India and other countries of the world from Swamiji. He commented that Swami himself was a living encyclopaedia.

Some essays and lectures and class talks (e.g. The Cosmos, Practical Vedanda, Cosmology, Conception of the Universe, The cosmos and the self, Evolution, The Ether etc.) of Swamiji testify to his good command of various branches of science. He explained the quantum field theory and astronomy from the Vedantic philosophical point of view and the scientific base of the Vedas.

It was only the beginning of the twenty first century when the scientists were able to have the basic idea of the origin and nature of at least all physical matters in the universe. Long before that it was Swamiji who confidently explained on the basis of the Vedantic science that all perceptible, tangible reality around us originates from the only source which is compeltely formless omnipresent invaritable and eternal. At that time modern science had limited idea of the universe.

> Swamiji discussed the riddle of creation, the relation between religion and science, transformation of all of animate and inanimate, gross and subtle into oneness; heat, light and electricity as the different state of the same energy etc. with the help of suitable examples. Before the publication of the theory of Response of Inorganic Matter to Electric by Sir Jagadish Chandra Bose an eminent scientist of India, he foretold about the existence of animation more or less even in the so-called inanimate substance.
>
> Nikola Tesla, a reputed electrical inventor was deeply impressed by the talk of Swamiji about the Vedantic *prana* (energy), *akasha*, and the *kalpas* (cycles)–which Tesla considered the only theories modern science could accept.
>
> Swamiji held that 'matter' and 'energy' were indifferent and sought for the answer from the eminent scientist who failed to reply. Interestingly, after ten years Albert Einstein, legendary scientist, mathematically proved that actually 'matter' and 'energy' are equivalent.

Swamiji was Hercules in strength, courage and determination, a human dynamo and wisdom personified. Principal William Hastie of General Assembly's Institution (now Scottish Church College) remarked about his student :

> Narendranath is really a genius. I have travelled far and wide but I have never yet come across a lad of his talents and possibilities, even in German universities, amongst philosophical students.[9]

The scriptures and culture of his motherland encouraged Narendranath at an early age to find out the truth for himself or in self-realization while the Western education taught him to accept nothing without reason or evidence. Dr. Brajendra Nath Seal, Narendra's fellow student and one of the erudite philosophers in India, wrote in an article in the Prabuddha Bharata of 1907. :

"Undeniably a gifted youth, sociable, free and unconventional in manners a sweet singer, the soul of social circles, a brilliant conversationalist, somewhat bitter and caustic, piercing with the shafts of a keen wit the shows and mummeries of the world, sitting in the scorner's chair but hiding the tenderest of hearts under that garb of cynicism, altogether an inspired bohemian but possessing what bohemians lack, an iron will; some what peremptory and absolute, speaking with accents of authority and withal possessing a strange power of the eye which could hold his listeners in thrall."[10]

Swamiji had mastery of all subjects. He said to Priya Nath Sinha, one of his disciples : "A nation that has no history of its own has nothing in this world. Do you believe that one who has such faith and pride as to feel, "I come of noble descent" can ever turn out to be bad? How could that be? That faith in himself would curb his actions and feelings so much so that he would rather die than commit wrong. So a national history keeps a nation wellrestrained and does not allow it to sink so low.... we have our own history exactly as it ought to have been for us. Will that history be made extinct by shutting your eyes and crying, "Alas! we have no history!" Those who have eyes to see, find a luminous history there, and on the strength of that they know the nation is still alive. But that history has to be rewritten. It should be restated and suited to the understanding and ways of thinking which our men have acquired in the present age through western education."

Researchers of Indian history may find some directives in the articles and lectures of Swamiji e.g. 'Historical Evolution of India.' 'Lectures from Colombo to Almora'. "The East and the West' etc. He said, "You will find there also that, hidden under the ashes of apparent death, the fire of our national life is yet smouldering and that the life of this nation is religion, its language religion and its idea religion, and your politics, society, municipality, plague-prevention work, and famine-relief work—all these things will be done as they have been done all along here, viz. only through religion, otherwise all your frantic yelling and bewailing will end in nothing, my friend!"[12]

Swamiji's 'Memoirs of European Travel' has more the appearance of history than of a travelogue in which he has analysed the causes of rise and fall of various dynasties, sects and nations and characteristics of some civilizations of the world. He wrote : "In the Vedas we find both names, "Sindhu" and "Indu" for the Indus; the Persians transformed them into "Hindu", and the Greeks into "Indus," whence we derived the words "India" and "Indian". With the rise of Mohammedanism the word "Hindu" became degraded and meant "a dark-skinned fellow", as is the case with the word "native" now.

"...ye labouring classes of India, as a result of your silent, constant labours Babylon, Persia, Alexandria, Greece, Rome, Venice, Genoa, Baghdad, Samarqand, Spain, Portugal, France, Denmark, Holland, and England have successively attained supremacy and eminence! And you?—well, who cares to think of you!...ye ever-trampled labouring classes of India! I bow to you."[13]

A voracious reader Swamiji was so sincere in exploring the truth about historical informations that when a librarian of the British Museum recommended him to read *Histoire Ancienne Orientale*, a voluminous history of the Egyptians and Babylonians by Maspero, a great savant and famous author on Egyptology, in original French for the translator of the book into English was a bigoted and distorted and twisted those passages wherever the author's researches hit Christianity in any, Swamiji who had already gone through the English version of the book, read it in French and discovered the meanness of the religious bigotry.

Swamiji's commentary on history cannot be called 'revivalist' or 'traditionalist'. His study of history of the world was guided by the principles of truth, neutrality and rationalism. Sister Nivedita wrote, "His (Her Master's) historic consciousness was extraordinarily developed."[14]

Swamiji disciple of a good artist Sri Ramakrishna, may not only be called a skilful artist but he was a great sensitive art-critic also.

Mahendranath Datta, brother of Swamiji said that his elder brother used to draw scene-sceneries for the theatrical stage in their house at the age of eleven or twelve. In his itinerant life Swamiji was acquainted with the historic pieces of art and architecture of the East and the West. In a letter to Miss Josephire MacLeod (Joe) on 24th July 1900 Swamiji explained the suggestive design on the Ramakrishna Math and Ramakrishna Mission seal made by him :

The sun = knowledge. The stormy water = work. The lotus = love. The serpent = yoga. The swan = the Self. The Motto = May the Swan (the Supreme Self) send us that. It is the mind-lake...(works, vol.8 p. 528)

Ranadaprosad Dasgupta founder of the Jubilee Art Academy (Kolkata), eminent artsit Nandalal Bose, historian Girijashankar Roychowdhuri, Dr. Kalidas Nag acknowledged the important contribution of the Swami to the Renaissance of the Indian art.

Maud Stumm the Art-teacher of Swamiji said, "once only did I have to tell him anything; his memory and concentration were marvellous, and his drawings strangely perfect and intelligent for a beginner. By the time he had taken his fourth lesson, he felt quite equal to a portrait; so...Turiyananda posed, like any bronze image, and was drawn capitally—all in the study of Mr. Leggett, with its divan for our seat, and its fine light to aid us. Many great ones may come to that room in its future years, and probably will, but never again that childlike man, toiling over his crayons, with as single a mind and heart as if that were his vocation. How often, he thanked me for the pleasure it gave him, and for the joy of learning even that! (Reminiscences of Swami Vivekananda, Advaita Ashrama, 3rd Ed. p. 180)

During class-talks and discourses on Art he commented :

"The secret of Greek Art is its imitation of nature even to the minutest details; whereas the secret of Indian Art is to represent the ideal...

"Art is—representing the beautiful. There must be Art in everything The difference between architecture and building is that the former expresses an idea, while the latter is merely a structure built on economical principles. The value of matter depends solely on its capacities of expressing *ideas*."[15]

He said to Priyanath Sinha, a friend of his childhood days and disciple :

They (the Japanese) are great as a nation because of their art. Don't you see they are Asians, as we are? And though we have lost almost everything yet what we still have is wonderful. The very soul of the Asian is interwoven with art. The Asian never uses a thing unless there be art in it. Don't you know that art is, with us, a part of religion?

"...The Westerner looks for utility in every thing, whereas with us art is everywhere."[16]

According to Swamiji "In art interest must be centred on the principal theme. Drama is the most difficult of all arts."[17]

Sister Nivedita in reference to their experience of visiting the Temple of the Pandrenthan famous for its 'quite classical' interior decoration, in Kashmir on July 19, 1898; wrote : "For all but the Swami himself, this was our first peep at Indian archaeology. So when he had been through it, he taught us how to observe the interior."[18]

Having been inspired by Swamiji's extraordinary sense of historic values and interest in art and architecture his disciple Nivedita analysed the artistic beauty of Ajanta, Ellora, Banaras etc. along with the beauty of everyday life of the village folks of the northern India in her books 'Studies from an Eastern Home' and 'The Web of Indian Life.'

Swamiji while visiting the Louvre museum in Paris, saw the statue of Venus de Milo and afterwards wrote to Mary Hale from

Darjeeling in 1897, "By the by, I saw the venus of what do you call it—and you are right—Isabelle's face is much like that statue. Of course her hands are better for the statue has only stumps—that is to say, to our uneducated taste..."[19] Without fair knowledge of sculpture he could not criticize such a famous piece of art.

Swamiji had great musical talent and melodious voice. He was taught music by Beni Ustad, Abja Ustad etc. since his boyhood and had mastery over the subject. Sri Ramakrishna was deeply moved by the songs sung by Narendranath in the house of Surendranath Mitra during their first meeting. The Master himself went to Narendra's maternal grandmother's house to hear his songs. Subsequcently he used to hear him often at Dakshineswar. He played well on tanpura (a musical instrument of four or six strings), mridanga (an instrument of percussion shaped almost like a tom tom) banya tabla, piano, sitar etc. Swami Abhedananda described how they, the brother disciples were taught music by their leader Swamiji. Swami Akhandananda reminisced about how Swamiji welcomed him when he (the former) at the fag end of a night knocked on the door of the latter, with a song :

Knocking knocking who is there?
Waiting, waiting, Oh brother dear!
Once for all — oh, brother receive me!
Once for all — oh, sinner believe me!
Unto the Cross thy burden fall;
Once for all — oh, once for all![20]

In July 1898 during a long conversation on music in Nilambar Mukherjee's garden-house Swamiji attested to his wide knowledge of the art and science of the Eastern and the Western musuc. In reply to the questions put by Swami Shivananda, "What is Western music like?" Swamiji said :

"Oh, it is very good; there is in it a perfection of harmony, which we have not attained. Only, to our untrained ears, it does not sound well, hence we do not like it and think that the singers howl like jackals. I also had the same sort of impression, but when I began to listen to the music with attention and study it minutely, I came more and more to understand it, and I was lost in admiration. Such is the case with every art. In glancing at a highly finished painting we cannot understand where its beauty lies. Moreover, unless the eye is, to a certain extent, trained, one cannot appreciate the subtle touches and blendings, the inner genius of a work of art. What real music we have lies in Kirtana and Dhrupada; the rest has been spoiled by being modulated according to the Islamic methods. Do you think that singing the short and light airs of Tappa songs in a nasal voice and flitting like lightning from one note to another by fits and starts are the best things in the world of music? Not so. Unless each note is given full play in every scale, all the science of music is marred. In painting, by keeping in touch with nature, you can make it as artistic as you like; there is no harm in doing that, and the result will be nothing but good. Similarly, in music, you can display any amount of skill by keeping to science, and it will be pleasing to the ear. The Mohammedans took up the different Râgas and Râginis after coming into India. But they put such a stamp of their own colouring on the art of Tappâ songs that all the science in music was destroyed."

In answer to other questions Swamiji commented : "...The music of the Westerners is much advanced. They have the sentiment of pathos as well as of heroism in their music, which is as it should be. But our antique musical instrument made from the gourd has been improved no further.

"Every Râga may be made martial if it is set in harmony and the instruments are turned accordingly. Some of the Râginis can also become martial."[21]

Swamiji made commendable remarks about music in class talks also : "There is science in Dhrupad, Kheyal etc., but it is in Kirtana, i.e. in Mâthura and Viraha and other like compositions that there is real music—for there is feeling. Feeling is the soul, the secret of everything. There is more music in common people's songs, and they should be collected together. The science of Dhrupad etc. applied to the music of Kirtana will produce the perfect musuic."[22]

It is interesting to note that Swamiji rightly realized that the folk songs rich in varied sentiments and notes bear the flavour of the communities concerned and those should be preserved properly. He appreciated the cadence in our music.

Swamiji was an efficient music composer who composed some popular devotional songs and hymns in Sanskrit and Bengali e.g. Khandana-bhava-bandhana, Hara Hara Bhutnath, Katvang shubhe, Mujhe bari Banoyari, Achandalapratihatarayo, Om hring etc. In reference to this it may be added that Swamiji, ignoring prejudice agreed to hear songs of a professional dancing-girl and songstress (Maynabai) and appreciated her devotional songs at the pleasure-garden of Ajit Singh, the Maharaja of Khetri (Rajputana).

Swami Nirbhayananda (Kanai Maharaj) one of the disciples of Swamiji recollected how the Swami showed him various forms of European dance in his room at Belur and how he refusing phaeton drawn by four horses—singing kirtan danced all the way to the new house of Nabagopal Ghosh at Ramakrishnapur, Howrah on the auspicious day (1898) of consecration of the image of Sri Ramakrishna by him there. (Foot note. Smritir Aloy p.271)

Asim Kumar Bose, initiated by Swamiji, wrote how he enjoyed his preceptor's acting the part of various characters of 'Romeo and Juliet' by Shakespeare and of the dramas by Girish Chandra Ghosh (his dear G.C.)

Swamiji was so judicious that he did not initiate Miss Margaret Elizabeth Noble (later, Sister Nivedita) as soon as she reached Kolkata (January 28, 1898) rather he waited two months until she was able to free herself from the British outlook and embrace the Indian mode of living and ideas. In the math in the garden of Nilambar Mukherjee Swamiji initiated Miss Noble into brahmacharya (celibacy) and gave her the name 'Nivedita' 'the Dedicated One' on March 25, 1898. Particilarly in order to destroy her blind nationalism and make her acquainted with the Himalayas, the Ganga and the tradition, diversity of nature and culture, rich heritage of this country and the Indian way of life he left Kolkata for the Northern India and Kashmir with his Western disciples on May 11, 1898.

Rejecting the proposals made by Jamshedji Tata and Kali Kamliowala Swamiji showed his prudence.

As a good cook Swamiji knew recipe of delicious veg and non-veg dishes and fed korma (a kind of highly spiced grilled curry of meat, clarified butter and curd) to his brother disciples at Merrut and pilau to his disciples Narasinhachari (GG), Bhupendranath Banerjee and others at Sikkimfrontier. Nareshchandra Ghosh an initiated disciple of the Mother and Swamiji's companion (9 December 1900-4 July 1902) described how he like a juggler tactfully prepared saruchakli (made of rice powder) veg soup etc. at Belur.

Swamiji, a mine of many accomplishments was very polite, affectionate, agile in body and mind, outspoken, courageous and protester against falsehood, wrongs and injustice. Swami Premananda one of his brother-disciples advised (25.4.1917) one of the devotees to go through the epistles of Swamiji to have an idea of his amazing manliness. Swami Turiyananda, another brother-disciple of the Swami said that Swamiji by nature was self-relient and self-supporting and did not like to keep himself alive by the recommendation of other. Another codisciple Swami Akhandananda referring to his diligence said that he himself scoured a huge urn shaped pot blackened with soot. Swami Sadananda, one of Swamiji's disciples said with overwhelming emotion, 'He was all Love.' He full of vigour and energy was never tired of learning or teaching. His portrait announces, 'Strength is life. Weakness is death.' He was very strict about punctuality, perfection and cleanliness. He himself off and on examined the rooms and beds of the disciples and celibates to see if those were free from dirts and bugs and their bed-sheets napkins etc. were spread out in the sun to dry regularly. He advised all to work with bulldog's tenacity. He did not compromise his principles and discipline. He introduced a rule that all the inmates of Belur Math would have to rise at four A.M. and attend the temple within five minutes failing which the late-comer would have to manage his meal of the day by begging. One day he asked his dear Tarak da (later Swami Shivananda) who was senior to him by nine years that as he was late in arriving the temple he as the rule, would have to live the day on alms. Shivanandaji admitted that he was late by ten minutes and at once left for begging. After food-offering made to Sri Ramakrishna all but Swamiji had lunch together. Swamiji sat on the verandah to the West of the Math and waited for Mahapursh Maharaj. When he returned, Swamiji with great delight was eager to see what his Tarakda had brought and told him that he had not taken food obtained by begging for many days and the two brothers lunched together joyfully. Despite being a world-famous personality he did not hesitate to clean service-latrine at Belur. One day the aforesaid Nareshchandra Ghosh saw him clean a drain attached to Jnan Maharaj one of his disciples, with a broom in his hand.

Swamiji was the high priest of nature. He had some pets those he nurtured with motherly affection and care and named each of them e.g. a chinese duck—Yashomati, a swan—Bombete, a goat—Matru, a she goat—Hamsi, two dogs —Bagha and Lion. Besides there were cows, sheep, cat, pigeon, an antelope and a large stork. Once his beloved Matru caught a fever. A veterinary surgeon was called in. He came and to his utter astonishment he discovered the patient under a costly blanket on the iron cot of his master. In a letter to Sister Nivedita on September 7, 1901 he wrote in details about his pets. On 12th November 1901 he wrote to Sister Christine: '...we have fenced in a lot of our grounds to protect our vegetables from our cows and goats and sheep...Two of my ducks are sitting on their eggs. As this is their first time, and the male does not help them a bit. I am trying my best to keep up their strength by good feeding...'

> Swamiji perfected the cultivation of hand head and heart. Swami Ambikananda commented that Swamiji had 'originality' in all respects. He transformed an ordinary gown into a coat by fitting with buttons and ribbon in front. He introduced a new pattern of the monkeyish cap generally put on by the Vaishnavas by making the back side cover flexible.

The Swami's sharp wit would disperse usually in both philosophical deliberations and humorous situations. Once in 1892

Haripada Mitra one of his householder disciple requested him to explain the scientific aspects of space and time. His answer was so precise profound and lucid that it can illumine the brains of the reputed scientists even today. He said, "There can be no two infinites." When Haripada said that time is infinite and so is space, Swamiji replied, "I can understand that space is infinite, but it passes my understanding how time can be infinite. In any case, I can understand that only one thing can be infinite. If there be two infinites, how would you demarcate their respective spheres? If you advance further, you will find that time and space get lost in each other. Still further advance will show you that all things are infinite, but those infinite things are one in essence and not two." (*Reminiscences of Swami Vivekananda,* His Eastern and Western Admirers, Advaita Ashram, Kolkata, 2004, p. 38)

One day an American said to Swamiji tauntignly, "If all things are one, what is the difference between a cabbage and a man?" He quipped, "stick a knife into your leg, and you will see the line of demarcation." (Ibid, vol-2. p. 496)

Swamiji had such an unquenchable thirst for knowledge that wherever and whenever he had any opportunity to learn, he tried to take that in order to enrich himself more. During his journey in India he became a pupil of the foremost Sanskrit grammarian of the time at Khetri. At Ahmedabad he gained more knowledge of Jain and Mohammedan culture. Despite his vow as an itinerant monk he stayed about nine months at Porebandar to perfect his philosophical and Sanskrit studies with reputed pandits and worked with a court pandit who translated the vedas.

> Professor John Henry Wright of Harvard University who was described as 'encylopedic' in the 'Dictionary of American Biography' recommended Swamiji to the authorities of the World's Parliament of Religions, Chicago as being "more learned than all our learned professors put together."[23]

Perhaps the remarks made by Mrs. Wright in a letter (August 29, 1893) to her mother, may be treated as valuable material for the estimation of genius of the Swami: "We have been having a queer time. Kate Sanborn had a Hindoo monk in tow as I believe I mentioned in my last letter. John went down to meet him in Boston and missing him, invited him up here. He came Friday! In a long saffron robe that caused universal amazement. He was a most gorgeous vision. He had a superb carriage of the head, was very handsome in an oriental way, about thirty years old in time, ages in civilization. He stayed until Monday and was one of the most interesting people I have yet come across. We talked all day all night and began again with interest the next morning. The town was in a fume to see him; the boarders at Miss Lane's in wild excitement. They were in and out of the Lodge [the Wright's cottage] constantly and little Mrs. Merrill's eyes were blazing and her cheeks red with excitement . Chiefly we talked religion, It was a kind of revival, I have not felt so wrought up for a long time myself!...

"He is an educated gentleman, knows as much as anybody...

He is wonderfully clever and clear in putting his arguments and laying his trains [of thought] to a conclusion. You can't trip him up, nor get ahead of him..."

Of course, the last word in this matter was uttered by Sri Ramakrishna himself. He spoke eloquently on the originality, distinction and multifaced genius of Narendranath.

On July 15, 1885 he said to M :

> "Narendra belongs to a very high plane—the realm of the Absolute. He has a manly nature. So many devotees come here, but there is not one like him.
>
> "Every now and then I take stock of the devetees. I find that some are like lotuses with ten petals, some like lotuses with sixteen petals, some like lotuses with a hundred petals. But among lotuses Narendra is a thousand-petalled one.
>
> "Other devotees may be like pots or pitchers; but Narendra is a huge water-barrel.
>
> "Others may be like pools or tanks, but Narendra is a huge reservoir like the Hāldārpukur.

"Among fish, Narendra is a huge red-eyed carp; others are like minnows or smelts or sardines. Tarak of Belghariā may be called a bass.

"Narendra is a 'very big receptacle', one that can hold many things. He is like a bamboo with a big hollow space inside.

"Narendra is not under the control of anything. He is not under the control of attachment or sense pleasures. He is like a male pigeon. If you hold a male pigeon by its beak, it breaks away from you; but the female pigeon keeps still. Narendra has the nature of a man, so he sits on the right side in a carriage. Bhavanath has a woman's nature; so I make him sit on the other side. I feel great strength when Narendra is with me in a gathering.[24]

A magnetic personality :

Bhaskar Setupati, the king of Ramnad, perhaps the most pious, erudite and intelligent of all rajas and maharajas of the-then India; himself drew the carriage carrying his Guru Deva (preceptor); some enthusiastic students of Kolkata drew his landau; a poor old woman did not hesitate to feed him bread; catching sight of seven thousand people rising to their feet as a tribute to him and scores of women walking over the benches to get near him, Mrs. S. K. Blodgett, an American lady one of the audiences in the opening session of the Parliament of Religions at Chicago on 11 September 1893, said to herself, "Well, my lad, if you can resist that onslaught, you are indeed a god.'[25] He was none other than Swami Vivekananda.

Swamiji was a man of robust optimism, indomitable self-reliance, progressive thinking and great strength of mind and character. Since his boyhood he had to fight adverse situation and opposition. The letter written from the U.S.A. on 9th July, 1895 to the Maharaja of Khetri is a convincing evidence to support our views : "...I am, as your Highness well knows, a man of dogged perseverance. I have planted a seed in this country; it is already a plant, and I expect it to be a tree very soon. I have got a few hundred followers. I shall make several Sannyâsins, and then I go to India, leaving the work to them. The more the Christian priests oppose me, the more I am determined to leave a permanent mark on their country... Each work has to pass through these stages—ridicule, opposition and then acceptance. Each man who thinks ahead of his time is sure to be misunderstood. So opposition and persecution are welcome. Only I have to be steady and pure and must have immense faith in God, and all these will vanish." He believed—'India must rise.'

Swami Bodhasarananda wrote, "Swamiji was, first and foremost a man of the Spirit, who had realized the ultimate Truth. This was the most prominent facet of his multisided personality." (Publisher's Note, The complete works of Swami Vivekananda, vol. I, Advaita Ashrama 1989).

Swami Vijnanananda said,

> Swamiji had a wonderful overwhelming personality. People felt inadequate in front of him. When we mentioned this to Swamiji he said, 'It is the play of that mad brahmin [meaning the Master]; he is working through me.' Swamiji was very simple and a man of renunciation. [Udbodhan. 45 : 224]

Swamiji was an embodiment of the watchwords of the Upanishads—strength, courage and freedom. He wrote on 28th May 1894 from Chicago to Alasinga Perumal, "The spirit, my boys, the spirit; the love, my children, the love, the faith, the belief; and fear not! The greatest sin is fear." He wrote to him on 6th May, 1895 from the U.S.A. "...I am the one man who dared defend his country, and I have given them such ideas as they never expected from a Hindu. There are many who are against me, but I will never be a coward like you." Again he wrote (on 1st July 1895) to this disciple, "...Cowardic is no virtue... Be brave, be brave! Man dies but once. My disciples must not be cowards."

In the poem, 'Kali the Mother' Swamiji wrote :

> Who dares misery love,
> And hug the form of Death,

Dance in Destruction's dance
To him the Mother comes.

In the poem, 'To the Awakened India' he said :

Yet strong and steady,
Blissful, bold and free. Awakener ever
Forward! Speak thy stirring words.

The monk-poet invoked his countrymen in his long poem 'And let Shyama dance there':

Break the harp! Forward, with the ocean's cry !
Drink tears, pledge even life—let the body fall.
Awake, O hero! Shake off thy vain dreams,
Death stands at thy head—does fear become thee?

To celebrate the anniversary of the American Declaration of Independence Swamiji composed a poem, 'To the Fourth of July' on the 4th of July, 1898 while travelling in Kashmir with sister Nivedita and some American disciples. Sister Nivedita wrote,

> I had recognized the heroic fibre of the man and desired to make myself the servant of his love for his own people. But it was his *character* to which I had thus done obeisance... I studied his teaching sufficiently to become convinced of its coherence, but never, till I had had experiences that authenticated them, did I inwardly cast in my lot with the final justification of the things he came to say. Nor did I at that time, though deeply attracted by his personality, dream of the immense distance which I was afterwards to see, as between his development and that of any other thinker or man of genius whom I could name.[26]

In fact, renowned personalities—professors, philosophers, scientists, national leader, artist, litterateur, singer, journalists, Rajas, Maharajas of home and abroad who came in contact with Swamiji or learnt about him were charmed by his captivating personality and they expressed their respective pleasure and wonder unequivocally. Sister Christine an American disciple of Vivekananda wrote about him :

> Blessed is the country in which he was born, blessed are they who lived on this earth at the same time, and blessed thrice blessed are the few who sat at his feet. He shares the life of those about him, enters into their Joys and sorrows rejoices with them, mourns with them but through it all he never forgets who he is, whence he came, or what the purpose of his coming. He never forgets his divinity. He remembers that he is the great, the glorious, the majestic Self. He knows that he came from that ineffable supernal region which has no need of the sun or moon for it is illumined by the Light of lights. He knows that he was long before the time when all the sons of God sang together for joy.[27]

Honourable Mr. Merwin—Marie Snell, president of the Scientific Section of the Parliament of Religions wrote of Swamiji as "beyond question the most popular and influential man in the Parliament,... [who] on all occasions...was received with greater enthusiasm than any other speaker, Christian or 'Pagan'".[28]

The most interesting word-picture of the Swami's personality was drawn by Harriet Monroe foundress of *Poetry: A Magazine of Verse*, in her autobiography, 'A Poet's Life':

'...It was the last of these, Swami Vivekananda the magnificent, who stole the whole show and captured the town...the handsome monk in the orange robe gave us in perfect English a masterpiece. His personality dominant, magnetic his voice, rich as a bronze bell, the controlled fervour of his feeling; the beauty of his message to the Western world he was facing for the first time-these combined to give us a rare and perfect moment of supreme emotion. It was human eloquence at its highest pitch.'[29]

Prince Wolkonsky, a free-lance delegate from Russia to the Parliament commented to Albert Spalding, an eminent violinist of America, on Swamiji's popularity :

"He made a — what do you call it? — sensational 'hit' in your country, especially with the Chicago ladies.'[30]

The malicious Christian opponents of Swamiji attributed his tremendous popularity among the American women (who were deprived of economic freedom, political voice and scope for the employment of their qualities and talents despite their leading role in education, religion, literature, art and culture) to the brilliant colour of his robe and turban. The fact was however stated by an American erudite woman Marie Louise Burke (Abhoyananda, disciple of Swami Asokananda) :

'Although the women, generally speaking, may have given more expression than the men to their admiration of Swamiji—for women were intent upon expressing themselves—men and women alike were drawn to him as to a magnet. The descriptions we have of Swamiji at the Parliament of Religions show him as colorful and dynamic, dominating the scene with the force of his personality and the utter purity of his message. He was glowing with the vigor of his youth, ready to face the entire world and to sacrifice his life for "the poor, the ignorant, the oppressed" of his motherland. And there was yet another reason for his phenomenal popularity. Never before, had the people of America seen one in whom spiritual truths had been fully realized. Though Swamiji's towering spiritual eminence was not consciously recognized by the hundreds who, as he later reminisced, "jostled with one another in the streets of Chicago to have a sight of this Vivekananda." who flocked to hear him speak, who waited interminable hours for even a few words, and who applauded him when he simply crossed the platform, the people through some inner knowledge seemed unerringly to recognize him for what he was and, from start to finish instinctively to sense that his very presence conferred a blessing. 'Darshan' was unheard of in America, but here at the Parliament was a spontaneous and unconscious manifestation of the attraction of the human soul to the spiritually great."[31]

Indeed the personality of Swamiji is like a prism through which rays of various virtues form a spectrum that holds us spellbound.

Subhas Chandra Bose wrote,

> I can not write about Vivekananda without going into raptures. Few indeed could comprehend or fathom him—

> even among those who had the privilege of becoming intimate with him. His personality was rich, profound and complex and it was this personality—as distinct from his teachings and writings—which accounts for the wonderful influence he has exerted on his countrymen and particularly on Bengalees. This is the type of manhood which appeals to the Bengalee as probably none other. Reckless in his sacrifice, unceasing in his activity. boundless in his love, profound and versatile in his wisdom, exuberant in his emotions, merciless in his attacks but yet simple as a child—he was a rare personality in this world of ours...
>
> Swamiji was a full-blooded masculine personality—and a fighter to the core of his being...[32]

Priya Nath Sinha a friend of Swamiji's childhood days and his disciple as well, reminisced about the personality of Swamiji and expression of restraint in his every work and attitude even in his boyhood.

A marvellous and impressive Orator :

In a lecture entitled 'The Powers of the Mind' delivered at Los Angeles, California on January 8, 1900 Swamiji commented : "Words, even thoughts contribute only one-third of the influence in making an impression, the man two-thirds . What you call the personal magnetism of the man—that is what goes out and impress you." Swamiji evidently possessed this powerful personal magnetism.

He who while a school-boy of the Metropolitan school fascinated even Surendranath Banerjee a great national leader and renowned orator by his eloquence, won the heart of the world by only a simple but touching phrasal address; not even a sentence!

With reference to that epoch-making maiden speech Swamiji wrote (on 2nd November 1893 from Chicago to one of his disciples Alasinga Perumal, "...And I who never spoke in public in my life to address this august assemblage!!...From that day I became a celebrity...Nearly all the papers paid high tributes to me, and even the most bigoted had to admit that "This man with his handsome face and magnetic presence and wonderful oratory is the most prominent figure in the Parliament." etc. etc. Sufficient for you to know that never before did an Oriental make such an impression on American society."

John Henry Barrows, pastor of the First Presbyterian Church of Chicago and Chairman of the General Committee of the Parliament of Religions commented : "When Mr. Vivekananda addressed the audience as 'Sisters and Brothers of America' there arose a peal of applause that lasted for several minutes."[33] In reference to the historic incident Swamiji himself told Marie Louise Burke and other devotees that 'a deafening applause of two minutes followed'.

Indeed, the Swami, blessed with a melodious voice, was an enchanting orator by 'divine right'.

The 'electrified' audiences heard from 'the lips of the arrestingly handsome Hindu Monk' :

"It fills my heart with joy unspeakable to the rise in response to the grand words of welcome given to us by you. I thank you in the name of the most ancient order of monks the world has ever seen, of which Gautama was only a member. I thank you in the name of the Mother of religions, of which Buddhism and Jainism are but branches; and I thank you, finally in the name of the millions and millions of Hindoo people of all castes and sects...

"I am proud to belong to a religion which has taught the world both tolerance and universal acceptance. We believe not only in universal tolerance but we accept all religions to be true. I am proud to tell you that I belong to a religion in whose sacred language, the Sanskrit, the word exclusion is untranslatable. (Applause) I am pround to belong to a nation which has sheltered the persecuted and the refugees of all religions and all nations of the earth...

"The present convention, which is one of the most august assemblies ever held, is in itself an indication a declaration to the world of the wonderful doctrine preached in the Gita : "Whosoever comes to Me, through whatsoever form I reach him, all are struggling through paths that in the end always lead to Me." Sectarianism, bigotry and its horrible descendant fanaticism, have possessed long this beautiful earth. It has filled the earth with violence, drenched it often and often with human gore, destroyed civilization and sent whole nations into despair. But its time has come, and I fervently believe that the bell that tolled this morning in honour of the representatives of the different religions of the earth, in this parliament assembled, is the death-knell to all persecution with the sword or the pen, and to all uncharitable feelings between brethren wending their way to the same goal, but through different ways."[34]

How amazingly Swamiji in his extempore and brief address highlighted the essence of all religions, the seniority and superiority of Hinduism, danger of religious dogmatism and robust optimism!

In the Parliament of Religions each orator spoke of the God of his sect. Swamiji alone spoke on behalf of all their Gods and greeted all in the spirit of tolerance and universal acceptance. Thus the message of Sri Ramakrishna broke down the barriers among religions through his most favourite disciple.

Marie Louise Burke commented,

> The applause that had punctuated Swamiji's talk thundered out at its close. The people had recognized their hero and had taken him to their hearts; thenceforth he was the star of the Parliament.[35]

Various journals and periodicals namely the *Boston Evening Transcript*, the *Messenger*, the *Critic*, the *Interior Chicago*, the *Rutherford American* the *Life* highly appreciated this and other lectures of Swami Vivekananda. Owing to his immense popularity as an orator he had to speak at least four times at the erudite Scientific Section besides more popular sessions of the Parliament and generally he had to address at the last in order to hold the audiences intact. With a view to reach the people with words and ideas meaningful to them, he intentionally spoke in language as simple and untechnical as possible. Of course his speeches were informative, genuine, evocative and spell-binding.

As a judicious and impartial speaker Swamiji focused on the problems and drawbacks of both the East and the West courageously. The *Chicago Inter Ocean* of September 21, 1893 read as follows :

"...It was but 9 O'clock and the main auditorium and galleries were full filled. There was an outburst of applause as they caught sight of the Hindoo monk, Vivekananda, sitting in his orange robe and scarlet turban upon the platform.

...Christian brethren of America, you are so fond of sending out missionaries to save the souls of heathens. I ask you what have you done and are doing to save their bodies from starvation? (Applause) In India, there are 300,000,000 men and women living on an average of a little more than 50 cents a month. I have seen them living for years upon wild flowers. Whenever there was a little famine hundreds of thousands died of starvation. Christian missionaries, come and offer life but only on condition that the Hindoos become Christians, abandoning the faith of their fathers and forefathers. Is it right? There are hundreds of asylums, but if the Mohammedans or the Hindoos go there they would be kicked out. There are thousands of asylums erected by Hindoos where anybody would be received. There are hundreds of churches that have been erected with the assistance of the Hindoos, but no Hindoo temples for which a Christian has given a penny.

...Brethren of America, the crying civil need of the East is not religion. We have more than religion enough; what they want is bread, but they are given a stone. (Applause). It is an insult to a suffering man dying of hunger to preach to him metaphysics. Therefore, if you wish to illustrate the meaning of "brotherhood" treat the Hindoo more kindly, even though he be a Hindoo and is faithful to his religion. Send missionaries to them to teach them how better to earn a better piece of bread and not to teach them metaphysical nonsense. (Great applause)

And then the monk said he was in ill health today and wished to be excused. But there were thunders of applause and cries of "Go on" and Mr. Vivekananda continued :

"...I am one of those monks who have been described as beggarly. That is the pride of my life (Applause). I am proud in that sense to be Christ-like. I eat what I have today and think not of tomorrow. "Behold the lilies of the field. they toil not, neither do they spin." The Hindoo carries that out literally. Many gentlemen present in Chicago sitting on this platform can testify that for the last twelve years I never knew whence my next meal was coming. I am proud to be a beggar for the sake of the Lord. The idea in the East is to preach or teach anything for the sake of money is low and vulgar, but to teach the name of the Lord for pay is such a degradation as would cause the priest to lose caste and be spat upon ...If the priests of China and India were organized there is an enormous amount of potential energy which could be used for regeneration of society and humanity. I endeavoured to organize it in India, but failed for lack of money. It may be I shall get the help I want in America.

But we know it is very hard for a heathen to get any help from "Christian people". (Great applause). I have heard so much this land of freedom , of liberty and freedom of thought that I am not discouraged. I thank you, ladies and gentlemen."

This and some other lectures of Swamiji were caustic but honest criticism that was received by the Catholics with sympathy. It was reported in the section of Barrow's history entitled "Introduction to the Parliament Papers" that on the eleventh day, Bishop Keane of the Catholic church who assured Swamiji during his speech that Americans would not be offended at honest criticism; said, "I endorse the denunciation that was hurled forth last night against the system of pretended charity that offered food to the hungry Hindus at the cost of their conscience and faith. It is a shame and a disgrace to those who call themselves Christians."[36]

Sister Christine who attended every public lecture delivered by Swamiji in Detroit, wrote in her 'Reminiscences' (p. 154) : "The power that emanated from this mysterious being was so great that one all but shrank from it. It was overwhelming."

Lucy Monroe in an article published in The '*Critic*' of October 7, 1893 wrote "...But eloquent as were many of the brief speeches of this meeting, whose triumphant enthusiasm rightly culminated in the superb rendering by the Apollo Club of the Hallelujah Chorus, no one expressed so well the spirit of the parliament, its limitations and its finest influence, as did the Hindoo monk. I copy his address in full but I can only suggest its effect upon the audience, for he is an orator by divine right, and his strong intelligent face in its picturesque setting of yellow and orange was hardly less interesting than these earnest words and the rich rhythmical utterance he gave them.

"...Perhaps the most tangible result of the congress was the feeling it aroused in regard to foreign missions. The impertinence of sending half-educated theological students to instruct the wise and erudite Orientals was never brought home to an English-speaking audience more forcibly. It is only in the spirit of tolerance and sympathy that we are at liberty to touch their faith, and the exhorters who posses these qualities are rare..."[37]

Miss Marguerite Cook, stolid and unimpressionable by nature and a teacher of German in a Detroit high school attended one of the lectures of Swamiji at the Unitarian Church and was deeply moved by his power. After his lecture she felt an irresistible urge to congratulate him. While shaking hands with him she was overwhelmed and confused. She reminisced about the memorable incident in her life to Sara Bard Field, the American poetess : "I shall never forget his searching look. I was so aware of his greatness and holiness that I couldn't bear to wash my hand for three days!"[38]

Swami Saradananda once said to Swami Yogananda, 'Yogin, I can't really follow all that Naren (Swami Vivekananda) says. In what a diversity of moods he talks! Whatever standpoint he takes up, he makes so much of it that the others pale into insignificance.' Holy Mother Sri Sarada Devi, Swami Gambhirananda, Sri Ramakrishna Math, Madras, p. 187)

On another occasion Swami Saradananda said, "To move one's hands and use facial gestures are great arts of oratory, and most speakers use those tools to make their lectures impressive. But Swamiji did not like it. He said : 'During a lecture one should remove one's ego and stand in front of the Master humbly and calmly. He will make you speak whatever he wants, and he himself will listen to it. Thus when one speaks surrendering fully, then only that lecture carries the messsage of God." (The Life of Swami

Vivekananda, *His Eastern and Western Disciples*, Advaita Ashrama, cal. 1979, 1 : 452) Swamiji had corrected Swami Saradananda's bad habit of moving hands and head while speaking in London.

As 'the cyclonic Hindu' Swamiji had to visit numerous places of America and Europe to deliver lectures or conduct classes those bore rich fruits and left lasting memories.

With reference to the impression of Swamiji as an orator in England, we are tempted to quote from 'The Life of Swami Vivekananda' by His Eastern and Western Disciples :

The lectures and talks of the Swami were sometimes thrilling and always illuminating. It might be the tense expression of his face or the sudden light of insight in his eyes, or an over powering consciousness of higher things revealed in a spontaneous and brilliant remark, or the fact that one lost sight entirely of his physical personality in his glowing and fervid portrayal of the beyond-body outlook —it must be one or all of such characteristics that carried the audiences off their feet. Probably no other instance sets forth his eloquence and spirit more clearly than that which occured in a Western drawing-room where he lectured one evening to a highly cultured audience, composed mostly of fashionable young, mothers. He was speaking on the greatness of the path of love, showing to what heights of selflessness it leads and how it draws out the very best faculties of the soul. In elucidating his remarks, he said, "Suppose a tiger should suddenly appear before you in the street. How terror-stricken you would be and how eager to fly for your very lives! But"—his tone changed, and his face of a sudden lighted up with that strength and fearlessness which the spiritual fire alone endows in fullest measure—"suppose there were a baby in the path of the tiger! Where would your place be then? At the mouth of the tiger—any one of you—I am sure of it." His hearers were carried away by this splendid remark, at once a compliment to the possibilities within them and a challenge charged with the power of arousing their very highest spiritual nature. It was such characteristics as these—his immense personal magnetism, his directness, his lucidity, his vision—which gave convincing force to his utterances and bound indissolubly to himself large groups of the very finest and the most devout disciples. The remarkable way in which he classified religious ideas, the great breadth of his intellectual and spiritual culture, the newness and profundity of his ideas, the great ethical import attached to all he said, and finally his strength, manliness and fearlessness of spirit, each and all of these were bound to create an indelible impression. (vol. 2 pp. 51-52)

Referring to the historic lecture of Swami Vivekananda at the World's Parliament of Religions Chicago, reputed poetess Miss Harriet Monro Wrote in her autobiography mentioned before, "It was human eloquence at its highest pitch."

An innovator of a new concept of religion : a champion expounder and experimenter of Vedanta

Swami Vivekananda once said, "Rare indeed are the persons who can give to the world new ideas and thoughts on any subject."[39]

Swamiji himself was one of those rare persons who gave to the world new ideas and thoughts on not only one but many subjects. He was deeply impressed by the analytic and scientific method of the West and wanted to apply it to the study of Hindu religious ideas. According to the Hindu theory religions belong to the supersensuous plane and come from within. Religion is a light which illuminates the absolute truth. He said, 'It is a vision, an inspiration, a plunge into the unknown and unknowable, making the unknowable more than known, for it can never be "known"[40] This inquiry into the beyond has been in the human mind from the dawn of civilization and it differentiates between man and an animal. He concluded that spiritual knowledge is the goal of all life. Amidst various forms of religion in the world there is harmony; there is a note of concord throughout these discordant sounds and he who is prepared to listen to it, will catch the tone.

Swamiji explicated the deepest truths of religion and science as if they were two sides of the same coin. He wrote to Miss Noble (Sister Nivedita) on 4th July 1897, "In India, lectures and teaching cannot do any good. What we want is Dynamic Religion.'

While lecturing on 'Ideal of a Universal Religion' on January 9, 1896 in New York Swamiji said,

> Religion is realisation, nor talk or doctrine nor theories however beautiful they may be. It is being and becoming, not hearing or acknowledging. It is not an intellectual assent. By intellectual assent we can come to a hundrred sorts of foolish things and change them next day, but this being and becoming is what is Religion.

Swamiji redefined religion for his occidental audience saying, "Religion is the idea which is raising the brute unto man, and man unto God...Take religion from human society and what will remain? Nothing but a forest of brutes. Sense-happiness is not the goal of humanity. Wisdom is the goal of all life."

Swami Vivekananda said that four Yogas or spiritual paths namely, Karma Yoga (the path of unselfish action), Bhakti yoga (the path of devotion), Jnana yoga (the path of knowledge) and Raja yoga (the path of meditation) help people to manifest the divinity already in them and to unite themselves with God or Brahman so they can overcome all problems and weakness in their lives and attain freedom and supreme bliss.

The Swami wrote to his trusted Indian disciple Alasinga Perumal (on 17tth February, 1896) from the U.S.A.

"Then you see, to put the Hindu ideas into English and then make out of dry philosophy, and intricate mythology and queer startling psychology, a religion which shall be easy, simple, popular and at the same time meet the requirements of the highest minds—is a task only those can understand who have attempted it. The dry abstract Advaita must become living—poetic—in everyday life, out of hopelessly intricate mythology must come concrete moral forms; and out of bewildering Yogi-ism must come the most scientific and practical psychology—and all this must be put in a form so that a child may grasp it. That is my life's work."[41]

India, the land of religion Eternal, was ravaged and exploited by various foreign invaders, traders and rulers and has become a breeding ground for hunger, poverty, illiteracy, disease and stupor.

In this state Swamiji considered that the first thing required was the worship of the Kurma (tortoise) Incarnation and the belly-god was this Kurma, as it were. He said to his disciple Sharat chandra Chakravarty, 'Until you pacify this, no one will welcome your words about religion.'

Swamiji said to his disciple that the masses in our country were like the sleeping Leviathan and the young Sannyâsins trained in the Math established by him, would make the people realise their pathetic condition by means of facts and reasoning and instruct them in the ways and means for their welfare and at the same time would explain to them as clearly as possible, in very simple and easy language the higher truths of religion. He said to his disciple, "Show me by your actions that your reading the Vedanta has been fruitful of the highest good. Go and tell all "In every one of you lies that Eternal Power, and try to wake It up." He considered that serving man was more important than personal meditation or salvation.

Swamiji advised his disciple to impress upon the minds of one and all in his motherland that they have the same right to religion as the Brahmins and initiate all even down to the Chandâlas (people of the lowest castes) in these fiery Mantras and to instruct them in simple words about the necessities of life and in trade; commerce, agriculture, etc. He said to his disciple, 'If you cannot do this then fie upon your education and culture, and fie upon your studying the Vedas and Vedanta!"[42]

Sri Ramakrishna used generally to teach dualism. But he initiated Narendra into the teachings of nondualistic Vedanta for he knew that Narendra was inclined to the path of knowledge. Once the magic touch of the Master made him feel that there was really nothing in the universe but God and accept the conclusions of the Advaita philosophy. Narendra himself experienced the Ultimate Reality. So he was able to make the truths of Vedanta understandable.

Swamiji wanted to uplift the masses through his 'man-making religion' He said, "The first step in getting strength is to uphold the Upanishads, and believe : "I am the Soul. I am the Omnipotent, I am the Omniscient.' Repeat these blessed saving words...These conception of Vedanta must come out, must not remain only in the forest not only in the cave, but they must come out at the bar and the bench, in the pulpit and in the cottage of the poor man."

The Swami in a lecture entitled "Indian Religious Thought' emphasised that true religion is positive and not negative; that it consists in a persisent performance of noble and beautiful deeds and not in merely abstaining from evil. We believe in one God, the omnipotent omnipresent omnoscient Father of us all. He is in us and we are in Him. He used the words 'man-making religion' to mean the man who realises something of that infinite presence in his own heart.

Swamiji the most favourite disciple of Ramakrishna Paramahamsa a perfect Sannyasin whose influence and ideas he fell under, remarked like his Master that nowhere is it said in the Vedas that man is born a sinner. To say so is a great libel on human nature.

Vedanta has been practised by mendicants in the forests and caves all through the ages. It was Swamiji who with the co-operation of his brother-disciples, monastics and by devotees established the Ramkrishna order (1 May 1897) with a view to carry the message of Vedanta all over the world. Thus he made Vedanta an organized religion.

Swamiji inspired people to organize in order to carry on the work of practical Vedanta. He bitterly opposed orthodox view about the Vedas nurtured by Lala Hansaraj, the leader of the Arya Samaj and preached the universal, eternal principles of Vedanta. He disliked religious fanaticism, dogmatism and personality cults those grow speedily and die quickly. He used to repeat his Master's great message of harmony : 'As many faiths so many paths.' A prophet is known by the path he shows. Christ is known for his path of love, Buddha for the eightfold path, Mohammad for his path of solidarity while Sri Ramakrishna and his illustrious disciple Vivekananda are known for renunciation harmony and being open to all paths to freedom.

The word 'religion' is derived from the Latin term *religare,* which means that which binds. Generally it means a set of practices that liberate a person. Thus the irony of religion lies in its very definition.

Swami Vivekananda stated a broad and cogent yet minimal definition of religion: 'Each soul is potentially divine. The goal is to manifest this Divinity within by controlling nature, external and internal. Do this either by work, worship or psychic control or philosophy–by one or more, or all of these—and be free. This is the whole of religion. Doctrines, or dogmas or rituals or books, or temples, or forms, are but secondary details.' A careful analysis of this definition reveals its relevance in the contemporary context. In contrast to the existing definitions of religion, both academic and popular, Swamiji's definition erases sense of bondage and stresses freedom.

German philosopher and economist Karl Marx (1818-1893) made a one-sided controversial comment: 'Die Religion...ist das Opium des Volkes'. The full quote from Karl Marx translates as, 'Religion is the sigh of the oppressed creature, the heart of heartless world, and the soul of soulless conditions. It is the opium of the people.'[43]

Actually the 'cocaine' of emotion of religion stirs up the masses and impels them to make or mar.

As magnanimous Swamiji himself said, "And thus we find that though there is nothing that has brought to man more blessings than religion, yet at the same time, there is nothing that has brought more horror than religion. Nothing has made more for peace and love than religion; nothing has engendered fiereer hatred than religion. Nothing has bred more bitter enmity between man and man than religion. Nothing has built more charitable institutions, more hospitals for men, and even for animals, than religion; nothing has deluged the world with more blood than religion. We know, at the same time, that there has always been an undercurrent of thought; there have been always parties of men, philosophers, students of comparative religion who have tried and are still trying to bring about harmony in the midst of all these jarring and discordant sets. As regards certain countries, these attempts have succeeded, but as regards the whole world, they have failed."[44]

According to Swamiji, the first lesson to learn is that what is meat for others may be poison for us. Every nation, like each individual, has one central theme or principal note round which all other notes come to form the harmony. In one nation like the English political power is its vitality, artistic life in another while religion is the lifeblood of many cultures particularly in India. He said, "In India, religious life forms the centre, the keynote of the whole music of national life; and if any nation attempts to throw off its national vitality–the direction which has become its own through the transmission of centuries– that nation dies if it succeeds in the attempt... To prevent this you must make all and everything work through that vitality of your religion. Let all your nerves vibrate through the backbone of your religion. I have seen that I cannot preach even religion to Americans without showing them its practical effect on social life. I could not preach religion in England without showing the wonderful political changes the Vendanta would bring. So, in India, social reform has to be preached by showing how much it will improve the one thing that the nation wants–its spirituality."[45]

Swami Vivekananda believed that an upheaval in religion and not in socialistic or political ideas was the first condition of India's, progress. Every one must know the most wonderful truths confined in our Upanishads, in our scriptures and in our Purânas. In fact, Swamiji wanted a reshaping of religion. His new religion which is his perspective on Vedanta or his realization of the essential, does not stress ritual, a rigid set of practices, theory, dogma, or doctrine. The living being and its reason is the centre of this religion.

Though there was nothing new in the Swami's lectures on Vedanta or Hinduism so far as the theme concerned; the novelty about his presentation was that every word he uttered was instinct with life and self-relience and optimism and its modern outlook and his application of Vedantic principles to the solution of existing social and educational problems. Infact, Hinduism was vindicated by him emphatically. Manabendra Nath Roy opined, "Declassed socially, possessing a keen intellect, he (Swami Vivekananda) made a spectacular plunge into the philosophical depths of Hindu scripture and discovered in his cult of Vedantism (religious Monism of Hindus) a sort of socialistic, humanitarian religion. He decried scathingly orthdoxy in religion as well as in social customs. He was the picturesque, and tremendously vigorous embodiment of the old trying to readjust itself to the new." (India in Transition, p.192) He planted the triumphant flag of new-Hinduism in America and Europe.

Swamiji said, "The alpha and omega of Vedanta philosophy is to "give up the world, giving up the unreal and taking the real. "[46]

The elixir of Advaita Vedanta is that Brahman or the Supreme Self alone is real and the individual selves are not different from Brahman. The essential oneness of all human beings is the essence of Advaita philosophy. It is non-dualism which constitutes the base of Swamiji's concept of universal religion and his philosophy of equality. Even those in America or elsewhere who declare themselves to be 'spiritual but not religious' may accept Swamiji's original idea– realizing one's own Divinity. In his lengthy lecture in San Francisco on April 8, 1900 Swami Vivekananda said, 'But God is the infinite, impersonal being—ever-existent, unchanging, immortal, fearless; and you are all His incarnations, His embodiments. This is the God of Vedanta and His heaven is everywhere. In this heaven dwell all the Personal Gods there are – you yourselves. Exit praying and laying flowers in the temples!

"...our whole idea of God, our praying, our worshipping, all are vitiated by our ignorance, our foolish idea of ourselves as body. You may not like what I am saying. You may curse me today. but tomorrow you will bless me...

"I am the servant of a man who has passed away. I am only the messenger. I want to make the experiment. The teaching of Vedanta I have told you about were never really experimented with before. Although Vedanta is the oldest philosophy in the world, it has always become mixed up with superstition and everything else.

"...The hour comes when great men shall arise and cast off these kindergartens of religion and shall make vivid and powerful the true religion, the worship of the spirit by the spirit."[47]

Referring to the practical Vedanta the Swami said in London on November 10, 1896. :

"Throughout the history of mankind, if any motive power has been more potent than another in the lives of all great men and women, it is that of faith in themselves... Faith in ourselves will do everything. I have experienced it in my own life, and am still doing so; and as I grow older that faith is becoming stronger and stronger. He is an atheist who does not believe in himself. The old religions said that he was an atheist who did not believe in God. The new religion says that he is the atheist who does not believe in himself. But it is not selfish faith, because the Vedanta, again, is the doctrine of oneness. It means faith in all, because you are all."[48].

The Swami's life's mission was to propagate the lofty teachings of the Vedanta, in the light of the realizations of Sri Ramakrishna, throughout the world and to regenerate his holy motherland in tune with her ancient tradition and intrinisic potentiality. He illuminated the eternal vigour and glory of the Sanâtana Dharma. Rightly said sister Nivedita, "What Hinduism needed amidst the general disintegration of the modern era was a rock where she could lie at anchor, an authoritative utterance in which she might recognise herself. And this was given to her, in these words and writings of the Swami Vivekananda...

"...to a great gathering in the West he says, "If one religion be true, then all the others also must be true. Thus the Hindu faith is yours as much as mine." And again, in amplification of the same idea : "We Hindus do not merely tolerate, we unite ourselves with every religion, praying in the mosque of the Mohammedan, worshipping before the fire of the zoroastrian, and kneeling to the cross of the Christian. We know that all religions alike, from the lowest fetishism to the highest absolutism, are but so many attempts of the human soul to grasp and realise the infinite. So we gather all these flowers, and binding them together with the cord of love, make them into a wonderful bouquet of worship...

"Of the Swami's address before the Parliament of Religions, it may be said that when he began to speak it was of " the religious ideas of the Hindus", but when he ended, Hinduism had been created.

"...He stands merely as the Revealer, the Interpreter to India of the treasures that she herself possesses in herself... Had he not lived, texts that today will carry the bread of life to thousands might have remained the obscure disputes of scholars. He taught with authority, and not as one of the Pandits..." (Works vol. 1. Intr. ix–xv)

> Religion will do nothing to him who is both physically and mentally weak. Referring to the Upanishads Swamiji commented in 'Vedanta in its application to Indian life' : 'Ay, it is the only literature in the world where you find the word "Abhih", "fearless", used again and again; in no other scripture in the world is this adjective applied either to God or to man.' And in the context he said to his countrymen 'Be strong, my young friends; that is my advice to you. You will be nearer to Heaven through football than through the study of the Gita.' This scripture does not talk of salvation, but of freedom and solidarity of this universe.

Schopenhauer, the great German philosopher, studying from a not very clear translation of the Vedas, prophesied at the beginning of the nineteenth century far before Swami Vivekananda's visit to the West that there would be the epochmaking impact of the Vedantic mysticism of the Upanishads on the thoughts of the coming ages. He said,

> In the whole world there is no study so beneficial and so elevating as that of the Upanishads... The world is about to see a revolution in through more extensive and more powerful than that which was witnessed by the Renaissance of Greek Literature. (works, vol.3 p 109)

His predictions came true through the emergence of Swamiji and through his interpretation of Advaita Vedanta which he called the 'Science of Religion' as the new holistic paradigm and philosophy of modern science.

Swamiji, working a good deal upon the cosmology and eschatology of the Vedanta clearly saw their perfect unison with modern science and remarked that the elucidation of the one would be followed by that of the other. He wrote Mr. Sturdy,"...It will take more study in physiology, on the relations between the higher and lower centres, to fill out the psychology of mind, Chitta (mind stuff) and Buddhi (intellect), and so on. But I have clear light now, free of all hocuspocus. I want to give them dry, hard reason, softened in the sweetest syrup of love and made spicy with intense work, and cooked in the kitchen of Yoga, so that even a baby can easily digest it." (Works, vol.5, pp. 103-104) His intention to write a book on the subject failed to materialise.

Swamiji said, "Art, Science and Religion are but three ways of expressing a single truth. But in order to understand this, we must have the theory of Advaita." (Works, vol. I, p. xvi) He insisted that Vedantic thought based on reason was not inconsistent with science rather the two would meet and shake hands. He said, "Modern science has really made the foundations of religion strong. That the whole universe is one is scientifically demonstrable. What the metaphysicians call "being", the physicist calls "matter," but there is no real fight between the two, for both are one. Though an atom is invisible, unthinkable, yet in it are the whole power and potency of the universe. That is exactly what the Vedantist says of Atman. All sects are really saying the same thing in different words.

"Vedanta and modern science both posit a self-evolving Cause. In Itself are all the causes..."(Works, vol.7, p. 50)

With reference to Swami Vivekananda's comments on the convergence of Vedanta and Science Dr. Raja Ramanna wrote:

"The discoveries of quantum mechanics and relativity have shaken the very foundations of epistemology. In spite of these violent changes it is only Vedanta which seems to be in a position to absorb the tremendous impact of the new science." (Vedanta, Science and Spirituality by Swami Jitatmananda, Ramakrishna Mission, Swami Vivekananda's ancestral house & cultural centre, Kol. p. 135.)

Before Swamiji no attempt had ever been made to reconcile the three philosophic systems –Advaita (Unism), Dvaita (Dualism) and Visishtâdvaita (Modified Unism). On reaching Madras (now Chennai) in 1897, Swamiji at one of his mid-day question-classes confidently declared that even the utmost realisations of Dualism and Modified Unism, were but stages on the way to Unism itself; and the final bliss, for all alike, was the mergence in One without a second. One of the audiences asked him why, if this was the truth, it had never before been mentioned by any of the Masters. The great gathering was surprised to hear the Swami's reply : "Becuase I was born for this and it was left for me to do!" (The Master as I saw him – Sister Nivedita, p.201.)

Thus Swamiji was the first to experiment and interpret the oldest religion of the world and introduce a new concept of it which is universally beneficial and acceptable to all amidst malice and strife, communal riot and terror in the name of religion.

Victor Hugo satirically said, "We are for religion against the religions." Thomas Fuller made a suggestive remark, "Religion is the best armour, but the worst cloak." Somerset Maugham commented ruefully, "What mean and cruel things men do for the love of God." In the context of the tense times of bigotry and blasphemy Swamiji's new religion is of great significance and importance. He succeeded in his quest for Universal Religion and may be regarded as the harbinger of the world religion of the future.

Swamiji said, "My religion is one of which Christianity is an offshoot and Buddhism a rebel child...There is no new religious idea preached anywhere which is not found in the Vedas.' (Works, vol. 6, p. 105). According to him, Indian thought, Indian philosophy and spirituality, Indian manners and literature should be preserved read and made them acquainted with the great principles underlying these ideas. 'Slow and silent, as the gentle dew that falls in the morning, unseen and unheard yet producing a most tremendous result, has been the work of the calm, patient, allsuffering spiritual race upon the world of thought.'(Works vol. 3, p.110)

The neo-religion being the synthesis of all worldly religions and bearing the message of oneness and equality may one day be the universal religion of the Holy Sri Ramakrishna Empire as has been foretold by an Arab erudite. The Swami himself said," Everything looks propitious, and Indian thought, philosophical and spiritual, must once more go over and conquer the world. The problem before us, therefore, is assuming larger proportions everyday. It is not only that we must revive our own country–that is a small matter; I am an imaginative man–and my idea is the conquest of the whole world by the Hindu race."(Works, vol. 3 p. 276)

The Swami said to Sturdy : "Vedanta teaches the basic philosophy of all religions; this philosophy is no monopoly of any particular religion. This is why Vedanta will become the universal religion convert it into universal treasure. The Vedanta must not remain as the closed preserve of a group of narrow-minded people." (The Life of Swami Vivekananda, By his Eastern and Western Disciple, p.109.

A mixture of opposites :

C.C. Calton said, 'Man is an Embodied paradox, a bundle of contradiction.'[49]

Swamiji's personality is an exceptional example of synthesis of sharp contrasts, multiple perspectives.

Swami Vivekananda a perspicacious and multifaceted creative genius imbued with the Western epistemology was naturally rational and sceptical about religious claims. At the same time his mind was flexible enough to realize the limitations of rationality as well as to submit to the call of the divinity emanating from a poor priest at the Kali temple of Dakshineswar. Sri Aurobindo remarked, "...it was when the flower of the educated youth of Calcutta bowed down at the feet of an illiterate Hindu ascetic a self-illuninated ecstatic and 'mystic' without a single trace or touch of the alien thought or education upon him that the battle was won."[50]

There are numerous examples of Swamiji's scientific bent of mind. In his father's chamber there were several hookahs meant for people of various castes and religions. In order to test the consequence of touching the hookahs of other communities, the young boy Narendranath took a whiff from each of the hookahs and then cheerfully told his father that nothing happened to him as he broke caste rules.

Sri Ramakrishna tried Narendranath in various ways. Similarly, Swamiji tested the strange stoic priest properly and having been satisfied, he accepted him as his Master and followed his teachings sincerely.

Swami Vivekananda was such a paradoxical personality that he like his Master, devoted himself with his brother-disciples to severe austerity and asceticism on the one hand and kept up down -to-earth humanism on the other.

At Ramnad Swamiji said, "There are the two great obstacles on our path in India, the Scylla of old orthodoxy and the Charybdis of modern European civilization. Of these two, I vote for the old orthodoxy, and not for Europeanised system; for the old orthodox man may be ignorant, he may be crude, but he is a man, he has a faith, he has strength, he stands on his own feet; while the Europeanised man has no backbone, he is a mass of heterogeneous ideas picked up at random from every source–and these ideas are unassimilated, undigested, unharmonised."[51]

But Swamiji himself was in many respects unorthodox. When his countrymen were chained by ignorance, superstitions, inhumane practices, abject poverty and political subjugation; he did not hesitate to execute prohibited activities such as crossing the seas, eating food from a Muslim vendor, respecting the pariahs or low-castes, smoking a chillum of tobacco prepared by a low-caste sweeper, bringing Western aspirants and devotees into high caste houses. He wrote to Shrimati Saralâ Ghosal, 'I am a humble mendicant, an itinerant monk;...' (Works. vol. 4. p. 486) But like the traditional itinerants mendicants he did not have for life matted locks, Kamandalu and shelter in the cave or forest which those words suggest.

One day Narendranath requested Sri Ramakrishna to pray to the Divine Mother *Bhavatarini* (the Saviour of the Universe) in the Dakshineswar temple on his behalf to save him from financial crisis. The Master advised him to go to te temple and pray to Her himself for help. He went to the temple and saw the image of Kali as living and conscious. Forgetting all about the world and the pitiable condition of his family he in ecstatic joy, prostrated before Her and prayed "Mother give me discrimination! Give me renunciation! Give me knowledge and devotion! Grant that I may have an uninterrupted vision of Thee!" Thrice he prayed the same instead of asking for something worldy.

Later Swamiji said to one of his Western Disciples : 'I used to hate Kali and all her ways. That was my six years' fight because I would not accept Kali.' But ultimately he accepted Her. He said, "Ramakrishna dedicated me to Her. And you know I believe that She guides me in every little thing I do and just does what She likes with me.'[52]

A bonafide nondualist Swamiji who once scolded his friend Rakhal (later Swami Brahmananda) when he saw him bowing down before the images; accepted the worship of God with form. The Master knew that the concept of God as Mother would make his disciple's spiritual life fuller and richer.

Swamiji composed beautiful poems on the Mother Kali.

Once Swami Vivekananda said to the students of a Calcutta art school, 'Why do you always have to represent Kali in exactly the same way : same pose, same ornaments, same expression; where is your creativity?'

Swami Vivekananda himself was a great prophet, a world-famous spiritual teacher yet he did not hesitate to say to some students in Madras : "First of all, our young men must be strong. Religion will come afterwards. Be strong, my young friends; ...you will be nearer to Heaven through football than through the study of the *Gita* ... You will understand the *Gita* better with your biceps, your muscles, a little stronger."[53]

The liberal Hindu monk did not try to curve any religious tenet; on the contrary, highlighted the merit of other religious doctrines. In a letter he wrote to one of his disciples Sarfaraz Hussain, a Muslim :

"Whether we call it Vedantism or any ism, the truth is that Advaitism is the last word of religion and thought, and the only position from which one can look upon all religions and sects with love. I believe it is the religion of the future enlightened humanity. ...I am firmly persuaded that without the help of practical Islam, theories of Vedantism, however fine and wonderful they may be, are entirely valueless to the vast mass of mankind. ...For our own motherland a junction of the two great systems, Hinduism and Islam—Vedanta brain and Islam body—is the only hope."[54]

Thus rationality and modernity of Swami Vivekananda who said, 'I vote for the old orthodoxy'; challenged baseless old ones and outmoded ideas. Describing Swamiji as 'Paradoxical Prophet', Swami Yogeshananda analyses this dichotomy :

"Swamiji was both a presever of the past and a harbinger of the future; truth for him did not depend on whether it was old or new."[55]

"It is often said that Hinduism is paradoxical due to its uncanny ability to seamlessly harmonize contradictory positions. Therefore, it follows that Swamiji, as the embodiment of Hinduism, would also be paradoxical, favouring broad integration, transcendence, and inclusivity over narrow, dogmtic and exclusionary fundamentalism. Creative mind shun the concrete and convergent for the abstract and the divergent,"[56]

The Swami played the role of a great monk and a fervent nationalist simultaneously. As a stern iconoclast Swamiji wrote to his disciple Alasinga Perumal, "No religion on earth preaches the dignity of humanity in such a lofty strain as Hinduism, and no religion on earth treads upon the necks of the poor and the low in such a fashion as Hinduism. The Lord has shown me that religion is not in fault, but it is the Pharisees and Sadducees in Hinduism, hypocrites, who invent all sorts of engines of tyranny in the shape of doctrines of Pâramârthika and Vyâvahârika."

It may sound snobery still he said in the aforesaid letter : "You would be astonished if I sent over to you the newspaper cuttings, but you already know that I am a hater of celebrity. Suffice it to say, that whenever I went on the platform, a deafening applause would be raised for me. Nearly all the papers paid high tributes to me, and even the most bigoted had to admit that "This man with his handsome face and magnetic presence and wonderful oratory is the most prominent figure in the Parliament." etc., etc. Sufficient for you to know that never before did an oriental make such an impression on American society."

Swamiji said those words not for self-advertisement but for assuring and inspiring his disciples and devotees of Madras particularly and others of his motherland as well.

In an aforesaid essay entitled "Swami Vivekananda' (in Prabuddha Bhāratā, July 1932) Subhas Chandra Bose wrote, "Reckless in his sacrifice, unceasing in his activity, boundless in his love, profound and versatile in his wisdom, exuberant in his emotions, merciless in his attacks but yet simple as a child— he was a rare personality in this world of ours."

Mahedranath related an unpleasant incident that occurred one evening at a lecture-meeting in London:

The Swami had just started a profound and inspiring lecture on Raja-Yoga. Goodwin was making himself ready to take notes; Swami Saradananda, Sturdy, Fox and Mahendranath were seated on the sofa at the other end of the hall. The Swami had hardly spoken for five munutes, when a retired Anglo Indian shouted from the audience with great derision, "Oh, thank you!" Many startled listeners turned toward the man but said nothing, for they were more interested in listening to the lecture. When the heckler repeated the same kind of jeering remark at intervals, the audience became visibly annoyed, but the Swami went on speaking unperturbed without wasting even a glance at him. Presently he assumed the role of critic. When the Swami eulogized the Buddha, he railed against the Buddha. Again, when the Swami claimed that even at the time of his speaking there were in India monks who had attained to high spiritual states, the man declared them to be thieves and burglars. Sturdy and Goodwin became furious but they could do nothing to stop the man, for the Swami went on without so much as a look at him. But a limit finally came. Somehow the heckler thought the speaker must be a Bengali Babu, and he tauntingly announced that during the Sepoy Mutiny the English had saved the Bengalis. And now, at last, the Swami turned toward him, his benign face grown fearful. For more than half an hour he went on cogently citing history, exposing the record of the English people's oppression and evil deeds in various countries of the world. One could not have thought of a more powerful and convincing impeachment, under the impact of which the man openly wept–and this so profusely that his three handkerchiefs became soaked with his tears.

Now, turning to the audience the Swami said in a calm and soothing voice, "Now I come to Pratyahara and Dharana." And he gravely took up his topic where he had left off, as though there had been no disturbance or excitement in the hall.

After the lecture was over the audience rose and greeted him, saying. "Swami, you have taught us a grand lesson in forbearance. Should anyone have insulted us in this manner, we could not have withstood it at all. You are a saint. You are a truly great man." (The Life of Swami Vivekananda–by His Eastern and Western disciples vol. II, pp 109-110.)

Like Iswarchandra Vidyasagar Swamiji was harder than thunder; softer than flower.

Sister Nivedita in her celebrated book 'The Master as I saw him' spoke of Swamiji, "His was the modern mind in its completeness...I see in him the heir to the spiritual discoveries and religious struggles of innumerable teachers and saints in the past of India and the world, and at the same time the pioneer and prophet of a new and future order of development.' (p.p. 79-80)

A Pioneer in the field of education :

Swami Vivekananda wrote on October 11, 1897 to his brother disciple Rakhal (Swami Brahmananda), "After all, what is the purpose behind all these–money and wealth, Maths and institutions, preaching and lecturing? There is only one purpose in the whole of life–education."

To define education Swamiji said : "Education is the manifestation of the perfection already in man.' Accroding to him education is the nervous association of certain ideas.

Swamiji wrote in reply ("The education that India needs') on April 24, 1897) to Sarala Ghosal, 'Education, education, education alone! Travelling through many cities of Europe and observing in them the comforts and education of even the poor people, there was brought to my mind the state of our own poor people, and I used to shed tears, What made the difference? Education was the answer I got. Through education comes faith in one's own self, and through faith in one's own self the inherent Brahman is waking up in them, while the Brahman in us is gradually becoming dormant.' He used to observe how the Irish colonists come–down-trodden, haggard-looking, destitute of all possessions at home, penniless, and wooden-headed held in contempt in their own country, were changed as soon as they landed in America and came in contact with the optimistic view of life. Nature herself spoke, as it were, "Arise, awake, and stop not till the goal is reached." (Katha Upanishad i. ii. 4)

Mentioning this experience Swamiji added in the aforesaid reply, "Likewise the education that our boys receive is very negative. The schoolboy learns nothing, but has everything of his own broken down–want of Shraddhâ is the result...Gradually in these main centres will be taught agriculture, industry etc. and workshops will be established for the furtherance of arts. To sell the manufactures of those workshops in Europe and America, associations will be started like those already in existence. It will be necessary to start centres for women, exactly like those for men."

The views of Swamiji about education was well thought-out and original. He criticised contemporary policy and system of education based on the so-called Downward Filtration Theory—aim of education, curriculum and method of teaching.

Regarding the defects of educational system prevalent at that time Swamiji said to his friend of childhood days and afterwards his disciple Priya Nath Sinha, "It is almost wholly one of defects. Why. It is nothing but a perfect machine for turning out clerks... What we want are Western science coupled with Vedanta, Brahmacharya as the guiding motto, and also Shraddhâ and faith in one's own self. Another thing that we want is the abolition of that system which aims at educating our boys in the same manner as that of the man who battered his ass, being advised that it could thereby be turned into a horse." (Works, vol. 5 P. 366)

Referring to the role of a teacher and religion he commented, "You see, no one can teach anybody. The teacher spoils everything by thinking that he is teaching. Thus Vedanta says that within man is all knowledge–even in a boy it is so–and it requires only an awakening, and that much is the work of a teacher. We have to do only so much for the boys that they may learn to apply their own intellect to the proper use of their hands, legs, ears, eyes etc, and finally everything will become easy. But the root is religion. Religion is as the rice, and everything else, like the curries. Taking only curries causes indigestion, and so is the case with taking rice alone. Our pedagogues are making parrots of our boys and ruining their brains by cramming a lot of subjects into them...It would be better if the people got little technical education so that they might find work and earn their bread, instead of dawdling about and crying for service." (Works 5 p. 367)

In reference to the limitation of the education policy of the imperialistic Government, Swamiji said to his disciple, "The education imparted by the present university system reaches one or two percent of the masses only. And even those who get that do not succeed in their endeavours of doing any good to their country. But it is not their fault, poor fellows! As soon as they come out of their college, they find themelves fathers of several children! Somehow or other they manage to secure the position of a clerk, or at the most, a deputy magistrate. This is the finale of education!'

Swamiji pointed out the lack of books well suited for the little boys. He suggested that we should compose some books in Bengali as also in English with short stories from the Râmâyana, the Mahâbhârata, the Upanishads etc, in very easy and simple language, and those were to be given to our little boys to read.

Swamiji told his disciple the story of Satyakâma from the Upanishads that teaches us that true education is gained by constant living in communion with nature. Emphasizing character building he remarked, "One should live from his very boyhood with one whose character is like a blazing fire and should have before him a living example of the highest teaching. Mere reading that it is a sin to tell a lie will be of no use. Everybody should be trained to practise absolute Brahmacharya, and then, and then only, faith–Shraddha–will come." (Works, vol. 5. pp. 365–369)

Swamiji believed that economic progress and all social transformation could be brought about through education–both secular education and spiritual education. He held that a Math in every town and in every village should be established and a well-educated sadhu (saint) should be at the head of that centre and under him there should be departments for teaching practical science and arts with a specialist Sannyasin (ascetic) in charge of each of these departments. He considered that none could master a thing perfectly in so short a time as the Tyagis (self-deniers) would. To meet the need of such teachers some young men with burning patriotism and renunciation were required.

Swamiji highlighted the freedom and honour enjoyed by women during the Vedic civilisation. Referring to the Aryan literature he mentioned that women in ancient times took the same share as men, and in no other literature of the world had such record. Women contributed large portion to the Vedas. In the 'Devi Sukta' (Rig-veda) God [as the Devi] speaks for Herself "I am the empress of the Universe, the Fulfiller of all prayers.' In those days girls had the right to officiate as priest or to choose their grooms. He said, "This Absolute being, of whom we can predicate nothing, has its *powers* spoken of as She– that is, the real personal God in India is She. This Shakti of the Brahman is always in the feminine gender.' (Works, vol. 9 p. 195) Reminding his countrymen of the ever memorable learned women namely Maitreyi, Gargi, Bachaklavi Swamiji harboured deep resentment toward degradation of the women of India and treating them as manufacturing machine in the subsequent period. Stressing the importance of women-education Swamiji said that India's well-being was impossible without the rise of her women.

In a letter addressed to Shashi (Swami Ramakrishnananda) he wrote from The U.S.A. in 1895 :

> There is no chance for the welfare of the world unless the condition of women is improved. It is not possible for a bird to fly on only one wing. (Works, vol. 6, p. 328)

Swamiji suggested that in the process of man-making education positive ideas should be imparted to all matters physical, mental or spiritual and brain and muscles of the learners should be properly developed. He said, 'Iron nerves with a well intelligent brain and the whole world is at your feet.' Rabindranath told Romain Rolland that if he wanted to know India he should read Vivekananda for 'in him everything is positive and nothing negative.'

The Swami persuaded his co-disciples and disciples to spread education and encouraged his spiritual daughter Nivedita in running her girls' school.

An attempt of making rational synthesis of the ancient and modern education and values of the oriental philosophy and occidental science is evident in the views of Swamiji on the education of India. His observations bore originality of his reflection and realistic approach to the problem.

Reformer of monasticism :

Swamiji successfully implemented his idea of reorganizing monastic life. The sannyasi, abiding by the old tradition of Hindu monasticism used to pend himself up in a solitary cave of a mountain or a cottage in a forest and spend his time in the contemplation of God. He never cared to feel any concern for society and people who porvided him food, clothing and sustenance. It was Swamiji who established monasticism on its true term. Swami Purnatmananda in his essay 'Swamis Brahmananda, Premananda, Turiyananda and Saradananda breaking new ground' (in 'The Story of Ramakrishna Mission, Swami Vivekananda's vision and fulfillment' p. 95) commented : "He (Swami Vivekananda) gave a new consciousness to monasticism and religion–infused new life into both, as it were. He established monasticism on its true ideal and added to it a new dimension, new significance, new import, new expansion, new depth and new mobility. Ascetic monasticism turned poetic and humane."

To quote from the booklet entitled 'Ramakrishna Math and Ramakrishna Mission History. Ideals. Activities' :

One of the significant achievements of Swami Vivekananda is the rejuvenation and modernization of Hindu monasticism...

...Although rooted in the three-thousand-year-old monastic tradition of India, and forming a part of the Ten Orders (dashanāmi) established by Shankaracharya in the 8th century A.D. the Ramakrishna Order represents a new pattern of monastic life which combines some of the best elements of the monastic traditions of the East and the West.

One of the main features of this new pattern of monastic life is the emphasis on service. All monks of the Ramakrishna Order when they are ordained as Brahmacharins (novices) take, apart from the vows of chastity and poverty a vow of service to the poor, the sick and the ignorant. The Ramakrisha Math centres are meant not only for the dwelling of monks but also for service to society.

Another feature of this new pattern of monastic life is its modern outlook. The emphais is on inner purity and detachment rather than on outer show...

Thirdly, the life of the monks, both individual and collective, is governed by definite rules and regulations originally framed by Swami Vivekananda...

Another feature of Ramakrishna Math is its universal outlook. It admits into its monastic fold not only people belonging to different castes of Hinduism but also people belonging to other religions. Not only Indians from various regions speaking different languages, but also Americans, South Americans Russians, Japanese and people of other nationalities – all live together in peace in Ramakrishna monasteries like children of the same parents.

Placing man before religion, Swami Vivekananda synthesised humanism and spiritualism. He stressed the importance of discipline and code of conduct of the monks He was eager to introduce a nation-wide educational programme involving hundreds of men and women teachers. But owing to the hostile political situation prevailing in India then, it was not possible for him to materialize his plan. So he encouraged his disciples in Madras and the heads of princely states such as Mysore and Khetri to take up social service campaign with the active co-operation of groups of trained and dedicated workers. He wanted to make his brother monks involved in such social welfare activities. Accordingly he wrote epistles to them at the Alambazar Math mentioning the importance of reorganizing moanstic life on a new pattern which is God-related and at the same time service-oriented.

Swamiji told his disciple Sharat Chandra Chakravarty that the people of Europe and America reached the climax of Bhoga (enjoyment) and getting no peace of mind. They wanted something else–balm of Yoga (renunciation). Thus the ground in the West was very fertile and fit for sowing seeds of the new religion of universal love and oneness. In India the ground should be prepared first by eradicating some burning problems the first and foremost of which was the evil of hunger and starvation. To remove that evil he decided to establish a Math to train young Sannyâsins who would go from door to door and make the people realise their pitiable condition by means of facts and reasoning, and instruct them in the ways and means for their welfare, and at the same time would explain to them as clearly as possible in very simple and easy language, the higher truths of religion. He said emphatically :

> 'Do you not see? The dawn has already appeared in the eastern sky, and there is little delay in the sun's rising. You all set your shoulders to the wheel!... Your duty at present is to go from one part of the country to another, from village to village, and make the people understand that mere sitting idly won't do any more. Make them understand their real condition and say, "O ye brothers, Arise! Awake! How much longer would you remain asleep!" Initiate all, even down to the Chandâlas (people of the lowest castes) in these fiery Mantras. Also instruct them in simple words, about the necessities of life, and in trade, commerce, agriculture, etc. If you cannot do this then fie upon your education and culture and fie upon your studying the Vedas and Vedanta! At your very threshold, Nârâyana Himself in the form of a poor beggar is dying of starvation! Instead of giving him anything would you only satisfy the appetites of your wife and children with delicacies? Why, that is beastly!
>
> ...Don't you see how sister Nivedita, a Britrish lady, has learnt to serve Indians so well, by doing even menial work for them? And can't you being Indians, similarly serve your own fellow countrymen?'[57]

Swamiji drew up guidelines on the mode of living and activities including some do's and don'ts in the Math. Reminding the inmates of the Master's repeated saying that the sapling must be hedged round, he stressed the importance of abiding by some rules at the immature stage and advised them to keep off vices namely any feeling of jealousy, egotism, gossiping, faction - mongering etc. He remarked 'Is it possible for those to establish cordial relations on earth who can not cordially live with one another for any length of time?'

Swamiji wrote about the management, the Governing Body, departments (study, propaganda, Religious practice), the Office Bearers and forbade the members huddling together in a room, chatting the whole day away with outsiders, reporting scandals about others, smoking outside a particular small room, using rude language, showing temper, residing in the Women's Math or allowing any woman to enter any other room except the Visitors' Hall and the Worship-room, harbouring jealousy, taking note of others' shortcomings and practising vile Vâmâchâra at the Math. He never compromised his principles and tolerated turpitude. He wrote "Better an empty fold than a wicked herd".

"Men of evil character shall be rigorously kept out. On no pretence shall their shadow even cross the threshold of my room. If anyone amongst you become wicked, turn him out at once, whoever he be. We want no black sheep. The Lord will bring lots of good people."

Swamiji advised the inmates to keep their rooms and clothing clean and cook sacramental food in clear and pure water. He wrote : "For the ordinary man and the beginner steady devotion (Nishthâ) to an ideal is of paramount importance. That is to say, teach them that all great Personalities should be duly honoured, but homage should be paid now to Ramakrishna. There can be no vigour without steady devotion. Without it one cannot preach with the intensity of Mahâvira (Hanumân) ... Now we have a new India, with its new God, new religion and new Vedas...

"...Moreover, please show this letter to Gouri-Mâ, Yogin-Mâ and others, and through them establish a Women's Math... They will manage their own affairs. They will not have to work at your dictation. I shall supply all necessary expenses for that work also...

"...Obedience is the first duty. Well just do with alacrity what I ask you to. Let me see how you carry out these few small things. Then gradually great things will come to pass."[58]

Swamiji wrote Rakhal (Swami Brahmananda) instruction to reply to Miss Noble according to these hints–that monks should be secular educators and be trained to build up character, to be obedient and fearless, to help the poor physically first and then work up to higher regions of mentality. More attention should be given to spiritual exercises than to anything else. Indians should be induced to use their own produce and get markets for Indian artware etc. in other countries. All castes were open to the influence of the Order. From the very start there was no distinction in charities or other good works between the different religions of India. He commented : "Wandering from place to place will be necessary till people come to education." The religious character of the wandering monks will carry with it a much greater weight than otherwise."[59]

Thus Swami Vivekananda outlined the aims and objectives and scope of activities of the Math and invariably those were distinctive and original in terms of a spiritual fold.

Dazzling patriotism :

Swami Vivekananda was a multi-faceted genius–an outstanding orator, brilliant litterateur, soulful singer, extraordinary motivator, a world-famous doyen of spiritualism, proficient organizer, social reformer of an unusual type and a charismatic leader of the Order. Above all, he was a great patriot monk, quite out of the ordinary run of patriots. Concern for his motherland was at the core of his thoughts and activities.

Swamiji was seized with over-mastering emotion pride and pain while extolling his holy motherland (in a lecture on 'The future of India) :

"This is the ancient land where wisdom made its home before it went into any other country, the same India whose influx of spirituality is represented, as it were on the material plane, by rolling rivers like oceans, where the eternal Himalayas, rising tier after tier with their snow-caps, look as it were into the very mysteries of heaven... It is the same India which has withstood the shocks of centuries, of hundreds of foreign invasions, of hundreds of upheavals of manners and customs. It is the same land which stands firmer than any rock in the world, with its undying vigour, indestructible life. Its life is of the same nature as the soul without beginning and without end, immortal; and we are the children of such a country."

The sub-continent of India which had been for centuries invaded, captured and subjected to extreme extortion and oppression by the alien imperialist powers was under the British during the lifetime (1863-1902) of Swamiji. He felt anguished and worried about the humiliation of bondage and miserable plight of his countrymen crippled by extreme poverty, gnawing illiteracy, superstitions, untouchability, caste-distinction, langour and so on.

The Swami's clarion-call still finds an echo in the hearts of his country men :

O India! With this mere echoing of others, with this base imitation of others, with this dependence on others, this slavish weakness, this vile detestable cruelty–wouldst thou, with these provisions only, scale the highest pinnacle of civilization and greatness? Wouldst thou attain, by means of thy disgraceful cowardice, that freedom deserved only by the brave and the heroic? O India! Forget not that the ideal of thy womanhood is Sita, Savitri, Damayanti; forget not that the God thou worshippest is the great Ascetic of ascetics, the all-renouncing Shankara; the Lord of Umâ; forget not that thy marriage, thy wealth, thy life are not for sense-pleasure, are not for thy individual personal happiness; forget not that thou art born as a sacrifice to the Mother's altar; forget not that thy social order is but the reflex of the Infinite Universal Motherhood; forget not that the lower classes, the ignorant, the poor, the illiterate, the cobbler, the sweeper, are thy flesh and blood, thy brothers. Thou brave one, be bold, take courage, be proud that thou art an Indian and proudly proclaim, "I am an Indian, every Indian is my brother." Say, "The ignorant Indian, the poor and destitute Indian, the Brahmin Indian the Pariah Indian is my brother." Thou, too, clad with but a rag round thy loins proudly proclaim at the top of the voice : 'The Indian is my brother, the Indian is my life, India's gods and goddesses are my God. India's society is the cradle of my infancy, the pleasure-garden of my youth, the sacred heaven, the Vârânasi of my old age," Say, brother : "The soil of India is my highest heaven, the good of India is my good." and repeat and pray day and night, "O Thou Lord of Gauri, O Thou Mother of the Universe vouchsafe manliness unto me! O Thou Mother of Strength, take away my weakness take away my unmanliness, and make me a Man!"[60]

On the eve of his departure from Lodon, an English friend (Eric Hammond) said to him, "Swami, how do you like your motherland after four years' experience in the luxurious glorious and powerful West?' He gave an unhesitating and significant reply : "India I loved before I came away. Now the very dust of India has become holy to me, the very air is now to me holy; it is the holy land, the place of pilgrimage."[61]

Returning from the West, Swamiji in his first public lecture in the East entitled 'India, the Holy Land' : in the evening of the 16th January 1897 in the Floral Hall, Colombo, Sri Lanka, said : "What little work has been done by me has not been from any inherent power that resides in me, but from the cheers, the goodwill, the blessings that have followed my path in the West from this our very beloved, most sacred, dear Motherland...If there is any land on this earth that can lay claim to be the blessed Punya Bhumi, to be the land to which all souls on this earth must come to account for Karma, the land to which every soul that is wending its way Godward must come to attain its last home, the land where humanity has attained its highest towards gentleness, towards generosity, towards purity, towards calmness, above all, the land of introspection and of spirituality–it is India.

"...Slow and silent as the gentle dew that falls in the morning, unseen and unheard yet producing a most tremendous result, has been the work of the calm, patient, all-suffering spiritual race upon the world of thought."[62]

The Swami's many other lectures too burst with tremendous emotion and excitement born out of his love of motherland and concern for his countrymen. In order to infuse consciousness, patriotism, self-confidence, sense of self-respect and courage into the arteries of the dozy nation he went on with usual fire and eloquence :

"I believe in patriotism, and I also have my own ideal of patriotism...Feel, therefore, my would-be reformers, my would be patriots! Do you feel? Do you feel that millions and millions of the descendants of gods and of sages have become next-door neighbours to brutes? Do you feel that millions are starving today, and millions have been starving for ages? Do you feel that ignorance has come over the land as a dark cloud? Does it make you restless? Does it make you sleepless? Has it gone into your blood, coursing through your veins, becoming consonant with your heartbeats? Has it made you almost mad? Are you seized with that one idea of the misery of ruin, and have you forgotten all about your name, your fame, your wives, your children, your property, even your own bodies? Have you done that? That is the first step to become a patriot, the very first step."[63]

The countrymen hard with bated breath the clarion call of Vedanta from the lips of the Swami : 'Arise! Awake ! And stop not till the goal is reached!' The great humanist and patriot monk said :

> ...so give up being a slave. For the next fifty years this alone shall be our keynote–this, our great Mother India. Let all other vain gods disappear for the time from our minds. This is the only god that is awake, our own race–"everywhere his hands, everywhere his feet, everywhere his ears, he covers everything." All other gods are sleeping. What vain gods shall we go after and yet cannot worship the god that we see all round us, the Virat? When we have worshipped this, we shall be able to worship all other gods. Before we can crawl half a mile, we want to cross the ocean like Hanuman! It cannot be ...The first of all worship is the worship of the Virat–of those all around us. ...These are all our gods–men and animals and the first gods we have to worship are our countrymen. These we have to worship; instead of being jealous of each other and fighting each other.[64]

The Swami tried to galvanise the people into wakefulness and action through his 'man-making religion' and 'man-making education'. He wrote to his disciple Alasinga Perumal, "...I do not believe in a God or religion which cannot wipe the widow's tears or bring a piece of bread to the orphan's mouth. However sublime be the theories, however well-spun may be the philosophy–I do not call it religion so long as it is confined to books and dogmas...

...Do you love your fellow men? Where should you go to seek for God– are not all the poor, the miserable the weak, God? Why not worship them first? ...India's doom was sealed the very day they invented the word MLECHCHHA and stopped from communion with others...."[65]

Swamiji like his predecessors Rammohan Roy, Iswarchandra Vidyaagar of Bengal, Justice Mahadev Govinda Ranade and Swami Dayaanda Saraswati of Mahârâstra etc. fought evil forces and vices of the society with dogged determination relentlessly. He fervently asked his countrymen to wash out the stain of caste-distinction, untouchability and all other superstitions, extortion and cowardice and to serve the ailing humanity. He said to his disciple Sarat Chandra Chakravarty :

"Don't you see why I am starting orphanages, famine-relief works, etc? Don't you see how sister Nivedita, a British lady, has learnt to serve Inidans, so well, by doing even menial work for them? And can't you, being Indians, similarly serve your own fellow-countrymen? Go, all of you, wherever there is an out-break of plague or famine or wherever the people are in distress, and mitigate their sufferings. At the most you may die in the attempt–what of that? How many like you are being born and dying like worms everyday? What difference does that make to the world at large? Die you must, but have a great ideal to die for, and it is better to die with a great ideal in life. Preach this ideal from door to door, and you will yourselves be benefited by it at the same time that you are doing good to your country. On you lie the future hopes of our country. I feel extreme pain to see you leading a life of inaction. Set yourself to work–to work!"[66]

The Swami even during his extremely active stay in the West, could not forget motherland for a moment. 'The Life of Swami Vivekananda' by his Eastern and Western disciples (vol. 1) has depicted a vivid picture of the Swami as patriot – his intense love for India shining out in his words and actions :

"But in the midst of all the immediate acclaim and popularity that his appearance at the Parliament had brought him, he had no thought for himself, his heart continued to bleed for India...On the very day of his triumph, he was invited by a man of great wealth and distinction to his home in one of the most fashionable parts of the city. Here he was entertained royally; a princely room fitted with a luxury beyond anything he could have conceived was assigned to him. But instead of feeling happy in this splendid environment, he was miserable. Name and fame and the approval of thousands had in no way affected him; though sumptuously cared for, he was the same sannyasi as of old, thinking of India's poor. As he retired the first night and lay upon his bed, the terrible contrast between poverty-stricken India and opulent America oppressed him. He could not sleep for pondering over India's plight. The bed of down seemed to be a bed of thorns. The pillow was wet with his tears. He went to the window and gazed out into the darkness until he was well-nigh faint with sorrow. At length, overcome with emotion, he fell to the floor, crying out, "O Mother, what do I care for name and fame when my motherland remains sunk in utmost poverty! To what a sad pass have we poor Indians come when millions of us die for want of a handful of rice, and here they spend millions of rupees upon their personal comforts! Who will raise the masses in India! Who will give them bread? Show me, O mother, how I can help them." (pp. 438-439) His heart was bleeding for the inexpressible miserable plight, humiliation and inertia of the subjugated nation as he wrote to Alasinga from the U.S.A.

"Many of the Western people think of you as a nation of half-naked savages, and therefore only fit to be whipped into civilisation. If you three hundred millions become cowed by the missionaries– you cowards–and dare not say a word, what can one man do in a far distant land? Even what I have done, you do not deserve.

"Why do you not send your defences to the American magazines? What prevents you? You race of cowards – physical, moral and spiritual! you animals fit to be treated as you are with two ideas before you– lust and money– you want to prod a Sannyasin to a life of constant fighting, and you are afraid of the "Saheb logs", even missionaries! And you will do great things, pish!"[67]

Swamiji realized that a worn out nation still having malice, hatred and discrimination among the people could never rise. That is why he reminded his countrymen of the great reformers, preachers namely Ramanuja, Shankara, Nanak, Chaitanya, Kabir and Dadu and their message of love, sacrifice, solidarity and liberality.

The Swami, always modern, proactive and positive in his approach, spoke of mass education going from door to door using maps, charts, magic lantern and so on. He advocated that the Western science and technology must be introduced to uplift the poor masses of this country. He was aware of the basic needs of his countrymen : food, clothing, shelter, education, employment opportunities and medical facilities. At the same time he was an exponent of equality fraternity and liberty. So he wrote to Alasinga Perumal unhesitatingly and emphatically :

"Liberty is the first condition of growth...

...Material civilization, nay, even luxury is necessary to create work for the poor. Bread! Bread! I do not believe in a God, who cannot give me bread here, giving me eternal bliss in heaven! Pooh! India is to be raised, the poor are to be fed, education is to be spread, and the evil of priestcraft is to be removed. No priestcraft, no social tyranny! More bread, more opportunity for everybody!... None deserves liberty who is not ready to give liberty."[68]

Sister Nivedita described (in 'The Master as I saw him' p. 247) how Swamiji was pleased to see his Brahmin disciples nursing low-caste patients through cholera and the industrial education carried on by the Orphange at Murshidabad.

The Swami's patriotism was modified by humanism and magnanimity. During the epidemic of 1899 a pandit came to see him and complained of not being able to talk to him of religion for he talked with the visitor about the wretched condition of the people. Swamiji replied, "So long as even a single dog in my country is without food, my whole religion will be to feed it."

Gandhiji said, 'I have gone through his (Swami Vivekananda's) works very thoroughly, and after having gone through them, the love that I had for my country became a thousandfold.'

Netaji Subhas Chandra Bose, describing Swami Vivekananda as 'the spiritual father of the modern nationalist movement' remarked,

"He was consequently a worshipper of *Sakti* and gave a practical interpretation to the Vedanta for the uplift of his countrymen."[69]

The Swami was more a philanthropist than a religious theorist or preacher. He coined some new words such as 'don't touchism', 'daridra-Narayana' or a "God in the poor and the lowly'. He said to sister Nivedita,' We Indians are MAN-worshippers, after all! our God is man !'[70] According to him, God and Man being the obverse and reverse of the same coin, it is the best to take the service of man as a form of serving God. His life and message inspired the freedom-fighters to dedicate themselves to the cause of their motherland.

Rightly has estimated Dr. R. C. Majumdar, "For the first time in the modern age he (Swami Vivekananda) boldly proclaimed before the world the superiority of Hindu culture and civilisation, the greatness of her past and the hope for her future. Instead of the tone of apology and a sense of inferiority which marked the Indian attitude towards European culture and civilization, a refreshing boldness and consciousness of inherent strength marked the utterances of Swāmi Vivekananda. This combined with his patriotic zeal, made him an embodiment of the highest ideals of the renascent Indian nation. He was, to quote the words of Sir Valentine Chirol "The first Hindu whose personality won demonstrative recognition abroad for India's ancient civilization and for her new-born claim to nationhood."[71]

> In the eyes of Swami Vivekananda his motherland is a living organism – his holy mother. The idea of God, more to say the beneficent, most merciful God, our father, our mother, our friend, the soul of our souls; was nowhere else ever so fully developed as in his motherland. Other races and their respective clan-Gods got into fight. Whenever and wherever he spoke of his motherland he did so with deep emotion, passion and devotion.

To Swamiji welfare of his motherland was a top-priority. Sometimes he did not hesitate to go to the length of subordinating religion to other interests of life. He laid the foundation for true nationalism in India by his message of brotherhood and synthesis of religions. He was born at the dawn of the Renaissance in Bengal and moulded the final shape of the Renaissance movement. The unleashing of freedom movement of India owed much to his spirited message.

Sister Nivedita wrote :

"These then–the Shâstras, the Guru, and the Motherland–are the three notes that mingle themselves to form the music of the works of Vivekananda."[72]

The Swami's letter dated June 5, 1896 to Mrs. Bull testifies to the powerful influence of his Master on him and his advanced ideas for the material betterment of India :

You know my brother Mohin is here in London for the last two months. He intends to become a barrister, He has also a liking, he says, for electrical engineering.

Now I do not like anyone of my blood would become a lawyer although my father was one. My Master was against it, and I believe that family is sure to come to grief where there are several lawyers... Again, what my nation wants is pluck and scientific genius. So I intend him to be an electrician. Even if he fails in life, still I will have the satisfaction that he strove to become great and really useful to his country.

...I want my brother to be daring bold and struggle to cut a new path for himself and his nation...pluck is what my nation wants and scientific education... (The Life of Swami Vivekananda – By his Eastern and Western Disciples, Vol. II p. 108)

Swamiji invested everybody who went to the Math at the garden-house of Nilambar Mukherjee on the sacred birthday of Shri Ramakrishna in 1898 with the holy thread. He said to his disciple Sharat Chandra Chakrabarty, 'These people have fallen from their true status, and the scriptures say that after proper expiation, those fallen in the way earn the right to investiture with the holy thread.' (Works, vol. 7 p. 107)

At the same time this ideal great patriot did not hesitate to criticise idleness, jealousy, cowardice, meanness, miserliness and many other short coming of his countrymen or to make caustic comments about them for their rectification e.g. "...we observe in Bengal almost always "Much cry but little wool." Secondly as I have written before, I do not expect anything from the rich people of India. It is best to work among the youth in whom lies our hope– patiently steadily, and without noise.

"Where, except in India, can be had millions of men who will cut the throats of their own fathers and brothers for six rupees?" (Works, vol. 4 p. 482)

The Swami wrote his brother-disciple Swami Shivananda, "Thousands honour Ramakrishna Paramahamsa, but nobody will give a cent – that is India..." (works, vol. 7. p. 482)

Robust Optimism :

Swami Vivekananda firmly believed that it was impossible that a highly civilized and intellectual and spiritual race like the Indians should acquiesce for centuries in playing the role of hewers of wood and drawers of water in the industrial world. India would certainly rise from the stupor in which she was cast by the spread of education and consciousness; by incessant country-wide campaign and infusion of fearlessness and self reliance into the nation.

The Swami wrote to his brother disciple Swami Ramakrishnananda 'For the last six months I have been saying, the curtain is going up, the sun is rising.

...'A movement which half a dozen penniless boys set on foot and which now bids fair to progress in such an accelerated motion– is it a humbug or the Lord's will? If it is, then let all give up party-spirit and jealousy, and unite in action. A universal religion cannot be set up through party-faction.' (Works, vol. 6. p. 284-285)

Coming back from the West for the first time Swamiji began his address at Ramnad with the words of hope and assurance :

"The longest night seems to be passing away, the sorest trouble seems to be coming to an end at last, the seeming corpse appears to be awaking and a voice is coming to us – away back where history and even tradition fails to peep into the gloom of the past, coming down from there, reflected as it were from peak to peak of the infinite Himalaya of knowldege and of love, and of work, India this motherland of ours – a voice is coming unto us, gentle , firm and yet unmistakable in its utterances and is gaining volume as days pass by, and behold, the sleeper is awakening!...

Let us all work hard my brethren, this is no time for sleep. On our work depends the coming of the India of the future. She is there ready waiting. She is only sleeping. Arise and awake and see her seated here on her eternal throne, rejuvenated, more glorious than she ever was – this motherland of ours."[73]

The Swami realised that the keynote of the whole music of India's national life was religion. He reminded his countrymen of the great ancient Masters namely, Ramajuja, Shankara, Nanak, Kabir, Chaitanya whom he described as the great originators of society, great givers of strength, and of purity, and of life and who always said positive : "O Hindus, what you have done is good, but, my brothers, let us do better." Following the ideas of those great teachers the Swami wanted to do most marvellous work like them and said to his countrymen, "Let all your nerves vibrate through the backbone of your religion."[74]

Romain Rolland in a letter written to Swami Asokananda informed that Rabindranath Tagore once told him these words : If you want to know India, study Vivekananda. In him, everything is positive and nothing negative.

In an article entitled 'The problem of modern India and its solution' written as an introduction to the *Udbodhana* started on the 14th of January, 1899 as the Bengali fortnightly (afterwards monthly) journal of the Ramakrishna Order, Swami Vivekananda narrated how the confluence of two great races the Aryas of India and the Yavanas of Greece led to the tremendous intellectual and spiritual progress and expansion of Christianity over half of the globe. Similar commingling resulted in the prosperity of Arabia and the foundation of modern European civilization. In this connection he had high hopes for his motherland and said :

"And perhaps, in our own day, such a time for the conjuction of these two gigantic forces has presented itself again. This time their centre is India.

"...Europe and America are the advanced children of the Yavanas, a glory to their forefathers, but the modern inabitants of the land of Bharata are not the glory of the ancient Aryas. But as fire remains intact under cover of ashes, so the ancestral fire still remains latent in these modern Indians. Through the grace of the Almighty Power, it is sure to manifest itself in time."

At the same time the Swami also warned his countrymen that unless they overpower and submerge their Tamas (ignorance and vice) by the opposite tide of Rajas (intense spirit of activity) they will never gain any temporal welfare in this life. He cautioned them against blind imitation of impracticable foreign ways ignoring our national customs and ideals; our most precious jewels, earned through ages of hard toil. He added that everyone of the masses should know about his own ancestral property and be liberal and brave to open his door to receive light from the four quarters of the earth. Reminding them of the evidence of history he stated that a nation in which the juxtaposition of Sattva (absolute purity of mind) and the Nitya (Eternal Reality) predominates, is as it were immortal.

The Swami realised the distinctive greatness and immortality of the nation and said : "It is the same India which has withstood the shocks of centuries of hundreds of foreign invasions, of hundreds of upheavals of manners and customs, It is the same land which stands firmer than any rock in the world, with its undying vigour, indestructible life. Its life is of the same nature as the soul, without beginning and without end, immortal, and we are the children of such a country."[75]

In almost every address to his countrymen Swamiji tried to analyse their draw-backs and prospects and to infuse new blood of hope and high spirits and active habits into them. In reply to the address of welcome at Kolkata he said :

"India must conquer the world, and nothing less than that is my ideal......every one of you knows that that little stir, the little life that you see in India, begins from the day when Raja Rammohan Roy broke through the walls of that exclusiveness. Since that day, history in India has taken another turn and now it is growing with accelerated motion. If we have had little rivulets in the past, deluges are coming, and none can resist them. Therefore we must go out and the secret of life is to give and take." According to him we can learn mechanism and many other things from the Westerners and teach them our religion.[76]

In a letter to his affectionate disciple Alansinga the Swami like a teenager wrote huffily, "...why should I waste my energies defending Hinduism if the Hindu all go to sleep? What are you three hundred millions of people doing there, especially those that are so proud of their learning etc?... What help does India send? Did the world ever see a nation with less patriotism than the Indian?" Interestingly, in the same letter the Swami added : "...I am the one man who dared defend his country, and I have given them such ideas as they never expected from a Hindu. There are many who are against me, but I will never be a coward like you. There are also thousands in the country who are my friends, and hundreds who would follow me unto death; every year they will increase, and if I live and work with them, my ideals of life and religion will be fulfilled. Do you see?"[77]

India as an extorted and neglected colony was passing through a state of inertia and decadence under the imperialist foreign ruler. Still she possesses some treasure and potentiality of her own. By virtue of those entities this holy seat of the oldest civilization would surely rise again, With firm conviction Swamiji said to his another disciple Sharat Chandra Chakravarty :

"Do you not see? The dawn has already appeared in the eastern sky, and there is little delay in the sun's rising. You all set your shoulders to the wheel!"[78]

Such inextinguishable optimism, will force and self-relience helped the indomitable monk overcome all sorts of obstacles on his way to reach the goal and awake his countrymen.

An embodiment of youth :

Swami Vivekananda was wise enough to realize the truth that neither the children nor the old could shoulder the resposibility of saving a dying nation. It was the youth only who could transmit elixir of life to the nation. He had a squad of youthful gurubhais (codisciples) and dedicated disciples and devotees at home and abroad.

Swamiji wanted to awaken his countrymen through his 'man-making education' and 'man-making religion'. He said, "Stand and die in your own strength, if there is any sin in the world, it is weakness; avoid all weakness, for weakness is sin, weakness is death."[79] He realised that a subjugated nation like the Indians might rise and gain strength to fight bondage and all other evils only if they had flame of fearlessness in their hearts. As an exponent of the Upanishads he said, "If their is one word that you find coming out like a bomb from the Upanishads, bursting like a bomb-shell upon masses... of ignornce, it is the word fearlessness. And the only religion that ought to be taught is the religion of fearlessness."[80]

Swamiji had a plan to start institutions in India, to train her young men as preachers of the truths of her scriptures in India and outside India. In reference to this plan of campaign he said, "Men, men, these are wanted; everything else will be ready, but strong, vigorous believing young men, sincere to the backbone, are wanted. A hundred such and the world becomes revolutionised. The will is stronger than anything else."[81]

The Swami appealed to the young men of India to respond to the call of the nation and to have a tremendous faith in themselves to revive their motherland. He reminded them of the words of the Vedas : "It is the young, the strong, and healthy, of sharp intellect that will reach the Lord." The freshest, the untouched and unsmelled flowers alone are to be laid at the feet of God. Similarly, the people, while they have the vigour and freshness of youth, should dedicate themselves to the benefit of the nation, to the welfare of humanity. In reply to the address of welcome in Kolkata Swamiji said :

"Young men of Calcultta, arise, awake, for the time is propitious. Already everything is opening out before us. Be bold and fear not. It is only in our scriptures that this adjective is given unto the Lord–Abhih, Abhih. We have to become Abhih, fearless, and our task will be done. Arise, awake for your country needs this tremendous sacrifice. It is the young men that will do it. "The young, the energetic, the strong, the well-built, the intellectual" – for them is the task."[82]

Swamiji diagnosed correctly the awful disease creeping into our national blood–the lack of seriousness, fear the greatest of all superstitions and the great cause of misery and loss of Shraddha. At the same time he pronounced, 'I have faith in my country, and especially in the youth of my country.'[83]

In a poem entitled 'Hold on yet a while, brave heart' written to Ajit Singh Maharaja of Khetri (Rajputana) the poet-monk wrote :

> Not a work will be lost, no struggle vain,
> Though hopes be blighted, powers gone;
> Of thy loin shall come the heirs to all,
> Then hold on yet a while, brave soul,
> No good is e'er undone.

Swamiji was an out-spoken rebel who uttered : "Expasion is life, contractionn is death...Do any deserve liberty who are not ready to give it to others? [84] In a letter (headed 'To my brave boys') he wrote : "Struggle, struggle was my moto for the last ten years, Struggle still say I. When it was all dark, I used to say, struggle, when light is breaking in, I still say, struggle. Be not afraid, my children... Liberty is the first condition of growth. Just as man must have liberty to think and speak, so he must have liberty in food, dress and marriage and in every other thing, so long as he does not injure others...."

Sri Aurobindo describing Swami Vivekananda as "the heroic soul destined to take the world between his two hands and change it' added : "Vivekananda was a soul of puissance if ever there was one, a very lion among men, but the definite work he has left behind is quite incommensurate with our impression of his creative might and energy. We perceive his influence still working gigantically, we know not well how, we know not well where, in something that is not yet formed, something leonine, grand, intuitive, upheaving that has entered the soul of India and we say, 'Behold, Vivekananda still lives in the soul of his Mother and in the souls of Her children."[85]

Swamiji had travelled India twelve years with the load of worries about the sufferings of his countrymen in his heart and the idea of rebuilding the nation in his head. He had crossed half the world seeking for help to his country with a bleeding heart. Regarding service and sacrifice to his motherland he trusted the meek and lowly but faithful youngmen instead of the so-called rich whom he called "more dead than alive.' In a letter to one of his disciple Alasinga Perumal the revolutionary-monk wrote :

"A hundred thousand men and women, fried with the zeal of holiness, fortified with eternal faith in the Lord, and nerved to lion's courage by their sympathy for the poor and the fallen and the downtrodden, will go over the length and breadth of the land, preaching the gospel of salvation, the gospel of help, the gospel of social raising up–the gospel of equality.

"...I may perish of cold or hunger in this land, but I bequeath to you, young men, this sympathy, this struggle for the poor, the ignorant, the oppressed... Vow, then, to devote your whole lives to the cause of the redemption of these three hundred millions, going down and down every day.'[86]

The Swami was dragged through a whole life full of crosses and tortures. He had to see the nearest and dearest die, almost of starvation. He had to fight against starvation, cold, hooting in the streets on account of his quaint dress, calculated vicious slander and above all abject poverty. With his youthful energy, indomitable spirit and unyielding will force the great hero had a pragmatic approach to those problems. His leonine courage and dogged determination flashed as he wrote to his another disciple Ajit Singh, the Maharaja of Khetri, '...The more the Christan priests oppose me, the more I am determined to leave a permanent mark on their country.'[87]

In a eulogy Subhas Chandra Bose said, "Swamiji was full blooded masculine personality–and a fighter to the core of his being. He was consequently a worsipper of *Sakti* and gave a practical interpretation to the Vedanta for the uplift of his countrymen... If he had been alive I would have been at his feet. Modern Bengal is his creation–if I err not."[88]

Though the Swami was not a politician in the ordinary sense of the term; he was one of the great founders of the national movement of India. The freedom-fighters, particularly the youths drew their inspiration from his stimulating teachings, writings and speeches. He provided his countrymen courage, self-confidence and strength the basic tenets of life India needed then most. Rabindranath Tagore said :

"Some time ago Vivekananda said that there was the power of Brahman in every man, that Nārāyana [i.e.... God] wanted to have our service through the poor. This is what I call real gospel...

"Vivekananda's gospel marked the awakening of man in his fullness and that is why it inspired our youth to the diverse courses of liberation through work and sacrifice."[89]

The inextinguishable flame of the 'roaring fire'–the mighty message of Swami Vivekananda still kindles abhih (fearlessness) and self-relience in the droopy hearts.

'a big banyan tree' :

A charismatic leader and an ideal organizer :

As an experienced jeweller can identify a real diamond; Sri Ramakrishna with his fascinating insight realized the worth, the divinity and potetiality of his most beloved disciple Narendranath.

Narendranath possessed such a treasure of extraordinary entities that his Master used to speak often eloquently on his distinctive qualities and originality.

During Narendranath's third visit to Sri Ramakrishna at Dakshineswar the latter said to the former. "O Narāyana, you have assumed this body for my sake. I asked the Divine Mother, "Mother, unless I enjoy the company of some genuine devotees completely free from "woman and gold', how shall I live on earth?" You came to me at night, woke me up, and said, "Here I am!"[90]

In the house of Balaram Bose on 'July 15, 1885 Sri Ramakrishna said to M (Mahendranath Gupta) :

Narendra belongs to a very high plane–the realm of the Absolute. He has a manly nature. So many devotees come here, but there is not one like him.

Every now and then I take stock of the devotees. I find that some are like lotuses with ten petals, some like lotuses with sixteen petals, some like lotuses with a hundred petals. But among lotuses Narendra is a thousand petalled one.

"Other devotees may be like pots or pitchers; but Nārendra is a huge Water-barrel.

"Other may be like pools or tanks; but Narendra is a huge reservoir like the Hāldārpukur.

"Among fish, Narendra is a huge red-eyed carp; others are like minnows or smelts or sardines. Tarak of Belghariā may be called a bass.

"Narendra is a 'very big receptacle' one that can hold many things. He is like a bamboo with a big hollow space inside.

"Narendra is not under the control of anything. He is not under the control of attachment or sense pleasures. He is like a male pigeon. If you hold a male pigeon by its beak, it breaks away from you but the female pigeon keeps still. Narendra has the nature of a man; so he sits on the right side in a carriage. Bhavanath has a woman's nature; so I make him sit on the other side. I feel great strength when Narendra is with me in a gathering."[91]

One day in the presence of Keshab Chandra Sen, Vijay Krishna Goswami, Narendranath and a number of Brahmo devotees at Dakshineswar Sri Ramakrishna commented : "If Keshab possesses one virtue which has made him world-famous, Naren is endowed with eighteen such virtues. I have seen in Keshab and Vijay the divine light burning like a candle flame, but in Naren it shines with the radiance of the sun."

Narendra, feeling embarrassed, later said to the Master, "Sir, people will think you're mad if you talk like that. Keshab is famous all over the world. Vijay is a saint And I am an insignificant student. How can you speak of us in the same breath? Please, I beg you, never say such things again."

"I can not help it," replied the Master. "Do you think these are my words? The Divine Mother showed me certain things about you, which I repeated. And She reveals to me nothing but the truth."[92]

"How do you know it was Mother who told you?" Narendra objected. "All this may be a fiction of your own brain. Science and philosophy prove that our senses often deceive us, especially when there's a desire in our minds to believe something. You are fond of me and you wish to see me great– that may be why you have these vision."[93]

The Master was at a loss and prayed to the Divine Mother for guidance. She said, "Why do you care what he says? In a short time he will accept every word of yours as true."

The Master discovered God in his disciple whom he moulded with great care and affection to make him his worthy messenger, an ardent expounder of his ideas and teachings in the world.

One day the Master wrote on a piece of paper, "Naren will teach people when he will address at home and abroad." Glancing at the paper Narendranath said, "I won't do any such thing." Thereupon the Master said, "Your very bones will do it."

The special purpose in his transmission of power to Narendranath was to accomplish much work through him. Later on Swamiji narrated that strange experience to his disciple Sharat Chandra Chakravarty :

"...two or three days before his leaving the body, he called me to his side one day, and asking me to sit before him looked steadfastly at me and fell into Samadhi. Then I really felt that a subtle force like an electric shock was entering my body! In a little while, I also lost outward consciousness and sat motionless. How long I stayed in that condition I do not remember; when consciousness returned

I found Sri Ramakrishna shedding tears. On questioning him, he answered me affectionately "Today, giving you my all, I have become a beggar. With this power you are to do many works for the world's good before you will return." I feel that that power is constantly directing me to this or that work. This body has not been made for remaining idle."[94]

Having been a victim of terminal throat cancer Sri Ramakrishna knew that his days were numbered. So he expedited the formation of his own monastic order by distributing ochre monastic robes among some of his young disciples including Narendranath and nominating him as the leader of the squad. He advised his disciples other than Narendranath to obey Narendra and take care of him. On the other hand, he said to Narendranath, "I leave them all to your care. See that they practise spiritual disciplines even after my passing away and that they do not return home."

On 23 May 1897 Goodwin wrote to Mrs. Ole Bull, 'When the Paramahamsa was passing away he called in all his disciples but Swamiji (Naren) and gave them an express command that they were always to pay every attention to Swamiji and never to leave anything undone that could add to his health or comfort. Then sending them out and calling in Swamiji he committed all his other disciples into his charge.' The source of this information was either Swami Vivekananda or some one of his brother-disciples.

One day Narendranath implored Sri Ramakrishna to enable him to experience nirvikalpa samadhi (a trance or profound meditation in which one is completely identified with or absorbed into the Infinite), the highest and most covetous realization of non-dualism. But the Master rebuked him :

> Shame on you! You are asking for such an insignificant thing. I thought that you would be like a big banyan tree, and that thousands of people would rest in your shade. But now I see that you are seeking your own liberation.

Since then Narendranath had no craze for nirvikalpa samadhi (though he was blessed by the Master to experience the same) and he advised his disciples afterwards to dedicate themselves to the welfare of the world instead of seeking their own liberation selfishly.

It was Narendranath only who understood the implication of the Master's words properly and who was selected as the leader of the squad by the Master himself and who was unanimously accepted as their leader and guide by his brother-disciples after the resurrection of the Master.

Indeed, subsequently, Swamiji with his multifarious activities appeared to be 'a big banyan tree'.

Sometimes in the middle of January 1886, elder Gopal (Gopal Chandra Ghosh, later Swami Advaitananda) wanted to distribute twelve pieces of ochre cloth, the garb of a monk and twelve rosaries to some monks on their way to attend Ganga Sagar Fair. Sri Ramakrishna, pointing to his young disciples, said to him "You won't find better monks than these. Give your cloths and rosaries to them." Gopal offered them to the Master and he himself distributed them among his eleven disciples and one ochre cloth kept for Girish Chandra Ghosh.Thus Sri Ramakrishna himself started his monastic Order. In a letter dated 13 July 1897 Swamiji wrote from Almora to Swami Brahmananda : All our associations centre round that garden of Cossipore. In reality that is our first Math." (Works, Vol. 8, p. 411)

After passing away of the Master, the Mother was anxious about the shelter and sustenance of her shocked and confused monastic children. Her continuous tearful prayer was an important factor in the formation of the Order.

Another factor at the genesis of the Ramakrishna Math and Ramakrishna Mission was Sri Ramakrishna's mandate to Narendranath : to do Mother's work and to save humanity. His words and activities cast a deep impact on the mind of zealous Narendranath and moulded the mission of his life. He realized that a permanent organization was inevitable in order to implement the Master's instruction to him : to preach India's spirituality all over the world and to work for the welfare of the world.

In the Rig Veda it was said that life is made for the *'Atmano mokṣhārtham jagat hitāya ca.* i.e. for the salvation of our individual self and for the well-being of all on earth. Swamiji's experience as an itinerant monk from 1888 to 1892 fortified his conviction to lay stress on the second half of the ideal (welfare of the world) too which was ignored in the traditional notion so long with regeneration. Romaind Rolland in his book 'The Life of Vivekananda and the Universal Gospel' wrote, "But this consciousness of his mission only came and took possession of him after years of direct experience, wherein he saw with his own eyes and touched with his own hands the miserable and glorious body of humanity-- his mother India in all her tragic nakedness." (p. 7)

After Sri Ramakrishna's passing away his intimate disciples were at a loss to determine what to do. On the 30th August, 1886 Jogindranath Roy Choudhury, Kaliprasad Chandra and Rakhturam (Latu) left for Vrindaban with the Holy Mother, Golap-Ma, Lakshmi Devi and Nikunja Devi, wife of Master Mahashay (M) to put up at the Kala Babu's grove belonging to Balaram Bose one of the greatest householder-devotees and suppliers of stores of the Master. Latu, Taraknath Ghosal, Kaliprasad Chandra, Gopal Chandra Ghosh etc. were either shelterless or resolved not to go back home. Tarak in advance went to Vrindaban and was engaged in asceticism at the Kala Babu's grove. Some of the young disciples returned home to resume studies or domestic duties. Some senior devotees namely Ramachandra Dutta held that excessive ascetic practice was unnecessary for those who had seen the Master. All of them except Balaram Bose, Surendranath Mitra, Master Mahashay and Chunilal Bose disowned the zealous disciples. On April 9, 1887 in the garden to the West of the monastery Narendranath said to M, "Whatever spiritual disciplines we are practising here are in obedience to the Master's command. But it is starange that Ram Babu criticizes us for our spiritual practices. He says, 'We have seen him. What need have we of any such practice?'"

It was a very crucial situation. Narendranath though bereaved, was fretfully busy with maintaining his poverty-stricken family, attending a lawsuit in which his family had been invloved and brooding over his future course of activities. In the meantime one day Surendranath Mitra (whom Sri Ramakrishna called 'Suresh') had a transcendental vision that Sri Ramakrishna said to him, 'What are you doing? My sons are wandering the streets. Do something before anything else.' He at once rushed to his neighbour Narendranath and narrating his vision requested him very intently to set up an abode where the vessel containing ashes and pieces of bone of the Master along with his picture and clothes might be kept and worshipped by his self-denying devotees who might live together there. He also assured him of regular financial help. Hearing about such co-operation Narendranath was overwhelmed with joy and started searching for a suitable and at the same time affordable house. He wrote to his gurubhai (co-disciple) Taraknath in Vrindaban asking him to make himself ready to leave for taking charge of the new monastery as soon as he would receive the wire. Accordingly Taraknath proceeded to Banaras and was awaiting his leader's second direction.

At last Narendranath and his friend Bhavanath (Chatterjee) of Baranagore found a two-storied decayed and deserted house inhabited by jackals, snakes and lizards at Baranagore between Dakshineswar and Kolkata and near the holy burning-ghat at Cossipore where the body of the Master had been cremated. The monthly rent for the house was eleven (according to Swami Virajananda, ten) rupees. The monastery at Baranagore was set up at the end of September or beginning of October in 1886.

The younger Gopal under the direction of Surendranath brought the bed and other articles of daily use of the Master from the garden house at Cossipore (or from Balaram's house for the garden house was left by the devotees at the end of August though it was not impossible to keep some articles there by arrangement with the owner of the garden). The relics of the Master had been brought from Balaram's house. The first permanent member was the elder Gopal. Tarak soon joined the monastery. Probably the elder Gopal, Tarak, Kali and Shashi were living in the monastery permanently when in the middle of December 1886, Baburam's mother Matangini Devi (mother-in-law of Balaram Bose) invited the intimate disciples of Sri Ramakrishna to her country home at Antpur (forty eight kms. from Kolkata) in the district of Hooghly. Accordingly a team comprising Narendra, Tarak, Baburam, Kali, Sharat, Shashi, Gangadhar, Niranjan and Sarada travelled to Antpur by train with musical instruments and Narendranath and others sang devotional songs along the way. One cold night, a bonfire was lit in front of Baburam's house. The disciples sat around it and were in deep meditation for a long while. Then Narendra told the story of Jesus emphasizing his great renunciation and the role of st Paul and other disciples of Jesus who by dint of their tireless endeavour and self-sacrifice and preaching expanded Christianity in the world. Then he invoked his brother-disciples to build their life as holy as that of Jesus and his disciples and dedicate it to the welfare of the world. They, deeply moved and inspired by the passionate and very appealing words of their leader, stood up lithely and took the vow of renunciation before the holy *dhuni* fire (a sacrificial fire en-kindled by ascetics). Later they discovered that it was Christmas Eve (24 December, Friday) an auspicious day and realized that it was the most propitious time to start a new life. After returning to Baranagore they including Rakhal took formal sannyasa, performing *Viraja homa* (a special fire ceremony) in the third week of January 1887 and Narendranath gave each of them a significant monastic-name. Gangadhar who was then travelling Tibet and Jogin and Latu who were then at Vrindavan and a few others had taken formal sannyasa later on.

One day Shashi's father (Ishwar Chandra Chakraborty) came to the monastery to persuade him to come home and said to M : "Narendranath alone is the cause of all the mischief. For a while all these young men returned home and devoted themselves to their studies."[95] On learning that his father had come, Shashi fled the monastery by another door instead of meeting him. In fact, Narendranath secretly used to meet those brother-disciples who under pressure and torture of their guardians were compelled to live with their families; and insisted them earnestly on living at the monastery rousing in them the spirit of renunciation by his fiery words. Gradually Shashi, Baburam, Niranjan, Rakhal, Sharat, Sarada and Subodh lived at the monastery. A few months later Latu and after a year Jogin (returning form Vrindavan with the Mother) joined the monastery. Gangadhar left home for the Himalayas and Tibet to practice austerity in the month of February 1887 and coming back he became a member of the monastery in the middle of 1890. Hari soon embraced the monastic life.

The monastic names of Sri Ramakrishna's intimate disciples who renounced the world soon after his death were given by Narendranath :

Narendranath Dutta–Swami Vividishananda / Swami Sachhidananda / Swami Vivekananda.

Rakhal Chandra Ghosh – Swami Brahmananda

Taraknath Ghosal – Swami Shivananda

Baburam Ghosh – Swami Premananda

Jogindranath Roy Chaudhury – Swami Yogananda

Nityaniranjan Ghosh – Swami Niranjanananda

Sharatchandra Chakraborty – Swami Saradananda

Shashibhusan Chakraborty – Swami Ramakrishnananda

Harinath Chattopadhyay – Swami Turiyananda

Rakhturam (Latu) – Swami Adbhutananda

Kaliprasad Chandra – Swami Abhedananda

Sarada Prasanna Mitra – Swami Trigunatitananda

Gopal Chandra Ghosh – Swami Advaitananda

Subodh Chandra Ghosh – Swami Subodhananda

Gangadhar Gangopadhyay – Swami Akhandananda

According to the direction of Narendranath Hari Prasanna Chattopadhyay took Sannyasa directly from the Master on 9 May 1899 with the traditional *viraja homa* and became known as Swami Vijnanananda.

Thus Surendra Nath Mitra was in a way the founder and chief patron of the Baranagore monastery and Narendranath was the leader of the monastic disciples of Paramahamsa Deva. He supervised the household. The only goal in life of the inmates of the monastery was the realization of God and they depended on him for their spiritual inspiration. He said to them, 'We must practise sādhanā; otherwise we shall not be able to realize God."

It was morning after Sivarātri, M who used to visit the monastery frequently to observe the spirit of intense renunciation of his brother disciples; discovered an impressive appearance of the leader :

"Narendra was clad in a new ochre cloth. The bright orange colour of his apparel blended with the celestial lustre of his face and body, every pore of which radiated a divine light. His countenance was filled with fiery brilliance and yet touched with the tenderness of love. He appeared to all as a bubble that had risen up in the Ocean of Absolute Existence and Bliss and assumed a human body to help in the propagation of his Master's message. All eyes were fixed on him. Narendra was then just twenty-four years old, the very age at which the great Chaitanya has renounced the world."[96]

The inmates of the monastery called themselves the 'danas' and the 'daityas'; the companions of Shiva to indicate their detachment from worldliness. They dedicated themselves round-the-clock to the practice of spiritual discipline japa, meditation and study of the scriptures. They often spent their evenings on discussing the teachings of their Master, Shankaracharya, Ramanuja and Jesus Christ and Hindu philosophy, European philosophy, the Vedas, the Puranas and the Tantras on the roof. Of course, Narendranath was the pivot of all these activities.

One day no sooner did Narendra arrive from Kolkata than Kali said to him, "What about the lawsuit?" Narendra replied sharply, "Why should you bother about it?" As an ideal leader Narendranath considered that the main focus of attention of his brother-disciples should not be changed.

One day Rakhal said to Narendra, "Many people think that it is enough not to look at the face of a woman. But what will you gain merely by turning your eyes to the ground at the sight of a woman?" Narendranath quipped : "Woman exists for a man as long as he has lust. Free from lust, one sees no difference between man and woman." M. at once exclaimed : "How true it is! Children do not see the difference between man and woman."

There were mutual love and respect and understanding among the brother-disciples. Swamiji tried to enrich them with knowledge of various subjects and to make them self-reliant regarding their personal spiritual progress and realization of God. He reprimanded them if needed. He said to M. "Kali has a craving for knowledge. I scold him for that. Is knowledge so easy to get? Let his bhakti first mature...."

...Again, one day he said to Prasanna, "...I scolded Kali, saying : 'You fool! Do you want to measure God with your tape and foot-rule?'

One evening at Belur Math Swamiji said to his disciple Sharat Chandra Chakravarty :

"After the passing away of Sri Ramakrishna we underwent a lot of religious practice at the Baranagore Math. We used to get up at 3 a.m. and after washing our face etc. –some after bath, and others without it—we would sit in the worship-room and become absorbed in japa and meditation. What a strong spirit of dispassion we had in those days! We had no thought even as to whether the world existed or not. ...

"...There have been days when the Math was without a grain of food. If some rice was collected by begging, there was no salt to take it with! On some days there would be only rice and salt, but nobody cared for it in the least. We were then being carried away by a tidal wave of spiritual practice. Boiled Bimba leaves, rice, and salt–this was the menu for a month at a stretch. Oh, those wonderful days! The austerities of that period were enough to dismay supernatural beings, not to speak of men."[97]

After the passing away of the Master the feeling of bereavement and helplessness was replaced by intense spiritual activities and to the credit of the leader there always hovered an air of peace and holiness despite inexpressible suffering in the monastery. In this connection M said to himself : "Everything is as it was before. The same Ayodhyā – only Rāma is not there."[98]

Swamiji spent much time in discussing, answering questions of his brother disciples, singing devotional songs and exhorting them to surrender themselves at His feet and to drink deep from the cup of Divine Bliss. Once (May 8, 1887) he said to himself : "My brain is heated by talking to these youngsters."

There goes a proverb, "The monk is pure who goes, and the river is pure that flows." Naturally the monastic disciples left the monastery to live as a penniless wandering monk.

On April 9, 1887 M. said to Narendranath, "...You have become the guardian of these young men. Yours is the entire responsibility. You have to bring up the brothers of the monastery." Owing to his sense of responsibility Narendranath was anxious as he heard that Prasanna (Swami Trigunatitananda) had left the monastery for an unknown destination (Vrindāvana) during his absence in Kolkata. He said to M. "You see what a lot of trouble I am in! Here, too, I am involved in a world of māyā. Who knows where this boy has gone?"

The inmates of the monastery practised spiritual disciplines in obedience to the Master's command though Ram Babu (Ramachandra Dutta) opined that they didn't need to do so as they had seen the Master.

As an ideal leader Narendranath knew well how to handle a tense situation. The Master exhorted his monastic disciples to realize God. Standing far from that realization they were at a loss what to do. When Rakhal (Swami Brahmananda) proposed that they should go to the Narmada, Narendranath said, "What will you achieve by wandering about? Can one ever attain Jnāna, that you are talking about it so much?" A member of the monastery feigning great suffering on account of his separation from God, said : "Ah! Please give me a knife. I have no more use for this life. I can't stand this pain any more!" Narendranath pretending seriousness said to him : "It is there. Stretch out your hand and take it." Everybody laughed. Thus with the help of convincing arguments, wit and love the paterfamilias tried to save his brothers from depression and restlessness and to create a convivial atmosphere in the monastery.

On May 9, 1887 M. listening to the hymns sung by Narendranath said to himself : "How intense Narendra's dispassion is! This is how he has infused the spirit of dispassion into the hearts of the other brothers of the monastery."

As 'a conscious dreamer' and vivacious organizer Swamiji asked Swami Shivananda to leave for Africa to look after the religious needs of the Indian emigrants there when Mr. Setlur of Girgaon, Mumbai requested the Swami and assured him of bearing all expenses regarding that. (Works Vol. 8, pp. 440 – 441)

The Swami wrote Rakhal : "By all the means in our power the Nivedita Girls' School in Calcutta should be put on a firm footing." (Works, Vol. 8. p. 455)

He used to strive for earning money by lecturing relentlessly as 'a cyclonic Hindoo' for the maintenance of the organization and conducting social services. He wrote Swami Shivananda, "In this terrible winter I am lecturing from place to place and fighting against odds, so that funds may be collected for Mother's Math." (Works, Vol. 7 p. 485)

As a competent general the Swami had intense love and sympathy for his band of brother-disciples. Sister Nivedita wrote : 'Suddenly news came that one of the brothers by name Yogananda, lying ill with small-pox at Allahabad and a party followed by the Swami, started to nurse him.' ('The Master as I saw him', p. 59)

On May 26, 1890 Swamiji, in a long letter to Pramadadas Mitra of Varanasi, wrote :

...1. I already told you at the outset that I am Ramakrishna's slave, having laid my body at his feet "with Til and Tulasi leaves"; I cannot disregard his behest. If it is in failure that that great sage laid down his life after having attained to superhuman heights of Jnana, Bhakti, Love and powers and after having practised for forty years stern renunciation, non-attachment, holiness, and great austerities, then where is there anything for us to count on? So I am obliged to trust his words as the words of one identified with truth.

2. Now his behest to me was that I should devote myself to the service of the Order of all-renouncing devotees founded by him, and in this I have to persevere, come what may, being ready to take heaven, hell, salvation, or anything that may happen to me.
3. His command was that his all-renouncing devotees should group themselves together, and I am entrusted with seeing to this of course, it matters not if any one of us goes out on visits to this place or that, but these shall be but visits, while his own opinion was that absolute homeless wandering suited him alone who was perfected to the highest point. Before that state, it is proper to settle some where to dive down into practice. When all the ideas of body and the like are dissolved of themselves, a person may then persue whatever state comes to him. Otherwise, it is baneful for a practising aspirant to be always wandering.
4. So in pursuance of this his commandment, his group of Sannyasins are now assembled in a dilapidated house at Baranagore, and two of his lay disciples, Babu Suresh Chandra Mitra and Babu Balaram Bose, so long provided for their food and house-rent.

…6. What greater regret can there be than this that no memorial could yet be raised in this land of Bengal in the very neighbourhood of the place where he lived his life of Sâdhanâ–he by whose birth the race of Bengalees has been sanctified, the land of Bengal has become hallowed, he who came on earth to save the Indians from the spell of the wordly glamour of Western culture and who therefore chose most of his all-renouncing disciples from university men.

…10. ...If you deem it proper to have some shelter erected on the banks of the Ganga in Bengal for Bhagavan Ramakrishna's sacred remains and for his disciples, I shall with your leave report myself to you, and I have not the slightest qualm to beg from door to door for this noble cause, for the sake of my Lord and his children. Please give this proposal your best thoughts with prayers to Vishvanatha. To my mind, if all these sincere, educated, youthful Sannyasins of good birth fail to live up to the ideals of Sri Ramakrishna owing to want of an abode and help, then alas for our country!

11. If you ask, "You are a Sannyasin, so why do you trouble over these desires?" —I would then reply, I am Ramakrishna's servant, and I am willing even to steal and rob, if by doing so I can perpetuate his name in the land of his birth and Sâdhanâ (spiritual struggle) and help even a little his disciples to practise his great ideals... (Works, Vol. 6, pp. 239 – 241)

The letter shows how dogged determined and eager the Swami was to set up a shrine of his Master and an abode for his monastic disciples. Of course, his first priority was to establish Mother's Math.

The monastery was shifted from Baranagore to Alambazar (1892) and then to the garden house of Nilambar Mukherjee at Belur village (February 1898) and finally to Belur (December 1898) adjacent to the garden on the Ganga.

In a letter written to his disciple Alasinga Perumal from New York on November 19, 1894, Swamiji advised him :

"Have fire and spread all over. Work, work. Be the servant while leading. Be unselfish, and *never listen to one friend, in private accusing another*. Have infinite patience, and success is yours.

"Now take care of this : Do not try to "boss" others, ...

"I want that there should be no hypocrisy, no jesuitism, no roguery... "No shilly-shally, no *esoteric, blackguardism*, no secret humbug, nothing should be done in a corner..."[99]

In a long and important letter from England addressing the members of the Alambazar Math Swamiji wrote :

"Let me write something for you all. It is not for gaining personal authority that I do this, but for your good and for fulfilling the purpose for which the Lord came. He gave me the charge of you all, and you shall contribute to the great well-being of the world–though most of you are not yet aware of it – this is the special reason of my writing to you. It will be a great pity if any feeling of jealousy or egotism gain ground among you. Is it possible for those to establish cordial relations on earth who cannot cordially live with one another for any length of time? No doubt it is an evil to be bound by laws, but it is necessary at the immature stage to be guided by rules; in other words, as the Master used to say that the sapling must be hedged round, and so on. Secondly, it is quite natural for idle minds to indulge in gossip and faction-mongering, and so forth. Hence I jot down the following hints. If you follow them, you will undoubtedly prosper but if you don't do so, then there is a danger of all our labours coming to naught."

Swamiji, not as a leader but as an elder-brother and not in an authoritative tone but benignly reminded his brother-disciples of the teachings of the Master and warned them of the piteous consequence of jealousy, egotism or factionalism. He drew up guidelines on the management, the governing body, departments, office-bearers etc. He knew how the intimacy of the Buddhist mendicant friars with the Buddhist mendicant nuns toppled the existence of Buddhism. So to safeguard the organisation he made some general remarks, apparently caustic :

1. If any woman comes to have a talk with a Sannyasin, she should do it in the Visitors' Hall. No woman shall be allowed to enter any other room – except the Worship-room.
2. No Sannyasin shall be allowed to reside in the Women's Math. Anyone refuse to obey this rule shall be expelled from the Math. "Better an empty fold than a wicked herd."
3. Man of evil character shall be rigorously kept out. On no pretence shall their shadow even cross the threshold of my room. If anyone amongst you become wicked, turn him out at once, whoever he be. We want no black sheep. The Lord will bring lots of good people.
4. Any woman can come to the class-room (or preaching hall) during class time or preaching hour, but must leave the place directly when that period is over.

5. Never show temper, or harbour jealousy, or backbite another in secret. It would be the height of cruelty and hard-heartedness to take note of others' shortcomings instead of rectifying one's own.
6. There should be fixed hours of meals. Everyone must have a seat and a low dining table. He will sit on the former and put this plate on the latter as is the custom in Rajputana.

Swamiji persuaded his brother-disciples to establish a Women's Math through Gouri-Mâ, Yogin-Mâ and others and assured them of supplying all necessary expenses for the Alambazar Math (only if his ideas and rules were followed) and the would-be Women's Math. The letter concluded with some authoritative words : "...He who is the servant of all is their true master. He never becomes a leader in whose love there is a consideration of high or low. He whose love knows no end, and never stops to consider high or low, has the whole world lying at his feet." (Works, Vol. 7 p. 498)

In another letter written to his brother-disciples at Alambazar monastery Swamiji gave them a new idea of imparting mass-education with the help of some teaching-aids namely cameras, maps, globes, some chemicals etc. instead of busying themselves with effete ceremonials and ringing bells. He told them that as children of Ramakrishna they should propagate his lofty character, his sublime life, his teaching, his new religion. To define the word 'organization' he said : "The term organization means division of labour. Each does his own part, and all the parts taken together express an ideal of harmony..." He strove for maintaining harmony and cautioned the members of the organization against backbiting and factionalism etc. In the aforesaid epistle Swamiji wrote : "What is wanted is a power of organization – do you understand me? Have any of you got that much brain in your head? If you do, let your mind work. ...We want some disciples – fiery young men – do you see? –intelligent and brave, who dare to go to the jaws of Death and are ready to swim the ocean across. Do you follow me? We want hundreds like that, both men and women. Try your utmost for that end alone. Make converts right and left, and put them into our purity-drilling machine." (Works, Vol. 6. 292)

Once Swamiji told his disciple Sharat Chandra Chakravarty that first some young men full of the spirit of renunciation are needed – those who would be ready to sacrifice their lives for others, instead of devoting themselves to their own happiness. With that object in view he would establish a Math (monastery) to train young Sannyâsins, who would go from door to door and make the people realize their pitiable condition by means of facts and reasoning, and instruct them in the ways and means for their welfare, and at the same time would explain to them as clearly as possible, in very simple and easy language, the higher truths of religion.

Sensing Narendra's eagerness for experiencing nirvikalpa samadhi, one day Sri Ramakrishna scolded him for his selfish-thought of seeking his own liberation. The Master thought that his beloved disciple would teach people and he would be like a big banyan tree to cater shade to thousands of people and would see God in all beings as well as to serve them in a spirit of worship.

Swamiji was eager to translate his Master's message to humanity into action :

"First make character – that is the highest duty you can perform. Know Truth for yourself, and there will be many to whom you can teach it afterwards; they will all come. This was the attitude of my Master. He criticised no one. For years I lived with that man, but never did I hear those lips utter one word of condemnation for any sect. I learned from my Master that the religions of the world are not contradictory or antagonistic. They are but various phases of one eternal religion."[100]

Swamiji felt the dire need of a monastic Order that would carry the message of his Master and of Vedanta as well all over the world. During his stay in America he thought, "To organize or not to organize? If I organize, the spirit will diminish. If I do not organize, the message will not spread."[101]

At a time when social reformers were busy with widow-remarriage and abolition of idol worship, Swamiji, travelling all over India as a mendicant monk for a few years realized that the burning problem of his motherland was the abject poverty, illiteracy, exploitation and lack of self-relience of the masses that caused the backwardness of the country. The poor people especially the down-trodden, low-born have-nots needed fearlessness and faith in themselves, secular and spiritual education, knowledge of improved methods of agriculture, rural industries and hygienic way of living. And for this purpose what was needed most was an organization 'a machinery which will bring noblest ideas to the doorstep of even the poorest and the meanest.'

The Master discerned the potentiality and qualities of an efficient organizer in his most beloved disciple Narendranath. Swamiji said in a class, "He (Sri Ramakrishna) was afraid about me that I might create a sect, if left to myself." (Work, Vol. 7, p. 414)

Swamiji wrote from Chicago to Dewanji (Haridas Viharidas Desai) on 20 June 1894 :

"Primarily my coming has been to raise funds for an enterprise of my own...

"...Every new religious wave requires a new centre... Now do you not think that you have already seen the nucleus of such a great movement, that you have heard the low rumblings of the coming tidal wave? That centre, that God-man to lead was born in India. He was the great Ramakrishna Paramahamsa, and round him this band is slowly gathering. They will do the work. Now Dewanji Maharaj, this requires an organization, money – a little at least to set the wheel in motion..."

The Swami had to swim across a sea of troubles on his way to raise some funds for setting up his work. First, the year 1894 was very bad year in America; thousands of their poor were without work. Secondly, the missionaries and the Brahmo Samajists tried to thwart all his views and slander his character. Referrining to the foul play of Mazoomdar he wrote to his brother monk Swami

Ramakrishnananda 'I am very sorry to hear of Mazoomdar's doings. One always behaves thus in trying to push oneself before all others. I am not much to blame. M – came here ten years ago, and got much reputation and honour; now I am in flying colours. Such is the will of the Guru, what shall I do? It is childishness on M's part to be annoyed at this.' (Works, Vol. 6, p. 282)

Thirdly, his countrymen could not even do so much for him as to tell the Americans that he was a real Sannyasin and not a cheat and that he represented the Hindu religion. Besides, sometimes he had to give as many as three lectures a day, moving on from one place to another and was exhausted. But he was able to continue such strenuous tour as 'the cyclonic Hindu' by dint of his amazing will-force and tenacity. He said to the aforementioned brother disciple, 'I depend on no one in Hindusthan. I shall try to earn the wherewithal myself to the best of my might and carry out my plans, or die in the attempt.' (Works, Vol. 6. p. 255)

The Swami, both as an organizer and a leader was a genius with farsightedness and indomitable spirit.

Swamiji wrote to his brother-disciple Swami Ramakrishnananda, 'A leader is born. Do you understand? And it is very difficult task to take on the role of a leader. One must be दासस्य दासः :- a servant of servants, and must accommodate a thousand minds. There must not be a shade of jealousy or selfishness, then you are a leader. First, by birth, and secondly, unselfish – that's a leader.' (Works, Vol. 6, p. 284) He told him that a true Swnnyasin made no distinction between householders and Sannyasins and took no pride in their monastic order when it was full-grown. Ultimately on I May 1897. Swamiji convened a meeting of the monastics and lay devotees of Shri Ramakrishna in the house of Balaram Bose at Bagbazar, Kolkata and discussed the importance of preaching the message of the Master and carrying on the work of practical Vedanta on an organized basis. Then he proposed to the monastic disciples and house holder devotees present that the organization should "bear the name of him in whose name we have become sannyasins, taking whom as your ideal you are leading the life of householders, and whose holy name, influence and teachings have within twelve years of his passing away, spread in such unthought-of way both in the East and in the West." The proposal was unanimously accepted by all the members and the Ramakrishna Mission Association was set up formally.

Swamiji was greatly delighted to see the enthusiastic response from his brother-disciples and householder devotees and the auspicious introduction of his work in India. He told his friend and disciple Priya Nath Sinha that he had more than three thousand disciples in the West. He succeeded in establishing some centres (e.g. the Vedanta Society of New York founded in November 1894) for the cultivation of Vedanta and the teachings of Sri Ramakrishna there. He encouraged his brother disciples to spread out all over India. He sent Swami Ramakrishnanda to set up a centre in Madras and deputed Swamis Trigunatitananda and Akhandananda to start extensive famine relief service in Murshidabad and Dinajpur. From May 1897 to the end of that year he, ignoring his illness and exhaustion travelled and lectured extensively in northern India. On 3 June 1897 he wrote to Christine Greenstidel : "As for myself, I am quite content. I have roused a good many of our people, and that was all I wanted. Let things have their course and Karma its sway. I have no bonds here below." He encouraged Mr. and Mrs. Sevier to build the Advaita Ashrama at Mayavati in the Himalayas in order to practise nondualistic Vedanta. On 9 July 1897 he wrote to Mary Hale : "Only one idea was burning in my brain – to start the machine for elevating the Indian masses, and that I have succeeded in doing to a certain extent. It would have made your heart glad to see how my boys are working in the midst of famine and disease and misery – nursing by the mat-bed of the Cholera-stricken pariah and feeding the starving Chandala, and the Lord sends help to me, to them, to all."

Swamiji spent most of the year 1898 training his Indian and Western disciples and striving to consolidate what he had already started. Several young men, inspired by the life and message of Swamiji, joined the monastery. A plot of land at Belur village on the Ganga was purchased (March 5, 1898) and on 9 December 1898 Behur Math was formally consecrated when Swamiji himself carrying the urn of relics and photo of his Master on his shoulder from the garden house of Nilambar Mukherjee installed those in its new shrine.

In this connection it may be recalled that once Sri Ramakrishna said to Narendranath; "I will go and live wherever you take me, carrying me on your shoulder, be it under a tree or in the humblest cottage."

Credibility and impartiality are the two principal principles of true journalim. As an ideal leader, friend, philosopher and guide Swamiji wrote to his most beloved disciple Alasinga :

"A letter you published from Kripananda in the *Brahmavadin* was rather unfortunate. Kripananda is smarting under the blows the Christians have given him and that sort of letter is vulgar, pitching into everybody. It is not in accord with the tone of the *Brahmavadin*. So in future, when Kripananda writes, tone down everything that is an attack upon any sect, however cranky or crude. Nothing which is against any sect, good or bad should get into the *Brahmavadin*. Of course, we must not show active sympathy with frauds. ..."[102]

Swamiji laid down some strictures against malice and rash comments and on maintaining decency and decorum in order to keep up the standard of the journals (*Brahmavadin, Prabuddha Bharata, Udbodhan*).

Swamiji wrote his brother disciple Shashi (Swami Ramakrishnananda) to save time by curtailing time of the worship of Sri Ramakrishna in order to hold classes and do some preaching. He requested him to educate two widowed daughters of Biligiri so that through them more such widowed women could get a thorough grounding in their own religion and learn a little English and Sanskrit. At the same time he cautioned him : "Don't enter into wrangles with anybody – always maintain a calm attitude. ...One has to be exceedingly careful before young women. Once you fall, there is no way out, and the sin is unpardonable. ...See that an atmosphere of perfect purity is always maintained, and that there enters not the slightest trace of Vâmâchâra."[103]

As a happy and confident organizer Swamiji who planned to train up numbers of young men, wrote Miss Noble (afterwards his disciple and spiritual daughter Sister Nivedita) : "I have sent some of my boys to work in the famine districts. It has acted like a miracle. I find, as I always thought, that it is through the *heart*, and that alone, that the world can be reached. ...

"It is true in one way that the people here have so little to give up– yet renunciation is in our blood. One of my boys in training has been an executive engineer, in charge of a district. That means a very big position here. He gave it up like straw!"[104]

Swamiji considered that the garden of Gopal Chandra Ghosh at Cossipore where Sri Ramakrishna passed his last days (December 11, 1885 - August 16, 1886) was in reality their first Math and believed that in future great works would be accomplished. For that he advised Swami Brahmananda to try to buy the historic plot quickly and secretly and as a realist leader added that the work would be spoiled if plans were not kept secret. He assured him of sending some money within seven weeks.

A farsighted organizer Swamiji considered the proposal made by Mr. Setlur of Girgaon (Bombay now Mumbai) for sending somebody to Africa to look after the religious needs of the Indian emigrants there. He felt that it was really the work for a perfect man to look after the Indians, and at the same time maintain cool-headedness to avoid quarrel with the white rulling class who disliked the emigrants. And considering Swami Shivananda worthy of shouldering the responsibility, requested him to take up the challenge. He realized, "No immediate result can be expected, but in the long run it will prove a more beneficial work for India than any yet attempted."[105]

Swamiji encouraged self-assessment and did not hesitate to criticise himself. He wrote to Rakhal (Swami Brahmanada), "I see very well that my policy is wrong, and yours is correct, regarding helping others; that is to say, if you help with money too much at a time, people instead of feeling grateful remark on the contrary that they have got a simpleton to bank upon."[106] In the same letter he wrote, Skilful management lies in giving every man work after his own heart. By all the means in our power the Nivedita Girls' School in Calcutta should be put on a firm footing." Regarding Master (M) Mahashay's proposal to start a college in Calcutta (now Kolkata) Swamiji advised his brother-disciple to do what they all considered best.

As an ideal leader and organizer Swami Vivekananda was anxious about the future of the nascent organization. After thirteen days of the aforesaid letter he wrote Rakhal, "My great anxiety is this : the work has somehow been started, but it should go on and progress even when we are not here; such thoughts worry me day and night. Any amount of theoretical knowledge one may have but unless one does the thing actually, nothing is learnt. I refer repeatedly to election, accounts, and discussion so that everybody may be prepared to shoulder the work. If one man dies, another– why another only, ten if necessary – should be ready to take it up. Secondly, if a man's interest in a thing is not roused, he will not work whole-heartedly; all should be made to understand that everyone has a share in the work and property, and a voice in the management. This should be done while there is yet time. Give a responsible position to everyone alternately, but keep a watchful eye so that you can control when necessary; thus only can men be trained for the work. Set up such a machine as will go on automatically, no matter who dies or lives. We Indians suffer from a great defect, viz we can not make a permanent organization – and the reason is that we never like to share power with others and never think of what will come after we are gone."[107]

These well-thought-out suggestions were goaded by the principles of democracy, liberalism and stern realism and prudence. He was so sincere and particular about morality that he frankly wrote in the aforesaid letter : "I am borrowing this amount from the Math and will pay it back to you with interest."

The Swami, in order to maintain congenial environment and cordial relationship used to value the opinion and proposal of his brother-disciples and would try to satisfy them by answering their questions or dispelling doubts. To mention an exemplary event : Miss Minnie C. Boock of America like some other fellow-students of Vedanta, considered a big city like San Francisco with all its amenities of luxury and comfort unsuitable for spiritual practice and offered Swamiji a property of 160 acres in northern California for a retreat fit for meditation and devoting to a life of renunciation. When Swamiji asked Swami Turiyananda to take up the project the latter hesitated to do so. Swamiji said to him, "It is the will of the Mother that you should take charge of the work there. Swami Turiyan anda amusingly quipped, "Rather say it is *your* will. Certainly you have not heard the Mother communicate Her will to you in that way. How can we hear the words of the Mother?" The Swami replied with great emotion, "Yes, brother, yes, the words of the Mother can be heard as clearly as we hear one another. It only requires a fine nerve to hear the words of the Mother."[108] Swami Turyananda was convinced and agreed to assume the responsibility. Shanti Ashram (on 2323 Vallejo Street, San Francisco, California) was set up.

While the Swami was putting up at the residence of Seth Shyamal Das in Delhi, his brother-disciples hailing from Meerut unintentionally and unexpectedly met Swami Vividishananda who was none but their beloved 'Naren' and naturally were happy to see him. But Swamiji said to them, "Brothers, I told you that I wanted to be left alone. I said that I had work to do. I asked you not to follow me. Now I insist that you obey me. I do not want to be followed. With this I leave Delhi. And he who follows me does so at his peril; for I am going to lose myself to all old association. Where the Spirit leads, there I shall wander, no matter whether it is a forest or a desert waste, a mountain region or a densely populated city I am off."[109] Actually Swamiji loved his brother-disciples and tried to enrich them with knowledge of various subjects whenever he got opportunity and persuaded them to study more. As a result, each of them despite having no such remarkable formal education, turned out to be great erudite and venerable personality. The Swami, as the leader of the fold wanted to make every brother-disciple self-relient and worthy disciple of the great Master instead of being a blind imitator or parasite. He encouraged them to illuminate their respective originality and ability.

The depth of mutual love, respect and understanding among the brother-disciples can be realised from the following narration :

"Shortly afterwards the brother-disciples left Delhi one after another. Saradananda went to Etawah; and because he was ill, Kripananda went with him. Brahmananda and Turiyananda left for the Punjab, Akhandananda made for Vrindavan; and the Swami set out for Rajputana (now Rajasthan). His brothers knew in which direction their leader had gone, but they dared not follow him. They knew that his soul was in the grip of a great restlessness to fulfill the mission for which he had been born; they knew that it was under the guidance of the Master, by the will of the Mother, that he wanted to be left alone. So, with moist eyes and anguish in their hearts, they had bidden him farewell and sought his blessings. But the Swami himself was glad to cut this last attachment of his soul– his love for his brother-disciples."[110]

It is said that he who is ready to offer his head, deserves to be the chieftain or leader. During his stay at the house of Major Ramchandraji, the Dewan to Mangal Singh the Maharaja of Alwar (Rajasthan) one day Swamiji said to the visitors, "Dear sons, I am ready to sacrifice my life for you, for you are willing to follow my advice and have the power to do so."[111]

One day Swamiji asked Swami Vijnanananda for an estimate expenditure on building a ghat and an embankment on the bank of the Ganga for the Belur Monastery. Swami Vijnanananda, fearing Swamiji might change his decision, understated the cost and said it would be roughly three thousand rupees. Swamiji consulting with Swami Brahmananda ordered to start the project. When he learnt that the expenses had already exceeded the original estimate and the work was still incomplete, he became angry with Brahmananda and rebuked him harshly. After a while Swamiji regretted his bad temper and hearing from Vijnanananda that Raja Maharaj was weeping he rushed to his room and embraced him and said tearfully, "Raja, brother, please forgive me. It is my fault that my temper is short and that I scolded you. Please pardon me." Seeing Swamiji weep, Brahmananda was deeply moved and said, "What does it matter? You have scolded me because you love me - that is all." Still Swamiji went on, "Brother, please forgive me. I know how much the Master loved you and never uttered a harsh word to you. And I on the other hand, for the sake of this petty work, have verbally abused you and given you pain. I am not fit to live with you. I shall go away to the Himalayas and live alone in solitude." Raja Maharaja said, "Don't say that, Swamiji, your scolding is a blessing. How can you leave us? You are our leader. How shall we function without you?" By degrees both of them turned calm.

With reference to that incident Swami Vijanananda commented "I shall never forget that scene in my life. I never saw Swamiji weeping so bitterly. What a bond of love existed between them! Swamiji loved his brother disciples like a mother, and that is why he could not bear any shortcoming in them. He wanted them to be as great as himself; nay, even greater than himself. His love was incomparable [Swami Vijnanananda by Swami Jagadiswarananda, Ramakrishna Math Allahabad, 1947, p. 244]

Swami Saradananda wrote in the *Udbodhan* (Vol. 35 No. 7, 1340 B. E), 'He (Swamiji) was the rock upon which the whole structure was to be built.'

Two days after the passing away of Swamiji Dr. J. C. Bose wrote to Miss J. MacLeod : India has lost her great son [in Swami Vivekananda]. But his has been a heroic life, and he carried the banner of glory. The next day Dr. Bose wrote to Mrs. Ole Bull : That great soul [of Swami Vivekananda] is released; his heroic deeds on earth are over. Can we realize what that work has been– how one man did all this? When one is tired it is best that he should sleep, but his deeds and teachings will walk the earth and waken and strengthen.

[Letters of Sister Nivedita Ed. Sankari Prasad Basu, Vol. 1, p. 478]

An introducer of a new concept of worship :

Sri Ramakrishna's life and teaching of *Shivajnane Jivaseva* (Service to Shiva in all human beings) taught Swami Vivekananda and his brother disciples how to apply spiritual excellence for removing human sufferings and promoting human conditions. The great Master said, "A great worship is going on all the time. Nothing should be neglected. One should think of God during all activities of life, such as eating, walking, moving, talking and sleeping. This is called true religion."

Referring to this new dimension of 'true religion' Swamiji said to a representative (Sister Nivedita) of *Prabuddha Bharata* :

"The history of the past has gone to develop the inner life of India and the activity (i.e. the outer life) of the West. Hitherto these have been divergent. The time has now come for them to unite. Ramakrishna Paramahamsa was alive to the depths of being, yet on the outer plane he was more active. This is the secret. Let your life be as deep as the ocean, but let it also be as wide as the sky.

"It is a curious thing," continued the Swami, "that the inner life is often most profoundly developed where the outer conditions are most cramping and limiting. But this is an accidental - not an essential - association, and if we set ourselves right here in India, the world will be 'rightened'. For are we not all one?" (Works, Vol. 5, p. 227)

Sri Ramakrishna's constant vision of God immanent in all beings, high or low brought forth Swamiji's futuristic vision of 'Immanent God'.

The Swami said in one of his long poems, 'TO A FRIEND' :

> Formulas of worship, control of breath,
> Science, philosophy, systems varied,
> Relinquishment, possession, and the like,

All these are but delusions of the mind–
Love, Love – that's the one thing, the sole treasure.

* * * * * * *

From highest Brahman to the Yonder worm,
And to the very minutest atom,
Everywhere is the same God, the All-Love;
Friend, offer mind, soul, body, at their feet.

These are His manifold forms before thee,
Rejecting them, where seekest thou for God?
Who loves all beings without distinction,
He indeed is worshipping best his God.

Thus the poem is keyed to the central theme of Swamiji's life, Brahmajnâna. He repeatedly spoke of the workship of the Virât – the Brahman in manifold forms.

In her widely, acclaimed book, 'The Master as I saw him' Sister Nivedita has quoted her Master : "Out of that old ancestor-*puja*, you might create Hero-worship.

"In the worship of the gods, you must of course use images. But you can change these. Kali need not always be in one position. Encourage your girls to think of new ways of picturing Her. Have a hundred different conceptions of Saraswati. Let them draw and model and paint their own ideas.

"...And never forget Humanity! The idea of a humanitarian man-worship exists in nucleus in India, but it has never been sufficiently specialised. Let your women develop it. Make poetry, make art, of it. Yes, a daily worship of the feet of beggars, after bathing and before meal, would be a wonderful practical training of heart and hand together. On some days, again, the worship might be of children, of your own pupils." (pp. 262 - 264)

Swamiji asked his brother-disciple Swami Akhandananda to try to develop spirituality and philanthropy amongst people, to teach them various subjects and to look upon the poor, the illiterate as God. He wrote to him, "No good will come of sitting idle and having princely dishes, and saying "Ramakrishna, O Lord!" – unless you can do some good to the poor. Go to other villages from time to time, and teach the people the arts of life as well as religion. Work, worship, and Janana (Knowledge) – first work, and your mind will be purified; otherwise everything will be fruitless like pouring oblations on a pile of ashes instead of in the sacred fire. ...The Geruâ robe is not for enjoyment. It is the banner of heroic work. You must give your body, mind, and speech to "the welfare of the world."[112]

The Swami reminded his beloved brother-disciples at Alambazar Monastery that this world is a place for action and wrote them :

> What I am most afraid of is the worship - room. It is not bad in itself, but there is a tendency in some to make this all in all and set up that old-fashioned nonsense over again – this is what makes me nervous. I know why they busy themselves with those old, effete ceremonials. Their spirit craves for work, but having no outlet they waste their energy in ringing bells and all that.
>
> "...We must electrify society, electrify the world. Idle gossip and barren ceremonials won't do. Ceremonials are meant for householders, your work is the distribution and propagation of thought-currents. If you can do that, then it is all right...."[113]

Swamiji considered that work was worship particularly to the children of Sri Ramakrishna and only meditation, uttering mystic and esoteric words, chanting prayers or acquiring knowledge were not sufficient for them. Their work included service to the poor and out-cast, spread of education and spirituality and formation of a band of young educated Sannyasins. Their worship was to take active role in forming character, making man and building nation.

In one of his famous lectures (entitled 'The future of India') Swamiji, emphasizing the importance of Chittashuddhi or purification of the heart, said to his countrymen :

> The first of all worship is the worship of the Virat – of those all around us. Worship it. Worship is the exact equivalent

> of the Sanskrit word, and no other English word will do. These are all our gods–men and animals; and the first gods we have to worship are our countrymen. These we have to worship, instead of being jealous of each other and fighting each other. It is the most terrible Karma for which we are suffering, and yet it does not open our eyes ![114]

Swamiji said to his disciple and spiritual daughter Sister Nivedita, "You do not yet understand India! We Indians are Man-worshippers, after all! Our God is man!" On another occasion he said to her :

"This idea of man-worship exists in nucleus in India, but it has never been expanded. You must develop it. Make poetry, make art of it. Establish the worship of the feet of beggars, as you had it in Mediaeval Europe. Make man-worshippers."[115]

Swamiji told his disciple Sharat Chandra Chakravarty that in order to hold the true eternal principles before the people for the benefit of our religion and our country, first of all, we had to introduce the worship of the great-souled ones namely Sri Ramachandra, Sri Krishna, Mahâvira and Sri Ramakrishna, among others. He realized that the subjugated and gasping nation mostly needed the ideal of a hero whose tremendous spirit of Rajas thrilling through his veins from head to foot; whose armour was renunciation and sword was wisdom. He said : "Keep aside for the present the Vrindâvan aspect of Shri Krishna and spread far and wide the worship of Shri Krishna roaring the Gita out, with the voice of a lion. And bring into daily use the worship of Shakti – the divine Mother, the source of all power." (Works, Vol. 5, p. 388)

The Swami wrote his brother-disciple Swami Shivananda :

"Without Shakti (Power) there is no regeneration for the world. Why is it that our country is the weakest and the most backward of all countries? Because Shakti is held in dishonour there. Mother has been born to revive that wonderful Shakti in India; ...Without the grace of Shakti nothing is to be accomplished." Drawing attention to the worship of Shakti by the Americans and the European though ignorantly through sense-gratification, he said to his co-disciple :

"Imagine then, what a lot of good they will achieve who will worship Her with all purity, in a Sâttvika spirit, looking upon Her as their Mother! ...Brother, I shall show how to worship the living Durga and then only shall I be worthy of my name..." (Works, Vol. 7, pp. 484-485)

From realistic and philanthropic point of view these are revolutionary and liberal utterances of Swamiji regarding the true way and object of worship.

Immeasurable devotion to the Master and Holy Mother :

In this land of unimaginable devout disciples like Aruni and Ekalabya........ Swami Vivekananda set another amazing example of devotion to his Gurudeva (the Master) and his consort (the Holy Mother).

Frantic with worries about his poverty-stricken family and agitated mentally with the question about the existence of God, Narendranath Dutta first met Sri Ramakrishna at Dakshineswar (1881) at the age of 18. Both of them tried each other in various ways. Having been impressed by the priest's stern renunciation, child-like simplicity, divinity and above all his bold declaration 'Yes, I have seen God...'; he took refuge at his feet and became his most beloved disciple.

Swami Prabhananda quoted from the books, 'Yuganayak Vivekananda' by Swami Gambhirananda and Biography of Swami Saradananda by Brahmachari Akshay Chaitanya an unbelievable incident in his book 'Shri Ramakrishner Antyalila' (footnote, p. 154) that when the Master had terminal throat-cancer, some of the devotees, fearing the disease to be infectious were found busy with self-protection. With a view to do away with such mentality Narendranath oneday (5th February 1886) after the 'Lord's supper' (as was written in the diary of M.) drank some portion of left-over barley mixed with spittle and 'Fresh blood' unhesitatingly. Niranjan (afterwards Swami Niranjanananda), Shashi (Swami Ramakrishnananda) and Sharat (Swami Saradananda) following him swallowed the remaining liquid.

Swami Premananda said, "After the Master's passing away Swamiji used to cry for him so much secretly at night that his pillow would get wet and I would put it in the sun in the morning to dry."[116]

Swamiji's letter written from the Baranagore Math on 19th Nov. 1888 to Pramadadas Mitra of Varanasi, help us presume that he had sent the addressee two photographs of his revered Master and two parts of some of his teachings as given in his homely style compiled, and published by a certain gentleman.

In a letter (dated 26th May, 1890) Swamiji wrote the aforesaid erudite : "I already told you at the outset that I am Ramakrishna's slave, having laid my body at his feet, "With Til and Tulasi leaves", I can not disregard his behest. If it is in failure that that great sage laid down his life after having attained to super human heights of Jnana, Bhakti, Love, and powers, and after having practised for forty years stern renunciation, non-attachment, holiness, and great austerities then where is there anything for us to count on? So I am obliged to trust his words as the words of one identified with truth.'[117]

In 1896 Swamiji lectured on his Master in New York and England. In those addresses he sketched the biography of his Master precisely and expressed his deep gratitude saying :

> Today the name of Sri Ramakrishna Paramahamsa is known all over India to its millions of people. Nay, the power of that man has spread beyond India; and if there has ever been a word of truth, a word of spirituality, that I have spoken anywhere in the world, I owe it to my Master; only the mistakes are mine.

Besides mentioning his Master's renunciation, practice of austerities, yearning for God-realization, overcoming the idea of sex, worshipping woman as the Divine Mother, his principles and messages, respect for all religions, etc. Swamiji extolled his uniqueness :

> To proclaim and make clear the fundamental unity underlying all religions was the mission of my Master. Other teachers have taught special religions which bear their names, but this great teacher of the nineteenth

> century made no claim for himself. He left every religion undisturbed because he had realized that in reality they are all part and parcel of the one eternal religion.

Simultaneously Swamiji held the Mother in high esteem : "The maiden was a pure and noble soul and was able to understand her husband's aspirations and sympathise with them. She quickly told him that she had no wish to drag him down to a life of worldliness; but that all she desired was to remain near him, to serve him, and to learn of him. She became one of his most devoted disciples, always revering him as a divine being. Thus through his wife's consent the last barrier was removed, and he was free to lead the life he had chosen."[118]

In his 'Inspired Talks' Swamiji remarked, 'The Guru is the conveyance in which the spiritual influence is brought to you... The Guru passes the thought power, the Mantra, that he has received from those before him; and nothing can be done without a Guru.'[119] '...intense love for the Guru makes rapid growth possible, he connects us with the internal Guru. Adore your Guru if there be real truth in him; that Guru-bhakti (devotion to the teacher) will quickly lead you to the highest.'

Sri Ramakrishna's purity was that of a baby. He never touched money in his life, and lust was absolutely annihilated in him. ...In Sri Ramakrishna Paramahamsa the man was all dead and only God remained; he actually could not see sin, he was literally "of purer eyes than to behold iniquity."[120] 'Have faith in Guru, in his teachings and in the surety that you can get free.'[121]

During class talks Swamiji discussed diverse aspects of his Master e.g. 'The significance of his life and teaching', 'on Sri Ramakrishna and his views,' 'Sri Ramakrishna : The nation's ideal'. He said, 'He (the Master) used to love me intensely, which made many quite jealous of me. ...I have a superstitious regard for the latter (the Master). "Love me, love my dog," as they say. I love that Brahmin priest intensely, and therefore, love whatever he used to love, whatever he used to regard!"[122]

In reply to the address of welcome presented at Calcutta (on 28 February, 1897) Swamiji said, "Brothers, you have touched another chord in my heart, the deepest of all, and that is the mention of my teacher, my master, my hero, my ideal, my God in life – Sri Ramakrishna Paramahamsa. If there has been anything achieved by me, by thoughts, or words, or deeds, if from my lips has ever fallen one word that has helped any one in the world, I lay no claim to it, it was his. But if there have been curses falling from my lips, if there has been hatred coming out of me, it is all mine and not his. All that has been weak has been mine, and all that has been life-giving, strengthening, pure, and holy, has been his inspiration, his words, and he himself. ...Through thousands of years of chiselling and modelling, the lives of the great prophets of yore come down to us; and yet, in my opinion, not one stands so high in brilliance as that life which I saw with my own eyes, under whose shadow I have lived, at whose feet I have learnt everything the life of Ramakrishna Paramahamsa."[123]

Describing his Master as a great spiritual hero and 'the most marvellous manifestation of soul-power', Swamiji added, "Judge him not through me. I am only a weak instrument. Let not his character be judged by seeing me. It was so great that if I or any other of his disciples spent hundreds of lives, we could not do justice to a millionth part of what he really was."

Swamiji composed some beautiful hymns to Sri Ramakrishna.

Swamiji wrote his brother-disciple Swami Shivananda, '...As to money, I have determined first to build some place for Mother, ...I can send nearly Rs. 7000 for a place for Mother.

...Whether Bhagavân Shri Krishna was born at all we are not sure; And Avataras like Buddha and Chaitanya are monotonous; Ramakrishna Paramahamsa is the latest and the most perfect – the concentrated embodiment of knowledge, love, renunciation, catholicity, and the desire to serve mankind. So where is anyone to compare with him? He must have been born in vain who cannot appreciate him! My supreme good fortune is that I am his servant through life after life. A single word of his is to me far weightier than the Vedas and the Vedanta तस्य दासदासदासोऽहम् —Oh, I am the servant of the servants of his servants....

> 'You have not yet understood the wonderful significance of Mother's life– none of you. But gradually you will know. Without Shakti (Power) there is no regeneration for the world. Why is it that our country is the weakest and the most backward of all countries? –Because Shakti is held in dishonour there. Mother has been born to revive that wonderful Shakti in India; and making her the nucleus, once more will Gârgis and Maitreyis be born into the world. Dear brother, you understand little now, but by degrees you will come to know it all. Hence it is her Math that I want first. ...Without the grace of Shakti nothing is to be accomplished...
>
> 'To me, Mother's grace is a hundred thousand times more valuable than Father's. Mother's grace, Mother's blessings are all paramount to me. ...Please pardon me. I am a little bigoted there, as regards Mother. If but Mother orders, her demons can work anything. Brother, before proceeding to America I wrote to Mother to bless me. Her blessings came, and at one bound I cleared the ocean. ...Brother, I shall show to worship the living Durga and then only shall I be worthy of my name. I shall be relieved when you will have purchased a plot of land and established there the living Durga, the Mother.'[124]

Once Swamiji had driven back a servant from the Monastery for stealing. But he had to take the man back as the Mother asked him to do so. He thought of selling the plot of land meant for the Monastery if needed during an out break of plague in Kolkata. But owing to the objection from the Mother, he gave up the idea. He, abiding by the order of the Mother, refrained from offering sacrifices to Goddess Durga at Belur Math.

Thus with great emotion and devotion to the Master and the Mother Swamiji was eloquent on their divinity, unequalled uniqueness and significance of their birth.

Great respect for women :

Medhas a great sage, told the King Suratha that when Sumbha, the great Lord of asuras was slain by Devi Kātyāyanī; Indra and other devas led by Agni, with their object fulfilled, cheerfully eulogised her :

All lores are your aspects O Devī; so are all women in the world, endowed with various attributes. By you alone, the Mother, this world is filled. What praise can there be for you who are of the nature of primary and secondary expression regarding (objects) worthy of praise?

—Caṇḍī, 11 : 6

Translated by Swami Jagadiswarananda

Swami Vivekananda as revealed in his statements loved his mother more than his father and loved Holy Mother more than the Master. On January 29, 1894, Swamiji wrote to Haridas Viharidas Desai, the Dewan of Junagarh State : '...You had been to see my poor mother and brothers. I am glad you did. ...If there is any being I love in the whole world, it is my mother.' Mrs. Ole Bull wrote : 'It was conspicuous in the Swami that wherever he went, he paid the highest tribute to his mother, whenever occasion arose.' He spoke often of his mother that she had wonderful self-control and had once gone without food for as many as fourteen days together. It was his mother who inspired him to this. He said, 'Her character was a constant inspiration to my life and work.' He tried his best to make his mother happy and having a premonition of his early death, he requested Swami Brahmananda to take care of his mother in his absence and also settle her legal suit. He also asked his brother-disciple to take her to various pilgrimage centres in northern India. He realized that woman is the very embodiment of Shakti (Power). In the afore-mentioned epistle he remarked that the cause of India's weakness and backwardness was the disrespect for and deprivation of women there and added : 'What do I find in America and Europe? –the worship of Shakti, the worship of Power. Yet they worship Her ignorantly through sense-gratification. Imagine, then, what a lot of good they will achieve who will worship Her with all purity, in a Sâttvika spirit, looking upon her as their mother! I am coming to understand things clearer every day, my insight is opening out more and more. Hence we must first build a Math for Mother. First Mother and Mother's daughters, then Father and Father's sons– ...'

Swmiji believed that making the Holy Mother nucleus ideal women like Gârgi,, Maitreyi would be born in the world. He said, 'Only let Woman and the People achieve education! All further questions of their fate, they would themselves be competent to settle.'[125] To him, an ideal Hindu wife would be trustful and devoted companion to her husband. The education that could not develop the spirit of true womanhood was useless. A modernized Indian woman must learn modern science but not at the cost of the ancient spirituality. He considered, 'True womanhood, like true monkhood, was no matter of mere externals.'

In one of the most interesting lectures at the Unitarian church on 'The Women of India' (on March 25, 1894) Swami Vivekananda reverted to the women of ancient India, describing in what high regard they are held in the holy books, where women were prophetesses. He said 'It is unfair to judge women in the East by the Western standard. In the West woman is the wife, in the East she is the mother. The Hindoos worship the idea of mother, and even the monks are required to touch the earth with their foreheads before their mothers. Chastity is much esteemed.'[126]

Swamiji during his stay in the West ruefully reflected on the difference between the women of his motherland and the West. He wrote (on 25th September, 1894) to his brother-disciples "Well, I am almost at my wit's end to see the women this country! ...They are like Lakshmi (the Goddess of Fortune) in beauty, and like Sarasvati (the Goddess of Learning) in virtues – they are the Divine Mother incarnate and worshipping them, one verily attains perfection in everything. Great God! Are we to be counted among men? If I can raise a thousand such Madonnas, Incarnations of the Divine Mother, in our country before I die, I shall die in peace. Then only will your countrymen become worthy of their name."[127]

Sister Nivedita in her book, 'The Master as I saw him' wrote :

The Swami felt that there was no task before India which could compare in importance with that of woman's education. His own life had had two definite personal purposes, of which one had been the establishment of a home for the Order of Ramakrishna, while the other was the initiation of some endeavour towards the education of woman. With five hundred men, he would say, the conquest of India might take fifty years : with as many women not more than a few weeks.

He exclaimed"...Revive the old arts. Teach your girls fruit-modelling with hardened milk. Give them artistic cooking and sewing. Let them learn painting, photography, the cutting of designs in paper, gold and silver filigree and embroidery. See that everyone knows something by which she can earn a living, in case of need." (pp. 260, 263)

In the context of child-widowhood in India the Swami advocated women's education and later marriage. He encouraged his disciple Nivedita to set up a girls' school and later (17th July, 1898) wrote Rakhal (Swami Brahmananda) : 'By all the means in our power the Nivedita Girls' School in Calcutta should be put on a firm footing.'[128]

He was so interested and sincere in women's education that while wandering with his party in Kashmir one day (July 24, 1898) he said to Sister Nivedita, "You never mention your school now, do you sometimes forget it? You see, I have much to think of ..." on August 12 or 13 1898 he worshipped an infant daughter of a Mohammedan boatman as Umâ. During the first Durgapuja (1901) at Belur Math he worshipped nine girls.

In an article entitled 'Modern India' (March 1899) Swamiji said, 'O India! Forget not that the ideal of thy womanhood is Sita, Savitri, Damayanti....,'

On January 18, 1900 in a lecture headed 'Women of India' Swamiji said, "Now, the ideal woman in India is the mother, the mother first, and the mother last. The word woman calls up to the mind of the Hindu, motherhood; and God is called Mother. As children, everyday, when we are boys, we have to go early in the morning with a little cup of water and place it before the mother, and the mother dips her toe into it and we drink it."[129]

Like his Master Swamiji too had great respect and sympathy for the fallen women. With reference to a letter from Ramdayal Chakraborty in which he had written that many public women attended the Ramakrishna anniversary festival at Dakshinewar which made many less inclined to go there. Swamiji wrote from Lake Lucerne, Switzerland on 23rd August, 1896 to his brother-disciple Shashi (Swami Ramakrishnananda) : "If public women are not allowed to go to such a great place of pilgrimage as Dakshineswar, where else shall they go to? It is for the sinful that the Lord manifests Himself specially, not so much for the virtuous.

...I pray to the Lord that hundreds of public women may come and bow their heads at His feet; it does not matter if not one gentleman comes. Come public women, come drunkards, come thieves and all – His Gate is open to all. "It is easier for a camel to pass through the eye of a needle than for a rich man to enter the kingdom of God." Never let such cruel, demonical ideas have a place in your mind."

Referring to Gour-Ma Swamiji wrote to his brother-disciple Swami Ramakrishnananda, 'We want a thousand such Mothers with that noble stirring spirit.' (Works, Vol. 6. P. 285)

Transcendental powers :

When Narendranath came to Dakshineswar for the second time, Sri Ramakrishna placed his right foot on his body and at once he had a wonderful experience. He saw that all the things of the room including the walls were swiftly spinning and receding into unknown region and his I-ness along with the universe was, as it were, going to disappear in the all-devouring great void. With a terrible fear he crying out said, 'Ah! What is it you have done to me? I have my parents, you know.' Hearing those words Sri Ramakrishna laughed and touching Narendra's chest with his hand said, 'Let it then cease now, it need not be done all at once, it will come to pass in course of time.'

Later on one day Sri Ramakrishna called Narendra aside to the Panchavati and told him that he was thinking of asking the Mother to impart all his supernatural powers acquired as the result of practising austerities, to him because she had told him that he (Narendra) would have to do much work for Her. If all those powers were transferred to him, he would be able to use them when necessary, he added. Narendra replied, "Sir, I have no need of these things. Let me realize God first and then it will be decided whether to accept them or not. If I obtain these wonderful powers now, and goaded by selfishness, forget the aim of life and happen to make improper use of them, it will be wholly ruinous to me."[130]

Three or four days before the passing away of Sri Ramakrishna, Narendra being alone with him, the Master stared at him and went into samādhi. Narendra felt the penetration of a subtle force like electric shock and lost all outer consciousness. Coming back to the normal state, he found the Master weeping. Sri Ramakrishna said to him, "Today I have given you my all and I am now only a poor fakir, possessing nothing. By this power you will do immense good in the world, and not until it is accomplished will you return."[131] Thus the Master made his most beloved Narendra fortified with his own miraculous power and lived in the disciple.

Swami Ambikananda disciple of Swami Brahamananda was fortunate to come in contact with Sri Ramakrishna and his monastic disciples. He told Swami Dhireshananda that Swamiji possessed originality in every sphere. In order to substantiate his notion he cited a number of examples.

One day Swamiji squatting on his haunches and playing on a tanpura (a stringed musical instrument) in the corner of a room adjacent to Visitors' Room at Belur Math, sang with so emotion and devotion ('Kailaspati Maharaj...Bhola') that Swami Ambikananda realized that day how worship of God could be done through classical music. He could sing the whole of the Chandi in correct modes.

Swamiji could play with human mind and once he said to Swami Ambikananda, 'Well, tell me where shall I throw your mind.' He transformed his gown into a coat fitting with buttons or ribbon. Besides, he gave a new pattern to monkey-cap usually put on by the Vaishnavas by making the back-cover flexible.

At the Barānagore Math the monastic disciples of Sri Ramakrishna had to suffer much from bitterly cold in winter as they had no warm clothes. It was too cold to sleep. Swamiji asked to bring a mridanga (a musical instrument of percussion shaped almost like a tom-tom) and went on singing Kirtan and dancing. Thus their spirit of renunciation won over biting cold or starvation and misery.

Patanjali, the great sage, says in his *yoga-sutras* (2/39) that all kinds of Yogic power are attained by observing continence and winning over worldly desires. The Chhandogya Upanishad mentions (8.2) that the aspirants who become free from all desires whatsoever and fully established in the Pure Consciousness Itself with the help of the non-dual mood, attains Jatismaratwa (ability to remember previous lives) and the resolves of such persons always come true. And their minds through Samadhi (ecstasy) can perceive any domain they prefer whether of gods or of ancestors or of any other beings.

Swamiji said to a man in the audience, 'I have met some who told me they did remember their previous life. They had reached a point where they could remember their former incarnations.'[132]

The Swami in 1901 at the Belur Math said to his much beloved disciple Sharat Chandra Chakravarty, 'Do you see, simply by the observance of strict Brahmacharya (continence) all learning can be mastered in a very short time– one has an unfailing memory of what one hears or knows but once...'[133]

Swamiji himself was a jatismara. On March 25, 1887 he said to M. at the Baranagore Math, "I have noticed a peculiar thing. Some men, objects, or places make me feel as if I had seen them before, in a previous birth. They appear familiar to me. One day I went to Sarat's house in Calcutta, on Amherst Street. Immediately I said to

Sarat, 'This house seems familiar to me. It seems to me that I have known the rooms, the passages, and the rest of the house for many, many days.'"[134]

Swami Saradananda described an incident of which he was an eye-witness.

> Once Shantiram, brother of Baburam Ghosh (Swami Premananda) and later on disciple of Swami Vivekananda, fell seriously ill and his life was at stake. His mother eagerly insisted Swamiji on doing something immediately to relieve her son. He asked for the water of the Ganga in a bowl. Then he stared at the water for some moments and the water grew hot and smoke billowed. He told her to feed him the water little by little and to store the remaining substance in order to administer it to a seriously ill patient of the family in future. Reproducing the fact Swami Saradananda remarked that Swamiji possessed enough Miracle though he did not use it every where. His Master forbade him to do so.

Swamiji once told Sister Christine that in the event of dire need of money, she would open the bag and have money. He cautioned her that misuse of opportunity would be fruitless.

Sister Christine, who attended every public lecture given by Swamiji in Detroit (U.S.A.) wrote, "The power that emanated from this mysterious being was so great that one all but shrank from it. It was overwhelming." [135]

Manmathanath Gangopadhyay a domestic-disciple of Swami Vivekananda and founder of the 'Brahmavadin Club' in Allahabad, described his strange experience. While he was lodging in the Math, one day Swamiji asked him to come to him after having a bath in the Ganges.' After bath as he entered the room of Swamiji, he saw him lying on his back on a sofa with a hand hanging loose. The Swami ordered him to keep on holding his hand. Accordingly Manmathanath held the wrist of the right hand of Swamiji with his right hand partially (for it was too wide to grip) for awhile. Swamiji lay motionless with his eyes closed for a considerable poeriod. Manmathanath completely fell under a magic spell and forgot all about time and place. Getting out of sofa Swamiji sat on a carpet and asked him to sit on another carpet. Then he told him he (Manmathanath) had a vision of the virgin image of the Mother and meditated the image of Shodashi (the Mother of the Universe; otherwise known as Tripura-sundari or Sri-vidya). Swamiji added that afterwards he (Manmathanath) had a vision of Lord Mahadeva holding a trident who initiated him by teaching the mantra he used to recite silently in prayers since then.

Manmathanath was astonished to listen to the words of the Swami as none but only he knew of the visions. He realised that Swamiji could see the mind as man can see his face on a mirror. 'What else other than God can we call him who is such competent to know other's mind?' –said he.

> Swamiji possessed a supernal power of accurate prediction. Before embarking for America, he had said to his brother-disciple Swami Turiyananda, "The Parliament of Religions is being organized for this," (pointing to himself). "My mind tells me so. You will see it verified at no distant date."[136] History says, Swamiji won the world starting from America.

To guess about the Swami's spiritual magnetism and super human power, Mme Calve's episode needs to be jotted down elaborately : Mme Emma Calvé, the famous French operatic singer was visiting Chicago with the Metropolitan Opera Company when she first met Swamiji. In the 1890s she enjoyed a tremendous success in Europe and America with her dramatic interpretation of the role of Carmen. She was stormy, sensuous and headstrong seemingly involved in frequent emotional attachments and was unhappy. Her only comfort was her daughter, whom she loved so much and who had accompanied her to Chicago.

Mme Calvé, confided more details of her first meeting with Swamiji to Mme Paul Verdier of Paris and San Francisco than her reminiscences published in her autobiography, 'My Life'. Mme Verdier took notes of Calvé's words.

Mme Verdier's Notes : She [Calvé] told me that one evening at the opera where she was singing Carmen her voice had never been so beautiful, and although she felt nervous going to the theatre, she had after the first act a tremendous success. ... Right after the second act, coming back to her dressing room she almost collapsed and asked the manager to announce she was ill. She was more depressed than before and had difficulty in breathing. The manager and people around her insisted so, that finaly she continued and was carried to the stage for the last act. She told me that at that minute she made the greatest effort of her life to finish the performance. She also said that it was the day she sang her best and the public gave her a tremendous ovation. She ran to her dressing room without waiting for the applause, and when she saw several people and the manager waiting for her with sad faces, she knew something tragic had happened.

The tragedy was that her daughter, who had been in a house of a friend that evening, was dead, having been burned to death during the performance of Carmen. Calvé collapsed.

Then came the period of days during which she wanted to commit suicide. Her friend Mrs. X was constantly with her, trying to comfort her, asking begging her to come to her house to see Swamiji. Calvé constantly refused. She told me that her only thought was to commit suicide by throwing herself in the lake, and each time as though in a daze she found herself on the road to Swamiji's house. She said it was like awaking from a dream, And each time she came back home. Finally, the fourth or fifty time, she found herself on the threshold of her friend's house, the butler opening the door. She went in and sat in a deep chair in the living-room. She was there for a while as in a dream, she said, when she heard a voice coming from the next room saying, "Come, my child. Don't be afraid." And automatically she got up and entered into the study where Swamiji was sitting behind a large table-desk.

With reference to the incident Mme Calvé wrote in her autobiography, 'My Life' : ...Before going I had been told not to speak until he addressed me. When I entered the room, I stood before him in silence for a moment. He was seated in a noble attitude of meditation, his robe of saffron yellow falling in straight lines to the floor, his head swathed in a turban bent forward, his eyes on the ground. After a pause he spoke without looking up.

"My Child," he said, "What a troubled atmosphere you have about you. Be calm. It is essential."

Then in a quiet voice, untroubled and aloof, this man who did not even know my name talked to me of my secret problems and anxieties. He spoke of things that I thought were unknown even to my nearest friends. It seemed miraculous, supernatural.

"How do you know all this?" I asked at last. "Who has talked of me to you?"

He looked at me with his quiet smile as though I were a child who had asked a foolish question.

"No one has talked to me," he answered gently. "Do you think that it is necessary? I read in you as in an open book."

...I left him deeply impressed by his words and his personality. He seemed to have emptied my brain of all its feverish complexities and placed there instead his clear and calming thoughts. I became once again vivacious and cheerful, thanks to the effect of his powerful will. He did not use any of the hypnotic or mesmeric influences. It was the strength of his character, the purity and intensity of his purpose that carried conviction. It seemed to me, when I came to know him better, that he lulled one's chaotic thoughts into a state of peaceful acquiescence, so that one could give complete and undivided attention to his words.[137]

Mme Calvé wrote : "It has been my good fortune and my joy to know a man who truly "walked with God", a noble being, a saint, a philosopher and a true friend."

The master of the house where Swamiji was staying in Chicago was a partner or an associate in some business with John D. Rockefeller, a powerful and strong-willed rich man and a hard man to advise. Many times talking about the extraordinary and wonderful Hindu monk, the householder invited Rockefeller to meet Swamiji; but he refused every time for one reason or another. One day having been driven by an impulse to meet Swamiji, he without waiting to be announced directly entered into the monk's room. He saw Swamiji behind his writing table not even lifting his eyes to see the visitor. After a while Swamiji told Rockefeller to his utter astonishment much of his past that was known to none but himself. He learnt a lesson on philanthropy from the Swami and echoed him in his biography 'John D. Rockefeller' by Barnie F. Winkleman "There is more to life than the accumulation of money. Money is only a trust in one's hands. To use it improperly is a great sin. The best way to prepare for the end of life is to live for others. That is what I am trying to do."[138]

Swamiji was sailing for India from the West. On 16 December 1896 at night when the ship 'Prince Regent Leopold' reached a particular place between Naples (Italy) and Port Said (Egypt) in the Mediterranean Sea, he had a vision of an old saintly man who introduced himself to be a Theraputi or a Buddhist monk and told him that he was then by the island of Crete (Greece) where Christianity originated. No sooner did the image disappear than the Swami came out of bed and on enquiring of an employee of the liner about her location, he came to know that it was dead of night and the ship was then fifty miles off the island of Crete.

Swamiji had not ignored the dream taking as cock and bull story rather he told his spiritual daughter Nivedita, Surendranath Sen and others about the vision. Besides, he wrote an archaeologist of England about it with a request to find out the truth about it. Accordingly after his passing away a team of British archaeologist had conducted excavation in the island and recovered ancient inscriptions those provide marvellous and important information about the origin of Christianity.

Swami Vijnanananda narrated an amazing incident. One night at Belur Math Swamiji woke up at 2 A.M. and had a stroll on verandah. Swami Vijnanananda asked him why he was not sleeping. Swamiji replied that while sleeping he suddenly felt something like a jolt and woke up. It occurred to him that a calamity had taken place somewhere causing great damage to people's lives, property etc. Considering this to be impossible Swami Vijnanananda smiled aside. But to his utter astonishment the next morning he read a news in a daily of volcanic eruptions in an island near Fiji claiming innumerable lives and causing indescribable suffering to people. He realized that the nervous system of Swamiji was more responsive to human miseries than a seismograph.

Sister Nivedita said, "Long, long ago, Sri Ramakrishna had told his disciples that the day would come when his beloved 'Noren' would manifest his own great gift of bestowing knowledge with a touch. That evening at Almora, I proved the truth of his prophecy. For alone, in meditation, I found myself gazing deep into an Infinite Good, to the recognition of which no egoistic reasoning had led me. I learnt, too, on the physical plane, the simple everyday reality of the experience related in the Hindu books on religious psychology. And I understood for the first time, that the greatest teachers may destroy in us a personal relation only in order to bestow the Impersonal Vision in its place."[139]

Gift of unerring prophecy :

(i) In 1897 Swamiji cautioned the Westerners that they were at the crater of a volcano that might erupt any moment. He prophesied that a terrible holocaust would break out in the West within next twenty years.

The Swami's prophecy proved to be true. It did not take twenty years. In 1914 the First World War broke out.

(ii) More astonishing to note that during his tour around Europe, Swamiji reaching the borderline between Germany and Austria foretold that the clash would start there. It happened so. To avenge the assassination of Archduke Franz Ferdinand (Sarajevo murder) on 28 June 1914 Austria attacked Serbia on 28 July 1914. Germany sided with Austria on 31 July and declared war on Russia, France and England on 1st, 3rd and 4th August respectively. Thus the Great War began in the zone earmarked early by Swamiji. The First World War ceased on November 11, 1918.

(iii) In the second half of the nineteenth century China, having been exploited by Japan and some of the Western powers; was gasping. Manmathanath Gangopadhyay wrote in the 'Udbodhan' that towards the end of the nineteenth century once he asked his Master if such an old civilized country like China would be destroyed. Remaining silent for a short while Swamiji replied that he had a vision – a large female elephant was gravid with offspring. It was born. But it was a lionet. The cub would grow up and then new China would be built.

In fact, China gradually rose to power. Now she has become one of the big powers of the world.

(iv) Manmathanath mentioned another prophecy made by Swamiji that within next fifty years India would be independent. He foretold also that India would win freedom by an unexpected means and not in the way other countries generally attain independence.

Swamiji told Kumudbandhu Sen also the same words in 1898 (1899 ?). Swami Lokeshwarananda told Swami Purnatmananda that he had heard that from Kumudbandhu himself.

Actually, India has won freedom within the period stipulated by the Swami and with the help of a new weapon – non-violent national struggle.

(v) Manmathanath wrote that swamiji prophesied that another war would inevitable if the Western countries did not forsake materialism.

Really, blind materialism and craving for earthly pleasures goaded the Western countries on competing for extending their market and colony abroad and indulging in political and commercial imperialism and led to the second World War (3 September 1939 –1 September 1945).

(vi) Further more Swamiji told Manmathanath independent India would gradually accept materialism of the West and would tarnish her old temporal glory. On the other hand, America and some other countries would gradually welcome spiritualism. Reaching the peak of materialism they had realized that mere materialism could not afford them peace.

This prophecy also appears gospel truth.

(vii) Returning from the West Swamiji had to leave for Darjeeling on his physician's advice to recover health on 30 March 1898. From there he wrote Miss Joe (Josephine MacLeod) on 29 April, 1898 :

...In case the plague breaks out in Calcutta, I must not go anywhere; ...

If the plague comes to my native city, I am determined to make myself a sacrifice; and that I am sure is a "Darn sight, better way to Nirvâna" than pouring oblations to all that ever twinkled.[140]

How surprising it is that no sooner did he despatch the letter, than he received a news from Calcutta. (now Kolkata) that plague had broken out in the city. He spent a silent anxious fasting whole day and came back Calcutta on May 3. Under his direction Sister Nivedita, Swamis Shivananda; Nityananda, Atmananda and all others of the Ramakrishna Mission devoted themselves to the service of plague-victims.

(viii) Sister Nivedita recollected that during their [members of the party were Swamis Vivekananda, Turiyananda, Niranjanananda, Sadananda, Sister Nivedita, Mrs. Ole Bull (Dhira Mâtâ), Miss Josephine MacLeod (Joe/Jaya), Mrs. Patterson wife of the American Consul General in Kolkata etc.] wandering in the Himalayas one day of May 1898 Swamiji made some accurate predictions about America at Almora :

Another morning he began by observing that as there were four main castes–Brâhman, Kshattriya, Bunea, Sudra, – so there were four great national functions, the religious or priestly, fulfilled by the Hindus; the military, by the Roman Empire, the mercantile by England to-day; and the democratic by America in the future, And here he launched off into a glowing prophetic forecast of how America would yet solve the problems of the Sudra – the problems of freedom and co-operation – and turned to relate to a non-American listener, the generosity of the arrangements which that people had attempted to make for their aborigines.[141]

The scenario of America in the next centuries justified Swamiji's prophecies.

(ix) In November 1900 Swamiji as a guest of Mme Emma Calvé toured Egypt with her and Miss Macleod and a French litterateur Monsieur Jules Bois. While visiting the Sphinx and pyramid, the Swami pondered over the futile efforts of the Pharaohs to make themselves immortal through those inanimate disgraced huge memorials. Suddenly he was deeply apprehensive that his beloved friend and disciple Sevier might no longer survive. At once he was extremely eager to leave for India in order to visit the Seviers at Mayavati.

Reaching Belur Math on 9 Decermber Swamiji came to learn that his favourite Sevier died on 28 October. Mrs. Sevier's letter bearing the heart-rending news failed to trace him as he was then visiting the Eastern Europe and Egypt and the redirected note came back to Belur Math on 26 December.

(x) Two days before his passing away Swamiji foretold that the spiritual power generated at Belur Math would get on for 1500 years and would be transformed into a great university. He added that it was not a fancy but a reality before his eyes.

In fact, the Ramakrishna Mission Vivekananda Educational and Research Institute set up on 4 July 2005 at Belur has been approved by the Central Government and the UGC as deemed to be University.

(xi) Lord Tennyson heard 'one clear call ' for him from his 'Pilot' three years before his death. Swamiji could hear footfall of death and used to prophesy it six to seven years before his passing away. On 9 July 1897 he wrote Miss Mary Hale from Almora : "... My time is short?"[142] The same day he wrote Mari Louise Burke (his disciple Abhayananda) that he was realizing that his works had been completed and the remaining part of his life was three to four years at most.

While sailing from London to America Swamiji wrote his disciple Sturdy from Port Said on 14 July 1899 :

... Moreover, I do not have much life left. At least I must go on with that supposition. ...[143]

The Swami wrote Mrs. Bull on 15 November 1899 :

... I want to hide for a time or for all time. How I curse the day that brought me celebrity![144]

Again on 18 April 1900 Swamiji wrote Joe (Miss Josephine MacLeod) :

...pray for me Joe that my works stop for ever, and my whole soul be absorbed in Mother....

I am well, very well mentally. I feel the rest of the soul more than that of the body. The battles are lost and won. I have bundled my things and am waiting for the great deliverer.

"Shiva, O Shiva, carry my boat to the other shore."

After all, Joe, I am only the boy who used to listen with rapt wonderment to the wonderful words of Ramakrishna under the Banyan at Dakshineswar. That is my true nature; works and activities, doing good and so forth are all super-impositions. Now I again hear his voice; the same old voice thrilling my soul. Bonds are breaking – love dying, work becoming tasteless – the glamour is off life. Only the voice of the Master calling –"I come Lord, I come." "Let the dead bury the dead, follow thou Me." —I come, my beloved Lord, I come."

Yes, I come. Nirvâna is before me. I feel it at times – the same infinite ocean of peace, without a ripple, a breath.

I am glad I was born, glad I suffered so, glad I did make big blunders, glad to enter peace. I leave none bound, I take no bonds, Whether this body will fall and release me or I enter into freedom in the body, the old man is gone, gone for ever, never to come back again! The guide, the Guru, the leader, the teacher has passed away; the boy, the student, the servant is left behind....[145]

Swamiji was as has been said in the Gita, (2 : 56), the soul enjoying perpetual mental calm through philosophic contemplation and conviction and realised the truth :

Beings are unmanifest before birth, O Arjuna; they are manifest in the middle state and again unmanifest after death. What is there to grieve over in all this?

Chapter II, 28
Srimat Bhagavad Gita

His eagerness to embrace death calmly is reflected in the aforementioned heart-rending epistle as his readiness to do so was evident in his subsequent sayings and doings.

On his way to Mayavati Swamiji told his disciple Swami Birajananda on January 2, 1901 that he had been at the fag end of his life. In April 1901 he declared in Dhaka that he would survive one year at best. Just six months before his passing away Swamiji told Bhavanicharan Bandyopadhyay (Brahmabandhab Upadhyay) that he would live no more and added that he had no leisure as he was busy doing the remaining works for smooth running of the Math.

On 28 March 1902 while Miss MacLeod was watching Sister Nivedita giving away prizes on the occasion of a sports competition at Belur through a window of the Swami's bedroom; he told her, 'I shall never see forty.' She knew that he was thirty nine then and told him that in Buddha's life all the great deeds were accomplished when he was in between forty and eighty and not before that. Swamiji replied that he had given what he had to and he would have to go must.

One week before his death the Swami fetched an almanac and fixed the date and time of his passing away. He selected a site by the Ganga for his cremation-ground three days before.

2 July 1902 Wednesday. It was the eleventh day of the lunar fortnight and the Swami observed fasting without drinking even a drop of water. He invited his spiritual daughter and disciple Nivedita and fed her rice, boiled potatoes and stones of jackfruit and milk. At the termination of dinner he poured water on her hand and wiped with a towel. Nivedita hesitatingly told him that she herself should do all those for him. Swamiji replied that Jesus washed the feet of his disciples. Nivedita fearfully thought to herself that that happened at his last stage.

On 4 July 1902 Friday at 9 : 10 p.m. Swamiji passed away at the age of thirty-nine years, five months, and twenty-four days, thus fulfilling the prophecy of his own death : 'I shall never see forty.'

(xii) Swamiji wrote from Almora on 9 July 1897 to Miss Mary Hale :

> ...I feel my task is done – at most three or four years more of life are left. I have lost all wish for my salvation. I never wanted earthly enjoyment. I must see my machine in strong working order, and then knowing sure that I have put in a lever for the good of humanity, in India at least, which no power can drive back, I will sleep, without caring what will be next; and may I be born again and again, and suffer thousands of miseries so that I may worship the only God that exists, the only God I believe in, the sum total of all souls – and above all, my God the wicked, my God the miserable, my God the poor of all races, of all species, is the special object of my worship.[146]

The 'machine' installed (on I May 1897) by the Swami is the Ramakrishna Math and the Ramakrishna Mission. People loosely use the name 'Ramakrishna Mission' to mean both the organizations. The Ramakrishna Math is a purely monastic institution while the Ramakrishna Mission is a Society open to monks as well as lay people. To fulfill the wish of the Swami for having an independent monastic order for women, the Sri Sarada Math and the Ramakrishna Sarada Mission were founded in 1959 and in 1960 respectively. The organizations follow the motto put before them by Swamiji, *Ātmano moksārtham jagaddhitāya cha* – doing good to the world with a spirit of worship and thus paving paths for one's own salvation. Though both the Math and the Mission continue philanthropic and Charitable activities, the former gives priority to spiritual upliftment of people and the latter lays emphasis on welfare activities e.g. to run educational, medical and other types of institutions, old-age homes and doing relief services in times of natural calamities like famine, drought, flood, epidemic of disease etc. The Ramakrishna Order carries out the ideals and messages of Shri Ramakrishna and the Holy Mother and Swami Vivekananda through its 177 (excluding sub-centres) branches in and outside India. As time passes, the Ramakrishna Movement is gaining strength and flourishing as a great power for peace and fraternity.

Thus Swamiji's machine is 'in strong working order' only to justify his prophecy.

(xiii) At the time of his departure from London for India. Swamiji said to Mr. Eric Hammond : "It may be that I shall find it good to get outside of my body– to cast it off as a disused garment; but I shall not cease to work! I shall inspire men everywhere, until the world shall know that it is one with God."[147]

How miracle it is that ever since the Swami's passing away, persons not fortunate to see him in his lifetime, feel his spiritualising influence by communing with him through the great utterances he left behind.

Incarnation :

Bhuvaneshwari Devi, Narendranath's pious mother had practiced austerities and prayed to Vireshwar Shiva of Varanasi to give her a child. The Lord granted her the prayer. Bhuvaneshwari Devi named her new born babe 'Vireshwar' the corrupted form of which was 'Bileh'. Whenever his restlessness appeared unmanageable, she used to pour water on his head saying 'Shiva Shiva' and astonishingly he would become quiet. She would say, 'I had prayed to Shiva for a boon of a son but He, instead of coming Himself, has sent one of his ghosts.' But Bileh was fond of meditation. One day he was meditating with his playmates when a cobra appeared. Other boys shouting a warning to him ran away fearfully. But he remained calm. Referring to that incident he said to his parents, 'I knew nothing of the snake or anything else. I was feeling inexpressible joy.' He was deeply moved by others plight and tried to help them. Thus the amusing anecdotes about Swamiji's boyhood appear quite different from those of other boys.

Sri Ramakrishna disclosed that he had a vision before the birth of Narendranath and later on as soon as he saw him, he recognized him to be one of those seven venerable sages (superior to gods in knowledge and holiness, in renunciation and love) whom he, as a divine child, clasping his neck with his lovely arms asked to go down with him.

Swamiji himself spoke of his super normal faculty : "From the earliest time that I can remember, I used to see a marvellous point of light between my eye-brows as soon as I shut my eyes to go to sleep, and I used to watch its various changes with great attention. That marvellous point of light would change colours and get bigger until it took the form of a ball; finally it would burst and cover my body from head to foot with white liquid light.

"As soon as that happened, I would lose outer consciousness and fall asleep. I used to believe that was the way everybody went to sleep. Then when I grew older and began to practise meditation, that point of light would appear to me as soon as I closed my eyes, and I would concentrate upon that."[148]

Narendranath, at the age of fifteen, on his way to Raipur in a bullock cart with his family catching sight of a large beehive in the cleft of a giant cliff realized with awe and reverence the Divine Providence and lost outer consciousness.

Regarding a vision during his student life Swamiji said : "While at school one night I was meditating behind closed doors and had a fairly deep concentration of mind. How long I meditated in that way I can not say. After the meditation was over I remained seated. Then from the southern wall of that room a luminous figure stepped out and stood in front of me. It was the figure of a *sannyasin* [monk] absolutely calm, with shaven head, and staff and *Kamandalu* [water pot] in either hand. He gazed at me for time, and seemed as if he would address me. I, too, gazed at him in speechless wonder. Suddenly a kind of fright seized me. I opened the door and hurried out of the room. Then it struck me that it was foolish of me to run away like that; perhaps he might say something to me. But I have never seen that figure since. I think it was the Lord Buddha whom I saw."[149]

While recalling his various meetings with Shri Ramakrishna, Narendranath told M. on 25 March 1887 at the Baranagore Math : "One day; during one of my early visits, the Master in an ecstatic mood said to me, 'You have come!' 'How amazing!' I said to myself. 'It is as if he had known me a long time.' Then he said to me, 'Do you ever see light?' I replied 'Yes, sir. Before I fall asleep I feel something like a light revolving near my forehead."[150]

Narendranath told M. that he used to see the strange light frequently. Many a time Sri Ramakrishna repeated to the devotees the same words referring to Narendrath : 'He will not keep his body if he knows who he is. But I have put a veil over his eyes.'[151]

Narendranath told M. that during the third visit with Sri Ramakrishna at Dakshineswar, the Master had gone into samadhi and begun to praise him as if he were God. He said to him, 'O Nārāyana, you have assumed this body for my sake. I asked the Divine Mother, "Mother, unless I enjoy the company of some genuine devotees completely free from 'woman and gold,' how shall I live on earth?" You came to me at night, woke me up, and said, "Here I am " But Narendranath did not know anything of that. He was sound asleep in their Kolkata house.

On listening to these words M. said to Narendranath :

"In other words, you may be both present and absent at the same time, It is like God, who is both formless and endowed with form."

Narendranath said to M. : "But you must not tell this to anyone else. At Cossipore he transmitted his power to me."[152]

Swami Prabhananda in his highly esteemed book, 'Antyalila' (Part II p. 239) mentioned experience of Tarak. One night Narendranath was sleeping with Shashi, Tarak and some others of his brother-disciples in a large mosquito-net in a room on the ground floor at Cossipore garden house. At dead of night Tarak woke up and to his utter awe and bewilderment discovered a white naked boy of seven or eight years having matted hair lying by him as Shiva in place of Narendranath and his body was beaming a stream of light. Finding no answer to the question, 'Was the figure real or just a hallucination?' he passed the night in meditation. At dawn he found Narendranath in sound sleep. In the morning when he disclosed his experience to Narendranath he simply chuckled.

Sister Nivedita wrote, "...they (the people of the Punjab) found in him (Swamiji) a rare mixture of 'Guru Nanak and Guru Govind', their first teacher and their last."[153]

No menial service e.g. fanning, the preparation of tobacco etc. to himself was permitted by Sri Ramakrishna from this particular follower Narendranath because of his divine entity.

When Swamiji with the members of his party was at Naini-Tal in May 1898 one day a Mohammedan gentleman said to him, "Swamiji, if in after-times any claim you as an *avatār*, an especial incarnation of the Deity–remember that I, a Mohammedan, am the first!"[154]

Suniti Kumar Chatterji, an internationally renowned linguist and luminary in the academic world, in a eulogy to Swamiji, remarked, "It is remarkable how in India in her days of political submission and spiritual inanity, when everything seemed hopeless, and the people had lost all confidence in themselves, a spirit calling us to action like Swami Vivekananda could come into being. That such a person could come at a time when the prospect was bleak, when we seemed to have lost all hope, indicated that God in His mercy never forsakes His people, and this in a way bears out the great idea behind this oft-quoted verse of the *Gitā*, that whenever righteousness is on the decline and unrighteousness is in the ascendant, God creates Himself as a great *avatāra* or Incarnation – as a Leader to guide men to the right path of salvation. And in that sense Vivekananda was an *avatāra*, a divinely inspired and God-appointed Leader, not only for Man of India, but also for the whole of Humanity in the present age."[155]

A great teacher :

The Master, a few months before his passing away, one day wrote on a piece of paper, "Naren will teach people." Glancing at the paper Narendranath said to him, "I won't do any such thing." Thereupon the Master said, "But you must. Your very bones will do it."

Swamiji tried to utilise every opportunity of teaching his brother-disciples various subjects or discussing problems with them so that they might overcome their short-coming and proceed confidently.

History has recorded how Swamiji devoted himself to the propagation of his Master's message to humanity relentlessly. As a wandering monk he travelled the length and breadth of India and preached people the Sanâtana Dharma and taught them the importance of self-reliance, courage, solidarity, literacy and liberal out look and love for others indiscriminately. He strove to enlighten his countrymen about the essential words of the Vedanta philosophy and vice of casteism and apartheid. He became world-wide figure and the Prophet of a New Dispensation at the Parliament of Religions held in Chicago, USA from September 11–27, 1893. While addressing at the Final Session on September 27, Swamiji, in a prophetic and luminous mood uttered some electrifying words :

> The Christian is not to become a Hindu or a Buddhist, nor a Hindu or a Buddhist to become a Christian. But each must assimilate the spirit of the others and yet preserve his individuality and grow according to his own law of growth....
>
> If the Parliament of Religions has shown anything to the world it is this : It has proved to the world that holiness, purity and charity are not the exclusive possessions of any church in the world, and that every system has produced men and women of the most exalted character. In the face of this evidence, if anybody dreams of the exclusive survival of his own religion and the destruction of the others, I pity him from the bottom of my heart, and point out to him that upon the banner of every religion will soon be written, in spite of resistance : "Help and not Fight", "Assimilation and not Destruction", "Harmony and Peace and not Dissension". (The Life of Swami Vivekananda, By His Eastern and Western Disciples p. 427)

The New York Herald spoke of the Swami :

He is undoubtedly the greatest figure in the Parliament of Religions. After hearing him we feel how foolish it is to send missionaries to this learned nation. (The Life p. 428)

In her introduction to the *Complete Works of Swami Vivekananda,* (Vol. 1, p. X) Sister Nivedita has with great insight best described the general import of her Master's historic address :

Of the Swami's address before the Parliament of Religions, it may be said that when he began to speak it was of "the religious ideas of the Hindus", but when he ended. Hinduism had been created.

History records his triumphant public career as the apostle of Vedantism during his sojourn in the West and the momentous significance of his ideas and of his work as the Spititual teacher of the World.

Swamiji was the true spokesman of Hinduism, the true bearer of his Master's message. He attended innumerable indoor-classes, discourses and open meetings as an itinerant monk in the West and spoke about not only Hinduism but various other topics also e.g. on Indian women – their past, present, and future, Law and freedom, Nature and man, Work and its secret, The powers of the mind, Ideals of womanhood, Manners and Customs in India, Buddha's message to the World, etc. With reference to one of his interesting lectures the Wisconsin State Journal commented on November 21, 1893 : "Pagan though he ('the celebrated Hindoo monk, Vivekananda) be, Christianity may well follow many of his teachings. His creed is as wide as the universe, taking in all religions, and accepting truth wherever it may be found. Bigotry and superstition and idle ceremony, he declared, have no place in "the religions of India."[156]

In his widely acclaimed lecture entitled 'My Master' Swamiji said, "He alone teaches who has something to give, for teaching is not talking, teaching is not imparting doctrines, it is communicating. Spirituality can be communicated just as really as I can give you a flower."[157] He succeeded in communicating his ideas and teachings to audience and impressing them.

Sister Nivedita, the 'most rebellious disciple' of Swamiji wrote, "Long, long ago, Sri Ramakrishna has told his disciples that the day would come when his beloved 'Noren' would manifest his own great gift of bestowing knowledge with a touch. That evening at Almora I proved the truth of his prophecy. For alone, in meditation, I found myself gazing deep into an Infinite Good, to the recognition of which no egoistic reasoning had led me. I learnt too, on the physical plane, the simple everyday reality of the experience related in the Hindu books on religious psychology. And I understood for the first time, that the greatest teachers may destroy in us a personal relation only in order to bestow the Impersonal Vision in its place."[158]

During his arduous lecture tour in the West this great teacher spoke of the merits of Hinduism and pleaded for universal acceptance of all religions and for love and emphasized the basic divinity of man. He had the guts to criticise the faults of his countrymen and those of the Westerners with impregnable arguments. He constantly tried to dispel a monumental ignorance of the Westerners of Hindu culture and erroneous ideas of Indian life. While replying to irritating questions he would sometimes retort with sarcastic humour. One day in Minneapolis a woman asked the Swami if Hindu mother threw their children to the crocodiles. He answered, "Yes, Madam! They threw me in, but like your fabled Jonah I got out again."[159]

At the beginning of 1894 Swamiji wrote to his brother monk Swami Remakrishnananda : I am amazed at His grace. Whichever town I visit, it is in an uproar. They have named me "the cyclonic Hindu". Remember it is His will– I am a voice without a form.[160]

Swamiji strove for restating the entire contents of the Sanâtan Dharma, remodelling the Indian thought-world and bringing about a religious revival in his motherland.

Wherever and whenever the Swami lectured on whatever subject; the impact on the listeners was same profound as has been written by Tirtha Ram Goswami (later known as Swami Ram Tirtha) then a professor of mathematics at one of the Lahore Colleges to Pandit Din Dayal Vyakhyana Vachaspati (on November 16 1897) : "...The listeners were so deeply engrossed, and it created such an atmosphere, that all idea of time and space was lost ... In short, it was such a grand success as is seldom seen. Whoever heard this lecture (listeners were in large number), for all of them – whether Englishmen, Christians or Muslims, or Arya Samajists, or Brahmo Samajists – it proved an eye-opener."[161]

During conversations, classes, visit to places of interest and sojourn the Swami's talks encompassed a wide range of topics – religion, philosophy, history, science, geography, anthropology, ethnology, literature art and architecture etc. His words were delightful and instructive experience for his disciples, devotees and companions.

Swamiji possessed the power of deep realization and intuition. During his second visit to the West (from the middle of 1899 to the end of 1900) he could see the darker side of occidental culture and felt that the West needed an infusion of Indian spirituality for its progress and survival though he was a great admirer of the Western spirit and its science and technology and its industrial advancement and its humanism. Previously Swamiji wrote to Alasinga from America on 31 August 1894 :

The whole world requires Light. It is expectant! India alone has that Light, not in magic, mummery, and charlatanism, but in the teaching of the glories of the spirit of real religion – of the highest spiritual truth. That is why the Lord has preserved the race through all its vicissitudes unto the present day. (Works, Book - 5, p. 43)

In fact, Swamiji gave his five most intense years to the Westerners to enrich them with Indian spirituality. Rightly has been estimated, by Swami Ranganathananda 'As a teacher of modern India and as her cultural and spiritual emissary to the West, Vivekananda has illuminated the horizon of national and international life, and this has no parallel in world history.' (The story of Ramakrishna Mission, Advaita Ashrama, p. 89)

None but Narendranath grasped the importance of his Master's historic utterance.

Some time in 1884 Sri Ramakrishna while explaining to the devotees the essence of the Vaishnava religion in his room at Dakshineswara, suddenly went into ecstasy. In a short time, regaining semi-normal consciousness, he muttered, "Talk of compassion for beings! Will you, all little animals, bestow compassion on beings? You wretch, who are you to bestow it? No, no; not compassion to Jivas but service to them as Siva."

It was Narendranath alone who realized the tremendous significance of that profound utterance of Sri Ramakrishna. On coming out of the room he said : "Ah, what a wonderful light have I got today from the Master's words ! In synthesizing the Vedantic knowledge, which was generally regarded as dry, austere and even cruel, with sweet devotion to the Lord, what a new mellowed means of experiencing the Truth has he revealed today ! In order to attain the non-dual knowledge, we have been told so long, one should have to renounce the World and the company of men altogether and retire to the forest and mercilessly uproot and throw away love, devotion and other soft and tender emotions from the heart.

Formerly when the aspirant tried to attain that knowledge in the old way, he regarded the whole universe and each person in it as obstacles to the path of religion and contracting therefore a hatred for them, he more often than not went astray. But, from what the Master in ecstasy said today, it is gaṭhered that the Vedanta of the forest can be brought to human habitation and that it can be applied in practice to the work-a-day world....

"...If the divine Lord ever grants an opportunity, I'll proclaim everywhere in the World this wonderful truth I have heard today. I will preach this truth to the learned and the ignorant, to the rich and the poor, to the Brahmins and the Chandalas." (Sri Ramakrishna the great Master, Swami Saradananda, Sri Ramakrishna Math, Chennai, 6th ed. p.p. 1163 - 1165)

Thus the great Master indirectly sowed the seeds of Ramakrishna Math and Ramakrishna Mission in the sub-conscious mind of his Chief disciple Narendranath that very day and towards the end of his life (August 1886) at Cossipore he distributed ochre cloths to Narendranath and some of his young disciples and two days before his passing away made Narendranath the leader of his boys saying, "I leave them all to your care. See that they practise spiritual disciplines even after my passing away and that they do not return home." After the passing away of Sri Ramakrishna Holy Mother Sri Sarada Devi had been deeply concerned about establishing a Sangha (Mission) to preserve and preach the ideals of the Master. She said, 'It is due to my prayer to Thakur [Sri Ramakrishna] that Naren later on established the Math, Mission and similar institutions,' These incidents led to the inception of the Ramakrishna Mission on 1 May 1897.

'The Life of Swami Vivekananda' by his Eastern and Western disciples rightly comments : "It was the Swami, among all the disciples of Sri Ramakrishna who saw in the Master not a person only, but a principle, not the apostle of realization and renunciation only, but that of service to humanity in the spirit of worship also. ...It was left to the genius of Swami Vivekananda to interpret Sri Ramakrishna's life and teaching from all angles. It was left to this his greatest disciple to bring out and emphasize the human side of his Master's nature and message and to clear away the misconception that prevailed in the minds of many, that Renunciation and Service were conflicting ideals which could not be combined without detriment to one or the other. And it is to the Swami's glory that he gave shape to these divine impulses by founding the Ramakrishna Mission. Renunciation and Service are, according to him, the twofold National Ideal of modern India. The institution that he started was to practise and preach this ideal in its national and international aspects. (Vol. 2, p.p. 250 – 251)

Chapter – 5

SWAMI BRAHMANANDA

While talking about 'The Master as I saw Him,' Sister Nivedita persuaded sister Devamata (Laura Glenn) to discuss the role of Swami Ramakrishnananda as she had done about Swamiji and added that each of the monastic disciples of Sri Ramakrishna should be highlighted so that they were not consigned to oblivion. On June 4, 1883 Sri Ramakrishna spoke of them, 'I know these youngsters to be Narayana Himself.'[1]

Sri Ramakrishna's spiritual child : divine entity

One day Sri Ramakrishna said to the Divine Mother, 'Certainly I shall not have any children, Mother. But it is my desire that a boy with sincere love for God should always remain with me. Give me such a boy.'[2]

A few days later Sri Ramakrishna had a vision of a boy. Again in his second vision he saw the Mother putting a child into his lap and saying. 'This is your son.' To his utter amazement he asked Her how it was possible for him who looked upon all women as his mother, to have a son. The Mother explained that it would be a spiritual child. In June or July 1881, he had another vision of boy Gopal dancing on a full-blown lotus on the Ganga with the same boy whom the Mother had previously placed on his lap. That very day Rakhal (literally 'cowherd boy', a playmate of Krishna) came to Dakshineswar from Konnagar, crossing the Ganga with his bride's brother Monomohan Mitra a devotee of Sri Ramakrishna. The Master at once recognised him as his spiritual child and said to Monomohan with a smile, 'A wonderful receptacle!'

Referring to the Master's anxiety about illness of Rakhal on March 29, 1883 M. jotted down : "He looked at Rakhal with infinite tenderness of a mother and affectionately uttered the name of Govinda. Did he see in Rakhal the manifestation of God Himself? The disciple was a young boy of pure heart who had renounced all attraction to lust and greed. And Sri Ramakrishna was intoxicated day and night with love of God. At the sight of Rakhal his eyes expressed the tender feelings of a mother, a love like that which had filled the heart of Mother Yaśodā at the sight of the Baby Krishna."

That day the Master said to Amritalal Bose and Trailokyanath Sanyal : "Youngsters like Narendra and Rakhal are ever-perfect. Every time they are born they are devoted to God. An ordinary man acquires a little devotion after austerities and a hard struggle. But these boys have love of God from the very moment of their birth. They are like the natural image of Siva, which springs forth from the earth and is not set up by human hands."

Swâmi Saradananda wrote in his introduction to Swami Brahamananda's book, 'Words of the Master' : "The present brochure is from the pen of one who was regarded by the Master as next to Swami Vivekananda in his capacity for realizing religious ideals. It is indeed the work of grateful love of the beloved disciple – one who, more than anyone else, lived constantly with the Master – to set the Master correctly before the public, seeing how his invaluable words are being roughly handled, deformed, and distorted nowadays at the hands of many."

M. wrote on June 4, 1883. 'Rakhal lay on the floor, resting his head on the Master's lap. For the past few days the Master had been regarding Rakhal as the Baby Krishna.'

On December 9, 1883 Sri Ramakrishna said to M, 'While listening to the Kirtan, I had a visiojn of Rakhal in the midst of Sri Krishna's companions in Vrindāvan.'[3]

A wonderful receptacle :

Docile, devotional and contemplative by nature Rakhal Chandra Ghosh (afterwards Swami Brahmananda) son of a wealthy landlord and businessman Anandamohan Ghosh and Kailashkamini of Sikra Kulingram in North 24 Parganas in his boyhood would meditate like a yogi during Durga and Kali puja and was fond of devotional songs.

While staying at Vrindāvan with Balaram Bose, Rakhal in his excited letters to M. described the holy place as the best of all places where peacocks danced around and one always heard and saw religious music and dancing and invited him to visit the place of an unending flow of divine bliss.

On September 19, 1884 Sri Ramakrishna said to the devotees, "Rakhal had his first religious ecstasy while sitting here massaging my feet. A *Bhāgavata* scholar had been expounding the sacred book in the room. As Rakhal listened to his words, he shuddered every now and then. Then he became altogether still.

"His second ecstasy was at Balaram Bose's house. In that state he could not keep himself sitting upright; he lay flat on the floor. Rakhal belongs to the realm of the Personal God. He leaves the place if one talks about the Impersonal."[4]

To divert Rakhal's mind from God to the world, his father Anandamohan married his son to Vishweshwari daughter of Bhubanmohan and Shyamasudari Mitra of Konnagar in 1881 and afterwards put him under lock and key. The more love for Sri Ramakrishna was obstructed the more intense it became. Both the Master and Rakhal longed for each other. Paramahamsadeva prayed to Goddess Kali, "Mother, my heart is breaking for Rakhal. Please bring him back to Dakshineswar." One day Rakhal quietly left home for Dakshineswar and his father was happy listening to Sri Ramakrishna's spiritual talk and the praise of his son : "Ah, what a nice character Rakhal has developed ! Look at his face and every now and then you notice his lips moving. Inwardly he repeats the name of God, and so his lips move.

"Youngsters like him belong to the class of the ever-perfect. They are born with God-Consciousness."[5] Rakhal, like the homā bird in the Vedas, was afraid of the world and eager to reach the Mother.

A mystical relation :

When Shyamasundari Devi visited Dakshineswar with his daughter Vishweshwari, Sri Rakakrishna examined the girl's physical features eagerly to see if she would stand in the way of Rakhal's devotion to God and saw that she bore an auspicious aspect of the Divine Shakti (power), He accepted her as their daughter-in-law and sent word to the *Nahabat* (i.e., to Sarada Devi) to give her a rupee and unveil her face as a mother in-law to welcome her daughter-in-law.

The Master as has been said earlier, looked at his spiritual son with tenderness and love like that which had filled the heart of Mother Yasoda at the sight of the Baby Krishna. On the other hand, Rakhal a boy of eighteen, behaved towards the Master as a little Child. Sometimes the Master fed him, played with him and carried him around on his shoulders.

Even after the passing away of the Master, he in his astral body was always with his spiritual son. In 1920 Pandit Kshirod Prasad Vidyavinod told Swami Brahmananda how, while a student, he missed a chance seeing Sri Ramakrishna. On his way to Dakshineswar at Alambazar he thought that he would be embarrassed if the omniscient Master exposed his secret thoughts publicly. That fear goaded him into returning home. Maharaj replied that since he had gone to Alambazar to see the Master, he certainly saw him. But Kshirod could not believe it and bending his head began to weep. No sooner did he lift his head that he saw to his utter astonishment Sri Ramakrishna seated in the place of Swami Brahmananda.

In 1918 one day at noon a girl who had lost her husband only two weeks after her marriage at the age of fourteen, came with her brother to see Swami Brahmananda at the house of Balaram Bose.

She told him how in that catastrophic state, she earnestly prayed to God to show her the way and after a year or so, one night Sri Ramakrishna appeared to her in a dream and said, "Don't weep. My son Rakhal is living in Baghbazar. Go to him. He will help you."

The widow had never heard of Sri Ramakrishna or Rakhal. Maharaj initiated her that day. Afterwards the girl became a nun and set up a convent. In 1895 Swamiji wrote Shashi (Swami Ramakrishnananda) from America. : "My special loving greeting to Rakhal and Hari. Take great care of them. ...Never forget that Rakhal was the special object of Sri Ramakrishna's love."

While practising intense spiritual disciplines and sadhana forgetting food and family under Sri Ramakrishna's guidance, Rakhal developed some supernatural powers. One day a worker in the temple garden became sick and there was none to take care of him. Rakhal served him cordially. One night the patient was groaning with pain. As he had no medicine, Rakhal sat near his head and began to repeat a mantra. A handsome girl of twelve appeared before him when he dozed off. Waking up he identified her as a goddess and said to her, 'Mother, will this patient be cured?' The girl replied 'Yes' and vanished. The patient was wonderfully cured the next day.

An *ishwarakoti, nityasiddha* – a mudfish :

Rakhal was an *ishwarakoti* (a godlike soul), *nityasiddha* (an ever-perfect soul) and a companion of Krishna in his past life.

On 16 April 1886 Sri Ramakrishna said to Girish Chandra Ghosh, "Rakhal has now understood what is good and what is bad, what is real and what is unreal. He lives with his family, no doubt, but he knows what it means. He has a wife. And a son has been born to him. But he has realized that all these are illusory and impermanent. Rakhal will never be attached to the world.

"He is like a mudfish. The fish lives in the mud, but there is not the slightest trace of mud on its body."[6]

Though Rakhal belonged to a well-off family and had a young wife and a child, he, within a very short period, through the grace of the Master eschewed everything for God. One day as he told Sri Ramakrishna that he could not get rid of lust, the Master touched him in the region of the heart muttering some words and all lust disappeared from him forever. M. observed "Rakhal had renounced the world, leaving behind his wife and child. A fire of intense renunciation burnt day and night in his heart."[7]

Intelligence of a king :

At the Cossipore garden house once Sri Ramakrishna remarked, "Rakhal has the keen intelligece of a king. If he chose, he could rule a kingdom." Accordingly Narendranath said to his brother disciples."Henceforth we shall call Rakhal our Raja, king."[8] In the Ramakrishna order Rakhal (Swami Brahmananda) is known as Maharaj or Great king.

As the head of the Order Swami Brahmananda made a strong impression of his commendable intellect, prudence and administrative competence.

Great yearning for the highest spiritual experience :

Rakhal used to practise intense spiritual disciplines and meditation and arrived in an ecstatic mood frequently. He had visions of the mother and experienced other transcendental incidents many a time. But he was not satisfied with a few momentary experineces or visions He practied so much austerity to know more about God and to realize spiritual truth. M. said to Rakhal, "I see that you too have become restless for God."[9] Once Swamiji said to his disciple Sharat Chandra Chakrovarty : "See for instance, Brahmananda, who is here–even I have not the spirituality which he has. Shri Ramakrishna looked upon him as his mind-born son; and he lived and walked, ate and slept with him. He is the ornament of our Math–our king."[10] Once a western gentleman met Swamiji with some spiritual questions. The Swami asked the visitor to see Swami Brahamanda saying "There is a dynamo working and we are all under him."[11]

Amazing administrative capacity :

1 May 1897 saw the historic incident of formation of the Ramakrishna Mission in the house of Balaram Bose one of the most beloved of the disciples of Sri Ramakrishna. Swami Vivekananda became the General President of the Mission and Swami Brahmananda became the President of the Calcutta (Kolkata) centre.

Brahmananda, extremely practical and endowed with immeasurable spiritual power, strong common sense, vast experience, unselfish love, sweetness of temper and powerful personality, had to take the helm of the Order after the passing away of Swamiji. It was a very crucial period when a void was left by the sudden and premature death of Swami Vivekananda; 'as if the whole HImalayan Mountains have disappeared from before my eyes!'– as was lamented by Swami Brahmananda. There were numerous problems the most burning of those was paucity of fund. As head of the Mission Brahmananda faced problems calmly and confidently.

After the passing away of Swamiji his disciple and spritual daughter Sister Nivedita owing to her love of India and her motherland Ireland both subjugated and exploited by the British and her genetic revolutionary spirit, became more interested in India's freedom movement than spiritual and other activities. The Ramakrishna Order being strictly a non-political organization, Brahmananda asked her to choose either to be a member of the Ramakrishna Order or of the freedom movement. She opted for the latter. A report was published to that effect on July 19, 1902 in the Amrita Bazar Patrika ('...her work shall henceforth be regarded as free and entirely independent of their sanction of authority.'). In order to silence the vilifiers she stated in the "Indian Mirror" on 31 July 1902 that the entire leadership of the Order rested on Swami Brahmananda and Swami Saradananda like whom spiritual personalities were rare. Swami Brahmananda had a great affection for Nivedita whom he asked to write a biography of Swamiji which was published entitled 'The Master As I Saw Him' in 1910. Besides, he was helpful in her educational work. Swamiji wrote Nivedita :

> I recommend you none–not one–except Brahmananda. That Old Man's judgements never failed–mine always do. If you have to ask my advice or to get anybody to do your business, Brahamananda is the only one I recommend, none else, none else; with this my conscience is clear.[12]

Swami Brahmananda encouraged her to set up a history-school at Buddha Gaya.

Though it was very difficult for Swmi Brahmananda to attend the trustee meetings of the Order for the whole world appeared shadowlike to him, he was surprisingly very alert about everyday life in the Order. Swami Ashokananda wrote : "He knew everything, kept watch over everything – not only the details of the external work, but the spiritual condition of the monks as well. He could guide them, and he would give those who were earnest as much help as they wanted."[13]

Swamiji relied much on Brahmananda's prudence and competency in guiding the Order. On 12 February, 1902 he wrote to his dear Rakhal "Don't ask my opinion on any other matter either. That makes me lose my temper. Just do that work for me–that is all...

"Continue doing your work as the Lord guides. Why bother about the opinion of this man and that?"[14]

Swami Saradananda said to a young monk : "When I say something you should judge and discriminate whether I am right or wrong, but when Maharaj says something you may safely accept it as true without the slightest doubt."[15]

Guts and Love :

Swami Brahmananda had the courage and determination to express his own opinion

On 27 April, 1896 Swamiji wrote the members of the Alambazar Math : "No doubt it is an evil to be bound by laws, but it is necessary at the immature stage to be guided by rules; in other words, as the

Master used to say that the sapling must be hedged round, and so on."[16] Accordingly he jotted down some hints regarding the management of the Math, the Governing Body, Departments and the Office-Bearers.

Kumud Bandhu Sen, a lay devotee witnessed an incident. Probably in 1897 a meeting of the disciples of Shri Ramakrishna was held at Balaram Bose's house to consider organizational matters. Swamiji had submitted a draft of regulations of conduct. All but Maharaj considered the table carefully and suggested changes and gave approval.

Then Swamiji asked, "Raja what is the matter? Why don't you say something? Don't you like it?" Maharaj replied, " No, Naren. I don't like so many rules and regulations. Then Swamiji took the draft of that section and without a word just tore it up and threw the pieces away.[17]

The Swami really valued the opinions of his beloved 'Raja' who on another occasion said to Swami Dhirananda, "Swamiji has already made the rules for us. We do not need to add any new ones. Add more love, attain more devotion and help others to move towards the ideal of God."

Swami Abhedananda spoke about his brother-monk Swami Brahmananda, "Love was the dominant theme of his character. As the first President of the Ramakrishna Order he enforced no other law but love; and by that sheer force of love he could dominate over one and all."[18]

Efficient Organizer :

Swami Brahmananda was innovative, practical and tenacious by nature. Before taking charge of the RamaKrishna Math and Mission he had to handle the accounts, supervise the monastery, keep the monastery's diary and give spiritual instructions to the novices.

Swami Brahmananda, during his presidency travelled from one part of the country to another to extend the ideas and ideals of Sri Ramakrishna and to organize the activities of the Order.

While in Varanasi in 1903 he collected some funds to help the Ramakrishna Advaita Ashrama set up by Swamiji with the financial help of the Maharaja of Varanasi and under supervision of Swami Shivananda in 1902. Swamiji inspired a group of young devotees who had established a small organization called 'Poor Men's Relief Association' with a view to provide destitute pilgrims with food, shelter and medical help. Swamiji named the institution 'Ramakrishna Home of Service.' Swami Brahmananda officially affiliated the institution with the Order and bought some land adjacent to the Home to construct some buildings on it. In April 1908 he laid the foundation stone of the hospital building of the Home of Service. In 1912 he showed Holy Mother the activities of the Home. She, with great pleasure, extolled, "Sri Ramakrishna is ever present in the place and Mother Lakshmi always casts her benign glance upon it." And as a mark of appreciation she donated a ten rupee note to the centre.

Swami Kalyanananda a disciple of Swamiji had started to serve sick monks in three thatched huts at Kankhal. Swami Brahmananda went there and in co-operation with a devotee of Kolkata bought fifteen acres of land and sent Swami Vijnanananda to supervise the construction of buildings. Again in March 1912 he visited Kankhal and introduced Durga Puja (the annual festival of the worship of goddess Durga) in the ashrama.

While at Bhubaneswar Swami Brahmananda was informed of the failure of Swami Turiyananda and Swami Saradananda to stop quarrel among the untrained monks of the Ramakrishna Advaita Ashrama and the Home of Service in Varanasi. Swami Brahmananda assured his brother-monks of going to see for himself. Reaching Varanasi on 20 January 1921 the President neither called any meeting nor asked any question regarding work or dissension but simply announced that all the monks from both centres would have to meditate with him in the morning and evening, and that devotional singing and questions and answers would follow meditation A few days later he initiated forty members of the two-wings into brahmachaya and sannyasa. He raised their minds to such a height that all of them forgot all their conflict and confrontation.

Swami Saradananda complimented the President on his victory in a battle without a fight :

> It would be proper for you to be a king rather than a monk. Where both Turiyananda and I could not figure out the solution, how easily you solved the crucial problem![19]

In 1908 Swami Brahmananda accompanied by Swami Ramakrishnananda visited Madras (Chennai) monastery located on the first floor of Castle Kernan (Ice House) and then Rameswaram, Madurai and Kanchipuram in South India. On 20 January 1909 the President inaugurated the Ramakrishna Ashrama in Bangalore. There he was so impressed with *Ramnam Sankirtan* (Choral singing in praise of Lord Ramachandra) that he introduced it to the Order.

In July Maharaj laid the foundation stone of the new monastery building in Madras. On 12 August he left for Bangalore and then he visited holy places of the South Namely Chamunda Devi in Mysore, Lord Padmanava in Trivandrum, Kanyakumari (the Virgin Goddess) at Cape Comorin, the birth place of Ramanuja at Perambudur, Lord Ranganath at Trichi, and Lord Balaji Venkateshwara in Tirupati.

In April 1921 Swami Brahmananda went to Madras with Swami Shivananda and inaugurated the Madras Students' Home. He arranged to have Durga Puja in the monastery. He spent the summer in Bangalore.

Maharaj accompanied by Swami Premananda and a few other monks on their way to Dhaka (now the capital city of Bangladesh) visited the holy temple of Kamakhya at Guwahati and stayed five days at Mymensing . On 13 February he laid the foundation stone of the Ramakrishna Math at Dhaka. He initiated many of the devotees and visited the ashrama of Vijaykrishna Goswami there and the birthplace of Durga Charan Nag a saintly disciple of Sri Ramakrishna whom the Master called a 'blazing light', at Deobhog (Narayangunj)

The President set up a monastery at Chakratirtha in Puri and another at Bhubaneswar. He handed over the management of the daily activities at Belur Math to Swamis Premananda and Shivananda. Though he was busy establishing new monasteries, initiating devotees and inspiring and guiding monks and was far from the headquarters most of the time and lived a God-intoxicated life, he knew what went on around him. During his stay at Belur Math he would check the cleanliness of the Shrine and the rooms of the monks and brahmacharins as well and would inquire about the health and spiritual progress of them and would supervise the care of the trees, plants, vegetable garden and dairy.

As a successful organizer and architect Maharaj held the praramount position for more than two decades (1900-1922).

Frequent ecstasy and vision :

Swami Brahmananda would remain in a highly spiritual mood in a holy place and would experience ecstasy while visiting the deities and would have visions quite often. Attending a Christmas festival in Madras he said to the arranger Sister Devamata (Laura Glenn, an American disciple of Swami Vivekananda): "I have had a great blessing here this afternoon . As you were reading the Bible, Christ suddenly stood before the altar dressed in a long blue cloak, He talked to me for some time. It was a very blessed moment"[20]

In the Meenakshi Temple at Madurai Maharaj fell into ecstasy and Swami Ramakrishnanda had to hold him up for nearly an hour and to chant the glory of the Divine Mother in the midst of a large crowd.

Referring to his vision in the temple he said : "When I stood in front of the deity, I saw the living image of Mother Meenakshi coming towards me and I lost outer consciousness."[21]

Maharaj used to talk about how the deities would manifest themselves to him during his visit to the holy places. He reminisced : "In Kanyakumari, I was about to burst into laughter out of joy. I saw the goddess, as an eight-or ten-year-old girl, giggling. It was a beautiful, awesome, living form."[22]

Swami Brahmananda miraculously and meticulously saw the Divine Mother in the image of Lord Balaji Venkateswara in Tirupati. He said to Swami Sharvananda : "I have distinctly seen the from of the Divine Mother. Please inquire about it."[23] It may be noted that later an inquiry revealed that it was originally an image of the Divine Mother which was converted into Lord Vishnu, perhaps under the influence of Ramanuja, the exponent of qualified nondualistic Vedanta, afterwards.

In Puri Maharaj often would fall into ecstasy while visiting the deities– Balaram, Jagannath and Subhadra (elder brother of Krishna, Krishna and their sister respectively) in the inner sanctuary of the holy shrine. One day he had a vision of a cowherd boy in place of the deities.

In February 1916 one morning at Dhaka Maharaj said : "Last night I saw the Master dancing here. The Master himself is preaching; we are only instruments."[24]

Swami Ashokananda commented : "Yes, he (Swami Brahmananda) was so close to God that we believed and with good reason that he was always in contact with Him. I have heard that he often saw God in the from of Sri Ramakrishna and in other forms as well."[25]

An ideal Guru–a friend, saviour of the fallen and redeemer of the sinners :

Swami Brahmananda was an ideal Guru who removed the darkness of ignorance of his disciples. Shri Chaitanya Mahaprabhu never wrote a single line but "Shikshastakam' but he made others compose beautiful hymns and devotional songs. Similarly Maharaj never spoke in public except the President's inaugural address in the Ramakrishna Ashram Bangalore (20 January 1909) but made his life his teaching. He demonstrated religion rather than preaching. Once Swami Ramakrishnananda said to V. Krishnaswami Iyer: "What is there in lectures? He (Maharaj) never gives lectures. Men such as he can impart religion by a mere look or touch."[26] He had the power to impart illumination or samadhi to anybody.

In her memoirs Tara an actress of Girish Chandra Ghosh described how Swami Brahmananda's blessings and love brought about a sea-change in her tormented and unbearable life : "I was impure–a fallen woman. And so when I touched the holy feet of Maharaj, I did it with great hesitancy, afraid to offend him. But his sweet words, his solicitude and love dispelled all my fear.

"Maharaj asked me, "Why don't you come here often"? I replied, 'I was afraid to come to the Math." Maharaj said with great earnestness : "Fear? You are coming to Sri Ramakrishna. What fear can there be? All of us are his children. Don't be afraid! Wenever you wish, come here. Daughter, the Lord does not care about externals : He sees our inmost heart. There should be no fear in approaching Him." "I could not hold back my tears. My lifelong sorrow melted as the tears fell from my eyes, and I realized : Here is my refuge. Here is someone to whom I am not a sinner, I am not an outcast."[27] Bashi Sen's brother Tabu (Matiswar Sen), a young devotee and dearly beloved of the Holy Mother and Maharaj as well committed an immoral act and Maharaj heard about it. Tabu was ashamed of showing his face to Maharaj who one day by chance came across him and said : "Look, if a mosquito sits on its horn, does the buffalo feel it or register any pain? Know us to be like that."[28] Maharaj meant to say that he did not mind his small mistake.

Once Swami Brahmananda said to a monk, "If you can't make a bad man good, why did you become a monk?" One day in Dhaka, when Swami Premananda told Swami Brahmananda that Swamiji was a saviour of the lowly and redeemer of the sinners; the addressee at once answered, "I am also a saviour of the lowly and a redeemer of the sinners."

Initially he, like his Master, was very selective regarding initiation But Holy Mother asked him to initiate more people as it was too hard for her to tackle all the aspirants. Moreover, in 1916 he as a spectator of a drama at the Minerva Theatre was deeply moved by the words of the guru of Ramanuja who told his disciple that whoever repeated the mantram would be liberated. Then he became more liberal in giving initiation.

Generally Maharaj taught the monks from his profound personal experience rather than by quoting from the seriptures and his spsiritual teachings were practical, direct and simple.

In 1921 a young monk at Varanasi told Maharaj that he had been practising japam and meditation mechanically and acquired no taste for them. Maharaj said : "Is it possible to get that taste in the beginning? you will have to struggle hard to attain it. Direct all your energy to that one pursuit...

"In the beginning it is good to make a routine and then follow it strictly. It does not matter whether your mind likes it or dislikes it. You must practise your japam and meditation as a daily routine...

You have received the precious mantram from your guru. Now dive deep into the ocean of Satchidananda. You have no self-reliance. Self-effort is indispensable in spiritual life. Do something for a period of at least four years. Then if you have not made any tangible progress come back and slap my face!"[29]

Silence is more eloquent. Hailing from Dhaka to see Maharaj at Udbodhana, once Swami Satprakshananda prostrated himself before him and sat at his feet. Maharaj's attendant Swami Dhirananda introduced him to Maharaj saying, "He has some questions." Swami Brahmananda glancing at him graciously said, "You have seen a holy man, have bowed down to him and touched his feet, what more questions can there be?" Swami Satprakashananda wrote, "Evidently he meant that this was enough to solve my problems and remove all doubts and difficulties from within."[30]

Regarding the infallible effect of holy company and spiritual words of the holy men, Maharaj said to the devotees : "A bumble-bee hiding in a fragrant flower offered in the worship touches the feet of the Lord. Similarly by the grace and association of a holy man, one surpasses even the gods and attains liberation."[31]

Devotees coming in contact with Maharaj experienced a positive change in their lives.

Swami Brahmananda was a compassionate guru, an affectionate father and at the same time a strict taskmaster. He taught the monks to keep three-fourths of their mind fixed on God, and with the remaining one-fourth do whatever they had to do. By following that method, they would be an ideal Karmayogi and would attain peace and joy. On the other hand if they got engaged in activities without practising meditation, they would be prey to pride and ego and meanness. Meditation or household duty everywork should be done with right spirit.

In December 1915 Swami Brahmananda made a rule in which it was mandatory for all monks and brahmacharins to rise at 4:00 a.m. to sit for japam and meditation by 4:30 a.m. for two to two and a half hours and to gather in the room of Maharaj by 7:00 a.m. and sing devotional songs for about an hour. Then he used to give spiritual instructions to all to elevate their mind six or seven steps.

Maharaj refused to compromise on moral standards and discipline.

Once in Madras (now Chennai) while Swami Prabhavananda accompanied his gurudeva Swami Brahmananda on a walk, the latter said to the former, "Just do one thing : always try to remember God. I also do that."[32] Maharaj said to him also "There are times when it becomes impossible for me to teach anyone. No matter where I look, I see only God wearing many masks. Who am I, the teacher? Who is to be taught? How can God teach God? But when my mind comes down again to a lower level, I see the ignorance in man and I try to remove it."[33]

Insight :

Hemantakumar Sarkar a freedom fighter and friend of Subas Chandra Bose wrote that the grace and advice of Swami Brahmananda the-then President of the Ramakrishna Mission brought about a significant change in the course of life of Subhaschandra.[34] While in Varanasi Maharaj told Subhas who in his student life was deeply attracted by the life of sannyasi and wanted 'to be a full-fledged sannyasi' and wrote 'If Swamiji had been alive today, he would have been my guru, that is to say, I would have accepted him as my

Master'[35] —that asceticism was not his field of business, his life was to be dedicated to the untiring service to the country. He told Subhas Chandra too that he would have to play a key role in the service to his motherland in future and despite his bent for spiritualism, patriotism would be the main inspiration. Lateron Subhas chandra admitted to his friend Dilip Kumar Roy the influece of Swami Brahmananda on his life.[36] Swami Brahmananda's prophesy turned out to be true afterwards.

Prudence :

As the supremo of the organization Swami Brahmananda was very judicious. A rich merchant after the death of his young wife came to Belur Math to live with the monks in order to assuage his bereavement. The holy company and ambience there solaced his heart and he decided to donate his entire possessions to the Ramakrishna Mission. At that time the Mission had been suffering from a paucity of funds. Swami Premananda satisfied with such generous gesture of the merchant, informed the President of the fabulous offer. Maharaj said to him, with folded hands: "Brother, having the company of the holy that man got renunciation, and having his company shall we be involved in the world?"[37] The farsighted Maharaj realized that the merchant's renunciation was utterly emotional and temporary and that it might put the organization to trouble if he accepted the donation.

As the President of the Calcutta centre of the Ramakrishna Mission and afterewards as the General President of the Order, Swami Brahmananda with his profound practical knowledge and strong common sense tried to implement Swami Vivekananda's plans regarding the management and philanthropic activities of the organization. Swamiji's letter (11 July 1897 from Almora)[38] to his disciple Swami Shuddhananda testifies to that.

Maharaj had an insight into human character and abilities and his frugality was remarkable. He considered that work is worship. One day in order to test the adherence of the monks to their morning meditation, he ordered each of them to peel a potato and bring it to him. While checking those potatoes Maharaj observed that Swami Shuddhananda removed the skin of the potato so neatly that no flesh was wasted. Holding up the potato he declared that the peeler of that one had had deep meditation.

Intense love for and loyalty to the leader :

Sri Ramakrishna himself selected Narendranath as the leader of his monastic disciples and asked him to guide them properly and ordered his monastic disciples to take care of Naren. Each of the monastic disciples gladly accepted Naren as the leader and loved and obeyed him.

M. heard Rakhal at the Baranagore Math say : "...when someone says, 'You have not realized God by renouncing home; then why all this fuss?' Narendra gives a good retort. He says, 'Because we could not attain Ram, must we live with Shyam and beget Children?" Ah! Every now and then Narendra says nice things. You had better ask him."(The Gospel of Sri Ramakrishna, p. 994)

"Many people think that it is enough not to look at the face of a woman. What will you gain merely by turning your eyes to the ground at the sight of a woman? Narendra put it very well last night, when he said : 'Woman exists for a man as long as he has lust. Free from lust, one sees no difference between man and woman."

Rakhal said to his brother disciple Prasanna (Sarada Prasanna Mitra i.e. Swami Trigunatitananda) who afraid of being drawn by the love of his parents wanted to flee to a distant place, "Where do you want to go, running away from here? Here you are in the company of holy men. Wouldn't it be foolish to run away from this? Where will you find another like Narendra?"(p.996)

Swami Brahmananda though coeval with the age of Swami Vivekananda regarded him as their leader and respected him deeply. Swamiji introduced a rule that every monk and brahmacharin must practise meditation in the shrine at dawn; absentees would have to beg for their food that day outside the monastery. One morning he discovered that Maharaj and some other monks were absent from meditation. He reminded them of the rule and went to Calcutta (now Kolkata) in order to avoid the sight of the miserable plight of his co-disciples. Abiding by the rule Maharaj went out for begging and managed to beg a square meal at a rich merchant's house in a village nearby . The leader was happy to hear it the next day.

Swamiji entrusted Swami Vijnanananda, an ex-engineer with the construction of a ghat and an embankment on the bank of the Ganga at Belur. The latter under estimated the cost but Maharaj took the risk of completing the project. On learning that the budget had been exceeded, Swamiji rebuked Maharaj severely and confining himself to his room wept bitterly. Later on Swamiji with tears in his eyes said to Maharaj, ''Brother please forgive me. I know how much the Master loved you and never said a harsh word to you. And I, on the other hand, for the sake of this petty work, have verbally abused you and given you pain. I am not fit to live with you. I shall go away to the Himalayas and live in solitude. Maharaj replied, "Don't say that Swamiji. Your scolding is a blessing. How can you leave us? You are our leader. How shall we function without you?'[39]

Swamiji with his deep faith in Maharaj's loyalty to him, used to say, 'Others may desert me, but Raja will stand by me till the last.' Crying like a child over their leader's body on the fateful day of 4 July 1902 Swami Brahmananda said to Swami Saradananda, 'It is as if the whole Himalayan Mountains have disappeared from before my eyes!'

One day after lunch at Belur Math Swamiji askd his disciple Sharat Chandra Chakravarty to give him a little massage. The disciple enthusiastically tried to utilise the opportunity of serving his gurudeva. But it did not comfort Swamiji for, Sharat Chandra, out of respect for his gurudeva, massaged him tenderly. Swamiji asked him to call Swami Brahmananda who had just then gone to rest. When Maharaj appeared, Swamiji asked him to give him a massage. Maharaj, as an experienced, massaged Swamiji vigorously for a couple of hours. When he returned to his room, Sharat Chandra to his utter amazement said : "Maharaj, I have come to you to resolve my confusion. I have heard that you are the spiritual son of the Master, and I have seen how much Swamiji respects you. I don't understand why Swamiji asked you to give him a massage." Maharaj replied : "What do you say? Don't you know he is the Lord Shiva Himself."[40]

Swami Brahmananda said to the monks and brahmacharins : "This is Swamiji's Math. If you cannot live according to his wishes, leave the monastery! Swamiji gave his very life to build this organization and to give you everything to facilitate your spiritual practice and growth. Try to realize the infinite love he bore for you."[41]

Unfathomable spiritual power :

Swami Brahmananda, God-intoxicated spiritual giant was endowed with god-gifted power. One day in Puri he said to his disciple Swami Sharvananda. "It is easy to get occult powers, but difficult to acquire purity of mind. It is this purity of mind that really matters."[42]

Girish Chandra Ghosh reminisced" "Compared to myself Rakhal is only a young boy. I know that the Master regarded him as his spiritual son, but that is not the only reason I respect him. Once I was suffering from asthma and various kinds of ailments. As a result, my body became very weak and I lost faith in Shri Ramakrishna. With a view to getting rid of that dry spell, I engaged pandits to read to Gita and the Chandi to me, But still I had no peace of mind... Then one day Rakhal came and asked me, "How are you?" I replied : "Brother I am in hell. Can you tell me the way out?" Rakhal listened to me and then burst into laughter. "Why worry about it?" said he "As the waves of the ocean rise high, then go down again, and again rise so does the mind. Don't be upset. Your present mood is due to the fact that it will lead you to a higher realm of spirituality. The wave of the mind is gathering strength."

As soon as Rakhal left my house my doubt and dryness disappeared and I got back my faith and devotion.[43]

In 1920 Pandit Kshirod Prasad Vidyavinod as stated earlier told Maharaj at Bhubaneswar how he while a student missed a possibility of seeing Sri Ramakrishna. On his way to Dakshineswar, at Alambazar he thought that if the Master who could read everybody's mind, exposed his secret thoughts in front of others, he would be embarrassed. Fearing that he went back home. Maharaj replied, "Since you went to Alambazar to see the Master, take it for granted that you did see him." "No Maharaj, I did not see him"—saying this Kshirod bending his head began to sob. After awhile he lifted his face only to find Sri Ramakrishna seated in Swami Brahmananda's place.[44]

Swami Umananda, a disciple of Swami Brahmananda, while working in Madras (Chennai), became ill with small pox and was admitted to the hospital. A couple of days before his death he told Swami Ramakrishnananda who visited him everyday that he was eager to see his gurudeva. Swami Ramakrishnanada communicated this to Maharaj who showed anxiety but did not go to his dying disciple thinking that the disease might be contagious. After the passing away of Swami Umananda Sri Ramakrisnananda said to his broter-disciple with teary eyes, "Maharaj" you are so cruel! Umananda wanted to see you once in his final hours, and you did not go!" Maharaj slowly replied, "Shashi, is it enough to see a person through the eyes? Have I not been there?" Swami Ramakrishnananda bowing down said, "Maharaj, please forgive me; I did not understand you."[45]

During her stay in Varanasi one day the Holy Mother visited Saranath where Lord Buddha had preached his first sermon after attaining nirvana, by a carriage. Swami Brahmananda with three other devotees followed her in another carriage. While returning to Varanasi, the Holy Mother, at the earnest appeal of Maharaj exchanged carriages with him. Maharaj's carriage met with an accident on the road, though none was seriously injured. Hearing about the incident the Mother said:"I was fated for this mishap, but Rakhal by force as it were took it on his own shoulders. I had several children with me, who know what would have happened to them?"[46]

Raja Maharaj appeared to Swami Bodhananda from the very beginning to be a man of different level! He commented that Maharaj and Hari Maharaj (Swami Turiyananda) cast a strong impression on others that 'they have got something already.'

Swami Chetanananda, on the basis of a diary of Swami Pabitrananda containing precious reminiscences of Swami Bodhananda, wrote in his book 'Prachin Sadhuder Katha,' (Part-I, 2nd Ed. p. 326, Udbodhan Office, Kolkata); that Hari Maharaj said that Maharaj could change the atmosphere in a minute. He possessed such power that he could mould the minds of those who lived within a certain area with him. If he would meditate, they too would meditate; if he smiled, they also did so; if he talked, they felt a tendency to talk.

Reputed writer Devendranath Bose was informed about the spirituality of Maharaj and had no respect for him. He had been suffering from family problems. One day he visited Maharaj in his room on the upstairs at Belur Math. Maharaj spontaneously passed his hand lightly and caressingly over his chest. He at once felt himself free from all sorts of worries. Since then he became a great devotee of Maharaj.

A true Mystic :

Kankhal, Varanasi, Vrindaban and Puri—these four holy places were favourite of Swami Brahmananda for meditation. As a true mystic he had delicate intuition and could monitor the time when the spiritual current flows in these places. He said :"Each place has its own time, when it is favourable for spiritual disciplines. The auspicious time in Vrindaban is midnight, in Varanasi, from 3:00 a.m. to dawn, in Puri, afternoon, in Bhubaneswar and Belur Math at 4:00 a.m."

Maharaj said about Kankhal : "It is a holy place. Here it does not take much effort to be asborbed in Japam and meditation. The very atmosphere is wonderful. The presence of the Mother Ganga and the Majestic Himalayas make the mind calm spontaneously. The unobstructed sound of Om is always vibrating in the air."About Varanasi he commented : "Kashi is beyond the universe—a great place saturated with consciousness. A person gets ten times the results if he practises spiritual disciplines here, and the mantram becomes living very quickly."[47]

Swami Brahmananda remarked about Bhubaneswar : "This place is very conducive to practising yoga. It is a place of Lord Shiva — a hidden Varanasi. Practising a little spiritual discipline here one can accrue immense results It is a healthy place. After getting tired from working in other places, the monks may come here to rest as well as practise meditation."[48]

Describing Belur Math as 'glorious monastery', Maharaj said : "This Belur Math is like Kailash [the abode of Shiva]. Here the guru and the Ganges are present. Swamiji also left his body here. This is Vaikuntha [the abode of Vishnu]."[49]

Swami Turiyananda who lived and practised japam and meditation punctually with Swami Brahmananda during their stay at Vrindaban in 1903, observed that Maharaj could create such an atmosphere around himself that everyone present would be filled with some of his spiritual mood.

Swami Saradananda wrote in his introduction to the book 'Words of the Master' by Swami Brahmananda,

> The present brochure is from the pen of one who was regarded by the Master as next to Swami Vivekananda in his capacity for realising religious ideals.

In the afternoon of the first day of January 1886 Sri Ramakrishna appeared before his householder devotees as the Kalpataru (the wish fulfilling tree) or in the words of Swami Saradananda, the "Self-revelation of Master" and said : "May you all be blessed with the spiritual awakening."

The Master's spiritual son Swami Brahamananda too appeared as the Kalpataru. One day Swami Premananda forcefully taking an obstinate and quarrel-some young monk to him said : 'Maharaj, this fellow is short-tempered, he quarrels with other monks and even with me. Please touch his head with your palm so that he can be freed from anger." Swami Premananda believed that Maharaj had the spiritual power to change not only the atmosphere of a place but the nature and life of a person also. Maharaj amusingly said: "Brother Baburam, today my palm is not good; you better put your palm on his head." But Swami Premananda, pushing the monk's head near Maharaj's feet persuaded him to bless. Maharaj rubbed the monk's head with his palm seriously. Then Swami Premananda placing his own head near Maharaj requested him to touch it. Maharaj did so. Swami Premananda loudly called to the other monks : "Hello! Please come and take the blessings of Maharaj. He has become Kalpataru today." Blessing all monks and servants who had rushed to him, Maharaj got up from his seat. Just then a doctor-devotee who was in the bathroom, arrived and Swami Premananda requested his brother-disciple to bless the doctor. Maharaj answered "The power that came has gone."[50]

'Green even when ripe' :

M. recorded in 'The Gospel of Sri Ramakrishna' that with reference to the amazing and amusing life and manners of an illumined soul, Sri Ramakrishna said to Pundit Shashadhar (on July 3, 1884) : "But the nature of the vijnani is quite different as was the case with Chaitanyadeva. He acts like a child or a madman or an inert thing or a ghoul. While in the mood of a child, he sometimes shows childlike guilelesseness, sometimes the frivolity of adolescence, and sometimes, while instructing others, the strength of a youngman." (p. 493)

As a man Swami Brahmananda was both grave and gay. He had a keen sense of humour and childlike simplicity. When his mind came down to sense plane, he, like his Master, used to joke and make fun with the monks and devotees.

Both the Swamis Vivekananda and Brahmananda were friends and had genuine mutual trust and understanding since their school life. Yet Maharaj did not spare his leader if his pets destroyed his flower and vegetable gardens in Belur Math. Their childish quarrel was very amusing to others.

Swami Prabhavananda remarked about Swami Brahmananda : "One of his favourite jokes was to have some fruits or sweets placed beside a disciple who was meditating. When the disciple had finished his meditation he would find his favourite dishes laid out before him. Later Maharaj would ask, "well, did you get the fruits of your austerities?"[51]

One day in the house of Balaram Basu Maharaj covering up himself with a bearskin appeared before Balaram's grand-children to scare them. They screamed in fear. After a little one little boy with tearful eyes said : "I know it's you, Maharaj, You can't frighten me! But why did you do it?" Then Maharaj laying the bearskin aside took the boy on his lap.

One morning while Swami Brahmananda was walking on the lawn of Belur Math, a young man politely said to him : "I want to meet Swami Brahmananda. I would like to be a monk." Pointing to Swami Shivananda, who was then taking tea, Maharaj said : "You see that heavy-set person at the table, he is Brahmananda." The young man bowed down to Shivananda and said: 'I have come to you." Seeing that unknown person, Shivananda asked "Could you tell me the name of the person whom you want?"

"Swami Brahmananda."

"He is walking there on the lawn," Said Shivananda.

"Sir, he has told me that you are Swami Brahmananda."

"No, I am not. Swami Brahmananda is walking there."

When the young man returned to Maharaj and reported everything, Maharaj said : "No, I am not Brahmananda. You see, great souls sometimes delude people and do not like to be caught. Go again and hold his feet firmly."

The young man again went to Shivananda, got a nice scolding from him and returned to Brahmananda again. Maharaj said to him : "I have already told you that great souls delude people, and even beat people, but you should not leave him. Hold his two feet firmly." The young man became confused, and tears came from his eyes. Then Maharaj compassionately said : "All right, you can stay in the monastery."[52]

On 1 January 1921 in the house of Balaram Basu Maharaj insisted Ramlal, nephew of Sri Ramakrishna to dress as a gypsy woman and dance and sing the songs those the Master used to sing.

One day Maharaj started dancing while Swami Chitprakashananda prayed to him for sannyasa.

One day at Belur Math Kali Maharaj (Swami Abhedananda) catching sight of attendants sitting around Rakhal Maharaj during his eating said, "Raja what are you doing? They will make you an idol, I fear? "I say brother Kali', replied Maharaj with a smile, 'they don't love me. (Pointing at the bowls of food) They are tempted by these and gather here. Now I can't eat much.' Kali Maharaj said, "All these are your joke and fun.' Maharaj answered, 'Mind brother Kali, these boys love brother Hari more than me. He says exciting and inspiring words about renunciation and apathy towards wordly interests and attracts them. If you do so, all these guys will go to you.'

In those days one had to wait for three years after one's joining the Math for formal continence. Kiranchandra Ghosal (Afterwards Swami Ashesananda) a disciple of Holy Mother who joined the Ramakrishna Mission in 1921 and acted as the secretary (1921-1927) to Swami Saradananda, reminiseed before Swami Chetananda (Prachin Sadhuder Katha, p. 336) that one day Sharat Maharaj sent him from Udbodhan to Brahmananda Maharaj at Belur Math for continence vows. Then Maharaj sat on an easy chair facing the Ganga on the eastern verandah on the first floor of the Math building. He said, 'Maharaj, I pray for your blessing. Kindly initiate me into continence on the holy birth day of the Master.' Musing on the subject, Maharaj said, 'well, I may grant you continence on condition that you will have to pay rupees 108 in advance as Gurudakshina (fees to a mentor) otherwise not.' Kiranchandra, utterly perplexed, said, 'Maharaj, I have no money. Besides, from where shall I get so much money? I have no means but your pity.'

Then Maharaj said seriously. 'I show you a way. Saradananda has plenty of money. The entire treasure of Udbodhan belongs to him and you are his attendant. You bring money from Saradananda.'

Kiranchandra stood still. Maharaj said to a Brahmachari, 'Govinda, you have come from Midnapore. I shall grant you continence if you can dance after Odissi style.' Govinda danced moving his arms legs and waist unhesitatingly. Maharaj, with a smile, approved of his continence.

Returning Udbodhan Kiranchandra reported all to Swami Saradananda who asked him to tell Maharaj that he (Swami Saradananda) was his servant and he (Swami Brahmananda) was the owner of the whole amount of money of Udbodhan. He would be paid what he demanded.

Going back to the Math Kiranchandra prostrated himself before Maharaj and told him all those were said by Swami Saradananda.

Shaking his head Maharaj loudly said, 'Empty words! I shan't be cajoled by these empty words. How shall I undrestand that he will keep his words? Have you brought from him written anything? Mind, you are secretary to him, I shall accept a draft of understanding signed by him regarding payment.

Learning all from his secretary Swami Saradananda assured him of visiting the Math with him the next day. The following day after brief prattle between two Swamis Swami Saradananda told Kiranchandra that he would be initiated into continence with others. It happened on the auspicious birth day of Sri Ramakrishna in 1922 which was the last initiation into continence under Maharaj.

Swami Vijoyananda one of the disciples of Swami Brahmananda, was an intelligent and erudite student of Chemistry of the University of Calcutta (now Kolkata). In order to test him one day Maharaj sending a phial of perfume wanted to know of the formula. Just smelling the scent he jotted down the formula and sent it to Maharaj by his attendant. The second day saw the same thing. On the third day when an attendant came to him with a phial, he himself went to Maharaj with the Phial and formula and said, 'Maharaj my balloon of egotism has already burst. Then why do you poke fun at that again?' Maharaj replied, 'My son, you should have understood before.'

Swami Prabhavananda reminiseed how Maharaj used to joke with Swami Premananda. One day while Swami Prabhavananda aged eighteen, was massaging feet and legs of Maharaj; the latter asked the former to give his brother disciple Baburam in the next room a massage. Accordingly Swami Prabhavananda began to massage the feet of Swami Premananda sleeping on a cot. He woke up and told him to go to Maharaj as he did not want rubbing and pressing. The more he resisted the more the attendant persisted in obeying the order of Maharaj. Ultimately Swami Premananda accepted his service and blessed him.

Swami Brahmananda said, 'Always meditae upon the smiling face of your Guru or tutelary deity. Dull meditation doesn't interest me. Ever complacent face is the manifestation of perfect meditation. Displeasure should never be expressed on the face and meditation should start from feet towards face and not from upwards to downwards.'

Thus the child in Maharaj would come out off and on to create a relaxed ambience around him.

There are many more stories about Swami Brahmananda's playful jokes. One day a devotee said: "Maharaj, people come to hear your spiritual talk, and you entertain them with funny jokes." Maharaj replied : "Look, householders are burning with miseries almost all the time, so I give them some momentary joy. There are very few persons in this world who want spirituality. Those who are sincere, I talk to them about God; and I know they will listen to my spiritual instructions and follow them. That is why I don't talk about spiritual matters to all. It is not so easy to practise spiritual disciplines — it needs good *samskaras* [tendencies] from a previous life.'[53]

Once Sri Ramakrishna spoke of his spiritual son : "Rakhal is like the kind of mango that look, green even when ripe." He meant that Swami Brahmananda possessed immense spiritual power that he kept hidden from the outside world.

Dazzling courage and manliness :

Christopher Isherwood wrote : "It has been said that Brahmananda was so entirely fearless that others could not feel fear in his presence. Once when he was walking with two devotees in the woods of Bhubaneswar a leopard appeared and came straight towards them. He stood still and confronted it calmly until it turned tail. Again, while he was going along a narrow lane in Madras, attended by two monks, a maddened bull came charging to meet them.. The young men tried to protect their guru, who was already an elderly man, by standing in front of him; but he pushed them behind him with extraordinary strength and fixed his eyes upon the bull. It stopped, shook its head from side to side, and then trotted quietly away."[54]

Paragon of love and compassion :

Swami Brahmananda showered his unconditional love and immeasurable compassion on all— human beings and animals, trees and plants. It is amazing how such a God-intoxicated person could regularly visit the cowshed, supervise the cows, feed the dog and nurture the flower and vegetable gardens of the monastery. Under his supervision North Indian flower and fruit trees were planted in South Indian centres. He taught the inmates how to fertilize and water the trees and how to control pests.

One day Maharaj visited the Basu Vijnan Mandir (Bose Research Institute) Kolkata to watch the sensitivity of plants to external stimuli with great interest and mused over it for long time. One day observing a brahmacharin at Belur Math plucking the big flowers in front of the garden, Swami Brahmananda advised him to pick the flowers hidden under the leaves and always leave some flowers in each tree as he realized that the trees also worshipped God with their flowers.

Outspokenness :

Swami Brahmananda did not hesitate to utter unpleasant truth. One day Bashi Sen playfully told Maharaj that he seemed a miser for he helped none see God though he could do so if he wished.

Maharaj turned serious and replied, "Who wants? Even monks and celebrates come and say, "Maharaj, kindly initiate, give us continence and asceticism. None say, 'Let me see God."'

In Madras (Chennai) one day Swami Sharvananda said, "Maharaj, why is there so much bad blood among our monks in the fields of activities?' Maharaj quipped, 'Because you don't love the Master.'

One day Swami Dhirananda requested Maharaj to introduce some rules for the new saints. Maharaj answered, "Swamiji has already laid down rules.' "Yes Maharaj,' said Swami Dhirananda, 'but we need some more rules.' Then Maharaj, replied 'Krishnalal, instead of increasing rules increase love in your heart.' Once he said, "Our monastic life is based on love and not on rules.'

Swami Brahmananda's life—a lesson

Maharaj like his spiritual father believed that religion is realization. He demonstrated religion rather than merely preaching it. He laid great stress on prayers. Usually his advice was dualistic perhaps because monistic propensity hinders work and does not differentiate between Guru and his disciple as was said by Shankaracharya (Tattvopadeshah, Sloka-87). Maharaj told his disciple Swami Vividisananda that if he went through worship, study, prayer and meditation his spiritual life would not be monotonous. He was an awakener of souls.

Manmathanath Gangopadhyay, a householder disciple of Swamiji wrote[55] that realization of God makes one lover of all creatures. It was very hard to get the direction of how work could be done possessing such all pervading love. He considered Rakhal Maharaj an ideal in this respect. It was astonishing that such a self-absorbed introspective man like him was attentive even to trifling matters such as laying leaves of banana for dinner or serving salt.

Shaileshwar Bose a neighbour of Balaram Bose and devotee of Swamiji reminisced[56] that one day in Nilambar Mukherjee's garden house in Belur village two bosom co-disciples Swamiji and Rakhal Maharaj had put on the garb of Lord Siva. So delightful they were.

Raja Maharaj had a strong sense of etiquette and utmost courtesy. Swami Bhaswarananda told Swami Chetanananda that when he prayed to Raja Maharaj for initiation, he giving him a rosary advised him to recite Gayatri mantra for a year and assured him of initiation after returning from Bhubaneswar. Coming back to Belur Math, Maharaj asked him to get initiation from Hariprasanna Maharaj (Swami Vijnanananda) who he attended to. But the unyielding youngman insisted Maharaj on initiating. Maharaj asked him to bring recommendation from 'Peshan' and Swami Vijnanananda sent him back to Maharaj. In fact, initially Swami Brahmananda was very choosy about initiating. After initiation he said to his dsiciple, 'You need not abide by so many advice. It is enough to observe truth and continence.'[57]

Swami Brahmananda used to keep an eye on the needs and problems of Holy Mother. He arranged for a palandquin for her to visit the Ramakrishna Mission Home of Service from Laskshimi Nivas in Varanasi in November 1912 as she had developed pain in her legs and had to limp.

At the Baranagore Monastery Rakhal (Swami Brahmananda) said to his brother disciple Prasanna (Swami Trigunatitananda) : "Can our parents love us as Gurumaharaj [meaning Sri Ramakrishna] did? What have we done for him, to deserve all this love? Why was he so eager for our welfare in body, mind and soul? What have we done for him to deserve all this?"[58] Thus since the dawn of his monastic life Swami Brahmananda devoted himself to be a worthy disciple of his Master and advised all that realisation of God should be our only motto.

A uinique teaching on the concept of the *Ista*, the Chosen Deity :

Swami Brahmananda the illustrious first President of Ramakrishna Math and Ramakrishna Mission suggested that the aspirant at the beginning of his spiritual practice, should meditate on his chosen Deity while thinking of him as effulgent conscious and blissful, recite his mantra and visualize him. Rajaji stated, "This kind of meditation gradually turns into meditation on the formless aspect of God. Your awareness will be filled with God-consciousness. Then, when the knowledge-eye opens, you will see God face to face."[59] The seeker should rely on a spiritual teacher to find the appropriate Chosen Deity. The Guru selects Chosen Deity and the mantra according to the nature of the disciple. Maharaj said, "There is much work involved in initiating a disciple. I have to meditate long hours to slelect the Chosen Deity of each disciple."[60] One of his conditions of initiating a person was to know his Chosen Deity in meditation. Thus it is an important and practical part of cognitive psychology.

The only man to shoulder the Herculean task :

Swamiji was not only a great prophet but also an extraordinary visionary and a meticulous planner. As an agile and self relient General President of the Ramakrishna Mission he said, 'My work must be quick as lightning and strong as the thunderbolt.' But he knew that his days were too numbered to implement his plans and ideas. This made him impatient and restless. He selected Swami Brahmananda the President of the Calcutta centre whom he considered his 'friend, philosopher, and guide', as his principal assistant to conduct the whole movement. In this context Swami Purnatmananda wrote, "There was none among the brother disciples except Swami Brahmananda who could cope with his tumultuous impulses and impatience. Swami Vijnanananda, another brother disciple of Swami Vivekananda who happened to be a district civil enginer before he embraced monasticism, was an eye-witness to such outbursts of Swamiji on Swami Bramananda. He narrated later how terrible and servere those outbursts had been. But Swami Brahmananda remained absolutely calm and unperturbed on such occasions. This state of poise and graceful balance was his nature, but at the same time it must also be remembered that such harshness in no way reflected the slightest change in Swami Vivekananda's tremendous faith and confidence in and profound love for Swami Brahmananda. Swamiji loved all his brother disciple more than anybody else on earth' as he himself said, and for Swami Brahmananda he had an extra-special love and fondness." [Swami Purnatmananda, The Story of Ramakrishna Mission, Advaita Ashrama, Kol. p. 97]

Swami Brahmananda dedicated himself to materialize various projects chalked out by Swamiji e.g. constructing brick steps from the bottom of the Ganga, clearing and levelling the uneven ground, planning and constructing new buildings including the shrine, and renovating the existing quarters, and maintaining a record of accounts and even conducting a lawsuit against the municipality of Belur which regarded the property of the Math as a garden-house instead of a monastery and imposed high tax on this religious and philanthropic institution. With reference to this Swami Ashokananda commented :

"A spiritual giant of the stature of Swami Brahmananda was not, according to any tradition, the person to engage in this kind of labour— supervising construction, conducting lawsuit, keeping accounts, and so on. But he stood by Swamiji in every respect... Not for a single moment did he differ from Swamiji, and Swamiji knew that even if all the others were to forsake him, Swami Brahmananda would stand by him with the utmost faith and loyalty— and on that faith and loyalty of his, stability of the Ramakrishna Order was based." [Swami Brahmananda, Swami Ashokananda San Francisco Vedanta Society of Northern California, 1970, p. 17]

In order to provide Swami Brahmananda with plenty of scope for thinking and acting freely, Swamiji resigned from the Presidentship of the Organization and Swami Brahmananda was elected President on 12 February 1901 and held the office till his passing away on 10, April 1922. Appreciating the great ability of his worthy successor as an architect and administrator of the Math Swamiji used to say :

"I have been stunned to see Raja's work. How nicely he is running the Math! About him Sri Ramakrishna used to say, 'He can rule a kingdom."

[The Life of Swami Vivekananda, His Eastern and Western Disciples, Advaita Ashrama, Kolkata, 7 ed. Vol. II p. 389.]

Significant enunciation :

In the *Indian Review* in its March 1910 number Swami Brahmananda wrote a well-throught article 'Ramakrishna Mission : The Scope and Method of It's Work' that has been described by Prof. Sankari Prasad Basu as 'effectively, *the manifesto of the Ramakrishna Order*.' Swami Brahmananda pointed out the common goal of the twin organizations the Math and the Mission set by Swamiji —ātmano mokṣārtham jagat hitya ca (to work out one's own liberation and to do good to the world) and the special features of the Ramakrishna Mission —its fight against 'fanaticism, bigotry and narrow-mindedness', its recognition of the 'harmony of religions' and 'Divinity of man', its denouncement of 'esoterism' and 'proselytisation', its emphasis on 'reason' and the 'practice of religion' and its enunciation of Vedanta as the basis of its religious ideas. In reference to the special distinction of the organization Swami Brahmananda wrote :

"Ramakrishna Mission is distinct from all other religious missions of the past and the present as it only had discovered the harmony, the common basis, and the necessity of all the various religions, whereas each of the other religious missions of the world asserts its infallibility, perfection and supremacy over all the rest."

Embodiment of the Masters message :

Swami Brahmananda regarded Sri Ramakrishna and Swamiji as the obverse and reverse of the same coin and believed that Swamiji was the true interpreter of his Master's message that man was potentially divine, service to man was service to God and work was worship. As a sincere follower of his Master and leader he made his life an example of a perfect balance between spiritual practice and work. He encouraged the monks to maintain such balance.

Chapter – 6

SWAMI SHIVANANDA

Once his attendant, as was ordered bought a big live catfish for making nice curry out of it. He asked him to release the fish into the Ganga only to enjoy the fish's joy of freedom.

Another day while his eyes fell on his own figure in a group photo in Swamiji's room at Belur, he burst out laughing and said, "Eh, who is this rogue, here? This one became a saint, having been with saints!"

He in order to save his father from paying the dowry for his youngest daughter had to marry against his wishes his brother-in-law's sister Nityakali who died within a year of the marriage.

One day at Dakshineswar while he was taking notes of Sri Ramakrishna's conversations, the Master said, "you don't have to do that. Your life is different."

He was none but Tarakanath Ghosal who was born of pious parents Ramkanai and Vamasundari on 16 November 1854, at Barasat Kolkata He was destined to live a different life— holy and dedicated life of a monk under the monastic name Swami Shivananda.

Ability to renounce the world in his younger days :

After the death of his wife in 1883 Tarak resigned from his job in the mercentile firm of Machinnon, Mackenzie, and company

Kolkata and determined to lead the life of a monk. He was the first among the disciples of Sri Ramakrishna to renounce the world in order to realize God.

He believed that he who had performed much austerity, God made him an instrument and worked through him. He lived mostly with Ramakrishna during the last three years of his Master's life. Sometimes he cooked his own food and practised meditation in some solitary places. He reminisced :

"I was so happy there all by myself. For lunch I used to procure from the neighbourhood a little rice and one or two simple dishes. For supper I prepared over the open *dhuni* fire [a fire used by wondering monks] a few pieces of unleavened bread and roasted an eggplant or a couple of green bananas. And I ate only these, washing them down with drinks of water. Day and night I used to be absorbed in my spiritual practice beside the dhuni fire, and right there snatched my sleep and rest. The fire would sometimes attract snakes, but for some reason or other they avoided me."[1]

Having sāttvic or good signs :

Sri Ramakrishna identified Tarak as one of his inner circles. one day the Master said to him, "Well, so many people come here. I seldom ask anyone about his home and family, or desire to know anything about these things. But when I first met you I felt that you belonged here, that I would like to know the particulars of your home, parents and the like. Can you tell me why? Where is your home and what is your father's name?" Hearing that Tarak's father was Ramkanai Ghosal, a highly developed spiritual aspirant whom he knew very well, he said, "Now I understand why the Mother aroused this desire in me for information about your home....

"Whenever he (Ramkanai Ghosal) came here, he would take his bath in the Ganges put on a red silk garment, and enter the Mother's temple... He meditated for long periods in the Mother's temple... Your father would be absorbed in meditation, with tears streaming down his cheeks. When he left the temple after meditation his face would be flushed with spiritual emotion and nobody would dare approach him."[2]

Tarak inherited his father's bent for spiritualism and a great yearning for God. He said, "Since my boyhood I didn't care for family life, and I had a spiritual inclination in my heart. I shall never be bound to this world by getting married—this idea was deep in my mind. I had an innate desire to travel to various holy places. I used to work for the railways and call on God.

"The idea of samadhi would agitate my mind. How to be absorbed in the bliss of samadhi forgetting the world—this keen desire occupied me most of the time. I was very fond of the meditation pose of Shiva and Buddha. I tried to attain samadhi month after month—I rarely slept at night. I had that one thought—how to attain samadhi."[3]

Lord Buddha's Compassion :

In April 1886 Narendra, Tarak and Kaliprasad captivated by Lord Buddha's renunciation, love, compassion and patience, spent a few days in meditation under the historic bodhi tree where Lord attained enlightenment at Bodh Gaya. On the third night Narendra feeling an intense longing for Buddha was overcome with emotion and with tears welling up in his eyes embraced Tarak engrossed in meditation next to him. It is said that Narendra saw Buddha enter into Tarak's body.

A married man with unbroken chastity :

As Tarak had to accept his wife as a bitter tablet, his nuptial life was disgusting to him. When he had to spend the night at home he used to repeat the name of the Lord. He prayed to Sri Ramakrishna for destroying his temporal bondage. The Master advised him to perform a certain ritual and think of him and assured that nothing adverse would happen to him as he would protect him. The Master said to him, "I am telling you that even if you sleep in the same room with your wife, you will be free from danger. You will see it will rather intensify your spirit of renunciation." Tarak went through the ritual as prescribed and his lust was extinguished for good. One day hearing about the incident from Tarak Narendranath to his utter astonishment commented, '"What do you say! It is the characteristic of a Mahapurush. You are certainly one" Since then Narendranath started calling him by the venerable name 'Mahapurush', and he became popularly known by the name (Mahapurush Maharaj) in the Ramakrishna circle.

Shiva-like nature :

Tarak's parents prayed to Lord Tarakeshwar Shiva for a son and performed austerities for a year. One night his mother had dreamt that Lord Shiva appearing before her said, "I am pleased with your devotion. I bless you. You will be the mother of a spiritual son."[4] Tarak's parents believed that the child was born by the grace of Tarakeshwar Shiva. So they named him Taraknath. An astrologer foretold in a horoscope of Tarak that the child would be either a monk or a king.

Tarak was deeply indrawn, contemplative and serious by nature. Narendranath named Tarak "Swami Shivananda' knowing his Shiva like nature. Here to repeat Tarak himself said, "I was very fond of the meditation pose of Shiva and Buddha."[5]

Intense love for and faith in the Master :

While working in Mughalsarai, UP, Tarak was haunted by an idea of being absorbed in the bliss of samadhi forgetting the world. He heard from his roommate Prasanna the name of Sri Ramakrishna of Dakshineswar who had experienced real samadhi. He returned to Kolkata and became a member of the Brahmo Samaj led by Keshab Chandra Sen. But this association could not satisfy his unquenchable thirst for God. In the meantime he had learnt much about Ramakrishna from Keshab Chandra Sen's paper *Dharmatattwa* and was eager to see him. One evening when Tarak arrived at the house of Ram Chandra Dutta, Sri Ramakrishna was on an ecstatic mood and was talking on Samadhi a subject in which Tarak was so interested. He saluted him and sat amid the crowd but got no chance to talk to the Master that day. A month later one Saturday evening Tarak and a friend visited Dakshineswar. He found the Master seated cross-legged in his room with three or four others on the floor in front of him. When Tarak bowed down to the Master, putting his head on the Master's lap, the latter affectionately caressed his head. Tarak recollected : "At once I felt a deep attachment for the Master. I felt as if I had known him a long time. My heart became filled with joy. I saw in him my tender loving mother waiting for me. So with the confidence, faith, and certitude of a child I surrendered myself to him, placing myself entirely under his care. I was certain that at last I had found him for whom I had been searching all these days. From then on I looked upon the Master as my mother."[6]

While President of the Ramakrishna Order one day Swami Shivanada commented : "The Master is an expert player. He can win the game with a valueless cowrie [shell coin in ancient India] What do I have? Neither have I learning nor intellect, neither am I a speaker nor am I good-looking; still the Master is using me as an instrument for doing his work."[7]

Swami Shivananda in various occasions described the Master as his 'Paramatman, the supreme self', 'none other than Vishwanath himself', 'the Soul of his soul'. Despite his old age and illness he monitored particularly the Master's service and other activities in the monastery. He asked the worshippers to fan the Master for some time after putting him to bed in the summer. One day no sooner had Swami Jnanadananda finished sweeping the courtyard of the Math near the mango tree than Swami Shivananda said: "Hello, what are you doing? The Master walks here. I still see dust and used match sticks on the courtyard. Clean this place with special care, so that the master can walk with joy and his feet won't get dirty."[8]

Once Swami Nikhilatmananda who used to mop the floor of the shrine daily, did not mop the southern veranda flooded with the rainwater. Observing it Swami Shivananda said to him: Look, is it the way to serve the Master? The Master can't walk on the veranda because of the rainwater His feet will get wet. What are you doing here? I see the Master walking on that veranda every afternoon. My child, always be careful so that the Master may not feel discomfort. He is the Soul of our souls, the Lord of the universe ...If he is pleased, the whole world will be pleased."[9]

Swami Shivananda believed that the Master himself was present in Belur Math because Swamiji installed him there. One day he said to Swami Brahmananda, "Raja, I see the Master even these days. Were it not so, it would be unbearable for me to live.[10]

Swami wrote from America in 1894 to his brother disciple Swami Shivananda "Oh, I am the servant of the servants of his servants."[11] On the other hand, Swami Shivananda, pointing to his pet dog Kelo, would say : "Kelo is my dog and I am the dog of the Master."[12]

Words and incidents like these reveal Mahapurush Maharaj's exceptional faith in the Master and phenomenal humility.

Unfathomable devotion to Holy Mother :

Holy Mother passed away on 21 July 1920. Swami Shivananda was deeply shocked at that news. But suppressing his own grief, he tried to console the lay devotees. On 12 August 1920 he wrote :

"He who feels more keenly the loss of the Mother will certainly see her more within, thereby enjoying genuine peace. She was not an ordinary woman or a seeker on the path— not even one of those who attained the goal. She was verily a manifestation of the Divine Mother—the Primal Energy, ever perfect. She is indeed the Mother of the universe, the same as the dormant spiritual power, the indwelling spirit in every living being. Blessed is the devotee who received initiaition from her and had a taste of her utterly selfless love. The devotee who even once felt the touch of her loving hands in belssing is bound to be spiritually awakened, if he is not already awakened. This is my sincere conviction."[13]

Love for and loyalty to the leader :

Swamiji perceiving the universality and potentiality of his Master's message and its impact on the West was encouraged to set up a permanent organization which would preach, preserve and pass on the legacy of Sri Ramakrishna to the future generations. Persuaded by the leader all of the ever-trusted brother disciples unitedly and zealously devoted themselves to the Herculean task of translating the vision of their uncomromising leader into reality. One of the apostles of Sri Ramakrishna Swami Shivananda once commented :

"Only after travelling over the globe from one end to the other and scrutinizing it closely did Swamiji found this Math and Mission to carry on activities beneficial to the world and particularly to India, according to the directions of the Master. One by one, Swamiji engaged us all in these activities. If we had so wished we could very well have lived a life of exclusive contemplation and meditation in mountains and forests. As a matter of fact, most of us had been away from the monastery in differennt places, doing that to some extent. It was Swamiji who called us together and engaged us in different forms of service—the service of God in humanity. Even in our old age we have been carrying on that work."[14]

Mahapurush Maharaj used to remind the monastics and devotees of Swamiji's message : "Make the poor of humanity your God. The service of these living gods is the religion of this age." He wrote to a monk :

> May the Lord give you indomitable enthusiasm and courage! Know for certain that the Ashrama is bound to flourish. Don't worry on that score. Never forget that Swamiji said regarding work. Whatever you do in connection with the monastery or in the way of service to the country is not inferior to spiritual practice. All that you do is His work—even Japam and meditation. Never doubt this. Even as repeating His name and thinking about Him is spiritual practice, so is the service of humanity when done selflessly. You are wholly mistaken, in fact irrational if you think that you have wasted your life in doing service. Spiritual practice is not of one kind only, it is various. It is true that work brings attachment; but this Order of the Master, Holy Mother and Swamiji is different. This Order does not stand exclusively for spiritual practices—the practice of renunciation and austerity only. This Order

> has a mission that will reestablish the religion of the age. Here one must perform action along with contemplation. Those who will work at our [the disciples of the Master] direction will never get attached, The Master himself will be responsible for them.[16]

Regarding Swamiji as the commentator of the Master Swami Shivananda tried to implement his message and instructions in his personal life and at the same time persuaded the monks to honour the contribution and the teachings of Swamiji.

'a great capacity for work within' :

When Swami Shivananda as an itinerant monk reached Madras (Chennai), the news of Swamiji's historic success at the world's Parliament of Religions in Chicago (11-27 Sept, 1893) had already electrified his countrymen. Swamiji's followers were highly delighted to have Mahapurush Maharaj in Madras. They showed him Swamiji's inspiring letters written to them from the U.S.A. He attended the birth anniversary festival of Sri Ramakrishna with zealous devotees of Madras.

Swamiji wrote to the brother-disciples at Alambazar monastery in 1894.

"...I do not take into any consideration whether people accept his (the Master's) name or not, but I am ready to lay down my life to help his teachings, his life, and his message spread all over the world...

I have heard everything about Brother Tarak from Madras. They are highly pleased with him. Dear Brother Tarak, if you go to Madras and live there for some time, a lot of work will be done. But before you go, start this work there first. Can't the lady devotees convert some widows into disciples? And can't you put a bit of learning into their heads? And can't you then send them out to preach Shri Ramakrishna from door to door, and impart education alng with it?...

...The day of gossip and ceremonials is gone, my boy, you *must work now*.

...What is wanted is a power of organization—do you understand me? Have any of you got that much brain in your head? If you do let your mind work. Brother Tarak, Sharat, and Hari will be able to do it."[17]

In the same year (1894) Swamiji wrote to his beloved brother-disciple Swami Shivananda :

"...And you too have done excellently in co-operating with the Madrasis. Dear brother, I expect much from you, you should organize all for conjoint work. As soon as you have secured the land for Mother, I go to India straight, It must be a big plot, let there be a mud-house to begin with, in due course I shall erect a decent building, don't be afraid."[18]

Swamiji felt that his brother-disciples would reap good harvest if they would live and continue activities in places where he had sown the seeds of their Master's ideals. In a letter to Rakhal (Swami Brahmananda) in 1895 he wrote :

"...But in my opinion if Brother Tarak goes on starting some societies in the Punjab and Madras, and you become organized, it will be the best thing...Let Brother Tarak, as an alternative, start a Himalayan Math at Almora and have a library there so that we may spend some of our spare time in a cool place and practise spiritual exercises...Brother Tarak has a great capacity for work within him. Hence I expect much of him."[19]

Swamiji advised Mahapurushji to set up a centre at Almora which was materialized in 1916 when Swami Shivananda was the Vice-President of Ramakrishna Math and Ramakrishna Mission. On 6 May 1897 Swamiji accompanied by Swami Shivananda left for Almora to rest. There the leader taught his brother-disciple how to read other people's minds and persuaded him to preach Vedanta in Sri Lanka. Swami Shivananda's classes there were attended by many educated Hundus and Europeans. He sent Mrs. Picket one of his serious Western students to teach Vedanta in New Zealand and Australia. After a stay for about seven to eight months in the island he returned to Belur Math in February 1898. In January 1901 during their return journey from Mayavati after consoling and inspiring Mrs. Sevier, Swamiji requested his companion Mahapurus at Pilibhit to propagate the Master's message in that region and to collect some money for the monastery. Accordingly Swami Shivananda visited various places in Uttar-Pradesh for almost a year and left for Kankhal to help Swami Kalyanananda towards the end of 1901. In compliance with the advice of Swamiji and with the help of the Maharaja of Bhinga Swami Shivananda etablished a centre named *Sri Ramakrishna Advaita Ashrama* in Varanasi in 1909. During his tenure as President several centres were opened in India [i.e. Nilgiri Hills, Bombay (Mumbai)] Singapore, Europe, North America and South America. He succeeded in consolidating the activities of the Order.

Having been requested by a devotee Mr. Setlur of Bombay to send someone to Africa to look after the religious needs of the Indian emigrants there, Swamiji wrote on 27 December 1897 to his 'Mahapurush' in reference to that :

"The work will not be congenial at present. I am afraid, but it is really the work for a perfect man. You know the emigrants are not liked at all by the white people there. To look after the Indians, and at the same time maintain cool-headedness so as not to create more strife—is the work there. No immediate result can be expected, but in the long run it will prove a more beneficial work for India than any yet attempted. I wish you to try your luck in this. If you agree, please write to Setlur, about your willingness and ask for more information, mentioning this letter..."[20]

Concern for the monks and disciples :

Swami Shivananda would take care of the monks like an affectionate mother. One day he said to a senior monk, "you know, the boys living here are like young cobras [which means they possess the same deadly poison as a mature cobra]. You should not belittle them. Those who have taken refuge in the Master are great."[21]

One day some monks went to prostrate themselves before Mahapurush Maharaj. Showing a yellow rose in a flower-vase on the table he told them that only a single flower with its beauty and fragrance had charmed the ambience of the room. Similarly a genuine monk could create spiritual environment in the ashrama and attract many people.

A monk in charge of the clinic at Belur Math recollected :

"There was no end to his (Swami Shivananda's) worries when anyone happened to be sick at the Math. He would insist on having reports twice or thrice a day, eager to know how the patients were doing. Ah! How concerned he was for us! How deep was his love for us!"[22]

During the malaria season Mahapurush Maharaj used to guide the cook in preparing a suitable diet for the sick monks.

Swami Shraddhananda wrote in his diary how Swami Shivananda cordially offered the remains of his sweetmeat to his disciple Swami Ashokananda and on the day of his leaving for America encouraged him and said that he had no doubt that he would do there very well.

Mahapurush Maharaj always thought about the well being of his disciples. One day his attendant asked him why he needed to meditate so much. He replied 'Not for myself, my child. I initiate many people into spiritual life, but not all can keep up the necessary practices. Others find it possible to do so, yet make little headway, When I concentrate their faces flash before me and I pray for them, removing the obstructions to their progress."[23]

The monks, his disciples and devotees found in him a great mentor and a true sympathetic guide. The queen of Balangir, while leaving bowed down and said to Swami Shivananda in tears : "Maharaj, you have many devotees like me, but I have none like you."[24]

Deep love for brother-disciples :

The monastic-disciples of Sri Ramakrishna looked like flowers in a garland made by the Master. They were bound with a cord of love, with a bond of friendship and fellow-feeling.

Having been assured by Surendranath Mitra of regular financial support, Narendranath enthusiastically wrote to his brother-disciple Tarak living then in Vrindaban that as soon as a house would be found he would wire him to come back and take charge of the new monastery. Tarak and the elder Gopal were the first to live full time in the Ramakrishna monastery at Baranagore (1886). While living there for about two and a half years Tarak dedicated himself to sprititual practies along with consolidating the new monastery, household work, nursing the ailing monks even cleaning the toilets. In reference to amazing fraternity and mutual understanding among the brother-disciples Swami Shivananda later commented :

"We had so much deep love for each other that we were ready to sacrifice our lives for each other."

Mahapurush Maharaj used to sit under a mango tree at Belur Math in the evening and keep sharp vigil whether the monks attended the vesper rituals and prayer in the temple. One day Swami Bhaswarananda who was then a new-comer Brahmachari (celebate) and was entrusted with the duty to kindle the lamp in the evening in the room of Swamiji, had left for eating mangoes in a devotee's house at Belur and failed to discharge his duty. Mahapurush Maharaj asked another monk to kindle the lamp. When the Brahmachari appeared before him he said, "See, you are newly arrived. Religious worship should not be neglected. Today you have not lit the candle in the Swamiji's room. It's a serious offence. If you commit this again, you will be sent back home. Purification of mind and devotion could be attained through such activities."

Once after vesper Swami Swaprakashananda prostrated himself before Mahapurush Maharaj. The latter said to the former, "Have you prostrated in the Swamiji's room?' 'No, I haven't. I'm doing it right now', replied the former. Maharaj said, "Pay obeisance to him at first and then here. There is Swamiji the Shiva incarnate!'

Indomitable longing to realise God :

Swami Shivananda had a spiritual inclination in his heart since his boyhood. He was goaded by the irresistible urge to attain samadhi and by the insatiable hunger for God. He used to cry and pray to God for Samadhi and hardly slept at night. He reminisced, "In those days I felt great restlessness and longing to realize God. While walking I would practise the recollectedness of God and pray to Him earnestly. I disliked the company of people and avoided roads ordinarily frequented by travellers. Towards evening I found shelter somewhere and spent the night absorbed in my thoughts. If a person lives this way, having no possessions, he develops full resignation to God. He becomes established in the idea that God alone is his protector in prosperity as well as in adversity."[25]

Swami Prabhavananda told Swami Chetanananda at Hollywood centre that one day at Belur Math Mahapurush Maharaj was going to bow down to one of his disciples just when the latter entered his room. Timorously the disciple said, 'What are you doing Maharaj? I am a disciple of you.'

Mahapurush Maharaj said, 'I see God first then man.'

Swami Vividishananda who took formal vow of monasticism to Swami Shivananda in 1923 wrote about this God-intoxicated soul:

"For over a decade the Swami travelled in different parts of India sometimes in the Himalayas, sometimes on the plains, and sometimes in deserts or forests, and always he lived a life worthy of a man of God... Mahapurush had experienced samadhi three times as a young man during the lifetime of the Master. The austerities and meditations of his itinerant period established him in that blessed state, enriching his life and giving him the necessary depth and strength to shoulder the responsibilities of the great task ahead of him. On the anvil of those years and the ones in which he began doing works of service were forged the character and personality later adored as Mahapurush, the head of the Order, who constantly lived in God and overflowed with love and blessings to all."[26] He used to lay much importance on meditation for successful execution of all work and believed that work without spirituality was sheer garbage.

Great zeal and zest :

A tireless rover Swami Shivananda perhaps said to himself : 'I cannot rest from travel :'[27]

Feeling an irresistible urge to lead the free indifferent life of an itinerant monk, the Swami left for two famous Himalayan holy places Kedarnath and Badrinarayan in the beginning of 1889. He stayed in both the places for a few days and enjoyed the panoramic and scenic beauty and meditated in tranquility. On the way to Srinagar he came across brother-disciple Gangadhar (later, Swami Akhandananda) who had come down from Tibet. On meeting each other after a long separation they embraced and wept for joy. While staying in Almora he talked about spiritual life to some sincere seekers of truth. Towards the end of that year he returned to the Baranagore Math. In October 1891 he went on a pilgrimage and visited Prayag at the cofluence of the Ganga and Jamuna, Omkarnath Shiva on Narmada, Panchavati on Godavari, Bombay (later Mumbai) and Poona. In the early part of 1892 he came back to Alambazar where the monastery was shifted. Towards the end of March 1892 Swami Shivananda and Swami Ramakrishnananda visited Kamarpukur, the holy birth place of Sri Ramakrishna. Hearing many stories about the Master's boyhood from some villagers who had personally known him and seeing the places associated with him made him alive in their minds. They rolled on the courtyard of the Master's parental cottage. Then they went to Jayrambati, the holy birth place of the Holy Mother and stayed there a few days with her.

At the end of 1892 Mahapurush Maharaj left Alambazar Math and visited Kurukshetra, Jwalamukhi, Saroe and other places for pilgrimage in the north western region. From the middle of 1893 he stayed several months at Almora

On 2 October 1893 Mahapurush Maharaj set out for Rameswaram in South India and on his way he visited Agra, Vrindaban, Jaipur, Abu, Bombay (later Mumbai) and Madras (later Chennai) where the followers of Swamiji were elated at the presence of one of Swamiji's brother-disciples and showed him Swamiji's inspiring epistles addressed to them from America. He left Madras for some holy places like Kanchi, chidambaram, Bangalore, Madurai, Rameswaram and Sri Rangam, He attended the Ramakrishna birth anniversary festival with the Madras devotees and came back to Alambazar Monastery.

In 1895 Swami Shivananda again left the monestery and visited Khanderao Baba at Brahmavarta (Vithur) in U.P. He also met great monk namely Trailanga Swami, Swami Bhaskarananda, Chameli Puri and Magniram Brahmachari in Benares. In February he returned to Alambazar Monastery. Later he recollected his strenuous spiritual journey :

"This body did a lot of mountain climbing visited many places, and practised much austerity. There were times when I did not have more than one piece of cloth with me. Many nights I slept under a tree. I had a feeling of great dispassion and never thought about physical comfort, finding joy in austerity alone. I wandered a great deal, carrying no possessions, but was never in any trouble. The master stayed by me and protected me from all dangers and difficulties, and I never went hungry."[28]

Obedience to Law :

Swamiji imposed a rule in the monastery that all monks would have to rise at 4:00 a.m. and then after washing, meditate in the shrine, failing that they would have to beg for alms that day. One day Swami Shivananda could not get up and meditate in time. Swamiji noticed this and reminded his Tarak-da of the rule. Mahapurush Maharaj said to him, "Of course, I am leaving the monastery right now for alms, and whatever I shall get that I will eat." He went out to beg for alms and Swamiji instead of lunching with others in the dining hall, awaited him on the western verandah. When Mahapurush Maharaj came back, Swamiji gladly said, "Tarak-da, what did you bring? I have not eaten any food obtained by begging for a long time. [It is customary in India for monks to live on food obtained by begging from door to door as bees collect honey from flower to flower]. Let us share the food and eat together."[29]

Sri Ramakrishna's monastic disciples learnt from him to be well organized in their activities and to keep things in their proper places. In Belur Math Swamiji made a rule that after smoking a hubble-bubble should not be left here and there and it should be put back in a particular place. One day Swamiji saw a hubble-bubble on the front verandah of the Math and was annoyed. He came to know that Swami Shivannda had left it there. Swamiji shouted loudly, "Tarak-da!' The thunderig voice of the Swami made all even Swami Shivananda scared. No sooner did Mahapurush Maharaj appear than Swamiji threw the hubble-bubble on the floor and broke it into pieces. Then he said to his borther-disciple. "Now you collect money, buy a new hubble-bubble, and keep it in its proper place."[30] The latter accepted the order tamely.

Phenomenal humility : A tree laden with fruits bends :

Swami Shivananda was a simple-hearted guileless humble monk. He was completely free from egoism and considered himself an instrument in the hands of Sri Ramakrishna. It was previously mentioned that while President of the Ramakrishna Order one day he commented : "The Master is an expert player. He can win the game with a valueless cowrie [shell coin in ancient India]. What do I have ? Neither have I learning nor intellect, neither am I a speaker nor am I good-looking; Still the Master is using me as an insturment for doing his work."[31]

While staying at Ootacumund in 1926 one morning Swami Shivananda accompanied by his attendant went for a stroll. On the way he saw a western woman who was a Christian missionary. He heartily said 'Good morning' to her. But casting him a scornful look and then turning her face she left the place without returning the greeting. The service of the Ramakrishna Mission among the poor in the Nilgiri Hills caused anger of the evangelists The attendant monk was unhappy and said, "Maharaj why did you greet her? She left, humiliating you!" Swami Shivananda replied, "It does not matter. One should respect women of all countries. The Divine Mother manifests in all women of the world."[32]

Love of nature :

The snow-capped Himalayas with its lofty peaks, amazing vastness, magnificent grandeur and all-pervading tranquility attract people particularly the monks in all ages. The holy places there though inaccessible are hospitable to them for realizing the truths of Vedanta in the midst of sublime beauty. While visiting the shrine of Kedarnath the beauty of the never-ending snow range overwhelmed Swami Shivananda who stayed there a few days. With reference to the beauty of Badrinarayan he wrote to Swami Brahmananda : "It has been fourdays since I arrived at Badrinarayan– a beautiful place situated right on the bank of the river Alakananda, surrounded by snow peaks. Here the Alakananda flows through snow. In certain spots the river is so wholly covered with snow that the water is not visible at all."[33]

Swami Shivananda's frequent visits (in 1889, 1893, 1894) to the Himalayas testifies to his special liking for the king of the mountains. While visiting the Ramakrishna Mission cnetre at Kankhal he was charmed by the superb panorama of the snow-clad mountains and commented : "For years I haven't seen snow. So Shiva, the Lord of the mountains, has been gracious to reveal himself in his white form today! Ah, how magnificent it is! Without snow the Himalayas do not look right."[34]

Magnanimous personality :

The enchanting personality and ideal spiritual life of Swami Shivananda made people more interested in the ideals and activities of the Order and many zealous young men deeply moved by his talks joined the Order. While staying at Almora in 1893 Swami Shivananda happened to meet an English theosophist E.T. Sturdy who was leading the life of a Hindu monk and practising yoga in that region. He was deeply impressed by the graceful personality of Mahapurush Maharaj.

Swami Shivananda tried to manage the Order through his spiritual power as well as his captivating personality. In Benares one evening a brahmachari was unwilling to work according to the Swami's advice. Later the young brahmacharin was repentant and said : "Maharaj, you alone know what is best for me. I am ready to do whatever you want me to do. " The Swami with great tenderness replied : "That's right. You have rightly understood. It will certainly be good for you if you listen to us and follow our instructions implicitly. Whatever we say comes directly from Sri Ramakrishna. These days I live wholly united with the Master."[35]

One day a senior monk requested Swami Shivananda to take disciplinary action against an unruly monk and expel him from the Order. The Swami listened to the allegations attentively and then said to the accuser, "Does he not have one or two good qualities?" When the complainant mentioned a couple of the monk's good qualities, the Swami gladly said, "That is enough!" The accused monk was exempted from punishment.

As a Vedantist Swami Shivananda was indrawn and contemplative by nature and at the same time resolute and impregnable He off and on intimated to the monks their vow and ideals: "Renunciation of lust and gold! If you can renounce lust of the flesh and the greed for wealth, everything will be right... Above everything, a monk should observe the vow of chastity and poverty...Purity and guilelessness should be your watchwords The Master forgives all failings except hypocrisy and self-deception. Those who play false and take to hypocritical ways do not belong here. The Master does not allow them to remain in the Order; he removes them. Only those who are genuine can stay."[36]

As a man Mahapurush Maharaj was affectionate and softhearted. During malaria season he used to go to the kitchen to guide the cook in preparing a suitable diet for the sick monks. Once a monk saw the President himself carrying an orange in his hand for a Western woman who was sick in the Belur guest house. Even animals and birds were not deprived of his motherly affection. He used to feed the cows and pat them and watch the birds eating grain on the roof adjacent to his room.

Mahapurushji was judicious and outspoken. Swami Prabhavananda persuaded by Sister Lalita (Mrs. Carrie Wyckoff) started a Vedanta Centre in Hollywood a part of Los Angeles (U.S.A). Swami Paramananda had already set up a centre in Los Angeles.

Sister Devamata (Laura Glenn) requested Mahapurushji to stop Swami Prabhavananda's activities in that same city. Mahapurushji replied "Paramananda does not own the city of Los Angeles."

Though Swami Shivananda was not a reputed orator, his on-the-earth simplicity and inspiring heart-to-heart talks roused spiritual hunger in the minds of the votaries. One day in Dhaka a devotee said to Mahapurushji then the Vice-President of the Order, "Maharaj, we are poor. Will you be kind enough to visit our home in spite of that?" Mahapurushji answered, "You are right. We don't go to the house of a poor person." The devotee left for home depressed. The next day the Swami with his attendant walked two miles to that devotee's house. The man was amazed by their generosity and rejoiced, "What great fortune! Maharaj, welcome to our poor home." Mahapurushji said smilingly, "We do not go to the house of a poor person. We visit the devotee's house that is God's dwelling place—and that is the house of the richest person."[37]

Swami Gahanananda remarked about Mahapurushji : "He stands as a shining personality among the monastic disciples of Sri Ramakrishna...."[38]

Free from egotism :

Though Swami Shivananda, with the help of his profound realization and experience could solve both scriptural questions and the monks' spiritual problems, considered himself an instrument of Sri Ramakrishna. One day in reply to a question about rebirth he said to Swami Nikhilananda, "I am not a scholar. I do not know the scriptures. Can you tell me what is the cause of rebirth? Is it not unfulfilled desires?"[39]

Mahapurushji was completely free from ego and guile. He wrote to a monk, "Spiritual practice is not of one kind only; it is various. It is renunciation of the ego or the self." He advised his disciples and devotees to be docile and submissive to the Master. Once Swami Satprakashananda said to Swami Shivananda, 'Maharaj, some take initiation from the Holy Moher and others from Swami

Brahmananda. Is there any difference between the two?" He replied, "No I do not see any difference whatsoever—the same Ganges water is coming out of two taps. The same grace of the Master is flowing out through the Holy Mother and Maharaj, the One Substance is in two receptacles. But look here, what do you mean by "taking initiation"? They receive it. It is given, it is given.'[40] Thus Mahapurushji taught Swami Satprakashananda who was initiated into sannyasa by the former in 1927 a lesson of submission and the latter admitted that as soon as he had heard those words his inner eyes were opened with regard to initiation and a great problem was solved for him. Swami Shivananda was so cautious about coinage.

Humanity :

Swami Shivananda was very concerned for each of the inmates of the Belur Math and was worried about those who fell ill. The monk in charge of the free clinic and dispensary at Belur Math reminisced :

"It was the rainy season. All around there was sickness, especially malarial fever. The number of outside patients visiting the clinic was growing fast. To make the situation worse the compounder [pharmacist] assisting me fell ill. I found it very difficult to manage the work alone. One day Mahapurush dropped in at the clinic and after hearing the report of the work said : " I see that you are having a hard time doing the work by yourself. Shall I help you a little?" In reply I said : " Why, Maharaj? No. That is not necessary. Please bless me that I may manage it myself."[41]

Once Swami Shivananda and his companions Swamis Shravananda and Bodhanada were invited for lunch by a devotee. While leaving Mahapurushji happened to notice some poor hungry people in the alley fighting for the leftover food. Deeply pained by the sight he asked his host to feed them and reminded him of the message of his leader Swamiji "Make the poor of humanity your God. The service of these living gods is the religion of this age."

Swami Shivananda advised the monks to devote more time to japam and meditation, simultaneously to serve ailing humanity.

Reminding a monk of Swamiji's message he wrote: "Whatever you do in connection with the monastery or in the way of service to the country is not inferior to spiritual practice."[42]

While staying in a retreat centre of the Ramakrishna Order at Jamtara (Jharkhand) for a few days in 1926 once the President Maharaj arranged a feast for the poor tribal people and was greatly delighted to see them enjoying their food. He exclaimed, "Ah! they are the veritable manifestations of the Lord."

The Swami from the upper verandah used to watch how Purna Haldar an old and feeble fisherman from Bally failed most of the time to catch sufficient fish in the Ganga to provide the members of his family with meagre meal The Swami's heartfelt sympathy would go out to him and he asked the monk in charge of the kitchen to buy whatever Purna caught and to pay him generously. Besides, the Swami often used to give him cloth and other things. Even as soon as Mahapurushji heard about his death, he immediately sent sufficient money and clothes to his widow so that she could perform obsequies for her deceased husband. Afterwards he sent money to the poor widow regularly.

One morning Mahapurushji asked the attendant to see if there was someone who wanted initiation. Going downstairs the attendant found a woman who wanted initiation. The young village-lady confessed that though born in a brahmin family, she had kept evil company and gave about herslf. She was eager to see Mahapurushji once. The attendant reluctantly said, "Maharaj, it is a lady who wants initiation, but..," Before the attendant could finish what he felt he must disclose, the Swami said, "What of that? Ask her to bathe in the Ganga and come to me after visiting the shrine. Sri Ramakrishna is the redeemer of the fallen. He came especially to uplift them. What will happen to them if he does not come to their rescue? One could not then call him the saviour of the fallen."

When after bath and visit to the shrine, the lady came to Swami Shivananda for initiation, he said, as if he knew everything about him "What is there to fear, my daughter? You will certainly be blessed, since you have taken refuge in Sri Ramakrishna our Master and saviour. Say this : 'Whatever sins I have committed in this life and in lives past I offer them here [i.e. to the Master] and I will sin no more.'

The forgiveness and blessing of the Swami brought about a sea-change in the nature and life of the lady.

One noon after lunch Swami Shivananda noticed a cobbler mending shoes under a mango tree in the monastery courtyard. Sensing his hunger the Swami asked his attendant to give him a good quantity of offered fruits and sweets. The Swami dropped a half rupee coin from the window for the poor man who overwhelmed with joy and gratefulness saluted him with folded hands and put the coin in his pocket. Besides the Swami scolded a monk for bargaining with the poor cobbler regarding the charge for the work done.

Maharpurushji forgave a thief who entered the room of Josephine MacLeod (Joe) an American devotee of Swamiji and snatched her locket reliquary containing hair of Swamiji.

Mind soaring up towards the absolute :

Swami Shivananda, a *Jivanmukta* (one who is free while living) who continuously lived in God-consciousness, had to strive to keep his mind on the relative plane so that he could help others. During the day he would have many things namely a stick, a musical instrument, the Gospel of Sri Ramakrishna, the Gita, the Chandi, Sanskrit texts and Bengali folk tales as well as much illustrated books. To satisfy the curiousity of the monks about such child-like practice he said : "My mind wants to rush towards the Absolute all the time. That is why I am trying with all these trifling diversions to hold my mind down. Just as a mother gives her child toys to keep it engaged, so I am also trying by various means to make my mind forget the Absolute."[43]

Conscious of the distinction of his own body :

Swami Shivananda whose mind was full of Sri Ramakrishna, was satisfied with the holiness and utility of his mortal body. One day he said to a monk pointing to his own body : "This is not just an ordinary body; it has its own distinction. God-realization has been attained in and through this body. This body had touched Bagavan Sri Ramakrishna, lived with him, served him. The Master has made this body a vehicle for the propagation of his message for this age. Otherwise this body is nothing but a cage of flesh and blood. ... Should he feel it necessary to maintain this body longer, he will do so. Else, I am ready to depart at his first call. I am waiting for his call."[44]

To sum up, Swami Gahanananda eulogised, "Swami Shivananda exemplified in his own life how intense inner spirituality and outer dynamism can be harmoniously blended. He stands as a shining personality among the monatic disciples of Sri Ramakrishna, in whom the 'Math' and 'Mission' aspects of the Order were harmonized in a very happy and potent fashion."[45]

Chapter – 7

SWAMI PREMANANDA

Sri Ramakrishna himself begged a woman for her son : "Will you give me your son? I want a pure-hearted boy to live here. I am greatly pleased even when he gives me a glass of water."

This very handsome little boy at the age of four or five would strongly protest against marriage if he were teased about it : 'Don't say that! Oh, don't make me marry! I would die."[1]

When he was eight, the boy used to fancy he would live in a hut with another monk and meditate on God in a beautiful wooded place by the Ganga.

This pure-hearted boy of religious inclination was Baburam second son of Taraprasanna Ghosh and Matangini Devi. He was born on 10 December 1861 in an aristocratic and well-off family at Antpur, Hooghly.

Auspicious signs of Spirituality :

During Baburam's first visit (probably on 8 April 1882) to Dakshineswar, Sri Ramakrishna after some introductory conversation caught hold of his hand and told him to go closer to the light. In order to judge his spirituality the Master examined his face hands and feet. Then he weighed the newcomer's forearm by placing it on his palm and felt it lighter than ordinary. Observing the auspicious signs the Master exclaimed in delight : 'Very good, very good.' On other occasions the Master identified Baburam as a *nityasiddha* (ever-perfect soul) and one of his six ishwarakoti (Godlike soul) disciples namely Narendra, Rakhal, Yogin, Niranjan and Purna. About Baburam's purity, he would say, "He is pure, pure to the very marrow of his bones."[2]

A part of Radha :

Sri Ramakrishna realized in an ecstatic mood that Baburam was a part of Radha, the spiritual consort of Lord Krishna. On 20 June 1884 he said to M (Mahendranath Gupta), "I noticed the other day that Baburam, Bhavanath and Harish have a feminine nature. In a vision I saw Baburam as a goddess with a necklace around her neck and with women companions about her. He has received something in a dream. His body is pure. Only a very little effort will awaken his spiritual consciousness... Baburam says that he too likes the womanly attitude."[3]

When Baburam, with some of his brother disciples took formal sannyasa performing *viraja homa* at the Baranagore Monastery in the third week of January 1887, Narendranath gave him the name 'Premananda' meaning "bliss of divine love' remembering the Master's comment that Sri Radha the goddess of love herself was partially incarnated in him.

In the last week of July 1918 seriously ill Premananda said to Swami Saradananda, "You know, I have a great desire to put on a cloth of pure yellow and to eat rice white as jasmine.' That is a symbolic description of Sri Radha and Swami saradananda realized the significance of the words and understood that his brother-disciple would depart soon.

The Master's love for Baburam :

On June 20, 1884 Sri Ramakrishna said to M. "Tell me, does Baburam intend to continue his studies? I said to him, 'Continue your studies to set an example to others.'...

"You see, I am having some diffficulty about my physical needs. It will be nice if Baburam lives with me..."[4]

Swami Premananda reminisced : "The Master used to cry whenever I left Dakshineswar to return to calcutta, Oh, how can I explain to you how much he loved us!... One day he was found waiting outside Balaram babu's house where I was staying. Balaram Babu was not at home, and the Master was hesitant to go inside, thinking he might not be welcomed. He had come to see me. Someone finally called him in. His love knew no bounds, and one drop of it completely filled us.'[5]

In fact, Swami Premananda had the treasure of his own to make him one of the beloved of the Master.

One day Pratapchandra Hazra was insisting some young boys including Baburam on pressing the Master to get some power, wealth etc from him. Hearing his words Sri Ramakrishna ordered Baburam to come to his room and forbade to listen to the calculating advice of Hazra. He said to him : "The beggar pesters the rich man, saying, 'Sir, give me a pice! Give me a pice'. Being disgusted with the beggar, the rich man throws a small coin to him, saying, 'Take this and get out of here.' you are my very own. You will not have to ask for anything from me. Whatever I have, it is all yours."[6]

Sri Ramakrishna could not normally take any food if it was cooked by a nonbrahmin or touched by an impure person. But one day he asked Baburam who was a nonbrahmin, to cook food for him and he ate from his disciple's hand.

One day Swamiji ordered his disciple to drag Swami Premananda from the bed as he was sleeping (perhaps he had no sleep last night) in the afternoon violating the rule. The disciple carried out the order. Premananda woke up and understood that Swamiji was the ringleader. So he did not scold the disciple. After vespers, seeing Swami Premananda Swamiji embraced him and said, "Brother, our Master used to treasure you in his heart, and I am such a person that I asked you be dragged from your bed! I am not fit to live here."[7]

Then he began to sob constantly.

Swami Premananda's love for the Master :

Baburam used to give personal service to Sri Ramakrishna such as massaging his body with oil before his bath, preparing tobacco and betel-rolls, making his bed, fanning him in need and sweeping the floor. He would accompany the Master whenever he visited the houses of the devotees or theatres in Kolkata.

One day Swami Premananda fell form a tree while plucking flowers and fractured his right wrist. But he forgot his pain by thinking of Sri Ramakrishna.

While living in Alambazar Monastery Swami Premananda left for Dakshineswar frequently to meditate and practise japam either in the Master's room or in the Panchavati for long hours forgetting food and rest as he lived in the memory of the Master.

Reminiscing about the past days in Alambazar Monastery, Swami Turiyananda wrote to Swami Premananda on 20 November 1915 : "The memory of all past associations with you gives me great joy. And why shouldn't it be so? You are so full of the Master that there is no room within you for anything else. This reminds me of an incident that took place at the Alambazar Monastery. As you spoke that day, you invoked the memory of the Master in all visible things. At that time I observed in you the truth of this saying, 'Wherever the eyes fall, there the Lord manifests.' You did not see anything that did not remind you of the Master. I don't know whether you remember it or not, but it is indelibly imprinted on my mind. That day I realized what it is to be merged in God."[8]

Swami Premananda's love for the Master was indescribable and unfathomable. Swami Rameswarananda recollected:

"His (Swami Premanada's) service to the Master was living, as if he could see the Master rising from bed, washing his mouth, eating his meals, resting in his bed, and walking in the garden. He would instruct the monks : cut the overgrowth of the thorny rose plants, otherwise they will stick to the cloth of the Master. Watch so that he may not find difficulty walking in the monastery compound. Don't put too much lime in the betel-roll-it will burn the tongue of the Master. He preferred to eat warm food; don't serve cold food to him. When you make sandalpaste for worship, there should not be any rough particles in it. In Dakshineswer the Master loved flowers and the sweet fragrance of incense; therefore, decorate the Master's shrine with flowers and burn incense. Putting the Master to bed, drop the mosquito curtain, and mentally massage his feet. Keep a glass of water on a stool next to the Master's bed, if by chance he gets up he may drink it. Change the cloth on the Master's picture on the altar every day.

"In 1916-17 I used to perform worship in the shrine. One day Swami Premananda asked me: "Is the clothing of the Master okay? My boy, look carefully. After offering a new cloth to the Master, I was about to put it on; then the Master told me through a vision, 'Baburam, you are going to have a new cloth, and my shirt is torn. Don't you love me any more?' Then both of us went to the shirne and found that the Master's shirt had been chewed by a mouse."[9]

How incredible Swami Premananda's love for the Master was!

Swami Premananda's love for the Mother :

Swami Premananda's love for and devotion to the Mother was legendary. Once Sri Ramakrishna complained to the Holy Mother that her indiscreet affection might destroy Baburam's future life by giving him six chapatis instead of four. The Mother firmly answred: "Why are you so much worried because he had a couple more chapatis? I shall look after his future. Please don't make an issue about his food." Thus Baburam received incessant blessing and assurance from the mother.

In 1896 while staying at Jayrambati for a couple of weeks once Swami Premananda during his walk, saw beautiful lotuses in a pond. Out of great devotion to the Mother he got into the water and picked some lotuses to offer to her. When he came out of the water, his companion Brahmachari Kalikrishna (later, Swami Virajananda) noticed that nearly twenty leeches were attached to his body to suck blood. He began to bleed as soon as they were removed. Learning about the incident the Mother was anxious and warned him never to do such a thing again.

Swami Premananda was one of the few fortunate disciples of Sri Ramakrishna having free access to the Mother who was very fond of him. Whenever any monk would go to visit her at Udbodhan, Premanandaji would send flowers, vegetables and milk for her asking the monk to convey his salutations to her. He believed that the Master and Holy Mother were like the two sides of one and the same coin and who differentiated between the Master and his consort would never make any spiritual progress. One day at Belur Math he said to the devotees : "We have seen that she had a much greater capacity than the Master. She was the embodiment of Power, and how well she controlled it! Sri Ramakrishna could not do so, though he tried. His power became manifest through his frequent ecstasies, which were seen by all. The Mother repeatedly experienced samadhi, but others did not know of it. What wonderful self-control she exercised! She covered herself with a veil, like a young bride in her husband's home. The people of Jayrambati thought she was busy day and night looking after her nephews and nieces."[10]

Swami Premananda wrote an emotional as well as substantial long letter to Surendra (Probably Surendranath Mitra, one of the house holder devotees and chief suppliers of stores of the Master) in which he placed Holy Mother before Sita, Savitri, Vishnupriya and Radha and admired her incredible greatness, sacrifice and indiscriminate affection.

Loyalty to and love for the leader :

According to one of the rules introduced by Swamiji in Alambazar Monastery, if a monk did not get up early in the morning, he had to beg for his food that day. One day Swami Premananda woke up late and said to Swamiji, "I am sorry I did not get up early today; brother, you made the rule that one should be punished for that reason. Please punish me." Swamiji replied, "Baburam, could you imagine that I would punish you?" Tears trickled down his cheeks. Swami Brahmananda negotiated the situation saying, "It is not a question of punishment. According to the rule, one is supposed to beg food that day that's all."[11] Swami Premananda left to abide by the rule.

Swami Premananda was so full of the Master that he would discharge the responsibility of the worship service with great care and caution. One day swamiji said to him, "Brother all these days you have been worshipping the Lord with flowers and sandal paste; now start worshipping the living gods Go to Belur village and serve the poor and the afflicted." Swami Premananda left for Belur village to obey his leader's order. There he offered an old sick widow treatment from the monastery's charitable dispensary but she refused his help. Then he brought a few unwashed children to the monastery, cleaned them with soap and water, fed them and sent them back to their homes. He said to Swamiji about his experinece: "When I was serving them, I felt I was actually serving the Master through living gods."[12]

In Belur once Sharat Chandra Chakrabarty, to materialise his dream, worshipped his Guru Swamiji's feet in the flower tray meant for the Master's worship. Swamiji had to acquiesce. Seeing Swami Premananda, Swamiji with uneasiness said to him, "Look what a sacrilege he has committed! With the articles of the Master's worship, he has worshipped me." Swami Premananda, smiling quipped, "Well done! Are you and the Master different?"[13]

Swami Brahmananda visited Varanasi several times. In 1914 Swami Premananda went to Varanasi to bring Swami Brahmananda back to Belur Monastery. But Maharaj was not willing to leave the city of Lord Shiva. Swami Premananda said, "But Maharaj, Swamiji is our Lord Shiva, and he resides in Belur,"

Love for brother disciples :

When Swami Brahmananda or any other direct disciples of Sri Ramakrishna were at Belur Monastery, Swami Premananda advised the young monks to meet and serve them. He said to the monks, "Having the company of God, they have become gods. They are not ordinary people. Your life will be blessed if you associate with them and serve them."

Once during Durga Puja in Belur Monastery the monks were singing devotional songs. Swami Premananda suddenly became God-intoxicated and elated by divine delight. He insisted Swami Saradananda on singing a song to complete that flow of joy. The latter protested that he had not sung for a long time. But he could not avoid his unyielding brother's earnest request and had to sing and dance with his heavy body. He commented, "Alas, Brother Baburam made me dance in my old age."[14]

Once during the Shivaratri festival Swami Premananda, addressing Swami Shivananda said, "This is our Lord Shiva! Brother Tarak is our Shiva!'

One day M, the chronicler of the Gospel of Sri Ramakrisha visited Belur Monastery to pay homage to the Master on his birth anniversary He was unwell. After saluting the Master he sat under the mango tree in the courtyard. He carried some puffed rice for refreshment and enquired of a young monk if there was any curd in the storeroom. The monk found a pot of curd in the storeroom but he could not give it to M. for it had not been offered to the Master. Learning from the monk that M. needed curd, Swami Premananda at once standing in front of the Master's picture in the shrine offered the pot of curd to him and then gave it to the monk to serve M. Swami Premananda emotionally said to a monk, "Today the Master saved me from a grave error. Do you know M. was an intimate companion of the Master? The Master eats food through the mouths of these devotees. Have you not read in the Gospel, where the Master says that if you feed one of them, you will attain virtue equivalent to feeding one thousand monks? In the Ramakrishna incarnation, M. is the Sage Vyasa (the recorder) and again the Sage Narada (the singer). Day and night the gospel of the Master comes from his lips like a fountain. The Master saved me today from a serious mistake,"[15]

In January 1916 while visiting East Bengal Swami Brahmananda and Swami Premananda stayed a few days at Agnes villa Dhaka.

One day Dinesh Chandra Das Gupta (afterwards Swami Nikhilananda) with two members of their revolutionary society went to them. Learning from Swami Premananda that they had become revolutionaries with a view to serve their motherland, Swami Brahmananda advised them to give up the method of violence, to follow the instructions of Swamiji and to first mould their character and only then to take up the service of India. He said, "If gunpowder is damp it will not explode. However you may try to ignite it, you will only be wasting match sticks. But if the powder is dry, one match will be enough to produce the explosion." "But sir" Dineshchandra interrupted, "You have not understood Swami Vivekananda. We read in his books that he wants us to shed our blood for India's freedom. That is what the revolutionaries are doing. You have not understood Swami Vivekananda's teachings." Swami Premananda could not bear with such insolent remark about his brother-disciple and roared, "You idiot! You do not know with whom you are talking. We knew Swamiji for over twenty years. We ate together, played together, talked together, and discussed our plans of work together—and we have not understood him! And you fools have read a few pages of his books and understood him completely!" Then addressing Swami Brahmananda, he said "Maharaj, did you hear that? He said that you did not understand Swamiji. Do you think he has the intelligence of a horse? Let me see if he can carry me on his back!" [16]

Leaving his bed Swami Premananda asked the young man to go down on all fours. He did as he was ordered. Sitting on his back, with his feet hanging down on both sides, Swami Premananda directed him to take him ronud the room. The revolutionist obeyed the order. After a minute or two getting off Swami Premananda told him that every thing would be all right. That very year (1916) he forsaking his connection with the revolutionary society, was initiated by the Holy Mother.

Letters of Swami Premananda manifest his love and respect for his brother-disciples. On 27 April 1916 he wrote to a disciple of the Holy Mother how in Baranagore Math he would feed good something to his brother disciples whenever he would have it and they also thrust it into his mouth holding his hands and legs tightly and how he would rush to Kolkata if he would miss Naren a day and how much attraction and affection for his brother disciples Swamiji showered. He wrote how he would feel distressd when Raja Maharaj left for somewhere. On 27 March 1917 he wrote to a devotee to write to Sri Hari Maharaj (Swami Turiyananda) whom he described as a "versed in scriptures' and "endowed with divine grace through austere religious practice." On 29 March 1917 he made almost the same comment about Swami Turiyananda in a letter to another devotee. In some letters he expressed deep anxiety over the illness of Hari Maharaj in Puri. He often reminded the monks and devotees of Swamiji's dream and message.

An embodiment of service :

Swamiji asked Swami Premananda to manage Belur Math, the headquarters of the Ramakrishna Order and the latter obeyed the leader. In fact, he had to take charge of Belur Math whenever Swami Brahmananda, the President of the Order visited other centres to give initiation and to strengthen the organization. Despite his fragile body, he spontaneously shouldered various responsibilities e.g. to worship regularly in the shrine, to train the monks, to entertain the devotees and visitors, to look after the sick monks, to set out for delivering lectures, to collect money for the maintenance of the Math, to supervise the kitchen, dairy and garden.

The Swami would up-root weeds from the courtyard, cut fodder for the cows and mix coal dust with cowdung to make balls for fuel. Like his Master he could not tolerate any wastage and would remind the monks that all necessaries were bought with the devotees' hard-earned money.

As a strict disciplinarian Swami Premananda lived a routine-life He would rise at 3:00 or 3:30 a.m. After washing, he would go to the shrine to perform the morning service to the Master and to meditate with the monks for a couple of hours. Then, if Swami Brahmananda was at Belur, he with them would go to his room to pay obeisance to him and join devotional singing. At 8:00 a.m. Swami Premananda would instruct the monks to do their respective duties. He himself would cut and clean vegetables with some monks for lunch. After having a bath in the Ganga he would worship the Master and then meditate for at least half an hour and offer flowers to the Mother Ganga. Then he would take some prasad and would talk about the teachings of the Master if there were any devotees and guests. At 11:30 a.m. he would offer food to the Master and then eat his lunch. After a little rest he would answer letters and give a class to the monks. In the afternoon he would go for a stroll and in the evening he would perform the vesper service and would dive deep in meditation Then he would join the monks and devotees in the visitors' room, where there was either devotional singing or reading and discussion from the works of Swami Vivekananda or he would reminisce about the Master. When the bell for food offering was rung, the Swami would go to the shrine to offer food to the Master and then closing the shrine for the day, he would eat supper. Before going to bed at 11:00 p.m. he would see if the visiting devotees had beds to sleep on and were properly cared for. Thus he taught more through the example of his duty-bound life than through his words. He would say, "All work here is sacred, whether you cut vegetables, whether you prepare cowdung balls, whether you go out to give lectures or worship in the chapel—everything is service unto the Lord. You have to learn to do every thing with an equal sense of reverence and sanctity in your heart."[17]

> Holy Mother said to the devotees, "Baburam was dearest to my heart. All the energy devotion and wisdom of Belur Math were embodied in my Baburam and walked there on the bank of the Ganges."[18]

Mother of Belur Math :

Sri Ramakrishna used to say, "Bhagavata–Bhakta–Bhagavan—the scripture, the devotee, and God—all three are the same." Swami Premananda told the monks that service to the Master and service to the devotees are not different. He considered it a great honour and opportunity for the monks to serve devotees with food and love and spirituality.

Swami Premananda as a true devotee of God, was devoted to the devotees of God. He received all devotees even who came to the Math at odd times cordially. He was hospitality personified. Devotees would sometime come after dinner was over and the Swami himself would go to the kitchen to prepare food for them. When the monks came forward to start cooking, he would say, "You have worked so hard, let me cook." Sometimes he gave his own food to the devotees coming at unsuitable time only to remain himself starving. Once some devotees came with a baby who was crying for food. The Swami at once set aside some milk for the Master's offering and gave the rest to the child. Once at midnight he noticed a devotee from Chennai sleeping on the upstairs verandah. He forthwith rigged up a mosquitonet over his bed and began to fan him. One day many devotees before entering the shrine left their shoes in the courtyard. In the meantime it started raining. A brahmacharin began to lift those shoes with his foot to bring them to the verandah. Catching the sight and realizing the Brahmacharin's superiority complex the Swami said to him, "Carry the devotees' shoes on your head."[19] If the young monks complained about the heavy load of work regarding hospitality; Swami Premananda would say, "Look, people suffer so much in the world. They come to Sri Ramakrishna's place to get some peace. It is your duty to make them feel welcome. It will be of great benefit to you, it will be of great benefit to them."[20]

Once in the meeting of the board of trustees Swami Brahmananda, learning from the financial report that there was a four hundred rupee deficit asked his brother-disciple Swami Premananda how they would tackle that deficit. The latter replied that he had spent that money for serving the devotees, so he would collect it by begging. On another occasion Swami Shuddhananda proposed to Swami Brahmananda that there should be some rules and regulations about the devotees' staying in Belur Math. Swami Premananda retorted, "Look Suddhananda, as long as we are alive, let it continue this way; when we die, you can open a hotel for the devotees.... It is the Master who brings the devotees and they bring everything for him. Likewise, it is the Master who is eating and also who is feeding the devotees. What can we say about it?"[21]

Swami Premananda, with his love, sympathy and spiritual power was able to change the nature and character of an aberrated young man who eventually renounced the world and became a monk of the Ramakrishna Order.

A few days before his passing away Swami Premananda said to Bahmachari Jnana who was then supervising the Math, "Remember, let there be no negligence towards the devotees."[22] The Swami's last wish testifies to his immeasurable love and concern for the devotees. M. described him as 'Sri Ramkrishna's love aspect'[23] while Swami Brahmananda lamented, "Belur Math has lost its mother."[24]

A good trainer :

When Baburam begged the Master to procure ecstasy for him, the devine Mother warned Sri Ramakrishna that Baburam was destined to have Jnana (knowledge) and not Bhava (emotional absorption in God). In the early days of the Order particularly after the passing away of Swamiji, Swami Premananda had to look up some jobs namely training and orientation and building up of character of the brahmacharins along with imprinting the ideas and spirit of practical Vedanta on their minds. Swami Premananda inspired the monks to practise this great ideal preached by Swamiji and build their character. In his time many young men joined the Order and accepeted the ideal of worship of God through the service of man. Many among them showed their marvellous efficiency and dynamic personality. For this astonishing achievement, 'at least fifty percent of the credit should go to him', commented Swami Ashokananda in his book 'Swami Premananda' (p.27)

Swami Premananda possessed love purity, renunciation and knowledge all the essential qualities of an ideal trainer of monks. Though he did not have much formal education his close association with the Master and Swamiji compensated the lack of formal education. Once he himself said to a young man, "My boy, whatever learning we needed, the Master gave us. We don't need any degrees."[25]

There goes a proverb : 'Example is better than precept.' Swami Premananda taught more through the example of his dedicated life than through his words. His magnetic personality not only attracted people to Belur Math but fascinated the monks also.

Swami Premananda tried to ignite the spirit of love, renunciation humanity and above all devotion to God into the monks. He said to them: "Never forget that the goal of human life is to realize God, to have his vision. That is why you have renounced hearth and home. Struggle hard to have love and devotion for him. Yearn for him with a longing heart. You are men. Be gods! Teach others by the example of your own life. I see very clearly that after we are gone, multitudes will come to learn from you young men."

When a young monk said to the Swami "who will listen to us?" he replied, "Don't think that you are inferior to us. You have received the grace of the Holy Mother. Do you think we have become great just because people take the dust of our feet? No! We first saw Sri Ramakrishna and then renounced the world; you are great indeed because you have renounced the world without seeing him !" He added : "The Master did not make us great, he made us 'nobodie's. You also have to become 'nobodies'. Wipe out all vanity from the mind. The Master used to say, 'When the ego dies, all troubles cease.' 'Not I, not I but Thou, O Lord,"[26] Thus he was an inspirer of souls. Swami Premananda tried to inculcate a sense of responsibility in the monks and laid great stress on humility and perfection of work. He said to the monks, "My boys, one day you will have to do very responsible things. If you don't learn the habit of responsibility in big things, You will cheat."[27]

As a good guide the Swami had to play the roles of an affectionate mother and a chastising father as well. He scolded the monks to correct their faults and carelessness or indifference towards their work. He did not take time to forgive and forget their shortcoming.

Swami Gnaneswarananda reminisced three incidents with reference to his stren attitude. One day as the former said that he had read the Bhagavad Gita Swami Premananda at once said to him, "My boy, say I am reading it. Never say I have read the Gita. One can never finish reading the Gita."

Once Gnaneswarananda with some other monks was weeding the Math garden. Swami Premananda noticed that one of them was not pulling the weeds out by the roots. He said to him, "My boy, you must pull the weed out by the roots, otherwise you are simply fooling yourself and wasting time. If you do not realize the necessity of rooting out weeds in the garden how can you weed out your old faults and tendencies? How can you understand the real meaning of spiritual life?"

Another day the Swami rebuked them for talking too much : "You talkative fools! You talk nothing but nonsence. Let not your tongue talk; let your character speak! Why do you buzz so much? You bees evidently heaven't yet found the honey,"[28] Swami Gnaneswarananda noted that Swami Premananda was loving to all.

Once Swami Premananda asked a brahmacharin to cut fodder for the cows. He started his duty with cutting his finger owing to overconfidence. Noticing the bleeding finger the swami said, "You are careless! I asked you to cut the fodder, not your finger. Didn't I? You can see your finger bleed. But do you know how it makes another's heart bleed? I thought you were a very clever boy, but you have proved yourself a fool and me a greater one. Shame on you! you considered the work very trivial![29] Saying that he took the boy to the dispensary and his finger was bandaged.

One day a monk in charge of the kitchen store, fell a few drops of oil on the floor while pouring. Swami Premananda saw it and said to him : "Why are you wasting the Master's oil? The devotees donate their hard-earned money for the Master's service. You will not have to work here anymore. I bow down to you." Saying this he bent his head and left the place. The monk was scared. Though he discharged his responsibilites, he ate nothing for a few days except for driking Ganga water. Learning about it the Swami embraced the monk and said : "Are you mad at me? Who else do I have other than you? If you do not do right, shall I not scold you? Know for certain, a monk's scolding purifies the mind." Then Swami Premananda gave him prasad and freed him from strain.

The swami encouraged the monks to practise all four yogas–Karma, Jnana, bhakti and raja. A monk said, "By his eloquent and impassioned appeals he would firmly impress upon the novitiates the high ideals of Sri Ramakrishna and Swami Vivekananda. As he held out vividly before their imagination the wonderful renunciation of the Master, his keen thirst for God-realization, his unheard-of devotion to truth, his strenuous religious practices and austerities, his wonderful realizations and his profound love and kindness for his disciples— he would appear to be lifted out of the mundane plane and his words would electrify the audience. Thus he moulded the young minds in the cast of a new ideal."[30]

Divine light emanating from body :

Sometimes unworldly halo or divine light disperses from the body of a holy person indicating his sacredness of soul and profound spiritual power.

In 1914 Swami Premananda went to Varanasi to bring his brother-disciple Swami Brahmananda the-then President of the Order back to Belur Math. During this trip a remarkable incident happened that was witnessed and later narrated by Swami Prabhavananda :

It was in Varanasi in October 1914. Swami Premananda used to visit the temples of Lord Vishwanath and Mother Annapurna after taking his bath in the Ganga. I would accompany him. One day after we finished worship in the temple of Annapurna, the head priest placed a garland of marigolds around Swami Premananda's neck. When the Swami was about to take the garland off to give it to me, I saluted him : "No Maharaj, keep it yourself. You look so beautiful." The word "beautiful" reminded the Swami of God's beauty and he went into ecstasy. His face flushed, and then a light began to emanate from his whole body. Walking slowly, he left the temple, and I followed him. The temple lane was crowded as usual, but on either side of us people stared at the Swami and made way. It was quite evident that everyone present saw him illumined. He was completely absorbed in the thought of God and oblivious of his surroundings. As we approached the outer gate of the monastery, Swami Nirbharananda, the abbot saw us from the verandah. He immediately ordered the monks to prepare a special welcome for Swami Premananda. We entered the monastery grounds to the sound of bells and conch shells. As the Swami got to the verandah, he took off the garland and placed it around the neck of the abbot. For a brief moment he danced in ecstatic joy. Gradually the ecstasy abated, and the divine light disappeared.[31]

A magnetic and impressive orator and preacher :

Swami Premananda started to note some of the Master's teachings down during his stay at Dakshineswar. But Sri Ramakrishna said to him, "That is not your tasks, Many beautiful words of wisdom will burst forth from your lips."[32]

One day Swami Premananda said to Holy Mother, "Mother, I do not have any learning, but people from various places invite me to speak. What shall I do?" Mother answred "My son, don't worry, The master will speak sitting on your tongue. He is with you."[33] Thus the Swami was blessed by both the Master and the Mother.

Swami Vivekananda while lecturing on 'The powers of the mind' said: 'A man comes; you know he is very learned, his language is beautiful and he speaks to you by the hour; but he does not make any impression. Another man comes, and he speaks a few words, not well arranged, ungrammatical perhaps; all the same, he makes an immense impression. Many of you have seen that. So it is evident that words alone cannot always produce an impression. Words, even thoughts contribute only one third of the influence in making an impression, the man, two-thrids, what you call the personal magnetism of the man—that is what goes out and impresses you."[34]

Swami Premananda possessed marvellous personal magnetism. He knew the recipe of articulation. He spoke from the core of his heart and on the basis of his experience.

In 1901, Swamiji after returning from East Bengal (now Bangladesh), had said to Swami Premananda, "I have left East Bengal for you.' How a prophetic utterance it was! Every year from 1913 to 1917. Swami Premananda visited East Bengal and made profound impact on people there. The Swami with his illumined soul and catholicity of the Vedic spirit was free from sectarian outlook. The Nawab Salimulla of Dhaka satisfied with the Swami's liberal attitude and indiscriminate love for all invited him to his palace where the Swami told the Begums (Muslim women of royal families) the life story of Sri Ramakrishna and his message of the harmony of religions. The Nawab's sister, Begum Akhtara Banu, donated some money for founding Ramakrishna Math in Dakha, in her father's memory. Later some Muslim women with great devotion to the Swami, visited Belur Math. Swami Ashokananda depicts tremendous enthusiastic interest of laymen in the personality and preaching of Swami Premananda : 'His visits were all epic events. Wherever he went, thousands of people—old and young, Hindus and Muslims–were attracted to him. And when he would leave a place, even after a visit of only a few days, people would run after him, crying. He probably would be going off in a horse carriage and they would run to keep up with him. For miles people would follow him like that, shedding tears as if someone very near to them were dying, These are the real miracles of the spirit. He would just pull their hearts out; he bought them up, as it were, with his love—Hindus and Muslim's alike."[35]

Swami Premananda's extensive preaching in East Bengal brought many youngmen to the fold of the Ramakrishna Order. Learning about his successful mission in East Bengal Swami Turiyananda wrote to him, "You are the precious jewel-casket of Sri Ramakrishna. As an embodiment of love, you are distributing love like the gopis of Vrindaban. Brother, save some love for us."[36]

Swami Ashokananda reminisced in his book 'Swami Premananda : "He became a fiery preacher of the teachings of Swami Vivekananda. A great missionary zeal came into him. He took every opportunity to go out and lecture and he would call to young men to come and dedicate themselves to Swamiji's cause. He became like a powerful magnet. He was often invited to speak in different parts of Bengal. Sometimes he would command audiences of several thousand people and give long talks. He would just speak fire.

"Even his appearance had become more spirited after his conversion to Swamiji's ideas."

Once Swami Brahmanada, considering the fragile body of Swami Premananda, warned him against overdoing preaching. Swami Premananda replied, ; "I am perfect, eternally free. I am a follower of Swamiji, and it is he who asked me to carry the message of Sri Ramakrishna to every village."[37]

Humility and purity personified :

As a man Swami Premananda was in a class of his own. He was so humble that one day he said to a monk, "The Master did not make us great, he made us "nobodies". He had some good qualities such as patience, forbearance and forgiveness. While coming down the stairs of the shrine after finishing his morning meditation, he used to repeat the mantram of the Master : 'Sha, Sha, sa—forbear, forbear, forbear. He who forbears survives; and he who does not perishes.' He did not indulge in pride and egotism and sometimes said to himself, "O Baburam, be careful! O Baburam, be careful!"

The Swami considered himself to be an instrument in the hands of the Master. In a letter written on 5 October 1917 to a votary he prayed to be a servant of a servant of a devotee.

When Swami Brahmananda or any other direct disciples of Sri Ramakrishna were at Belur Math, Swami Premananda would advise the young monks to serve them and associate with them. He said to them : "Having the company of God, they have become gods. They are not ordinary people. Your life will be blessed if you associate with them and serve them."

The Master himself was very humble and taught his disciples to be so. Swami Premananda was a strict vegetarian and occasionally expressed his antipathy to those who ate fish. One night the Master told him in a vision : "Look Baburam, my children eat a little fish. Why do you make so much fuss about it? Do you think that you have achieved everything because you don't eat fish?" The next morning the Swami first touched his tongue to the fish-cutting knife in the kitchen and said to himself. "I am Baburam, why should I hurt others' feelings?" Then he sent someone to the market to buy good fish. He cut them, cooked and served them to the monks himself. After lunch he said to the monks, "The Master used to say, 'The poison of the big cobra and the little cobra is the same' I beg forgiveness from all of you. I must not say anything that could hurt others' feelings."[38]

Swami Prabhavananda was an eye-witness of the following incidents : Once Swami Turiyananda and Swami Premananda prostrated themselves at each other's feet when they had met after few years. The former told the latter that none would be able to surpass him interms of humility.

One day Swami Premananda said to Swami Brahmananda, "Let's relieve ourselves of this ochre. This is nothing but an advertizement of our asceticism." In him the spirit of renunciation grew so intense that he considered the ochere cloth conventional symbol of asceticism, hindrance to perfect self-effacement.

Swami Premananda was pure in heart. He was one of those fortunate souls who were allowed by the Master to touch him during samadhi or when necessitiated. He reminisced : "Sri Ramakrishna was the embodiment of purity... During the Master's samadhi we had to hold him so he would not fall, but we were afraid, we thought that if we were not pure enough, then, when we touched him during samadhi, he would publicly cry out in pain. So we prayed for purity. It was the Master's grace that I was allowed to live with him."[39]

The Master would say about Swami Premananda's purity: "He is pure, pure to the very marrow of his bones."[40] The master described him as a *nityasiddha* (ever-perfect soul) and an *ishwarakoti* (godlike soul). He did not fall into the clutches of woman and gold.

Once Swami Brahmananda said to the monks : "Listen, if you can follow sincerely one or two thing that Premananda says, your lives will be blessed. Is he an ordinary man? He is so pure that in whatever direction he looks, everything in that direction becomes pure."[41]

A Part of Radha :

Swami Premananda very handsome, slim and having a complexion like pure gold, was twenty when he first visited Sri Ramakrishna. In the beginning he used to meet the Master only on holidays so that his studies were not neglected. During these first visits the Master came to know in an estatic mood that Baburam had been born as a part of Radha, the spiritual consort of Lord Krishna. On 20 June, 1884 Sri Ramakrishna said to M. : "I noticed the other day that Baburam, Bhavanath and Harish have a feminine nature. In a vision I saw Baburam as a goddess with a necklace around her neck and with woman companions about her. He had received something in a dream. His body is pure. Only a very little effort will awake his spiritual consciousness."[42]

Swami Bodhananda recollected that during Swami Premananda's stay in Vrindaban he used to say "Radhe Radhe while saluting an outsider saint there."

One day in the last week of July 1918 Swami Saradananda came from Udbodhan to see Swami Premananda suffering from deadly Flu in the house of Balaram Bose. The latter said to the former, "You know, I have a great desire to put on a cloth of pure yellow and to eat rice white as jasmine." Swami Saradananda realized that that is a symbolic description of Radha of whom the Master had said he was a part. On his death bed Swami Premananda became aware of his real identity as Swamiji did.

In late January 1887 Swami Vivekananda gave Baburam the significant name Premananda meaning bliss of divine love, recollecting the Master's remark that Sri Radha herself the goddess of love, was partially incarnated in him. Radha stands for all-pervading love. Towards the end of his life swami Premananda wrote to someone : "I feel a desire now to love everybody. This is a disease which has now possessed me."

Blessed with visions of the Master :

Swami Premananda said to the lay members of the Mission, "Grow into Gods. Only then will the work of the Mission prosper. This is my earnest prayer to you all."[43] He himself grew into his Master. In 1915 while visiting Rarikhal in Dhaka one day the Swami very busy lecturing and talking to the people after a sleepless night owing to the attack of bedbugs, said to someone who requested him to take rest : "My body does not get tired talking about the Master."[44]

During his stay in Alambazar Monastery Swami Premananda quite often left for Dakshineswar to practise japam and meditation either in the Master's room or in the Panchavati. He would live on the memory of the Master forgetting food and rest.

Once Swami Premananda fell from a tree while picking flowers and fractured his right wrist but he forgot his unbearable pain by thinking of Sri Ramakrishna.

Love is reciprocal. Swami Premananda loved his Master so much. The Master also did so and called him 'daradi' (the companion of his soul). On various occasions he appeared in his disciple's visions.

Swami Premananda's service to Sri Ramakrishna was living, as if he could see the Master doing his routine activities as usual. One day he asked Swami Rameswarananda who used to perform worship in the shrine in 1916-1917, if the clothing of the Master was okay and advised him to look carefully. Then he narrated an incident : "After offering a new cloth to the Master, I was about to put it on; then the Master told me through a vision, "Baburam, you are going to have a new cloth, and my shirt is torn. Don't you love me anymore? Then both of us went to the shrine and found that the Master's shirt had been chewed by a mouse."[46]

Sri Ramakrishna used to teach his disciples to wipe out ego which separates human mind from God and to be polite. Even after his passing away, he kept watch on his disciples. A strict vegetarian Swami Premananda bore antipathy to the fish-eaters in the monastery and this attitude occasionally would become obvious in his manner. One night the Master said to him in a vision : "Look, Baburam, my children eat a little fish. Why do you make so much fuss about it? Do you think that you have achieved everything because you don't eat fish?" The next morning Swami Premananda touched his tongue to the fish-cutting knife in the kitchen and said to himself : 'I am Baburam; why should I hurt other's feelings?' Later on he sent someone to the market to buy good fish and then cut and cooked them and served them to the monks himself. He apologized to them after lunch.

Swami Premananda used to take care of the devotees and visitors in the monastery and advise the monks and brahmacharins to serve them cordially. One day he gave a pumpkin from the monastery garden to a poor brahmin. On seeing this Swami Brahamananda said to Swami Premananda, "If you freely distribute the vegetables in this way how shall we manage the Master's service here?" Swami Premananda was crestfallen. Deciding to leave the Belur monastery for ever he walked towards the gate. As he reached the gate, the towel on his shoulder was suddenly snatched from him and tightened around his neck immediately. He turned and found the figure of his beloved Master who said to him, "Where are you going my child? How can you go away, leaving me here?" Overcome by the incredible experience, the Swami went back to Swami Brahmananda and prostrated himself at his feet.[47]

Conflict and Catharsis :

In the West Swamiji spoke about Sri Ramakrishna publicly in two lectures probably but he never preached his Master or his life. He never said that Sri Ramakrishna was an Incarnation of God. He mainly talked about the monistic aspect of Vedanta there. Besides, Swamiji in his letters repeatedly told his brother disciples that they should minimize ritualistic worship of the Master and try to serve the sick, the hungry, the illiterate, looking upon them as veritable images of God. But some of his brother disciples including Swami Premananda considered that Swamiji had forgotten his Master and was going his own way because Sri Ramakrishna had principally taught *bhakti* or devotion and said that the path of *jnana* or knowledge and monism of Vedanta were not suitable for the common people.

Swamiji wanted to translate his words into action. One day he said to Swami Premananda, "Brother all these days you have been worshipping the Lord with flowers and sandal paste, now start worshiping the living gods. Go to Belur village and serve the poor and the afflicted." Swami Premananda obeyed his leader's order unhesitatingly.

One afternoon Swamiji was holding a class for the junior monks, which continued till evening. Finding none in the shrine for the vespers, Swami Premananda, going to the classroom said to the monks, "What are you doing? Aren't you coming to vespers? Finish the class and come," Swamiji at once grew angry with his brother disciple and said rudely : "Is it your idea that what I am doing here is not wosrhip? When you ring the bell in the shrine, is only that worship?" Swami Premananda was disappointed.

In fact, initially Swami Premananda and some of his brother disciples could not understand the well-devised role of their leader in the West. Sri Ramakrishna an incarnation of God came to the world to establish the eternal religion and made his most favourite monastic disciple Narendranath a vehicle to carry out his mission. Few days before his passing away he wrote on a piece of paper, "Naren will teach people." Swami Vivekananda only whom the Master taught monism, talked about the Advaitic or monistic aspect of Vedanta in the West without uttering the name of his Master frequently. Swamiji realised that once the West was familiar with these grand ideas, it would be easy to present the person embodying them. Actually Swami Premananda and few others could not understand that without mentioning the name of the Master Swamiji in fact, preached the Master, because Sri Ramakrishna embodied those very principles on which Vedanta was based.

Ultimately the cloud of misunderstanding and doubt dispersed because Swami Premananda and others of the confused fraction recollected their Master's words about Narendranath" Just follow him. As you would follow me, follow him."[48] Besides, there was a bond of mutual love, respect and faith among the brother disciples. Regular discussion with Swamiji helped them realize their mistake.

Considering the activities of Swamiji on the last day of his life (4 July 1902) it was obvious that Swami Premananda was the only fortunate who learnt about Swamiji's final dreams, plans and his experiences in the West from him. Swami Premananda took more than a decade to be converted into an ardent advocate of Swamiji and his ideal. One day in the autumn of 1913 he said to Jogeshchandra Dutta (afterwards Swami Ashokananda) and two of his college friends : "But as time has gone on, I have become convinced that unless we look at Sri Ramakrishna through the eyes of Swamiji we will not know what he was, what he wanted us to do. I am a disciple of Swamiji now. If you ever want to understand Sri Ramakrishna, read the works of Swamiji. Think about him..."[49] He accepted the ideal of worship of God through the service of man and trained the monastics according to the mould and ideal of Swamiji whom he once said : ""Do you think you are different from Sri Ramakrishna? We look upon you as the same as our Master."[50]

With reference to the impact of reading the works of Swamiji and this metamorphosis and Swamiji-consciousness of Swami Premananda Swami Purnatmananda wrote : "And this efflorescence in the life of Swami Premananda was not an isolated event in the history of the Ramakrishna Mission. It contributed enormously to the consolidation and growth of the whole movement and its ideal on the one hand, and to the sustenance and strength of the organization on the other. That is indeed a fantastic story..."[51]

Chapter – 8

SWAMI YOGANANDA

He would often be possessed of spiritual feelings even at the age of five. He was identified by Sri Ramakrisna as an *ishwarakoti* (a godlike soul) and in his previous life Arjuna, the hero of the Mahabharata.

'He' was Jogindra Nath Roy Chaudhury who was born on 30 March 1861 into an aristocratic family at Dakshineswar. He was the eldest son of Navin Chandra Roy Chaudhury.

Characteristics of spiritual greatness :

Jogindra Nath developed a mystic bent of mind very early in life. While playing suddenly a serious thought would strike him and losing all interest in play he would retire to a quiet corner and looking at the sky soliloquise : "Where am I? Certainly, I don't belong here. These are not my playmates–I have other friends and companions. I must have come from one of those stars. But which one? I don't know. And why am I here if I belong to another world? Is this all a dream?"[1]

During their second meeting Sri Ramakrishna recognized Jogindra as one of his inner circle and said to him : "It is wonderful that we have come to know each other now. You must come often. You have been born into a noble family and possess many characteristics of spiritual greatness. You will easily advance on this path."[2]

Strong independence and continence :

Jogindra resolved not to marry. But the passionate appeal and tears of his mother weakened him for the time being and he had to marry. But his strong independence could not accept the forced marriage. He began to chant God's name in the bridal chamber immediately after the wedding ceremony ignoring taunt of the bride's female companions. He never slept in the same bed with his wife. Soon after the marriage one day in the father-in-law's house Jogindra went to the roof after supper and walked there the whole night and came back home at dawn.

Although born into a well-off family and married, Jogindra demonstrated how to practise continence and renunciation. Swami Vivekananda commented, "If there is anyone amongst us who has conquered lust in all respects, it is Jogin."[3]

Artless credulous and tender-hearted :

Yogananda was very simple-natured and tended to believe in everything and everybody. One day Sri Ramakrishna heard that Yogananda had bought an iron pan and returning home he discovered that the pan had a crack. The Master said to him. "Because you are a devotee of God, does that mean that you should be a fool? You think any shopkeeper opens a shop to practise religion? Why did you not examine the pan before you purchased it? Never act so foolishly again. When you go out shopping, first determine the usual price of the item by going around to several shops and then thoroughly examine the thing you want to buy. And do not fail to demand the little extras where allowed." He advised his disciples to use their discrimination both in the spiritual field as well as in worldly matter and not to believe others blindly.

Yogananda was very soft-hearted. Sometimes people while practising religion become so tender that their kindness may cause their deviation from the path of righteousness and spirituality. Once on seeing a cockroach in a clothes-chest, the Master asked

Jogin to take it outside and kill it. When he learnt that the latter instead of killing the insect let it go, scolded him saying : "I told you to kill the cockroach, but you let it go. You should always do as I ask you to do. Otherwise, later in more serious matters also you will follow your own judgement and come to grief." The master thus wanted to make such kind hearted boy firm and resolved. He rebuked him when he heard that Jogin had not even protested against false accusations against him made by a boat-passenger. The Master taught Jogin to defend the truth. Other occasion he advised him to ignore gossips (such as fabricated by some villagers of Dakshineswar about an ill famed woman and Sri Ramakrishna) of worldlly people, because otherwise, it would spoil his concentration on God.

Humanity :

Another remarkable aspect of Jogindra's nature was his deep feeling for suffering people. When a man of his village died in a train accident, his family was left completely destitute. Jogindra was deeply moved by the plight of the widow and her children. He told his brother disciples about the incident. Tarak nath Ghosal (afterwards, Swami Shivananda) gave him forty rupees to take to the helpless family.

During his last illness, Swami Yogananda suffered from fever and blood dysentry. Swami Adbhutananda came to see him at Holy Mother's house in Bosepara Lane, Kolkata. Swami Yogananda said to him : "This illness will never be cured. The doctors advised me to take pomegranate juice, luchi (fried bread) and catfish soup. They have no sense. How can a monk procure such expensive food like that meant for rich aristocrats? They have money and people to prepare such delicacies but we are monks—we have none except God. We live on alms, so that kind of luxury does not befit us. What do you think?"[4]

Though born into an aristocrat family Swami Yogananda lived a very simple saintly life and remembering the pale faces of the starving masses he hesitated to eat costly diet.

Courage to test Sri Ramakrishna :

After his first visit to Sri Ramakrishna while Jogindranath was returning home, he reflected : "This man must be a saint who has seen God. People do not understand that and therefore they laugh at him. How else can one account for such words of devotion, such divine love and such ecstasy in the name of God? However, let me watch him closely."[5]

Sri Ramakrishna used to ask his disciples to test him; to test whether his words and actions were in perfect accordance; as money changers test their coins. Jogindranath, like Narendranath, had the guts to try the godlike priest of the Dakshineswar Kali Temple. One evening Sri Ramakrishna was pleased to learn that Jogindranath was willing to spend the night with him in order to serve him if needed. After dinner the Master went to bed and Jogindranath lay down on his bed on the floor and soon fell asleep. He was all along a light sleeper. Waking up at midnight he did not find the Master in his bed. He found the water pot used by the Master for washing in its particular place. He thought that the Master might be walking outside, but could not find him there. Suddenly a horrible suspicion cropped up in his mind : "Has the Master gone to *nahabat* (concert tower) to be with his wife? Can it be possible that his actions are contrary to his teachings?"[6]

Determined to find out the truth, Jogindranath at once going out of the room stood by the *Nahabat* fixing his eyes on the door of the Mother's room. He heard the clattering of slippers coming from the side of the Panchavati. After a few minutes Sri Ramakrishna appeared before Jogindranath and said to him. "Hello, why are you standing here?" Deeply ashamed of his doubt about the Master's character, Jogindranath with his head hung, was unable to utter a single word. On reading his mind the Master reassured him : "Well, you are quite right—you must examine a *sadhu* (holy man) by day and by night before believing in him."[7]

The first initiated disciple of the Mother :

One day at Cossipore Sri Ramakrishna said to the Mother, "See, the people of Calcutta appear to be crawling about like worms in the dark. Do look after them." The mother replied, "I am a woman. How can that be?" The Master pointing towards his body said, "What after all has this one done? You'll have to do much more."[8]

Even a few weeks after passing away, the Master invited the Mother openly to shoulder the responsibility. During pilgrimage the Mother, with her party including Jogindranath was in Vrindaban where she had the first direct intimation of her future mission. One day the Master appeared infront of her and told her to give Jogindranath formal initiation. He also mentioned the mantram with which she should initiate him. The Mother considered it a hallucination, but she had the same vision the next two days. On the third day she said to Sri Ramakrishna, "I do not even speak to Jogin. How can I initiate him?" The Master told her to have Jogin-ma with her at the time of initiation. Jogindranath also had a vision and received the Master's advice regarding his initiation. Shortly, he was initiated by the Mother and became her first disciple.

Some days before getting Holy Mother as his mantra-guru, Jogindrnath happened to see the holy face of the Mother. It was three O'clock in the morning. The Mother was absorbed in deep meditation on the verandah of the nahabat at Dakshineswar. A light wind blew away her veil and the light of the full moon fell on her face. The Master went to the pine grove and Jogindranath followed him with a water pot. Both saw her in that state.

Afterwards Swami Yogananda, owing to his close association with the Mother as a disciple, attendant and caretaker was fortunate to treasure numerous experiences of her spiritual life. He said : "During such periods of ecstasy, her manner of speech, her voice, her way of taking food, her way of walking, and her general behaviour were exactly like those of the Master. We have heard that in deep meditation the worshipper and the worshipped become one. The scriptures mention a spiritual state known as *todatmya-bhava*—being at one with God. We have read in the Bhagavata how the gopis (shepherd girls of Vrindaban), unable to bear separation from Krishna, became so deeply absorbed in the thought of him that for the moment they forgot their own individualities and behaved as though they were Krishna. In the same manner the Mother, too, forgot her own separate existence and acted just like the Master, feeling her oneness with him. When I asked her some complex questions about spiritual matters shortly after her states of samadhi, she replied in a God-intoxicated mood, very much like Sri Ramakrishna; that is in the same manner characteristic of the Master, even using his same easy style of expression with metaphors and parables.

"We all were surprised to see the spirit of Sri Ramakrishna united with hers. It was unique. We then realized that the Master and the Mother were one in essence, though appearing in separate forms. Is it not said in the scriptures : "Lord, thou art man, thou art woman"? The Master told me many times that there was no difference between him and the Mother.

"...She was then in such a blissful state of mind that at times her yearning for Krishna's presence and her utterance of his name with intense love reminded us of Radha. I have heard from her women companions that the Mother at times spoke frankly of herself as Radha!"[9]

Saved by the Master :

Each of the monastic disciples of the Master was blessed and protected by him even after his passing away.

Once Jogindranath, along with the Mother and her party went from Vrindaban to Hardwar by train. On the way he caught a high fever. During his unconscious state, a frightful form appeared before him and said : "I would have put an end to your life, but I am helpless. On the order of your guru, Paramahamsa Deva, I am leaving you. However, you must offer some *rasagollas* (juicy cheese balls) to this woman (pointing to a goddess wearing a red cloth)."

Jogindranath came round the next morning and a few days later while visiting the Govinda Temple he discovered Sitala wearing a red cloth, the goddess of disease whom he had seen while he was unconscious. Buying some rasagollas he offered those to the deity.

Taking formal monastic vows of renunciation in 1887 at the Baranagore Monastery Jogindranath became Swami Yogananda. He was very handsome and robust. While travelling in Central Province once he was alone in a train car. At a station a beautiful courtesan got into the same car and was completely besotted with the Swami as soon as she saw him. She said to him : "I offer my every thing to you, please accept me." The stoical attitude of Swami Yogananda made her furious and impatient. She threatened him : "If you don't listen to me right now, I shall pull the alarm chain to stop the train, and I shall complain to the guard that you had molested me." The Swami didn't respond. She began to drink wine to incite herself and soon became unconscious. He got off the train unharmed the next station. Thus Swami Yogananda was saved by the grace of the Master.

In 1891 while Swami Yogananda was living in a small cottage in a solitary garden in Varanasi, he spent most of his time in meditation. One night, when he was chanting the name of Sri Ramakrishna an evil spirit tried to harm him. The Swami at once shouted out, "Jai Ramakrishna" (Victory to Ramakrishna). Getting scared, the spirit said to him : "I shall never again come to disturb you. Henceforth this place is yours."[10] Thus by the grace of Sri Ramakrishna his life was saved once again.

Robust Optimism :

Once in the Baranagore Monastery the monastic disciples of Sri Ramakrishna read from the Bible : "For there are some eunuchs which were so born from their mother's womb;...and there be eunuchs which have made themselves eunuchs for the kingdom of heaven's sake."[11]

When one of the brother disciples jokingly called Swami Yogananda a eunuch, he laughingly answered : "You will see—just wait. Jesus left a group of eunuchs who shook the world. We will do the same thing."

Sense of humour :

Mahendranath Dutta stated few incidents related to Swami Yogananda's sense of humour in his book, 'Srimat Vivekananda Swamijir Jivaner Ghatanavali.'

Once some village women while carrying water from the Ganga, saw Swami Yogananda seated under a banyan tree. The Swami's appearance, though lean due to intense austerity, impressed them and they felt love and sympathy for him. They questioned him about his background. In order to avoid them the Swami answered in Hindi as if he didn't know Bengali. The women thought he was either a Hindustani hemp smoker or a cheat and left.

One day Swami Yogananda as a mendicant went to beg for food. In Alambazar he arrived at a thatched cottage where a poor woman was sweeping. As she saw the young monk begging food, she rudely said, "Get away from this place! You are a young man, why don't you work and make money? You come in the disguise of a monk at daytime to check the houses and will return at night to steal." Saying this she hit her broomstick on the ground. Returning to the monastery the Swami mimicked the woman out of fun and his brother-disciples rolled on the floor with laughter. Swami Yogananda had a good sense of humour.

Extreme austerity :

Swami Yogananda was a so highly evolved soul that he would have given up everything—even his body for the sake of God. He preferred japam and meditation for long time in solitude to study. He was a serious monk with burning renunciation. Regarding eating, working and sleeping he was an extremist. Sometimes at Balaram Bose's house in Kolkata he used to repeat his mantram day and night continuously which caused severe headache. In 1891 while living in a small cottage in a solitary garden in Varanasi, he spent most of his time in meditation. He would go out to beg for food once a day; sometimes he would eat dry bread soaked in water for two or three days. Due to such nominal meal or intense fasting his digestive system collapsed and his robust health was reduced to lean. Sister Nivedita wrote on Aug. 1899 to Miss J. MacLeod and Mrs Ole Bull : 'But as to the other monks—Jogindra was an awful ascetic.' (Letters of Sister Nivedita, Col. & Ed. by Sankari Prasad Basu, Vol. 1. p. 175)

Guts and Greatness :

Swami Yogananda had the guts to expose his doubts and ask their leader Swami Vivekananda if some of his activities were contradictory to the teachings and ideals of Sri Ramakrishna.

On 1 May 1897 Swamaji inaugurated the Ramakrishna Mission at Balaram Bose's house in Kolkata. After the resolutions had been passed office-bearers were appointed. Swamiji himself became the General President, and made Swami Brahmananda and Swami Yogananda, President and Vice-President respectively, of the Kolkata centre. When the meeting had broken up and most of the lay members had departed, Swamiji said to Swami Yogananda : "So the work has now begun in this way. Let us see how it succeeds, by the will of Sri Ramakrishna."

To quote from "The Life of Swami Vivekananda" :

Swami Yogananda : "You are doing these things by Western methods. Would you say that Sri Ramakrishna left us any such instructions?" The Swami : "How do you know that these methods are not in keeping with his ideas? Shri Ramakrishna was the embodiment of infinite ideas : do you want to shut him up in your own limits? I shall break those limits and scatter his ideas broadcast all over the world. He never instructed me to introduce worship of him, and so forth. The methods of spiritual practice, concentration and meditation, and the other higher ideals of religion that he taught—those we must realize and teach to all men. Infinite are the ideas and infinite are the paths that lead to the Goal. I was not born to create a new sect in this world, too full of sects already. Blessed are we that we have found refuge at the feet of our Master. It is our duty to give the ideas entrusted to us freely to the whole world."

Swami Yogananda did not dissent, and so the Swami continued : "Time and again I have received in this life marks of his grace. He himself is at my back and is making me do all these things in these ways. When I used to lie under a tree, exhausted, smitten with hunger; when I had not a strip of cloth even to tie my Kaupina (loin-cloth) with, when I had resolved to travel round the world penniless; —even then, through his grace, I received help in every way. Then again, when people in crowds jostled with one another in the streets of Chicago to have sight of this Vivekananda, I was able, through his blessings, to digest without difficulty all that honour, a hundredth part of which would have turned the head of any other man. By the will of the Lord, victory has been mine everywhere. Now I intend to do something for this country. Do you all give up doubts and misgivings and help me in my work; and you will see how, by his grace, wonders will be accomplished."

Swami Yogananda : "Whatever you will, shall come about. We are always ready to follow your leading. I clearly see that the Master is working through you. Still, I confess, doubts do sometimes arise in the mind, for, as we saw it, his method of doing things was so different, and so I am led to ask myself whether we are not straying from Shri Ramakrishna's teachings."

The Swami : "The thing is this : Shri Ramakrishna is far greater than his disciples understand him to be. He is the embodiment of infinite spiritual ideas capable of development in infinite ways. Even if one can find a limit to the knowledge of Brahman, one cannot measure the unfathomable depths of our Master's mind! One gracious glance of his eyes can create a hundred thousand Vivekananda at this instant! But if this time he chooses, instead, to work through me, making me his instrument, I can only bow to his will."[12]

Swami Yogananda felt how deep devotion Swamiji bore to his Master and was satisfied with the convincing words and arguments of the Swami and gradually all his doubts and conflicts were dissipated.

Devotion to the Master :

Jogindranath resolved to overcome lust and not to marry. His father Navin Chandra made arrangements for his son's marriage as an antidote to his bent for spiritualism. He turned down his father's proposal. Then his mother begged him with tearful eyes to marry and save his father's reputation and added, "Even if you are unwilling, marry for my sake, dear." His mother's passionate appeal and tears undermined his firm resolution and he had to marry. Seeing Jogindranath's apathy towards the world, one day his mother said, "If you don't care to earn money, why did you marry?"

Jogindranath answered : "Didn't I tell you again and again that I had no intention of marrying? But I had to give way to your tears."

His mother indignantly said : "What do you mean? How could you marry unless you had the desire to do so?"

To his utter amazement and dismay Jogindranath said to himself "Gracious God! I committed the act to please my mother, and now she talks like this! Fie on the world! Sri Ramakrishna is the only person I have met whose words and thoughts are in perfect accordance." He sought solace in the company of Sri Ramakrishna and spent his days and sometimes nights in the temple garden. He liked to stay with the Master at night in order to serve him in need.

One day Sri Ramakrishna said to Jogindranath, "What do you think of me?" The latter replied, "You are neither a householder nor a sannayasin." He infact, regarded the Master as God. Sri Ramakrishna greatly satisfied with the reply exclaimed "What an extraordinary statement you have just made!"[13]

Sri Ramakrishna fell terminally ill with cancer in the middle of 1885 and in December he was taken to Cossipore garden house. One day he asked Jogindranath to buy *palo* pudding (a kind of custard made from the zedoary root) from a particular shop in Kolkata.Jogindranath thought out of his love for the Master and cautiousness about his well-being that the pudding from the market might be adulterated and that it might harm his health. So he went to the house of Balaram Bose and returned with the homemade pudding late in the afternoon. The Master had to lunch without pudding. Hearing all from Jogindranath he said : "I wanted to eat the pudding from that particular shop, so I asked you to buy it from there. Why did you bring this pudding, giving trouble to the devotees? Moreover, this pudding is very rich and hard to digest. I shall not eat it." Jogindranath was so embarrassed.

Jogindranath dedicated himself to serve the Master. But his severe austerity and negligence to his body caused serious illness. Sri Ramakrishna advised him to eat at the proper times and take sufficient rest.

It was Jogindranath whom Sri Ramakrishna asked to bring the almanac and read the events of each day and the positions of the stars eight or nine days before his passing away. When Jogindranath finished reading about 16 August 1886, the Master told him to stop and to put the almanac back in its proper place.

Once Swami Yogananda said about the advent of the Master whom he regarded as an avatar or divine incarnation. "There have always been various religious paths, countless scriptures, and holy places in every country. In spite of that why is there a decline in religion? Because in the course of time all ideals become lost. Therefore God incarnates Himself to explain the hidden mystery of religion and to show the ideal."[14]

On a separate occasion Swami Yogananda said : "By the grace of the Master I have attained so much knowledge and devotion that I am unable to express it all."[15]

Once Swami Yogananda, on his death bed, said to Girish Chandra Ghosh : "All right, Let the Master's will be done. I am his servant. Whatever he asks me to do. I will do."[16] The Swami's total submission to Sri Ramakrishna was remarkable. His passing-words were : "Yes, I remember the Master more—even more—much more."[17]

Devotion to the Mother :

Swami Yogananda was the first initiated disciple of the Mother. In 1892 he returned from Varanasi to Alambazar Math to stay there for some months. Then he devoted himself to serve Holy Mother as her attendant and caretaker until his passing away. He was among the three or four monastic disciples of the Master who had free access to the Mother. The Master appointed him to do earrands for the Mother as he was pure like the ever-free soul Shukadeva son of Vedavyasa.

Holy Mother said : "Nobody loves me as Yogen did. If anybody gave him so much as eight annas, (formerly 16 annas = 1 rupee) he kept it by saying, "Mother will go out on pilgrimages, etc. and then she will need it." He was always by my side. Because he lived in the midst of women, the boys taunted him. Yogen told me, "Mother, you will call me "Yoga'...Sarat (Swami Saradananda) and Yogen—these two belong to my inner, circle."[18] The Mother described Swamis Yogananda and Saradananda as her 'burden bearers'.

Swami Yogananda used to carry the load of rice, coarse flour etc from market on his shoulders while the Mother stayed in the garden-house of Nilambar Babu. Once she was hurt as she saw him from the roof carry the load and said sadly that she did not like to eat. The Swami's dedicated service to the Mother for more than twelve years (autumn of 1886 to spring of 1899) distinguished him among the disciples of Sri Ramakrishna.

Swami Yogananda's respect for the Mother was legendary. He never saluted her by touching her feet. When the Mother would leave the place, he would touch that spot with his head. The Swami asked about such strange behaviour, answered : "What ! I don't have the audacity to keep the Mother standing and waiting for me so that I can bow down to her."[19]

Swami Yogananda was one of the first monastic disciples of Sri Ramakrishna to discover the light under a bushel— the amazing spiritual greatness of Holy Mother hidden under the veil of rustic simplicity. One day Swami Saradananda said to Swami Yogananda: "Brother, I do not always understand Swamiji. He speaks in various moods. Whatever stand he takes, he makes so much of it that the others pale into insignificance." Swami Yogananda replied: "Sharat (Swami Saradananda's premonastic name), I tell you one thing : Cling to Holy Mother. Whatever she says—that is right,"[20]

Pivot—'a brick', 'a beam' :

The brother disciples of Swami Yogananda were quite fond of him. When Swami Yogananda fell ill, Swami Vivekananda said : 'Jogin, you get well, let me die instead." Swami Niranjanananda once said; "Jogin you are our crest jewel."[21] During the last years of his life Swami Yogananda used to visit Girish Chnadra Ghosh, and talk about the Master. Once Girish Chandra said to the Swami on his deathbed : "Brother don't you know that you have been suffering terribly these last six months? Your pain is causing pain to all of us. Please agree to the will of the Master. Don't refuse to come back with the Master," Though initially Yogananda denied to be born again, ultimately he completely resigned himself to the Master.

At dawn of the 28th March, 1899 the Mother saw that the Master had come to take her Yogen. At 3:10 p.m. catching the sound of wailing of Brahmachari Krishnalal the Mother lamented, "My Yogen has left me—who will now look after me?' She nextday said with a long sigh : 'A brick has slipped off the structure; now the whole thing will come down.' Rightly has pointed out Swami Gambhirananda : "From the subsequent talks and action of the Mother we can have an idea of the depth of her affection for this son of hers, and the extent of her dependence on him. In her reminiscent moods she said at different times, 'Nobody loves me as Yogen did.'[22]

Swamiji waved the light and offered flowers and sweets in accordance with the ritual before the corpse of Swami Yogananda was taken to Kashi Mittra's cremation ground. He was too stunned to join the funeral procession; even to go to his Master's shrine for three days. He commented : "A beam is down and now the rafters will fall one after another."[23]

The Master as well as the Mother regarded Swami Yogananda as Arjuna who came down again with Sri Ramakrishna to establish the Kingdom of Heaven on earth.

This first incident of premature death of a monastic disciple of the Master was an irreparable loss to the nascent order.

Chapter – 9

SWAMI NIRANJANANANDA

The boy, in order to cherish their achievement tried hard with his maternal uncle Dr. Pearychand Mittra, to mesmerize Sri Ramakrishna by using their psychic powers in vain and was embarrassed.

Immediately at first sight the Master commented, 'This boy is very good—extremely guileless.'

The boy applied his psychic powers to cure a moneyed man of Kolkata suffering from insomnia for long eighteen years. Later he said : "Finding the man suffering so much in spite of all his riches and wealth, I was seized with a feeling of the emptiness of all the worldly things."[1]

This boy endowed with a broad chest, beautiful bright eyes and a tall, strong, handsome physique was Nityaniranjan Ghosh (who later was named as Swami Niranjanananda by Swami Vivekananda) son of Ambika Charan Ghosh and was born in 1862 at Rajarhat-Vishnupur in the district of North 24 Parganas.

An *ishwarakoti* :

Sri Ramakrishna identified Niranjan as an *ishwarakoti* or a godlike soul who was born perfect and free from maya or illusion. One day the luminous form of Niranjan playing with a bow and arrows appared before Sri Ramakrishna in a vision. The Master considered Niranjan a partial incarnation of Sri Ramachandra and one of his inner circle.

Ability of discretion : Ascension from a crude medium to a refined medium :

In his maternal uncle's house Niranjan was employed by his uncle and other spiritualists as a medium for contacting spirits. Ultimately dispassionate for the world and disillusioned with spooky business of spiritualism, he left for Dakshineswar in his quest for spirituality.

One day Sri Ramakrishna touched Niranjan. As a result of that holy touch he could not sleep for three days and three nights and had the incessant vision of a mysterious light and kept repeating the Lord's name. He could not abstain from saying japam for another three days. The Master humourously said to him. "Now, my boy, another ghost—the Holy Ghost—is upon you. However much you try, you will not be able to dismiss Him."[2]

Sattvic :

Niranjan had impressed the Master with his purity and dispassionateness so much that the latter could not bear with his separation of two or three days only and was so concerned about his spiritual welfare. On seeing Niranjan he rushed to him and grasping his arms exclaimed in delight "O Niranjan my boy, the days are flitting away. When will you realize God? This life will be in vain if you do not realize Him. When will you devote your mind wholly to God? Oh, how anxious I am for you!" The Master's words of unselfish and unconditional love and concern for him won his heart and occupied all of his thoughts.

Free from lust : 'seated on a light' :

Sri Ramakrishna used to advise his would-be monastic disciples to renounce 'woman and gold'. On 25 May, 1884 he said to Vijaykrishna Goswami, M (Mahendranath Gupta) and the others : "A sannyāsi associated with 'woman and gold' is like a beautiful damsel with a bad odour. The odour makes her beauty useless. ... The sannyāsi must renounce' woman and gold' for his own welfare. Even if he is unattached, and consequently not in danger, still, in order to set an example to others, he must not keep 'woman and gold' near him. The sannyāsi, the man of renunciation, is a world teacher. It is his example that awakens the spiritual consciousness of men."[3]

Niranjan was fortunate enough to earn the Master's affection and attention. On 15 July 1885 the Master, with tears in his eyes said to himself : "O Niranjan! O my child! Come! Eat this! Take this! When shall I make my life blessed by feeding you? You have assumed this human form for my sake."[4]

The Master was highly delighted when Niranjan said to him, "A woman never enters my thoughts." On that same day he praised Niranjan to the devotees including M. Balaram Bose and a few others : "Look at Niranjan. He is not attached to any thing. He spends money from his own pocket to take poor patients to the hospital. At the proposal of marriage he says, 'Goodness! That is the whirlpool of the Visālākshi! I see him seated on a light."[5]

Absolute dependence on and devotion to the Master :

Sri Ramakrishna was aggrieved as he learnt that Niranjan had accepted a job with an indigo planter at Murshidabad. But a few days later he felt relieved to see Niranjan and know that he had to accept the job to maintain his old mother. The Master said to Niranjan, "Ah, then it is all right. It won't contaminate your mind. But I tell you, if you, had done so for your own sake, I could not have touched you. Really it was unthinkable that you would stoop to so much humiliation. Did't I know that my Niranjan had not the least trace of impurity in him?"

The Master's great yearning for Niranjan led him to resign from the job and visit the Master.

Once in an ecstatic mood, Sri Ramakrishna said to Niranjan, "You were living in an indigo-house of such a place; on this particular day you rode on your deputy's horse; you stood in such a place with a bow and arrow."

Realizing that the Master was an omniscient Niranjan submitted himself to him and said with tearful eyes : "Sir, all these days I could not recognize you."

On 23 December 1885 Sri Ramakrishna said to Niranjan, "Please tell me how you feel." Niranjan replied, "Formerly I loved you, no doubt, but now it is impossible for me to live without you."

Niranjan's great devotion to and love for the Master made him worried about his illness. Sensing this once the Master said to him : "Niranjan, if I were cured of this disease, what would you do?" Flushing with excitement Niranjan answered, 'Master, I would uproot that date palm tree from the garden!' Sri Ramakrishna commented : "Yes, you could do that'.

On 18 Dec. 1946 Swami Achalananda, a disciple of Swamiji wrote to Swami Bamdevananda the then Manager of the Advaita Ashrama of Varanasi : "Swami Niranjanananda believed that Sri Ramakrishna was the infinite God incarnated in human form, and he who took refuge in him would not have to worry in life...He believed one should sincerely serve the Master— thinking of him as a living, conscious being, our very own. This is the supreme worship."

Overwhelming devotion to Holy Mother :

Swami Niranjanananda had a high estimation of the Mother. With reference to this Swami Achalananda said : "He believed that by the grace of the Mother, he could do anything."

In 1888 Harish Kundu a devotee of Sri Ramakrishna who was mentally ill, visited the Mother living alone at Kamarpukur and began to disturb her peace. On hearing about the problem from the Mother, Swamis Niranjanananda and Saradananda rushed from the Baranagore Monastery to Kamarpukur. No sooner did Harish see Swami Niranjanananda than he became so scared that he left for Vrindaban.

In 1894 Swamiji wrote from the U.S.A. to Swami Shivananda : "Niranjan has a militant disposition, but he has great devotion for Mother and all his vagaries I can easily put up with. He is now doing the most marvellous work."[7]

Loyalty to the leader :

Swamiji wrote from the U.S.A. on 22 October 1894 to his brother disciple Swami Ramakrishnananda : "Our object is to do good to the world, and not the trumpeting of our own names. Why doesn't Niranjan learn Pali in Ceylon, and study Buddhist books? I can not make out what good will come of aimless rambling."[8] Swamiji was impressed with Swami Niranjanananda's preaching mission in Sri Lanka.

Swamiji returned from the West to India via Sri Lanka and Swami Niranjanananda jubilantly left for Colombo to receive him on 15th January 1897. He arranged for Swamiji to stay at Kali Krishna Tagore's garden house in Varanasi. In February 1902 he and Swami Shivananda escorted ailing Swamiji to Belur Math and at his earnest request Swamiji took ayurvedic medicine for three weeks.

Swami Achalananda wrote about Swami Niranjanananda : "He had tremendous faith in the doctrine of service as established by Swami Vivekananda and he encouraged people to serve human beings as manifastation of God."

The Master's unrestrained love and concern for Niranjan and others :

Niranjan was fortunate enough to receive spontaneous love of the Master. In the garden house at Cossipore on the morning of 23 December 1885, Sri Ramakrishna said to Niranjan, "You are my father; I shall sit on your lap."[9]

One dark night Niranjan with a few of his brother disciples walked in the direction of a date palm tree near the southern boundary of Cossipore garden to get juce from it. They did not know that there was a very ferocious black cobra nearby the tree. The Master, who then needed help even to change his position in bed, rushed to the spot by a different route to drive away the venomous snake in order to save the boys.

Heroic type :

The character of Swami Niranjanananda was a unique mixture of opposites— of sternness and tenderness. Swamiji mentioned about Swami Niranjanananda's 'militant disposition'. He possessed some innate divine qualities—simplicity, fearlessness, purity, renunciation, truthfulness and steadiness. At the sametime he had a violent temper that was harnessed by the Master. One day while he was coming to Dakshineswar in a public ferry, some of his fellow passengers began to vilify Sri Ramakrishna. Finding his protest in vain, he began to rock the boat, threatening to sink it in mid stream. That had frightened the offenders who kept mum. When he reported the incident to the Master, the latter scolded him for his inability to curb his anger.

The Swami was stubborn. During the winter one day heating a large vessel of water for the Master's bath, Niranjanananda carried the whole vessel of water to the Master and said, "Sir I don't have enough sense to know how much water you need. Since I have brought it, you will have to use it." The Master was pleased by Niranjan's simple and fearless behaviour."[10]

Niranjan was one of the Master's monastic disciples who vehemently protested against Ramchandra Dutta's suggestion for installing the Master's relics at Kankurgachi Yogodyana, his retreat house. He and some others secretly shifted the major amount of the Master's relics to a separate urn and secretly kept at the house of Balaram Basu. Later (on 9 December 1898) Swamiji installed this second urn in the shrine at Belur Math.

The Swami had a great sense of humanity. Once he was carrying some sweets for the Master's offering. A little boy who holding his poor mother's hand was walking in the same direction, saw the packet of sweets and cried out, "Mother, I want to eat sweets'! She tried in vain to control her child. Niranjanananda said to the boy, "Please eat these sweets." The mother said, "Father, no. You are carrying these sweets for the Lord. It would be inauspicious if my son were to eat them." Niranjanananda replied, "No, mother, it would be all right. His eating would be the same as the Lord's eating."[11] He handed the packet to the boy and went back to the market to buy sweets for the Master.

Niranjanananda did not put too much stress on rituals and mantras. He was so large hearted that he would help Holy mother or brother-disciples in need. One day Swami Saradananda while bathing in a pond suddenly slipped from a step and fell into deep water. His life was at stake. Niranjanananda, risking his life, jumped in and rescued him. He served Swamis Yogananda and Adbhutananda suffering from small pox and pneumonia respectively. He helped Balaram Basu and Ramchandra Dutta two foremost lay disciples of the Master up to the time of their deaths. He took Girish chandra Ghosh while he was suffering from severe depression to the Mother who awakened optimism and spirits in him. Swami Achalananda wrote about Swami Niranjanananda: "He was extremely generous. Without any misgivings, he would take care of anyone who asked help from him."

Sincere gatekeeper :

Niranjan acted as a gatekeeper in the retreat of Sri Ramakrishna at Syampukur in 1885. He was fooled by an eminent actress Binodini whom he did not allow to meet the Master fearing that if Sri Ramakrishna talked too much or if he were touched by impure people his disease would be aggravated. One evening Binodini in disguise of a European gentleman was introduced to Niranjan by Kaliprasad (afterwards Swami Abhedananda) as his friend and met the Master who gave her some spiritual instructions and permitted her to touch his feet with her forehead.

At Cossipore garden house towards March-April 1886 Sri Ramakrishna's body because of terminal cancer became very emaciated. During those days of agony and anxiety of his disciples and devotees, once the Master said to Niranjan, "Look I am now in such a state that whoever sees me in this condition will attain liberation in this life by the grace of the Divine Mother. But know for certain that it will shorten my life." On hearing this from the Master, Niranjan who used to keep a watchful eye on him, became more alert like a sentinel on duty. He sat at the gate day and night with a turban on his head and a stick in his hand to keep the visitors off the Master. Sometimes he had to hurt people for the sake of the Master's life.

One day a psychotic woman who used to sing for Sri Ramakrishna at Dakshineswar, came to Cossipore at noon to see him. As Niranjan stopped her at the gate, she behaved hysterically. Hearing her cries, the Master asked Sashi (Later Swami Ramakrishnananda) to escort her to him and he blessed her. Then she began to visit more frequently. Niranjan prevented her visiting the Master time and again and finally she paid no further visits. Feeling sympathy for the woman, Rakhal (Later Swami Brahmananda) said "We all feel sorry for her. She causes so much annoyance and for that she suffers too." At once Niranjan commented, "You feel that way because you have a wife at home," Rakhal said sharply, "Such bragging! How dare you utter such words before him [Sri Ramakrishna]?"[12] Remaining silent on the issue Sri Ramakrishna recognized Rakhal's sympathy for an ailing humanity and Niranjan's sincere service to him as well.

Once Ramchandra Dutta came to see the Master. But Niranjan did not allow him. It hurt Ramchandra for he was one of the prominent devotees of Sri Ramakrishna. He then requested Latu (Afterwards Swami Adbhutananda) to offer his flowers and sweets to the Master and bring a little prasad for him. Latu who was shocked at this, said to Niranjan, "Brother, Ram Babu is our very own; why are you putting such restrictions on him?" Still Niranjan remained unyielding. Then Latu said to him bluntly, "At Shyampukur you allowed the actress Binodini to visit the Master and now you are stopping Ram Babu, who is such a great devotee." The caustic comments made Nirajan feel guilty about the incident and he allowed Ramchandra to meet the Master. Later when Latu went to the Master, the omniscient avatar said to him : "Look, never find faults with others : rather see their good qualities." Latu was embarrassed and coming down he apologized to Niranjan saying : "Brother, please don't mind my harsh remark. I am an illiterate person."[13]

Another day, Atul Ghosh, brother of Girish Chandra Ghosh wanted to visit the Master, but Niranjan stopped him at the gate. Atul was so hurt that he took a vow that he would not come to Sri Ramakrishna again unless someone personally came to his house and took him to the Master. Once Sri Ramakrishna asked Niranjan to bring Atul to check his health. Niranjan, at once, rushed to Atul's house and brought him there. On 20 February 1899 Sister Nivedita wrote from Kolkata to Miss J. MacLeod : And I wish you had been with me over that dead girl the other day when I heard the ring of Niranjanananda's voice. "A soldier and a gentleman"—that was what it felt like. "I heard that Sister Nivedita was here" he said, "and of course I came at once." And there he mounted guard, and it was just lovely...the ring of strength and that exquisite chivalry. It was too lovely.[14]

On the birthday (18 February) of Sri Ramakrishna Swami Niranjanananda became gatekeeper of Swami Vivekananda who had been suffering from diabetes and kidney disease, to prevent the general public from disturbing him. A young brahmacharin, a disciple of Swamiji hailed from Mayavati to visit him. Since Swami Niranjanananda did not know the brahmacharin, he stopped him at the gate. But while the Swami was talking to someone else, the young man crawling through his legs entered Swamiji's room. Learning about it from Swamiji, Swami Niranjanananda was not displeased with the clever brahmacharin, rather he appreciated resourcefulness and dedication of the young man.[15]

A major role in formation of Ramakrishna Mission Home of Service.

When Swami Niranjanananda was in Raipur, Suraj Rao an army officer met him and hearing about the wonderful life and message of Sri Ramakrishna was greatly inspired. Later he resigned from his job and was initiated by Swamiji. Afterwards he became known as Swami Nischayananda.

Sudhir an initiated disciple of Swamiji was greatly impressed and initiated into Sannyasa and was named as swami suddhananda by Swami Niranjanananda on 16 September 1898 at Almora. They left for Varanasi and stayed a few months at the garden house of Banshi Dutta and lived on alms, without possessions, depending solely on God. A group of young men were deeply moved by severe austerities and graceful personality of Swami Niranjanananda. The Swami inspired them to embrace spiritual life and to devote themselves to the service to all. This group observed the birthday celebration of Sri Ramakrishna under his guidance in 1899. Swami Kalyanananda, a disciple of Swami Vivekananda encouraged the youngmen namely Charuchandra Das (leader of the group, afterwards Swami Shubhananda), Kedarnath Moulik (later Swami Achalananda), Haridas Odedar (Later Swami Sadashivananda) Jaminiranjan Mazumdar, Vibhutiprakash Brahmachari, Haridas Chattopadhyay, Jnanendranath Singha and Pandit Shibnath Bhattacharya to practise the ideal of service. Accordingly they set up an organization named 'Poor men's relief association' in June 1900. Swamiji visited Varanasi in February 1902 and named it as "Ramakrishna Home of Service' because still then Ramakrishna Mission was not registered officially. In time it became famous as the Ramakrishna Mission Home of Service. Some youngmen of the group were initiated into sannyasa by Swamiji.

Response calmly to the clarion call :

Owing to hard austerity Swami Niranjanananda's health began to break down like those of Swamis Premananda and Yogananda. He suffered from chronic dysentery during the last few years of his life. Possibly he had a premonition that his days were numbered and resolved to spend the remaining days at Hardwar as the climate and water there were better than those of the Belur Math. He visited the Mother to receive her blessings and implored her to cook for him and feed him. She fulfilled his wishes. Washing her feet with tears he silently went off.

He lived in a rented cottage at Hardware and continued his meditation though dysentery was constantly emaciating his body. As an extra trouble, he was laid up with cholera. Taking shelter on the bank of the Ganga he surrendered himself to God. He refused his attendant's service saying, "Don't you want me to die in peace?"[16] He heroically embraced death in meditation on 9 May, 1904.

On 15 July, 1885 Sri Ramakrishna said to Balaram Basu : "Do you know what these youngsters are like? They are like certain plants that grow fruit first and then flowers. These devotees first of all have the vision of God; next they hear about His glories and attributes; and at last they are united with Him. Look at Niranjan. He always keeps his accounts clear. He will be able to go whenever he hears the call."[17]

Chapter – 10

SWAMI RAMAKRISHNANANDA

In his boyhood he worshipped Mother Durga in autumn for twenty-four hours at a stretch without leaving his seat. Such a phenomenal worship can not be possible without tremendous will-power, physical discipline, profound spiritual absorption, divine intoxication and above all orthodox upbringing. He himself disclosed the mystery, "Devotion can accomplish anything."

He, when young, threw all his Persian text books into the Ganga for fear of losing devotion to God.

After studying *Chaitanya Charitamrita* by Krishnadas Kaviraj, he decided to be a vegetarian for the rest of his life.

Buying a piece of ice he wrapped it with a paper and then with a towel. While walking over six miles from Kolkata to Dakshineswar, the scorching sun blistered his body but strangely could not melt the ice which his guru was fond of.

He was Shashi Bhusan Chakrabarty (later Swami Ramakrishnananda) born on Monday 13 July 1863 in Ichapur village (Hooghly District, W.B.). He was the eldest of eight children of his parents Ishwar Chandra Chakrabarty a court pandit of Raja Indra Narayan Singh of Paikpara and well versed in Tantra scriptures and disciplines and Bhavasundari Devi, a pious woman.

Multifaceted genius :

As a meritorious student Shashi won a scholarship in the Calcutta University Entrance examination. After passing his First Arts examination from the Albert college he entered the Metropolitan College (now Vidyasagar College) for his B.A. He left a commendable record in college before giving up his studies in order to serve his guru Sri Ramakrishna.

During the trying period of the begining of the Ramkrishna Movement, Swami Ramakrsihnananda worked as a teacher in the Baranagore High School for two hours daily after lunch forsaking his rest. He had to do this for three months to support the Baranagore monastery suffering from paucity of fund.

Some Bengali Christians from the Salvation Army used to visit Baranagore Monsastery frequently with the hidden intention of converting the monks who revered Jesus and celebrated Christmas Eve at the monastery. Once they dared to make a proposal of conversion to the monks saying that none but Christ could grant salvation. Swami Ramakrishnananda, well versed in the Bible, argued with Christian missionaries confidently and proved the fallacy of their dogmatic arguments.

Swami Ramakrishnananda, like his Master, was not an insipid ascetic. He was interested in literature. After dinner he used to roar with laughter along with other listeners while reading dramatically Mark Twain's 'The Innocents at Home' and 'The Innocents Abroad'. Besides, he had a bent for mathematics. Sometimes after his rest at noon he would work on the mathematics on a slate or piece of paper and enjoyed solving mathematical problems. Sometimes young students used to visit the monastery and some of them would stay there during their vacations. The swami would teach mathematics to those who were weak in that subject. One of the students was Haripada (later, Swami Bodhananda) who used to visit the monastery in 1890.

One day Girish Chandra Ghosh, a devotee of Sri Ramakrishna extolled the devotion and perseverence of Swami Ramakrishnananda:

"Shashi is *asana-siddha* [perfect in sitting]; otherwise it is impossible for anyone to worship Mother Jagaddhatri at a twenty-four hour stretch sitting in one place."[1]

Swami Ramakrishnananda could speak and write in Bengali, Sanskrit, English and Tamil. He was a prolific author who translated some teachings of Swami Ramakrishna into Sanskrit and some of the writings of Swamiji from Bengali into English and vice-versa. He contributed many substantial article to the Bengali magazine *Udbodhan*. He wrote *Sri Ramanuj Charit*, an authoritative biography of Ramanuja in Bengali. He was an author of some repository books in English—*God and Divine Incarnation, The Message of Eternal wisdom, Sri Krishna : Pastoral and King-maker, For Thinkers on Education, The Ancient Quest, Sri Ramakrishna and His Mission,* and *Search After Happiness.*

The Swami composed a beautiful Sanskrit hymn on Swamiji and wrote Sanskrit mantras for the Brahmacharya vows of the Ramakrishna Order. Besides, he introduced and systematized the ritualistic worship of the Master, which is now more or less followed by the centres of the Order.

Superhuman devotion to the Master :

Swami Ramakrishnananda's love for his guru was legendary. Once he said to Devamata (Laura Glenn), "The true devotee never thinks of himself. He is so full of the thought of God that his own self is forgotten. This body is only an instrument, a passive instrument, and an instrument really has no existence of its own, for it is wholly dependent on the one who uses it. Suppose a pen were conscious, it could say, 'I have written hundreds of letters,' but actually it has done nothing, for the one who holds it has writen the letters. So because we are conscious we think we are doing all these things, whereas, in reality we are as much an instrument in the hand of a Higher power as the pen in our hands and He makes all things possible."[2] The Swami considered himself an instrument in the hand of his guru.

Shashi's father left no stone unturned to detach his son from Sri Ramakrishna but failed. The furious father, it is said, criticised

Paramahamsa Deva in front of Shashi who immediately was about to stab him, saying "Who is my father?" Ishwar Chandra gladly said to his son, "Yes, your devotion to your guru is geniune."[3]

Sri Ramakrishna then suffering from terminal cancer, was taken to the Cossipore garden house on 11 December 1885. Since then Shashi dedicated himself to serve his guru for last eight months. He had a conviction that service to the guru was the highest form of religion and to serve the guru was his holy pilgrimage. So instead of practising meditation, asceticism or any other spiritual discipline and travelling holy places he, forgetting his personal needs, food or rest devoted himself to serve the Master.

> Once in the dead of a cold night Shashi wearing only a thin cloth left the Master's room to clean the commode. On returning he saw a pathetic sight that his guru who was too weak to rise or walk, somehow crawled across the room and was fetching a shawl hanging on a clothes horse. Shashi repented that in his hurry he had forgotten to cover his guru sufficiently, so probably he was cold and was trying to get a shawl. Shashi said to him in a rebuking tone, "What are you doing, sir? The air is very chilly, and you should not be up. Why did you not ask me for the shawl?" Holding out his shawl the Master said, "I felt cold as you went out almost barebodied on such a cold night, so I picked up this shawl for you. Please take this."[4] Thus reciprocal love captivated each other.

Ramchandra Dutta a prominent domestic devotee of Sri Ramakrishna and an author of the authentic book 'Sri Sri Ramakrishna Paramahamsa Dever Jeevan Vrittanta' took almost two pages (169-170) of his thin book to admire Shashi's service to his Master which he described as 'incomparable and imitable'.

Swamiji gave the name 'Swami Ramakrishnananda' to Shashi as he knew that Shashi's devotion to the Master was second to none.

Even after the passing away (16 August 1886) of the Master, Swami Ramakrishnananda continued service of his guru with great care and interest. Since 1887 some of his brother disciples began to travel as itinerant monks and practise austerities in the Himalayas or other holy places of India. Sometimes they would return to the monastery. During this period Swami Ramakrishnananda never went out.

Treating his guru as though he were physically living he tried to offer the choicest food and other necessaries. Swamiji said to his disciple Sharat Chandra Chakravarty : "After the passing away of Sri Ramakrishna we underwent a lot of religious practice at the Baranagore Math. We used to get up at 3 a.m. and after wahing our face etc.—Some after bath, and other without it—we would sit in the worship-room and become absorbed in japa and meditation. What a strong spirit of dispassion we had in those days! We had no thought even as to whether the world existed or not. Ramakrishnananda busied himself day and night with the duties pertaining to Sri Ramakrishna's worship and service, and occupied the same position in the Math as the mistress of the house does in a family. It was he who would procure, mostly by begging, the requisite articles for Sri Ramakrishna's worship and our subsistence."[5]

One day four monks went out for alms but received nothing. The monastery store also lacked provisions. The brother disciples, giving up hope for food, became absorbed in devotional singing. In order to save his guru from starvation, Swami Ramakrishnananda secretly went to the house of a friendly neighbour to beg for some rice, potatoes and little ghee (clarified butter). Although other members of his family had no sympathy for the young monks; he gave the Swami a half pound of rice, some potatoes and a little ghee. The Swami cooked food and offered it to his guru.

Swami Adbhutanada spoke of an incident about Swami Ramakrishnananda's uncompromising atitude of service to the Master :

One day brother Shashi aked the old swami [Swami satchidananda] to put a fresh twig, stripped of leaves and bark, in the shrine early in the morning to be offered to the Master for use as a toothbrush. The old swami did not know that one end of the twig was to be gently beaten to softern the fibers and make them brushlike. He brought a whole twig, unbeaten, as most people would use. During the breakfast offering Shashi saw this, and he rushed up to the old swami and scolded him bitterly. "You rogue, you have caused the Master's gum to bleed today. I will teach you a good lesson." I cried out to the old swami : "Don't just stand there looking at him, brother. Run away!" So he fled and the situation calmed down immediately. Shashi got another twig, properly beaten to soften the fibres, and threw away the first one."[6]

Swami Adbhutananda reminisced : once a householder devotee said "You fellow do nothing but act as priests to the photograph of the Master, burning incense and waving lights before it, just as orthodox priests do before the stone image of Goddess Sitala." These words irritated swami Ramakrishnananda who said bluntly : "The money of such a householder should not be touched with a barge pole! It is cursed."

Swami Ramakrishnananda spent the whole summer night fanning his guru with a palm leaf fan.

Swami Satchidananda who was the helper of Swami Ramakrishnananda for some time in the Alambazar monastery recollected : One day Swami Ramakrishnananda told me, "Before you sweep the room, first sprinkle a little water on the floor, otherwise the dust will go on the body of the Master." Another day he asked me to prepare betel-rolls for the Master; he chewed one and said, "You have put in too much lime. It will burn the Master's mouth." He entrusted me to put the Master to bed, to fan him for some time, and drop the curtain. When I went to take my supper, he aked, "Have you dropped the curtain?" "Yes, Swami," I replied.

Afterwareds he never aked me to put the Master to bed, because I had not fanned the Master for a sufficient time. One morning he went to prepare *halua* [farina pudding] for the Master, and found the pan dirty. When he learned that Latu Maharaj had fried gram with oil and chili in that pan, the Swami scolded him, but later he felt pained because he had hurt his brother.

Sri Ramakrishna used to chew spices, so Swami Ramakrishnananda used to keep those spices in a small bag near the Master's bed. He used to dry them after washing them, and clean them one by one so that there would not be any tiny stone particles in them. He would check my cleaning and ask me not to hurry ...

One night the Swami could not sleep because he was shivering from cold. He thought perhaps he had forgotten to put the quilt over the Master's picture. He immediately opened the shrine and found that his guess was correct. He covered the Master's picture with the quilt, then slept peacefully..[7]

Once Swami Ramakrishnananda, pointing to the picture of the Master in the shrine, said to Brahmachari Tejnarayan (later, Swami Sharvananda) : "Look here, my boy, don't consider that a mere picture of Sri Ramakrishna. He is actually present here. Try to feel his living presence and do your services accordingly."[8]

Swami Sharvananda reminisced about a touching incident.

> One day in the Madras (later, Chennai) Monastery Swami Ramakrishnananda came to know at 3:00 p.m. that there was no food in the storeroom to offer the Master at 4:00 p.m. Instead of being displeased with the monks for not informing him in time, the Swami aired his grievance against his guru saying : "You want to test me? I will eat sand and do Swamiji's work here. Sirrah! You are testing me, I know. But you should also know my grim resolve. I would rather die and perish here than budge an inch from this place. Do your worst, if you will." Miraculously at 3:30 p.m. Mr. Kondiah Chetty, an old student of the swami came with some of flour, ghee, sugar candy and dried fruits. He also offered five ruppes as a donation. Overwhelmed with joy Swami Ramakrishnananda at once prepared some refreshment in co-operation with the monks and offered it to the Master at 4:00 pm.

The first building of the Madras Monastery cracked in several places and water would come down through the craks in the roof when it rained. At such times Swami Ramakrishnananda would go into the shrine to check if water was leaking through the ceiling. One night the Swami, to his dismay, saw that rain water began to drip inside the shrine right on the Master's picture. He did not remove the picture to a safer place for that would wake his guru from sleep at an untimely hour. Rather he stood by the picture holding an umbrella till the rain ceased in the morning.

The Swami firmly believed that the prasad of Sri Ramakrishna had purifying power and whoever partook of a little prasad would be purified of all sins and blessed with unwavering faith and devotion.

Besides, there were such numerous incidents ('sublime spectacle's as has been said by Swami Sharvananda) to testify to Ramakrishnananda's matchless love for and devotion to his Master.

Exuberant devotion to the Holy Mother :

While staying in Madras since 1897 Ramakrishnananda earnestly wanted to get the Holy Mother there for he firmly believed that the whole of the South India would be purified by the holy touch of the blessed feet of the Mother. When the Swami was informed of the Mother's decision to go on a pilgrimage to Rameshwara where her father-in-law (Khudiram Chattopadhyaya) had made a pilgrimage on foot; he cordially invited her intimating his willingness to shoulder all responsibility. In the middle of February 1911 the Mother with her party reached Madras (later, Chennai) station where the Swami and a number of devotees gave a fitting reception to the Holy Mother raising a loud cry of joy and elation. The Swami had rented a two-storeyed house near the Ramakrishna Math at Mylapore where the Mother and her companions were accommodated. There she lived for about a month and visited various places of interest. Then she, with her party (excluding the aunt of Ramakrishna Babu, son of Balaram Bose owing to her illness) visited Madurai on their way to Rameshwara. Swami Ramakrishnananda himself accompanied them to see personally to their comfort and conveniences. The Swami procured for the Mother one hundred and eight golden bel leaves to worship Shiva the presiding Deity of the famous Rameshwara temple. When the temple staff communicated to the

Mother the wishes of Bhaskar Setupati, the Raja of Ramnad and a disciple of Swami Vivekananda to show the temple jewellery to her and present her any piece that she might ask for. She said : 'What can I need? Whatever was necessary has been arranged for by Shashi (Swami Ramakrishnananda).'[9]

While staying at the Ramakrisha Ashrama at Bangalore for about a week one day at dusk the Mother climbed a small hillock behind the Ashrama along with one or two companions to enjoy the beauty of the sunset. Hearing of this Swami Ramakrishnananda to his utter astonishment said : 'Indeed! The Mother has become *Parvata-vasini,* (a dweller on the mountain, an epithet of Mother Durga)!' He hurried to the Mother and laying his head on her feet chanted three well-known verses from the *Chandi,* begining with *Sarva-mangala-mangalaye*—the *mantras* for the salutation of the Divine Mother. He prayed 'Grace! grace'. The Mother caressed his head till he felf himself fully blessed.

Owing to overwork, lack of proper food and strenuous life in Madras Swami Ramakrishnananda became seriously ill with diabetes and tuberculosis and his body gradually was reduced to a skeleton. Towards the end the Swami was eager to see Holy Mother who was then at Jayrambati, her bithplace. Swami Dhirananda went there to bring her. But she could not come perhaps because she knew that it would be unbearable for her to witness Swami Ramakrishnananda's premature death. To quote Swami Gambhirananda : 'But after full deliberation, the Mother decided not to go. The tireless service that the Swami rendered to her in the South was still fresh in her mind. How could the Mother bear the sight of the passing away of such a devoted son?' After receiving the news of Swami Ramakrishnananda's passing away Holy Mother remarked with tearful eyes : "Alas, Shasi is gone. My back is broken."

The 'roof-tree' of the Order in early years :

If there were no Shashi (Swami Ramakrishnananda), there perhaps might be no monastery and none of his brother-monks who renounced the world. Swami Vivekananda would be prodigal while recalling the unparalled contribution of his diciple-brother Swami Ramakrishnananda to sustain the nascent monastery and its inmates.

Towards the beginning of 1902 Swamiji said to Sharat Chandra Chakravarty : "After the passing away of Shri Ramakrishna we underwent a lot of religious practice at the Baranagore Math. We used to get up at 3 a.m. and after washing our face etc.—some after bath, and others without it—we would sit in the worship-room and became absorbed in Japa and meditation. What a strong spirit of dispassion we had in those days! We had no thought even as to whether the world existed or not. Ramakrishnananda busied himself day and night with the duties pertaining to Shri Ramakrishna's worship and service, and occupied the same position in the Math as the mistress of the house does in a family. It was he who would procure, mostly by begging, the requisite articles for Shri Ramakrishna's worship and our subsistence. There have been days when the Japa and meditation continued from morning till four or five in the afternoon. Ramakrishnananda waited and waited with our meals ready, till at last he would come and snatch us from our meditation by sheer force. Oh, What a wonderful constancy of devotion we have noticed in him! ...

"Owing to want of funds I would sometimes fight for abolishing the Math altogether. But I could never induce Ramakrishnananda to accede to the proposal. Know Ramakrishnananda to be central figure of the Math."[11]

While living at the Baranagore monastery, Swamiji felt his attachment to the brother-monks as an obstacle to the progress to the realization of God. Therefore he persuaded his brother-disciples to go on pilgrimage so that they might have their own experiences of the new wandering life which would make men of them, absolutely bold and unconquerable and spiritually independent and thus they would become 'giants'. One by one all the brother-disciples, except Swami Ramakrishnananda, went on pilgrimage. In later years Swamiji used to say about him :

> I used to fire them (his brother-disciples) to break it up and go about the world begging. But on no account could I make Shashi yield. He would hear of nothing of the kind. You must know him to be the backbone of our Math.[12]

In fact, Swami Ramakrishnananda's love and respect for his brother monks almost bordered on worship.

Love for the leader :

Swamiji and his brother-disciples had reciprocal love and repect. There were a number of instances highlighting Swami Ramakrishnananda's love for their beloved leader.

One day in 1897 some pandits from West India came to the Alambazaer Monastery to test Swamiji's knowledge of the Vedas. Swami Ramakrishnananda seated in the shrine in meditation posture was counting his beads while their discussion was taking place. He said later on that he was praying whole heartedly to the Master so that Swamiji might win the debate.

One day Swamiji said to Swami Ramakrishnananda who was extremely orthodox : "Shashi, I want to put your love for me to the test. Can you buy for me a piece of English bread from a Muslim shop at the corner of Chitpore Road?"[13] A conservative Hindu would not even touch that kind of food. But Swami Ramakrishnananda obeyed the order of their leader unhesitatingly.

Swamiji knew well that Swami Ramakrishnananda preferred worshipping the Master and keeping vigil over the Master's remains to going on pilgrimage. Still he asked Swami Ramakrishnananda to go to Madras (later, Chennai) and found a monastery there in the name of Sri Ramakrishna. The sweepingg victory of Swamiji in the West caused a great sensation among the people of Madras who requested him to send one of his brother monks to set up a monastery there. Swamiji considered Swami Ramakrishnananda fit for the job. The latter, without raising any objection or pleading any excuse left for Madras in the last part of March 1897 to carry out the order of the leader.

Swamiji left Calcutta for America a second time, with Swami Turiyananda and Sister Nivedita in June 1899. Swami Ramakrishnananda and a large number of devotees gathered at the Madras harbour to meet Swamiji. But the Steamer was quarantined in the Madras harbour and was anchored far from the jetty because there was a plague in Calcutta. Swami Ramakrishnananda prepared single handedly salty (*nimki*) and sweet (*gaja*) snacks for Swamiji which he carried with him in serveral large cans. He took a boat with some devotees and the cans to the steamer. Swamiji greeted his brother monk and talked to him, leaning from the deck. Presents like food, fruits, flowers were drawn up in baskets and the Ganga water brought in a big jar by Swamiji for Swami Ramakrishnananda was lowered to them in the same basket.

Then Swami Ramakrishnananda said to his companion: "Please ask the boatman to take us right around the steamer. Let us at least make a *pradakshinam* [a religious rite to encircle the deity] of the two great souls whose feet we have not been able to touch today."[14]

The world saw a marvellous sight of love and respect for the great leader.

On the night of 4 July 1902, Swami Ramakrishnananda said to Swami Satchidananda, "I saw Swamiji standing before me and he said to me, 'Look here, Shashi, I threw away this body like spitting out spittle.' and he spat twice or thrice."[15] Both Swamis groped for the meaning of that vision throughtout the sleepless night. The next day when the Swami received a cable from Belur Math infoming of the passing away of Swamiji he and Swami Satchidananda cried for their beloved leader and arranged for a big memorial meeting in Madras.

Swami Shankarananda highlighted an instance of Swami Ramakrishnananda's unfathomable love for his leader :

One summer morning (between 1902 and 1903) Swami Ramakrishnananda returned from his classes by 10:30 a.m. in a hackney carriage. After entering his room he stripped himself, sat on the edge of his cot and began to fan himself. Seeing him in such a plight owing to the summer heat the brahmacharin began to fan him from behind. After a minute or so the Swami threw away his fan and with clenched fists threw out his arms as if to fight with somebody. He began to say, "It is for you that I suffer so much. See, what suffering I go through." The next moment he fell flat on the floor with outstretched hands and joined palms, and began to rub his face on the carpet, saying, "No brother, no brother, excuse me, excuse me. What you have done is perfect. It is all right, it is all right." He got up with flowing eyes and blissful countenance and cast a divine look around before he sat again. All this was with Swami Vivekananda, who had sent him to Madras to live the life as moulded by Sri Ramakrishna.[16]

Swami Vishuddhananda reminisced : Once I saw Swami Ramakrishnananda praying before an oil painting of Swami Vivekananda after his return from a lecture tour. I overheard his fervent prayers as he bowed down before him : "O my beloved brother, you are verily the accredited representative of Sri Ramakrishna and it is you who have sent me over here to propagate his message. I am only carrying out your commands. I beseech you to see to it that no pride or self-esteem enters my heart, no thirst for name or fame disturbs my mind. All the burden and the reponsibility that you have placed upon me are verily yours. Bless me so that I may carry on the work of our Master only as an instrument in his hands and that I may offer all the fruits of work into him. Guide me always in the right path." What a glorious example of self--surrender and dedication to God and his work![17]

Once in Ernakulam, South India, upon entering the house of Mr Duraiswami Aiyar, a reputed lawyer, Swami Ramakrishnananda said to him, "I have heard that Swami Vivekananda stayed in your house in his itinerant days. This is a holy place. I wish to see first the exact place or room where he stayed. Mr. Aiyer replied, "He was seated, when he came in, even where we stand now." At once Ramakrishnananda rolled on the floor and kissed the ground, for to him the very dust of the place where his leader had been was sacred.[18]

Swami Ramakrishnananda composed a beautiful Sanskrit hymn on Swamiji and translated some of the writings of Swamiji from Bengali into English and vice versa. He had so much love and esteem towards his leader that when he heard that Pandit Pramathanath Tarkabhusan had corrected Swamiji's Sanskrit compositions, he became disappointed and remarked: "Those words were composed by a *rishi* [a seer of truth]"[19]

Organizing power :

In many of his epistles Swamiji stressed organization. On 25 September, 1894 he expressed his pleasure in a letter from the U.S.A to his brother-diciples to learn that 'Shashi and others are making a stir.'[20] The same year he wrote to them: "What is wanted is a power of organization—do you understand me? ... Shashi (Ramakrishnananda) is executive to a degree ...

"We must electrify society, electrify the world. Idle gossip and barren ceremonials won't do. Ceremonials are meant for householders, your work is the distribution and propagation of thought-currents. If you can do that, then it is all right."[21] The next yerar Swamiji wrote a letter in which the addressee was Swami Ramakrishnananda exclusively and he wrote : "Now, let me give you some insructions. This letter is meant for you ..... but now we want organization ..... The reason why I give you these few instructions is that there is an organizing power in you—the Lord has made this known to me—but it is not yet fully developed. Through His blessings it will soon be. That you never lose your centre of gravity is an evidence of this, but it must be both intensive and extensive."[22] Considering Swami Ramakrishnananda's efficiency, Swamiji took him away from worship room in order to send him to Madras to start a monastery there. In 1897 the Madrasi devotees of Swamiji received Swami Ramakrishnananda cordially and rented Flora cottage for him. Shortly afterwards, Biligiri Iyengar, a leading lawyer and the owner of Castle Kernan (the Ice House), offered the first floor of that castle to the Swami to start his work. The Swami first set up the shrine in a room and installed a picture of Sri

Ramakrishna. Then he started to conduct worship and give classes on the Upanishads, Gita and Bhagavata in different parts of the city. He tried to inspire and train some young people. In addition, he had to cook and do all the household duties. He lived a strenuous life alone for most of the first four years undergoing indescribable suffering from financial crisis and starvation. After the death of Mr. Bhiligiri Iyengar in 1906 the Ice house was sold and the Swami had to take shelter temporarily in the gatehouse of the same compound. Since 1898 Swami Ramakrishnananda started to celebrate the birth anniversary of Sri Ramakrishna and many local people attended. The Swami and the devotees felt a dire need of a permanent home for the Master. The votaries began to collect donation to their building fund and in 1906 a student of the Swami donated a piece of land in Mylapore, Madras. On an auspicious day the Swami conducted the religious ceremonies and Swami Abhedananda laid the foundation stone. On 17 November 1907 the Swami dedicated the building where the new ashrama was set up shortly afterwards.

At the Swami's instance Ramaswamy and Ramanujachariar started a free boarding-house for poor students. This later developed into a large residential institution providing education, food and other necessaries free of cost to deserving students. Following this a number of educational institutions were set up in Madras city. Thus Swami Ramakrishnananda was the initial inspiration behind all academic activities conducted by the Ramakrishna Mission in Madras.

On the invitation of the Vedanta Society of Ulsoor, Bangalore, the Swami went there on 19 July 1903 and stayed there for a fortnight. His lectures and interviews attracted large numbers of devotees who were interested in starting a permanent centre in Bangalore. The Swami himself went from door to door collecting money to start it. On 20 January 1909 Swami Brahmananda opened a centre at Bangalore.

Once Swamiji said, 'Mysore in time will be a great stronghold.' Swami Ramakrishnananda visited Mysore in October 1903 and delivered lectures at Rangachari Hall and an address in Sanskrit to the pundits at the Sanskrit college. Thus he prepared the ground so as to fulfill the prophecy of Swamiji.

In Trivandrum the Swami encouraged the devotees to establish a Vedanta Society for continuing the work initiated by him.

The Swami's visits to Rangoon and Bombay were also very successful in establishing permanent centres there in course of time.

Swami Gahanananda wrote in an essay 'The other Apostles of Sri Ramakrishna' : "Ramakrishnanada's life of 14 years in Madras (1897-1911) marked the beginning of a great epoch in spreading the Ramakrishna Movement in South India, and he was rightly called 'Sri Ramakrishna's Apostle to the South."[23] At Puri on hearing the sad news of passing away of Swami Ramakrishnananda, the grief-stricken brother-monk Swami Brahmananda lamented: 'The guardian angel of the South has passed away. The southern side is, as it were, covered with darkness.'[24]

The great organizer was too polite to claim credit for his glorious achievement in the South. He remarked, 'It is no credit of mine. The Master's grace and Swamiji's command are mainly responsible for the success of my work in the South.'[25]

An ideal preacher and teacher :

Once Swami Ramakrishnananda said to Swamiji, 'How can one be a good preacher?' Swamiji first touching his head said, 'One needs good intellect.' Then touching his face, he said, 'One should have good looks.'Touching his lips, he said, One should have a sweet tongue.' Touching his chest, he said, 'One should have a broad, catholic heart, otherwise people won't listen to you. I achieved more through my loving heart than through my sharp intellect.' At last, pointing to his sex organ, he said, 'One should have self-control. This chastity is the most vital aspect in a preacher's life.'[26] Swami Ramakrishnananda possessed each of those qualities mentioned by Swamiji.

The Swami visited all over South India preaching the Hindu religion and philosophy as well as the message of Sri Ramakrishna and Swamiji for 14 years tirelessly. Wherever he went he, with his melodious voice, serene look and extensive lectures and cordial manners was able to arouse a tangible sensation among a lot of people and their interest in the message of Sri Ramakrishna.

During his short stay in Rangoon Swami Ramakrishnananda once visited the Shwedagon Pagoda where he met an Irish Buddhist monk who believed that Buddhism alone was true and catholic while all other religions were insubstantial and narrow. He wanted to know about the specialty of Sri Ramakrishna's teaching. The Swami said to him : He (Sri Ramakrishna) realized and preached the harmony of religions. Buddha, christ, Muhammad and other world teachers—each proclaimed that the religion taught by him is the only way to salvation. The difference between Sri Ramakrishna and other prophets is that he himself preached no new religion, but practised all religions in his life and experienced the universal truth underlying them all. His message can be summed up in the sentence : 'As many faiths so many paths.'

The impact of the Swami's visit and lectures in Rangoon took shape twenty years later in the form of the Ramakrishna Mission Hospital and the Ramakrishna Mission Library and Cultural Centre.

On May 25, 1884 Sri Ramakrishna said to Vijaykrishna Goswami: "The sannyasin, the man of renunciation, is a world teacher. It is his example that awakens the spiritual consciousness of men."[27] Like all other brother-monks Swami Ramakrishnananda too was an embodiment of amazing renunciation. Once he said to an American devotee : "Man must give up everthing to God, then alone he thrives. If you study all the personal religions, you will find that all preach renunciation. Renunciation is their fundamental teaching."[28] He taught; 'Those who give up the world for spiritual life are giving up the uncertain for the certain, the passing for the permanent. All our power comes from renunciation. Only when we have given up our lives do we begin to live. At present we are like prisoners. We may get a glimpse of freedom now and then but the world falls upon us when we are off our guard and drags us back once more into our prison cells. As soon as a man finds out, however, that these little pleasures of the flesh are nothing compared with the infinte pleasures of the spirit, he wants to renounce; not for the sake of renunciation but because he has found something better.' He had realized the hollowness of the enjoyments of the world and can be satisfied only with higher enjoyment. Renunciation means giving up a lesser thing for a greater.'[29] Another time the Swami said : "So long as we are selfish our work must be fruitless. We may deliver fine lectures, we may gain name and fame, but the actual results will be nil. The moment, however that our little self disappears, at that moment our real work begins. Then we may live an obscure life and go nowhere, but we shall accomplish wonders .....

"The word 'selfishness' is not always understood. When by 'self' I understand the body or the little self and I do something for that self, I am selfish. But there is a Self which is beyond this physical body; when I do something for that Self, that is wroshipping God. The man who lives in that higher Self is never selfish. Try to feel God inside yourself and you will overcome all selfishness."[30]

Once Swami Ramakrishnananda said to someone who came with words of condemnation on his lips : "Never find fault with any form of religion. Differences are all in the external customs. That which makes up the external is the shell. It may be hard and rough and perhaps not to our liking, but it holds a valuable kernel. The kernal of every religion is God. To whatever religion a man belongs, he has to worship the same God. The essential parts of religion are everywhere the same. It is only in the nonessential parts that differences are found...'[31]

The Swami used to correct the habits obstructive to spiritual progress of the students. One day he said to a student sitting in his class with his chin resting on the palm of his hand "Do not sit like that; it is a pensive attitude." Another day he found a student gently shaking his legs while sitting on a bench. He at once said to him, "Stop shaking, it is not good and conducive to well-being." He advised the students who drank water while standing to sit and drink. Thus the Swami took so much interest in the spiritual welfare of his students and tried to regulate their habits.

The Swami would talk to the inmates of the monastery how his Master was careful about every little thing in his room and how he would correct doubts and misgivings of his disciples and used to make mimicry of other persons at Dakshineswar.

The Swami did not like to have the ambience of the monastery contaminated with worldly talks and gossip with delight of the wordly visitors. He said to them, 'You can do that anywhere. Here you should try to think of God.'[32]

The humanistic awareness nurtured by Sri Ramakrishna and Swamiji was illustrated as Swami Ramakrishnananda said to Sister Devamata (Laura Glenn) : "Work for others is self-amelioration. We need to serve others in order to lift ourselves up out of the state of degradation and selfishness into which we have fallen. We should be grateful to the needy for making it possible for us to raise ourselves. That is the only real good that comes out of all that we do for others; we merely better ourselves."[33]

Once the Swami said to Sister Devamata : "Mind is like a big mirror which gives a perfect reflection but which has been so thickly covered with dirt that nothing can be seen in it. The more you can rub off that dirt the more you will be able to see youself in it. The more you can remove the least speck of dust the more you can get a perfect image of your true self. What is the dirt that hides the image? Selfish desire. Be free from every selfish desire. That is purity. Purity means singleness. Desire is a very dangerous thing. Sometimes we think we have killed all selfish desires; but somewhere in our mind there lingers some remnant, and as from a spark left in the corner of the hearth may come again a big fire, so out of that small remnant may spring a huge fire of desire."

One evening someone asked Swami Ramakrishnananda how one should practise meditation. The Swami replied : "Meditation means complete self-abandonment. Meditation requires complete annihilation of self-consciousness. You know that before a great light, lesser lights disappear so before the effulgent glory of God, the little glory of the ego will completely vanish, as stars vanish when the sun rises. You must therefore practise the presence of God inside you. You may say, 'I cannot see Him with these eyes of mine. I can not hear Him with these ears. How then am I to perceive Him?' You can never perceive Him in this way. To go to the Creator you must throw aside these instruments which take you directly to the creation. You must go beyond your mind and senses, then meditation will come of itself. This is the only way to get inner vision. These senses are made for creation, not for the Creator."[34]

Thus the Swami taught in lucid language and used appropriate examples as his Master did to impress the listeners.

Unique definitions of avatar and religion :

Swami Ramakrishnananda explained the meaning of the phrase avatar Sri Ramakrishna to Brahmachari Tejnarayan (later, Swami Sharvananda) in the language of mathematics : "Swami Vivekananda and all his lectures and writings plus all the disciples of the Master and their works plus the infinte—are equal to Sri Ramakrishna."[35]

In Madras in his inaugural lecture on 'Necessity of Religious Education in Youth', Swami Ramakrishnananda said : "Religion takes a man to God by making God of a man. ... Religion is the highest chemistry, for it analyzes the compound man into the elements, ego and nonego, the self and the nonself, the soul and the body. Religion is the burning furnace in which is burnt up all the dross of his heart."

Sister Devamata worte, the Swami defined religion as 'the struggle of spirit against matter.' Once he told her : "Science is the strugle of man in the outer world. Religion is the struggle of man in the inner world. Science makes man strugle for Truth in the outside universe, and religion makes him struggle for Truth in the inner universe. Both strugles are great, no doubt, but one ends in success and the other ends in failure. That is the difference. Religion begins where science ends. The whole scientific method is based on observation and experiment but the moment man realizes that there is something beyond observation and experiment he will give them up and leave material science behind. Science will always have to deal with finite bodies; and God is infinte."[36]

Strong personality :

Swami Ramakrishnananda carried masculine spirit in his veins. Shashi carried the urn containing the ashes and bones of the Master on his head to the Cossipore garden house. After the passing away of the Master, the next day Ramchandra Dutta a prominent householder devotee of the Master visited the garden to advise the disciples of the Master to return to their homes and disclosed to them that he had a plan to enshrine the relics of the Master at his garden house at Kankurgachi and establish a monastery there. But Shashi and Niranjan refused.to his face to give the reclics as they would continue the worship service of the Master. Consulting with Narendranath and other disciples they secretly put the greater portion of the relics into an urn and kept it at Balaram Basu's house for the time being. Afterwards the relies were brought to Baranagore monastery.

Once some Bengali Christians visited the Baranagore monastery and audaciously made a proposal of conversion to Swami Ramakrishnananda and others who had love and admiration for Jesus Christ; saying that none but Christ could grant salvation. Swami Ramakrishnananda was well versed in the Bible and with strong arguments proved the fallacy of the dogmatic statement of the Christian missionaries. After losing the debate, the crooked missionaries tried to tempt the monks, saying that if they became Christians they would be provided with European wives! At these offensive words the Swami became furious and asked them to leave the monastery.

In 1897 when the people in Madras requested Swamiji to send one of his brother monks to start a monastery there; Swamiji, keeping Swami Ramakrishnananda in his mind, said to them : "I shall send you one who is more orthodox than your most orthodox brahmins of the South and who is at the same time incomparable in performing worship, scriptural knowledge, and meditation on God."[37]

Swami Ramakrishnananda was an uncompromising task master. A routine framed by him was strictly followed by the monks in the Madras Monastery. He stressed the importance of punctuality. He had an affectionate mother's heart. If he would scold a brahmacharin or a monk for any kind of mistake or dereliction of duty; after a short while he would console him saying : "Do you know what Sri Ramakrishna used to say? A blacksmith first puts a lump of iron into the fire; when it becomes red hot, he puts it on the anvil and beats it into shape? That is how an unformed lump of metal is shaped into a useful article! All of you are like that unformed lump, and it is for your good that you are put to the forge and beaten into shape on the anvil by such scoldings."[38]

Swami Ramakrishnananda was a strict disciplinarian and true to his word. One drizzly afternoon the Swami acompanied by a brahmacharin went to Geroge Town by a hackney carriage to give class. But the room was desolate. He waited for about fifteen minutes but none turned up. He then began to read and explain his Upanishad enthusiastically. After an hour he closed his book and rode the carriage to return. On the way the brahmacharin said to the Swami, "How is it that you gave the class for fully one hour though nobody turned up." Swami Ramakrishnananda answered : "I have not come to teach anybody. I only fulfill the vow I have taken."[39]

The Swami never compromised the truth. Referring to the teachings of Sri Ramakrishna he taught his students that purity and renunciation are essential in spiritual life and 'God and Mammon' cannot be worshipped simultaneously. On hearing such words a few influential figures of the city (Madras) were displeased and feared that their boys would leave family in order to become monastics. They threatened to withdraw financial support if the Swami continued those tecahings. Swami Ramakrishnananda had guts to tell a votary : "Am I to preach other than what I learned from my Master? Certainly I won't do that. I don't care a fig for the bigwigs. They are at liberty to do whatever they like. If I am ousted today from the castle, I shall very gladly find accommodation in a room of one of my students' houses. I am a sannyasin and do not know where my next meal will come from."[40]

Swami Ramakrishnananda visited the famous Meenakshi Temple at Madurai with Swami Brahmananda. While coming out of the temple the former saw an image of Shakaracharya the great teacher of Vedanta in the front hall. As he went to touch his feet with his head, the priests obstructed him Shoving them aside he roared : "Who can prevent my worshipping the Great One?"[41] His immeasurable devotion kept the priests mum and he fulfilled his desire.

Swami Ramakrishnananda was a powerful orator and monk of spotless character. Sister Devamata wrote : "If Swami Ramakrishnananda was a conservative in his mode of worship, he was essentially a liberal in his religious conviction. Tolerance, universality of outlook, freedom from all prejudice—these formed the keystones of his thought structure."[42] His whole mind was fully occupied with thoughts of God. He had in him an amazing perfection of four yogas.

The Swami had a sense of humour. Sometimes he talked to the monks about the amusing gestures Sri Ramakrishna used to make or the mimicry of other persons at Dakshineswar even without any reservation with regard to the use of abusive language.

On the occasion of birthday celebration of the Master Swami Ramakrishnananda was distributing Khichudi (Hotchpotch) from a pail. Dharmapal, a Buddhist monk said to him, "What are you doing? Give them spiritual food." The Swami quipped, "Yes, but now I am giving them material food." In "Smritir Aloy Swamiji' edited by Swami Purnatmananda, Haricharan Mallick reminisced the event (P. 263).

Christ's disciple :

On 23 December 1885 Sri Ramakrishna said to M. at Cossipore garden house : "The Divine Mother used to reveal to me the nature of the devotees before their coming. ... In a vision I saw that Shashi and Sarat had been among the followers of Christ."[43]

Sister Devamata wrote : "He (Swami Ramakrishnananda) knew the Bible from cover to cover and expounded it in a spirit and with an understanding which are rare even in Christian countries. ... When Good Friday came, he talked on the Crucifixion... My whole being was stirred by the living reality of his words and as we drove home I asked how he could make them so real and living. He sat silent for a moment, then he said quietly and simply. 'My Master used to tell me that in a previous life Saradananda and I were Christ's disciple.'[44]

During his last days the Swami became inspired when he, forgetting his suffering, talked about the Master and Christ. He would recall how Sri Ramakrishna had regarded him as Christ's companion in his previous life.

One evening the Swami accompanied by Swami Paramananda and P.M. Mudaliar a devotee went to Saidapet in order to respond to a dinner invitation by one of his students. After pertaking of dinner he visited a church at the summit of Saint Thomas Mount near by to keep an appointment with the pastor of the church. As the gate was opened, the Swami, to the amazement of his companions went straight to the altar, knelt before it as a Christian would do and prayed. Despite being orthodox Sri Ramakrishnananda possessed catholicity.

Rightly wrote Sisiter Devamata : "What Saint Paul declared in his Epistle to the Galatians, 'Yet not I, but Christ liveth in me,' prefectly described Swami Ramakrishnananda's attitude towards himself and towards that one whom he called guru. He was dead wholly to himself and alive only in Sri Ramakrishna."[45]

Sister Nivedita eulogised Swami Ramakrishnananda in a letter to Miss J. MacLeod in 21 December 1902 : "How strong Swami Ramakrishnananda! My soul is full of that peace which comes only where worship is constant."[46] Further she wrote to the same addressee on 29 December 1902 : "Swami Ramakrishnananda has been more than good. He has given his strong quiet presence and support to every lecture and every conversation."[47]

> The remarkable contribution of Swami Ramakrishnananda to the Ramakrishna Order is his tireless service to the Master both during his illness at Cossipore and also at the Baranagore monastery through the worship of his relics. Later this worship of Sri Ramakrishna, in some form or other was introduced in almost every centre of the order. Another imprssive contribution was the Swami's commitment to take care of the monastery and its inmates duirng its inception at Baranagore. Swami Gahanananda said : "Sri Ramakrishna sowed the seed of the monastery, Vivekananda transplanted the seedling to Baranagore and Ramakrishnananda nourished it with all his motherly care. And this he did at great personal sacrifiece. ...Thus his contribution to the Organization is marked both by its extensity and intensity."[48]

Chapter – 11

SWAMI SARADANANDA

He used to save his pocket money to help his deserving classmates buy books, papers or something else and would give his used clothes, shoes and so on to his poor friends. He tried utmost to save the life of his neighbour's maid servant who was a victim of cholera and was sent to the roof uncared for by her master fearing contagion. He miraculously survived drowning one evening in a sudden storm on the Ganga in 1905. He was 'among the followers of Christ'.

He was Sharat Chandra Chakrabarty (later Swami Saradananda) born in Kolkata on 23 December 1865 as a son of Girish Chandra Chakrabarty and Nilmani Devi belonging to a well-off family. He was a meritorious student of Albert School and later of Hare School and used to take a leading role in his school's debating society. He was admitted to Calcutta Medical College but did not continue his studies. He was very robust thanks to regular exercise and nutritious food. Romain Rolland said, "He (Sri Ramakrishna) was very particular about perfect health. The chief disciples—Vivekananda, Brahmananda, Saradananda, Turiyananda, etc.—seem to have been of athletic build, tall and broad and possessing rare physical strength."[1]

Tremendous Yearning for God :

Swami Saradananda inherited a strong religous inclination from his pious mother. In 1883 in his room at Dakshineswar Sri Ramakrishna at first sight identified Sharat as his own and sensing his spirit of renunciation, he said to him "Bricks and tiles, if burnt with the trademark on them, retain those marks forever. Similarly you should enter the world after advancing a little in the path of spirituality. Then you will not sink in the mire of worldliness."[2]

One day at Dakshineswar when Sharat told sri Ramakrishna that he liked the character of Ganesha very much and Ganesha was his ideal; the Master, in order to rectify his attitude said, "No Ganesha is not your ideal. Your ideal is Shiva. In you lie dormant the attributes of Shiva. Always think of yourself as Shiva and me as your Shakti [power]. I am the ultimate repository of all your powers."[3]

With a view to practise spiritual disciplines under the guidance of the Master Sharat started staying at night at Dakshinewar. One day first appearing as a Kalpataru (wish fulfilling tree) Sri Ramakrishna said to him, "How would you like to realize God? What divine vision do you prefer to see in Meditation?" Sharat replied, "I do not want to see any particular form of God in meditation. I want to see Him in all beings. I do not like visions." The Master said with a smile, "That is the last word in spiritual attainment. You cannot have it all at once." "But I won't be satisfied with anything short of that," replied Sharat, "I shall strive my best until I am able to attain it." At last the Master blessed him saying, "Yes, you will attain it."[4] His blessing came true in this disciple's life.

On April 9, 1887 at the Baranagore monsatery Narendranath said to M., "He (the Master) has given me charge of Sharat. Sharat is now yearning for God, the Kundalini is awakened in him."[5]

Organizer :

One day at Dakshineswar Sri Ramakrishna sat upon the lap of Sharat in an ecstatic mood and later said to the inquisitive devotees, "I was testing how much weight he could bear."[6] In fact, Sharat afterwards carried the heavy weight of responsibility of the nascent Ramakrishna order for nearly thirty (1898–1927) years.

Swami Saradananda possessed all the qualities of an ideal organizer: sound judgement, evenmindedness, tenderness of heart, mental poise, diligence, steadiness and so on. Besides, he was familiar with Western methods of organization. As a far-sighted leader Swamiji knew that Swami Saradananda would play an important role in the life of the organization founded by him. He selected this brother-disciple as the general secretary (executive chief) of Ramakrishna Math and Ramakrishna Mission. In a letter[7] to his brother-disciples at Alambazar monastery Swamiji expressed his confidence in the power of organization of Saradananda three years before the foundation of the Ramakrishna Mission Association (on 1 May 1897). His humanity and humility helped him succeed as an organizer. He acted as the mother of the Order.

Swami Saradananda knew human nature very well. He adopted three basic methods to rectify the attitude of the monks who were not docile and took shelter in Udbodhan being banished by other centres. The methods were to give them liberty, to love them and to rely on them. In 1919 the Swami wrote to the head of a centre who faced problems with some monks : "Each soul is eternally free, so each person desires to be free in every respect of his life. A real leader never obstructs others' freedom, rather he teaches how one should enjoy freedom properly even in the field of action."[8] He was experienced enough to realize that the causes of unrest and conflict in the monastery were hatred, bad temper, intolerance for others' mistakes, incompatibility between the mind and the speech and above all, an attempt to control the monks through tricks and politics in lieu of selfless love.

The message of Swamiji 'Service to man is service to God' and 'work is worship' was embodied in the activities of Swami Saradananda. Under his guidance the Ramakrishna Mission conducted relief service immediately whenever there were natural calamities namely flood, famine, earthquake, epidemic etc. His great qualities of head, heart and hand together with his acquaintance with Western methods of organization were what that the new organization needed most at that point of 'breaking new ground' for its consolidation, development and onward march. He was democratic in his style of governance and treated everyone, even the junior most member of the Order as his equal.

After the passing away of Swamiji, Swami Brahmananda and Swami Saradananda had to face and solve numerous problems—Sister Nivedita's dissociation from the fold, crisis of management of *Udbodhan*, the Bengali organ of the Order, following Swami Trigunatitananda's departure for America, permanent residence for the Holy Mother in Kolkata and the problem of a permanent house for *Udbodhan* office etc.

As the fearless secretary of the Ramakrishna Order, Swami Saradananda accorded permission to former revolutionaries Debabrata Basu and Sachindra Nath Sen (1909) and Priyanath Dasgupta (1912) afterwards known as Swami Prajnananda, Swami Chinmayananda and Swami Atmaprakashananda respectively. He knew well that to accept them into the Order was to invite displeasure and suspicion of the British government and the police. But as a patriot and judicious person he could not refuse admission to the sincere spiritual aspirants simply because of their past political activities. The police summoned Swami Saradananda and Atmaprakashananda for questioning. The Swami, ignoring discourtesy of the police official gently assured him that the Ramakrishna Order is a non-political philanthropic and religious organization and the young men who joined the Order had given up all political activites. The British government was annoyed with the Order about the works of Swami Vivekananda when the police found Swamiji's books in the houses of the revolutionaries and understood that they had been inspired by the patriotic writings and lectures of Vivekananda. In Dhaka on 11 December 1916 during his Durbar speech Lord Carmichael, the governor of Bengal made some offensive remarks against the Ramakrishna Mission which tarnished public image of the Mission.

The general public avoided the Mission fearing that they might be harassed or tortured by the police. Besides the government might impose total ban on the activities of the Mission. In order to dispel doubt and misunderstanding the Swami wrote a memorandum, containing twelve points, to Lord Carmichael on 23 January 1917. Mr. Gourlay, the Governor's secretary, and Mr. Denham the police chief visited Belur Math to see Saradananda on 2 March. The Swami was invited on 10 March to the Governor's house where he discussed the role of the Mission and change of attitude of the former revolutionaries with the governor for an hour and convinced him of the fact. As a result of Saradananda's persuasion on 26 March the governor withdrew his statement—a historic event during the British rule in India. He wrote to the Swami :

> Dear Sir,
>
> I thank you for having come to see me and for the trouble you have taken to tell me about the origin of the Ramakrishna Mission and its aims and objects.
>
> I read with great interest the memorial which the Mission authorities submitted to me sometime ago. I regret very much to hear that words used by me at the Durbar in December last regarding the Mission should have led in any way to the curtailment of the good religious, social and educational work the Mission has done and is doing. As you, I know, realize my object was not to condemn the Ramakrishna Mission and its members. I know the character of the Missions's work is entirely non-political, and I have heard nothing but good of its work of social service for the people. ...
>
> Yours Very sincerely,
> (Sd.) Carmichael[9]

Public's fear disapperaed when this letter was published. The police survellance was also withdrawn. Thus Swami Saradananda overcame the crisis calmly. Swami Chetanananda rightly wrote about Swami Saradananda : "He was a wonderful troubleshooter."[10]

In 1926 Swami Saradananda convened the first convention (1 April 1926-8 Ap.) of the Ramakrishna Math and Mission in Belur Math. It was attended by many monks and devotees from all over the world. He delivered two important speeches those were considered to be the guidelines of the Ramakrishna Order. He realized that the Master's direct disciples were passing away one after another (Swamis Yogananda, Vivekananda, Niranjanananda, Advaitananda, Trigunatitananda, Premananda, Adbhutananda, Ramakrishnananda, Brahmananda), so the next generation of the fold should come forward to shoulder responsibility. A working Committee was formed for the conduct and control of all the activities of the organization. Thus Swami Saradananda manifested his farsightedness and respect for democratic principles.

One day Holy Mother said to one of her disciples : "Look at Sharat! He works so much, he faces so many problems, yet he remains calm and never complains. He is a *sadhu* [holy man]. Why does he undergo all these things? If he wishes he can remain absorbed in God day and night. It is only for your good that he is living on this earthly plane."[11]

Swamiji said : "The Master brought Sharat for his work."

Like Leader like Soldier :

Selected by Swamiji as his assistant in England and America :

While propagating the messsage of vedanta in England and America for several years, 'the cyclonic Hindu' Swamiji urgently needed an assistant to hold the momentum and asked Swami Saradananda to come to England. Initially he was hesitant about responding to the call but when he sought for the Mother's advice, she said to him : "My son, be not afraid. You should go to the West. The Master will protect you, and will be with you wherever you go.'[12]

On 1 April 1896 Swami Saradananda reached England. He was the guest of Mr. E.T. Sturdy, a vedanta student in London. Swamiji arrived there at the end of April and was very happy to see him and to hear about the activities of his brother disciples in India.

From May 1896 Swamiji busied himself with giving five classes a week, Jnana Yoga lectures on Sundays and meeting new people. Swami Saradananda had no previous experience in public lecturing. So he atteneded Swamiji's lectures and learned how to lecture in the West. He gave some classes on the Gita. Prof. Maxuller, a reputed German orientalist and writer of an article on Sri Ramakrishna entitled 'A Real Mahatman' in the 'Nineteenth Century', asked Swamiji to furnish him with enough material so that he could write about Sri Ramakrishna in details and authentically. Swamiji asked Swami Saradananda to undertake the job immediately. The Swami laboured much to gather all the incidents in the life of the Master and his teachings and showed the manuscript to Swamiji. In reference to this Swami Saradananda recounted :

"I thought Swamiji would edit it and make extensive corrections. He didn't do that. He simply changed a few words for fear of exaggeration and sent the whole manuscript to Professor Muller. As I remember, Professor Muller incorporated the complete manuscript in his book' *The Life and sayings of Sri Ramakrishna* and published it without making any alterations."[13]

In 1894 Swamiji set up the Vedanta Society of New york. In June 1896 he asked Saradananda to go to America with his English disciple and stenographer J. J. Goodwin, to continue discourse on vedanta. Sensing his nervousness about lecturing, Swamiji encouraged him, "Look I have already lectured there. You just teach them a little Gita and Upanishad, and answer their questions. That is all."

A hearty welcome was given to Swami Saradananda by the Vedanta Society of New York on January 16 at the New Century Hall. At the meeing Dr. E. G. Day spoke as follows :

"... I wish to assure you that his (Swamiji's) mantle has fallen on worthy shoulders in the person of the Swami Saradananda who will now teach the Vedanta studies among us. I am sure that I voice your sentiments when I say that we are ready to extend to him the love and loyalty we had for his predecessor. Let us extend to the new Swami a hearty welcome."[14]

Swami Saradananda's lucid explanation of the Vedanta philosophy and graceful personality won the heart of the audiences. He was invited to lecture at the Green Acre Conference of Comparative Religions in Maine. There he gave classes on Yoga. He delivered lectures in Brooklyn, New York and Boston and used to give classes regularly in Montclair and New Jersey. He lectured at the Cambridge Conferences. Dr. Lewis G. Janes, director of the Cambridge Conferences appreciating Swami Saradananda's contribution wrote to the editor of the *Brahmavadin* :

"In Cambridge; the classes in the Vedanta philosophy, constituting a single feature in the broad field of comparative study outlined for the Cambridge Conferences, attracted large and intelligent audiences, in part made up of professors and students of Harvard University. The Swami's exposition of the principles of the Advaita doctrine, in just comparison with other views which are held in India, was admirably lucid and clear. His replies to questions were always ready and satisfactory ... In Boston, Waltham and Worcester, Masachusetts, Swami Saradananda conducted a series of lectures which were largely attended and which everywhere manifested a sustained interest in his subject."[15]

Swamiji was delighted to learn about the progress of his brother disciple's work in America. While Saradananda was gaining ground as a popular exponent of Vedanta in America, Swamiji called for him to help him organize the Ramakrishna Mission at Belur. After having stayed two and a half years in America, Swami Saradananda handing over the charge of the Vedanta Society to Swami Abhedananda sailed with Mrs. Ole Bull and Miss MacLeod for India on 12 January 1898.

A good shepherd :

An Ideal spiritual teacher :

On December 14, 1882 Sri Ramakrishna said to Vijaykrishna Goswami, a leader of the Brahmo Samaj : "The task of a religious teacher is indeed difficult. One cannot teach men without a direct command from God. People won't listen to you if you teach without such authority. Such teaching has no force behind it. One must first of all attain God through spiritual discipline or some other means. Thus armed with authority from God, one can deliver lectures.

After receiveing the command from God, one can be a teacher and give lectures anywhere. He who receives authority from God also receives power from Him. Only then can he perform the difficult task of a teacher.'[16]

Swami Saradananda was a knower of Brahman. The unique synthesis of noble character, decent behaviour, intense spirituality, intellectual acuity and acumen, graces of head, hand and heart and love for man made him an ideal spiritual teacher. Considering his impaired health once some monks asked him to abstain from giving initiation. Swami Saradananda said, "Do not say that. I consider myself blessed that people come to me to hear the Lord's name. It is not they but I who have to be thankful for this. I am fortunate indeed that I have been given the privilege of telling them of the Lord."[17]

The Swami was in the language of the Gita *Sthita-prajna, Sthitadhi* :

"He whose mind is not perturbed in pains, who has no longing in pleasures, who is free from desire, fear and anger is called a sage of firm wisdom." [2 : 56]

One of the main criterions for assessing a spiritual teacher's ability is steady wisdom.

Swami Saradananda once said to Swami Aseshananda who took sannyasa from Swami Saradananda and was Secretary (1921-27) to him and others : "It is not easy to give initiation. You will have to work for your disciples. An illumined guru has to perform special japam for their inner growth and spiritual welfare. The relationship between the guru and disciple is established by God. The real guru has to take the burden of his disciples. He works for them through silent prayer and meditation. He has no rest until all of them have become illumined."[18]

As a real teacher Swami Sardananda was truthful. One day after a terrible thunderstorm was over, he visited Belur at night as he sent word to his brother disciple Swami Premananda in the morning that he would be in the monastery in the afternoon. Swami Premananda said, "Like guru like disciple. If any word would come from the lips of the Master, he always kept it."[19]

As an ideal teacher Swami Saradananda tried to remove the doubts of his disciples. Once a disciple said to the Swami : "X instructs his disciples not to practise japam without taking a bath etc. Are such observance compulsory?"Swami Saradananda replied, "The Master came to make religion easy. People were being crushed under the weight of rules and regulations. To repeat the Lord's name or to worship Him, no special time or place is necessary. In whatever condition one may be, one can take His name. The Master never gave too much importance to these external observances ..."[20]

The Swami advised his disciples to think of the Master before meditation and to practise regularly in order to attain strength and pleasure. He said, "May God who is the creator, sustainer, and dissolver of the Universe, remove my sorrows.' This is the significance of all mantras. Have faith in God; otherwise even thousands of explanations will be of no use. Pray to Him and love Him."[21]

Many monks and devotees used to come to Swami Saradananda to solve their spiritual as well as other problems. His constant effort to develop proficiency of his disciples and aspirants in attaining inner realization reminds us of the beautiful saying of Jesus Christ that a good shepherd has no rest until the last sheep has been brought to the fold.

A born leader :

Three or four days before his passing away looking lovingly at Narendranath Sri Ramakrishna said to him ecstatically, "Today I have given you my all and am now only a poor fakir, possessing nothing. By this power you will do immense good in the world and not until it is accomplished will you return."[22]

Long before that one day at Dakshineswar Sri Ramakrishna said to Sharat : "Always think of yourself as Shiva and me as your Shakti [power]. I am the ultimate repository of all your powers."[23]

Sri Ramakrishna considered that the true disciples were to be leaders and have the charge of others souls.

The mystical utterance of the Master was fulfilled later in Saradananda's life. He was democratic and impartial in his dealings. He was judicious and even-minded and disliked slander. He considered even the youngest member of the Order his equal. He used to take part in domestic and menial tasks along with other members of the monastery when needed. He possessed one of the loftiest religious and philosophical minds in India. He organized plague relief in Kolkata and supervised foreign visitors. All these made him an ideal executive head of the Order. His judicious, bold and calm leadership helped him solve numerous problems and take the organization in the right direction with dignity without compromising its principles.

Saradananda was one of the greatest intellectual disciples of Sri Ramakrishna and the most learned in Hindu metaphysics.

As a real leader the Swami never obstructed other's freedom, rather, he taught how one should enjoy freedom properly. Swamiji wrote to Shashi (Swami Ramakrishnananda) from U.S.A in 1895, "I have got Sarada's letter—he is doing good work..." In many fields Saradananda helped the Order by way of contributing to its growth, development and consolidation. He actualized a balance of all the Yogas within himself. Swami Gambhirananda described him as "the most balanced man in the whole Order.'[24] Swami Saradananda was one of the great architects of the Order who devoted himself completely to building the organization physically, ideologically and spiritually as well.

Devotion to the Master :

From the very beginning Sharat was tremendously attracted to Sri Ramakrishna. He used to visit the Master at Dakshineswar on Thursdays, a college holiday and stay at night there in order to practise spiritual disciplines under his guidance.

On 1 January 1886 Sharat and Latu saw the historic event from the roof of Cossipore garden house when the Master appearing as a *Kalpataru* (wish--fulfilling tree) blessed many devotees, saying, "Be illumined'. Later somebody asked Sharat why he did not go to the Master for blessings. He answered, "I did not feel any necessity for that. Why should I? Was not the Master dearer than the dearest to me? Then, what doubt was there that he would give me, of his own accord, anything that I needed?"[25]

Miss Laura Glenn (later, Sister Devamata), an American devotee of Swamiji met Swami Saradananda at Udbodhan (Kolkata) and wrote in her memoirs about him: "No disciple ever *served* his Master's cause with greater fervour and steadfastness than did he."[26]

Swami Saradananda was more deeply versed in the intellectual make-up of his Master than any who came near him. He said, "All through my life I worked, envisioning the faces of the Master and Swamiji. I had no time to pay any attention to others' opinions."[27]

Referring to his Master Swami said, "We are mere instruments in his hands.'[28]

Devotion to the Mother :

In the Ramakrishna Order Swami Saradananda's devotion to Holy Mother was legendary.

After Swami Yogananda and Swami Trigunatitananda Swami Saradananda had been the Mother's care-taker (from 1904 to 1920). It was pathetic to him that the Mother had no house of her own either in Kolkata or in Jayrambati. So she could not conduct spiritual activities of her own accord. Though a monk, he borrowed money and built a house for the Mother and the Udbodhan office. He built another house for her in Jayrambati.

Despite his diverse activities and duties as the executive head of the Order, Swami Saradananda dedicated himself to serving the Mother. Besides, he took care of the welfare of her relatives, nursed her dying younger brother (Abhaycharan), attended his widow Surabala and their daughter Radhu both insane and made provisions for Radhu's future financial security. He often visited Jayrambati especially when the Mother was ill and accompanied her on her several pilgrimages.

Swami Saradananda was indispensable to Holy Mother who said : "I shall have no difficulty as long as Sharat lives. I do not see anybody else who can shoulder my burden." If anyone spoke of her going to Calcutta when the Swami was not there she would say : "I simply cannot think of going to Calcutta when Sharat is not there. While I am in Calcuta, if he says that he wants to go elsewhere for a few days, I tell him : "Wait a while, my child. First let me leave the place and then you may go." The Swami sometimes sang to entertain her and when her body was burnt with high fever he placed her tender hands on his bare body and thus cooled her. Her confidence in the Swami was total.[29]

The Swami looked upon Holy Mother as the Divine Mother Herself and served her as her *dwari* (door-keeper) and *bhari* (burden-bearer). The Mother described him as her Vasuki, a mythical snake, who protected her with his thousand hoods. She used to speak of him, "Wherever water pours, he spreads his umbrella to protect me."

Once a devotee prayed to the Mother for initation. She, owing to her illness, asked him to come a few days later. But as he insisted she asked him to speak to Swami Saradananda about it. He arrogantly said "I do not know anybody else. I have come to you; please initiate me." The Mother said, "What do you mean? Sharat is the jewel of my head. What he says will be done."

In order to fulfil the Mother's wish the Swami built two temples; one on the spot where the Mother's body had been cremated in Belur Math and the other was on the spot where she was born in Jayrambati. It is said that during her last illness, Mother once uttered, "I am tired of this life. I shall now depart with Sharat in my arms and take him wherever I go."

Swami Saradananda was fotunate enough to serve and come close to Holy Mother for more than fifteen years yet he said,

> What can we understand of Mother? This, however, I can say : I have never seen such a great mind; and I do not hope to see one. It is not within our capacity to comprehend the extent of Mother's glory and power. I have never seen in anyone else such attachment; nor have I seen such detachment.

One day a devotee said to Swami Saradananda that he could not believe in the divinity of Holy Mother. The Swami said to him, "Do you mean to say that God married the daughter of a woman who maintained herself by gathering cowdung?"[30]

The Mother's confidence in the ability of Swami Saradananda was so high that before her passing away she said to one of her disciples : "My child, I am leaving Sharat behind."

Loyalty to the leader :

The strength of mutual love, respect, faith and understanding of the brother-diciples was the Key to the solidarity and steady propagation of the Order. The monastic disciples of the Master obeyed his instruction to accept Narendranath as their leader.

Swami Saradananda demonstrated in his own life and activities the great message of Swami Vivekananda—'Service to man is service to God' and 'Work is worship' which constitutes the cornerstone of the Ramakrishna Mission. He was absolutely loyal to Swamiji and to his ideal of service, philanthropic activities and work known as 'Practical Vedanta'. He as noted earlier, said : 'All through my life I worked, envisioning the faces of the Master and Swamiji. I had no time to pay any attention to others' opinions'.[31]

Swamiji convened a meeting in Belur Math to felicitate Swami Saradananda for his marvellous achievement in America. Swami Saradananda in response to that jovial recognition said humbly: "What have I done? I have simply followed the foot-prints of our illustrious leader."[32]

After the passing away of Swami Brahmananda (10 April 1922) in accordance with the rules of the Order an election was held in order to fill up the vacant position of the President. There were two nominees : Swami Shivananda and Swami Saradananda. The monks cast their votes. It was found that Swami Saradananda had received ninety-five percent of the votes. Naturally his name was announced as the President. But he refused saying : "Swamiji appointed me the Secretary. I shall never give up the post." He himself proposed Swami Shivananda's name as the President of the Order and remained Secretary until his passing away (19 August 1927). Sister Nivedita wrote to Miss J. MacLeod on 11 October 1902. "But Swami Sarada has most intellectual realization of Swamiji's real meaning and at the same time most courage—so I wd. back *him* rather than any." [Letters of Sister Nivedita, col. & ed. S. P. Basu, Vol. 1, p. 464]

Charismatic Personality :

Swami Saradananda with his sweet and gentle personality and mastery of Vedanta philosophy and other scriptures was very attractive. He was one of the greatest intellectual disciples of Sri Ramakrishna. In May 1896 Swamiji wrote to Mary Hale about him: "We have a nice little family, in the house, with another monk from India. Poor man!—a typical Hindu with nothing of that pluck and go which I have, he is always dreamy and gentle and sweet!"[33] Swami Saradananda learned from Swamiji how to sing and play drums (tabla). When he would recite the Chandi and other hymns with his melodious voice, the listeners felt spiritually uplifted. He was a man of spotless character and intense spirituality and gifted head, hand and heart.

When Sri Ramakrishna heard from Sharat about his meeting with Narendranath and sprouting of their intimacy, he realized that Sharat would be to some extent a match for Narendranath at spiritual aspect and with delight said, "A housewife knows which lid will go with which cooking pot."[34]

Swami Saradananda possessed intense love of nature. Referring to his stay in Puri for six months he recollected : "The seaview would make my mind limitless. Sitting on the sea-coast at Swargadwara I would spend the night fearlessly."[35] He was charmed by the beauty and diversity of the perpetual snow range of the Himalayas.

Swami Saradananda, a knower of Brahma knew no fear. In 1896 on the way to England the Swami's ship was knocked severely by a hurricane in the Mediterranean sea. He reminisced: "All the passengers were in a great panic. Some were crying some were running here and there in fear; some were shaking out of nervousness. The whole scene was frightening, but I was not afraid in the least. My mind was as steady and calm as the needle of a compass."[36] Once Swami Brahmananda was suffering from an abscess and needed minor surgery. Swami Saradananda accompanied Dr. Kanjilal, a disciple of the Mother, and left from Kolkata for Belur Math by boat. In the middle of the Ganga, a heavy storm arose and the boat began tossing violently. The Swami was smoking his hubble-bubble calmly. The frightened doctor angrily threw the hubble-bubble into the river and said to the Swami, "You are a strange man! The boat is about to sink, and you are enjoying your smoke!" "Is it wise to jump into the water before the boat sinks?" replied the Swami calmly. Then he advised the boatman to put the sail down. The storm abated gradually and the boat reached the Belur ghat safely. He remained calm during a terrible accident on his way to Srinagar by a tonga (horse carriage). These incidents justify the remarks of Mrs. Ole Bull : Swamiji was like the brilliant scorching sun and Saradananda, the cool refreshing moon.

Miss Laura Glenn (later, Sister Devamata) saw Swami Saradananda at Udbodhan and sketched a portrait of his magnetic personality : "I saw at once why he called forth so much love wherever he went in the west. He seemed to possess an exalted gentleness, a graciousnes and courtesy which made a direct appeal. His was the highest breeding of all—the breeding, not merely of manner or of culture, but of spirit. It was the outgrowth of Divine, rather than of human relations ..."[37]

The Swami was patience personified. Once Swamiji sent him to Kolkata on an errand. When he learned that it had not been carried out, he scolded him with harsh language which Swami Saradananda bore with calmly and began to take tea as if nothing had occurred. Swamiji remarked : "Sharat's veins carry the blood of fish, it will never warm up."[38]

While a school-student Swami Saradananda helped his poor classmates buy books, paper and so on; served a neighbour's maid servant stricken with cholera; afterwards while walking down a one-mile slope in the Himalayas he risking his own life gave his own stick to an old woman who did not have a walking stick and was losing her balance. He prayed to the Master and the Mother to mitigate the suffering of the people. It was Swami Saradananda who convinced Lord Carmichael the Governor of Bengal to withdraw his offensive statement and who untied the shoes of Lord Ronaldshay the Governor of Bengal (1919) before taking him to the shrine in Belur Math. When the Swami went to Belur Math on his last birthday in 1927, a devotee greeted him with a garland. He said with a smile : "I am a doorkeeper of the Mother's house. You are decorating me with a garland? Does a doorkeeper deserve such an expensive garland?"[39] There are so many instances of his humanity and humility.

The Swami was outspoken. When a probationer he said to Sri Ramakrishna, 'I do not want to see any particular form of God in meditation. I want to see Him in all beings. I do not like visions'. The Master smilingly said, 'That is the last word in spiritual attainment. You cannot have it all at once.' Sharat Chandra replied, 'But I won't be satisfied with anything short of that. I shall strive my best until I am able to attain it.'[40] One day the Master said to him, 'Whom do you love most of all?' Sharat Chandra replied, 'Well, Sir, I don't think I love anyone.' He was scolded by the Master for his narrowness and he rectified his outlook. In order to bind Sharat to the world his father Girish Chandra wanted to get his son married and requested Sri Ramakrishna to ask his son to marry. Sharat retorted : "Do you think I shall obey if the Master asks me to marry? In no way shall I deviate from my duty, even if the Master requests me to do so."

Swami Saradananda had a keen sense of humour. Once he was staying at Ridgely Manor, the country home of Mr. Francis Leggett, then President of the Vedanta Society. Every morning Miss Josephine MacLeod, sister-in-law of Mr. Leggett, used to say to the Swami, 'Did you sleep well?' One Sunday when the Swami was lecturing, Miss MacLeod fell asleep. While shaking hands after the lecture, he said to her, 'Did you sleep well?' Both laughed heartily.

A great author :

The magnum opus 'Sri Ramakrishna the Great Master' (Sri Ramakrishna Lila-prasanga', the original Bengali biography of Sri Ramakrishna) by Swami Saradananda is the most authentic comprehensive and critical estimate of the life, sadhana and teachings of the Master whom his chief disciple Swami Vivekananda described as 'the spirit of the Upanishads living in human form', 'the reformed and remodelled manifestation of all the past great epoch-makers in religion.'

Once Girish Chandra Ghosh had asked Swamiji to write a biography of Sri Ramakrishna. Swamiji replied, "Shall I make the image of a monkey while trying to make that of Shiva?" On another coccasion he said, "Sharat will write."[41]

After receiving the Master's command and having the permission and blessing from the Mother Swami Saradananda started writing (in 1909) the book on the basis of his extraordinary spiritual experiences and memoirs. He collected all materials about the Mother in the book directly from her and would read the manuscript to her when she was in Kolkata. When she was in Jayrambati someone else used to read it to her. She certified, "Everything has been written correctly in Sharat's book." When one of her disciples praised the 'wonderful book' of Sharat Maharaj, Holy Mother replied, "Yes, it needs learning and intellect to understand Sharat's book."[42]

Swami Nirvedananda rightly remarked :

> *Sri Ramakrishna Lila prasanga*, the original Bengali biography of Sri Ramakrishna, based as it is on first-hand observation,

> assiduous collection of materials from different sources, patient sifting of evidence by way of an earnest effort for precision, and backed up by lucid interpretation of all relevant intricate problems connected with religious theories and practices, may easily be ranked as one of the best specimens of hagiographic literature.[43]

This book is a classic in Bengali literature. Romain Rolland cogently commented :

> Incomplete though the work remains, it is excellent for the subject. Saradananda is an authority both as a philosopher and as an historian. His books are rich in metaphysical sketches, which place the spiritual appearance of Ramakrishna exactly in its place in the rich procession of Hindu thought.[44]

The family guru of Swami Saradananda Jaganmohan Tarkalankar was a reputed pandit and tantric yogi. His uncle Ishwar Chandra Chakraborty was an adept tantric. Obtaining permission from the Mother and Swami Brahmananda the President of the Order Swami Saradananda practised tantric sadhana under the guidance of his uncle. This sadhana of japam, meditation and perfomance of tantric rituals for long hours revealed to him the mystery of Shakti worship which is the realization of the Divine Mother (Supreme Goddess) in all. On the basis of this experience the Swami wrote in Bengali a repository book *Bharate Shakti Puja,* (Mother Worship in India) : "By whose gracious glance the author has been able to realize the revelation of Divine Motherhood in every woman—to Her lotus feet the work is dedicated in all humility and devotion."[45]

Chapter – 12

SWAMI TURIYANANDA

A teenaged boy saw a crocodile floating near him in the Ganga still he continued his bathing.

The dying father foretold that his youngest son belonged to the world and the world belonged to him. This prophecy came true.

He in his teens used to wrestle, could do 100 push-ups and 500 knee-bends at a stretch to keep his body fit for bearing severe austerity.

Sometimes in the evening he would recite the scriptures and cry for God on the bank of the Ganga.

This boy was Harinath Chattopadhyay (later Swami Turiyananda) the youngest child of Chandranath and Prasannamayi, born on 3 January 1863 in North Kolkata.

Natural trend of mind :

Swami Turiananda was innately drawn to the Brahmin ideals of orthodoxy and asceticism. During his sacred thread ceremony he was initiated into the Gayatri mantram. Since then he used to bathe three times a day, practise japam and meditation, sleep on the floor and eat vegetarian food regularly. He sincerely practised continence.

Swamiji had indelibly imprinted the truths of Vedanta on the mind of his brother-disciple : 'Self-knowledge together with renunciation is the means of immortality.'[1] The Swami had a natural bent for austerity and wandering. So after a stay of about two years he left the Baranagore monastery for Rishikesh in 1889. He and Swami Saradananda visited Gangotri and Kedarnath the next year. They lost their way in a jungle and had to starve three days. He met Swamiji and some other brother disciples at Rajpur on the Mussoorie Hill. Then they all went to Rishikesh where Swamiji became very sick. Swami Turiyananda served him. They stayed six weeks at Merrut until Swamiji recuperated completely. When Swamiji left for Delhi alone, Swamis Turiyananda and Brahmananda went out to visit Jwalamukhi, Gopinathpur, Baijnath, Pathankot, Multan, Gujranwala, Montogomery, Bombay (Mumbai), Mount Abu, Pushkar, Jaipur and Vrindaban. Swami Turiyananda realized that only experience of travelling was not sufficient for an itinerant monk. He said, "Though I travelled much, I also studied much all along. At Vrindaban I studied a great deal of devotional scriptures. It is not good to wander much if you do not at the same time continue your spiritual effort."[2] Leaving Vrindaban they visited Lucknow and Ayodhya and returned to Alambazar monastery in 1895. Swamiji asked him to give classes on the scriptures to the monastics which he agreed to do. But after a stay of more than a year, he again embraced a life of an itinerant mendicant monk and went to Allahabad and then travelled towards Narmada. Feeling that the atomosphere of the mountain region of Girnar conducive to meditation he lived in a cave for some months. He visited Delhi, Hardwar and Rishikesh on his way to Uttarkashi. He carried no money and lived on alms. At Srinagar Ghat he spent time doing meditation Japam and comitting eight Upanishads to memory. He returned to Kolkata towards the end of 1896. Thus he frequently led a life of amazing austery and toilsome wandering. In fact, he was one of the most austere monks amongst the disciples of Sri Ramakrishna.

Courage and Candour :

Swami Turiyananda's American student Gurudas (later, Swami Atulananda) described him as "sometimes gentle, sometimes the roaring lion of Vedanta." While practising sadhana alone at Rajpur, on the Mussoorie Hill, a police officer suspected him to be an anarchist in disguise of a monk and asked him all sorts of questions. Showing his vexation the Swami replied fearlessly. The officer said to him, "How dare you talk that way! Are you not afraid of the police?" Swami boldly replied : "I afraid! I am not frightened even of Yama, the god of death, what to speak of the police?" Then the officer realized that the Swami was a genuine monk, and afterwards became his devotee.

In the Himalayan region in Tihiri-Garhwal, Swami Turiyananda took shelter in a thatched hut that had a broken door. One night he caught the cry of the villagers, 'Tiger! Tiger!' He at once put some bricks behind the door to save himself. Just then he recalled a mantra of the Taittiriya Upanishad that declares : "One is not subjected to fear at any time if one knows the Bliss that is Brahman, failing to reach which, words, along with the mind, turn back.'[3] He ignored the body idea and was aware of the Atman. He removed the piles of brick and sat for meditation.

Swami Turiyananda was a free soul and guided only by God. He tried to rectify the shortcoming of his students openly. One day, sensing their dissatisfaction he said, "Yes, you people in the West always try to cover up and hide your mistakes. But how can the wound be treated unless the bandages are removed? You hide your real character behind a smooth and polite exterior, but the sore festers in the heart. The guru is the physician, and once the disease is diagnosed he must not fear to apply the lancet, if necessary. Sometimes a deep clean incision is the only remedy. You are so sensitive, always afraid of being scolded or exposed. When I flatter a little, you say, "Swami is so wonderful; but when I utter a harsh word you run away."[4]

In Boston Swami Turiyananda became the guest of a moneyed woman. She helped him discuss Vedanta. But she was quite bossy. Once a difference of opinion cropped up betwen them and she said to him, "If you do not accept my viewpoint, I shall stop helping you." The Swami politely replied, "I am a monk. God will help me. I shall not mind at all if you throw me out on the streets of Boston." The woman realized her mistake and continued to help him.

In Los Angeles, Swami Turiyananda became a guest of a woman, owner of a large oil company. She wanted to keep him under her control and curb his freedom. The Swami had the guts to protest against unjust act. He boldly said to her, "Madam, you have helped me with a few dollars, but that does not mean I have sold my head to you."[5]

The Swami's frankness in pointing out a person's defects sometimes would hurt him and lead to misunderstanding between them. One day he found a verse of the Bhagavata : "Realizing the universe as one in the aspect of Purusha and Prakriti, never praise or blame the action of others" (11.28.1). Then he read the commentary on that verse, "If accidentally the teeth bite the tongue, hurt and cut it, do people take a piece of stone and break the teeth? No, because the teeth belong to the same person to whom the tongue belongs. Since the one Lord who is in me also resides in others, it is improper to find fault with them." He was deeply impressed with the verse and learnt to rectify himself and be tender in correcting students in his charge.

Special power :

Swami Turiyananda was very free and frank about the struggles and experiences of his mystical life. He said to the spiritual aspriants :

> Formerly my nerves were very fine, and I had great powers of explaining things. Whenever anyone asked me a question, I could see everything from its very origin to its outer expression—I could see from what motive he spoke and why. And there was a flood of light in a single word of mine.
>
> "I used to observe absolute silence during the Navaratri. I would feel a sort of intoxication and the mind would be one-pointed."[6]

Owing to the difference between Eastern and Western upbringing and culture, sometimes misunderstandings develop between the two. Swami Turiyananda was an intuitive monk. When the students of the New York Vedanta society complained that he did not understand them, the Swami replied, "I know you better than you know yourself, because I can look deep into your mind. What is hidden to yourself, is revealed to me. In time you will realize that what I tell you is true."[7]

There are numerous examples of the amazing power of forbearance of Swami Turiyananda. A knower of Brahman or true Vedantin is supposed to be beyond body consciousness, physical pain and pleasure and mental agony. In the Shanti Ashrama in northern Carolina (America) one day a poisonous insect bit the Swami in the meditation cabin. He did not open his eyes to see what beetle had bitten him. He just flicked it aside and was again absorbed in meditation. The students anxiously saw that the following morning the Swami's whole arm was badly swollen. But he remained calm. The nearest physician was fifty miles away, and they had no transportation but a horse and a two-wheeled cart. Miraculously a young doctor from New York reached there after having walked fifty miles. He at once operated on his hand and administered medicine. The students were astonished to see the Swami's power of patience. This doctor afterwards became one of his most devoted disciple like his student Gurudas (later, Swami Atulananda).

While staying in Puri Swami Turiyananda suffered some trouble with his eyes. One morning as soon as his attendant Sharvananda put eye drops prescribed by the doctor, in his eyes, he said : "I think you have given me the wrong medicine. See what you have used!" The attendant found that it was diluted nitric acid. He was shocked and began to cry. Someone else washed the acid out of the Swami's eyes. The Swami kept calm and quiet and later he consoled his attendant, "You see, as soon as you put the drops in my eyes, I felt a terrible burning sensation covering my whole body. I thought : 'O Mother, what can I do if you want to take away my eyes? May Your will be done?"[8]

Swami Turiyananda underwent several surgeries without administering chloroform. During operation he dispelled his body consciousness and showed no sign of pain.

In Varanasi, when a surgeon operated on Swami Turiyananda's finger he remained composed. The attendant said to him, 'Don't you feel any pain?' The Swami replied : "Look, the mind is like a child, we must hold it tight. But like a youngster it will go on crying, 'Let me go! Let me go!' Once in the midst of surgery I let my mind get loose. Immediately I felt intese pain. The surgery was not finished. So I had to catch hold of the mind once more." Turiyananda was silent for some time. Then he continued : "Do you know how it is? In the Bhagavad Gita we read : 'Wherein established in the bliss of his inmost being he is not shaken even by the heaviest sorrow.' (6 : 22). This verse is explained by Shankara as follows, 'A man of realization is not shaken even by the pain caused by the application of a sharp weapon.' Two ideas are brought out here. First, Shankara shows that a perfect yogi has extraordinary control over his mind. Secondly, he shows that such a man remains in a state far beyond the control of nature."[9] Swami Turiyananda was the embodiment of forbearance.

A spiritual dynamo :

The great sage Vyasa said : "He who wishes to think upon the Lord after all his duties have been finished is like the fool who wishes to bathe in the sea after the waves have subsided."[10] Swami Turiyananda was fond of this wise saying and often uttered it. He said to the spiritual aspirants that his aim was to make his life pure. He was an illumined monk full of spiritual wisdom, purity and renunciation. His students in America or devotees in India saw to their utter astonishment how relentlessly the Swami spoke of spiritual subjects in the class, while walking, eating or sitting. One day, students of the New York Vedanta Society enquired of him about how it was possible for him to continue spiritual conversation without getting exhausted. The Swami replied : "You see, I have lived this life from my youth, it has become part and parcel of me.

And Divine Mother keeps the supply filled up. Her store can never be exhausted. Whatever goes out, she at once fills up again."[11]

Instead of showing intellectual snobbery Swami Turiyananda tried to make his lessons lucid and comprehensible. In Oakland he said in a class : "No matter about philosophy, or even the Gita. The thing to do is to know Mother. That is the whole of religion. Nothing else counts. Take all your troubles to Mother. She will right all wrongs."[12]

While leading an itinerant life Swami Turiyananda's spiritual impetus would rise high sometimes in suitable solitary places. While staying in a hut on the bank of the Ganga in Nangol, a small village surrounded by forests where wild beasts roamed freely, about sixty miles below Hardwar he, renouncing body consciousness and forgetting food and clothing remained absorbed in God-consciousness.

Before his departure leaving Swami Atulananda in full charge of Shanti Ashrama, Swami Turiyananda said to him, 'Don't you know yet, my boy, that it is life that counts? Life creates life.' He himself demonstrated a shining example of a true seeker of God through his life.

Sri Ramakrishna once said about Swami Turiyananda, "He comes of that transcendent region whence name and form are manufactured."[13]

Vedanta personified :

Swami Turiyananda said : "I used to read a great deal, eight or nine hours daily. I read many Puranas and then Vedanta, and my mind finally settled on Vedanta."[14]

The Swami preached the Vedanta in New York for a year (since August 1899). One of his American students Gurudas wrote, "He talked with fire and enthusiasm, and he would lose himself entirely in his subject, forgetting everything else for the time being." The zealous audience were infused with wonder and new thought as they heard from the Swami the uncompromising vibrant message of Vedanta: "Brahman alone is real, everything else is unreal; the human soul is that Brahman. We are bound by the delusion of ignorance. Tear away the delusion and be free. All power is within you, for you are the Atman. Assert your divine nature."[15] Gurudas wrote in his book that one day while walking on the street in New York, the Swami shouted to him "Be a lion! Be a lion! Break the cage and be free!"

After one lecture of the Swami a woman told him that she could not understand how the soul could be God and the world unreal. The Swami replied : "It took me many years to realize this, but once it is realized the work is done." She further described Christianity as much easier to grasp than Vedanta. The Swami answered :

> Yes, Vedanta is not an easy, comfortable religion. Truth is never cheap. So long as we are satisfied with glass-beads we don't search for diamonds. It is hard work to delve into the earth, remove the stones and rocks, and go to great depths to find the precious stone. Vedanta is the jewel among religions.[16]

As a true Vedantin Yogi Swami Turiyananda had no desire for enjoying temporal pleasure or visiting places of interest in America; rather he preferred to remain absorbed in spiritual matter. With an intention of giving the Swami a break from his routine life, one evening Gurudas said to him "Swami, there is a fine concert tonight. It is an oratorio and you will like it. You have never heard our Western music. Let us go." The Swami replied "But why should you care for those things? You have had enough of that now. Let us stay here and read something nice and have good talk. These amusements we must give up now if we want Mother."

In Shanti Ashrama when there was talk of the possibility of someone leaving, Swami Turiyananda said : "Where will they go? Vedanta is the essence of religion. When you have seen the full moon in all its glory, who cares to look at a candle?"[18]

Gurudas as stated earlier described his teacher as "Sometimes gentle, sometimes the roaring lion of Vedanta."

While leaving San Francisco, Swami Vivekananda said to the students of the Vedanta Society : "I have lectured to you on Vedanta; in Turiyananda you will see Vedanta personified. He lives it every moment of his life. He is the ideal Hindu monk, and he will help you all to live pure and holy lives."[19]

Devigiri, a well-known monk of Uttarkashi commented: "How shall I describe him? Only on rare occasions do we come across such a great vedantin and a man of renunication. He was an illumined soul and worthy of respect."[20]

Formal rule and planning :

Swami Turiyananda had original idea about formal rules and planning. In Shanti Ashrama an informal daily routine was followed. One day someone proposed that formal rules be imposed. The Swami said, "Why do you want rules? Is not everything going on nicely and orderly without formal rules? Don't you see how punctual everyone is—how regular we all are? No one ever is absent from the classes or meditation. Mother has made her own rules. Let us be satisfied with that. Why should we make rules of our own? Let there be freedom but no license. That is Mother's way of ruling. We have no organization but see how organized we are. This kind of organization is lasting, but all other kinds of organization break up in time. This kind of organization makes one free; all other kinds are binding. This is the highest organization, it is based on spiritual laws."[21]

The Swami had implicit trust in God alone. He strongly opposed to all planning. He said to his students, "Why do you plan? Why are you scheming? Why do you look so far ahead? Let Mother plan. Her plan comes true. Human planning is all in vain if She does not consent. She knows what will happen. The future is an open book to Her. Live in the present; make the best of your time and opportunities. Don't think of the future. Know for certain that Mother's will shall come to pass. Trust in Her. Only try to love Her sincerely. Give yourself to Her. Let Her do with you as She wishes." He on another occasion said "Trusting in Mother does not mean idleness. Try to know Her will, and then be up and doing like a man. Don't you see, I am never idle. The mind must be occupied in some way or other. If you don't do physical work you must use your mind—read, study or meditate. And don't spend your time in idle gossip. Gossip breeds mischief. If you talk, talk of the Lord."[22] The Swami had firm faith in divine providence.

Organizer :

Swami Vivekananda put his brother disciple Hari Maharaj (Swami Turiyananda) to acid test when in New York he said to him, "Brother, I don't have any money. I am going to San Francisco. Now you find a means of supporting yourself." Swami Turiyananda was baffled for he was a new comer to America. Swamiji added, 'Don't be frightened when I say you have to conduct classes and lectures. Whatever you say will do good to the people. Show them what spirituality is."[23]

Swami Turiyananda left for Montclair where there was a Vedanta Society and began to give classes and conducted classes on Saturday and Sundays in New York in absence of Swami Abhedananda.

Afterwards Swamiji sent Swami Turiyananda to take charge of the Vedanta Society in San Francisco founded by him as a resident Swami. Some of the students of the society considered that a big city with all its attractions and comforts was not suitable for spiritual practice. So they wanted a lonesome place where they might devote themselves to a life of austerity and renunciation. Miss Minnie C. Boock, a student of the Society donated a property of 160 acres in San Antonio Valley in northern California for a retreat. Swamiji accepted the gift and asked Swami Turiyananda to set up a centre there. Overcoming primary hesitation the Swami agreed to assume the responsibility.

On 2 August 1900 the Swami, with a dozen zealous men and woman left for their new destination. It was a desolate remote rugged Hamilton mountain area inaccessible and inhospitable. How to establish a retreat there was a serious challenge to him. There was no electricity, no running water and no bathroom facilities. There were tarantulas, scorpions, snakes and other poisonous insects. There was no town or market nearby. The nearest source of supplies was at least thirty miles in every direction. The place was at least one mile from the nearest road, fifty miles from a railway station, three miles from the post office. The inmates had to bring water from a distance of six miles and lived on vegetarian food. He felt utterly depressed as he could not think how to live under such primitive conditions with his students who were depending solely upon him. He complained to the Divine Mother, "Mother, what have you done? What do you mean by this? These people will die. No shelter, no water—what shall they do?" Mrs. Agnes Stanley at once said, "Swami, why are you dejected? Have you lost faith in Her? You have less faith than even Baby [Ida Ansell]." So saying, she emptied her purse in his lap. The Swami was deeply impressed by her generosity and bold words. He said to her : "You are right. Mother will protect us. How great is your faith! Your name henceforth will be Shraddha [one who has firm faith in God]."[24]

The women students would prepare food while the men were engaged in various tasks, such as carrying water from the well chopping wood, planting vegetables, building wooden cabins and canvas dining tent. First they built a simple one-room cabin only 12 feet by 16 feet in size for meditation and classes and gradually built more cabins for the students. The Swami took great interest in everything and he himself participated heartily in manual labour. An informal daily routine was followed in the ashrama. He named the retreat 'Shanti Ashrama'. The Swami considered, "This is the highest oranization; it is based on spiritual laws."[25]

Thus as a skilled organizer Swami Turiyananda accomplished a Herculean task of establishing an ashrama in a desolate place with the co-operation of a group of enthusiastic students inspired with the fire of his spirituality. But the health of the architect of Shanti Ashrama could not withstand the demands of outgoing activity and deteriorated. Swamiji brought him back to India and sent Swami Trigunatitananda to replace him.

Humility :

"A tree when it has no fruit to offer, remains erect. But when the tree is laden with fruit, it bends down."

Swami Turiyananda was a great yogi, a living example of Vedanta. His spiritual treasure did not indulge in sprouting egoism or pride rather made him polite and patient.

One day a wealthy and bossy woman said to the Swami, "If you do not accept my viewpoint, I shall stop helping you." Instead of showing displeasure the Swami calmly replied, "I am a monk. God will help me. I shall not mind at all if you throw me out on the streets of Boston."

Before his departure Swami Turiyananda leaving Gurudas in full charge of Shanti Ashrama, said to him : "Life creates life. Serve! Serve! Serve! That is the great teaching. Be humble. Be the servant of all. Only he who knows how to serve is fit to rule."

In Puri one morning the Swami's attendant Sharvananda put diluted nitric acid instead of prescribed drops in his eyes by mistake. He calmly bore with the severe pain and did not lose temper. He consoled the attendant, "You see, as soon as you put the drops in my eyes, I felt a terrible burning sensation covering my whole body. I thought : 'O Mother, what can I do if you want to take away my eyes? May your will be done!'

Loyalty to the leader :

Swami Turiyananda was one of the most austure monks amongst the monastic disciples of Sri Ramakrishna. He cherished the traditional notion that his main motto in life should be try to attain liberation of the self and their sevices for the welfare of the world should be restricted to giving people spiritual instruction and explaining scriptures to them. On the contrary, Swamiji wanted to implement his Master's instructions to him : to preach India's spirituality all over the world and to work for the welfare of the world. In Darjeeling one day Swamiji said to Swami Turiyananda, "Brother Hari, I have made a new path and opened it to all. Up till now it was thought that liberation could be attained only by meditation, repetition of God's name, scriptural discussion and so forth. Now young men and women will attain liberation by doing the Lord's work."[26]

Swami Turiyananda wanted to spend his days in spiritual disciplines. Once Swamiji interfered emotionally : "Brother, can't you see I have been laying down my life, inch by inch, in fulfilling the mission of the Master, till I am on the verge of death? Can you merely stand looking on and not come to my help by relieving me of a part of my great burden?"[27] Shaking off personal preference Swami Turiyananda responded to the call of their great leader and got on a ship bound for the West with the leader and Sister Nivedita in June 1899.

In June 1900 Swamiji accepted a property of 160 acres in northern California for a retreat donated by Miss Minnie C. Boock, a student of Vedanta. He asked Swami Turiyananda to take up the project. But the latter was devoted to meditation and austerity and did not like to plunge into work. So he hesitated to accept the challenge. Swamiji said to him, "It is the will of the Mother that you should take charge of the work there." At this the brother-disciple said humorously, "Rather say it is your will. Certainly you have not heard the Mother communicate Her will to you in that way. How can we hear the words of the Mother? "Yes, brother", said the Swami with great emotion, "Yes, the words of the Mother can be heard as clearly as we hear one another. It only requires a fine nerve to hear the words of the Mother."[28] Swamiji had uttered the words with so fervour that his brother-disciple as a disciplined soldier obeyed the instruction taking it as the expression of the will of the Divine Mother.

While receiving Swami Turiyananda cordially, the members of the Vedanta Society of San Francisco told him what Swami Vivekananda had said, "I will send you a real Hindu monk, who lives what I talk about." Swami Turiyananda replied, "I am a row boat : I can take two or three to the other side of this ocean of the world. But Swamiji is an Atlantic liner : he can take thousands."[29]

In Shanti Ashrama the students had to read the works of Swami Vivekananda along with other scriptures. Swami Turiyananda said to them, "... Swamiji has taught you that every soul is potentially divine. Realize your own divinity, then you will realize that all souls are divine."[30]

With intense love for Swamiji and deep emotion Swami Turiyananda used to say that if he were present then, he would see how Swamiji could pass away. He added also that before leaving for foreign land he considered Swamiji a very intelligent and scholar but going to America he realized that he was a prophet.[31]

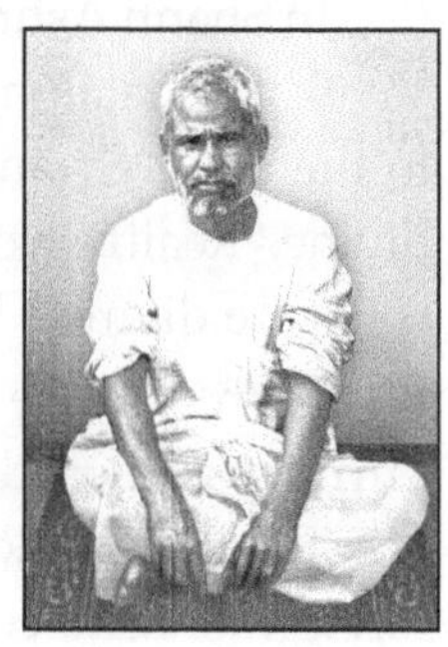

Chapter – 13

SWAMI ADBHUTANANDA

He was literally an illiterate unsophisticated village boy. He used to wander freely with the cowherd boys. He was a servant in Dr. Ramchandra Dutta's house. Sri Ramakrishna himself fanned him and went in search of his missing shoes.

He was Rakhturam, the first monastic disciple of Sri Ramakrishna. The story about his childhood is obscure. He was born into a poor family in a village in the Chapra district of Bihar perhaps after the middle of the nineteenth century. His parents died before he was five years old. He was brought up by his prodigal uncle who was compelled to leave for Calcutta (now Kolkata) to find a means of livelihood and with the help of his village neighbour Phulchand who worked in the Calcutta office of Dr. Ramchandra Dutta, put Rakhturam in the house of Dr. Dutta as a servant. Hearing about Sri Ramakrishna and his teachings from his employer who was one of the first disciples of Sri Ramakrishna, Rakhturam was eager to see him. One Sunday (either in late 1879 or early 1880) he went to Dakshineswar with Ramchandra. During their first meeting both of them impressed each other. Ramchandra sent Rakhturam to serve the Master in place of Hriday a nephew and attendant of Sri Ramakrishna who left Dakshineswar in June 1881.

Rakhturam's nickname was Latu. Sri Ramakrishna with his village accent used to call him affectionately, 'Leto' or 'Noto'.

Unique :

Sri Ramakrishna said : "The knowledge of those who are ever-free souls only needs to be unveiled, as it were. They are like underground springs which remain covered until a stonemason digging in the earth removes a particular rock. Then the water begins to flow."[1]—saying this he touched Latu and the boy fell into an ecstatic mood. From that day onwards the Master gradually changed the course of Latu's life through his divine grace, intensive supervision, necessary training, teaching and nurturing the rustic boy's innate spiritual entity. Thus he moulded an unpolished village boy into a great mystic—an illumined saint.

Once Swamiji eulogized :

> Latu is Sri Ramakrishna's greatest miracle. Having absolutely no education, he has attained the highest wisdom simply by virtue of the Master's touch.[2]

In fact, the absence of formal education of Latu made him unique among Sri Ramakrishna's monastic disciples. As a very simple, docile, pure-hearted village lad Latu sincerely obeyed the instructions of his Master without any doubt or question. Sri Ramakrishna demonstrated to the modern world that spiritual wisdom and realization of God depend not on the study of scriptures and books or academic qualification but on self realization—the inward abundance of vital and digested riches, called 'spirituality'.[3]

Swami Turiyananda said : "Many of us had to go through the muddy waters of knowledge before we attained God, but Latu jumped over them, like Hanuman."[4]

Romain Rolland commented in the same tune about the distinction of Latu : "... the example of Latu is significant, although it may be said that he was the exception to prove the rule. A humble and ignorant servant, a peasant of Bihar and a stranger to Bengal, he was awakened to eternal life by one glance from Ramakrishna, for he possessed unwittingly the same genius of heart as the Master."[5]

Devotion to the Master :

Swami Adbhutananda, though very poor and destitute, gave up his job in order to serve Sri Ramakrishna and to hear him about God. Absolute obedience to the Master moulded his life.

One day Sri Ramakrishna said to Latu. "Be careful about wine and about lust and gold. These things are obstacles that create doubts about God. A person who meditates after taking intoxicants and a Yogi who is attached to women are both hypocrites and only deceive themselves." Once Latu's mind became restless while passing a wine shop on the road from Dakshineswar to Ramchandra Dutta's house in Kolkata. Returning to Dakshineswar when he told the Master about it he said, "The odour of the wine caused restlessness in your mind. Avoid it from now on." Following the Master's advice literally Latu walked eight miles to kolkata (instead of normal distance of four miles) by some roundabout route. Learning that from Dr. Dutta Sri Ramakrishna said, "Latu, I asked you not to smell wine; I didn't forbid you to walk down the street where it is sold. It won't hurt you to pass near the shop. Remember this [pointing to his own body], and no intoxicant will be able to disturb you."[6]

Latu tried to start the day with first seeing the Master and saluting him. One morning he did not see the Master and shouted, "Where are you?" Sri Ramakrishna replied, "Wait a minute—I am coming. Latu waited closing his eyes until the Master came. Then taking away his hands from his eyes he bowed down to his feet. Latu's incomparable devotion was rewarded by his Mater's immeasurable affection and love for him. One morning Latu did not see the Master and requested him to come to the room. The Master asked him to come outside. Latu saw the Master in the flower garden to the West of his room and asked him what he was doing. The Master replied: "Yesterday a devotee brought a pair of sandals for you, and I can find only one of them. A jackal may have taken the other, so I am looking for it." Latu requested him to stop searching for that sandal. Sri Ramakrishna answered : "But I shall feel sorry if you can't wear these new sandals, since it was only yesterday that the devotee brought them." Latu seriously said : "Sir please stop. If you keep looking for my sandal, it will be harmful for me. My whole day will be spent in vain." (The disciple is expected to serve the guru. The reverse is not only unusual, but is even considered inauspicious for the disciple.) Ramakrishna responded : "Do you know what day is really spent in vain. That day when the Lord's name is not chanted."[7]

On learning that the Master wished to have a picture of Sri Chaitanya for his room, the next day Latu had gone to Dr. Dutta's house and brought from his wife a picture of Mahaprabhu Sri Chaitanya for the Master.

Despite his dog-tiredness and drowsiness owing to hard toil all day Latu one night was fanning the Master a long time. Observing this Sri Ramakrishna said : "Leto, can you say whether God sleeps or not?" Latu replied that he didn't know. Then the Master added : "Everyone in the world sleeps, but God does not, for if God slept, the universe would be plunged into darkness and would disssolve. God must remain awake day and night taking care of his creatures, so that they can sleep without fear."[8]

Once Sri Ramakrishna noticed Latu sleeping early evening. He woke him up and scolded him.

Fighting for two years Latu won sleep over and never again slept at night. Swami saradananda said : His life was a literal example of the teaching of the Gita : "In that which is night to all beings, the man of self-control is awake; and where all beings are awake there is night for the sage who sees. (2 : 69)."[9]

In the early days at Dakshineswar Latu used to wrestle and had a large appetite. One day a devotee fed Latu an exceptional quantity of food and the next day he praised Latu's power of consuming food before the Master. Later, Sri Ramakrishna said to him : "Look, it is not good to eat excessively by competing with others. During lunch, you may eat as much as you wish; but at night, don't eat too much." Obeying his Master's advice Latu gradually reduced his meals to such an extent that his health deteriorated rapidly. Observing this the Master said to him : "Look, you have gone to the other extreme. Please eat the amount that will keep your body in fit condition. Otherwise, if you eat too little you won't be able to focus your mind during meditation."[10]

Latu Maharaj was Sri Ramakrishna's personal attendant-cum-disciple. At Cossipore owing to throat-Cancer the Master's body became emaciated and he was too weak to walk to the toilet. One day as he asked Latu to clean his commode, Latu gladly responded: "Master, whatever you will order me to do, I will do. I am your sweeper and servant."[11] Afterwards Latu recollected : "Serving the Master was our worship. We didn't need any other spiritual disciplines. The Master taught us : 'During worship, one should think that his Chosen Deity is in front of him. You are washing His feet, bathing Him, decorating Him, feeding Him and placing Him in your heart, offering flowers at His feet.' At Cossipore we did that to the Master."[12]

Devotion to Holy Mother :

One day Latu had been meditating on the Divine Mother Kali on the bank of the Ganga. Sri Ramakrsihna said : "Look here, Leto, the one on whom you are meditating is now sweating over the flour." Then taking Latu to the nahabat (concert tower) where the Mother was living, said to her : "This boy is a pure soul. He will knead the flour and flatten the chapatis for you. Whenever you need any help, please ask him."[13] Since then Latu Maharaj used to render personal service to Holy Mother at Dakshineswar. After the passing away of the Master he would occasionally stay at Balaram Bose's house. In 1907 the Mother spent a few days there. One day standing at the door of Latu Maharaj (then Swami Adbhutananda) she said : "How are you Latu, my child?" Latu said : "Go away, you are an honourable lady. Why have you come to the outer apartment to speak to me? Please go upstairs right away. I will not speak to you here. You could have sent for me, and I would have gone to see you. I am your servant, you know." The Mother left with a smile.

While living in Balaram's house the Mother used to send a little prasad for Latu Maharaj.

One day when the Mother was leaving for Jayrambati, the devotees but Latu Maharaj went upstairs to take the sacred dust of her feet. Coming down the Mother stopped at the door of Latu Maharaj and heard him repeating the words : "Who is mother or father to a monk? He is free from all maya." She said : "My child, you don't have to accept me." At once Latu Maharaj fell at her feet and wept. Then he began to wipe tears of the Mother with his cloth and said : "You are going to your father's house, Mother, don't weep. Sharat will bring you back. Is it proper for one to cry when one departs?" All present there were deeply moved by his devotion to the Mother and childlike simplicity.

Referring to the eventful day when the Master's body was carried to the cremation ground at Cossipore and he stayed at the garden house, Latu Maharaj commented: "Only once did I hear Holy Mother weeping; after that she was silent. Never have I seen a woman with such strength."[14]

An illumined Soul :

"Sometimes he appears to be a fool, sometimes a wise man, sometimes he seems splendid as a king. Somtimes he wanders calmly and sometimes behaves like a motionless python, which waits for food to come to it. Somtimes he is honoured, sometimes insulted, sometimes unknown. That is how the illumined soul lives, always absorbed in the highest bliss."—says Shankaracharya in the 'Vivekachudamani' (verse 542)

Swami Adbhutananda's life is a glowing manifestation of an illumined soul. He appeared to be inactive though he was very active. He preferred solitary place and tranquility suitable for meditation. In the mornings and evenings people for a little while could meet him and he used to talk with them about spiritual matters. He was illiterate but wise. He did not like to live in the monastery or to obey rules there. He spoke with such intelligence that Ajit singh, the king of Khetri could not know that Latu Maharaj had no formal education at all.

The story of Jatila told by the Master was indelibly imprinted on the mind of Latu. He realized that sincere prayer does not go in vain. M. experienced on December 14, 1883 as he proceeded toward the Panchavati at three O'clock in the morning. Suddenly he heard a distant sound as if someone were wailing piteously, "Oh, where art Thou, Brother Madhusudana?" The light of the full moon streamed through the thick foliage of the Panchavati, and as he proceeded he saw at a distance one of the Master's disciples sitting alone in the grove, crying helplessly, "Oh, where art Thou, Brother Madhusudana?"[15]

The disciple was none but Latu.

One day Sri Ramakrishna said to Latu : "If you want to realize God, you will have to be a brahmacharin. Without practising brahmacharya, or continence, one cannot concentrate steadily on God. From brahmacharya comes intellectual conviction and then comes faith in the power of Brahman. Without this faith, one cannot feel that he lives in Brahman ... Practise japam and meditation day and night. This is the way one can get rid of attachment for lust and gold."[16] Latu, tried to avoid women on principle and there are so many examples of his strict adherence to this principle. In 1897 while Swami Adbhutananda was visiting Kashmir with Swamiji and other monks, one day he first got on a rented houseboat and as soon as he saw a woman, he jumped out. He agreed to get on the boat only when Swamiji assured him that no harm would happen to him. Another day Swamiji, as a joke, asked the boatman's young daughter to carry a betel-roll to Swami Adbhutananda. No sooner did Latu Maharaj see the girl than he jumped into the icy water though he did not know how to swim. Swamiji with the help of the boatman save his life. Thus Latu Maharaj tried to stick to his principles so sincerely.

But Latu Maharaj was not a misogynist. Once he said to a group of male devotess : "Some men abuse women, but you should never raise your hand against them. You do not know how much they bear—they are forbearance itself. If you abuse them, where shall they turn? They are aspects of the Divine mother, and if the Mother is insulted, the Lord is displeased. Thus your well-being lies in making them happy."

Girish Chandra Ghosh said about Latu Maharaj that he had never seen such a stainless monk and his air purified others.

Fortunate in having various experiences :

One day at noon Sri Ramakrishna asked Latu to meditate in a Shiva temple. The Master sent his nephew Ramlal to see about him as he had not returned in late afternoon. Ramlal saw Latu sitting motionless, deep in meditation and bathed in perspiration and reported that to the Master who went to the temple and fanned his disciple. Regaining consciousness Latu cried : "What are you doing, sir! Won't this disgrace me? It is I who should be serving you." The Master affectionately said to him : "No, my boy, it is not you I am serving, but the Lord Shiva inside you. He was uncomfortable in such unbearable heat. Did you know that He had entered you?" Latu answered : "No, I knew nothing. I was gazing at the *lingam* [the image of Shiva] and saw a wonderful light. I remember only that the light flooded the whole temple. After that I lost consciousness."[17]

One day at Dakshineswar Latu lost outer consciousness during meditation and fell flat on his face, and began to groan. Learning from elder Gopal about the incident the Master hurried to him and putting his knee on his chest began to massage him. Gradually Latu regained consciousness. The Master said to him : "Haven't you seen Mother Kali today? Don't talk about it. If you speak out, people will create a furore here."[18] Latu kept mum about what he'd seen and afterwards his face, eyes and chest turned red during meditation.

While practising tantric sadhana in the Beltala one night Latu was deeply absorbed in meditation. In the morning the Master went there in search of him and found him guarded by two dogs as he meditated. He said to Latu : "I saw two *bhairava* [guardian spirits] protecting you disguised as two dogs. You are very fortunate! The Divine Mother sent those spirits to protect you."[19]

Latu was fortunate enough that he got the opportunity to live with Sri Ramakrishna and serve him and the Mother for more than six years. With gratitude to the Master he said : "Did you know that the Master snatched me from the snares of the world? I was an orphan. He flooded me with love and affection! If he had not accepted me, I would have been like an animal, spending all my days working like a slave. My life would have been worth nothing. I am an unlettered man. He used to tell me, 'Always keep your mind spotless. Don't allow impure thoughts to enter it. If you find such desires tormenting you, pray to God and chant His name. He will protect you. If the mind still will not remain calm, then go to the temple of the Mother and sit before Her. Or else come here (pointing to himself)."[20]

It was only by the grace of the Master that Latu as the personal attendant of him day and night saw the dazzling life of his Master and heard his teachings. He said : "I saw the Master in samadhi many times, but one day I saw his beautiful unique form. His body complexion was changed, and his face radiated fearlessness and compassion. I shall never forget that form of the Master."[21]

Latu and M. were fortunate to see the Master's divine form on Sunday, August, 3, 1884. M.recorded the incident in his magnum opus : "Presently the Master left them, going in the direction of the pine-trees. After a few minutes M. and Latu, standing in the Panchavati, saw the Master coming back toward them. Behind him the sky was black with the rain-cloud. Its reflection in the Ganges made the water darker. The disciples felt that the Master was God incarnate, a Divine child five years old, radiant with the smile of innocence and purity. Around him were the sacred trees of the Panchavati under which he had practised spiritual disciplines and had beheld visions of God. At his feet flowed the sacred river Ganges, the destroyer of man's sins. The presence of this God-man charged the trees, shrubs, flowers, plants and temples with spiritual fervour and divine joy."[22]

Latu gained various kinds of spiritual experiences e.g. visions of divine forms, unworldly light, ecstasy etc. but at Cossipore he experienced the highest samadhi. Once he said to a devotee : "You see, it is nothing spectacular to see light during meditation, it only strengthens faith. When body consiousness goes away and the mind becomes pure, one realizes a realm behind the light, which neither can be known through the intellect nor can it be expressed by words. One day at Cossipore I was rubbing the Master's head, then that transcendental realm opened to me. My senses failed to grasp that Infinite, but I realized It through and through."[23] That time Shashi (later, Swami Ramakrishnananda) was present in the room and testified to the validity of Latu's words.

Extraordinary life :

Swami Adhbhutananda's unusual manner of living did not follow any rules or routine. At Vrindaban he had no fixed times for meals. He would come at odd hours to the Mother or her companions and ask for food. Sometimes he would feed the monkeys his own bread and would ask for more food to eat himself. Sometimes he would disappear for a few days to meditate by the Jamuna without intimating it to the Mother and caused anxiety to her.

While taking formal monastic vows one, according to custom, performs one's own *Shraddha* ceremony (funeral rites) in order to remove oneself from all ties with one's family and the world as well. During the Shraddha ceremony Latu, instead of repeating the Sanskrit mantras, followed his own unconventional method. He simply evoked his departed ancestors in Hindi-Bengali mixed accent while offering food and other articles to them, saying : 'Ai, ai, baith, baith, puja ley, pinda ley' (Father dear, do come here, take your seat, accept my worship, take this food and drink.')

With his bent for spiritualism since childhood, strange behaviour, distinct way of thinking, guilelessness and amazing renunciation Latu was unique among the disciples of Sri Ramakrishna. Once Swami Abhedananda said to Swami Siddhananda : "You are right. We, the brother-disciples consider that Latu Maharaj is a miracle created by the Master. A high-souled man like him is very rare in the world.'[24] Therefore Swamiji gave him the monastic name Swami Adbhutananda, to mean, he who finds bliss in the wonderful nature of the Atman.

Swami Adbhutananda was an exceptional monk who did not like to go on pilgrimage (except a few, once with the Mother and later with Swamiji and other monks in 1895 and in 1909 visited Puri) and to take active part in philanthropic work. Though his guru Sri Ramakrishna constantly taught his monastic disciples, house holder disciples and devotees two historic, liberal and universal message that made him utterly different from other prophets of the world : 'As many faiths, so many paths.' and 'No, no, not compassion to jivas (beings) but service to them as Siva (God)' He emphasized both spiritual rituals and service to the beings as God equally.

Swami Vivekananda persuaded his brother disciples to perform social service along with spritual disciplines. One day Swami Adbhutananda said to Swamiji, "Brother, why have you started all these activities? Won't these interfere with our meditation and prayer?" Swamiji replied : "How would you understand why I am introducing all those work? You are a dumbbell. At the sight of *Ka* you shed tears like Prahlada. You are all devotees. What do you understand of this? You can only whine like babies. You think you can attain liberation through crying, that on the last day the Master will come to take you to heaven, and there you will enjoy to your heart's content. And those who are studying the scriptures for knowledge, who are working to educate people in the path of righteousness and serve the diseased and distressed, will all go to hell because all these works are maya ..." He said to another brother disciple who supported Latu Maharaj's view : "Ah, what you call devotion is sentimental nonsense that only weakens man ... You know, one day I foolishly asked the Master for this kind of devotion and liberation, and he rebuked me and called me selfsih and small-minded. Should I be misled by your words? I will work as he has told me." After this, Vivekananda burst into tears and left the room. The brother monks realized Vivekananda's greatness and why the Master had made him their leader. The next day Latu Maharaj privately told Swamiji :

"Brother, I am a fool. Please don't take my words to heart."[25] Notwithstanding Latu Maharaj amazingly believed in the old conservative way of renouncing the world and the company of men altogether and uprooting love, sympathy and other tender emotions from the heart in order to attain the non-dual knowledge and self-liberation. After the passing away of Swamiji two western atheist philanthropist women came to meet Latu Maharaj at Balaram Bose's house and enquired of him about the humanitarian activities of the Ramakrishna Mission. Latu Maharaj replied "... To do good to others is, after all, only a social activity, It has nothing to do with God-realization. Moreover, philanthropic works may bring good to others but what about you? Can you explain to me what benefit working for others will bring you?"

But we should remember what Sri Ramakrishna said to Swamiji severely while he begged the Master for the experience of nirvikalpa Samadhi the highest realization of Advaita Vedanta : "Shame on you! You are asking for such an insignificant thing. I thought that you would be like a big banyan tree, and that thousands of people would rest in your shade. But now I see that you are seeking your own liberation." Latu Maharaj perhaps had not forgotten what the Master said to Holy Mother at Cossipore : 'See, the people of Calcutta appear to be crawling about like worms in the dark. Do look after them.' The Mother said : 'I am a woman. How can that be?' Sri Ramakrishna pointing towards his body replied : 'What after all has this one done? You'll have to do much more.'

He stayed at Baranagore Math for a year and a half. Afterwards he preferred to stay elsewhere instead of monastery such as by the bank of the Ganga, in Balaram Bose's house, at the home of various house holder devotees of the Master or in the Basumati office. He said to a devotee : "When I went to take leave of Lord Jagannath, I asked for two blessings : First, that I would not have to wander here and there, but could settle in one place and plunge into meditation on the Lord; and Second, that whatever I ate I would be able to digest."[26]

Intensity of meditation :

A mystic exceeds body consciousness through love and longing for God. Swami Adbhutananda was contemplative. Swami Ramakrishnananda spoke of the tremendous intensity of meditation of Swami Adbhutananda : "We often had to call Latu back to normal consciousness and virtually force him to take food. There were many days when we called him again and again but with no response, so we would place his food in his room and leave. The rest of the day would pass. When we went to call him for supper, we would find the noon meal still where it had been placed, untouched and stale, and Latu lying down in the same straight posture as before, completely covered with a thick cotton chadar. We had to resort to many tricks just to force a little food down his throat."[27]

Swami Saradananda said to Mahendranath Dutta, brother of Swamiji, "You see, at night that rascal Leto doesn't sleep at all. During the first part of the night he pretends to be asleep and even snores, but he keeps his rosary with him, and when the others are asleep he sits up and starts counting his beads..."[28]

Swami Adbhutananda's mind would think of God almost all the time. Regarding his practice of rigorous austerity even in his old age the Swami said to a devotee : "You know, merely seeing the Master and serving him are not enough for the attainment of the Highest. It is not that easy. Both self-effort and divine grace are necessary to realize God. Without self-effort how can one attain grace..."[29]

Swami Adbhutananda was so often deeply engrossed in meditation that he had no fixed time for meals. Biharilal Sarkar, a district court judge of Kolkata and a devotee of the Swami wrote : "There was such irregularity in his daily life that one could not say whether he was living in a city or in a forest. Today he might take his meal at 10:00 p.m, tomorrow at twelve midnight, and the next day at 3:00 a.m. His routine was very uncertain. His attendant had to be always alert for the moment when he would get up from meditation and ask for a meal to be prepared..."[30]

Swami Turiyananda one of the brother disciples of Swami Adbhutananda said : "Many of the brother monks were leaving the monastery at Baranagore to practise austerity. I too felt an urge to meet holy men in other places of India. As I was thinking this over, a voice said from within me, "Where will you find such a sadhu as he?" Startled, I turned my gaze and saw Latu Maharaj lying down covered with a thick cloth, deep in meditation. Immediately the thought came, "Where, indeed, will I find a sadhu like him?" The very same moment Latu Maharaj spoke out : "Where will you go? It is better to engage yourself in tapasya here." That time I stayed at the monastery.[31] While staying at the Ramakrishna Mission Home of Service at Varanasi Swami Turiyananda would often visit him and find him almost always in deep meditation. So he used to sit in silence for some time and enjoy his holy company.

A monk of steady wisdom :

When a man renounces all the desires of the mind, O Arjuna, when he is satisfied in the Self alone by Self, then he is called a man of firm wisdom.

He whose mind is not perturbed in pains, who has no longing in pleasures, who is free from desire, fear and anger, he is called a sage of firm wisdom. [Gita, Chapter-II : 55-56]

Swami Adbhutananda was a sage of firm wisdom as he was free from anxiety over pain and longing for pleasures, from desire, fear and anger. Once Girish Chandra Ghosh said to a devotee : "If you want to see a monk such as the Gita describes, go and see Latu. I see you have not read the second chapter of the Gita. The nature of a man of steady wisdom is described there. You can see all those qualities exemplified in Latu's character."[32]

Sri Ramakrishna himself tried to impart at least a rudimentary education to his unlettered disciple Latu. But his experiment for three days was in vain. He said to Latu, 'No more book-learning for you.' Lack of book learning was not a hindrance to his spiritual realization. Once the Master said to him in an ecstatic mood :

"One day the gems of the Vedas and Vedanta will pour forth from your lips."[33]

Considering the words of wisdom of Latu whom Sri Ramakrishna, with his village accent, would call 'Leto' or 'Noto'; Swamiji used to call him 'Plato'.

Distinctive teaching style :

Swami Adbhutananda, as a man was very simple. His teachings were also so simple, convincing and practical and were based on his own experience.

One day a devotee said to Latu Maharaj : "How can one overcome lust?"The Swami replied : "Keep a picture of Sri Ramakrishna with you. Whenever lustful feelings arise, you should look at the picture intently. You will find that the senses will gradually be gathered in and the mind will be freed from lust."[34] Once a devotee said to him : "How can we love God or surrender to Him, without seeing Him?" Maharaj responded : Don't you send your application for a job to the manager of a company without ever having seen him? Your interview with the manager depends upon sending your application to him. You wirte the application thus : "Sir, please appoint me for the job; I shall be extremely happy to serve you; I promise my unswerving obedience to you," and so on. And you write all this without having seen the manager, don't you?

Similarly, you can send an application to the Lord. However, this application is not to be written on paper, but on the pages of one's mind : "O Lord, may I never forget your name. I take refuge in You. Please assign me to your service and destroy my ego and doubts. You are my master, guru, father, mother and all in all. I am your child. Make me your instrument. Do not delude me with your bewitching maya. O my sweet Lord, I have not seen you, I have only heard your name. Please make me your own." You will have to pray like this daily. Only then will He choose to bestow His grace on you.[35]

Evidently Latu Maharaj followed his Guru's method of teaching in colloquial or native tongue with the help of suitable examples and stories and sometimes he used to quote words of his Master or Swamiji.

Once a devotee had done something wrong and had a guilty conscience. Hearing about it Latu Maharaj called for the repentant devotee and said to him : "Look here; my son, just because you have made one or two mistakes, you should not give up your spiritual practices and brood over your lapses and feel hopeless. To err is human. Call on God. He will give you the strength to overcome weaknesss and destroy your delusion. He is the compassionate one. However great your sins might be, the current of His mercy will not be kept from you. How little is your sin, and yet you are so depressed! ... Do you know what Brother Vivekananda used to say? 'Don't worry about a little spot of ink on the body. It is nothing. If one bathes in God's infinte ocean of mercy, the stains of a thousand inkspots will be washed away. So I am telling you, do not grieve. Pray unceasingly. Your bad tendencies will go away in a short time."

Yet the devotee was so ashamed of his conduct that he could not raise his head. Seeing this, Latu Maharaj said : "Before he commits a sin, a man's conscience fills him with shame, yet he brushes it aside. But divine law is such that after the sin is committed shame overwhelms him again and he cannot raise his head in front of others."

Even these words could not shake the devotee free from his sense of guilt. Latu Maharaj continued : "What are you ashamed of, my son? The Lord has seen everything you have done. You cannot hide anything from Him. Since He knows all of it, why should you still be so melancholy? Instead engage yourself in harder spiritual disciplines, keep the company of holy men, and come here now and then." These words helped the devotee regain his mental strength, and he began to practise spiritual discipline more vigorously.[36]

Latu Maharaj, an unschooled person, never studied the Gita, the Upanishads and other scriptures. How amazing it is that he would answer abstruse questions about those philosophy at ease. Sri Ramakrishna's teachings and Swamiji's classes were the main sources of his being acquainted with the scriptural knowlege perhaps. Once Shashadhar Ganguly, a teacher from Malda said to him : "Can the Atman be an object of knowledge?"

Latu Maharaj : An object is something that cannot be known without the help of something else, but the Atman is self-revealing. So you cannot say the Atman is an object of knowlege."

Shashadar : "Then why should we want to know the Atman?"

Latu Maharaj : "Because the Atman is our real nature."

Shashadhar : "If the Atman is our real nature, then why are we not aware of it?

Latu Maharaj : "Listen, can anyone devitate from his real nature? If he does, it cannot be called his real nature; for it is changeable. Man's real nature is covered by a dense cloud of ignorance, and consequently he appears to be something different, but that does not mean he has deviated from his real nature. ... Haven't you seen those polishing shops at Mechuabazar in Calcutta where they have glass jars filled with coloured liquids? The metal worker takes a tarnished brass pot and dips it into a jar, and instantly all the tarnish goes away and the pot starts to glitter. Then he dips it into another jar and it turns a golden colour. Similarly dip your mind in the jar of the Lord's name, and all the unclean stuff will be washed away. Then dip it in the jar of the Lord's grace. You will see how beautifully your real nature will shine forth."[37]

The teachings of Latu Maharaj were comprised of jokes, rebuke or silence. Once a devotee said : "Maharaj, your scoldings are like chocolates in the shape of bayonets, they are so sweet and loving. Parents scold for the good of their children, but your scoldings are sweeter still, for parents could never give us so much love."[38]

Strange Personality :

Swami Adbhutananda was a man of uncommon personality to some extent different from other contemporary monks of the Ramakrishna Order.

Lack of education and sophistication did not hinder Rakhturam from being honest, simple and frank. He was an energetic and faithful servant in the house of Dr. Ramchandra Dutta. Oneday a friend of Ramchandra suspected that Rakhturam had stolen some coins from the household shopping money and said to him : "My boy, tell me honestly—how much did you pocket today?" Rakhturam reported sharply, "Sir, I am a servant, not a thief." The boldness of this reply offended the man and he complained to his master. But Dr. Dutta supporting the boy said : "He is not a thief. Whatever he needs he asks from my wife."[39]

Latu was guileless and emotional by nature. So Sri Ramakrishna encouraged him to take part in Kirtan and in other devotional songs. Ramlal, the nephew of Sri Ramakrishna narrated how Latu had sung and danced with his guru and some devotees who came from Konnagar to Dakshineswar.

Latu's direct and uncompromising approach to spiritual life was astonishing. One day Sri Ramakrishna rebuked him sharphy for sleeping at the auspicious time of early evening instead of meditation. Latu said : "How can I express the deep sorrow that seized me at the Master's words! 'What a wretch I am" I said to myself, "that having the rare blessing of such holy compnay, I should be wasting my time.' I started walk briskly along the bank of the Ganges. When my body became overheated I returned and sat near him. Again I dozed, and again I went out for a walk. Thus I fought the whole night. The struggle continued the next night also. It was a terrible fight. Sleep would overcome my eyes during the day, but I did not give up. The battle went on day and night. Finally, night sleep came under control, but not day sleep."

Latu was able to conquer sleep after two years of struggle and never again slept at night. Swami Saradananda wrote : "Latu was invariably seen praying and meditating the whole night and sleeping during the day."[40]

Girish Chandra Ghosh said about Swami Adbhutananda : "Latu would often come to my place and listen eargerly to every word about Swamiji's triumphant activities in America. His attitude was like a child's, full of faith and enthusiasm. When I told him that Swamiji's speech had been considered the best, he laughed gleefully like a boy and said : "It is bound to be so. Didn't the Master say that in him eighteen powers were working in their highest form? It cannot be otherwise. Can the Master's prediction be false?"[41]

Swami Adbhutananda used to lead plain living and austere life even while living in a devotee's home. Sister Devamata (Laura Glenn) recollected : "My first meeting with Latu Maharaj was in Calcutta at Balaram Babu's house ...Latu Maharaj was a person of few words. He was also a person of few needs. His room bore witness to it. It lay immediately to the right of the house entrance; the door was nearly always open, and as one passed, one could see the large empty space with a small thin mat on the floor, at the far end a low table for a bed; on one side a few half-dead embers in an open hearth, and on them a pot of tea. I suspect that that pot of tea represented the whole of Latu Maharaj's concession to the body."[42]

Sometimes Swami Adbhutananda seemed whimsical. One day he told a devotee about his idea of brass-plating the wooden cot of the Master. The devotee at once agreed to provide money for the project and a few days later when the devotee came to confirm the plan, the Swami said : "Our Master could not touch metal. To brass-plate the cot wouldn't be right, so let us drop the matter."[43]

Besides naturalness and childlike simplicity Swami Adbhutananda possessed humanity. Once at midnight a man in drunken state came to him and persuaded to take some food so that he could take it as prasad. Though the stranger was aggressive, he accepted the food calmly and the man was contented and left. The Swami remarked : "Such people want a little sympathy. Why should we not give it to them?"[44] Latu Maharaj showed love and sympathy for guileless simple people and avoided hypocrites.

Swami Adbhutananda was very humble. One day Swami Vivekananda's disciple Sharat Chandra Chakrabarty sought for permission from Swami Adbhutananda to write his biography. Latu Maharaj said : "Sir, plesae do not write anything about me. I am an insignificant person. If you wish to write anything, then write about Sri Ramakrishna and Swami Vivekananda. That will benefit humanity."[45]

Swami Premananda said to one of Swami Adbhutananda's devotees "You have nothing to fear.You have received the grace of Latu Maharaj. Such a loving monk is rarely seen. By the very touch of the air he moves in you will be purified and blessed."[46]

Swami Adbhutananda was quite outspoken. One day at Dakshineswar a devotee did not behave well. The Swami rebuked him rudely. The Master taught him to be humble. Swamiji introduced a rule at the monastery that the monks must rise at 4:00 a.m. and after washing quickly, sit down to meditate in the shrine. Latu Maharaj did not like the rule, so without telling anyone he was leaving the moanstery with his cloth and towel. Swamiji stopped him and when he heard that his brother disciple was leaving for Calcutta he wanted to know the cause. Latu Maharaj retorted : 'You have recently returned from the West and are introducing new rules and regulations. It will not be easy for me to abide by them. I do not have that degree of control over my mind that it will quiet down to meditate when a bell is rung. Who knows when my mind might become absorbed? I have not yet reached that state. If you can do it, that is fine.'

Then Swamiji said : 'All right. You can go.' But hardly he had reached the gate, Swamiji called him back and said : 'You don't have to observe this rule. You should do as you like. These rules are meant for the novices." Latu Maharaj replied : "I am glad you said that."[47]

Swami Adbhutananda formally initiated nobody and would say : "Do you think that one man whishpers a mantram into the ear of another and then he becomes the guru and the other fellow his disciple? And does the disciple attain illumination immediately? Is it that easy? The guru can give a lot of advice, but everything is in the hand of God just as the lawyer says that he has pleaded his case as best he can, now everything is in the hands of the judge."[48]

Once the Swami said : "Do you think that a monk is your sweeper who will keep sweeping your mind for you day after day? He may clean your mind once, after that it is up to you to keep it clean. If you don't have any motivation, what can a monk do? Can a holy man erase your past impression, or do you think he will carry you to the Lord on his shoulders? He will show you the path, but you will have to walk it yourself. That is the only way to reach God."[49]

Literary genius Kali (later Swami Abhedananda) well versed in oriental and occidental philosphies confined himself to a room (Kali Tapasvi's Room) in the Baranagore Monastery and spent his time in meditation, studying the scriptures, composing Sanskrit hymns etc. During leisure he would debate with Narendranath who used to silence him very easily. Once Kali said to Latu ruefully "I could not defeat Loren for a single day!" Latu replied, "Brother it is bound to be so. Brother Loren is our leader. How can you surpass him?"[50]

When Swamiji was staying at Balaram Bose's house Swami Adbhutananda challenged him to prove how his western conception of serving the poor and the diseased, his ideas of organization and of patriotism could be reconciled with the teachings of Sri Ramakrishna who insisted on Bhakti (devotion) and on meditation for the realization of God. Swamiji at first took the observations of Swami Adbhutananda lightly and replied jokingly but within a few minutes he burst out seriously to convince his brother disciples that he did nothing contrary to the teaching of the Master and his love for him was no less than their love for him. Later Swami Adbhutananda said to a devotee : "I was stunned to hear all these things; and when some other brother-monk tried to say something taking up the thread of our talk, Vivekananda grew more and more serious, and thundered on."[51]

Swami Adbhutananda had no craze for power or pelf. Swamiji asked him to become one of the trustees when a board of trustees was formed for the Ramakrishna Order early in 1901. Swami Adbutananda said, "I don't want position or authority. Please, brother, don't get me involved. Swamiji insisted : "Brother Latu, please obey me. Put your name down as a trustee. Don't refuse." Swami Brahmananda also persuaded him to agree. But Latu Maharaj replied firmly : "I don't want to be entangled in anything."[52]

Swami Adbhutananda was a man of ready wit. One day a devotee with several friends attended the birth anniversary festival of Sri Ramakrishna at the Belur Monastery and came to visit Latu Maharaj in Kolkata. Maharaj said to him, "How much did you give as an offering to the Lord in the shrine?" When he heard that though the devotee had offered, his friends had offered nothing, he said with a smile : "Your friends want religion by "bearing post." The devotee did not understand. Latu Maharaj clarified that they wanted their letters to reach their destination without putting any stamps on them; thus the recipient must pay the postage. The devotee commented, "Maharaj, you have coined a wonderful phrase."

While sailing from the rented monastery at Alambazar to Ramakrishnapur in Howrah on the occasion of installation of an image of Sri Ramakrishna in the newly built house of Nabagopal Ghosh, a devotee of the Master in 1898 in two boats, the monastic disciples of the Master were playing a game of making words ending with 'fy'. The brother-disciples added many words. e.g. Ramify, Verify, Justify, Clarify, Magnify, Glorify, Beautify, Vilify etc. When the game was over, Latu Maharaj to the utter astonishment of his brother-disciples uttered 'Stultify'.

Swami Adbhutananda sometimes apperared to be unpredicatable for his strange behaviour. When Swamiji returned from the West to Kolkata on 18 February, 1897, all of the disciples and devotees of Sri Ramakrishna except for Swami Adbhutananda gathered to greet him. Swamiji inquired about him and at last found out him amidst large crowd outside the house. Swami Adbhutananda said to a devotee : "When Swamiji returned from the West, some of his western disciples were with him. Thinking Swamiji might have developed some sort of egotism at having Westerners as his disciples, I did not go to meet him. But Swamiji sought me out and talked with me. He asked me, "All the others came; why didn't you come?" I replied : "You have Western disciples now, men and women. I wondered whether you would remember me. He caught hold of my hand and said : "You are my same old Brother Latu and I am your same old Brother Loren." Then I knew that he regarded us the same as before, that fame and position had not lessened his love for us ..."[53]

Swamiji returned from the West for the second time on the evening of 9 December 1900 to Belur Math without any prior intimation. All the monks were overwhelmed with joy to see their beloved leader. On that particular hour Swami Adbhutananda sat alone by the Ganga. A devotee told him about Swamiji's arrival, but instead of reacting to the news he said to the devotee : "Why be so excited? This is a good hour for meditation. Sit down right here. Look, how calm is the Ganges! Meditate." After supper Swamiji came to the ghat to meet Latu Maharaj : They embraced each other. Swamiji said, "Leto what's the matter? Everyone came to meet me except you. Are you annoyed with me?" "Why should I be annoyed?" replied Latu Maharaj. "My mind wanted to be here, so I was here." "I heard that you have not been staying at the monastery. How have you maintained yourself?" asked Swamiji. Latu Maharaj replied : "Upen Babu helped me. On days when food didn't come unasked for, I used to stand near his shop. He would understand at once and give me some coins." At this Swamiji gazed upward and said, "O Lord, bless Upen." After a few more minutes of conversation, Swamiji retired inside the Monastery. Latu Maharaj remained sitting where he was and soon became absorbed in meditation."[54]

Swami Adbhutananda did not participate in the day-to-day activities or philanthropic work of the Order.

A role model :

The contributions of Swami Adbhutananda was so subtle that he might go unnoticed on superficial observation. Though he, despite his leader's persuasion, did not devote himself to the multifarious activities of Ramakrishna Math and Ramakrishna Mission; his life itself was a great contribution to the organization.

In spite of his lack of formal education or book-learning, Swami Adbhutananda possessed a deep understanding of scriptures. His simple and austere life of meditation as well as simple teachings with profound spiritual and philosophical impact are precious treasure to Ramakrishna Order.

Pundit Vishnu Tarkaratna said :

> Hearing this unlettered Latu Maharaj explaining in a simple way the reality of God, we feel blessed that we too can understand the great life of Ramakrishna Paramahamsa and his spiritual experiences. Latu Maharaj's words were not parrot-like from book-learning, but of inner realization born out of his guru's grace and his own austerities. Hence people found solace and satisfaction in life after hearing him, and many educated people would come and sit at his feet for hours to listen to his words. His deep realizations and his extraordinary capacity to awaken and inspire others is a wonder to behold and true to his name, a life lived fully.

Swamiji commented : "Coming from such surroundings Latu approached Sri Ramakrishna unlettered, and unlike others who were all educated and refined. Latu has no other resort except the one method of japa and meditation to follow and uplift himself from the bottom to the heights of great spiritual wealth. This shows the great power hidden inside Latu and the Master's extraordinary grace on him."

Swami Gahanananda said of Swami Adbhutananda: "His utterly simple and austere life has become a role model to be emulated by the members of our Order, for simplicity is the hallfmark of his monastic life. He showed in his exemplary life that complete surrender to Sri Ramakrishna and taking refuge in him would bring everything one needs in spirital life."[55]

Once the Mother said to a monk, "It will do you good if you live with him."[56]

Chapter – 14

SWAMI ABHEDANANDA

While a primary student he studied classical Sanskrit literature and composed poems in Sanskrit.

Despite his skill in painting he cherished an ambition to become a philosopher for, as he said to his art teacher : "... A painter studies the surface of things but a philosopher goes below the surface and studies the causes of things. So I want to be a philosopher."[1]

His father once took away the Bhagavad Gita from him considering it too difficult a book for a boy fourteen years old and hid it in his room. But he found out the book and in the dead of night he read it by the light of an oil lamp.

He was extremely inquisitive and in order to satisfy his thirst for knowledge he used to attend the lectures of political personalities namely Surendranath Banerjee, Brahmo leaders Keshab Chandra Sen, Pratap Chandra Majumdar, Christian evangelist Reverend Kali Charan Banerjee, Hindu leaders Pandit Shashadhar Tarka chudamani and others.

He was Kali Prasad Chandra son of Rasiklal Chandra an English teacher in the Oriental Seminary and Nayantara Devi a pious woman. He was born on 2 October 1866 at 21 Nimu Goswami Lane, Ahiritola, North Kolkata.

'A great Yogi' :

With a view to find a competent guru to learn Yoga from him Kali went to Dakshineswar and met Sri Ramakrishna Paramahamsa Deva in June 1884. When he told Sri Ramakrishna that he had a desire to learn Yoga, the Master said : "It is a good sign that you have a desire to learn Yoga at this young age. You were a Yogi in your previous life. A little was left for perfection. This will be your last birth. Yes, I shall teach you Yoga ..." The next morning the Master wrote a mantram on Kali's tongue with the middle finger of his right hand and advised him to meditate on Kali, the Divine Mother. Kali sat in deep meditation and felt an indescribable joy. After some time the Master brought him back to outer consciousness by touching his chest. Kali was deeply moved by the Master's overwhelming joy and compassion. He left for home and his father reached Dakshineswar and requested Sri Ramakrishna to advise his son to get married and become a householder. The Master replied: "Your son is a great Yogi, As he does not want to get married, what good would it be to force him to marry?"

While practising spiritual disciplines under the guidance of the Master, Kali, through his grace, was blessed with wonderful visions of gods and goddesses. One day he had the vision of the omnipresent eyes while meditating at home. Another day he rushed to the Master to narrate his experience of seeing various gods and goddesses and divine incarnations Krishna, Christ, Chaitanya and others—merge one by one into luminous form of him. The Master said : "Ah, you have seen *Vaikuntha* [the abode of Lord Vishnu]! Henceforth you will no longer have these visions. You have risen to the formless state."[2] From then on, while meditating Kali's mind was absorbed in the realm of the infinite—the impersonal Brahman He was fully convinced that the Master was an avatar (incarnation).

Fortunate to observe Sri Ramakrsihna's super human power and to realize truth :

While suffering from a sore throat Sri Ramakrishna accompanied by Golap-ma, Kali and Latu visited Dr. Druga Charan of Kolkata.

When he was returning to Dakshineswar by boat at about 1:30 p.m. he was hungry and asked Kali to buy some sweets. Golap-ma had four paisa with her which she gave Kali. The Master took the packet of sweets and ate them all without sharing any sweets and drank some water from the Ganga with his hands. As soon as his hunger was relieved, amazingly the three hungry companions felt their stomachs full. The Master began to make jokes with a smile.

In the Mahabharata once Krishna eating a few particles of rice and a little cooked spinach and drinking a glass of water from Draupadi during their exile filled the stomachs of the sage Durvasa and his twelve hundred disciples.

Kali realized that it was a miracle that taught him the truth: "If God is pleased the whole world becomes pleased."

Devotion to the Master :

Kali would give personal service to Sri Ramakrishna whenever he went to Dakshineswar. He would carry his towel and water pot when he went to the pine grove to answer the calls of nature. Sometimes the Master would walk around the Panchavati with his hand on Kali's shoulder. Kali wrote in his autobiography : "I would really feel immense bliss in my heart to hear the teachings of the Master ...

Watching his God-intoxicated state we were amazed. We felt that the Master was in communion with the Divine Mother, that he was talking to Her, and that the Mother was answering his questions. We realized that Sri Ramakrishna was not a human being. He was God."[3]

Whenever Sri Ramakrishna visited the devotees' home in Kolkata, Kali would go there to hear the Master's wonderful conversations.

At Cossipore Kali would attend the Master two hours during the day and again two hours at night. He used to bathe him with warm water.

Kali wrote : "With tears in her eyes my mother asked me to have supper and to stay for the night. But within half an hour I felt uncomfortable at home. I felt as if I were in hellfire. My heart was restless and thoughts of the Master haunted me." When the Master wanted to know the cause of his return from home so soon Kali replied : "I went with the idea of staying at home tonight. My parents also begged me to stay. But I felt great agony while I was there. My mind longed to return to you. While there I felt as if I were in hell. So I ate a few sweets and hurried back here after saying goodbye to them. My mind was pacified only after arriving back here."

"In fact I always felt peace and joy when I was around the Master. Parental affection seemed insipid compared to the Master's pure love."[4]

It was only by the grace of the Master that Swami Abhedananda survived. On 6 May 1915 he went to the booking office to purchase a ticket from London to New York on the S. S. Lusitania. When he was about to buy the ticket, he heard a clear voice forbidding him to buy it. As he again went to the counter, the samething happened. He returned to the apartment without buying any ticket. The next morning he saw in the newspaper : "S.S.Lusitania Is No More'. The British liner along with one thousand one hundred ninety-eight passengers was destroyed in the Atlantic Ocean by a German submarine on 7 May 1915 during the World War 1. The Swami said, "I was overwhelmed. Tears rolled down my cheeks. I realized that the Master had saved my life."

During his stay in America Swami Abhedananda became so popular that some christian missionaries, out of jealousy, fabricated scandalous stories to defame his character. Referring to those slanders the Swami said to his disciples : "When I was in America, I would try to forget my sorrows and sufferings by singing or praying to the Master ... I don't care even if the whole world stands against me. I am holding onto the Master." [*Jeman Suniyachi,* Swami Sambhuddhananda, Ramakrishna Ashrama Howrah, 1970, II p. 170]

On the occasion of Sri Ramakrishna's centenary celebration, Swami Abhedananda spoke on All India Radio, Kolkata :

"... Salutation to Ramakrsihna, the perfect embodiment of the Eternal Truth that manifests Itself in various forms to help mankind. He is an incarnation of the Supreme Lord and is worshipped by all. Peace, Peace, Peace."

He said to one of his disciples : "I am only an instrument in the blissful sportive play of the Master, and the moment my life's mission is over, I shall not wait even for a second longer."[5]

Blessed by the Mother :

While living in the monastery at Baranagore Kali composed beautiful Sanskrit hymns on Sri Ramakrishna and Holy Mother. One day he visited the Mother at her residence at Nilambar Babu's garden house in Belur, and read a hymn that he had composed about her :

Prakritim Paramām abhayām varadaṁ
nararupadharām janatapaharām |
Saranagatasevakatosakarīm
pranamāmi parāṁ jananīṁ Jagatam || ...

[It is sung at many centres of the Ramakrishna Order, as the fourth hymn of the evening prayer. His meditation-hymn on Sri Ramakrishna is included in the daily worship of Sri Ramakrishna.]

After listening to the hymn, the Mother was very pleased and blessed him saying : 'May the Goddess of learning ever dwell on your tongue.' This blessing was fulfilled when Swami Abhedananda left for the west in 1896, responding to the call of Swamiji from London. She gave him a rosary.

Learning about Swami Abhedananda's illness in America Holy Mother advised him to take fish and not to mortify his body with severe austerities.

'The boy is lucky' :

At Cossipore Narendranath pestered Sri Ramakrishna for the experience of nirvikalpa samadhi, the highest realization of Advaita Vedanta. Though the Master discouraged him from meditating for that experience, by his grace Narendra while meditating one evening became aware of a light at the back of his head. It gradually became more dazzling until finally it deemed to explode. Having been engulfed by that strange light he lost body consciousness and remained immersed in samadhi, forgetting space and time. After regaining normal consciousness when he went to the Master, the latter said to him : "Now the Mother has shown you everything. But this realization, like the jewel locked in a box, will be hidden away from you and kept in my custody. I will keep the key with me. Only after you have fulfilled your mission on this earth will the box be unlocked, and you will know everything as you have known now."[6]

During *Shivaratri* in March 1886 after the first worship all but Narendra and Kali left the room. Narendra in order to use Kali to test his power to transmit superconsciousness, said to him : "Please touch me for a while." Kali touched Narendra's right knee and his hand trembled rapidly. After a few minutes Narendra opened his eyes and said : "How did you feel?" Kali replied, "When I touched your body I felt something like an electric shock coming to my body."[7]

When Narendranath went to the Master, the latter said: "What is this? Expenditure with hardly any accumulation! Allow it first to accumulate well in yourself, then you will know where and how to spend it. Mother Herself will teach. Don't you see what harm you have done to him by injecting your attitude of mind into him? He has been progressing till now with a particular mental attitude, the whole of which has now been destroyed, like a miscarriage during the sixth month of pregnancy. What's done is done. Don't act so thoughtlessly from now on. The boy, however, is lucky that greater harm has not be fallen him." Swamiji said afterwards, "I became completely flabbergasted. The Master could know whatever we did at the time of the worship! What else could I do but remain silent when he scolded me like that?"[8]

Swamiji transmitted some of his much coveted spiritual power to his brother-disciple Kali that brought about a visible change in his attitude. (In his autobiography Swami Abhedananda made contradictory statements about the incident. Vide 'Amar Jivankatha' p.p.96-97). He began to argue against other's ideas about blind faith in God. One day he told the Master that he did not believe in God and did not accept the validity of the scripture. He said to him, "Sir ... As long as I do not realize that God exists and that the Vedas are true how can I blindly accept these things? If you kindly enlighten me and give me spiritual insight, I shall aceept them all. Sri Ramakrishna was impressed by Kali's sincerity and said joyfully, "A day will come when you will know and accept everything but don't be one-sided. I don't care for one-sidedness."[9]

Inquisitiveness :

Swami Abhedananda was very inquistive from his boyhood. In order to satisfy his thirst for knowledge he used to ask to his father's astonishment various questions. He would spend his savings to buy books instead of luxury goods or refreshments. He used to attend lectures of political and religious leaders. He would visit Kalibar Vedantabagish every morning while he was given oil massage before bath, to hear Patanjali's Yoga Aphorisms. He learnt the disciplines of various Yogas from *Shiva Samhita.* His eagerness to learn the scriptures was phenomenal.

At his first meeting with the Master Kali said to him, "I have a desire to learn Yoga. Will you kindly teach me?"

Hearing an exaggerated story from Vijay Krishna Goswami, a religious leader and devotee about a hatha yogi living with his disciples in a cave of the Barabar Hills in Gaya, Kali telling none left for Gaya. While passing the night in an inn at the foot of the Hills, he copied the monastic vows of Shankaracharya's Order including the *presh mantram,* [a special mantram], *math* [monastery] *madi* [sect] and *yogapatta* [name] from the note-book of a monk of the Dashnami-Puri sect. Ignoring the warning given by the villagers and risking his life he met the man only to discover that his knowledge of yoga was limited and one of his disciples had been suffering from asthma and returned to Cossipore.

On April 9, 1887 Narendra said to M. at Baranagore math : "Kali has a craving for knowlege. I scold him for that. Is knowledge so easy to get? Let his bhakti first mature ..."[10] With reference to the interior of the math building M wrote : "The southern most room of the second floor was used for meditation, contemplation, and study, and was known as Kali Tapasvi's room, since Kali used to shut himself in there most of the day."[11] One member of the Baranagore monastery once complained that Kali was not taking part in the household work, Narendra said : 'Let one of the brothers be a scholar and I'will do the dishes myself.'

Swami Abhedananda wrote in his diary : "I went to Tibet and Kashmir crossing the Himalayas on foot, to study the manners, customs, the Buddhistic philosophy, and Lamaism which prevail among the Tibetan Lamas." He had read N. Notovitch's *The Unknown Life of Christ*, which was based on a Tibetan manuscript preserved in the Hemis Monastery which was about twenty-five miles north of the city of Leh, the capital of Ladak. The Swami had translated some pages with the help of a lama and wrote about Christ and his adventurous journey in his book *Journey in Kashmnir and Tibet.*

During the summer recess in 1903 Swami Abhedananda visited Italy, Switzerland, and Belgium in order to be acquainted with the social and cultural life of the common people of those countries. Thus his curiosity and a thirst for knowledge goaded him on travelling different places in India and the West as well.

Partial manifestation of Krishna :

One day Sri Ramakrishna said to Kali, "There is a partial manifestation of Krishna in you." A couple of weeks after the passing away of Sri Ramakrishna, Holy Mother, accompanied by Lakshmi, Golap-ma, M's wife Nikunja Devi, Jogin, Latu and Kali left for a pilgrimage in September 1886. After visitng Deoghar, Varanasi and Ayodhya the party reached Vrindaban and stayed at Balaram Basu's retreat house familiar as Kala Babu's Kunja. Kali visited many temples and meditated on Krishna for long hours.

While circumambulating Vrindaban with other Vaishnava pilgrims Kali walked 168 miles in 21 days. He used to beg from door to door with the Vaishnava anchorites who misunderstood him to be an atheist who did not accept Krishna, tried to avoid him. But when they heard from him melodious recitation of GopiGita : 'Na Khalu Gopikanandano Bhaban...;'[12] they were charmed and realized that he was a great devotee of Krishna and requested him to abstain from begging and allow them to serve him. He visited all the venues of sports of Krishna and realized the grace of Krishna. Returning to the Mother he narrated his experience of circumambulation.

Ascetic, 'an extraordinary intellect' :

Kali's brother-disciples would call him 'Tapasvi' for he sincerely perfomed 'tapas' or austerity secluding himself in a room in the Baranagore Monastery during most of the day. One day Mahendranath Datta, one of Narendra's brothers, was upset to see Kali lying like a dead person in the sun on the dusty floor of the verandah. Jogin assured him with a smile: 'He is not dead. The rascal meditates that way.'[13]

Kali was a vegetarian and wore no shoes and avoided peoples' company.

Kali never liked an easygoing life and always kept himself busy either practising meditation or studying the scriptures. During his extensive travel on barefoot and without money or possessions, he visited many temples and places of interst and met a number of scholars and mystics and gained various spiritual experiences.

The great austere Vedantin Swami Abhedananda said to his disciples : "Tapasya or austerity enhances willpower. Have self-confidence. Have faith in yourself. Think : I am a child of Immortal Bliss. The infinte power is playing within me. If you have this conviction, you will conquer the world."[14]

While travelling to the pilgrimage sites of North India with Tulasai (Swami Nirmalananda), they resolved that they would go barefotot and (Narendranath forbade him to travel barefoot in Junagad) wear only loin cloths and live on alms. They also decided that they would not carry any money or pass the night in anyone's house. They, as itinerant monk, carried only a blanket, a water pot, a staff and an extra loin cloth.

In Gazipur Swami Abhedananda helped Sisir Chandra Basu, a judge of the Gajipur court who was then translating Panini's Sanskrit grammar and Shankara's commentary on the Isha Upanishad into English. There the nondualist Swami defeated a dualist Sanskrit scholar in a debate within an hour.

After visiting Varanasi, Ayodhya, Lucknow, Hardware and Rishikesh they walked hundreds of miles in the high altitudes of the Himalayas to visit almost inaccessible places namely Devaprayag, Joshimath, Badrinath, Kedarnath, Uttarkashi, Gangotri and Jamunotri.

During his stay in Rishikesh, he studied the *Brahma Sutras* with Shankara's commentary under Dhanaraj Giri, the abbot of Kailash Math and an authority of the six types of Indian philosophy. Afterwards when Swamiji visited Rishikesh he asked Dhanaraj Giri about Swami Abhhedananda, the abbot described him as 'an extraordinary intellect.'

When Swami Abhedananada arrived at the Alambazar Monastery a private room on the first floor was arranged for his meditation and study. This room was known as 'Kali Vedanti's Room'.

At the Cossipore garden house one day Sri Ramakrishna said to Kali, 'I consider you to be one of the most intelligent of the boys ...' Kali was a prodigious scholar.

A great philosopher :

Young Kali was inspired when he had studied the life and works of Shankaracharya, the great exponent of Vedanta in Wilson's *History of India*. From that time he cherished an ambition of becoming a philospher and scholar like him.

Swami Abhedananada was assured of his place in the field of modern Indian philosophy by his scholarly interpretation of

Vedanta, making it consistent with modern science and acceptable to the modern mind following the footsteps of his brother-disciple Swami Vivekananda.

Kali at the age of sixteen or seventeen attended the lectures of Pandit Shashadhar Tarkachudamani on the six systems of Hindu philiosophy in Albert Hall, Kolkata and learnt the explanation of *Yoga Sutras,* from reputed scholar Kalibar Vedanta Vagish. Above all, he learnt the essence of the Vedanta and idolatry from Sri Ramakrishna who taught his disciples a scientific religion (the keywords of which are, 'As many faiths, so many paths') and said to Kali, '... don't be one-sided. I don't care for one-sidedness.' Swami Abhedananda wrote in his *autobiography 'Amar Jivankatha'* :

'I would really feel immense bliss in my heart to hear the teachings of the Master.' Sri Ramakrishna discussed Brahman, illusion, cosmology, Yogas, idolatry and faith in fromless God, etc. The Swami wrote, 'Sri Ramakrishna Deva's knowledge of and adherence to the Vedanata was strange.'[16] Besides, Narendra's discussion with his brother-disciples about the Vedanta and other subjects enriched him. He was a voracious reader of particularly scriptures and was well versed in both Eastern and Western philosophies. He is included among the contemporary Indian philosophers.

Orator and preacher :

Swami Abhedananda narrated in his autobiography (p.p. 91-92) that in the Cossipore garden house one night when Kali was reading John Stuart Mill's logic philosophy and essays on religion; Sri Ramakrishna said to him. "It is you who have introduced the habit of reading among the boys. You should know that book-learning is of no value. If you want to kill yourself, a nail-cutter can serve the purpose. But if you are to kill others, you need swords shields, and other weapons. Study is necessary for that purpose. Those who will teach people are to read books."

Responding to the call of the leader Swami Abhedananda reached London towards the end of September 1896 to assist

Swamiji in propagating the Vedanta movement in the West. Swamiji bought new clothes for his brother disciple, visited some notable places, introduced him to his friends and devotees and made him acquainted with Western culture and way of life. A month after his arrival Swamiji announced that Swami Abhedananda would speak on Hinduism. At first Swami Abhedananda felt nervous and hesitated to speak. Swamiji inspired him with spirited words : "Depend on the Master who has ever given me strength and courage in all the trials of my life ... 'Out of the fullness of the heart the mouth speaketh'" These words gave him courage and confidence. Swamiji was highly satisfied with the maiden speech delivered by Swami Abhedananda before the learned audience of the Christo-Theosophical Society at Bloombury Square in London on 27 October 1896 and commented : "Even if I perish on this plane, my messsage will be sounded through these dear lips and the world will hear it."[17]

Realizing that Swami Abhedananda would be able to carry on the Vedanta work efficiently in his absence, Swamiji left for India in December 1896. Swami Abhedananda gave classes and lectures in various churches and religious and philosophical societies in London and its suburbs for one year.

Having been asked by Swamiji Swami Abhedananda went to the U.S.A to take charges over from Swami Saradananda on 9 August 1897. Besides New York city he gave talks in different places namely, Philadelphia, Washington, Virginia, New Paltz. The Vedanta Society of New York founded by Swami Vivekananda in 1894, organized a lecture series at Mott Memorial Hall in New York. Swami made his first lecture on 29 Spetember 1897 on 'What is Vedanta?' Swami Atulananda, a disciple of Swami Abhedananda and a western monk as well wrote about that first lecture in his book : "Puncutally at three O'clock a Swami entered the hall. He was dressed in a robe and turban of an orange colour. He went straight to the platform and without a moment's delay began to deliver his lecture... . The discourse was lucid, convincing, and impressive. There was not much flourish, not much eloquence, hardly any gesticulation. It was a straight forward, well-reasoned-out exposition of Vedanta philosophy, delivered in a calm, dignified manner... Young, tall, straight, good-looking, the Swami had his appearance in his favour ... I was told that the Swami I had listened to was Swami Abhedananda, another disciple of Sri Ramakrishna."[18]

On 2 October, 1897 Swami Abhedananda started giving classes on Swamiji's *Raja Yoga* twice a week, on Wednesdays and Saturdays. On Mondays he gave lectures and classes at Montclair, New Jersey. A monthly bulletin was issued by the Vedanta Society of New York in 1905. Dr. Elmer Gates a famous scientist and psychologist was suitably impressed by the Swami's talks and considered Raja Yoga to be very rational and scientific. The Swami was the guest speaker at the annual festival of the Free Religions Association, held on the evening of 27 May 1898 at the Parker Memorial Building. Professor William James the author of *The Varieties of Religious Experience and Pragmatism* invited the Swami to speak on 'Unity in Variety' in his house. Professor James admitted the acceptability of Monistic philosophy. The Swami tried to dispel misconception about Indian religion and culture and inspired many to accept Vedanta as their way of life.

The Swami delivered a lecture before the Outlook Club, a women's organization in Lynn, Massachusetts and tried to wipe out misunderstandings about the position of women in India. In August 1898 he lectured at the Green Acre Conference in Maine. On 2 April. 1899 Swami Abhedananda initiated six students into the vows of brahmacharya. Gurudas (later Swami Atulananda) was among them. In April 1899 he gave a lecture entitled 'Hindu Religion' in Worcester, Massachusetts and on 7 May he lectured on 'Immortality', at the Cambridge Confernece. In August 1899 he spoke on 'Reincarnation' before an audience of 7,000 at a Spritualistic Camp Meeting At Lily Dale.

On 4 March 1900 the *New York Herald* reported on how Swami Abhedananda trained the American children :

Every Saturday afternoon a class of Young boys and girls gathers together in the rooms of the Vedanta Society in East Fifty-fifth Street, to speak an hour or so with Swami Abhedananda and drink in the teachings of the Hindu philosophy, which is expounded to them in the most fascinating way. The young people came in with beaming, expectant faces, and draw their chairs around the handsome Oriental figure of the Swami, who sits in the circle wearing a robe of rich red, and holding in his hand an ancient Sanskrit book, the *Hitopadesha*, or book of 'good counsels'. This book is one of the oldest pieces of literature in the world. It dates back to the thirteenth century B. C. and is the source of all of our fables of animals, our tales and fairy stories.[19]

The number of students in Swami's yoga class increased so much that he had to give the class twice a day. To accommodate the overflowing audiences, the Vedanta Society of New York rented Carnegie Lyceum for the Swami's lectures. The *New York Sun* reported on the lecture given by the Swami on the first Sunday of 1901 :

Swami Abhedananda lectured in the Carneigie Lyceum yesterday afternoon on the "Religious Need of the Twentieth Century'...

"The twentieth century needs a religion", he said, "with no scheme for salvation, no need for heaven or hell, no fear of eternal punishment. The twentieth century needs a religion free from sacerdotal institutions and free from all books, scriptures and personalities.

The twentieth century needs a religion with a concept of God, not personal, not impersonal but beyond both, a God whose supreme aspect will harmonize with the ultimate Reality of the Universe. The twentieth century religion must accept the ultimate conclusions of all the philosophies of the world."[20]

On 6 September 1901 Swami Abhedananda said in a lecture on 'Vedanata', philosophy at the University of California at Berkeley : "On one side, Vadanata philosophy gives expression to the highest ideal of all philosophy, and on the other, it gives a foundation to a system of religion which is the most rationalistic of all systems and it harmonizes with the ultimate conclusions of modern science and philosophy." Another Vedanta centre was set up in Brooklin and he formed an Indo-American club in New York in 1909 so that Indian students could get together and come in close contact with American friends.

Travelling and giving lectures and classes extensively in Europe and America for twenty-five years Swami Abhedananda left America on 27 July 1921 leaving behind a glorious record of innumerable commendable resourceful lectures there. On the way he delivered 'popular lectures' at Shanghai, Hong Kong, Canton, Manila, Singapore, Kualalumpore and Rangoon and reached Kolkata on 10 November 1921.

Oh hearing Swami Abhedananda's maiden speech in London, Swami Vivekananda said to him delightfully, 'You have a resonant voice which has carrying Power too.'[21] Swami Abhedananda's eloquence, his lucid exposition of Vedanta philosophy and his depth of spiritual realization made a profound impression even on the distinguished audiences. On august 1901 the *San Francisco Chronicle* reported : "Swami Abhedananda, who arrived here on Monday from New York, was the guest of honour at a reception given last evening at the residence of Dr. M.H.Logan. The Swami is a dignified intellectual-looking East-Indian ... He speakes English fluently, and his thoughts as he gives them utterance are so framed as to form an axiom."[22]

A prolific author :

Swami Abhedananda's collected works containing his repository writings and lectures on a variety of subjects such as psychology, religion, history, philosophy etc. run into eleven large volumes. He introduced a Bengali monthly called *Vishwavani* which is still being published from Sri Ramakrishna Vedanta Math, Kolkata. His hymns on Sri Ramakrishna and Holy Mother are so popular that they are regularly sung in almost all the centres of the Ramakrishna Order.

With reference to Swami Abhedananda's literary contribution, Swami Gambhirananda wrote : "He was not only a powerful speaker, but also a prolific writer. If his spoken words moulded the lives of hundreds of persons, his printed thoughts influenced a wider circle of people in different countries. His writings contain deep philosophy with a great wealth of infromation couched in a very popular style. As such, they have been of immense help in broadcasting the philosophical and spiritual ideas of India. As a matter of fact, they constitute a valuable legacy to the spiritually inclined souls all the world over."[23]

In this connection it may be added that during his tour (29 June 1905–26 October) with professor Herschel C. Parker of Columbia University, then president of the New York Vedanta Society, Swami Abhedananda met in Mexico city a Spanish gentleman who had read his books and surprised the Swami by showing him a copy of his book *Reincarnation* that he kept in his pocket.

An efficient Organizer :

Swami Abhedananda was a multifaceted genius. While living in America he activated the Vedanta Society of New York vigorously. The publication department was organized and a monthly bulletin was issued early in 1905. Besides giving classes and lectures he devoted himself to write books the sale of which became a steady source of income and made the Society financially self-supporting. In 1907 he reorganized the activities of the Society. He sent Swami Bodhananda to take charge of the Pittusburg (Pennsylvania) Vedanta Centre and asked Swami Paramananda to carry on services at the New York centre. He devoted himself to lecture in different places and to infuse a new life into the Vedanta movement in the UK.

One 2 March 1907, a five-storey building at 105 west 80th Street in New York city was bought for the Vedanta Society. Two rooms on the ground floor were converted into a single room that served as the lecture hall while some rooms of the upstairs were rented to others with a view to raise funds of the Society. After a few days of the same month a plot of 370 acres in the Berkshire Hills 107 miles from New York was purchased to set up a retreat site for students of Vedanta. While inaugurating Swami Abhedananda commented: 'The ashrama looks like Fairyland'.

The Swami established a Vedanta Society in Paris in April 1909. He founded an Indo-American club in New York in 1909 so that Indian students could get together and come in close contact with American friends.

Returning to India Swami Abhedananda needed a separate establishment, if not altogether a separate organization outside the Order in order to carry on his own activities almost freely and to store up his books, manuscripts, furniture etc. Accordingly he established the Ramakrishna Vedanta Society in a rented house at 45 B. B. Mechuabazar street (Now Keshab sen Street) in Kolkata on 20 February 1923 and again on 1 May 1923 he moved to Eden Hospital Road. Sri Ramakrishna Vedanta Math is situated at 19 A & B, Raja Rajkrishna Street, Kolkata.

In 1924 Swami Abhedananda established the Ramakrishna Vedanta Ashrama, a primary school, a charitable dispensary and a memorial building at Derjeeling in the name of Sister Nivedita who had died there in Roy-villa on 13 October 1911.

Swami Vivekananda represented Hinduism at the World's Parliament of Religions in Chicago (11th September, 1893–27 September, 1893) and as an unrivalled orator became internationally famous. Observing his amazing success and popularity the Christian missionaries and Pratap Chandra Majumdar a Brahmo leader out of jealousy began to vilify him by telling the American that he was not a true representative of Hinduism and tried to tarnish his character. To protest against this baseless fabricated propaganda and heinous conspiracy, Swamiji, a leonine monk, wrote his brother-diciples at Alambazar monastery, "Hold a public meeting in Calcutta approving of my activities in America and mentioning that I am accredited to represent Hinduism and send a letter of thanks to Dr. Barrows [chairman of the Parliament] with a copy to me."[24]

The monastic disciples and the devotees of Sri Ramakrishna took special interest and care in this 'sacred task'. Under the leadership of Swami Abhedananda, Swami Saradananda, Swami Ramakrishnananda and other brother monks they organized a very large meeting presided over by the Honourable Raja Peary Mohan Mukhopadhyay and attended by prominent religious leaders, reputed writers and scholars, high government officials, distinguished journalists, other eminent community leaders and innumerable laymen on 5 September 1894 in the Calcutta Town Hall. An excerpt from the unanimous resolutions was as follows: "This meeting desires to record its grateful appreciation of the great services rendered to the cause of Hindusim by Swami Vivekananda at the Parliament of Religions at Chicago, and his subsequent work in America."

The resolutions of the meeting were forwarded to Dr. John Henry Barrows, Merwin-Marie snell (President of the scientific section) and Swami Vivekananda. The procedings and lectures of the Calcutta Meeting greatly pleased the Swami, "He was moreover exceedingly happy to learn that behind the success of the meeting were the untiring efforts of his brother-disciples—Swami Abhedananda, Swami Ramakrishnananda, and others."[25]

Dynamic personality :

Swami Abhedananda during his stay for about a quarter century in the West was always conscious of the legendary popularity and influence of Swami Vivekananda and the irreparable void left by his absence there. Still he tried his best to propagate the message of Sri Ramakrishna and continue the Vedanta movement vibrantly by giving lectures and classes tirelessly, installing centres, writing books, meeting erudites and distinguished personalities and wandering.

Once Swami Abhedananda went to meet the famous scientist and inventor (of motion picture, camera, phonograph, dictaphone, autographic printer and so on) Thomas Edison and discussed Vedanta and India with him. He met Mckinley the President of the United States who cordially received him and inquired about the Vedanta movement in the United States and the British rule in India.

He also met John G. Brady, the Governor of Alaska who invited him to visit Alaska during the summer.

On 25 January 1898 the Swami was invited for dinner by Reverend Heber Newton a reputed minister of All Souls' Episcopal Church in New York, a liberal and influential man who was attracted to the universal message of Vedanta and Indian philosophies. Reverend Newton often sent his followers to listen to Swami Abhedananda. Dr. Elmer Gates, a famous scientist and psychologist was impressed when he discussed raja Yoga with the Swami and considered it to be very rational and scientific. During his stay in London Frank Dvorak, a famous Czechoslovakian artist came to see him on 7 May 1909 and painted oil portraits of Ramakrishna and the Mother at the request of the Swami.

While at Darjeeling Mahatma Gandhi, Chittaranjan Das, Lord Lytton, the then Governor of Bengal, the Nawab of Dhaka and others came in contact with him. The Swami said to Gandhi : "You are doing the work started by Ramakrishna and Vivekananda along the lines of removing untouchability and encouraging cottage industries. Therefore I bring to you blessings."[26]

Swami Abhedananda was not only a great scholar, a reputed orator, fond of music and playing on tabla, a prolific author, a practical person but also very diligent who taught his students to harmonize action and contemplation in their lives. The Swami was a highly spirited man. Some Christian missionaries, out of jealousy of his tremendous popularity began to slander him and defame his character. Such dirty attacks made a pioneering soul like him more strong and confident. As a worthy brother of a worthy leader Swami Abhedananda was undaunted and paid the scandalous stories no heed and went on working with his usual zeal and zest and sweetness of temper. He said to his disciples about how he faced the trials and troubles in his life :

> When I was in America, I would try to forget my sorrows and sufferings by singing or praying to the Master. I would spend my time practising japam and meditation, or studying books. There was none with whom I could

> open my heart, so I lived in my own world ... If a person uphold the truth, he encounters more obstacles; but one should never give up the truth. One should hold the post [i.e. God] with might and main. Don't you see how I have confronted the storms of obstables? I don't care even if the whole world stands against me. I am holding onto the Master.[27]

This statement, like a mirror, reflects various facets of the speaker's dynamic personality that kept him active till the last day of his life.

Love for the leader :

The Master taught his monastic disciples a scientific religion. In Cossipore one day Narendra while discussing Hindu prejudices about food and the knowledge of Brahman with Kali, Jogin, Sharat and Tarak; said to them : "After attaining self-knowledge, food can be taken from anyone's hand. Then one cannot look down upon anyone. As long as prejudices persist, Brahman has not been fully realized. Come, let me break your predudices today." In the evening Narendra took Kali, Sharat and Niranjan to a Muslim (Piru's) restaurant on Beadon street and ordered Chicken curry. Kali who became a vegetarian afterwards, accepted Narendra's proposal and coming back when he related the incident to the Master, he with a smile said, "It is all right. You are now free from all prejudice."[28] In his autobiography (p.p 82–83) Swami Abhedananda wrote that Narendranath was senior to him by about four years and he looked upon and loved him as his elder brother and Narendranath too loved him as his brother. He also wrote that he always obeyed his orders and was often attached to him like his shadow and imitated him in all respects. He recollected everlasting close relationship between them.

In March 1886 during Shivaratri Narendra had used Kali to test his power to transmit super consiouness and Kali felt as if a current were entering into him.

Swamiji gave his brother disciple Kali Prasad Chandra the significant monastic name 'Swami Abhedananda' (having the bliss of realization of oneness). He fondly used to call him 'Kalua' and Swami Saradananda 'Bhulua'.

Kali used to spend his time in studying the scriptures, composing Sanskrit hymns and meditation in a room known as 'Kali Tapasvi's Room in the Baranagore Monastery. When someone complained that Kali was not taking any responsibility for the household work, Narendra said : "Let one of the brothers be a scholar and I'll do the dishes myself." Learning about a conspiracy of a brother disciple to drive him out of the monastery for his enthusiastic interest in studies Kali decided to leave the monastery and never to return. During itineary he happened to meet Swamiji in Junagad and told him all about the incidents at the monastery along with his decision. Swamiji told him with a deep sigh that he was son of Sri Ramakrishna and the monastery was set up for them. It would have no utility if they did not visit there. The leader affectionately consoled him and the tears welled up in Kali's eyes and he changed his decision. (Amar Jivankatha, Swami Abhedananda, p.p. 165, 168). In this connection it may be noted that in the Alambazar Monastery a room was named 'Kali Vedanti's Room' for the same reason.

Swami Abhedananda as stated earlier took the lead in organizing a very large public meeting on 5 september 1894 in the Calcutta Town Hall in order to approve of Swamiji's activities in America and mention that he was accredited to represent Hinduism and to send a letter of thanks to Dr. Barrows (Chairman of the Parliament) with a copy to him.

Responding to the call of the leader Swami Abhedananda left for London to assist him in organizing Vedanta movement there. Swamiji encouraged him to be self-confident and self-supporting and to depend on the Master. Listening to his maiden speech Swamiji was highly pleased and said before the audiences, "Even if I perish on this plane, my message will be sounded through these dear lips and the world will hear it.'[29]

When Swami Abhedananda came back to India for six months after ten years from the West, a memorable reception was given for him at the Town Hall on 12 September 1906. In reply Swami Abhedananda paid deep homage to the leader Swamiji :

"Swami Vivekananda was not an ordinary man. He was the patriot-saint of modern India; he may be called an incarnation of divine wisdom in this age of commercialism. It was he who turned the table of commercialism in a foreign land like America ... He was the pioneer, the first preacher, the first Hindu sannyasin who went to the United States, carrying his Master's message and the gospel of Truth as taught by our ancient rishis. Vivekananda represented the Vedic religion, the *Sanatana Dharma*, which we may call a universal religion. He achieved great success because he preached nothing but the Eternal Truth.'[30]

Swami Abhedananda, like his leader, a great austere Vedantin and optimist said in his resonant voice on the eve of leaving San Francisco for India :

"The East and the West will unite—such is God's will. The signs of the times greatly encouage me, and my visit and prolonged stay in this country have clearly convinced me that it is possible to make the world our home, and to love all as brothers and sisters. God's spirit is working everywhere. Blessed is he who sees the work, and realizes the Divine spirit."[31]

Chapter – 15

SWAMI TRIGUNATITANANDA

On the second day of Entrance examination his precious gold watch had been stolen while he was having refreshments and repented his carelessness. He was so shocked that he could not concentrate on his studies and could not pass in the first division. Noticing his depression the Headmaster of his school brought him to Dakshineswar only to help him realize that the spiritual treasures were more valuable than a gold watch.

He could commit from memory 108 hymns and salutation mantras on different gods and goddesses and could also chant the Upanishads, the Gita and the Chandi in a rich melodious voice before he was fourteen .

He was the son of a rich landlord. He ate some tender grass to satisfy his hunger. Overcome by hunger and very tiredness he lay down to sleep in the rain by the side of the road at night while travelling in the Northern India.

An astrologer prdicted that he would be a great Yogi and a man of wisdom.

He was Sarada Prasanna Mittra, (later, Swami Trigunatitananda) son of Shivakrishna Mittra of Nandan Bagan, Kolkata, a religious man devoted to worship and the study of the scriptures. He was born on 30 January 1865 in a spiritual ambience.

Wonderful experiences :

Though Sarada was a disciple of Sri Ramakrishna, he was formally initiated by Holy Mother. He gained many wonderful experiences associated with the Master. He, despite his eagerness and practice, considered it too difficult to eradicate sexual desire. Once during meditation he felt that the idea of sex disappeared by the grace of Sri Ramakrishna.

Hearing from his mother that his father had finalized arrangement for his marriage, thinking this might divert his mind he was stunned. Sri Ramakrishna's words found an echo in his heart : "Why should you marry just now? (To M.) Sarada is now in a very good state of mind. Formerly he had a hesitant look; now his face beams with joy."[1] He left home for Puri and got no food for two days. He had lost his path and entered a dense forest at night. He climbed up a big tree to save himself from wild animals and began to chant Sri Ramakrishna's name and prayed to God for help and fell asleep; Sarada narrated his strange experience to his parents: "Suddenly I heard a man's voice, saying : "Hello, holy man. Here are some sweets. Please come down and appease your hunger." After a short while he brought a jug of water and disappeared in the darkness. I was impressed with his sympathy and received that food and drink as the grace of the compassionate God. At day break I searched for that man in the forest, but I couldn't find any human being or any village nearby."[2]

One night while the other brother disciples slept at the Baranagore Monastery Trigunantita was silently leaving for the cremation ground to perform some tantric rituals there. To his utter amazement and disappointment, he heard Swami Vivekananda calling out : "Where are you going? Sri Ramakrishna appeared to me in my sleep and told me where you were going. He said that you should not go, that he has done all these things for us, and that it is quite sufficient for us to keep our minds fixed on him." After this Swami Trigunatitananda never practised tantric disciplines.

While going on one of the most difficult pilgrimage to Mount Kailas and Manas sarovar (a holy lake) in Tibet, one evening Swami Trigunatitananda reached the bank of a river with no access to cross except by going over an old dilapidated dam. He decided to cross the river by jumping from one rock to another in the moonlight. When he reached the middle a dark cloudlet covered the moon and made him unable to move forward for one false step meant to fall into the icy water of the strong current. While chanting the name of Sri Ramakrishna, suddenly he heard a voice say, 'Follow me'. Obeying the order he reached the other side safely and realized that the Master's grace and assuracne of safety were always with him.

A pure soul :

While the disciples of Sri Ramakrishna living at the Baranagore monastery having been invited by Baburam's mother Matangini Devi to visit her native village, decided to visit Antpur, the birth place of Baburam Ghosh (later, Swami Premananda) for a retreat in the middle of December 1886, Sarada Prasanna receiving a secret message from the leader Narendranath left home to join the group. There on Christmas Eve nine disciples (Narendra, Baburam, Sharat, Shasi, Tarak, Kali, Niranjan, Gangadhar and Sarada) took vows of renunciation in front of a sacrificial fire. They vowed that they would never go back to family life. After a week they returned to the monastery and Sarada Prasanna stayed there.

With the intention of diverting Sarada Prasanna's mind from spiritual to temporal thoughts, his elder brother Binay secretly arranged an esoteric sacrificial ceremony. Twelve brahmins performed the ceremony for one month and twelve days. At the end of the ceremony they told Binay that it was impossible to bring his brother back to the world. They added also that he was praying intensely to realize God by embracing monastic life. Therefore, that sacrifice was not capable of bringing a pure soul to the lower plane. Hearing about his brother's secret plan, Sarada Prasanna was disgusted and stopped visiting home completely. In the third week of January 1887 Sarada Prasanna with some other brother-disciples perfomed the Viraja-homa in the Baranagore Monastery in front of the Master's picture and took his final monastic vows and was named Swami Trigunatitananda by Swami Vivekananda.

An occult power :

Swami Trigunatitananda's eating habits were very unusual. On his way to Navadwip, the birthplace of Sri Chaitanya on foot with Swami Saradananda and Swami Shivananda, he satisfied his hunger with eating some tender grass. One day he went to Dr. Bepin Ghosh for treatment of his stomach trouble. The doctor, a devotee and Swami Premananda's cousin entertained him with rasogollas more than two dozen which he finished quickly. Learning that the Swami visited him for treatment of stomach trouble, the doctor to his utter astonishment exclaimed, 'My goodness! Why then did you eat these rasagollas?' The Swami replied, 'You offered them with love, so what else could I do?'[3]

Swami Trigunatita had a strange capacity for food. As a glutton he could eat enormous amount of food, and again like an austere monk could fast for days at a stretch. Swami Premananda said about his brother-disciple's eating habits : "He had an occult power. Once I thickened seven and a half sers [seven and a half litres approximately] of milk and served him the whole quantity. He ate it all without stopping. On another occasion he stayed under the bel tree of Belur Math for several days, eating only one banana a day."[4] Once Swami Premananda's mother invited three of the Master's disciples to Balaram Basu's house. She cooked various dishes, but owing to unavoidable circumstances only Swami Trigunantitananda was able to pay a visit to the host in response to her invitation. She was upset that much food would be wasted. The Swami, much to her surprise finished the entire quantity. She was scared, thinking that the Swami would be sick. The next day when she saw the Swami well, she remarked : "It is amazing how Sarada eats! He has travelled over many mountains and learned many mantras so he can make any amount of food vanish. Otherwise it is not posssible for a human being to eat so much."[5] Once deciding to reduce his food intake the Swami began to eat two ounces of rice and two ounces of chilies each day for a month. Again, having just eaten a regular meal in a devotee's house, he consumed the food meant for four persons in Balaram's house in order to save wastage.

Superhuman will power : Amazing endurance :

While travelling in the Himalayas, Swami Trigunatitananda took shelter in a dilapidated temple on the outskirts of a village. The villagers warned him that dense clouds of mosquitoes would descend on the temple compound and any one who stayed at night would surely bleed to death. Covering himself with a thin blanket the Swami endured the pain with his amazing will force. The next morning the anxious villagers were surprised to see the Swami still alive. He had to stay in the village for a week to recover from the mosquito bites.

While staying in Kolkata, Swami Trigunatitananda developed a fistula, which needed surgery. Dr. Matilal Mukherjee intimated to him that since the operation would be painful and would take some time, he would use chloroform to lessen his feeling of pain. The Swami told the doctor to operate without chloroform and that he would bear with the pain. The surgeon and nurses saw to their utter astonishment that the Swami remained calm and without any change in his face during removal of the fistula cutting nearly six inches.

Swami Trigunatitananda had been suffering from rheumatism and Bright's disease for the last five years of his life. But he followed his routine and did not reduce his workload. He said to a disciple :

> A number of times during moments of excruciating pain I would think, "Let the body go, and end it all.' But I could not do it—the thought would come that the Mother's work must go on, and I set my will to force the body to carry on. This body has become a mere shell and may go to pieces at any time. For three years now I have held the body together by sheer force of will."[6]

On Friday, 25 December 1914 Swami Trigunatitananda conducted the all-day Christmas service from 6:00 a.m to 9:00 p.m consisting of his three lectures, chanting, singing, reading and explaining the scriptures. His amazing force of will made his pain-racked body endure anguish and pressure for long fifteen hours.

On Sunday afternoon, 27 December 1914 while Swami Trigunatitananda was lecturing in the Hindu Temple in San Francisco, suddenly an insane young man Louis Vavra, a former student of the Swami threw a bomb onto the rostrum. The assailant was killed and the Swami received severe injuries. On his way to the Affiliated Colleges Hospital the Swami inqruied : 'Where is Louis, poor fellow!' Lying in bed in a critical condition the Swami had thought not of his own pain but of the temple and asked Mrs. Peterson to arrange the repair of the damage to the temple. One of the nurses of the hospital remarked : 'I have never seen such calm, uncomplaining, and enduring patient in my life.'

Strange manners :

Sometimes Swami Trigunatitananda's activities and behaviour appeared to be peculiar and hard to understand. While suffering from blood dysentery and living on barley, one day he visited a devotee's house and ate a large amount of sweets. Later he told the doctor that the excessive eating had cured his disease. In the winter sometimes he would cover his body with a piece of thin cloth and sometimes with two blankets. Once he bathed with cold water when he was shivering with fever and ate plenty of meal and recuperated. Acutally he had very little body consciousness.

The Swami visited many deserted houses but found no ghost. So he was sceptical about the existence of ghosts. Once someone told him that he could see a ghost at midnight in a dilapidated haunted house near Baranagore Monastery. The Swami, telling none, went there before midnight and waited for the ghost. All of a sudden a faint light appeared in the corner of the room. The light grew brighter and an eye appeared in the centre of the light. It approached to harm him and he was about to faint while Sri Ramakrishna holding his hand said, "My child, why are you so foolishly taking chances with certain death? It is sufficient for you to keep your mind fixed on me."[7] The Swami's drooping spirit revived and his curiosity about ghosts satisfied forgood.

Once Swami Trigunatitananda decided to repeat his mantram day and night to reach to the goal—God-realization or death by starvation. Swami Shivananda was worried about his insistence and persuaded him to come out of his room. It was decided that while the young brother monk ate, Swami Shivananda would touch him and repeat a mantram on his behalf. He quickly took his meal and continued his japam.

Thirst for knowledge :

Sarada Prasanna was a brilliant student of the Metropoliton Institution in North Kolkata. Afterwards in the monastery while studying the Vedanta scriptures, he concentrated all his energy on it. He would then forget food and rest. He used to study Sanskrit literature and European philosophy unitl midnight. He had a bent for astrology and palmistry and would study those subjects day and night with dogged perseverance. In 1887 he practised Vaishnava sadhana with all the traditional body marks wearing a tulsi rosary around his neck and carrying a picture of his Chosen Deity in Puri.

Guts to confess :

Narendranath was in charge of the Baranagore monastery. On May 7, 1887 he found that during his absence Prasanna had gone away from the monastery leaving a letter for him : "I am going to Vrindavan on foot. It is very risky for me to live here. Here my mind is undergoing a change. Formerly I used to dream about my parents and other realtives. Then I dreamt of woman, the embodiment of māyā. I have suffered twice. I had to go back to my relatives at home. Therefore I am going far away from them. The Master once told me, 'Your people at home are apt to do anyting : never trust them.'

M. recorded Prasanna's mental state at that stage : "Rakhal said : There are the reasons for his going away. Once he remarked: Narendra often goes home to look after his mother, brothers and sisters. And he supervises the family's lawsuit. I am afraid that I too may feel like going home, following his example."

The next day Prasanna returned to the monastery from Konnagar as he was unable to manage railway fare.

"Rakhal (to Prasanna) : where do you want to go, running away from here? Here you are in the company of holymen. Wouldn't it be foolish to run away from this? Where will you find another like Narendra?

Prasanna : My parents live in Calcutta. I am afraid of being drawn by their love. That is why I want to flee to a distant place ...

Prasanna (to Rakhal) : Don't you yourself feel like running away from here?

Rakhal : Yes, now and then I have a fancy to spend a few days on the bank of the Narmada. I say to myself, 'Let me go to a place like that and practise sādhanā in a garden'. Again I feel a strong desire to practise the panchatapā for three days. But I hesitate to live in a garden that belongs to worldly people.[8]

Inquisitive mind :

As a rational person Swami Trigunatitananda had an analytical mind and left no claim of miraculous power without testing. While travelling in the Himalayas once he reached a place where a small spring flowed over the top of a rock. A fakir living nearby claimed to be able with the help of his occult power to make the water flow at will—for a small sum of money. Many people paid to see the water run at the fakir's order. But the Swami was a man not to be so easily convinced and was very sceptical about such claim of supernatural power. He climbed up around the rock and discovered a sporadic spring.

Innovator of a journal :

Swami Trigunatitananda knew that Swamiji had been eager to bring out a Bengali journal to propagate vedic culture and the message of Sri Ramakrishna and he wrote him that he was ready to take up the task. Swamiji had confidence in potentiality and hidden possibility of his brother disciple. In 1895 he wrote to Swami Brahmananda and on 26 January 1896 to Swami Yogananda requesting them to help Swami Trigunatita's endeavour. Swamiji 'a conscious dreamer' as he described himself, in order to encourage his brother disciple wrote from America in January 1896 : 'Dear Sarada, ... your idea of the paper is very good indeed. Apply yourself to it heart and soul... Never mind the funds. There are many to preach Chirstianity and Mohammedanism—you just go through the preaching of your own country's religion.'[9]

Udbodhan appeared on 14 January 1899 as a fortnightly paper. Ten years later it became a monthly journal. Swamiji named the magazine '*Udbodhan*', 'The Awakening'. The first editor and publisher was Swami Trigunatitananda who remained in that position over three years. He was also the manager, supervisor of the press, collector of subscriptions and article and when the typesetters were sick, he had to compose the type also.

Kumud Bandhu Sen a reputed writer and orator who came in close contact with all the monastic disciples of Sri Ramakrishna and the Mother while they lived at the Alambazar Monastery, has drawn a pen-picture of Swami Trigunatitananda's unparallel dedication and great energy put forth in making a distinguished journal which has been running uninterruptedly for 124 years (2021) :

> I call him the 'founder' because following Swami Vivekananda's direction and help, he and he alone shouldered the responsibility of editing and publishing the paper, doing tremendously hard work. I have seen him working in starving or near starving condition for days together, in winter, summer and rain. ... Even all this tremendously hard work could not remove the smile from his happy face—and there was no trace of weariness visible in him. Most of the compositors lived in the slums. Without hesitation he entered the places in search of them. I saw him many days drinking water in the afternoon at the residence of Manindra Krishna Gupta, a disciple and devotee of Sri Sri Thakur (Sri Ramakrishna). I gathered from him that till then he had not taken any food.

(Vivekananda O Samakalin Bharat Varsha, Sankari Prasad Basu, III : 53-54)

From the very beginning *Udbodhan* enriched with the writings of Swamiji, Swami Saradananda, Girish Chandra Ghosh, Haraprasad Shastri, Pramathanath Tarkabhusan, Kshirod Prasad Vidyabinod and many other reputed litterateurs, historians, educationists, Sanskritists, linguists, archaeologists etc identified itself as a very resourceful and popular magazine. Sankari Prasad Basu wrote : "In India, however, Trigunatitananda's great achievement as the first editor of *Udbodhan* earned him a secure place in the history of Bengali journals."[10]

Here is an excerpt from *From the Diary of a Disciple* by Sharat Chandra Chakrabarty, a disciple of Swamiji :

Disciple : "Sir, it is impossible for any other man to exert himself as Swami Trigunatita is doing for the Magazine."

Swamiji : "Do you think these Sannyasin children of Sri Ramakrishna are born simply to sit for meditation under trees lighting dhuni-fires? Whenever any of them will take up some work, people will be astonished to see their energy. Learn from them how to work. Here, for instance, Trigunatita has given up his spiritual practices, his meditation and everything, to carry out my orders, and has set himself to work. Is it a matter of small sacrifice? ... He will not stop short of success!"[11]

Devotion to the Master :

Sarada Prasanna's first visit to Sri Ramakrishna with his Headmaster M was on 27 December 1884 when he was nineteen. That day the Master probably talked about some important aspects of human life. His attaraction for the Master gradually began to increase. As a result, though he made good marks in the first year in Metropolitan college, he frequently visited Dakshineswar instead of attending classes. He lost interest in secular learning. The Master gave him spiritual instructions, fed him and asked Holy Mother to pay his carriage fare for Sarada used to visit Dakshineswar secretly avoiding his father's vigilance.

One hot day when Sarada reached Dakshineswar, Sri Ramakrishna told him to bring some water and wash his feet. Sarada amid his friends felt embarrassed at that command for he considered himself above all sorts of menial tasks done by servants and maids at home. He hesitated to carry out the order of the Master. But the Master repeated the request and Sarada could not but obeyed it. He realized that thus the Master wiped out his aristocratic pride for good and infused the spirit of service and humility. In September 1885 Sri Ramakrishna moved from Dakshineswar to Shyampukur in Kolkata for Cancer treatment, and in December 1885 he was moved again to Cossipore. Despite his father's scoldings and prohibition Sarada continued his visits to the Master, serving him during his last days.

Afterwards Sarada (Swami Trigunatitananda) wrote in an article 'Brahmacharya' :

> The only way to conquer lust is to look upon all women as your own mother, as images of the Divine Mother ... Sri Ramakrishna used to say, 'When a man succeeds in the conservation of his sexual energy, his intellect reflects the image of Brahman, even as a glass gives a perfect image when its back is painted with silver nitrate. The man who carries this image of Brahman in his heart is able to accomplish everything— he will succeed wonderfully in whatever action he engages himself.[12]

Devotion to the Holy Mother :

Sarada was Sri Ramakrishna's disciple. One day the Master sent him to the Holy Mother for spiritual instruction and made him aware of her divine power, quoting a Bengali couplet to put faith in him:

> Radha's infinite power of maya is beyond description,
>
> Millions of Krishnas and Ramas evolve, abide, and dissolve in it. [13]

Swami Trigunatitananda was formally initiated by the Mother. His faith in and love for her was phenomenal. He was her attendant while she was staying at the garden house of Nilambar

Mukhopadhayay in Belur. He was so attentive to her needs to the minutest detail that he used to spread a clean cloth below a *shephālikā* (weeping nyctanthes, an autumnal white fragrant flower) tree so that the flowers falling from it might not get spoiled by touching the ground. He collected the flowers for the Mother's morning worship.

After the passing of Swami Yogananda in 28 March 1899 Swami Trigunatitananda took charge of the Mother's physical needs. He busied himself with the Herculean task in connection with the fortnightly periodical *Udbodhan* the whole day and stayed in the Mother's house at night to meet her needs. A little over four months after the demise of Swami Yogananda her youngest brother Abhay a medical student waiting for the result of the final examination, died of cholera. The bereaved Mother finding little solace in Kolkata left for Jayrambati in October 1899. After crossing the river Damodar she got into a bullock cart. Swami Trigunatitananda was walking in front of the carriage as her bodyguard, with a heavy stick on his shoulder. It was past midnight. Suddenly he saw a wide breach in the road caused by a flood so that if the cart passed over the breach it might overturn or get a terrible jolt that might distrub the Mother's sleep or even might hurt her. At once he lay down on the depression and ordered the driver to drive the cart over his strong mascular body. Luckily the Mother woke up and looking ahead in moonlight sensing danger got down at once and walked over the spot and scolded her disciple for his rash act. The Swami's devotion to the Mother reminds us of the unforgetable devotion of Aruni and Eklavya to their respective guru.

Once Yogin-ma, a disciple of Sri Ramakrishna, asked Swami Trigunatitananda to buy some hot chillies for Holy Mother. In order to get the hottest chillies he walked from Baghbazar to Barabazar, a distance of about four miles tasting the chillies at every market. At last he got the best, the hottest ones at Barabazar. But by then his tongue had become red and swollen. Hearing about it the Mother remarked, 'What devotion to the guru!'

Even later when the Swami went to America he remembered

her and sent some money every month to her. It is rightly said : "His (Swami Trigunatitananda's) zeal to serve her (the Mother) appeared to be almost an obsession."[14]

Loyalty to the leader :

The brother disciples obeyed Swamiji's orders as they had Sri Ramakrishna's. Swami Trigunatitananda alike other brother disciples was very loyal and respectful to their leader Swami Vivekananda. At Belur monastery Swamiji introduced a rule that any monk who didn't go to the shrine for meditation at 4:00 a.m. would have to beg for his food outside the monastery that day. One day Swamis Shivananda and Trigunatitananda were late attending meditation. Swamiji asked them to live on alms that day. They left for alms politely and when they came back with food from Belur village, Swamiji gladly shared the food with them.

As stated earlier once in 1899 Sharat Chandra Chakravarty a disciple of Swamiji commented that it was impossible for any other man to labour for the Bengali fortnightly magazine, *Udbodhan* in the way Swami Trigunatitananda did. Swamiji replied : "... Trigunatita has given up his spiritual practices, his meditation and everything, to carry out my orders and has set himself to work. Is this a matter of small sacrifice. What an amount of love for me is at the back of this spirit of work, do you see?"[15]

In 1902 Dr. M. H. Logan, the president of the Vedanta Society of San Francisco wrote to Swamiji requesting him to send another Swami for Swami Turiyananda decided to return to India owing to a serious deterioration of his health. Swamiji asked Swami Trigunatitananda to set off for America to release Swami Turiyananda. Swami Trigunatitananda was then very busy with publication of the journal *Udbodhan*. Besides, he was a bonafide vegetarian and believed that vegetables might not be available in America and decided to live on bread and water if needed. In the mean time Swamiji passed away on 4 July, 1902. Still obeying the order of the leader and ignoring personal inconvenience or choice Swami Trigunatitananda handed over charge of the magazine to Swami Shuddhananda and sailed for America in the early part of

November and reached San Francisco on 2 January 1903.

When Swami Vivekananda returned to Kolkata from the West for the first time on Friday, February 19, 1897, he and his party were given a grand reception. The members of the Reception committee conducted the Swami and his compainions Mr. and Mrs. Sevier and Goodwin to a phaeton. When the huge procession was making its way to the destination, Swami Trigunatitananda standing behind the unharnessed carriage drawn by students shouted : 'Jai Ramakrishna', 'Jai Swamiji' with great delight.

Builder of the first Hindu temple in the West and other Contributions :

In order to accommodate the large crowds the Vedanta Society of San Francisco rented a spacious house at 40 Steiner Street in March 1903. But soon it appeared to be insufficient to meet the needs. Swami Trigunatitananda who by nature was up and doing felt the Society should have a suitable house of its own. Accordingly a committee was appointed to look for a suitable site and a meeting was held. The funds were quickly raised and a plot of land was bought on the corner of Webster and Filbert Streets. The cornerstone was laid ceremoniously on 25 August 1905. The Swami placed there pictures of Sri Ramakrishna, Holy Mother and others within a metal box.

Swami Trigunatitananda was innovative. While planning the temple he synthesized ideas from a Hindu temple, a Christian church, a Muslim mosque and an American residence. Joseph A. Leonard an architect designed it in a style generally known as Pointed Architecture of Grecian and Roman origin. Moorish style was followed in the construction of the mouldings, ornaments and the arches of the Verandah. The points of the domes, towers, and pinnacles directed upwards to the sky have a spiritual significance as was noted in the journal *voice of Freedom*—moving towards God, or rising higher and higher until one reaches the very highest.[16]

The temple was dedicated on 7 January 1906 and the first services were performed there on Sunday, 15 January 1906. This was the first Hindu Temple in the Western World. Swami Trigunatitananda said, "Believe me, if there is the least tinge of selfishness in building the temple, it will fall; but if it is the Master's work, it will stand." Amazingly the terrible earthquake and fire of 1906 destroyed much of the city but did no harm to the temple.

The Swami set up a monastery. Ten young American students being inspired to live the life of brahmachārins, became the inmates of the monastery and were engaged in various occupations to earn their own living and to contribute their share of the expenses of the monastery. Afterwards he started a nunnery at the cordial request of some women disciples. He also introduced a monthly journal there called *Voice of Freedom* in April 1909 in order to combine the thoughts and culture of the East and the West through that periodical which became very popular.

In 1911 Swami Trigunatitananda purchased some 200 acres of land to establish a model community accross San Francisco Bay. He planned to build a temple with attached library, a home for aged and helpless devotees, a hospital, sell plots of land to interested devotees who might build their houses and thus to form a community of devotees there. But these ambitious plans did not fully come to fruition.

The Swami succeeded in making the Shanti Ashrama a fully equipped and functioning establishment. Thus through multifarious activities he played a significant role in propagating the teachings of the Vedanta and Sri Ramakrishna in America.

Distinctive method of teaching :

After coming back to Kolkata from pilgrimage in the latter part of 1895, Swami Trigunatitananda began to study Vedanta literature exrtensively on the other hand, gave classes at various places in the city on the Gita and Upanishads. He set up three centre in Kolkata to teach morality and spirituality to young people.

In America the Swami taught his students to be engaged in various occupations and to earn their own living in the monastery. They had to obey discipline strictly. The Swami firmly believed that discipline forms a strong character which is indispensable for a foundation for spiritual life. The inmates had to rise early in the morning, meditate regularly and do household work such as sweeping, cleaning, gardening etc. The Swami himself took part in doing the household duties and cooked meals for the students so that they might eat pure and sattvic food, which is essential for spiritual growth. The meals started with a chant and ended with a few minutes of silent meditation. Each student in turn had to read from one of the scriptures and this was followed by questions, with answers by the Swami. He taught them that all works connected with the temple were holy and if done in the proper spirit, would purify their minds and condense their meditation.

The Swami liked to use forceful proverbs. Some of the mottoes hanging in every room of the monastery were : "Live like a hermit, but work like a horse." "Do it now", "Watch and pray", "Do or die but you will not die".[17] He considered singing a devotional exercise and led his young male disciples in hymns and chants up on the roof of the temple or down by the harbour at dawn.

Swami Trigunatitananda, born with a silver spoon in his mouth, was an uncompromising ascetic. He believed, 'Example is better than precept.' He was an embodiment of punctuality and regularity. He used to go to bed last of all and rise first of all. There was no bed in his office-cum-bedroom. He used to spread one blanket on the carpet and put another blanket over his body and used the upper part of right arm as his pillow.

Swami Trigunatitananda used to live at Shanti Ashrama for one month every year with his thirty or forty students. In the retreat the students in their rigorous routine life were busy with chanting, meditation, scripture classes, along with chopping wood, carrying water, cooking, cleaning, and maintenance from 3:45 a.m. to 10:00 p.m. The Swami provided sufficient recreation in order to relieve the students from any monotony or strain. Wednesday and Saturday afternoons were declared holidays. At night he used to tell stories about Sri Ramakrishna, as well as stories about varied experiences in his own life. Students attending the classes at Shanti Ashrama were deeply impressed with the spirituality of the Swami and could hardly forget their special experiences.

Swami Trigunatitananda acted with his students like an affectionate mother and a chastising father as well. He trained them to give lectures, and tried to bring out the best in them.

Charismatic personality :

Swami Trigunatitananda was a man of dynamism, undeterred spirit, unflagging zeal and indomitable energy. His activities and behaviour, like his food habits, were curious and sometimes unintelligible. He studied the Vedanta so attentively that he forgot hunger and thirst and sleep. With his unquenchable thirst for knowledge he used to study Sanskrit literature and European philosophy until midnight and practised spiritual disciplines with unswerving devotion. He bore with rebuke and criticism stoically.

The Swami was not a cloistered monk. He was a very likeable man who made friends with many known neighbours as well as with many distinguished people e.g. the Mayor of San Francisco.

The Swami, like his Master, was a man of truth. In San Francisco once he was invited to a dinner by a clergyman who was a good friend and an admirer of him. After dinner the host asked the guest, "Is the food all right?" The Swami at first hesitated to comment but when the clergyman insisted on knowing the Swami's opinion, the latter answered, "It is hard for me to tell you the harsh truth. Truly, I don't relish this kind of food." Though the clergyman was a little shocked, he appreciated the Swami's frankness and love for truth. He said to the Swami : "I know you will not deviate from truth, even for the sake of social etiquette or friendship. But let me tell you, if you are invited by somebody in the future, please don't say such a harsh truth, otherwise, they will criticize you. The Swami afterwards refused dinner invitation in order to avoid awakward situation."[18]

In 1897 a terrible famine broke out in the district of Dinajpur (now East Dinajpur is in Bangladesh and West Dinajpur is in

West Bengal). Swami Trigunatitananda responding to the call of humanity rushed to the affected area and organized relief work. He worked hard day and night to distribute food to starving people. He himself lived on alms or without food.

Deeply concerned about the hungry millions around him, the Swami wrote a monograph on famine. The comprehensive article was published in the *Udbodhan*.

On 27 December 1914 afternoon Swami Trigunatitananda was delivering a lecture in the auditorium of the Hindu Temple. Suddenly Louis Vavra an insane former student of the Swami exploded a bomb killing himself and severely wounding the Swami. On his way to the hospital the Swami in the midst of excruciating pain, inquired in a compassionate voice, "Where is Louis, poor fellow?" ...Thus the great saint like a martyr wrote lessons of love, humanity, catholicity and forgiveness with his sacred blood on the pulpit of the temple.

With his originality, innovation and special characteristics Swami Trigunatitananda made an immense contribution to the Ramakrishna Order and society as well and left some immortal and relevant message : Discipline yourself. Build your character. Work hard. Endure to the end. Realize yourself. And be free.

Chapter – 16

SWAMI ADVAITANANDA

Generally people take refuge in spirituality as an antidote to three kinds of affliction—physical and mental, terrestrial and supernatural. He lost his wife at the age of fifty five and bereavement changed the course of his life.

He felt chest pain for the pang of separation from the very man who looked at him with cold eyes at first sight.

He was eight years older than his guru.

He was Gopal Chandra Ghosh (later Swami Advaitananda) son of Govardhan Ghosh born in 1828 at Rajpur in North 24 Parganas.

Organized and methodical :

Owing to his depressing experience of the first meeting with Sri Ramakrishna, Gopal Chandra was not at all interested in him. But persuaded by his friend Dr. Mahendra Pal, a devotee of the Master, to visit the Master frequently, he went again to him and that time the Master gave him an infallible antidote for his intense agony. He told him that the world being unreal the only way to be free from bereavement is dispassion. The Master's words left a lasting impression on his mind and he decided to renounce the world and to serve the Master.

Once while the Master was strolling alone in the temple garden of Dakshineswar, Gopal kneeling down before the Master and holding his feet began to cry. The Master holding his arms lifted him up and the magic touch of the Master converted him into a great spiritual aspirant. After the passing away of Sri Ramakrishna Gopal took to monastic life and became Swami Advaitananda.

Sri Ramakrishna accepted him as his disciple and would address him as 'the elder Gopal' or 'Overseer'. The Mother needed a suitable person who would shop and run errands for her. The Master introduced that new disciple to her. He admired Gopal's managerial efficiency in household affairs and his decent behaviour. By temperament he was methodical and orderly. He was organized, neat and clean.

The Master's nurse, the Mother's messenger :

Gopal accompanied Sri Ramakrishna while he left for Shyampukur in Kolkata for cancer treatment in September 1885. He served the Master like a nurse, washing his sore throat, giving him medicine and proper diet. On the other hand, he acted as the Mother's messenger. Both of them were free with each other. Holy Mother did not cover her face with a veil in front of him. When the food was ready, she used to send Gopal or Latu to inform the Master. When the doctor prescribed any special diet for the Master, Gopal would take notes in details and convey them to the Mother,

On 11 December 1885 Sri Ramkrishna was moved to the Cossipore garden house from Shyampukur. Gopal continued his service to the Master sincerely. "On the morning of 23 December Ramakrishna gave unrestrained expression to his love for the devotees... His love this day really broke all bounds. He wanted to bless Gopal of Sinthi and said to a devotee, "Bring Gopal here."[1]

At Cossipore Gopal took responsibility for giving medicine to the Master. One day when the time for taking medicine had passed, the Master said to another disciple, 'Where is that old man?' Learning that Gopal was sleeping, he remarked compassionately, "Oh, how many sleepless nights he has passed! Let him sleep. Please don't call him. You had better give me the medicine today."[2]

Virtuous acts :

At Cossipore Gopal with a number of his brother disciples were taking turns attending to the needs of the Master. One day, instead of serving the Master Gopal meditated for a long time elsewhere. Hearing about this Girish Chandra Ghosh commented, "The one upon whom Gopal is meditating with closed eyes is suffering on a sickbed, and fancy, he is meditating upon him!" Gopal was called for. When he entered the Master's room the Master told him to stroke his legs. Then he said to Gopal, "Do you think I am asking you to stroke my legs because they are aching? Oh, no! In your previous births you did many virtuous acts; therefore I am accepting your service."[3]

Thus the consequences of noble activities of previous births of Gopal had begun to take effect. A God-man accepted his service, gave him blessing wilfully and transformed his life of a householder into an allrenouncing monk.

Significant gift to Sri Ramakrishna's monastic disciples :

In 1886 Gopal wanted to acquire virtue by offering cloths to holy people on the auspicious day of makar-sankranti (in the middle of January). Every year monks and pilgrims from all over India visit Gangasagar, the confluence of the Ganga and the Bay of Bengal, for a holy bath on the auspicious day. Many monks and pilgrims go by boat from the Jagannath Ghat of Kolkata. Gopal bought twelve pieces of cloth and twelve rosaries of rudraksha beads to distribute among the monks. He dyed the cloths in the ochre colour himself. When he mentioned this to Sri Ramakrishna, the Master said to him, "You will attain a thousand times more virtue if you present those ochre cloths and rosaries to my children rather than giving them to the monks of Jagannath Ghat; Where else will you find such all-renouncing monks? Each of them is equal to a thousand monks." This changed Gopal's mind.

On Tuesday 12 January 1886 (makar-sankranti) Gopal gave the ochre cloths and rosaries to the Master who touched them and sanctified them with a mantram. Then he himself (though Swami Abhedananda wrote in his book 'Amar Jivankatha' that the Master asked Gopal to distribute ochre cloths and rosaries among his eleven children and Gopal obeyed his order) distributed them among his young disciples. They put on the saffron cloths and prostrated themselves before the Master who was happy to see them in monastic cloth and blessed Narendra, Rakhal, Niranjan, Baburam, Shashi, Sharat, Kali, Jogin, Latu, Tarak, and Gopal. The Master asked to set aside the twelfth cloth and rosary for Girish Chandra Ghosh who afterwards touched them to his head and felt the Master's special blessing.[4]

Swami Gahanananda remarked, "Thus in a way, Gopal became instrumental in sowing the seed of the future Ramakrishna Order."[5]

Second to none in carrying out responsibilities :

Swami Advaitananda was the first inmate at the Baranagore Monastery. He was a diligent and sincere worker. He helped the brother monks with household work. In 1898 a plot of land was purchased at Belur for the permanent home of the Order and Swami Advaitananda was entrusted to make the uneven land ready for construction. Early in the morning after breakfast at Nilambar Mukherjee's garden house, he would go to the new plot and engage the Santal labourers who had been hired to level the ground. He scolded them if they neglected duty. One day their leader said to Swami Vivekananda, "O dear Swami, don't come to us when we work—our work stops when we talk to you. Later the old father [Swami Advaitananda] scolds us." At noon he used to bathe in the Ganga and sitting under a tree ate his lunch sent from the monastery.

Besides levelling the ground and other construction work, the Swami started a vegetable garden and a dairy farm. He considered the vegetable gardening work as the worship of Sri Ramakrishna. Swami Adbhutananda said : "without Gopal-da the monks of Belur Math would not have had vegetables along with their rice.

He worked so hard to produce various kinds of vegetables in the monastery garden."[6]

One day Swami Advaitananda went to see the Mother in Kolkata and told her that despite his rheumatic pain he worked hard to grow various kinds of vegetables garden and sometimes he sent some vegetables to her but he did not get much help from the boys. Holy Mother said to her devoted attendant, "My son, you are an old-timer; your life is different from the modern boys, who generally don't care for household matters. The monastery is like a family home where you need food, clothing, and other necessities. Without these things how can you live there? So it is your duty to take care of the Master's children."[7]

The Swami was a perfectionist to the letter. The inexperienced and unskilled novitiates coming from schools and colleges were not accustomed to manual labour and had to swallow mild scoldings of the Swami but they considered his criticism as a token of affection. One day the Master had shown him that it was he manifested through all. So there was none to blame or to criticise. Since then the Swami stopped to find fault with others. Swami Turiyananda said : "We are much indebted to Gopal-da because we learned the secret of work from him. He was organized and concentrated in everything he did. And he was very methodical in his habits. Until his last day he regularly practised meditation."[8]

A role model :

Gopal tried to absorb Sri Ramakrishna's teachings and way of life. One day Gopal and Dr. Mahendra Pal his friend and a devotee of Sri Ramakrishna walked into the garden path in Dakshineswar with the Master. A woman sweeper was coming towards them, carrying on her head a tub of excrement from a privy, about five or six yards away. When the Master saw her he prostrated before the poor woman stretching fully on the ground, saying, "Mother, who can do this work except you?' Gopal learnt to love and respect a low-born person instead of looking down him. He understood that the Master disliked carelessness in people because he believed that if a person is forgetful in minor things, he will be forgetful in the major aspects of life. On 25 May 1884 Sri Ramakrishna went to the Panchavati where arrangement for *Kirtan* (devotional song) had been made. Gopal carried an umbrella for Sri Ramakrishna. Suddenly the rain poured down. The Master returned to his room with the devotees and asked Gopal if he had brought the umbrella. Gopal replied that he had not brought the umbrella for he had forgotten all about it while listening to the songs. Saying this he rushed to the Panchavati to bring back the umbrella.

The Master said : "I am generally unmindful about the world, but not to that extent. Rakhal also is very careless. Referring to the date of an invitation, he says 'the eleventh' instead of 'the thirteenth'. And Gopal—he belongs in a herd of cows!"[9]

Once a physician prescribed the juice of three lemons for the Master's upset stomach. Gopal was asked to collect them. Gopal brought more than three lemons. But Sri Ramakrishna accepted only three lemons and asked him to return the extras. Gopal realized that the Master himself followed his advice (Never tell a lie) to the letter. He learnt from Sri Ramakrishna that words should be congruous with action. He followed his teaching to the letter and inspired others to do the same. He started his spiritual journey late but by virtue of sincerity and implicit devotion to the Master he attained fulfillment at the end of his life. He observed keenly likings and dislikings of the Master and forbade the monks to bang doors or tear new cloth with a shrill noise for Sri Ramakrishna could not bear it. He learnt from his Master lessons of etiquette and renunciation. Sri Ramakrishna made Gopal's life a role model for elderly seekers of God and his lay disciples to follow.

An exemplary life for the future generations of monks to follow :

Gopal won over age and sluggishness. He was a man of indomitable spirit and unflagging energy. He was older than the Master and the oldest of all other brother monks. Still he tried to keep the same pace as the other young disciples. On 4 January

1886 getting permission of the Master Gopal left for Dakshineswar at 9:00 p.m. with Narendra to meditate under Panchavati. Gopal tried very hard to follow the ideal the Master set for his monastic disciples.

Gopal was the embodiment of amazing will-power and self-relience. On 5 April 1884 the Master learning about Gopal's desire to go for a pilgrimage, said to him and the other devotees : "As long as a man feels that God is 'there' he is ignorant. But he attains knowledge when he feels that God is 'here'."

Then Sri Ramakrishna told a story about a man having a lighted lantern in his hand went to a neighbour's house at the dead of night to light his charcol for smoking. Pointing at the lighted lantern the neighbour made the unmindful smoker aware of his idiocy.

In the midst of laughter the great prophet added : "What a man seeks is very near him. Still he wanders about from place to place."[10]

After the passing away of his most beloved Master Swami Advaitananda while living at the Baranagore Monastery felt an irresistible urge to travel to various places for pilgrimage in India. It is said: "By the grace of Lord Krishna a dumb becomes garrulous a lame can cross a mountain."[11]

Swami Advaitananda set out for travelling towards the end of 1887 at the age of about sixty and visited many holy places namely Varanasi, Kedarnath, Badrinath, Vrindaban, Gaya, Merrut, Hardwar and returning to the cottage of Banshi Datta's garden house Varanasi he passed five years there practising austerities and being deep in meditation. In 1896 once while walking through the street in varanasi barefoot, a thorn pricked his foot, causing a lot of pain. He slowly recuperated through the active intervention of Swami Shivananda and sincere service of Pramadadas Mittra and other devotees. In 1897 Swami Advaitananda visited Raipur Central India, Kanyakumari, Rameswaram and other places for pilgrimage in South India. In 1899 he visited Kamakhya and Darjeeling and travelled to Dwaraka and other holy places of Western India in 1900. Responding to Swamiji's call he reached the Alambazar monastery and devoted himself to physical labour to make a plot of land ready for construction of Belur monastery. Swamiji made him one of the trustees of the Ramakrishna Math and Ramakrishna Mission. Afterwards he became the vice-president of the Order. Thus the vibrant octogenarian Swami set an amazing example of renunciation, austerity, devoting to spiritual disciplines, tenacity of extensive pilgrimage, manual labour and executing administrative duties sincerely breaking the barrier of age.

As a Man :

Swami Virajananda, a disciple of Swami Vivekananda gave a pen-picture of Swami Advaitananda as a man :

"In September 1895 I stopped at Varanasi on my way to Vrindaban and stayed with Gopal-da at Banshi Datta's house. His room was small but neat and clean. He was very methodical and economical. Very early in the morning, even in the cold winter, he would bathe in the Ganga and return to his cottage chanting the Sanskrit hymns of gods and goddesses. He practised japam and meditation until 9:00 a.m. and then he would go to beg alms from door to door. He was extremely punctual about his spiritual disciplines, eating, sleeping walking and other activities. Though his belongings were very few, everything was kept in its proper place. This indicated his great taste and orderliness. In the afternoon during our walk he would show me the important places of Varanasi. Gopal da, Swami Satchidananda and I circumambulated Panchakoshi [the holy city of Varanasi] in four days and covered forty-four miles. We walked until noon and then we cooked, ate, and took rest. At night we slept under a tree by the side of the road."[12]

Swami Advaitananda was healthy and liked to do his own work. He believed that a monk should be self-relient, depending only on God and no one else. He was fond of music and would play tabla when Swamiji or other brothers sang devotional songs. In leisure hours he would copy the scriptures in his beautiful hand-writing. He would chant the Gita every day.

Though Swami Advaitananda was senior to Swamiji by thirty five years, he had deep love and respect for thier leader. Swamiji too held him in high regard for his abilities.

Swamiji wanted that the monks of the Order should know the Sanskrit scriptures; so he asked Swami Advaitananda to study *Laghu Kaumudi.* (Sanskrit Grammar). Swami obeyed the leader's advice zealously.

At one time during his Sadhana, the Master prayed and said to the Mother, "Mother, don't make me a dry and austere monk, keep me above want."[14] His monastic disciples also liked merriment instead of living mundane mechanical life despite hardship in the monastery.

Swami Advaitananda was an old waggish monk who relished banter and fun. Swamiji composed a comical verse to tease Swami Advaitananda who enjoyed it and felt the warmth of affectionate respect of the composer for him. Swamiji stung him : 'You are like an old bull; breaking off your horns, you have joined the young calves."[13] Once Swamiji said, "Gopal-da, you are getting old day by day. Be careful. Now you must start taking milk and fruits, which will give you new life and then your bones will not be rusted. After all, you are the oldest among us, so tommorow we shall wash you ceremoniously with milk." The next day Swamiji and other monks poured ten seers of milk on Swami Advaitananda's head and then washed him with Ganga water. Then a new cloth and different kinds of nutritious fruits were offered to him. Swamiji said delightfully to him, "Brother, from today you are the abbot and the responsibility of the monastery is yours."[15]

There are so many examples of Swami Advaitananda's sense of humour. On 7 September, 1901 Swamiji wrote from the Belur Math to Sister Nivedita, one of my ducks unfortunately died Yesterday. She had been gasping for breath more than a week. One of my waggish old monks [Swami Advaitananda] says, "Sir, it is no use living in this Kali-Yuga when ducks catch cold from damp and rain, and frogs sneeze!"[16]

Swami Advaitananda did not like tea while Swami Subodhananda was fond of it. Oneday the former said to the latter, "Look, don't drink tea; you will get blood dysentery." The latter replied confidently, "Gopal-da, each drop of tea produces a drop of blood." "All right brother, drink more," Advaitananda said jokingly. All laughed.[17]

There was dearth of money, food and all other necessaries in the initial stage at the Belur monastery. But there was fun and laughter among the brother disciples. Swami Vijnanananda depicted an incident :

Gopal-da and Swami Nityananda were together at Belur Math along with several monks and brahmacharins. Nityananda asked the young monks, "Brothers, come with me and till this plot of land; I shall grow eggplant and potatoes." The young monks immediately started the project. Gopal-da noticed it. He went to them and said: "Oh! how hard you are working here! One should not load such a strenuous task on the young ones. You boys, come, with me." Gopal-da took them to his plot and said to them with affection : "Now, brothers dig this plot for a flower bed. The soil of the other plot is harder than this plot." Swamiji and other monks had a hearty laugh when they heard the story of Gopal-da's loving sympathy for the young monks."[18]

At the Baranagore Monastery most of the disciples used to sleep in a large room. One night when Swami Advaitananda went to the bathroom, Swami Akhandananda replaced his pillow with a brick. Returning from the bathroom Swami Advaitananda discovered his brick-pillow and said to Swami Akhandnanda with a smile : "Ganga [Gangadhar, the premonastic name of Swami Akhandananda], I know you have done this mischief. Brother, I shall use your precious gift tonight as my pillow." Swami Akhandananda was deeply moved and throwing away the brick at once brought back the pillow. Apologizing to Swami Advaitananda Swami Akhandananda said; "Brother, you are a real monk—free from anger and ego."[19]

Swami Gahanananda observed, "His (Swami Advaitananda's) life was a role model for young novitiates in the formative period of their monastic life.

"He started his spiritual life when he was quite advanced in age. He came from an ordinary merchant community, probably without much religious background. By the grace of the Master and by his own strenuous efforts he was transformed into a great spiritual personality instilling hope, especially in the elders. He will ever be remembered in the circle of monastics as well as devotees of the Order."[20]

Chapter – 17

SWAMI SUBHODHANANDA

Who is the Greatest?

18:1. At that time the disciples came to Jesus and asked, "Who, then, is the greatest in the kingdom of heaven?"

2. He called a little child to him, and placed the child among them.

3. And he said : Truly I tell you, unless you change and become like little children, you will never enter the kingdom of heaven.[1]

He was a guileless child who behaved like a boy all through his life and became a great spiritual personality. A God-man used to call him *Khoka* (little boy).

Though a brilliant student he intentionally got poor marks on the examination to resist his father arranging his marriage.

He was afraid of the dark and of riding in a boat because he did not know how to swim.

He was Subodh Chandra Ghosh son of Krishnadas and Nayantara of Kolkata. He was born on 8 November 1867. His family was rich and owned the Siddheswari Kali Temple of Thanthania which Sri Ramakrishna often visited as he stayed at Jhamapukur.

Innate treasure of spirituality :

Though Krishnadas was a devout Hindu, he used to take his children to the Brahmo Samaj services and buy religious books for them. In the evening Subodh's mother would tell him stories from the Bhagavata, the Ramayana and the Mahabhrata. When he was young he would read the biographies of holy people and would observe how their lives were transformed. Thus a religious inclination was created in him from his very childhood.

Subodh had a premonition that he would not live at home and would travel alone like an itinerant monk. In his teens Subodh said to his father, "Please don't insist that I get married. If you force me to marry, I shall obey you. But I will leave home, family life is not for me. Please don't entangle me."

Subodh was impressed by reading Sri Ramakrishna's teachings and went with his friend Kshirod to see the great man at the age of seventeen only in August 1885. Sri Ramakrishna said to him, "I knew you would come. Well, the Divine Mother sends here those who will attain sprituality. You belong to this place," Holding Subodh's hand and closing his eyes for a few minutes Sri Ramakrishna then said to him, "You will attain the goal. Mother says so."

On the following Saturday when Subodh and Kshirod met Sri Ramakrishna, he took them to the stairs leading to the Shiva temples and asked them to unbutton their shirts and stick out their tongues. The Master first wrote something with his finger on Kshirod's tongue and stroked his body from the navel to the throat. He did the same to Subodh, saying, "Awake, Mother, awake!" Then he told them to meditate. No sooner did Subodh begin to meditate than his whole body trembled and he felt a current rushig along his spinal cord to his brain. He saw with great delight a strange light within him in which images of numerous gods and goddesses flashed. In deep meditation he lost all sense of personal identity. After a while the Master stroked his body in the reverse direction, from the head downwards. Subodh could concentrate so easily because he would think about gods and goddesses since he heard of them from his mother.

Irresistible attraction for Sri Ramakrishna :

Subodh had intense love and respect for Sri Ramakrishna from the very beginning of their meeting. In order to avoid his parents Subodh sometimes on weekdays used to run away from school and return home before dusk after visiting Sri Ramakrishna at Dakshineswar.

Even when Sri Ramakrishna was moved to Shyampukur in North Kolkata in September 1885 for cancer treatment, Subodh utilized every opportunity to visit him secretly. That year on the day of Kali Puja M. the chronicler of The Gospel of Sri Ramakrishna visited the Siddheswari Kali Temple of Thanthania to offer worship on behalf of the Master. Subodh regretted that he was unable to go with M. to see the Master on that auspicious day. He decided that that night when the members of his family would be busy in their temple's worship service; he would go to the Master secretly.

The devotees worshipped Sri Ramakrishna as the Divine Mother on that auspicious night at the Shyampukur house. Subodh hurried to the Master at dawn and said to him, "Yesterday I couldn't come with M. to see you, since then my heart has been restless to see you. I didn't sleep at all last night. Now after seeing you I feel peaceful." The Master was pleased to hear his words and said to his attendants : "Listen to what this boy says! He was longing to see me and so spent a sleepless night! Please give him some prasad."

Considering from his own experience that drinking tea might heal up sore throat, Subodh with affinity told the Master that if he liked he would bring some good tea from his house. But hearing from Rakhal that hot tea might aggravate his throat pain, the Master consoled Subodh, "Hot tea will not suit me."[2] Subodh was deeply moved by the childlike simplicity of the Master.

At Cossipore garden house oneday Sri Ramakrishna asked Subodh to copy a devotional song composed by Saint Tulasidas. But he refused to do so by saying that his handwriting was not so good. The Master persuaded : "Please copy that song. It does not matter whether your writing is good or bad." When Subodh still declined, the Master said "You are really a dumbbell. Neglecting your studies you only played with your friends." Being thus severely rebuked, Subodh smiled. The Master said with a smile : "My boy aren't you upset that I scolded you?" Subodh answered, "Sir even your scoldings are sweet."[3] The Master said with delight : "Boys, listen to what this boy says. He says that even my scoldings are sweet." The Master blessed Subodh by touching his head while he was leaving for home.

The Master and Subodh had reciprocal love and feeling of kinship between them. Swamiji said : "The only true teacher is he who can immediately come down to the level of the student, and transfer his soul to the student's soul and see through the student's eyes and hear through his ears and understand through his mind. Such a teacher can really teach and none else."[4]

Subodh liked more to spend time with Sri Ramakrishna or in meditation than studies. He walked from school to Dakshineswar in hot sun in order to serve the Master and felt no tiredness while fanning him standing for a long time. The Master asked him to sit on his bed and like an affectionate father at times himself fanned Subodh. One day the Master touched Subodh's body and blessed him saying : "Today I have taken away the lust from your mind."[5]

On 31 August 1885 Monday evening Sri Ramakrishna said to M. at Dakshineswar : "Two boys came here the other day. One of them was Subodh. He is Sankar Ghosh's great grandson. The other, Kshirode is his neighbour. They are nice boys. I told them I was ill and asked them to go to you for instruction. Please look after them a little."[6]

Initially Subodh was reluctant to receive spiritual instruction from a householder but finally when he visited M. he was satisfied with his talks.

Learning from Subodh about his fear of ghosts, Sri Ramakrishna once pressed his thumbnail between Subodh's eyebrows. Since then he used it see a soft light over his forehead and he became free from his fear of ghosts for ever.

At Cossipore oneday Subodh begged the Master for his blessing so that he could realize God. Patting Subodh's back thrice affectionately Sri Ramakrishna said to him : "Yes, Yes you will realize God; and in the future many people will learn from you."[7]

Hearing of the Master's passing away on 16 August 1886, Subodh cried out and then fell unconscious.

In 1931 Swami Subodhananda contracted terminal tuberculosis and his body began to deteriorate. He wrote in a letter, 'only the Master knows how long he will work through this body. I have no objection whether my body remains or dies.' Even towards the end he did not forget his Master's advice, 'Think of me twice a day." In the morning and at night he would lift his head with much effort and looking at the picture of the Master behind his head saluted him with folded hands. If anybody asked about his pain, he answered, "When I think of the Master, I forget all physical suffernig." An hour before his death. (3:05 p.m. 2 December 1932) he looked intently at the picture of his guru and his face flashed with a smile.

Devotion to the Holy Mother :

After the passing away of the Master Subodh overcome with grief felt lonesome and sought solace in visiting the Holy Mother in Balaram's house everyday. He went to Kamarpukur to see the Mother and was happy to visit the birth places of the Master and the Mother. He again visited Jayrambati in 1891 with Girish Chandra Ghosh and Swami Niranjanananda.

Swami Brahmananda arranged a grand reception for the Mother when she visited Belur Math after her pilgrimage to South India in 1911. Swami Brahmananda forbade the monks and devotees to break the line or rush to take the dust of her feet while the Mohter walked onto the monastery grounds. All of a sudden Swami Subodhananda took the dust of the Mother's feet and vanished into the crowd.

Referring to Sri Ramakrishna and the Holy Mother Swami Subodhananda wrote in a letter : "If they don't want to reveal themselves, who can recognize them?"[8]

Swami Subodhananda initially was not interested in giving spiritual instructions to devotees. If anybody requested him for initiation, he used to say : "What do I know about initiation? I am a Khoka. You go to Swami Brahmananda or Holy Mother—they are highly spiritual." One day the Mother said : "Why does Khoka not initiate people? As long as the Master's disciples are alive, let the people receive their grace."[9] The Master also blessed him that in the future many people would learn from him. So he began to initiate devotees in 1915.

Love and respect for Swamiji :

Performing the traditional *Viraja home* at Baranagore Monastery Subodh took final monastic vows and was named Swami Subodhananda by Swami Vivekananda. As he was one of the youngest among the disciples of Sri Ramakrishna, Swamiji lovingly called him "Khoka' (little boy) and was known as "Khoka Maharaj' in the Ramakrishna Order.

One night at Belur Math Swamiji finished his meditation and waking up Subodhananda asked him to bring a pipe to smoke. Subodhananda did so. Swamiji granted him a boon that he would never, for the rest of his life, miss his daily cup of tea. The boon was not in vain. Swami Subodhananda would get tea unexpectedly.

Swami Subodhanada's love for Swamaji was second only to his love for the Master. Swamiji also loved him and selected him as one of the trustees of Belur Math in 1901. Afterwards he was elected treasurer of the Ramakrishna Mission and later he became the vice President of the Ramakrishna Math and Mission. Sometimes Swamiji would become so serious that none but Khoka Maharaj dared to approach him and interrupt his mood.

Swami Subodhananda used to avoid women devotees and did not talk to them. One day Swamiji said : "Khoka, women devotees come to hear about the Master; please talk to them. If you avoid them where will they go? They are the manifestations of the Divine Mohter. Treat them as your mother or daughter."[10] Swami Subodhananda obeyed the instruction of the leader and addressing the women devotees as "Mayi' or "Mother' talked to them.

One day on his way to Kolkata from Belur Math by steamer, Swami Subodhananda heard a few young men criticizing Swamiji. The Swami boldly said to them : "Do you give any donation to Belur Math? If so, please stop it from today. What will you gain by criticizing Swamiji? Neither will your criticism make Swamiji's hands fall off, nor will your praise help him grow two more hands." When he heard that those Young men did not help Belur Math, the Swami said : "Then why do you criticize unnecessarily? Can you appreciate the monks? You work like slaves under English officers and you are supposed to flatter them; if you make any mistake, they will kick you out with their boots." A few days later, one of those young men came to Belur Math and apologized to Subodhananda : "Maharaj, the other day out of sheer ignorance, we did wrong. Your words came true. One of us was kicked out of the office by an English Officer."[11]

Swami Subodhananda's devotion to Swamiji was touching. Despite his weakness he used to walk with a cane to Vivekananda's temple at Belur Math every day. He said to the monks : "The Master said that Swamiji was Lord Shiva Himself. To respect him is equivalent to worshipping Lord Shiva."[12]

Motto : renunciation for God-realization :

One day Krishnadas gave his son Subodh a book, *Sri Sri Ramakrishna Paramahamser Ukti* (The Sayings of Sri Ramakrishna) compiled by Suresh Chandra Datta in December 1884. During their first meeting Subodh said to Sri Ramakrishna : "I am impressed by reading your teachings. They are really remarkable. You are such a great man and so famous! Therefore we have come to see you." Holding Subodh's hand and closing own eyes for a few minutes Sri Ramakrishna said "You will attain the goal. Mother says so."

Swami Subodhananda possessed innate passion for God and dispassion for the world, In his teens as stated earlier he was more interested in spending with Sri Ramakrishna at Dakshineswar or in meditation, prayer and japam the name of God than studies. Subodh bluntly said to his father, "Please don't insist that I get married. ...If you force me to marry, I shall obey you. But I will leave home; family life is not for me. Please don't entangle me." Though a brilliant student Subodh intentionally received poor marks in order to avoid marriage. The Master was pleased to see Subodh so stern in his renunciation.

At Cossipore one day Subodh prayed to Sri Ramakrishna to bless him so that he could realize God. The Guru granted him his prayer.

Swami Subodhananda said to the devotees : "One day I asked the Master : "I have read about gods and goddesses in books and heard about them from various people. Can one really see them?' Sri Ramakrishna replied : "One can see God as one sees two persons talking together or walking. But one should call on God from the bottom of one's heart. Pray and cry for him. Demand His vision from Him as children demand toys from their parents with loud cries. Remove all worldly desires from the mind. Always remember : I have a Mother and I am Her son."[13]

Another day Sri Ramakrishna said : "Those who shall attain spritual experience will feel comfortable with my ideas and teaching. He who has faith in me, has faith in God; and again, he who does not have faith in me, does not have faith in God either."[14]

Though Subodh was not allowed by his parents to live with Sri Ramakrishna all the time like some of the other disciples; he observed his Guru's life minutely. Sri Ramakrishna had kindled the fire of renunciation which was intensified after his passing away. His longing for God was so strong that he felt his life was useless without God-realization. In search of mental peace he left home for Varanasi. Later he narrated his experience of this journey in a letter which manifests the degree of his renunciation : "I began my journey heading towards the western part of India on foot without carrying any money with me. If anybody wanted to talk to me on the way, I would talk only of God. As a result, no worldly thought would enter my mind. Some times I stayed at night under a tree or in a meadow or on the bank of a river. At noon I ate whatever I got by begging from door to door like the mendicants. I had no extra clothing or shoes or umbrella.

In the rain my clothes would get wet and they would eventually dry from my body heat."[15]

Though his relatives brought Subodh back to Kolkata, he could no longer live at home and he joined the Ramakrishna Monastery at Baranagore and performing *virajahoma,* took monastic vows.

Swami Subodhananda's personal needs were few and belongings were almost nil. He would accept only that what was absolutely necessary for him. He ate whatever came with equal relish. He laid great stress on self-surrender to God. His complete dependence on God infused this great spirit of renunciation into him and it was evident in his manners and talks.

In 1897 Swami Subodhananda delivered a lecture to the Young Men's Hindu Association in Madras (now Chennai) on "Sannyasa and Brahmacharya' : "Sannyasa is the renunciation of all selfish motives and desires...

"Our Master used to say that if we wanted to pass a thread through the eye of a needle all the scattered fibres of the thread should be brought to a point and then alone could we make it go through the needle; otherwise, if the fibres were allowed to point in all directions they would prevent the thread from passing through the eye; similarly, if we want to lift our mind up towards God, we must bring it back from all external things and concentrate it on one point..."[16]

Relationship with God natural; worship informal :

Another aspect of originality of Swami Subodhananda in his concept of God and his Guru : He like his Guru said : "God can be realized much more tangibly than one feels the presence of a companion with whom one is walking." He used to speak of God in such a way that it seemed that God was a greater reality to him than his own earthly relatives.

The nature of the Swami's personal worship was absolutely free from rigid ritualistic observances. He considered God one of his close relatives and there was no distance of awe or wonder between them. While performing worship in the shrine he like his Guru, did not care to recite memorized texts or make traditional gestures.

The Swami believed the Master to be alive. He used to teach the new monks how to prepare betel-rolls and tobacco for offering to the Master in the shrine. He, with the help of the young boys, would uproot the thorny bushes from courtyard so that his Guru could walk safely. One day he went to the person in charge of the kitchen to ask him why the lunch bell was late and learned that there was a special food offering for the Master. Swami Subodhananda said to him : "The Master did not like to have his lunch after twelve noon. It is better to offer regular food to the Master at the right time and then arrange for special food later."[17] One day Subodhananda performed the worship in the shrine. While he was offering the fruits and sweets, the Master appeared before him and pointing to the sliced cucumber, said, "Please add a little salt to it."[18]

He realized the grace of his beloved God and was always optimistic in his views. That's why his words infused cheer and confidence into the dejected and tired souls. "Intellectual snobs or philosophical pedants were bewildered to see the coviction with which he talked on problems which they had not been able to solve, all their pride and self-conceit notwithstanding."[19]

Miraculous experience–saved by the Master many a time :

During his stay in Vrindaban one day when Swami Subodhnanda was circumambulating the playground of Krishna alone a woman infatuated with him attacked him from behind. Scared the Swami prayed aloud to his guru for protection. In no time, the perverted woman fell on the ground, unconscious.

While Swami Subodhaanda was practising austerities in Hardwar, the following incident took place :

I had been suffering from fever for two months. I was so weak that I could not lift my water pot to pour water into my mouth.

One night when I went near the water pot to quench my thirst, I fell down on the floor unconscious. When I regained consciousness, my feelings were hurt and I cried : "Master, I am suffering terribly. There is none to look after me. You didn't give me sufficient strength even to drink a glass of water by myself." Thinking thus I fell asleep. Then I saw [in a dream or vision] the Master stroking my body with his hand said : "Why are you anxious? Don't you see I am always near you? What do you want—attendants or money?" I replied, "I don't want either of those things. I can't avoid disease as long as I have a body. May I never forget you : that is all I want. Be with me wherever I go."

Early in the morning I heard a voice from outside, "Swami, please open the door." I got up and opened the door. A young monk told me. "Please tell me what you need. I shall beg food for you." I said to him, "I don't want anything. When I asked how he knew about me, he said that he had arrived there a couple of days earlier to perform a religious rite at the Brahmakunda. The previous night Mother Durga had appeared to him in a vision and said, "you will get more virtue by serving that sick monk in the cottage than by performing this religious rite." So early in the morning he came to my cottage and realized that his vision was true. Tears trickled from my eyes. I controlled myself and asked the young monk to let me live alone.

On the same day another monk received fifty rupees by money order. He came to me and said : "You are suffering from fever. You need food and medicine. Please use this money." I declined his offer. Early the next morning the young monk came again and told me that at night Mother Durga had exhorted him to serve me as before. Then I told him politely that I really didn't need any service and that perhaps Mother Durga had asked him to serve someone else. The young monk left. Then I prayed to the Master : "Please don't tempt me anymore. I am glad that you have crushed my pique." The Young monk also came on the third day but never again.[20]

Swami Subodhananda described a life-threatening experience during his practising austerities in Gaya :

"It was the month of August. I saw a person wade through the Phalgu River and reach the other side. It was waist -deep, so I decided to cross. My companion knew how to swim, but I didn't. Suddenly the river swelled with a strong current because of heavy rain. When I had crossed a certain distance, I suddenly found myself in throat -deep water. I realized that there was very little chance of saving my life so I said to my companion : "I don't know where the current will take me. There is little chance for my life. Please convey my salutations to my brother disciples." Then I prayed to the Master, "Please accept my last *pranam* [salutation]." As soon as I said that, I was completely submerged. I felt that someone held my hand and pulled me through the gushing stream to the other side of the river."[21]

The Swami described another horrible experience. During his itinerant period one night he slept under a banyan tree while passing through Bihar or Uttar Pradesh. After a while he had a dream. He saw an old woman telling him : "You get up, Because of you the snakes are unable to get out of their holes. Go forward a little, and you will find a police station. You can spend the night there." The Swami asked her if they would allow him to stay. She said 'Yes, they will allow you to sleep there. When you knock at their door, they will ask, "Who are you?" Say to them, "I am a mendicant." He got up and went to the police station where he got shelter in the verandah. The next morning he went to check the ground under the banyan tree and found many holes and learned from the local people that the place was infested with cobras. The Swami believed the old woman the Divine Mother.[22]

All these miraculous and awesome happenings manifest the Master's keeping an alert eye constantly on his disciples as an affectionate father and a saviour; simultaneously intensity of devotion to and faith in the Master, austerity tenacity and will power of Swami Subodhananda.

A multifaceted personality :

(a) Outspoken :

In his teens Subodhananda was a spirited outspoken boy. In August of 1885 during their first meeting at Dakshineswar Sri Ramakrishna said to him : "...I knew you would come. Well, the Divine Mother sends here those who will attain spirituality. You belong to this place." At once Subodh aged seventeen quipped : "Sir, If I belong to this place, why did you not call me earlier?" When the Master asked him to sit on his bed Subodh said, "No, Sir, I can't sit on your bed. This is my school clothing, it is not fresh. Moreover, I have touched people on the way and my feet are dusty." The Master forced him to sit on his bed, saying : "You are my very own. What does it matter whether your cloth is clear or not?" But after a while Subodh sat on the floor.

Considering that Subodh and his friend Khisord were too young to walk a long distance from Dakshineswar to their home, Sri Ramakrishna insisted Subodh to take carriage fares. But Subodh refused to accept money saying : "Sir, we are young, if we do not walk now then when shall we walk? Moreover, you are a holy man; where will you get money?" Sri Ramakrishna, with a smile, replied : "Some people donate money for this place. You will not have to worry about that. Please take some money and go by carriage." None of his would-be monastic disciples but Narendranath dared argue with or disobey him like Subodh, a docile boy but relentless in this case. The Master asked Kshirod to take the money but Subodh forbade his friend : "Don't accept the money. We shall go on foot." Thus Subodh's disobedience indicates his diligence, zeal and zest above all his love for the Master whose money he did not want to spend.

One day Sri Ramakrishna asked Subodh to see his neighbour Mahendranath Gupta(M). Subodh replied "He hasn't been able to renounce his family. What could I learn about God from him?"[23]

One day the Master said to Subodh "What do you think of me?" Subodh replied, "People say many different things about you.

I won't believe any of them until I find clear proof."[24] The Master said : "Very well. As a money changer checks a coin, likewise accept me after testing."[25]

As Subodh came closer and closer to the Master, his faith in Sri Ramakrishna's divinity gradually gained ground.

One day when Sri Ramakrishna advised Subodh to practise meditation, he replied : "Sir I won't be able to do that. If I have to practise meditation, why should I come to you? I may as well go to some other guru."[26] Understanding his inner feeling, the Master said : "All right, you will not have to practise meditation. But think of me in the morning and evening."[27] As a true teacher Sri Ramakrishna could come down to the level of the student, and transfer his soul to the student's soul.

At Cossipore one day Sri Ramakrishna asked Subodh to copy a devotional song composed by Saint Tulasidas. Subodh refused by saying that his handwriting was not good. The Master persuaded, "Please copy that song. It does not matter whether your writing is good or bad." Still Subodh did not agree. The Master said : "You are really a dumbbell. Neglecting your studies, you only played with your friends." Paying no heed to the rebuke Subodh smiled. The Master said : "My boy, aren't you upset that I scolded you?" Subodh replied : "Sir, even your scoldings are sweet."[28]

(b) the best jockey :

The inmates of the Alambazar Monastery had to suffer from acute financial crisis. One day Swamis Saradananda and Subodhananda went to Girish Chandra Ghosh a steadfast devotee "Bhairav' of Sri Ramakrishna. When they approached him for money; he bluntly said, "Where is any money?" Swami Subodhnanda jokingly said : "Sharat Maharaj will grab you and I shall take the money breaking your box. "Extending his hand to Swami Subodhananda robust Girish Chandra said : First try to bend my finger." When Khoka Maharaj failed to bend his finger, the great actor, director, and playwright ordered his secretary to give all money of the box to the monks. After feeding the Swamis he said to Swami Sobodhananda :

"I am a wild horse; only the best jockey can handle me. Khoka, I see you will be able to deal with me,"[29] Sri Ramakrishna was an ideal Guru who knew that mere words or restrictions could not change nature or habits of Girish a devotee of heroic type but the silent influence of his love and sympathy worked miracles, unfolded the disciple's inner life. When the Master learnt that Girish was unable to submit to any routine of spiritual discipline, he said to him : "All right, give me your power of attorney. Henceforth I assume responsibility for you. You need not do anything." Ultimately Girish was engrossd in the thoughts of Sri Ramakrishna who as a skilled jockey knew how to tame a wild horse or control turbulent spirit.

In order to appreciate the spirit of Swami Subodhananda Girish made the aforsaid remark.

(c) Wit :

Swami Subodhananda's presence of mind was admirable. One night Swamiji was reading a book attentively while lying on his stomach. He did not hear the dinner bell. The monks were waiting for him but none dared to call him. Swami Brahmananda asked Swami Subodhananda to call Swamiji. Swami Subodhananda silently went to his room and looking at the page number abruptly closed the book. Swamiji said angrily, "Khoka, you rascal! Why did you close my book? Now how shall I know where I was reading?" Khoka Maharaj at once opened the book and showed him the exact place. Then he requested Swamiji to go for supper and added that the food would be cold and all were waiting for him. Swamiji went to the dining room to eat with all.

(d) Sense of humour :

The dreary, dilapidated and deserted two storeyed building of Baranagore monastery had a reputation of being haunted by evil spirits. The ground floor was infested with snakes, lizards and insects. The monastic disciples of Sri Ramakrishna lived in the first floor.

Swami Subodhananda knew that Swami Adbhutananda (Latu Maharaj) used to practise meditation at night under his mosquito curtain when all were asleep. One night Swami Subodhananda mischievously put a wet cloth on the top of Swami Adbhutananda's curtain. As the water began to drip, he got scared for the Baranagore Monastery was haunted. After discovering the culprit, he said: "Sharat! Look, this rascal Khoka is frightening me!"[30]

(e) Childlike nature :

In 1911 after her pilgrimage to South India when Holy Mother visited Belur Math Swami Brahmananda abbot of the Math arranged a grand reception for her. Monks and devotees stood in queue. Swami Brahmananda forbade to break the line to salute the Mohter by touching her feet. All of a sudden Swami Subodhananda breaking the line took the dust of Mother's feet and disappeared into the crowd. Swami Brahmananda amusingly said, 'catch him, catch him. Who's that, who's that?'[31] Every body laughed, seeing Swami Subodhananda's child like nature.

Then Swami Subodhananda was sixty one and suffering from tuberculosis. One day Swami Shivananda said to the visiting physician, "Have you seen that boy? How is he?" The doctor and the monks could not understand whom he was talking about. Then Mahapurush Maharaj added, "I mean that Khoka who lives in the room adjacent to mine. He is truly a child. He does not know how to take care of himself. Please check him carefully and arrange for proper medicine and diet."

(f) Humanity :

Swami Subodhananda did not forget Swamiji's message, "Make the poor of humanity your God. The service of these living gods is the religion of this age." He was a man of very tender heart. In 1899 plague broke out in an epidemic form in Kolkata. Swami Saradananda with the hearty co-operation of Sister Nivedita and his brother disciples organized plague relief in the city. Swami Subodhananda was one of the active members of the squad. Risking his life he worked hard to relieve the suffering of the poor, helpless, panic-stricken people. Sometimes he begged money from others to help poor patients with medicine and food. He saved a deserving family near Belur Monastery from starvation. No sooner did he hear that anyone needed help or was sick, than he would go to help him or her.

Swami Subodhananda devoted himself to the relief work during severe famine in the Chilka region of Orissa in 1908. He collected and distributed rice, lentils and clothes among the famine-affected people. While toiling day and night, he did not take care of his own food and rest. As a result he became sick. Sri Ramakrishna in a vision said to him : "You will not have to do this work anymore."[32] But the Swami continued the relief service until the plight of the people decreased. He nursed with cordial care a young student suffering from small pox of a very malignant type.

Swami Subodhananda was impartial. He looked upon literate rich upper class devotees and outcasts with same affection and gave initiation indiscriminately.

The Swami used to nurse sick monks like an affectionate mother. Swami Subodhananda came from a well off family which owned the Siddheswari Kali Temple of Thanthania. Once his relatives proposed sharing property owned as a hereditary right. But he refusing to accept it said to them : "I am an all-renouncing monk, I don't need any money. Please serve the poor and the mendicants with that money."

The Swami was not ostentatious and easy of access. Everybody felt very free with him and he despite his great spiritual wealth also could mix freely with all. Many persons initially reluctant to religion, were drawn to him simply by his love and later on were interested in spiritual life.

The young novices and monks of the Order found in Khoka Maharaj a great sympathizer and spokesman. The brahmacharins sometimes had to do such work that they did not know how to do that. On such occasions Swami Subodhananda used to come forward to help them solve their problems with advice and guidance and to rectify their shortcoming. One day a brahmacharin committed a serious mistake. He was asked to live outside the monastery and to get his food by begging. By begging he got nothing but a small quantity of fried gram and came back to the gate of the monastery in the evening. But he did not dare to enter the monastery. Learning about the punishment of the brahmacharin the Swami persuaded on behalf of him to forgive. Swami Gahanananda said :

> Subodhananda's contribution in providing a role model for the humanitarian activities of the Mission can never be exaggerated.[33]

Strict adherence to the principle :

Once a devotee invited Swami Subodhananda to dine. When the swami wanted to know about the menu, the devotee politely replied" "What could we offer you, Swami? We have arranged simple food—rice and lentils." Entering the dining room the Swami found that actually the devotee had made arrangements for him various delicacies. But he ate rice and lentils only. Despite the devotee's earnest request he stuck to his decision and said to him : "The Master taught us that one should hold to the truth and keep the word."[34]

A monk mentioned an incident highlighting guts and sticking to principles of Swami Subodhananda :

"One day the bell was rung, but nobody came to cut the vegetables. Khoka Maharaj therefore cut five kinds of vegetables for the Master and asked the cook to offer those five items to him. He arranged to have rice, lentils and boiled potatoes cooked for the monks. In the dining room, Swami Saradananda was pleased to have this simple menu. Then he asked, "Have you not offered any vegetables to the Master?' Khoka Maharaj replied : 'Yes, five kinds of vegetables were offered to the Master; but since the monks did not come to cut the vegetables, I arranged this simple menu for them.' Immediately Swami Saradananda said in front of the monks 'Tomorrow I shall come to cut the vegetables.' This took care of the problem."[35]

Swami Subodhananda was self-reliant. He advised that one should help oneself as far as possible. He would not accept personal service from disciples, devotees or others and avoided it until it became absolutely inevitable. In Hardwar as aforesaid he had been suffering from fever for two months and was too weak to lift his water pot to quench his thirst. Yet when the Master said to him, "What do you want—attendants or money?" the Swami replied, "I don't want either of those things. I can't avoid disease as long as I have a body. May I never forget you : that is all I want. Be with me wherever I go." The Swami despite his illness and dire need refused help from monks sent by Mother Durga and the Master. He strictly adhered to this principle in his daily life.

The "baby monk' was a great mystic and may be called the ideal model of a divine child of Sri Ramakrishna. On the previous night of his passing away he uttered his last words : "My last prayer is that the blessings of the Lord be always on the Order." With reference to this prayer Swami Gahanananda remarked.

> This prayer, issuing from a loving heart with absolute sincerity and concern, is a great contribution to the Ramakrishna Order, because he had poured his whole life into it.

Chapter – 18

SWAMI AKHANDANANDA

When a small child he mastered the English alphabet in one day. He told the doctor to operate on his large abscess between his eyebrows without anesthesia. The doctor was amazed at such stoicism and tolerance of a boy aged only eight.

He in his teens worked hard to make his character strong and pure.

He used to bathe four times a day in the Ganga without applying any oil to his skin.

He was a vegetarian and cooked his own food.

This wonder-boy was Gangadhar Gangopadhyay (later Swami Akhandananda) son of Srimanta Gangopadhyay and Vamasundari. He was born on 30 September 1864, in the Ahiritola area of western Kolkata.

Deep spiritual inclination :

Gangadhar probably inherited spritual trend from his father who was a priest, Sanskrit teacher and who practised yoga and Tantra. While an intelligent student of the Oriental Seminary he lost interest in formal education. He was attracted to the wandering life of the mendicants and their stories about the holy places of India. He was eager to see the Himalayas and the ashramas of the ancient sages. He was invested with the sacred thread at the age of twelve and he repeated the Gayatri mantram thrice a day. Very often he would make an image of Lord Shiva out of clay and worship Him with bel leaves and Ganga water. At the fascinating sight of the Master in samadhi at Dinanath Basu's house in Baghbazar Gangadhar's spiritual inclination intensified. Sometimes he would go to a cremation ground to meditate and by observing the impermanence of human life he was imbued with a desire for renunciation. At twelve, Gangadhar visited a monk at the Sarvamangala Temple in Cossipore and left home with him without informing his parents. But he returned home for the monk told him that he was too young for monastic life.

Firm Conviction :

At nineteen, Gangadhar met Sri Ramakrishna at Dakshineswar. During his second visit the Master initiated him by writing a mantram on his tongue. Whenever he approached the Master he would ask him : "Did you shed tears at the time of prayer or meditation?' When he answered in the affirmative, the Master was very happy. While teaching him how to pray he cried out : 'Mother dear, grant me knowledge and devotion. I don't want anything else. I can't live without you.' He then looked like a small boy. Profuse tears rolled down his chest and he passed into deep samadhi.

Gangadhar's extreme orthodoxy once prompted Sri Ramakrishna to call him 'oldish.' The Master told him that most of his habits, such as taking only self-cooked food, being a vegetarian, practising austerity, chewing mycrobalam and so on were for old people. Gangadhar gave up all those habits.

One morning the Master took Gangadhar into the holy room of the Kali Temple of Dakshineswar and showing him the face of Lord Shiva said : "Look, here is the living Shiva." With reference to this incident Gangadhar recalled : "I felt that Lord Shiva was conscious and breathing. I was astonished. How potent were the Master's words! Up to that time I had thought that this image was just like all the other Shiva images I had seen.

"...When we left the temple he was reeling like a drunkard. He was escorted to his room with difficulty and remained for some time in samadhi. I cannot describe the details of that day—the joy the Master poured into my heart cannot be communicated..."[1]

Sri Ramakrishna told Gangadhar and other would-be monastic disciples that those who were attached to lust and gold would never have God-vision. One day in Dakshineswar when a beggar came to the Master's door, the Master, pointing to four paise, asked Gangadhar to give them to the beggar. As he had done that, the Master asked him to wash his hands with Ganga water. Gangadhar learnt that money is dirt and a true monk should be free from lust and gold.

Dedication to spirituality :

In the middle of 1885 Sri Ramakrishna developed throat cancer. Gangadhar began to serve the Master whenever he could. He used to meditate by the Ganga at night. Gangadhar's father, observing his son's lack of interest in completing his education found a job for him in a merchant's office. Working there a few days Gangadhar quit his job. He then completely devoted himself to spiritual disciplines and service to the Master who was moved from Dakshineswar to Shyampukur for treatment and then to Cossipore. Gangadhar would wash the dishes at the Cossipore garden house and did all sorts of errands.

Sri Ramakrishna forbade his disciples to misuse any articles or be extravagant for the devotees supported him with their hard-earned money. One day one of his disciples said : 'I know'. The Master commented : "What do you say? you know? Never say that. Say, "As long as I live so long do I learn."[2] Gangadhar learnt a new lesson.

Sri Ramkrishna gave ochre cloths (the symbol of monasticism) to Gangadhar. On Christmas Eve of 1886 Gangadhar with some brother disciples took vows of renunciation at Antpur.

A Yogi :

At Bodh Gaya, Gangadhar stayed at the house of Durgashankar, a devotee of Sri Ramakrishna. One day Durgashankar said to him:

"I talked to you such a long time and I noticed your eyes never blinked. It is a sign of a divine nature. You are truly a disciple of Sri Ramakrishna."[3]

In Varanasi Gangadhar was an invited guest of Pramadadas Mittra a reputed landlord as well as a great Sanskrit scholar who taught the young yogi how to correctly chant the Upanishads and Sanskrit hymns in a melodious way. Gangadhar went to see the great saint Trailanga Swami and received his blessing. Then he met Swami Bhaskarananda who was a great Sanskrit scholar. He wanted to teach the Vedas to Gangadhar. The young man replied, "The power of sight which I would use for attaining knowledge by reading books, please turn it inward so that I can experience the Atman." Swami Bhaskarananda, to his utter astonishment said, "I see you are a yogi."[4]

In Rishikesh Gangadhar practised meditation in a thatched hut on the bank of the Ganga. The manager of the *Chatra* (a resting place for monks and pilgrims where monks are given free meals) would ring a bell once a day to call the mendicants there for food. Somedays Gangadhar was so absorbed in meditation that he did not hear the bell and had to beg food from villagers in the afternoon.

Two distinct phases in his life :

Gangadhar's originality and vibrancy were illuminated in two different arenas in his life—earlier as a mendicant rover and afterwards as a great social worker.

In Bodh Gaya once Gangadhar said to the famous yogi of the Natha sect Gambhiranath who affectionately told Gangadhar to stay with him : "My Master used to say that one cannot have a glimpse of the Infinite without seeing the Himalayas or the ocean. So I am eager to see the Himalayas." In Jamnagar an old abbot of a prosperous temple wanted to offer Gangadhar his position as well as all of his wealth. Gangadhar refused, quoting a Hindi couplet : "The water is pure that flows, and the monk is pure who goes."[5]

In February 1887 Gangadhar taking the ochre cloth given by Sri Ramakrishna secretly left the Baranagore monastery for the

Himalayas. His father who gave his consent came to Howrah station to see him off. He blessed his son : "Go my son. Fulfill your mission in life. This world is unreal. I bless you. May you attain unflinching devotion to God."[6]

Gangadhar wandered fourteen years all over India as a penniless monk, never touching money. He believed that one can learn more from a saint than from a library of a million books. He visited Bodh Gaya, Varanasi, Ayodhya, Lucknow, Naimisharanya Hardwar. In Hardwar he told Kamraj, a tantric saint about what he wanted :

He who does not rejoice nor hate, nor grieve, nor desires, renouncing good and evil—dear to me such a devotee. [The Gita, 12:17]

Gangadhar's wanderings included Rishikesh, Gangotri, Jamunotri, Chandravadani, Kedarnath and Badrinath. He goaded on by irresistable curiousity about the mysteries of Tibet particularly about Lhasa, went to Tibet thrice risking his life. He visited Mount Kailas and Manas Sarovar.

In June of 1890 Gangadhar returned to the Baranagore Monastery. Swamiji noticed that the skin of his dear brother disciple 'Ganges' had been burnt with cold. So he sometimes called him 'Ice Father'. Abiding by the advice of the leader Gangadhar took final monastic vows before the picture of the Master, in the first week of July 1890 and was named Swami Akhandananda by Swamiji.

In mid July Swami Akhandananda again left for the Himalayas with Swamiji to practise austerities. They visited Bhagalpur, Baidyananth, Gajipur, Varanasi, and Ayodhya. At Nainital one day Swami Akhandananda bathed in the ice-cold water of a lake, as a result he caught a severe cold associated with chest pain. At Almora they met Swami Saradananda and Vaikuntha Nath Sanyal. At Karnaprayag Swami Akhandananda had a high fever and Swamiji also became sick. At Tehri a physician examined Akhandananda and diagnosed bronchitis and advised him to go to the warm climate of the plains as early as possible. They arrived at Dehra Dun and met Swami Turiyananda. Swami Akhandananda with his attendent Kripananda stayed there for medical treatment, under Dr. Maclaren while Swamiji and the others went to Rishikesh to practise spiritual disciplines. In late 1890 Swami Akhandananda had slightly improved and he left for Meerut for further treatment. Swamiji had become very sick in Rishikesh and he with his companions went to Meerut. Swamis Brahmananda and Advaitananda joined them. They lived there as the guests of Dr. Trailokya Nath Ghosh for nearly six weeks. Meerut became a second Baranagore Monastry.

One day Swamiji told his brother disciples that he had received the command of God regarding his future, and was going to leave them in order to become a solitary monk. On the eve of the Swamiji's departure, Swami Akhandananda said to him, "It was for you that I cancelled my plan of going to Central Asia, and came to Baranagore Math; and now you are going away leaving me here!" Swamiji replied, "The company of the brother-disciple is a great hindrance to spiritual practices. Just see, it was because of your illness that I could not practise any spiritual disciplines at Tehri. It is not possible to perform any spiritual disciplines, unless the Maya [bondage] of the brother-disciples is given up. Whenever I plan to practise disciplines, the Master puts some obstacle in my way. Now I shall go alone. I shall not tell anyone where I am staying." Swami Akhandananda said, "Even if you go to Patal [the nether region], I shall hunt you out."[7]

One morning in the latter part of January 1891, Swamji leaving his devoted brethren journeyed on to Delhi by himself.

Swami Akhandananda visited numerous places namely Delhi, Agra, Vrindaban, Etawah (where he studied Sanskrit grammar and Shridhara's commentary on the Gita), Ajmere, Abu, Ahmedabad, Baroda, Narmada, Junagad, Prabhas, Dwaraka, Kachha-Mandavi, Narayan-Sarovar (on the way badly beaten and stripped off his belongings by robbers). Mandovi (where he met Swamiji), Bhuj, Porbandar, Jamnagar, Baroda, Bhavnagar, Bombay, Khetri, Jaipur,

Chittor, Udaipur and many other villages of Rajasthan. Towards the end of 1895 Swami Akhandananda returned to the Alambazar Monastery.

It was quite natural that he who in his childhood gave his own shirt to a poor classmate and used to give food to beggars secretly; would be a great philanthropist. While visiting some parts of India Swami Akhandananda was deeply moved by the miserable plight of the downtrodden people and tried to solve their problems to the best of his abilities.

An austere monk turned revolutionary :

Sister Nivedita wrote about Swamiji : "And when he would lose himself, in splendid scorn of apology for anything Indian, in fiery repudiation of false charge or contemptuous criticism or in laying down for others the elements of a faith and love that could never be more than a pale reflection of his own, how often did the habit of the monk seem to slip away from him and the armour of the warrior stand revealed!"[8]

Swamiji's brother-disciple Swami Akhandananda was outwardly a composed mendicant mystic but inwardly a spirited defender of human rights.

Swami Akhandananda drew inspiration for his humanitarian services from five persons—Sri Ramakrishna, Swamiji, Jhandu Bhat Vithalji, Florence Nightingale and Booker T. Washington. Sri Ramakrishna said on March 23, 1884 to Ram, "It is God Himself who plays about as human beings. If God can be worshipped through a clay image, then why not through a man?"[9] In 1884 with reference to the essence of the Vaishnava doctrine, the Master said : "No no, not compassion to jivas but service to them as Siva,"[10]

Sri Ramakrishna himself initiated philanthropic work on at least two occasions. He was deeply moved by the plight of the people while going through a village near Vaidyanath at the time of his pilgrimage to Varanasi, Vrindavan and other holy places with Mathuranath Biswas, son-in-law of Rani Rasmoni and the first and the foremost supplier of his provisions. The Master said to

Mathur, 'You are but a manager of the Mother's estate. Give these people sufficient oil to cool their heads and each a piece of cloth to wear and feed them to their fill once.' Mathur did as "Father' had asked him to do. The Master's disciple Swami Saradananda wrote another incident in his magnum opus "Sri Ramakrishna the great Master'(p. 654). "We are told that the Master went on another occasion with Mathur to a certain village in his estate near Ranaghat where he was seized with a similar compassion to see the miserable plight of the villagers and he made Mathur do likewise once again."

In March or April 1894 Swamiji wrote to Swami Akhandananda from Chicago :

"...The Geruâ robe is not for enjoyment. It is the banner of heroic work. You must give your body, mind and speech to the welfare of the world. ...The poor, the illiterate, the ignorant, the afflicted—let these be your God. Know that service to these alone is the highest religion."[11]

Swami Akhandananda was greatly influenced by the dedicated life of Jhandhu Bhat Vithalji, an Ayurvedic physician at Jamnagar in Gujarat. His house was full of patients. He provided them with prescription, medicine and diet. He would go out in a horse-carriage to visit his patients free of charge. Bhatji used to chant verses of Rantideva :

Na tvaham kamaye rājyam na svargam na apunarbhavam; kāmaye duhkhataptanam praninām ārtinasanam.[12]

I covet not any earthly kingdom, or heaven, or even salvation. The only thing I desire is the removal of the miseries of the afflicted. Swamiji once commented : "I have seen many benevolent persons, but none can compare with Jhandu Bhat Vithalji.[13]

Swami Akhandananda stayed at Bhatji's place for several months. He remarked : 'serving and loving man is the highest good. This I have learned especially by seeing it practised in Bhatji's life.'[14] Besides he was inspired by Florence Nightingale's and Booker T. Washington's spirit of service.

While living in Rajasthan for nearly eight months the Swami was deeply shocked at the sharp class-distinction between the haves and the have-nots—shameless luxury of a few rulers and landlords as well as the most wretched condition of the masses. Drawing the local rulers' attention to the suffering of the downtrodden he asked them to eliminate the problems. He wrote a letter to Swamiji seeking for his advice. In the aforesaid epistle Swamiji wrote :

Go from door to door amongst the poor and lower classes of the town of Khetri and teach them religion. Also, let them have oral lessons on geography and such other subjects. No good will come of sitting idle and having princely dishes, and saying "Ramakrishna O Lord!"—unless you can do some good to the poor. Go to other villages from time to time, and teach the people the arts of life as well as religion. Work worship, and Jnana (Knowledge) —first work and your mind will be purified; otherwise everything will be fruitless like pouring oblations on a pile of ashes instead of in the sacred fire...[15]

Swami Akhandananda started his campaign against poverty in 1894. He realized that the root of all evils was the shocking ignorance of the masses. So his prime objective was to spread education. He moved from door to door to make the residents of khetri conscious of the need to educate their children. By his tireless striving he succeeded in raising the enrollment of the local high school from 80 to 257 as well as improving the teaching staff. He set up five primary schools in the villages around Khetri. Ajit Singh, the Maharaja of Khetri and Swamiji's disciple as well, made an annual grant of 5,000 rupees for the promotion of education in his territory. He took the initiative in converting the Sanskrit school at Khetri into a Vedic School. He collected money to buy books for the poor students. He persuaded Maharaja Ajit Singh to allow his poor subjects to meet him on *durbar* (official reception) days, so that they could tell him directly about their problems.

Swami Akhandananda had the guts to ask the king to rectify his bad habits. He said : "The Maharaja of Khetri would rise late.

One day I told him that those who eat too much and rise late can never attain prosperity. From then on the Maharaja would rise early—even earlier than I. I would get up and find him standing and smiling at me. Some days he would be walking on the roof; and some days I would find him reading in the library with the help of a light."[16]

While visiting Jaipur, Chittor, Udaipur and many other villages of Rajasthan, Swami Akhandananda induced the local rulers to establish schools, distribute food among the poor, and help people set up cottage industries. The king of Udaipur became annoyed when the Swami refused to take food from the royal priest unless the poor people were fed first. The Shylocks and proud aristocrats did not like the Swami's revolutionary ideas and activities. Some of them threatened his life. Still he was enthusiastic and determined despite difficulties and opposition to continue his mission. He succeeded in founding several schools and performing other philanthropic activities in Rajasthan.

The indomitable spirit of adventure, the irresistible curiosity about the mysteries of Tibet particularly of the forbidden city Lhasa goaded youngish Gangadhar to travel to Tibet ignoring warning, danger and humiliation. During that dangerous and arduous journey he fell unconscious on the ice before reaching the Tholing Monastery. A monk rescued him the next morning and carried him to the monastery where the lamas saved his life by warming him. While staying there for three months Gangadhar observed painfully luxury and hankering after money, food and dress of the lamas. As he spoke to them on behalf of the poor, he was imprisoned and tortured by the lamas. One lama hit him on his shoulder with a sword into a sheath. The poor people loved him. Once some of them told the lamas of Gangadhar's sympathy for them. As a result the lamas were furious with daring Gangadhar and he was called for. The lamas warned him that they would cut open his jaw or keep him in lifelong imprisonment if he continued to stand by the farmers. But with the help of some friendly traders Gangadhar fled to Badrinath. The next year he again went to Daba in Tibet. He was arrested on the way to Lhasa. He was so crazy about visiting Tibet that he seemed mesmerized by the mysteries of Lhasa. He went to Tibet a third time in July 1889 with a view to visit Lhasa. But many of the Tibetans suspecting him of being a spy of British Government objected to his going. His trader-friends advised him to leave Tibet as early as possible. While returning to Kashmir Via Ladhak he was arrested by the British Government. When it was confirmed that he was a bonafide monk and had no political motive, he was released. Gangadhar was aequainted with the Tibetan people and their language, religion, culture and customs. So the British Government offered him a post of consul in Tibet, but he turned the proposal down. He returned to the Baranagore Monastery in June of 1890. In September 1894 with reference to the pioneering spirit of the monastic disciples of Sri Ramakrishna, Swamiji wrote from America mentioning Swami Akhandananda :

> Say not that you are weak. The spirit is omnipotent. Look at that handful of young men called into existence by the divine touch of Ramakrishna's feet. They have preached the message from Assam to Sindh, from the Himalayas to Cape Comorin. They have crossed the Himalayas at a height of twenty thousand feet, over snow and ice on foot, and penetrated into the mysteries of Tibet. They have begged their bread, covered themselves with rags; they have been persecuted, followed by the police, kept in prison, and at last set free when the Government was convinced of their innocence.[17]

A great organizer : 'a great hero'

"Distribute yourself among others and bring other souls within yourself. You will see how much joy you will get from it. On the other hand, if you are always busy with yourself, you will be entangled within yourself. You will kill your self and you will die.'—said Swami Akhandananda, (Udbodhan 52:381) the embodiment of service to humanity as the living image of God. He was the one who responded the most to Swamiji's call to serve the poor as God.

The Ramakrishna Mission's first organized relief services were started by Swami Akhandananda in Mahula and several other villages in the district of Murshidabad on 15 May 1897, two weeks after the Mission was founded by Swamiji on 1 May 1897. It was a historic event which marked a new phase in the Ramakrishna Vivekananda movement.

Swami Akhandanada left the Alambazar Math for visiting Navadwip, Murshidabad and a few other places of interest in North Bengal. A severe famine was then raging in the districts of Nadia and Murshidabad. One morning when he was about to leave Bhabda village for Behrampur, he heard a voice say thrice : "Where will you go? You have many things to do here."[18] He decided to give up his journey and to settle down there to serve the starving people. A teacher of the Bhabda school invited the Swami to attend the Annapurna (the goddess of food) worship in Mahula, an adjacent village in the Murshidabad district. He earnestly prayed to the Mother Annapurna to save the lives of the poor people. The villagers offered him a room in the temple complex. He started giving classes on the Gita to the villagers and they fed him. Every morning and evening he prayed to a picture of the Master with tears to enable him to serve the famine-stricken people. One day he heard the Master's voice say : "Wait and see what happens." Swami Akhandananda sent three letters to swami Premananda at Alambazar Math giving detailed descriptions of the calamity and asking for help. Swami Brahmananda advised him to come back to the Math. Swami Ramakrishnananda, on hearing about those letters, wrote to him from Madras (now Chennai) : "You are a penniless sannyāsin. It is impossible for you to arrange food for thousands of people. Therefore you should return to the Math.'[19] But Swami Akhandananda as a devoted disciple of Sri Ramakrishna and a sincere stalwart of Swamiji had the ultimate of the Vedantic experience i.e. to see God in all beings. Responding to the call of his conscience he resolved not to move from there until he could do something for those hapless victims of famine and poverty.

Swamiji returning from Darjeeling became anxious on going through his brother-disciple's letters giving a graphic description of the famine. He immediately sent two monastic workers and Rs. 150/- with the instruction to start work at once.

Being attracted by the appeal for relief in the newspapers, the Mahabodhi Society and some generous people of Chennai and Kolkata sent money to the Swami. Mr E. V. Levinge the district magistrate, and Mr. Panton, the district judge, also came forward to assist in Swami Akhandananda's relief work.

In response to an appeal for financial help, Pramadadas Mittra of Varanasi wrote to Swami Akhandananda that it was better for a monk to travel, study and practise meditation and japam than to get involved in social service. The Swami replied on 19 October 1898 :

"I am delighted that you have reminded me about my olden days. Those days are gone, and now a new era has sprung up. The Atman never changes, but life changes. Now I don't enjoy travelling anymore.

"When I first went to the Himalayas, I was a different person, Now I wonder upon seeing myself. At that time I would avoid seeing human beings, and leaving the village, I loved to live in the secluded caves of the Himalayas surrounded by ferocious animals. In this way I lived for some years. Now I see God living in all human beings, and I have realized that service to man is service to God. God, as it were, is whispering in my ears, "Verily these human beings are the Vedic sages, they are divine incarnations like Rama and Krishna—they are everything."[20]

The letter indicates how the great mystic Swami Akhandananda was a true humanist, progressive and outspoken.

Swami Akhandananda initiated the first relief work of the Ramakrishna Mission on 15 May 1897 with the distribution of rice among 18 famine-stricken families at Mahula. The distribution of rice was continued for several months and it included many families in the neighbouring villages as well. A severe earthquake followed by an out break of cholera rocked Mahula and surrounding villages only to make the situation worse. Finally the relief service was concluded after a mass feast and distribution of a large number of clothes. It may be added here that many of the beneficiaries of this first relief operation were Muslims.

Swamiji asked Swami Akhandananda to send the reports of relief operation to the Press for publication. But the latter was repulsed by the very idea of publicity. But when Swami Brahmananda told him that Swamiji's instruction must be obeyed he sat down to write a report and realized that service needed public support and the public must know about the income and expenditure and stock and what it would be asked to support.

Appreciating Swami Akhandananda's tireless striving for saving the starving people Swamiji wrote to him on 15 June 1897 from Almora :

> I am getting detailed reports of you and getting more and more delighted. It is that sort of work which can conquer the world. What do differences of sect and opinion matter? Bravo! Accept a hundred thousand embraces and blessings from me. Work Work, Work—I care for nothing else, Work, Work, Work even unto death! Those that are weak must make themselves great workers, great heroes—never mind money, it will drop from the heavens... It is the heart the heart that conquers, not the brain. Books and learning, yoga and meditation and illumination—all are but dust compared with love. It is love that gives you the supernatural powers, love that gives you Bhakti, love that gives illumination, and love, again, that leads to emancipation. This indeed is worship, worship of the Lord in the human tabernacle.[21]

The encouraging letter of Swamiji increased Swami Akhandananda's spirit of service as he reminisced :

"I read his letters over and over again and gained fresh strength within me. *Mantram va sadhayeyam shariram va patayeyam*—I shall either carry out my purpose or lay down my body —this mantram filled my heart. Oh into what a current of activity did I then submerge myself!"[22]

Swami Akhandananda set up an orphanage and a school for the children. He nursed the ailing persons and taught the villagers the basics of hygiene. Simultaneously he continued his preaching and talked with the villagers about the teachings of Sri Ramakrishna.

Swamiji pointing out the limitations and loopholes of such relief operation wrote a letter to one of his disciples Swami Shuddhananda on 11 July 1897 from Almora :

...Akhandananda is working wonderfully at Mahula, but the system is not good. It seems they are frittering away their energies in one little village and that only doling out rice. I do not hear that any preaching has been done along with this helping. All the wealth of the world cannot help one little Indian village if the people are not taught to help themselves. Our work should be mainly *educational* both moral and intellectual. I have not learnt anything about it—only so many *beggars are helped*.!...[23]

On 22 February 1898 Swami Akhandananda reached Nilambar Babu's garden house at Belur to attend the festival of Sri Ramakrishna's birth anniversary. He carried from Behrampur two pantuas (sweetmeat made mostly of fresh cheese fried in ghee and soaked in syrup) which weighed sixty four pounds (fifty six kilo grams) and had been presented by a rich devotee. When the prodigious pantuas were shown to Swamiji, he said to offer them to the Master in the Chapel. Making Swami Akhandananda the subject of his remarks, Swamiji said to his disciple Sharat Chandra Chakravarty "Mark you, what a great hero he is in work! Of fear, death and the like he has no cognisance—doggedly going on doing his own work —'work for the welfare of the many, for the happiness of the many."

The disciple commented, "Sir, that power must have come to him as the result of a good deal of austerities." Swamiji replied : "True, power comes of austerities; but again, working for the sake of others itself constitutes Tapasyâ (practice of austerity). The Karmayogins regard work itself as a part of Tapasyâ..."[24]

In 1898 a plague broke out in Kolkata. Swami Akhandananda risking his life distributed pamphlets written by Swamiji and devoted himself to extensive relief work with Sister Nivedita, Swami Sadananda and other monks.

During a devastating flood in Bihar in October 1899 Swami Akhandananda in cooperation with the local people operated the relief work for two and a half months, serving fifty villages in the Ghogha area in the Bhagalpur district.

Madhusundari Barman, a rich landowner, impressed with Swami Akhandananda's activities, donated one and a half acres of land to him for the ashrama and offered him her office building in Shivnagar. The Swami managed the orphanage and the ashrama activities from that office building for over twelve years. But the land being insufficient for the ashrama he bought about thirteen acres of land in August 1912 in Sargachi village on Krishnanagar Road, 9.6 kms south of Behrampur. The ashrama was permanently moved to Sargachi and ran a full-fledged industrial school, teaching weaving, carpentry, sewing and sericulture. He established a library and a charitable dispensary. There was an arrangement for regular practical schooling for the orphan boys and he taught the illiterate adult villagers at night.

As a guileless sincere organizer Swami Akhandananda was able to impress many a dignitary namely, Mr. E. V. Levinge the district magistrate, Mr. Panton, the district judge of Murshidabad, Mr. Caming the district magistrate of Bhagalpur, some other European officials, Maharaja Manindra Chandra Nandi of Kashimbazar, Raja Yogendranarayan of Lalgola along with people from all social strata.

A true worshipper of living gods in the remote village Swami Akhandananda transformed himself from a monk into a farmer. Putting aside the monastic ochre cloth, he put on half-pants, and tied his head with a handkerchief and tilled the ground like the farmers. Moreover, he lived on a farmer's diet—mixing lime and salt with rice put in water. He started to weave cloth on a spinning wheel.

When Swami Akhandananda became the president of the Ramakrishna Order in 1934 he lived in both Belur Math and Sargachi; but spent most of his time in Sargachi. In fact, Sargachi was to Swami Akhandananda what Shantiniketan was to Rabindranath Tagore.

A Vivacious personality :

Gangadhar and his friend Surendra Ghosh, a son of the famous play wright and actor Girish Chandra Ghosh formed an amateur theatrical party in North Kolkata. Gangadhar became popular as an actor. But he was more interested in spirituality than acting or formal education.

It's hard to find enough superlatives to describe the austerity of Gangadhar's life. He walked hundreds of Kilometers barefoot in the dangerous mountains of the Himalayas without carrying any money or any extra clothing, depending only on God. On the eve of his going on an expedition to Gangotri and Jamunotri a monk of the Mussoorie Hills offered some money and blankets to him, but he declined and accepted only a staff.

Gangadhar possessed a wonderful memory and intellect. He learned Vedic chanting after hearing it only once from Pramadadas Mittra in Varanasi and learned the Tibetan language in fifteen days.

Gangadhar's adventurous life highlights a number of instances of fearlessness. He said, "At one time in a Himalayan village I took shelter in a house and spent the first part of the night along with others and their cattle. But at midnight a tiger roared, and they were shivering out of fear. I silently got up and thought : 'What! I am a monk, Am I afraid of death?' I left the house and spent the rest of the night in meditation under a tree."[25] In Rajasthan he devoted himself to help the poor exploited and illiterate masses under threat from rich landlords. He dared visit Tibet thrice in order to save the starving farmers from the grasp of the heartless lamas risking his life. He had to tackle the enmity of some rich selfish people of Sargachi who out of jealousy tried to oust the Swami.

The spirit of service was deeprooted in Gangadhar's nature. While on the way to Jamunotri he had found a sick monk whom he carried to the nearest village with another person's help but failed to save his life. Once in a cave at Gangotri he came across a brahmin starving for two days while fulfilling a vow to recite the Gayatri mantram continually. Gangadhar at once collected food from some pilgrims and gave it to him.

Under his monastic garb, Swami Akhandananda was a revolutionary, patriot, and philanthropist. He absorbed the spiritual heritage of India from her holy places and saints. Besides he was a voracious reader and a great learner. As a result he had encyclopedic knowledge. He was a fine orator, a humourous conversationalist. He was a self-made self-relient man. His memoirs (Smriti katha) and travelogue (Tibbater Pathe Himalaye) testify to his writing skill.

The Swami made a judicious evaluation of Sri Ramakrishna and Swamiji :

> The Master and Swamiji are really one; the one spirit as it were, manifested in twin personalities. What we find in the Master in the form of a seed, becomes fully developed in Swamiji. Swamiji is to Sri Ramakrishna what the commentrary is to the *Vedanta Sutra*. The one is commentary to the other. They are in fact inseparable—the obverse and reverse of the same coin.[26]

On 24 February 1936 the farsighted and optimist president of the Ramakrishna Order Swami Akhandananda gave a significant and prophetic inaugural message of Sri Ramakrishna centenary :

The dawn of the New age is breaking over the world—the blessed day that will illumine our hearts with the glory of its effulgence is at hand.

Knowingly or unknowingly the human race is moving forward along the path of liberation inspired by Sri Ramakrishna's message of the harmony of all religions and by his unique realization of the essential oneness of Karma [action], jnana [knowledge], bhakti [devotion] and yoga [psychic control]. The day is not far off when the whole world will witness the establishment of a universal kingdom of peace, and when in loving response to the call of the Master, all people, forgetting their religious differences, will unite together and glorify the Master's message, "As many faiths, so many paths." Then only will the meridian light of the Master's advent illumine the hearts of humanity.

May the citizens of the world, on this blessed day, understand the meaning of the Master's coming and be hallowed. This and this alone is my fervent prayer. Peace, peace and peace be unto all.[27]

Swami Akhandananda's life was a burning example of great power of original thinking and intense activity and service based on spiritual realization.

Chapter – 19

SWAMI VIJNANANANDA

While wrestling with the God-man the young man felt a sort of electric current coming out of his hands and entering into him. He lost all his physical strength and went into ecstasy. The God-man said with smile, "Well, you are the winner."[1]

Later the God -man spoke about the young man, "He wrestled with Krishna in his previous incarnation, he is not an ordinary person."[2]

When he was about fourteen once his mother falsely accused him of something and scolded him. He protested strongly but his mother didn't believe a word of her son. The innocent boy was so hurt that tearing off his sacred thread he cried out, "If I tell a lie, I am not a brahmin." His mother realized that what she had said was wrong and feared that some misfortune might befall the family. The very next day a cable from Quetta (Afghanistan) brought the news of her husband's death.

During the British period at the Poona College of Science those students who secured first and second places in their examinations would immediately get jobs either in the state Government of Mumbai or in the Government of India. He, a brilliant student knew that he would secure one of the top positions but one of his classmates, Radhika Prasad Roy, a meritorious poor student needed a job badly. So a few days before the final examination he said to Radhika Prasad, "Brother, the financial condition of your family is not good. If you can get one of the two top positions in the examination, you will definitely get a government job. So I have decided not to appear for the examination this year."[3] He kept his word. Though Radhika Prasad could not secure first or second position he remembered the greatness of his friend.

The interesting anecdotes refer to Hari Prasanna Chattopadhyay (later, Swami Vijnanananda) son of Taraknath Chattopadhyay and Nakuleswari Devi. He was born on Friday, 30 October 1868 in Etawah (U.P.) where his father worked in the commissariat of the British Government.

Hariprasanna was fortunate enough to see strange physical changes and various moods and manners of Sri Ramakrishna while staying with him. At the age of seven he first saw Sri Ramakrishna in the garden house of Jaygopal Sen in Belgharia. The second time he saw him immersed in samadhi at the house of Dewan Govinda Mukhopadhyay in Belgharia. He was deeply moved by the Master's face shining with a heavenly lustre. He said, "Another thing that struck me has remained imprinted in my memory for ever. From the base of the Master's spine right up to his head the whole column had become inflated like a thick rope. And the energy that rose upward towards the brain seemed to be spreading its hood and swaying its head like a snake dancing in joy."[4]

One day Sri Ramakrishna drew a figure on the tongue of Hari Prasanna with his finger and his whole body began to tremble. He, intoxictated with joy from the Master's touch, moved with difficulty towards the Panchavati to meditate there. Following the advice of Swamiji Hari Prasanna took his final monastic vows from the Master with the traditional *viraja homa* ceremony in the Sri Ramakrishna's shrine and became known as Swami Vijnanananda on 9 May 1899.

Swami Vijnanananda was the most junior and of course an exceptional monk in the fold.

Converted from a civil engineer to a spiritual engineer :

After graduating in civil engineering in 1892, Hari Prasanna was appointed district engineer at Gazipur in the North-Western Provinces and the Varanasi-Gazipur Road was built under his super vision. Besides he worked at Etawa Bulandsahar, Merrut and other places in U. P. During his service life he was in constant touch with his brother-disciples and used to send sixty rupees every month to the Ramakrishna Monastery. He joined the Ramakrishna Monastery at Alambazar in 1896 as Brahmachari.

Realizing the importance of a temple in people's religious life, Swamiji conceived of the idea of a temple of Sri Ramakrishna at Belur Math. Long before he went to the West he, standing on the Baranagore ghat, said to some of his brother-disciples : "Something tells me that our permanent Math will be in this neighbourhood across the river."[5] His prophecy was fulfilled. A piece of land, over seven acres in extent, together with a building on the West Bank of the Ganga at Belur was secured on 4 March 1898. Swami Vijnanananda had to take on responsibilities to remodel the main building by adding some more rooms above, as well as one on the southern side. Another building, with the couple of rooms above to serve as a shrine and prayer hall, and with a kitchen, store and a diningroom below, had to be completed before the monastery could be shifted there.

During his travels in western and northern India in 1897 with 'Peshan' (Swami Vijnanananda) Swamiji discussed the architecture of the future Ramakrishna Temple with him and told about his own ideas as to how the temple should look like and how it should harmonize the architectural styles of various Hindu temples as well as the styles of a church, a Buddhist cave temple and a mosque. Swamiji earnestly wanted to have the relics of Sri Ramakrishna permanently housed in an imposing, enduring and magnificent temple that would be a combination of Eastern and Western styles of architecture and would inspire people for ages. On their return to the monastery, Swami Vijnanananda drew a sketch of the Ramakrishna Temple on the basis of the ideas of Swamiji and consulted with Mr. Guithar a reputed architect. Swamiji gladly approved of the third sketch and remarked "This temple will certainly come up, but I may not live to see it…I will see it from on high."[6]

The foundation stone for the second time was laid by Swami Vijnanananda on 16 July 1935 and the temple was almost complete by the end of 1937 and was opened ceremoniously by Swami Vijnanananda on 14 July 1938.

While dedicating the temple Swami Vijnanananda felt that, Swamiji true to his word, was blessing the occasion from the region where he was with some of his brother disciples Rakhal Maharaj, Mahapurush Maharaj, Sharat Maharaj, Hari Maharaj, Gangadhar Maharaj and others standing in the southwest corner in the inner sanctum. In the tenth General Report of the Mission the dignity and distinction of the temple were described thus : In point of beauty and grandeur, as well as strength, it may be considered the most remarkable temple of its kind in Northern India. Swamiji had wanted the temple to represent some of the best architectural features of various regions of India as well as the characteristic architecture associated with the major religions of the world. In fact, the temple symbolizes in stone the spirit of harmony of Sri Ramakrishna. The Vivekananda Temple, a ghat and an embankment on the bank of the Ganga for the Belur Monastery, a Ramakrishna Monastery and a charitable homeopathic dispensary in Allahabad, the Ramakrishna Mission Home of Service in Varanasi, buildings of the Order at Kankhal and some other places were constructed under the supervision of Swami Vijnanananda. It is covetable to quote Swami Gahanananda :

> Swami Vijnanananda had been an expert civil engineer. Later he became a spiritual engineer, surveying the landscape of the inner regions of the personality and building spiritual edifices within himself and helping others to do so by giving them blue-print of spiritual architecture.[7]

Initially no preaching the teachings of Sri Ramakrishna :

It is interesting to note that at least in one respect Swami Vijnanananda differed from the rest of the monks of the fold. It is curious that though he belonged to the Order as a direct disciple of Sri Ramakrishna and set up a Ramakrishna Monastery in Allahabad, he did not try to preach the message of the Master during his thirty eight years of stay in Allahabad. He was engaged with practising spiritual disciplines and going through Vedanta literature and writing books instead of preaching which was against his nature.

The Master's teachings are very useful and relevant to people in all ages. The world heard the short but significant utterances —"As many faiths so many paths", "To serve jiva as Siva" first from his lips.

Of course, Swami Vijnanananda's meeting (1933) with ailing Swami Shivananda changed his motto in life. He said : "That day Mahapurush [Swami Shivananda] laid his hand on my head; his touch changed my mental attitude. He passed on to me his great desire to help people spiritually and to assume responsibility for them. I now feel that as long as I live and have the least strength in my body I shall do the same and give the Master's name to all."[8] After becoming Vice-President the Swami initiated many people. He commented on initiation : "When people come to me for a mantram, I take them to the Master's shrine and introduce them to him. Afterward the Master will do what is necessary."[9]

Strictness about women :

In another respect Swami Vijnanananda was quite exceptional in the fold. He used to steer clear of women rigidly.

On 24 August 1882 Sri Ramakrishna said to M. "Some are born with the characteristics of the Yogi, but they too should be careful. It is "woman and gold' alone that is the obstacle; it makes them deviate from the path of Yoga and drags them into worldliness."[10]

During his initial stage of sadhana in Allahabad Swami Vijnanananda was very strict about women. He allowed no woman to visit the Brahmavadin Club. One day the sweeper had to go somewhere so he sent his young daughter to clean the privy of Swami Vijnanananda. Seeing the girl the Swami was displeased and said to her, 'Starting tomorrow I don't need anybody to clean my privy.' Hearing the Swami's, words from his daughter the sweeper hurried to the Swamiji in the evening and apologized. The Swami said to him, "I don't need anybody. I shall go to the public privy.' Afterwards, out of compassion, he said to the sweeper. "If you want to serve me please come, but don't send anyone else."

In the charitable homeopathic dispensary when the female patients tried to tell him their physical problems, the Swami forbade them to talk about their disease and asked them to take the medicine and go home. Once he said to a monk in Allahabad, "I have never seen any woman even in my dreams...In my fifty-three years of life, the Divine Mother has never shown me Her bewitching form.'[11] Considering his antipathy to women Swami Shivananda once said, "Even a she-fly has no entry in Hari Prasanna's ashrama."[12]

Despite his respect for the Holy Mother Swami Vijnanananda seldom visited her in Kolkata. One day he went to Balaram Bose's house with Swamiji to see the Mother. Learning that his affectionate Peshan did not salute the Mother, Swamiji asked him to go to her to bow down. On seeing him bow down to her bending his head to the floor Swamiji indignantly said to him : "What is this, Peshan? Does anybody salute the Mother in this way? Bow down to her by prostrating yourself on the floor. The Holy Mother is the Mother of the universe."[13] Saying this he prostrated himself to the Mother and Swami Vijnanananda followed him.

Once at Belur Math Swami Vijnanananda being curious about Swamiji's relationship with Western women said : "Swamiji, while you were in the West you associated with the women there; but didn't the Master teach the contrary in this respect? He used to say, "A monk should not even look at the portrait of a woman. He emphatically told me not to be close to women, however devoted they might be. So I am wondering why you did so." After pacifing his anger Swamiji said : "Well, Peshan, do you think that what you have understood about the Master is all that he is? What do you know about the Master? Do you know that the Master eradicated the idea of the difference between male and female from my mind? Is there any distinction of sex in the Atman? Moreover, the Master came for the good of the entire world. Did he come to liberate only men? He will save all—both men and women. You people want to belittle the Master by measuring him with the yard stick of your own intellects. Whatever the Master told you is true; you follow that implicitly. But to me his instructions were different. He not only gave me instructions, he clearly showed me everything. He holds my hands—whatever, he makes me do, I do."

Noticing Peshan's embarrassment, Swamiji added calmly : "Can a nation rise or become great unless the primordial energy that lies dormant in women is awakened? I have travelled all over the world and found that women are neglected more or less everywhere but this is particularly deplorable in India. That is why our nation has been degraded to such an extent. As soon as there is an awakening in women, you will see that the whole nation will rise up in its pristine glory. For that reason the Holy Mother has come. With her advent there has been a stir among the women of all countries. This is just a beginning, you will see many more things later."[14]

Actually Swami Vijnanananda was not a misogynist. Once his sister came to visit him in Allahabad. He arranged for her to stay in an inn. He arranged for his mother to stay in the ashrama guest house and served her carefully when she visited Prayag in 1918 for a pilgrimage and holy bath during *Purna Kumbha*. As the President of the Ramakrishna Order he initiated many women and was kind and compassionate towards them. One day he said to a woman devotee "Call on the Holy Mother, you will achieve everything. The Master is very strict about bestowig his grace, but the Mother is very compassionate. I have achieved everything by her grace."[15]

The Master in the Swami :

Noticing Hari Prasanna's long absence from Dakshineswar Sri Ramakrishna sent for him. Learning from him that he felt no urge to visit the Master and failed to meditate; the Master drew a figure on his tongue with his finger. The young man's whole body began to quiver and he felt an indescribable bliss within. He sat for meditation at Panchavati. When he regained his ordinary state of mind and told the Master that his meditation was very good, the Master assured him from then on he would always have deep meditation. That day he gave Hari Prasanna many spiritual instructions. The latter said : "I was overwhelmed by the Master's love and compassion for me. I had not realized before that he had so much feeling for me. Sri Ramakrishna's grace was boundless. On that day the Master said to me : "Never get involved with women. Always be careful. Let there be no stain on your character. Never look at a woman, even if she is made out of gold. Do you know why I am saying all this to you? You belong to the Divine Mother, and you will have to do a lot of work for Her. A pecked fruit cannot be offered to the Mother. So I tell you, be careful."[16]

In 1885 Hari Prasanna after passing the First Arts examination at Saint Xavier's College, Kolkata entered Patna college in Bihar to study for a B.A. degree. As a result he was unable to spend much time with the Master. But he was not deprived of the Master's love. He had the vision of the Master standing in front of him on the day (16 August 1886) of his passing away. He remarked : 'I can not express how much love the Master had for us. We don't have that capacity to love others. We became intoxicated seeing the Master and now people are intoxicated just by hearing his name. How blessed they are!'[17]

Swami Vijnanananda; as an ideal monk followed his Master's advice without compromise. He used to lead his life according to the ideal of the Master. One day Swamiji said : 'I cannot say anything to Peshan because I see the Master in him.' Swami Vijnanananda replied, 'The Master dwells in every being. It is no wonder that you see the Master in me through your divine sight.' Swamiji said : 'No Peshan, it is not like that. I see distinctly that the Master has made his habitat in you nicely.' Swami Vijnanananda politely responded, 'Swamiji, you see whatever you want to, but I don't understand it.'[18]

The Bishop of Allahabad :

Prayag or Allahabad is an old historic city. It is a holy place of pilgrimage because the confluence of three rivres—the Ganga, the Jamuna and the Saraswati—is located there. After the completion of the Belur Monastery, Swamiji advised Swami Vijnanananda to start a centre in Allhabad.

The Swami went to Allahabad in 1900 and stayed there thirty eight years. He practised severe austerities fifteen hours a day for ten years while at the Brahmavadin Club. He spent mornings and afternoons in worhship, japam, meditation and study in the shrine room. In the evening he gave classess on the Gita to club members in the library hall. He bought a house and a vacant plot in the Muthiganj area of Allahabad. The house was turned into a Ramakrishna Monastery and another house was built on the vacant plot for a charitable homeopathic dispensary. In Allahabad he did not preach the teachings of Sri Ramakrishna and seldom went outside the club. Yet his simple, austere God centred life attracted people. Pandit Madan Mohan Malavya was deeply moved by the Swami's interpretation of Vedanta.

At that time Swami Vijnanananda had not started to initiate. So he had no disciples to help him. There were only a few devotees who subscribed to the ashrama. Allahabad has an extreme climate. The ashrama had no electricity. It being very close to the main rail line in Muthiganj was very noisy. Initially it suffered financial crisis. Despite these hardships the Swami calmly continued all works of the ashrama. He kept on practising his sadhana in solitude as the Master had advised : 'Meditate in the mind, in the corner of the room, and in the forest.' He tried to elude public life. But gradually people became aware of his spiritual greatness and began to visit him for his advice.

Even when (1937) Swami Vijnanananda became president, he preferred Allahabad to Belur Math the head quarters of the Order and passed away there. Considering sincere activities of the Swami in Allahabad Swamiji called him 'the Bishop of Allahabad'. Bishop is a senior priest in charge of the work of the Church in city or district. Swami Vijnanananda was the abbot of the Ramakrishna Monastery in Allahabad.

According to him, Belur Math was a holy place which had been sanctified by the touch of the Mother and all sixteen of Sri Ramakrishna's direct disciples. Once he commented, "Mother Annapurna [the goddess of food] is everpresent in Belur Math. It is a place of mendicants who have no money. But people bring food and all sorts of things. It is the grace of the Mother that the monastery store is always full...Anybody who lives in Belur Math and practises japam and meditation intensely in solitude will attain spiritual experiences."[19] In January 1938 when Swami Vijnanananda, the president of the Ramakrishna Order visited Belur Math for the dedication of Sri Ramakrishna's temple, he remarked, "Allahabad is a nice place. I have sufficient privacy there, and not too many people come to me. But in Belur Math I am surrounded by a crowd almost continually—I can hardly breathe..."[20]

A hidden knower of Brahman :

The Bhagavan said : When a man renounces all the desires of the mind, O Arjuna, when he is satisfied in the Self alone by Self, then he is called a man of firm wisdom.

He whose mind is not perturbed in pains, who has no longing in pleasures, who is free from desire, fear and anger, he is called a sage of firm wisdom.[21]

Swami Vijnanananda was a sage of firm wisdom—a real Yogi free from all desires, fear and anger. Swami Brahmananda once spoke of this stoic brother-disciple : "Vijnanananda is a hidden knower of Brahman."[22]

The Bhagavata has described the way of life of an illumined soul thus : "Though wise, he plays like a child unconcerned about status; though highly intelligent he behaves like a fool without any plans, though learned, he speaks like one who is mad to avoid popularity; though established in the truth taught by the Vedas, he roams about like cattle with absolute unconcern for all established codes of conduct."[23] In order to discover the true identity of Swami Vijnanananda his nature and activities should be considered from this perspective.

One day Swami Brahmananda said to some of his disciples : "Hari Prasanna Maharaj has come from Allahabad : Have you met him? Please go and pay your obeisance to him. He is a knower of Brahman; and having attained the supreme state of beatitude, he is calm and silent. It is difficult to recognize him, he generally eludes people."[24]

Swami Brahmananda himself was a great spiritual teacher yet he used to send those brahmacharins who had special spiritual aptitude to Allahabad to grow under the guidance of Swami Vijnanananda.

An avadhūta :

In some Indian religions 'Avadhūta' a Sanskrit term indicates a type of mystic or saint who is beyond egoic-consciousness, duality and common worldly concerns and acts wihout consideration for standard social etiquette. Avadhūta is a jivanmukta who gives his insight to others and teaches them about his realization of the true nature of the ultimate reality (Brahman) and self (Atman) and takes the role of a guru to show the path of moksha (emancipation) to others. Some Avadhūta also achieves the title of Paramahamsa.

Swami Vijnanananda a hidden knower of Brahman lived like a true avadhūta. He was unconventional in his conduct. He used to put on queer attire—a long loose shirt (either woolen or cotton) with many pockets, a piece of dhoti (cloth) reaching his knees, a couple of pairs of sock (even in the hot summer), worn-out shoes and a cap that covered his ears. While travelling by *ekka,* (a one horse carriage), people on the street would look at him curiously. The Swami used to make fun of them : 'What are you looking at ? A monkey? Yes, I am a monkey devotee of Lord Ramachandra.'[25]

In 1933 one day at the Madras Math while Swami Vijnanananda was taking off his coat, sweater, shirt and T-shirt the young monks were watching him curiously. One of them said : "Maharaj, Sri

Ramakrishna compared the ego to an onion. If anyone removes the layers of an onion one after another, there will be nothing left. We see you are also removing your clothing like that." The Swami said with a smile, "Five sheaths are within the body and I put seven or eight more coverings over that, otherwise people will see my Atman."[26]

In this way a mystic like Swami Vijnanananda hid his true stature from the gaze of the public. But he could not hide himself for long. Ultimately scholars namely Pandit Madan Mohan Malavya and laymen were charmed by his spiritual greatness and started to come to him for his guidance.

Peculiar hobbies :

The mind of a knower of Brahman always soars high. In order to serve the mankind he cultivates some hobbies or desires to bring his mind down to the sense plane. Swami Vijnanananda had some interesting hobbies. He had a large collection of fountain pens and most of them were very costly. Swami Shivananda presented him with a good fountain pen and a flashlight.

In 1934 after the passing away of Swami Shivananda it was proposed that Swami Vijnanananda become a trust and the vice-president of the Ramakrishna Math and Ramakrishna Mission. Knowing that his brother-monk Swami Vijnanananda's favourite hobby was fountain pen collection, Swami Akhandananda, the president wrote to him "Brother, please give your consent and sign your name, and I shall present a fountain pen to you." Swami Vijnanananda replied "Brother, when you send me the pen, I shall sign my name with it." Swami Akhandananda sent him a pen and the Swami signed and became the vice-president of the Ramakrishna Order.[27] He liked to collect tea-sets. During his stay in Belur Math he bought a German cup and saucer and while visiting Rangoon he bought a cup and dish set made of ivory. He had a good collection of various types of pocket watches and pocketknives.

One day in Belur Math as the Swami heard that Swami Suddhananda had ridden in an aeroplane, he at once expressed his desire to fly in the sky. Accordingly an arrangement was made and he flew over the Belur Monastery.

Visions bestowed upon the Swami :

Swami Vijnanananda was blessed by visions of gods, goddesses, incarnations and brother-disciples.

In 1909 the Swami who was an expert engineer in his service-life, went to Varanasi to supervise the construction of the Ramakrishna Mission Home of Service. While riding from the rail station to the destination, the Swami's horse carriage suddenly overturned, and one of his legs was twisted inside a wheel. Bearing severe pain he at once pulled out his leg and reached the ashrama by another carriage and was treated by a physician. That night suffering from a high temperature and a splitting headache, he thought to himself : 'Lord Vishwanath, I have come to your city to work for the Master. This is an unselfish action! Why has this accident happened? The Master's work will suffer." Thinking thus, he fell asleep. Later the Swami described the following experience :

It was 1:00 or 2:00 a.m. I saw Lord Shiva with matted hair and smiling face appear before me. I said : "Lord, have you come to take me? But I cannot go now; I have to complete the Master's work first." He didn't listen to me. Smiling, he came forward and then embraced me. Immediately my body became as cold as ice. I then said to him, "Good-bye now, Lord. I shall have to do the Master's work." Lord Shiva laughed and left. Strangely enough in the morning I felt no fever and also my wounds were healed to some extent. Even now, sometime I see that calm, smiling form of Lord Shiva.[28]

Later, while visiting the temple of Vishwanath in Varanasi Swami Vijnanananda thought to himself : "Why have I come here? To look at a stone?" Then the same vision opened up. It was as if Vishwanath were telling me, "The light is the same here as there–Truth is one."—said the Swami.[29]

Swami Vijnanananda narrated the following experience of a vision of Lord Shiva in the Art studio of Kolkata :

I went alone to the studio and saw a beautiful picture of Lord Shiva. He was in a standing posture and had matted locks and a beard. A standing portrait of Shiva is rare. I gazed at it intently and was soon filled with ecstasy. The picture became living to me, and I felt that Lord Shiva would talk to me. I still vividly remember that sweet divine mood and I feel joy whenever I think of that picture.[30]

Swami Vijnanananda described a mystical experience which he had while visiting Kalighat in Kolkata :

I was taken inside the temple. I saw and touched the Divine Mother's image; then while I was circumambulatig the deity, the Mother out of Her infinite mercy, revealed Herself unto me. She roused my *kundalini* [the serpent power that resides at the base of the spine] to the *sahasrara* [the thousand petalled lotus on the crown of the head] and illumined it quickly.[31]

Swami Vijnanananda narrated his experience while visiting Sarnath :

While I was there, a guide informed me that there was a stone image containing carvings of Buddha's entire life story from his birth to mahaparinirvana [death]. The guide accompanied me there. While looking at the image I had a wonderful vision. I saw a formless ocean of light, and the whole universe was gradually merging into it. Like a speck, I was watching that blissful glow with wonder, standing on the shore of the ocean of light. I was beside myself. Then in the twinkling of an eye the universe completely disappeared, and from the ocean of pure consciousness the compassionate, loving form of Buddha appeared. What a joy! Even now while describing it, I feel that joy. I was in that state for some time. Then I heard the guide's voice, "Let us go forward—let us go forward." Gradually I regained my normal consciousness. The guide thought that I had fallen asleep. I followed the guide but I was extremely intoxicated...[32]

Swami Vijnanananda narrated the following experience of visiting the famous reclining image of Buddha at Pegu (in Burma) on 11 December 1936 :

Today Lord Buddha has graciously vouchsafed me his vision. I clearly saw that the reclining image of Buddha was living, as it were. How magnificent was the beauty of his luminous form![33]

The consecration ceremony of Ramakrishna temple took place on 14 January 1938. After installation of the relics of Sri Ramakrishna on the alter of the new temple and worship as Swami Vijnanananda returned to his room, his attendant asked him if he had said anything to Swamiji. The Swami replied : "Yes, I said to Swamiji, 'You told me that you would watch from on high. Please see now that the Master is seated in the new temple.' Then I vividly saw Swamiji, Rakhal Maharaj, Mahapurush Maharaj, Sharat Maharaj, Hari Maharaj, Gangadhar Maharaj and others standing in the south west corner watching the consecration ceremony."[34]

On the day (4 July 1902) of Swamiji's passing away Swami Vijnanananda, while meditating in the shrine of Brahmavadin Club (Allahabad), had a vision of Swamiji seated on the lap of Sri Ramakrishna.

In 1938 when Swami Vijnanananda was seriously ill, oneday a monk asked him if he saw the Master even then. Pointing to the picture of Sri Ramakrishna, the Swami said. "The Master is there. He is always near me. Of course I see him, whenever it is necessary. He is guiding me."[35]

One day after his bath in the *Triveni* (the confluence of three holy rivers—the Ganga, the Jamuna and the Saraswati) in Allahabad, while reciting a hymn to the Mother Ganga, Swami Vijnanananda had a vision. The goddess Mother Triveni appeared as a beautiful young girl with three braids hanging down her back and then disappeared again into the water. When he began to walk towards the ashrama he saw Mother Triveni walking in the same direction with her braids dangling. Hearing about the vision Swami Brahmananda confirmed it as genuine. Swami Vijnanananda commented :

The test of a true vision is this. It leaves a lasting spiritual impression on the mind that generates awareness and bliss. I still get joy when I think of that virginal form of the Divine Mother.[36]

In fact, Swami Vijnanananda's life verified that God is not a myth.

Distinctive Sayings :

On various occasions Swami Vijnanananda uttered well-thought of proverbial words for the propagation of his spiritual realization and the teachings of Sri Ramakrishna.

In 1931 The Swami said to the devotees in Madras : "The goal of human life is to realize God because only that can give us real and permanent peace. Truly it is the ego, a product of ignorance, which has covered our God-vision. Once someone asked Sri Ramakrishna, 'Why can't we see God?' He immediately covered his face with a towel and asked : 'can you see my face? No. Because this towel is the barrier; Yet I am seated infront of you. Similarly, remove the veil of ignorance, which is between you and God and you will see Him everywhere."[37]

In 1935 the Swami one day said to the devotees in Barisal in Bangladesh : "Only a few people can realize or understand God. This is not possible without purity of the heart. One should be extremely careful. Bad thoughts are like poison."[38]

Another day the Swami said to some spiritual aspirants : "Chant the Lord's name; you will get peace. The Soul is not matter. The Soul is beyond birth and death. The Soul is eternal. The individual soul is subservient to the Supreme Soul [Paramatman].[39]

In 1936 in Rangoon one afternoon a monk said to Swami Vijnanananda, 'How can we still the mind?' The Swami replied : 'It is quite essential to practise japam and meditation regularly every day. Then gradually the mind will be calm and steady. Try to live alone. A real holy man lives in solitude. It is no use listening to too many spiritual instructions at one time. It is far better to hear and concentrate on a few instructions and practise them. Often some people take too many instructions but do not follow any at all—that does not bear any results. What good advice you have heard, try to translate into action.'[40]

On 12 December 1936 Swami Vijnanananda heard that Prince Edward VIII had renounced the throne of England in order to marry an American woman. The Swami remarked : "Look, the prince gave up such a vast empire, wealth, honour and everything just for a woman! So a woman is greater than an empire, and again God is greater than a woman. Who renounces anything for God? God is the greatest of everything—upon gaining him one knows that there is no greater gain. But it is extremely difficult to attain him. The prince's renunciation of the empire is praiseworthy. Renunciation of any kind is good; it increases mental strength and dispassion. Today he has renounced the empire, perhaps in the future he may give up that woman."[41]

The Swami referring to the story of the British Prince said to his attendant : "There is little hope of making any progress in spiritual life without renunciation."[42]

One day the Swami said to the devotees : "Devotion is great to a bhakta and knowledge is great to a jnani. In the initial stage an aspirant experiences a difference, but after attaining perfection, he realizes that knowledge and devotion are the same."[43]

On 5 February 1938 Swami Vijnanananda said to the monks and devotees in the Ramakrishna Mission home of Service, Varanasi: "The Master is Rama and Krishna, and the Mother is Sita and Yogamaya. As the king visits his subjects sometimes in royal dress and sometimes in disguise to evaluate their needs, so the Master came this time in disguise...It is true : the Master will come back soon."[44]

Queer method of therapy :

On a Sunday in February 1882 Sri Ramakrishna said to a devotee, "Furthermore, he (a worldly person) should practise discrimination and pray to God, 'Give me faith and devotion'. Once a person has faith he has achieved everything. There is nothing greater than faith."

With reference to the tremendous power of faith the Master said to Kedar : "If a man has faith in God, then even if he has committed the most heinous sins—such as killing a cow, a brahmin, or a woman—he will certainly be saved through his faith. Let him only say to God, 'O Lord, I will not repeat such an action,' and he need not be afraid of anything."[45]

Swami Vijnanananda had firm faith in God and his Master. He wholeheartedly believed that all works of the Ramakrishna Monastery in Allahabad and of the charitable homeopathic dispensary attached to the Monastery belong to God. The Swami faced a difficult situation when the doctor of the dispensary resigned. He did not get a doctor at once and worried about the poor patients. One day he reflected : "Well, it is the Master's work; I shall give medicine chanting his name," The Swami had no knowledge of medical science. Yet he used to attend the dispensary every morning. He gave homeopathic medicine to the patients without asking about their physical problems or diseases. If any female patient tried to tell him her physical problem, he said : "Don't talk about your disease. Take the medicine and go home."

It was strange that each drop of homeopathic medicine the Swami gave cured every patient and none had to visit for the next dose. The more the miraculous news spread, the more patients appeared. The Swami found it difficult for him to tackle the crowds and brought in a doctor form Varanasi in order to relieve himself of the responsibility. The doctor while checking the stock of medicine, discovered to his utter astonishment that even the nitric acid bottles were empty. He fearfully and anxiously said to the Swami, "Maharaj, you have cleared even the nitric acid!" The Swami calmly replied : "I have given medicine in the name of the Master and the patients got well. There is no credit for me; I did as he asked me to do."[46]

During Swami Vijnananada's last visit to Belur Math (26 February— 8 March 1938) he had been suffering from dropsy. His attendant insisted him on taking medicine. The Swami replied : "I have no faith in doctors." A monk proposed that the Swami should consult the eminent physician who had treated Swami Shivananda. The Swami asked : "Is there any doctor better than this one?" The monk replied : "Yes, there is one—Dr. Nilratan Sarkar." The Swami again asked : "Is there anybody greater than him?" The monk answered, "No, there is none. He is the best doctor here." Then Swami Vijnanananda said : "Yes, there is one better still, and he is the Master himself. I am under his care."[47]

A week before the Swami passed away, a monk suggested that the Swami consult an ayurvedic physican. The Swami quoted a Sanskrit couplet : "Ganges water is the medicine and the Lord is the physican." He had strong antipathy to allopathic medicine. Thus keeping his faith in the will and care of the Master Swami Vijnanananda endured his pain calmly and spent his last days almost without treatment. The corpse of Latu Maharaj was immersed (jalasamadhi) in the Ganga in Varanasi. Swami Vijnanananda lay forgood on the riverbed at the confluence of the Ganga and Jamuna on Tuesday 26 April 1938.

Publication of repository books :

Swami Vijnanananda had no idle leisure in his busy life. When he was not practising his spiritual discipline or supervising any construction, he would either study Vedanta literature or write books. In 1904 he translated *Sri Ramakrishna's Life and Teachings.* by Suresh Chandra Datta from Bengali into Hindi under the title *Paramahamsa-Charita.* His later publications included : *Jalsarvaraher karkhana,* an engineering and waterworks manual in two volumes in Bengali, translations of Varahamihira's *Brihajjataka,* and *Surya-siddhanta,* two ancient Sanskrit astrological and astronomical works, the first into English and the second into Bengali and translations of *Devi Bhagavata,* and *Narada Pancharatra,* two notable Hindu scriptures, from Sanskrit into English. His translation of Valmiki's *Ramayanam* from Sanskrit into English was left incomplete owing to his illness and passing away. He said, "When I sit down to translate the *Ramayana,* I forget the world. I see Rama, Lakshmana, Sita and Mahavirji in fornt of me."[48]

Illustrious personality :

Swami Vijnanananda was a graceful personality. One day Sri Ramakrishna asked Hari Prasanna then a student of Saint Xavier's college Kolkata, why he had been absent for so long; he was so simple, truthful and outspoken that he said to the Master's face : "Sir I didn't feel like coming. Moreover, I try to meditate, but I find I can not" That day Hari Prasanna was initiated by the Master.

Once in the Poona College of Science a Christian missionary professor of geology had made caustic comments on the Hindu belief in reincarnation. Hari Prasanna had the guts to protest the remark of the fanatic professor. As a result, the professor gave him a lower mark in geology than he really deserved. Due to this injustice he placed second in lieu of first in his final examination.

As a man he was so compassionate and great that he did not appear for the examination in order to help his poor classmate Radhika Prasad Roy get a job by securing first or second position.

Hari Prasanna was generous. During his years of service as district engineer in Uttar Pradesh, he used to keep in contact with his brother disciples and donate sixty rupees every month to the Ramakrishna Monastery. He served the ailing disciples who visited him with sincere care.

Hari Prasanna joined the Ramakrishna Monastery at Alambazar in 1896 He was economical in speech and did not like chatting and joking. He lived a plain and simple monastic life dedicated to japam and meditation most of his time.

Swami Vijnanananda followed exactly the advice of a Vedanta scripture : "If you want the knowledge of Brahman, shun crowds like a snake, good food like poison, and sex like the devil." While staying in the Brahmavadin Club in Allahabad he, in order to avoid crowd, seldom went outside the club. His meals were very simple—rice, lentils and a vegetable. He was very strict about women and did not allow any woman to visit the Club. He lived a simple, austere, God-centred life according to the ideal of Sri Ramakrishna.

His unconventional way of life is remarkable. He used to put on queer dress—a piece of dhoti(cloth) reaching the knees, a long loose shirt with many pockets, a couple of pairs of socks, worn-out shoes and a cap that covered his ears. In this way as a true stoic mystic he tried to hide his identity from the public eye. He was quite indifferent to temporal pleasure. Once, seeing the Swami's worn-out water pot, Pandit Madan Mohan Malavya a great scholar and founder of the Varanasi Hindu University, commented; "It needs replacing.[49] Pandit Malavya was astonished at the Swami's mastery over Vedanta literature and considered him the living representation of Vedanta.

In the Gita Lord Krishna said to Arjuna :

In this world a twofold way of yore taught by me. O Arjuna : that of the Sankhyas with the path of knowledge, and that of the Yogins with the path of selfless work. [3.3]

Swami Vijnanananda devoted himself to severe austerities and study and establishment of monastery, supervision of construction of building in various places simultaneously. Thus he synthesized successfully the yoga of spiritual knowledge and the yoga of selfless works in his dynamic life.

The Swami was very punctual. During the daytime he used to give interviews to aspirants, but if anybody arrived even one minute late, he would not meet him. He was calm and reserved but he had a sense of humour. While supervising the construction of the Vivekananda Temple at Belur Math, one day he told Swami Brahmananada that his work was suffering owing to a shortage of materials. The president assured him that the materials would reach by boat before the next morning. Swami Vijnanananda doubted this. Thereupon a bet was laid and both retired for the night. At dawn when the Swami did not see the boat, he was very glad at the prospect of winning the bet and went to his bed. A little later Swami Brahmananda went out and saw the boat tied-up and returned to his room. In the morning Swami Vijnanananda going to the President claimed with an impish grin his winnings. Swami Brahmananda said to him, 'What for? Swami, Vijnanananda felt embarrassed as he found the boat and said to Swami Brahmananda : "Well I have no money; you must pay it for me."[50]

At the Madras (now Chennai) Math one day the young monks watched with great curiosity how Swami Vijnanananda was removing his coat sweater shirt and T-shirt. One of them said, "Maharaj, Sri Ramakrishna compared the ego to an onion. If anyone removes the layers of an onion one after another, there will be nothing left. We see you are also removing your clothing like that." The Swami answered with a smile, "Five sheaths are within the body, and I put seven or eight more coverings over that, otherwise people will see my Atman."[51]

Once the Swami made a fun by using a pun. He said to a disciple, "Have you ever seen a *bhut* [ghost]?" Receiving a negative reply the Swami said, "There are five ghosts in your body. Do not fear. Chant the name of Rama, all the ghosts will run away. Where Rama's name is chanted, no ghosts can live."[52] Actually, the Bengali word *'bhut'* bears double meanings—ghost and element. The Swami made a pun by saying *panchabhut,* i.e. five elements—earth, water, fire, air and space—that constitute the human body, as well as everything else in this universe.

One day Swami Bhahmananda arranged a meeting on the verandah so that a young monk could fulfil his desire to give a lecture. He asked all monks of Belur Math to be present. The zealous speaker put on formal dress along with a beautiful turban. Then the president Maharaj announced, "I propose that Swami Vijnanananda take the chair and preside over the meeting." Immediately Swami Vijnanananda got up and announced, "I now dissolve the meeting." All laughed and the meeting ended.[53] Thus the monastic disciples of the Master sometimes used to make fun with the young monks to ease the rigid routine of the monastery.

One day Swami Vijnanananda wrote a letter from Belur Math to his servant Beni a pure, guileless faithful boy and asked a monk to write the address of the Allahabad Ashrama on the envelope. According to the Swami's dictation the letter was addressed to Dr. Beni Madhav, M.A., B.L.,L.L.D. The monk curiously said, "Maharaj, who is he?" The Swami only smiled. Another monk told him that it was Beni, the Swami's servant. All burst out laughing. Besides these there are so many instances of Swami Vijnanananda's sense of humour.

Swami Vijnanananda made significant comments on the Master and the Mother. On 26 November 1883 Hari Prasanna, having been invited by Sri Ramakrishna, attended the festival at Mani Mallik's house in Kolkata. He returned home late at night. Later he described what happened : "My mother scolded me. When she heard that I had gone to see Sri Ramakrishna, she said, "My goodness! You went to that brahmin! He has deranged the brains of three hundred and fifty young men!' It was indeed mental derangement! Even now my brain is hot. I did not pay any attentaion to my mother's scolding.'[54] Referring to that incident the Swami would remark :

> 'Derangement of brain indeed! The brain is still deranged. Had I not been caught in the influence of that mad man, who knows where I should have been now—wallowing in the welter of the world?"[55]

Once the Swami said to a woman devotee : "Call on Holy Mother; you will achieve everything. The Master is very strict about bestowing his grace, but the Mother is very compassionate. I have achieved everything by her grace."[56]

On the day of initiation the Master after giving some advice said to Hari Prasanna : 'Do you know why I am saying all this to you? You belong to the Divine Mother, and you will have to do a lot of work for Her. A pecked fruit cannot be offered to the Mother. So I tell you, be careful."[57]

Swami Vijnanananda, a man of stainless character, an embodiment of austerities obeyed his Master's order by teaching and inspiring many people more through his ideal life than through lecturing. Swami Gahanananda observed.

> He (Swami Vijnanananda) combined in his life intense spiritual discipline, intellectual study, a simple and unostentatious demeanour and hard work, along with missionary zeal. This type of life is best suited to members of a monastic Order. Thus his life can be a role model for spiritual aspirants in the Mission."[58]

Chapter – 20

'WE'RE IN THE SAME BOAT BROTHER'

Sri Ramakrishna, regarded as an Avatar or Incarnation of God by innumerable devotees even during his lifetime, a prophet of the new age; once declared :

"There was no limit to the longing I felt at that time. During the day-time I somehow managed to control it. The secular talk of the worldly-minded was galling to me, and I would look wistfully to the day when my own beloved companions would come. I hoped to find solace in conversing with them and relating to them my own realizations. Every little incident would remind me of them, and thoughts of them wholly engrossed me. I was already arranging in my mind what I should say to one and give to another, and so on. But when the day would come to a close I would not be able to curb my feelings. The thought that another day had gone by, and they had not come, oppressed me. When, during the evening service, the temple rang with the sound of bells and conch-shells, I would climb to the roof of the kuthi in the garden and writhing in anguish of heart, cry at the top of my voice : 'Come my children! Oh, where are you? I cannot bear to live without you.' A mother never longed so intensely for the sight of her child, nor a friend for his companions, nor a lover for his sweetheart, as I longed for them. Oh, it was indescribable"[1]

Shortly after that period of yearning his children came to him one by one at Dakshineswar. They were his sixteen would-be monastic disciples destined to create history. Sri Ramakrishna became busy training them to bear his spiritual treasure and carry out his mission. At Cossipore garden house when the Master heard that Gopal Chandra Ghosh (later, Swami Advaitananda) would distribute twelve pieces of ochre cloths and rosaries of rudraksha beads among the monks on the auspicous day of *makar-sankranti* he said to Gopal : .

> You will attain a thousand times more virtue if you present those ochre cloths and rosaries to my children rather than giving them to the monks of Jagannath ghat. Where else will you find such all-renouncing monks? Each of them is equal to a thousand monks.[2]

On Tuesday, 12 January 1886 Gopal gave the ochre cloths and rosaries to the Master who sanctified them with a mantram and himself distributed them among eleven disciples—Narendra, Rakhal, Niranjan, Baburam, Shashi, Sharat, Kali, Jogin, Latu, Tarak and Gopal. The twelfth cloth and rosary were set aside for Girish Chandra Ghosh who later touched them to his head with great devotion. Earlier the Master made metamorphosis internally by instilling in their hearts the burning fire of renunciation; that day he changed them externally with the colour of monasticism and thus he himself founded the Ramakrishna Order indirectly.

He made his most beloved disciple Narendra the leader of his group of children and asked them to take care of him. He said to Narendra : "I leave them all to your care. See that they practise spiritual disciplines even after my passing away and that they do not return home," Narendra afterwards tried to take on the responsibilities to the letter.

Their whole hearted love for the Master, service to him day and night, their practice of spiritual disciplines together, above all, divine intoxication by the Master's grace forged a bond of love for each other and mutual understanding among the monastic disciples.

After the passing away of the Master most of the monastic disciples lived at Baranagore Math 1886. In the middle of December, 1886 Baburam's (later, Swami Premananda) mother, Matangini Devi, invited the young monks to visit Antpur the birthplace of Baburam, during the Christmas Vacation. Narendra with eight other companions went to Antpur. One night they made a huge Dhuni (sacred fire) in the compound and sat around it for meditation. When meditation was over after a long time, Narendra began to tell the story of Christ's love, renunciation and his self-sacrifice for the good of humanity. Standing before the sacred fire, they took the vows of renunciation. Returning to their rooms someone discovered that it was holy Christmas Eve and all felt doubly blessed. Coming back to Baranagore Math they took formal monastic vows with the traditional *viraja homa* ceremony in the early part of 1887 and each of them was given a monastic name by Narendra.

Among the disciples of Sri Ramakrishna it was Narendra who was first aware of the universality of his Master's message—'To serve Jiva as Siva' and the strong humanistic impulse enshrined in it. Swami Saradananda observed : "It was Narendranath alone who, coming out of the room at the end of the Master's ecstasy said, "Ah, What a wonderful light have I got today from the Master's words! In synthesizing the Vedantic knowledge, which was generally regarded as dry, austere and even cruel, with sweet devotion to the Lord, what a new mellowed means of experiencing the Truth has he revealed today! In order to attain the non-dual knowledge, we have been told so long, one should have to renounce the world and the company of men altogether and retire to the forest and mercilessly uproot and throw away love, devotion and other soft and tender emotions from the heart. Formerly when the aspirant tried to attain that knowledge in the old way, he regarded the whole universe and each person in it as obstacles to the path of religion and contracting therefore a hatred for them, he more often than not went astray. But from what the Master in ecstasy said today, it is gathered that the Vedanta of the forest can be brought to human habitation and that it can be applied in practice to the work-a-day world...Thus serving the Jivas as Siva, he will have his heart purified and be convinced in a short time that he himself is also a part of God, the eternally pure, awake and free and bliss Absolute.

"...If the devout aspirant serves the Jivas as Siva or Narayana, he, it is superfluous to say, will see God in all, attain true devotion and have the aim of his life fulfilled in a short time....If the divine Lord ever grants me an opportunity, I'll proclaim everywhere in the world this wonderful truth I have heard today. I will preach this truth to the learned and the ignorant, to the rich and the poor, to the Brahmins and the Chandalas."[3]

Swamiji realized that his Master's message was relevant to an individual and welfare of mankind. He spent four years (July 1893–December 1896) in the West and established the Vedanta Movement there and sowed the seeds of his Master's message and power in the belief that "wherever the seed of His power will find its way, there it will fructify—be it today or in a hundred years."[4] His second visit to America and Europe was on and from Aug. 28, 1899 to Nov. 26, 1900.

Born leader Swamiji knew the spiritual worth of his brother-disciples and in order to make them perfect in every respect and commendable instruments for the fulfillment of Sri Ramakrishna's mission he sometimes spoke so mercilessly. In 1894 he wrote a long letter to his brother-disciples from America :

> ...There is no hope for our nation. Not one original idea crosses anyone's brains, all fighting over the same old, threadbare rug —that Ramakrishna Paramahamsa was such and such—and cock-and bull stories—stories having neither head nor tail. My God! Won't you do something to show that you are in any way removed from the common run of men! —Only indulging in madness!...Today you have your bell, tomorrow you add a horn, and follow suit with a chowry the day after; or you introduce a cot today, and tomorrow you have its legs silver-mounted, and people help themselves to a rice-porridge, and you spin out two thousand cock-and-bull stories–in short, nothing but external ceremoials. This is called in English

> imbecility. Those into whose heads nothing but that sort of stillness enters are called imbecile...
>
> If you want any good to come, just throw your ceremonials overboard and worship the Living God, the Man-God—every being that wears a human form—God in His universal as well as individual aspect...."[5]

Swamiji wanted that his brother-disciples should try to bring out their original ideas consistent with the teachings of Sri Ramakrishna and serve the ailing humanity instead of only performing external rituals mechanically.

The brother-disciples of Swamiji had access to express their opinion or doubts before him. It was an eventful day—May 1, 1897—the foundation day of Ramakrishna Mission. In the meeting Swamiji made Swami Yogananda vice-president of the Calcutta centre. When the meeting was over, Swami Yogananda said to Swamiji, "You are doing these things by Western methods. Would you say that Sri Ramakrishna left us any such instructions?"

The Swami : "How do you know that these methods are not keeping with his ideas? Sri Ramakrishna was the embodiment of infinite ideas; do you want to shut him up in your own limits? I shall break those limits and scatter his ideas broadcast all over the world. He never instructed me to introduce worship of him, and so forth...It is our duty to give the ideas entrusted to us freely to the whole world."...

Swami Yogananda : "Whatever you will, shall come about. We are always ready to follow your leading. I clearly see that the Master is working through you. Still I confess, doubts do sometimes arise in the mind, for, as we saw it, his method of doing things was so different and so I am led to ask myself whether we are not straying from Sri Ramakrishna's teachings."

The Swami : "The thing is this : Sri Ramakrishna is far greater than his disciples understand him to be...one gracious glance of his eyes can create a hundred thousand Vivekanandas at this instant! But if this time he chooses, instead, to work through me, making me his instrument, I can only bow to his will."[6]

One day at Balaram Basu's house Swami Adbutananda complained that Swamiji's ideas of starting Maths and Homes of service for the public good, his ideas of organization and of patriotism were western in conception and were incompatible with the teachings of Sri Ramakrishna. Outburst of emotion and thundering talks of Swamiji and his works dispersed the cloud of doubt and debate on this matter.

Swami Premananda was one of the monastic disciples of Sri Ramakrishna who reached a hasty conclusion that Swamiji had forgotten his master and was going his own way. After reading 'The complete works of Swami Vivekananda' Swami Premananda said : "I have become convinced that unless we look at Sri Ramakrishna through the eyes of Swamiji, we will not know what he was, what he wanted us to do. I am a disciple of Swamiji now. If you ever want to understand Sri Ramakrihna read the works of Swamiji. Think about him. Do what he asked us to do. That is the only way!"[7]

While in America Swamiji felt the need of a monastic order that would carry the message of Vedanta all over the world and would preserve and pass on the legacy of Sri Ramakrishna to the future generations. On 24 January, 1894 he wrote to his disciples in Madras (now Chennai) from Chicago : "...My whole ambition in life is to set in motion a machinery which will bring noble ideas to the door of everybody, and then let men and women settle their own fate..."[8]

Accordingly returning to India Swamiji called a meeting aforesaid of the monastic and lay devotees of Sri Ramakrishna at the Kolkata residence of Balaram Basu on 1 May 1897 and convincing them of the dire need of forming an organization he proposed to the members present that the association should "bear the name of him in whose name we have become sannyasins, taking whom as your ideal you are leading the life of householders, and whose holy name, influence and teachings have within twelve years of his passing away, spread in such unthought-of ways both in the East and in the West." Swamiji's proposal was passed unanimously and the Ramakrishna Mission Association was formed. The Ramakrishna

Mission a social service society and the Ramakrishna Math, a purely monastic Order, became two distinct legal entities from 6 February 1901.

The Ramakrishna Movement meticulously free from politics and based on the ideology of Practical Vedanta, looks upon religion as essentially a science of being and becoming. The three main fields of work of Ramakrishna Math and Ramakrishna Mission are—spirituality, social welfare and propagation of faith. In this stupendous task Swamiji heavily banked on considerable cooperation from his brother disciples.

There is an adage : Many men, many minds. There were marked differences in pedigree, academic qualification, taste and temperament, age etc. among the brother disciples. Despite these and many other differences each of them possessed extra ordinary entity and ability. They had the qualities of adjustment, creative thinking, implementation of new ideas or plans without defying the rules and regulations of the organization.

Swamiji tried to rectify shortcoming of his brother disciples and make them self-supporting. He, with the members of the Baranagore Math often spent their evenings on the roof where they devoted a great deal of time to discussion of the teachings of Sri Ramakrishna, Shankaracharya, Ramanuja, and Jesus Christ, and of Hindu philosophy, European philosophy, the Vedas, the Puranas, and the Tantras. Wherever and whenever he had any opportunity he used to give classes on history, culture and manners of the East and of the West. Under the spell of Swamiji's personality each of them had undergone an amazing metamorphosis from one of the Master's disciples to robust spiritual stalwart...

Swamiji like a magnet attracted his brother disciples to the Baranagore Math and steadily guided and inspired them knitting the brothers together. The inmates of the Math called themselves the 'danas' and the 'daityas' i..e the ghosts and the demons, the companions of Shiva because of their utter indifference to wordly comfort and relationship. "The blazing fire of Naren's personality by its heat welded the heterogeneous elements to be found among the boys into a homogeneous whole of one body and one soul, as it were. They were twelve in number, every one of them a tower of strength in consecration and single-minded devotion."[9]

Each of his brother disciples was able to be worthy assistant to his worthy leader and showed his efficiency in his respective field of work and sincerity in practising spiritual disciplines....

Originality or innovative power of the apostles mattered most to the propagation of ideals of the Master and Swamiji at the genesis of the Ramakrishna Mission. Ramakrishna movement known as Vedanta Movement in the West started with Swamiji's appearance at the world's Parliament of Religions (11-27 September 1893) in Chicago and his subsequent work in the U.S.A. America played the dominant role in the spread of Ramakrishna Movement outside India. During the early phase (1893-1920) there the Movement was initiated by Swamiji and nurtured by Swami Turiyananda, Swami Abhedananda, Swami Saradananda and Swami Trigunatitananda. They preached Vedanta and strengthened and expanded organization there by their tremendous and tireless striving and agility.

Swami Shivananda once remarked :

> Only after travelling over the globe from one end to the other and scrutinizing it closely did Swamiji found this Math and Mission to carry on activities beneficial to the world and particularly to India, according to the directions of the Master. One by one, Swamiji engaged us all in these activities. If we had so wished, we could very well have lived a life of exclusive contemplation and meditation in mountains and forests. As a matter of fact, most of us had been away from the monastery in different places, doing that to some extent. It was Swamiji who called us together and engaged us in different forms of service—the service of God in humanity. Even in our old age we have been carrying on that work.[10]

Once Sri Ramakrishna himself mentioned about originality, novelty and distinction of his beloved children to Balaram Basu :

"The youngsters are yet untouched by 'woman and gold.' That is why I love them so dearly...

"The youngsters' minds are not yet coloured by worldliness. That is why they are so pure in heart. Besides, many of them are eternally perfect; they have been drawn to God from their very birth. It is like a garden in which, while cleaning it, you suddenly discover water-pipes. The water gushes forth without any effort on your part."

"Do you know what these youngsters are like? They are like certain plants that grow, fruit first and then flowers. These devotees first of all have the vision of God; next they hear about his glories and attributes; and at last they are united with Him..."[11]

Once Swamiji scolded Swami Brahmananda harshly for spending extra money while building a ghat and an embankment on the bank of the Ganga for the Belur Monastery under the supervision of Swami Vijnanananda. Learning from Swami Vijnanananda that Swami Brahmananda was crying, Swamiji rushed to his room and embracing his brother disciple said tearfully "Raja, brother, please forgive me. It is my fault that my temper is short and that I scolded you. Please pardon me." Seeing Swamiji weep, Swami Brahmananda was also moved and said, "What does it matter? You have scolded me because you love me—that is all." But Swamiji went on "Brother please forgive me. I know how much the Master loved you and never uttered a harsh word to you. And I, on the other hand for the sake of this petty work have verbally abused you and given you pain. I am not fit to live with you. I shall go away to the Himalayas and live alone in solitude." Swami Brahmananda said, "Don't say that, Swamiji, your scolding is a blessing. How can you leave us? You are our leader. How shall we function without you?" Both of them regained composure.

With reference to that incident Swami Vijnanananda commented : "I shall never forget that scene in my life. I never saw Swamiji weeping so bitterly. What a bond of love existed between them! Swamiji loved his brother disciples like a mother, and that is why he could not bear any shortcoming in them. He wanted them to be as great as himself; nay, even greater than himself. His love was incomparable."[12]

It may be said that the first phase of Ramakrishna movement srarted in 1872 when the tenacious spiritual practices of Sri Ramakrishna for twelve years had culminated in various divine revelations about himself and his life's mission. Swami Saradananda wrote in his magnum opus 'Sri Ramakrishna the great Master' (p.p. 344-345) 'The divine Mother, for Her part, took upon Herself all his responsibilities and with a view to accomplishing a particular purpose of Hers, cast him, without his knowledge, into quite a new mould. By the decree of the universal Mother, the Master came to know that particular purpose of his life at the end of all his Sadhanas. And it was because of this knowledge that he bore with delight the great responsibility of doing good to humanity, thus thrust upon him by the divine Mother with whom he was fully one in love and for whose sake he kept himself just a little separate from Her." Sri Ramakrishna realized that as an instrument in the hands of the Mother of the Universe he would have to found a new community especially fitted for the liberal faith revealed in his own life.

The Mother said, "The Master had the power to die at will. He could have easily given up the body in samādhi. But he would say, "It will be nice if I unite all these youngsters together in a close bond of love..." That is why the Master did not give up the body early, inspite of so much suffering."[13]

Mahendranath Gupta (M.) remarked : "Here (at Cossipore on December 23, 1885) he (Sri Ramakrishna) predicted that a band of young disciples, with Narendranath as their leader, would in due course renounce the world and devote themselves to the realization of God and the service of humanity.[14]

The omniscient Master's prediction proved to be true. After his passing away his beloved children did not take much time to overcome depression for they soon realized that the Master had not left them and his spirit was always with them. Under the leadership of Narendranath they became united and busy with establishing monastery, practising spiritual discipline, travelling and preaching the vedanta. Thanks to these potential sannyasins, particularly their mentor, the Master's holy name and the influence of his unique life and teachings had within twelve years of his demise spread in an unthought-of way both in the East and the West.

Swamiji a great visionary and a prophet with the genius of an amazing planner wrote to Rakhal (Swami Brahmananda) : "But I have all along been like a hero. I want my work to be quick like lightning, and firm as adamant. Likewise shall I die also."[15]

But the Swami knew that his days were numbered. He had a special love and fondness for his 'Raja'(king) Swami Brahmananda whom he looked upon as his 'friend, philosopher and guide' and selected him as his principal assistant to monitor the whole movement. Swamiji trained Raja Maharaj in every possible way so that he might shoulder the entire responsibility as his worthy successor. In order to give him scope to work more freely Swamiji resigned from the presidentship of the organization and Swami Brahmananda was elected president on February 10, 1901 and held the office for over two decades. On seeing Swami Brahmananda's efficiency in streamlining the activities of the organization Swamiji remarked :

"I have been stunned to see Raja's work. How nicely he is running the Math! About him Sri Ramakrishna used to say, 'He can rule a Kingdom.'"[16]

Swamiji had great faith in Swami Brahmananda's love and loyalty and said, "Others may desert me, but Raja will stand by me till the last." Swami Brahmananda cried like a child over the still body of Swamiji and when Swami Saradananda lifted him up, Swami Brahmananda said : "It is as if the whole Himalayan Mountains have disappeared from before my eyes!"

Though the premature passing away of Swamiji was an irreparable loss and unbearable blow to his brother disciples, Swami Brahmananda held the helm of the Order with his profound experience, indomitable self-relience and with the personality of a spiritual giant under the guidence of the Holy Mother the supreme spiritual authority whose words were mandatory for the direct disciples and other monks. In the first phase of Ramakrishna

Movement (1872-1905) the tenure of the combined administration of spiritual head Swami Brahmananda (President 1901–1922) and executive head Swami Saradananda (General Secretary 1898–1927) saw the golden period in which the Movement was consolidated and expanded. In the second phase (1906–1936) the movement continued its progress under the enlightened leadership of Swami Shivananda (1922–1934) and Swami Akhandananda (1934–1937) with the co-operation of other nine direct disciples of Sri Ramakrishna whom Swami Vimalatmananda described as the 'lighthouses of the Movement.'[17]

Swami Vijnanananda, (President 1937–1938) the last but one (Swami Abhedananda) surviving direct monastic disciple of Sri Ramakrishna, laid the foundation stone of the Sri Ramakrishna Temple for the second time on 16 July 1935 and the new temple was opened for all by the Swami on 14 July 1938.

The more the Movement showed through different activities its all-round progress—spiritual, cultural, educational, medical and general; the more our countrymen were interested in the Movement which was regarded as one of the well-organized nation-building movements in India. By this time the monastic disciples of Sri Ramakrishna set up seventy-three branch centres through-out the world and attached to these were nine sub-centres. With the passing away of Swami Vijnanananda the baton of conducting the movement was handed over to the descendants.

In the previous chapters the uniqueness of the Master and the Holy Mother in various aspects has been discussed and subsequently the intrinsic originality, austerity, renunciation, sprituality, firm faith in the ideal, stainless character, universal outlook, devotion to work, sincerity, obedience to the leader, graceful personality and absolute dependence on Sri Ramakrishna and the Mother of sixteen apostles have been elucidated meticulously. The monastic disciples of the Master contributed much to the spontaneous growth of the Movement and gave the Order an international identity.

Swamiji spoke about his ever-trusted brother disciples : "Look at that handful of young men called into existence by the divine touch of Ramakrishna's feet. They have preached the message from Assam to Sindh, from the Himalayas to Cape Comorin. They have crossed the Himalayas at a height of twenty thousand feet, over snow and ice on foot, and penetrated into the mysteries of Tibet. They have begged their bread, covered themselves with rags; they have been persecuted, followed by the police, kept in prison and at last set free when the Government was convinced of their innocence."[18]

Each of the monastic disciples bore individual distinctive entity and had developed into robust spiritual stalwart. Swamiji realized that the universal message (To serve Jiva as Siva') of Sri Ramakrishna was directly relevant to the individual and collective welfare of mankind. He was eager to set up a permanent orgaization which would activate the message in practical field and preserve and pass on the legacy and spiritual lessons of Sri Ramakrishna to the future generations. In this Herculean task he earnestly banked on substantial cooperation from his beloved brother-disciples who dedicated themselves to the task of translating the vision of Swamiji into reality. To quote Swami Gahananda, "Even a cursory glance at the lives of some of these apostles gives us an idea of the unique role each one of them played in promoting the ideas and ideals of the Mission."[19]

In 1899 one day at Nilambar Mukherjee's garden Math during conversations Swamiji's disciple Sharat Chandra Chakravarty said: "Sir, it is impossible for any other man to labour for this magazine in the ways Swami Trigunatita does."

Swamiji replied : "Do you think these Sannyasin children of Sri Ramakrishna are born simply to sit under trees lighting Dhuni-fires? Whenever any of them will take up some work, people will be astonished to see their energy. Learn from them how to work. Here, for instance, Trigunatita has given up his spiritual practices, his meditation and everything, to carry out my orders, and has set himelf to work. Is this a matter of small sacrifice? What an amount of love for me is at the back of this spirit of work, do you see? He will not stop short of success! Have you householders such determination?

"...You have not yet got the capacity to make any enterprise stand on its legs. That is reserved only for these all renouncing Sannyasins to do. They will work themselves to death, but never yield. Whereas a little resistance or just a trifle of criticism is bewildering to you.

"...Well, Sri Ramakrishna is our centre. Each one of us is a ray of that light-centre..."[20]

In March 1875 the Brahmo leader and scholar Keshab Chandra Sen realized that Sri Ramakrishna was a great spiritual luminary. To share his discovery with others he mentioned about the saint in his sermons and in his writings for journals e.g., 'We met not long ago Paramahamsa of Dakshineswar, and were charmed by the depth, penetration and simplicity of his spirit. The never-ceasing metaphors and analogies in which he indulged, are most of them as apt as they are beautiful. The characteristics of his mind are the very opposite to those of Pandit Dayananda Saraswati, the former being so gentle, tender and contemplative, as the latter is sturdy, masculine and polemical."[21] The Brahmos, people belonging to various faiths, householders and youths from different strata of society started to visit Sri Ramakrishna in Dakshineswar, particularly on weekends and holidays. Brahmos and Hindus invited him to their houses and temples. His charming talks, child-like simplicity, devotional songs, dancing in joy and ecstasy were of prime attraction for the people. So his every visit turned into a festival. The number of his devotees began to increase gradually. In this way the Movement had a humble beginning. Among the monastic disciples of the Master it was Swami Abhedananda who passed away last in 1939. During this genesis period (1875-1939) the Master, the Mother and their sixteen children played important role in consolidating, intensifying and extending the movement both at home and abroad. Swamiji sent Swami Ramakrishnananda to Madras (now Chennai). to start a monastery there. It was mainly due to Swami Ramakrishnananda that the message of Sri Ramakrishna spread far and wide in South India. Swamiji sent Swami Vijnanananda to open a centre at Allahabad. Swami Akhandananda devoted himself to run a multi-functional ashrama in Sargachi. On the other hand, Swamis Saradananda, Turiyananda, Abhedananda and Trigunatitananda helped their leader continue his mission of spreading the message of Vedanta in England and America. Swamiji was so impressed by the enthusiastic performances of those brother-disciples that he commented : "Even if I perish on this plane, my message will be sounded through these dear lips and the world will hear it."[22]

Each of the brother-monks was able to study situation properly, take up challenges confidently and solve problems along with preaching and performing philanthropic work without distorting the basic tenets of the organization. They gave topmost priority over two cardinal principles of the Master i.e., love for the highest spiritual goal and fraternity among the monastic disciples besides of course over formal adherence to rules and regulations in the twin organizations–the Ramakrishna Math and the Ramakrishna Mission.

Ramakrishna-Vivekananda movement made a profound impact on the renaissance of India. Sri Ramakrishna taught 'As many faiths, so many paths', 'To serve Jiva as Siva' and thus established religion on the broader concept of tolerance, acceptence and humanity. On the other hand, Swamiji placed before the monks of the Ramakrishna Mission a twofold motto : *ātmano moksārtham jagat hitāya ca* as has been said in the Rig Veda— for one's own salvation and for the good of the world. The second part i.e. welfare of the humanity of this age-old ideal of monasticism was ignored for ages by the Sannyasins who were eager for their own salvation by means of performing spiritual disciplines and meditation isolating themselves from the society.

Swamiji emphasized the importance of the second part also. The mission of the Ramakrishna Mission was in the words of the Swami, 'evolving a God out of the material man'. The Ramakrishna Math and the Ramakrishna Mission cherished another aspect of practical Vedanta—the philosophy of the equation of work with worship. This movement built a bridge between the East and the West, between ancient and modern ideals, between two millennia.

Besides practice of spiritual disciplines and study of scriptures the moanstic disciples of the Master tried to make people aware of rationalism and humanity those are the main characteristics of renaissance. Their sacrifice and service to humanity kindled a fire of patriotism in the hearts of their countrymen.

It would not be possible for Swamiji and his brother-disciples to make their revolutionary movement so popular and extensive within a short period of only sixty five years without their individual originality and innovative skill and dedication. To quote a judicious comment : "...the monks of the Ramakrishna Order have often shown—quite apart from their scrupulous honesty and unfailing dedication—a degree of organizational, managerial and administrative ability that could well be the envy of professional specialists in different spheres of activity."[23]

The primary architects of the Ramakrishna Order built its foundation so strong and durable that Swami Gambhirananda an illustrious historian of the Order could optimistically comment recently (2015?) :

> We fervently hope and wish that future historians will continue to record the illustrious story of the further growth and development of the various activities of this dynamic, profoundly spiritual and universally esteemed twin organizations, and also truly assess its expanding impact and influence upon India and the world.[24]

We may refer to the evaluation of some special traits of Swamiji and his brother-disciples by Sister Nivedita : "For the Swami was nothing, if not a breaker of bondage. And it was essential that there should be those about him who understood the polar difference between his breaches of customs and those of the idly self-indulgent. Nothing in the early days of my life in India struck me so forcibly or so repeatedly as the steadiness with which the other members of the Order fulfilled this part of the mission laid upon them. Men whose own lives were cast in the strictest mould of Hindu orthodoxy, or even of asceticism, were willing to eat with the Europeans whom their leader had accepted. Was the Swami seen dining in Madras with an Englishman and his wife? Was it said that while in the West he had touched beef or wine? Not a quiver was seen on the faces of his brethren. It was not for them to question, not for them to explain, not even for them to ask for final justification and excuse. Whatever he did, wherever he might lead, it was their place to be found unflinching at his side. And surely none can pass this spectacle in review, without its being borne in upon him, that meaningless as would have been the Order of Ramakrishna without Vivekananda, even so futile would have been the life and labours of Vivekananda, without behind him, his brothers of the Order of Ramakrishna. It was said to me lately by one of the older generation that "Ramakrishna had lived for the making of Vivekananda." Is it indeed so? Or is it not rather impossible to distinguish with such fixity between one part and another, in a single mighty utterance of the Divine Mother-heart? Often it appears to me, in studying all these lives, that there has been with us a soul named Ramakrishna-Vivekananda, and that, in the penumbra of his being, appear many forms, some of which are with us still, and of none of whom it could be said with entire truth that here ends, in relation to him, the sphere of those others, or that there begins his own."[25]

J. J. Goodwin wrote to Mrs. Bull on May 23, 1897 : "When the Paramahamsa was passing away he called in all his disciples but Swamiji (Naren) and gave them an express command that they were always to pay every attention to Swamiji and never to leave anything undone that could add to his health or comfort. Then sending them out and calling in Swamiji (Naren) he committed all his other disciples into his charge." Thus the Master brought his holy children closer together with mutual love and respect and understanding without harbouring malice, egoism or complex. It was interesting to observe how they enjoyed fun, indoor games and sometimes differed in their opinions on work, and how quickly they were able to reconcile their difference.

"Previously Sri Ramakrishna had said to Narendranath "My Siddhis [powers] will manifest through you in time." One day the Master almost unable to speak, wrote on a piece of paper, "Narendra will teach others." His most beloved disciple at once replied, "I won't do that." But the Master replied, "You shall have to do it." Another day the Master transmitted his spiritual power to Narendra by steadfastly looking at him and said : "O Naren, today I have given you my all and have become a Fakir, a penniless beggar. By the force of the power transmitted by me, great things will be done by you; only after that will you go where you came from."[26]

Every word of the Master came true. His monastic disciples with their original resources and bent under the leadership of Swamiji grew into an indomitable power. Secondly Swamiji taught the world an international religion of humanity. And thirdly, he, in the cooperation with his worthy stalwarts had done 'great things' by introducing a historic and revolutionary movement throughout the world.

There goes a proverb : 'Like guru like disciple'. It is amazing to think that Sri Ramakrishna was such a superhuman teacher possessing originality that he took only about six years (1880–1885) to train sixteen apostles who by dint of their individual originality prowess and leonine spirit introduced a non-political international spiritual and philanthropic movement.

In this age of 'the fret and the fever' the historic proclamation of Sri Ramakrishna— 'As many faiths, so many paths' and his other teachings are the antidote to fanaticism, narrowness and intolerance towards different religions.

Swamiji and his brother disciples helped people realize that religion was essentially a science of 'being and becoming' and not performing rituals merely. Victor Hugo said, 'Nothing is more powerful than an idea whose time has come.' The strength of the Ramakrishna Movement lies in its ideas and ideals. During the genesis period the stalwart monks, with their innate qualities had succeeded in spreading these ideas those produced silent but inevitable impact on the minds of the people like a catalyst transforming their outlook.

Sticking strictly to the teachings of the great trio–Sri Ramakrishna, the Holy Mother and Swamiji and the fundamental principles and ideals of the Order each of the monastic disciples exerted his personal entities, his verbal and mental dexterity in order to expedite the unprecedented movement as the moon exerts a force on the earth that causes the tide.

REFERENCES

INTRODUCTION

1. The complete Works of Swami Vivekananda, Vol. 7, Advaita Ashrama, Kol., 2012, henceforth Works, P. 491.
2. Works, Vol. 5, P. 140.
3. Works, Vol. 4, P. 168.
4. **Hamlet, Prince of Denmark** — Shakespeare (The Tudor Edition of William Shakespeare, The complete works, Ed. Peter Alexander, The Eng. Book Agency and Collins) P. 1047.

CHAPTER - 1 SRI RAMAKRISHNA

1. Sri Sri Ramakrishna Paramahamsadever Jibanvrittanta — Ramchandra Dutta, Udbodhan office. 8th Ed. Preface P - 2.
2. My Master — Swami Vivekananda, Works, Vol. 4, P.P. 170 - 171.
3. Ramakrishna as We saw Him — Ed & trans. Swami Chetanananda, Vedanta Society : St. Louis 1990, P. 99
4. God Lived With Them — Swami Chetanananda, (Advaita Ashrama, Kol. 2011, henceforth God lived with them) P. 535.
5. Straight Talk on Religion : Excerpts from the Complete Works of Swami Vivekananda (internet)
6. My Master — Works, Vol. 4, P.P. 165, 167 - 168.
7. The Gospel of Sri Ramakrishna — Trans. by Swami Nikhilananda, Sri Ramakrishna Math, Madras henceforth the Gospel, P.P. 13 - 14.
8. Ramakrishna and His Disciples — Christopher Isherwood, Methuen & Co. London, 1974, P. 85

9. My Master — Works, P. 184.
10. Isherwood, P. 209.
11. My Master — Works, Vol. 4, P. 171.
12. Ibid, P.P 171 - 172.
13. The Gospel, P. 31
14. Ibid, P. 35.
15. My Master — Works, Vol. 4, P. 179.
16. God Lived — P. 537.
17. The Gospel, P. 726.
18. Ibid, P. 881.
19. Works, Vol. 7, P. 413.
20. God Lived — P. 137.
21. Works, Vol. 8, P. 84.
22. God Lived — P. 449.
23. The Master As I Saw Him — Sister Nivedita, Udbodhan Office, 1962, P. 285, Henceforth The Master.
24. Swami Prajnanananda, Man O Manush (Ramakrishna Vedanta Math, Calcutta 1959) P. 331.
25. The Gospel, P. 980.
26. Swami Vividishnanda, A Man of God (Ramakrishna Math, Madras, 1957) P. 262.
27. The First Disciples of Sri Ramakrishna, Spiritual Talks (Advaita Ashrama, Calcutta 1968) P.P. 99 - 100.
28. Sri Ramakrishna, The Great Master — Swami Saradananda, Trans. by Swami Jagadananda (Ramakrishna Math, Madras, 1979) II, P. 933, hence forth The Great Master.
29. Sri Sri Latu Maharajer Smritikatha — Chandra Sekhar Chattopadhyay (Udbodhan Office, Calcutta, 1953) P. 400.
30. Ramakrishna as We Saw Him — Ed. & Trans. by Swami Chetanananda (Vedanta Society : St. Louis, 1990) P. 218.
31. The Master — P.P. 287 - 288.
32. Ibid, P. 289.
33. Works, Vol. 7, P.P. 411 - 412.
34. Gospel — P.P. 101 - 102.
35. Ibid, P. 111 - 112.

36. Ibid, P. 128 - 129.
37. Ibid, P. 133 - 135, 137 - 138.
38. Ibid, P. 138.
39. Ibid, P. 155.
40. Ibid, P. 157 - 158.
41. Ibid, P. 191.
42. Ibid, P. 246.
43. Ibid, P. 261, 264 - 265.
44. Ibid, P. 392 - 393.
45. Ibid, P. 429.
46. Ibid, P. 449.
47. Ibid, P. 514.
48. Ibid, P. 548 - 549.
49. Ibid, P. 689.
50. Ibid, P. 699.
51. Ibid, P. 701.
52. Ibid, P. 719.
53. Ibid, P. 723,
54. Ibid, P. 729, 731.
55. Ibid, P. 776 - 777.
56. Ibid, P. 817.
57. Ibid, P. 844.
58. Ibid, P. 846.
59. Ibid, P. 862, 867.
60. Ibid, P. 874.
61. Ibid, P. 899.
62. Ibid, P. 917.
63. Ibid, P. 956 - 957.
64. Swami Premananda : Teachings and Reminiscences - Ed. & Trans. by Swami Prabhavananda (Vedanta Press : Hollywood, 1968) P. 114.
65. Ramakrishna as We Saw Him — Ed. & Trans. by Swami Chetanananda (Vedanta Society : S. Louis, 1990) P. 102.
66. My Master — Works, Vol. 4, P. 183.
67. The First Disciples of Sri Ramakrishna, The Message of Our Master (Advaita Asrama, Calcutta, 1944) P. 43.

68. My Master — Works, Vol. 4, P. 185.
69. Ibid, P. 187.
70. Gospel P. 47.
71. God Lived — Swami Chetanananda, Advaita Ashrama, Kol., P. 7.
72. Gospel, P.P. 1023 - 1024.
73. My Master — Works, Vol. 4, P. 178.
74. Isherwood, P. 195.
75. Conversations and Dialogues — Works, Vol. VII, P. 206 - 207.
76. The Life of Vivekananda and the Universal Gospel — Romain Rolland (Advaita Ashram, Kol.) P. 100.
77. Vivekananda : The Yogas and Other Works -— Swami Nikhilananda (Ramakrishna Vivekananda Centre, New York, 1953) P. 146.
78. Amar Jivankatha — Swami Abhedananda (Ramakrishna Vedanta Math, Calcutta. 1964) P. 88.
79. Life of Sri Ramakrishna (Advaita Ashrama, Kol. 1943) P. 401.
80. Ramakrishna as We Saw Him — Ed. & trans. Swami Chetanananda (Vedanta Society : St. Louis, 1990) P. 178.
81. The Gospel, P. 440.
82. *Sri Sri Latu Maharajer Smritikatha* — Chandra Sekhar Chattopadhyay, P.P. 165 - 166.
83. Men I Have Seen (Sadharan Brahmo Samaj, Calcutta, 1966) P.P. 66 - 67.
84. The Gospel, P. 72.
85. Ibid, P. 983.
86. Ibid, P. 195.
87. Ibid, P. 312.
88. Ibid, P. 390.
89. Ibid, P.P. 418 - 419.
90. God Lived, P. 519.
91. *Life of Sri Ramakrishna* (Advaita Ashrama, Kol., 1977) Foreword, XI.
92. The Great Master — P. 804.
93. Ibid, P. 804.
94. Gospel, P. 3.
95. The Great Master — P. 805.
96. Ibid, P. 333.

97. Works — Vol. 7, P. 411 - 412.
98. The Life of Ramakrishna — Romain Rolland, Advaita Ashrama, Kol., P. XXII.
99. The Great Master — P. 1281.

CHAPTER - 2 HOLY MOTHER

1. Holy Mother —Swami Nikhilananda (Ramakrishna -Vivekananda Center : New York, 1962) P. 2.
2. Devi Mahatmyam — English Trans. by Swami Jagadiswarananda, Sri Ramakrishna Math, Mylapore, Madras.
3. Holy Mother Sri Sarada Devi — Swami Gambhirananda, Sri Ramakrishna Math, Mylapore, Madras, P. 66.
4. Padaprantey — Part-I (1st Ed.) P. 2.
5. Holy Mother Sri Sarada Devi — P. 73.
6. God lived with them — Swami Chetanananda, Advaita Ashrama, Kol., P. 189.
7. Holy Mother Sri Sarada Devi — P. 216.
8. Ibid, P.P. 102-103.
9. Ibid, P. 46.
10. Works — Vol. 7, P.P. 484 - 485.
11. Holy Mother Sri Sarada Devi — P. 97.
12. God lived with them — P. 487.
13. Holy Mother Sri Sarada Devi — P. 336.
14. Ibid, P. 337.
15. Ibid, P. 345.
16. Ibid, P. 345.
17. Ibid, P. 345.
18. Ibid, P. 346.
19. Ibid, P. 347.
20. Ibid, P. 347.
21. Ibid, P. 350.
22. Ibid, P. 355.
23. Works — Vol. 7, P.P. 484 - 485
24. Prabuddha Bharata or Awakened India, January 2014, Vol. 119, No. 1, P. 188.

25. Holy Mother Sri Sarada Devi — P. 137.
26. The Gospel of Sri Ramakrishna, Sri Ramakrishna Math, Madras — P. 73.
27. Holy Mother Sri Sarada Devi — P. 137.
28. Ibid, P. 309.
29. Ibid, P. 311.
30. Ibid, P. 58.
31. Ibid, P.P. 115 - 116.
32. God lived with them — P. 189.
33. Ibid, P. 209.
34. Ibid, P. 232.
35. *Matri Sannidhey*, Swami Ishanananda, Udbodhan Office, Kol. — P. 230.
36. Sri Sarada Devi and her divine play — Swami Chetanananda, Vedanta Society of St. Louis, P. 674.
37. Ibid, P. 677 - 679.
38. Swami Nikhilananda, Holy Mother, Ramakrishna - Vivekananda Center : New York, 1962, P. 261.

CHAPTER - 3 'JEWELS OF CHILDREN'

1. *Holy Mother Sri Sarada Devi*, Swami Gambhirananda, Sri Ramakrishna Math, Madras, P. 126.
2. *The Gospel of Sri Ramakrishna*, P. P. 230–231.
3. *Works*, Vol. 4, P. 186.
4. *Works*, Vol. 8, P. P. 80, 83–84.

CHAPTER - 4 SWAMI VIVEKANANDA

1. The Life of Ramakrishna — Romain Rolland, Advaita Ashrama, Kol., P. P. 169 - 171.
2. The Life of Vivekananda and the Universal Gospel — Romain Rolland, Advaita Ashrama, Kol., P. 2.
3. Ibid, P.P. 2 - 3.
4. Sri Ramakrishna the Great Master — Swami Saradananda, Sri Ramakrishna Math, Mylapore Chennai, P. 1031, Henceforth, the Great Master.

5. God lived with them — Swami Chetanananda, Advaita Ashrama, Kol., P. - 21.
6. The Great Master — P. 1024.
7. Ibid, P. 1025.
8. Ibid, P. 1025.
9. The Life of Swami Vivekananda — His Eastern and Western Disciples, Advaita Ashrama, Calcutta, 1979, I : 48.
10. Ibid, Vol. 1, P. 107.
11. The Complete Works of Swami Vivekananda — Advaita Ashrama, Kol., Vol. 5, P.P. 365 - 366, Henceforth Works.
12. Ibid, Vol. 5, P. 461.
13. Ibid, Vol. 7, P.P. 357 - 359.
14. The Master As I Saw Him — Sister Nivedita, Udbodhan office, Kol., P. 74. Henceforth, the Master.
15. Works — Vol. 5, P.P. 258 - 259.
16. Ibid, P.P. 372 - 374.
17. Ibid, Vol. 7, P. 407.
18. Notes of Some Wanderings with the Swami Vivekananda - Sister Nivedita, Udbodhan office, Kol., P. 73. Henceforth Notes.
19. Swami Vivekananda in the West New Discoveries — Marie Louise Burke Part-1, Advaita Ashrama, Kol., P. 281 (Henceforth, Discoveries).
20. Smritir Aloy Swamiji (Beng.) — Ed. Swami Purnatmananda, Udbodhan office, Kol., P. 15.
21. Works — Vol. 5, P.P. 361 - 363.
22. Works — Vol. 7, P. 407.
23. Discoveries — P. 27.
24. Gospel — P.P. 810 - 811.
25. The Life of Swami Vivekananda, Vol. 1, P. 418.
26. The Master — P. 10.
27. Reminiscences of Swami Vivekananda — P. 454.
28. Discoveries — P. 85.
29. Ibid, P. 86.
30. Ibid, P. 100.
31. Ibid, P. 101.

32. 'Swami Vivekananda' — Prabuddha Bhārata, July, 1932, P. 352.
33. Discoveries — P. 81.
34. Ibid, P.P. 83 - 84.
35. Ibid, P. 84.
36. Ibid, P. 126.
37. Ibid, P. 137.
38. Ibid, P. 305.
39. The Great Master — P. 1026.
40. Works — Vol. 4, P. 203.
41. Works — Vol. 5, P.P. 104 - 105.
42. Works — Vol. 5, P. 381.
43. The introduction of Marx's work, A contribution to the Critique of Hegel's Philosophy of Right.
44. Works — Vol. 2, P. 360.
45. Works — Vol. 3, P.P. 220 - 221.
46. Works — Vol. 2, P. 259.
47. Works — Vol. 8, P.P. 134 - 135, 141.
48. Works — Vol. 2, P. 301.
49. Lacon : or Many things in a few words (1820) - Charles Caleb Calton
50. Sri Aurobindo — Vol. 2, 1972, P. 37.
51. Works — Vol. 3, P. 151.
52. Nivedita Lokamata — Shankari Prasad Basu, Ananda Publishers, Calcutta 1968, P.P. 320 - 321.
53. The Life of Swami Vivekananda — 2. 206.
54. Ibid — 2. 333.
55. Paradoxical Prophet — Swami Yogeshananda, <http. : //vedanta-atanta.org/article-archive/essays-on-swami-vivekananda/swami-vivekananda-paradoxcal-prophet > accessed 30 October 2013.
56. Swami Vivekananda : A Creative Genius - Dr. Gururaj Karjagi, Prabuddha Bharata Jan. 2014, Vol. 119, No. 1, P.P. 64 - 65.
57. Works — Vol. 5, P.P. 381 - 383.
58. Works — Vol. 7, P.P. 491 - 497.
59. Works — Vol. 8, P. 425.
60. Works — Vol. 4, P.P. 479 - 480.
61. Works — Vol. 3, P. 309.

62. Works — Vol. 3, P.P. 104 - 110.
63. Works — Vol. 3, P.P. 225 - 226.
64. Works — Vol. 3, P.P. 300 - 301.
65. Works — Vol. 5, P.P. 50 - 52.
66. Works — Vol. 5, P.P. 383 - 384.
67. Works — Vol. 5, P. 80.
68. Works — Vol. 4, P.P. 367 - 368.
69. Swami Vivekananda, *Prabuddha Bhārata*, July, 1932, P. 352.
70. The Master — P. 175.
71. An Advanced History of India — Dr. R. C. Majumdar, Macmillan & Co. Ltd. P. 886.
72. Works — Vol. 1, Sister Nivedita, Introduction, P. XVII.
73. Works — Vol. 3, P.P. 145 - 146, 154.
74. Works — Vol. 3, P. 220.
75. Works — Vol. 3, P. 285.
76. Works — Vol. 3, P.P. 316 - 317.
77. Works — Vol. 5, P.P. 80 - 81.
78. Works — Vol. 5, P. 381.
79. Works — Vol. 3, P. 151.
80. Works — Vol. 3, P. 160.
81. Works — Vol. 3, P.P. 223 - 224.
82. Works — Vol. 3, P. 318.
83. Works — Vol. 3, P. 320.
84. Works — Vol. 4, P. 366.
85. Sri Aurobindo —Vol. 17, 1971, P. 332.
86. Works — Vol. 5, P.P. 15 - 16.
87. Works — Vol. 5, P. 91.
88. 'Swami Vivekananda' — Prabuddha Bhārata, July, 1932, P. 352.
89. 'Vivekananda' — Udbodhan, Ashwin, 1348 issue.
90. Gospel — P. 985.
91. Ibid, P.P. 810 - 811.
92. Vivekananda : The Yogas and Other Works - Swami Nikhilananda, Ramakrishna Vivekananda Center : New York, 1953, P. 15.
93. Ramakrishna and His Disciples — Christopher Isherwood, Methuen & Co. : London, 1965, P. 20.

94. Works — Vol. 7, P.P. 206 - 207.
95. Gospel — P. 994.
96. Ibid, P. 979.
97. Works — Vol. 7, P.P. 248 - 249.
98. Gospel — P. 990.
99. Works — Vol. 4, P. 369.
100. Ibid, P.P. 178, 180.
101. Prabuddha Bharata, 1978 — P. 125.
102. Works — Vol. 7, P. 490.
103. Works — Vol. 8, P.P. 397 - 398.
104. Ibid, P. 406.
105. Ibid, P. 441.
106. Ibid, P.P. 454 - 455.
107. Ibid, P.P. 456 - 457.
108. Reminiscences of Swami Vivekananda — His Eastern and Western Admirers, Advaita Ashrama, Calcutta, 1983, P. 258.
109. The Life of Swami Vivekananda — P. 263.
110. Ibid, P. 263 - 264.
111. Ibid, P. 271.
112. Works — Vol. 6, P. 288.
113. Ibid, P. 289, 293.
114. Works — Vol. 3, P. 301.
115. The Master — P. 175.
116. *Swamijir Smriti Sanchayan* —Swami Nirlepananda, Karuna Prakashani, Kol. 1967, P. 12.
117. Works — Vol. 6, P. 239.
118. Works — Vol. 4, P. 173.
119. Works — Vol. 7, P. 63.
120. Ibid, P. 85.
121. Ibid, P. 92.
122. Ibid, P.P. 413 - 414.
123. Works — Vol. 3, P.P. 312 - 313.
124. Works — Vol. 7, P.P. 482 - 485.
125. The Master — P. 238.

126. Works — Vol. 3, P. 505.
127. Works — Vol. 6, P. 272.
128. Works — Vol. 8, P. 455.
129. Ibid, P. 57.
130. The Great Master — P. 1126.
131. The Gospel — P. 72.
132. Works — Vol. 1, P. 327.
133. Works — Vol. 7, P. 224.
134. The Gospel — P. 981.
135. Reminiscences of Swami Vivekananda, -His Eastern and Western Admirers — 1st Ed. 1961, (Sister Christine) P. 154.
136. Spiritual Talks by The First Disciples of Shri Ramakrishna (1955) Published by Swami Vireswarananda — Advaita Ashrama, Mayavati — P. 254.
137. Discoveries — P.P. 484 - 486.
138. Ibid, P. 488.
139. The Master — P.P. 88 - 89.
140. Works — Vol. 8, P.P. 450 - 451.
141. Notes — P. 19.
142. Works — Vol. 5, P. 137.
143. Works — Vol. 8, P. 464.
144. Ibid, P. 480.
145. Works — Vol. 6, P.P. 431 - 432.
146. Works — Vol. 5, P.P. 136 - 137.
147. The Life of Swami Vivekananda — Vol. II, P. 147.
148. Ramakrishna and His Disciples —Christopher Isherwood, P. 188.
149. Meditation and its Methods — Ed. Swami Chetanananda, Vedanta Press, Hollywood 1976, P. 19.
150. Gospel — P. 980.
151. Ibid, P. 981.
152. Ibid, P. 985.
153. The Master — P. 76.
154. Notes — P. 12.
155. Swami Vivekananda Centenary Memorial Volume — P. 233.

156. Works — Vol. 3, P. 481.
157. Works — Vol. 4, P. 177 - 178.
158. The Master — P. 88.
159. The Life of Swami Vivekananda — Vol. I, 454.
160. Works — Vol. 6, P. 283.
161. The Life of Swami Vivekananda — Vol. II, 293.

CHAPTER - 5 SWAMI BRAHMANANDA

1. The Gospel — P. 231.
2. Ibid, P. 332.
3. Ibid, P. 331.
4. Ibid, P.P. 534 - 535.
5. Ibid, P. 192.
6. Ibid, P. 957.
7. Ibid, P. 996.
8. Swami Chetanananda, *God Lived with them* — Advaita Ashrama, Kol. 2011, P. 86.
9. The Gospel — P. 994.
10. Works — Vol. 7, P. 258.
11. Swami Bhrahmananda —Udbodhan Office, Calcutta 1941, P. 180.
12. Works — Vol. 5, P. 175.
13. Swami Ashokananda, *Swami Brahmananda* — Vedanta Society, San Francisco, 1970, P.P. 26 - 27.
14. Works — Vol. 5, P. 176.
15. *The Apostles of Sri Ramakrishna* — Comp. & Ed. Swami Gambhirananda, Advaita Ashrama, Calcutta, 1967, P. 98.
16. Works — Vol. 7, P. 491.
17. *Vedanta and the West* — Hollywood, 108 : 43
18. *The Eternal Companion* — Swami Prabhavananda, Vedanta Press, Hollywood, 1960, P. 59.
19. Swami Prabhananda, Brahmananda Charit — Udbodhan Office, Calcutta 1982, P. 255.
20. Sister Devamata, *Days in an Indian Monastery* — Ananda Ashrama, La Crescenta, 1927, P. 161.

21. Swami Narottamananda, *Raja Maharaj* — Udbodhan Office, Calcutta, 1954, P. 90.
22. Brahmachari Akshay Chaitanya, *Brahmananda Lilakatha* — New Bharat Publisher, Calcutta, 1972, P. 171.
23. Swami Mukteswarananda, *Smritikatha* — Calcutta, 1970. P. 156.
24. *Udbodhan* 62 : 36.
25. Swami Ashokananda — P.P. 48 - 49.
26. *The Story of a Dedicated Life* — Ramakrishna Math, Madras, 1959, P. 141.
27. *The Eternal Companion* — P. 158.
28. *Smritikatha* — P. 141.
29. Swami Chetanananda, Trans., *A Guide to Spiritual Life*, (Vedanta Sociaty) St. Louis, 1988) P.P. 123 - 125.
30. Swami Satprakashananda, *Sri Ramakrishna's Life and Message in the Present Age* (Vedanta Society, St. Louis, 1976) P. 130.
31. Swami Chetanananda, *Swami Adbhutananda : Teachings and Reminiscences* (Vedanta Society, St. Louis, 1980) P. 100.
32. *The Eternal Companion* — P. 163.
33. Ibid, P. 87.
34. Hemanta Kumar Sarkar, *Subhaser sange baro bachhar : 1912 - 24*, 1946, P. 36.
35. *Udbodhan*, Ashwin, 1354, P. 459.
36. Dilip Kumar Roy, *Smriticharan*, 1367, P. 335.
37. *Brahmananda* — P. 226.
38. Works — Vol. 7, P. 507.
39. Swami Jagadiswarananda, *Swami Vijnanananda*, Ramakrishna Math, Allahabad, 1947, P. 243.
40. *Udbodhan*, Vivekananda Centenary Number; P. 262.
41. *Swami Brahmananda* — P. 35.
42. Swami Yatiswarananda, *Meditation and Spititual Life*, Ramakrishna Ashram Bangalore, 1979, P. XIX.
43. *A Guide to Spiritual Life* — P.P. 22 - 23.
44. *Lilakatha* — P. 81 - 82.
45. *Smritikatha* — P. 93.

46. Swami Nikhilananda, *Holy Mother,* Ramakrishna Vivekananda Center, New York, 1962, P. 309.
47. *Brahmananda Charit* — P.P. 314 - 315.
48. *Brahmananda* — P. 281.
49. *Udbodhan,* 48 : 13; *Ramakrishna Parikar,* P. 126.
50. *Smritikatha* — P.P. 81 - 83.
51. *The Eternal Companion* — P. 78.
52. *Lilakatha* — P. 184.
53. Sri Sri Ma O Sri Ramakrishna Parsadganaer Smritikatha — Ramakrishna Shivananda Ashrama, Barasat, 1965; P.P. 30 - 31.
54. Christopher Isherwood, Ramakrishna and His Disciples, Methuen & Co., London, 1965. P.P. 329 - 330.
55. Smritir Aloy Swamiji, Ed. Swami Purnatmananda, Udhodhan Office, P. 119.
56. Ibid, P. 242.
57. Prachin Sadhuder Katha (1st Part) — Swami Chetanananda, Udbodhan Office, 2nd Ed. P. 189.
58. The Gospel — P. 996.
59. *A Guide to Spiritual Life : Spiritual Teachings of Swami Brahmananda*, Trans, by Swami Chetanananda [St. Louis : Vedanta Society, 1988] P. 119.
60. Ibid, P. 50.

CHAPTER - 6 SWAMI SHIVANANDA

1. Swami Vividishananda, *A Man of God*, Ramakrishna Math, Madras, 1957, P.P. 20 - 21, hereafter A Man.
2. Swami Chetanananda, *God lived with them*, Advaita Ashrama, Kol., 2011, P. 135.
3. Swami Apurvananda, *Mahapurush Shivananda*; Udbodhan Office, Kol., 1949, P.P. 16 - 18, Hereafter *Mahapurush.*
4. Ibid, P. 9.
5. Ibid, P. 18.
6. Swami Chetanananda, ed. & trans., *Ramakrishna as We Saw Him* Vedanta Society : St. Louis, 1990, P. 117.

7. *Mahapurush* — P. 228 - 229.
8. Swami Apurvananda, Comp. *Shivananda Smritisangraha*, Ramakrishna Shivananda Ashrama, Barasat, 1968, Vol. 1, P. 206.
9. Ibid, Vol. III, P.P. 39 - 40.
10. Ibid, Vol. I, P. 17.
11. *The Complete Works of Swami Vivekananda*, Advaita Ashrama, Kol., Mayavati Memorial Ed. 2012, Vol. VII, P. 483, hereafter Works.
12. *Mahapurush* — P. 350.
13. *Mahapurushjir Patravali*, Udbodhan Office, Kol., 1953, P. 106, hereafter *Patravali*.
14. *For Seekers of God*, Advaita Ashrama, Kol., 1975, P. 10.
15. *A Man* — P.P. 152 - 153.
16. Patravali — P. 268.
17. Works, Vol. 6, P.P. 289 - 292.
18. Ibid, Vol. 7, P. 485.
19. Ibid, Vol. 6, P. 341.
20. Ibid, Vol. 8, P. 441.
21. *A Man* — P. 78.
22. Ibid, P. 99.
23. *The Voice of India* (San Francisco) 1946, P.P. 337 - 338.
24. *Smritisangraha* — Vol. I, 262, Pravrajika Prabuddhaprana.
25. *A Man* — P. 55.
26. Ibid, P.P. 55 - 56.
27. Lord Tennyson *Ulysses*.
28. *A Man* — P. 55.
29. *Udbodhan*, Vivekananda Centenary Number, 262; *Shivananda Vani* (1955). 1 : 163 - 164.
30. Gurudas Gupta's Diary (Told by Swami Ambikananda)
31. *Mahapurush* — P.P. 228 - 229.
32. Ibid, P.P. 278 - 279.
33. *A Man* — P. 41.
34. *Mahapurush* — P. 231.
35. *A Man* — P.P. 167 - 168.
36. Ibid, P. 219.

37. From Gurudas Gupta's Diary (Told by Swami Jnanatmananda) Reproduced by Swami Chetanananda in *God lived with them*, P. 157 Advaita Ashrama, Kol..
38. *The Story of Ramakrishna Mission*, Advaita Ashrama, Kol., P. 133.
39. *Swami Shivananda : Reminiscences*, His Devotees : Monastic and Lay, Bharatiya Vidya Bhavan, Bombay, 1971, P. 51.
40. Sri Ramabrishna's Life and Message in the Present Age, Swami Satprakashananda Vedanta Society, St. Louis, 1976, P.P. 178 - 179.
41. *A Man* — P. 99.
42. Ibid, P. 152.
43. The Voice of India, 1946 : 339.
44. Swamis Vividishananda and Gambhirananda, trans. *For Seekers of God*, Advaita Ashrama, Kol., 1975, P. 223.
45. The Story of Ramakrishna Mission, Advaita Ashrama, Kol. 1st Ed. 2006, P. 133.

CHAPTER - 7 SWAMI PREMANANDA

1. Swami Ashokananda, *Swami Premananda*, Vedanta Society : San Francisco, 1970, P. 3.
2. Ibid, P. 1.
3. M. *The Gospel of Sri Ramakrishna*, trans. by Swami Nikhilananda, Sri Ramakrishna Math, Chennai, 2013, P.P. 458 -459.
4. Ibid, P. 458.
5. Swami Chetanananda, Ed. & Trans. *Ramakrishna as We Saw Him*, Vedanta Society, St. Louis, 1990, P. 102.
6. Swami Chetanananda, *They Lived with God*, Vedanta Society, St. Louis, 1989, P.P. 182 - 183.
7. Swami Ashokananda — P. 21.
8. Swami Chetanananda, Trans. & Ed. *Spiritual Treasures : Letters of Swami Turiyananda*, Vedanta Society, St. Louis, 1992, P. 126.
9. Brahmachari Akshay Chaitanya, *Premananda Premakatha*, Navabharat Publishers, Kol., 1975. P.P. 51 - 52.
10. Swami Nikhilananda, *Holy Mother*, Ramakrishna Vivekananda Centre, New York, 1962, P. 261.
11. Swami Gambhirananda, *Bhakta Malika*, Udbodhan Office, Kol., 1963, Part - I, P.P. 200 -201.

12. Udbodhan 52 : 291 - 292.
13. The Complete Works of Swami Vivekananda, Advaita Ashrama, Kol. 2012, Vol. 7, P. 143.
14. Bhakta Malika, 1 : 209.
15. Swami Nityatmananda, *Srima Darshan*, General Printers and Publishers, Kol., 1972, XII : 105 - 106.
16. Swami Prabhavananda, ed. & trans., *Swami Premananda : Teachings and Reminiscences*, Vedanta Press, Holywood, 1968, P.P. 92 -94.
17. Swami Ashokananda — P. 32.
18. Ibid, P. 52.
19. *Udbodhan*, 48 : 420.
20. Swami Ashokananda — P. 37.
21. *Swami Premananda*, Ramakrishna Premananda Ashrama, Antpur, 1965, P.P. 142 -143.
22. Ibid, P. 139.
23. *Udbodhan*, 33 : 572.
24. Ibid, 37 : 240.
25. Swami Premananda (Antpur), P. 152.
26. Swami Prabhavananda — P.P. 115 -116.
27. Swami Ashokananda — P. 32.
28. Swami Prabhavananda — P.P. 14 -15.
29. *Prabuddha Bharata* 1933 : 596.
30. Ibid, 1941 : 564 - 565.
31. Swami Prabhavananda — P.P. 23 -24.
32. From Gurudas Gupta's Diary (Swami Chetanananda, *God lived with them*, Advaita Ashrama, Kol. 2011, P. 210.
33. *Swami Prabhavananda* (Antpur) — P. 29.
34. Works, Vol. 2, P. 14.
35. Swami Ashokananda — P. 48.
36. *Swami Premananda* (Antpur) — P. 105.
37. Ibid, P. 111.
38. Ibid, P. 41.
39. *Ramakrishna as We Saw Him* — P.P. 102 - 103.
40. Swami Ashokananda — P. 1.

41. Swami Kamaleswarananda, *Sri Ramakrishna, Parikar Prasanga,* Kol., 1977, P.P. 164 - 165.
42. *The Gospel* — P. 458.
43. The First Disciples of Sri Ramakrishna, *Spiritual Talks,* Advaita Ashrama, Kol., 1968, P. 82.
44. *Swami Premananda* (Antpur), P. 40.
45. Swami Chetanananda, trans. & ed. *Spiritual Treasures : Letters of Swami Turiananda,* Vedanta Society : St. Louis, 1992, P. 126.
46. *Premakatha* — P.P. 51 - 52.
47. Swami Prabhavananda, P. 17, Premakatha, P.P. 199 - 200.
48. Swami Ashokananda — P. 18.
49. Ibid, P.P. 27 - 28.
50. Ibid, P. 21.
51. *The Story of Ramakrishna Mission : Swami Vivekananda's Vision and Fulfilment,* Advaita Ashrama, Kol., P. 115.

CHAPTER - 8 SWAMI YOGANANDA

1. *Life of Sri Ramakrishna,* Advaita Ashrama, Kol., 1943, P. 393.
2. Ibid, P. 394.
3. *Udbodhan,* 21 : 139 - 140.
4. Chandra Sekhar Chattopadhyay, *Sri Sri Latu Maharajer Smritikatha,* Udbodhan Office, Kol., 1953, P. 339.
5. *Life of Sri Ramakrishna,* Advaita Ashrama, Kol., 1943, P. 394.
6. *God lived with them,* Swami Chetanananda, Advaita Ashrama, Kol., 1998, P. 226.
7. *Life of Sri Ramakrishna* — P. 400.
8. *Holy Mother Sri Sarada Devi,* Swami Gambhirananda, Sri Ramakrishna Math, Chennai, P.P. 120 - 121.
9. *Vedanta and the West* — 201 : 40 - 41.
10. Vaikuntha Nath Sanyal, *Sri Ramakrishna Lilamrita,* Kol., 1936, P.P. 311 - 312.
11. *The Bible* — Matthew, 19 : 12.
12. *The Life of Swami Vivekananda,* By his Eastern and Western disciples Advaita Asharama, Kol., Part - II, P.P. 249 - 250.
13. *Vedanta and the West,* Hollywood, P. 187 : 58.

14. Swami Apurvananda, Comp. *Shivananda Vani*, Udbodhan Office, Kol., 1964, P. II : 193.
15. Swami Jagadiswarananda, *Navayuger Mahapurush*, Orient Book Company, Kol., 1949, P. 104.
16. Her Devotee - Children, *The Gospel of the Holy Mother*, Ramakrishna Math, Chennai, 1984, P. 111.
17. *Sri Sri Mahapurushjir Katha*, Udbodhan Office, Kol., 1934, P. 109.
18. *Holy Mother Sri Sarada Devi* — P.P. 185 - 186.
19. Swami Bhumananda, *Sri Sri Mayer Jivankatha*, Ramakrishna Sarada Math, Kol., 1986, P. 148.
20. *Holy Mother Sri Sarada Devi* — P. 187.
21. *Sri Sri Mahapurushjir Katha* — P. 109.
22. *Holy Mother Sri Sarada Devi* — P.P. 185 - 186.
23. Swami Nirlepananda, *Swamijir Smriti Sanchayan*, Karuna Prakashani, Kol., 1967, P. 28.

CHAPTER - 9 SWAMI NIRANJANANANDA

1. Swami Gambhirananda, comp. & ed. *The Apostles of Sri Ramakrishna*, Advita Ashrama, Kol., 1967, P. 161.
2. Sri Chandra Sekhar Chattopadhyay, *Sri Sri Latu Maharajer Smritikatha*, Udbodhan Office, Kol., 2016, P.P. 363 - 364.
3. M. *The Gospel of Sri Ramakrishna*, trans. by Swami Nikhilananda, Sri Ramakrishna, Math, Chennai, P.P. 442 - 443.
4. Ibid, P. 809.
5. Ibid, P. 810.
6. Tattwamanjari — Vol. 8, P. 95.
7. *The complete Works of Swami Vivekananda*, Advaita Ashrama, Kol., Vol. 7, P. 485.
8. Ibid, Vol. 6, P. 278.
9. *The Gospel* — P. 932.
10. Vaikuntha Nath Sanyal, *Sri Ramakrishna Lilamrita* (Cal., 1936) P.P. 312 - 313.
11. Swami Gambhirananda, Sri Ramakrishna : Bhakta Malika, 3rd. Ed. 1962, Vol. 1, P. 238.
12. Ibid, P.P. 236 - 237.

13. *Sri Sri Latu Maharajer Smritikatha* — P. 227.
14. *Letters of Sister Nivediata*, Coll. & Ed. by Sankari Prasad Basu, Advaita Ashrama, Kol., 2017, Vol. 1, P. 54.
15. *Bhakta Malika* — Vol. 1, P. 245.
16. Ibid, Vol. 1, P. 248.
17. *The Gospel* — P. 813.

CHAPTER - 10 SWAMI RAMAKRISHNANANDA

1. *The Story of a Dedicated Life*, Ramakrishna Math, Madras, 1959, P. 47.
2. Sister Devamata, *Days in an Indian Monastery*, Ananda Ashrama : La Crescenta, 1927, P. 27.
3. Swami Kamaleswarananda, *Sri Ramakrishna Parikar Prasanga*, Cal., 1977, P. 64.
4. *The Story* — P.P. 32 - 33.
5. *The Complete Works of Swami Vivekananda*, Advaita Ashrama, Kol., 2012, Vol. 7, P. 298.
6. Swami Chetanananda, *Swami Adbhutananda : Teachings and Reminiscences*, Vedanta Society : St. Louis, 1980, P. 66.
7. *Ramakrishna Parikar* —P.P. 40 - 46.
8. Swami Tapasyananda, *Swami Ramakrishnananda, the Apostie of Sri Ramakrishna to the South*, Ramakrishna Math : Madras, 1986, P. 226.
9. Swami Gambhirananda, *Holy Mother Sri Sarada Devi*, Sri Ramakrishna Math, Mylapore, Chennai, P. 245.
10. Ibid, P.P. 254 - 255.
11. *Complete Works* — Vol. 7, P.P. 248 - 249.
12. *The Life of Swami Vivekananda*, His Eastern and Western Disciples, Advaita Ashrama, Kol., 1989, Vol. 1, P. 211.
13. Swami Gambhirananda, Comp. & Ed., *The Apostles of Sri Ramakrishna*, Advaita Ashrama, Kol., 1967, P. 233.
14. Swami Tapasyananda — P. 130.
15. *Ramakrishna Parikar* — P.P. 48 - 49.
16. *Vedanta Kesari*, 1951, P.P. 91 - 92.
17. Swami Tapasyananda — P.P. 214 - 215.
18. Ibid, P. 132.

19. *Ramakrishna Parikar* — P.P. 54 - 55.
20. *Complete Works*, Vol. 6, P. 268.
21. Ibid, P.P. 292 - 293.
22. Ibid, P.P. 326 - 327.
23. *The Story of Ramakrishna Mission — Swami Vivekananda's Vision and Fulfilment*, Advaita Ashrama, Kol., P. 137 - 138.
24. Ibid, P. 137.
25. *The Story* — P. 110.
26. *Udbodhan* — 64 : 635.
27. *The Gospel of Sri Ramakrishna*, Trans. by Swami Nikhilananda, Sri Ramakrishna Math, Mylapore, Madras, P. 443.
28. *Days in an Indian Monastery* — P. 32.
29. Swami Tapasyananda — P.P. 175 - 176.
30. Ibid, P. 172.
31. Ibid, P.P. 181 - 182.
32. Ibid, P. 183.
33. Ibid, P.P. 190 - 191.
34. *Days in an Indian Monastery* — P.P. 92 - 94.
35. *Udbodhan* — 48 : 536.
36. *Days in an Indian Monastery* — P.P. 19 - 20.
37. Swami Gambhirananda, *Bhakta Malika*, Udbodhan Office, Kol., 1963, 1 : 359.
38. *The Story* — P. 68.
39. Vedanta Kesari — 1951, P. 92.
40. Swami Tapasyananda — P.P. 140.
41. Ibid, P. 127.
42. Ibid, P. 181.
43. *The Gospel* — P. 934.
44. *Days in an Indian Monastery* — P. 22.
45. Swami Tapasyananda — P. 168.
46. Letters of Sister Nivedita, Col. & Ed. by Ssnkari Prasad Basu, Advaita Ashrama, Kol., Vol. I, P. 476.
47. Ibid, P. 476.
48. The Story of Ramakrishna Mission, Advaita Ashrama, Kol., P. 139.

CHAPTER - 11 SWAMI SARADANANDA

1. *The Life of Ramakrishna*, Romain Rolland, Advaita Ashrama, Kol., P. 149.
2. *Life of Sri Ramakrishna*, Advaita Ashrama, 1943, P. 472.
3. *Prabuddha Bharata* — 1927, P. 438.
4. *Bhakta Malika*, Swami Gambhirananda Udbodhan Office, Kol., 1997, Vol. I, P. 306 - 307.
5. *The Gospel of Sri Ramakrishna*, Originally recorded in Bengali by M. trans, by Swami Nikhilananda, Sri Ramakrishna Math, Madras, P. 985.
6. The Apostles of Sri Ramakrishna, Swami Gambhirananda (Comp. & Ed.) 1967, Advaita Ashrama, P. 169.
7. The Complete Works of Swami Vivekananda — Advaita Ashrama, Vol. 6, P. 292.
8. *Bhakta Malika*, — Vol. I, P. 332.
9. *Swami Saradananda*, Brahmachari Prakash, Basumati, Kol., 1936, P. 298.
10. *God lived with them*, Swami Chetanananda, Advaita Ashrama, P. 338.
11. *Swami Saradanander Jivani*, Brahmachari Akshay Chaitanya, Model Publishing House, Kol., 1955, P. 30.
12. Glimpses of a Great Soul, Swami Aseshananda, Vedanta Press, Hollywood, 1982, XII.
13. Ibid, P. 20.
14. The Life of Swami Vivekananda, By His Eastern and Western disciples, Advaita Ashrama, Vol. 2, P. 212.
15. *Glimpses of a Great Soul* — P. 24.
16. Gospel — P. 168.
17. *Prabuddha Bharata*, 1927, P.P. 442 - 443.
18. *Bhakta Malika*, Vol. I, P. 342. Akshay, P. 225.
19. *Udbodhan* — 37 : 84 - 85.
20. The First Disciples of Sri Ramakrishna, *Spititual Talks*, Advaita Ashrama, Kol., 1968, P. 355.
21. Ibid, P. 383.
22. *The Life of Ramakrishna*, Romain Rolland, Advaita Ashrama, Kol., P. 213.
23. *Prabuddha Bharata* — 1927, P. 438.

24. *History of Ramakrishna Math and Ramakrishna Mission*, Swami Gambhirananda, 3rd Ed. 1983, P.P. 124 - 125.
25. Swami Aseshananda — P. 13.
26. Prabuddha *Bharata* — 1932, P. 554.
27. *Jeman Dekhiachi*, Swami Bhumananda, Udbodhan Office, Kol., 1928, P. 316.
28. Swami Aseshananda — P. 23.
29. *Holy Mother*, Swami Nikhilananda, Ramakrishna - Vivekananda Center, New York, 1962, P. 267.
30. Ibid, P. 269.
31. *Jeman Dekhiachi* — P. 316.
32. *Smritir Aloy Swamiji*, Ed. Swami Purnatmananda, Udbodhan Office, Kol., P. 262.
33. The Life of Swami Vivekananda, By His Eastern and Western Disciples, Advaita Ashrama, Kol., Vol. II, P. 96.
34. *The Apostles* — P. 175.
35. Brahmachari Prakash — P. 47.
36. Swami Aseshananda — P. 19.
37. *Prabuddha Bharata*, 1932, P. 552.
38. *The Apostles* — P. 184.
39. *Sri Sri Ma O Sri Ramakrishna Parshadganer Smritikatha*, Ramakrishna Shivananda Ashrama, Barasat, 1965, P. 76.
40. Bhakta Malika, Part - I, P. 307.
41. From Gurudas Gupta's Diary *(God lived with them)* Swami Chetanananda, Advaita Ashrama, Kol., P. 335.
42. Akshay — P.P. 150 - 151.
43. *Sri Ramakrishna the great Master*, originally written in Bengali by Swami Saradananda, Trans. by Swami Jagadananda, Sri Ramakrishna Math, Chennai, P.P. 1281 - 1282.
44. *The Life of Ramakrishna*, Romain Rolland, Advaita Ashrama, Kol., P. 234.
45. Holy Mother — P. 270.

CHAPTER - 12 SWAMI TURIYANANDA

1. *The Brhadaranyaka Upanisad*, trans. Swami Madhavananda, Advaita Ashrama, Mayavati, Ch. - 4, Sec. V, P. 771.

2. The First Disciples of Sri Ramakrishna, *Spiritual Talks,* Advaita Ashrama, Kol., 1968, P. 125.
3. *Taittiriya Upanisad,* trans. Swami Gambhirananda, (Eight Upanisads). Advaita Ashrama, Vol. I, P. 334.
4. *With the Swamis in America,* A Western Devotee (Atulananda) Advaita Ashrama, 1946, P.P. 71 -72.
5. *Swami Turiyananda,* Swami Jagadiswarananda, Udbodhan Office, Kol., 1964, P. 110.
6. *Spiritual Talks* — P.P. 123 - 124.
7. *With the Swamis in America* — P. 72.
8. *Swami Turiyananda,* Swami Ritajananda, Ramakrishna Math, Madras, 1973, P.P. 131 - 132.
9. Ibid, P.P. 175 - 176.
10. *Spiritual Talks* — P. 192.
11. *With the Swamis in America* — P. 52.
12. *Prabuddha Bharata,* 1923, P. 225.
13. Ibid, 1922, P. 331.
14. *Spiritual Talks* — P. 124.
15. Ibid, P. 70.
16. Ibid, P.P. 70 - 71.
17. Ibid, P. 56.
18. *Vedanta and the West,* 1952, P. 141.
19. *Prabuddha Bharata,* 1927, P. 414.
20. Swami Ritajananda — P. 91.
21. *With the Swamis in America* — P.P. 97 - 98.
22. Ibid, P.P. 108 - 109.
23. Swami Ritajananda — P. 49.
24. Ibid, P. 57.
25. *With the Swamis in America* — P.P. 97 - 98.
26. Swami Ritajananda — P. 180.
27. Ibid, P. 43.
28. *The Life of Swami Vivekananda,* by His Eastern and Western disciples, Advaita Ashrama, Kol., 2016, Vol. II, P. 534.
29. *Vedanta and the West* — P. 135.

30. *With the Swamis in America* — P. 111.
31. Udbodhan, February, 2019.

CHAPTER - 13 SWAMI ADBHUTANANDA

1. *Sri Sri Latu Maharajer Smritikatha,* Chandra Sekhar Chattopadhyay, Udbodhan Office, Kol., 1953, P. 31.
2. *The Apostles of Sri Ramakrishna,* Comp. & Ed. Swami Gambhirananda, Advaita Ashrama, Kol., 1967, P. 271.
3. The Life of Ramakrishna, Romain Rolland, Advaita Ashrama, P. 150.
4. Ibid, P. 150.
5. Ibid, P.P. 149 - 150.
6. *Sri Sri Latu Maharajer Smritikatha* — P.P. 173 - 174.
7. Ibid, P.P. 204 - 205.
8. Ibid, P. 98.
9. Ibid, P.P. 179 - 180.
10. Ibid, P. 176.
11. Ibid, P. 241.
12. Ibid, P. 241.
13. Ibid, P. 96.
14. *Swami Adbhutananda : Teachings and Reminiscences,* Swami Chetanananda, Vedanta Society, St. Louis, 1980, P. 53.
15. *The Gospel of Sri Ramakrishna,* originally recorded in Bengali by M. trans, by Swami Nikhilananda, Sri Ramakrishna Math, Madras, P. 340.
16. *Sri Sri Latu Maharajer Smritikatha* — P.P. 181 - 182.
17. Ibid, P. 222.
18. Ibid, P. 225.
19. Ibid, P. 229.
20. Ibid, P.P. 70 - 71.
21. Ibid, P. 211.
22. The Gospel — P. 504.
23. *Sri Sri Latu Maharajer Smritikatha* — P. 248.
24. *Adbhutananda - Prasanga,* Col. Swami Siddhananda, Udbodhan Office, Kol., P. 151.

25. *Sri Sri Latu Maharajer Smritikatha* — P.P. 314 - 316.
26. Ibid, P.P. 305 - 306.
27. Ibid, P. 329.
28. Ibid, P. 329.
29. Ibid, P. 446.
30. Ibid, P. 446.
31. Ibid, P. 293.
32. Ibid, P. 334.
33. *Sri Sri Latu Maharajer Smritikatha* — P. 491.
34. Ibid, P. 190.
35. Ibid, P. 192.
36. Ibid, P.P. 419 - 420.
37. Ibid, P.P. 425 - 427.
38. *Swami Adbhutananda* — P. 93.
39. *Sri Sri Latu Maharajer Smritikatha* — P. 17.
40. Ibid, P.P. 179 - 180.
41. Ibid, P.P. 301 - 302.
42. Prabuddha Bharata, 1932, P.P. 506 - 507.
43. *Sri Sri Latu Maharajer Smritikatha* — P.P. 433 - 434.
44. Ibid, P. 439.
45. Ibid, P. 9.
46. Ibid, P. 500.
47. Ibid, P.P. 355 - 356.
48. Ibid, P. 450.
49. Ibid, P.P. 450 - 451.
50. *Swami Adbhutananda : Teachings and Reminiscences,* Swami Chetanananda, (Vedanta Society, St. Louis, 1980) P. 64.
51. *The Life of Swami Vivekananda,* by His Eastern and Western disciples, Advaita Ashrama, Kol., P. 252.
52. *Sri Sri Latu Maharajer Smritikatha* — P.P. 353 - 354.
53. Ibid, P. 309.
54. Ibid, P.P. 352 - 353.
55. *The Other Apostles of Sri Ramakrishna,* Swami Gahanananda, The story of Ramakrishna Mission, Advaita Ashrama, Kol., P. 143.

56. *Holy Mother*, Swami Nikhilananda, Ramakrishna - Vivekananda Center : New York, 1961, P. 263.

CHAPTER - 14 SWAMI ABHEDANANDA

1. *Amar Jivankatha,* Swami Abhedananda, Ramakrishna Vedanta Math, Kol., 1957 (1364), P. 13.
2. Ibid, P. 42.
3. Ibid, P. 35.
4. Ibid, P.P. 97 - 98.
5. *Bhakta Malika,* Swami Gambhirananda, Udbodhan Office, Kol., 1963, 1 : 418.
6. *Vivekananda : The Yogas and Other Works,* Swami Nikhilananda, Ramakrishna - Vivekananda Center, New York, 1953, P. 34. *Life of Swami Vivekanda* By His Eastern and Western Disciples, Vol. I, Advaita Ashrama, Kol., P. 178.
7. *The Gospel of Sri Ramakrishna,* M., trans. by Swami Nikhilananda,, Sri Ramakrishna, Math, Madras, P. 985. Amar Jivankatha (2015 edi.) P. 96.
8. *Sri Ramakrishna The Great Master,* Swami Saradananda, Trans. by Swami Jagadananda, Sri Ramakrishna Math, Chennai, Part II, P. 106.
9. Amar Jivankatha — P.P. 87 - 88.
10. The Gospel — P. 986.
11. Ibid, P. 991.
12. Amar Jivankatha — P. 115.
13. *Bhakta Malika,* Swami Gambhirananda, Udbodhan Office, Kol., 1963, 1 : 395.
14. *Jeman Suniyachi,* Swami Sambuddhananda, Ramakrishna Ashrama, Howrah, 1970, I & II, 236, 183.
15. *Amar Jivankatha* — P. 84.
16. Ibid, P. 57.
17. The Apostles of Sri Ramakrishna, Swami Gambhirananda Comp. & Ed. Advaita Ashrama, Kol., 1967, P. 259.
18. *With the Swamis in America,* A Western Disciple (Swami Atulananda) Advaita Ashrama, Kol., 1946, II, P. 13.
19. *Swami Abhedananda in America,* Sister Shivani (Mary Le Page) Ramakrishna Vedanta Math, Kol., 1991, P. 105.

20. Ibid, P.P. 107 -108.
21. *Smritir, Aloy* Swamiji *Swami* Abhedananda, Ed. Swami Purnatmananda, Udbodhan Office, Kol., 1990, P. 23.
22. *Swami Abhedananda in America* — P. 109.
23. *The Apostles of Sri Ramakrishna* — P. 263.
24. *Amar Jivankatha* — P. 177.
25. Life of Swami Vivekananda — P. 505.
26. *Swami Abhedananda* — P. 423.
27. Jeman Suniyachi, II, P. 170.
28. *Amar Jivankatha* — P.P. 83 - 84.
29. *Smritir, Aloy Swamiji* — P. 23.
30. *Swami Abhedananda* — P. 337.
31. Ibid, P. 376.

CHAPTER - 15 SWAMI TRIGUNATITANANDA

1. *The Gospel of Sri Ramakrishna*, M., Trans. by Swami Nikhilananda, Sri Ramakrishna, Math, Madras, P. 803.
2. *Udbodhan* — 35 : 344.
3. *Bhakta Malika,* Swami Gambhirananda, Udbodhan Office, Kol., 1964, II, 10.
4. Ibid, II : 10.
5. *Srimat Vivekananda Swamijir Jivaner Ghatanavali,* Mahendra Nath Datta, Mahendra Publishing Committee, 1964, II : 124 - 125.
6. Prabuddha Bharata — 1928, P. 525.
7. *Udbodhan* — 35, P. 402.
8. The Gospel — P.P. 988 -989, 996.
9. The Complete Works of Swami Vivekananda, Advaita Ashrama, Kol., VI, P. 355.
10. *Journals of the Ramakrishna Order the Early Years,* The Story of Ramakrishna Mission, Advaita Ashrama, Kol., Sankari Prasad Basu, P. 812.
11. *Conversations and Dialogues (From the Diary of a Disciple),* Shri Sharat Chandra Chakravarty, Works, Vol. VII, P. 168.
12. The Message of Our Master, Advaita Ashrama, Kol., 1944, P.P. 55, 43.

13. *Srima Sarada Devi*, Swami Gambhirananda, Udbodhan Office, Kol., P. 161.
14. *God lived with them*, Swami Chetanananda, Advaita Ashrama, Kol., 1998, P. 502.
15. Complete Works — VII, P. 168.
16. *Voice of Freedom*, (San Francisco) May 1909, VI - VIII.
17. *Prabuddha Bharata*, 1928, P. 162.
18. *Udbodhan* — 37 : 303.

CHAPTER - 16 SWAMI ADVAITANANDA

1. *The Gospel of Sri Ramakrishna*, M., Trans. by Swami Nikhilananda, Sri Ramakrishna, Math, Madras, P. 932.
2. *Sri Sri Latu Maharajer Smritikatha*, Chandra Sekhar Chattopadhyay, Udbodhan Office, Kol., 1953, P. 257.
3. *The Gospel of the Holy Mother*, Her Devotee-Children, Ramakrishna Math, Madras, 1984, P. 164.
4. *Amar Jivankatha*, Swami Abhedananda, Sri Ramakrishna Vedanta Math, Kol., Part - I, P.P. 93 - 94.
5. *The Other Apostles of Sri Ramakrishna*, Swami Gahanananda, The Story of Ramakrishna Mission, Advaita Ashrama, Kol., P. 145.
6. *Latu Smriti* — P. 434.
7. *Sri Ma*, Ashutosh Mitra, Kol., 1944, P. 206.
8. *Vedanta and the West* — P.P. 131 : 22.
9. *The Gospel* — P. 440.
10. Ibid, P.P. 425 - 426.
11. *Srimad Bhagavad Gita*, Ed. by Jagadish Chandra Ghosh, Presidency Library, Kol., (Preface) P. 1.
12. Udbodhan — 49 : 206.
13. From Gurudas Gupta's Diary (Collected by Swami Chetanananda)
14. *Sri Ramakrishna The Great Teacher*, Swami Saradananda, Sri Ramakrishna Math, Chennai, P. 919.
15. *Swamijir Smriti Sanchayan*, Swami Nirlepananda, Karuna Prakashani, Kol., 1967, P. 62.
16. *Complete Works of Swami Vivekananda*, Advaita Ashrama, Kol., 2012, Vol. VI, 442.

17. *Bhakta Malika*, Swami Gambhirananda, Udbodhan Office, Kol., 1997, Vol. I, P.P. 513 - 514.
18. *Satprasange Swami Vijnanananda,* Comp. Swami Apurvananda, Ramakrishna Math, Allahabad, 1953, P. 71.
19. *Srimat Vivekananda Swamijir Jivaner Ghatanavli*, Mahendra Nath Datta, Mahendra Publishing Committee, Kol., 1964, Vol. I, P.P. 94 - 95.
20. *The Other Apostles of Sri Ramakrishna*, Swami Gahanananda, The Story of Ramakrishna Mission, Advaita Ashrama, Kol., 2006, P. 146.

CHAPTER - 17 SWAMI SUBODHANANDA

1. *The Bible,* Mathew 18 : 1 –3.
2. *Sri Ramakrishna Charit*, Gurudas Barman, Kol., 1909, P. 345.
3. Ibid, P. 346.
4. *The Complete Works of Swami Vivekananda*, Advaita Ashrama, Kol., Vol. IV, P. 183.
5. *Khoka Maharaj* : Swami Subodhananda, Comp. Abani Gupta, Kol. I : 28.
6. *The Gospel of Sri Ramakrishna*, M., Trans. by Swami Nikhilananda, Sri Ramakrishna Math, Madras, P. 839.
7. *Khoka Maharaj* — I : 37.
8. *Swami Subodhanander Jivani O Patra*, Ramakrishna Math, Sonarga - Dhaka (1935) P. 79.
9. Bhakta Malika, Swami Gambhirananda, Udbodhan Office, Kol., 2nd Ed. 1964, II : 81 - 82.
10. Ibid, II : 83.
11. *Khoka Maharaj* — II : 97.
12. *Udbodhan* — 35 : 64.
13. *Swami Subodhananda* — P. 102.
14. Ibid, P. 69.
15. Ibid, P. 115.
16. *Prabuddha Bharata* — November 1898.
17. *Bhakta Malika* — II : 83.
18. *Khoka Maharaj* — I : 57 - 58.
19. *The Apostles of Sri Ramakrishna*, Comp. & Ed, by Swami Gambhirananda, Advaita Ashrama, Kol., 2nd Imp., 1972, P. 377.

20. *Udbodhan* — 40 : 316 - 317.
21. Ibid, 35 : 48.
22. Ibid, 88 : 626.
23. *Ramakrishna and His Disciples,* Christopher Isherwood, Methuen & Co. London, 1965, P. 234.
24. Ibid, P. 234.
25. *Udbodhan* — 88 : 624 - 625.
26. *The Apostles of Sri Ramakrishna* — P. 369.
27. *Bhakta Malika* — II : 69.
28. *Sri Ramakrishna Charit* — P. 346.
29. *Khoka Maharaj* — I : 60 - 61.
30. Ibid, I : 55.
31. *Holy Mother Sri Sarada Devi,* Swami Gambhirananda, Sri Ramakrishna Math, P. 250.
32. *Khoka Maharaj* — P. 58.
33. *The Other Apostles of Sri Ramakrishna,* Swami Gahanananda, The Story of Ramakrishna Mission, Advaita Ashrama, Kol., P. 160.
34. Punya Smriti, Swami Jnanatmananda, Udbodhan Office, Kol., 1977, P. 104.
35. From Swami Dhireshananda's Diary, *God Lived With Them,* Swami Chetanananda, Advaita Ashrama, Kol., P. 551.
36. *The Other Apostles of Sri Ramakrishna* — P. 159.

CHAPTER - 18 SWAMI AKHANDANANDA

1. *Ramakrishna as We Saw Him,* Ed. & Comp., Swami Chetanananda Vedanta Society St. Louis, 1990, P.P. 234, 238.
2. Smriti-Katha, Swami Akhandananda, Udbodhan Office, Kol., 1937, P. 20.
3. Ibid, P. 28.
4. Ibid, P. 29.
5. Ibid, P. 87.
6. Ibid, P. 26.
7. *The Life of Swami Vivekananda,* By his Eastern and Western Disciples, Advaita Ashrama, Kol., Vol. I, P. 261.
8. *The Master as I saw him,* Sister Nivedita, Udbodhan Office, Kol., P. 44.

9. *The Gospel of Sri Ramakirshna,* M. trans. by Swami Nikhilananda, Sri Ramakrishna Math, Madras, P. 407.
10. *Sri Ramakrishna the great Master,* Swami Saradananda, trans. by Swami Jagadananda, Sri Ramakrishna Math Chennai, P. 1163.
11. *The Complete Works of Swami Vivekananda,* Advaita Ashrama, 2012, Vol. 6, P. 288.
12. *Smriti Kathta* — P. 105.
13. Quoted in Swami Annadananda, *Swami Akhandananda,* trans. by N. C. Bhattacharya, Advaita Ashrama, Kol., 1993, P. 92.
14. *Swami Akhandananda* — P. 92.
15. *Complete* Works, Vol. 6, P. 288.
16. *The Call of the Spirit,* Swami Niramayananda, Ramakrishna Math, Madras, 1984, P. 28.
17. *Complete Works,* Reply to the Madras Address, Vol. 4, P. 352.
18. *Smriti Kathta* — P. 231.
19. Ibid, P. 229.
20. Swami Akhandananda, P.P. 158 - 159.
21. *Complete Works,* Vol. 6, P.P. 400 - 401.
22. *Smriti Kathta* — P. 241.
23. *Complete Works,* Vol. 7, P.P. 507 - 508.
24. Ibid, P. 110.
25. *Swami Akhandanander Smriti-Sanchaya,* Swami Niramayananda, Udbodhan Office, Kol., 1976, P.P. 61 - 62.
26. *The Ramakrishna Math & Mission Convention,* Belur Math, 1926, P. 85.
27. Prabuddha Bharata, 1936, P. 281.

CHAPTER - 19 SWAMI VIJNANANANDA

1. *Ramakrishna as We Saw Him,* Ed. & Trans. Swami Chetanananda Vedanta Society St. Louis, 1990, P. 247.
2. *Udbodhan* — 53 : 311.
3. *Swami Vijnanananda,* Swami Jagadiswarananda, Ramakrishna Math, Allahabad, 1947, P.P. 5 - 6.
4. *Swami Vijnanananda* : His Life and Sayings, Swami Vishwashrayananda, Ramakrishna Math, Chennai, 1980, P. 8.

5. *The Life of Swami Vivekananda,* By His Eastern and Western Disciples, Advaita Ashrama, Kol., Vol. II, P. 309.
6. *Satprasange Swami Vijnanananda,* Swami Apurvananda, Ramakrishna Math, Allahabad, 1953, P. 11.
7. *The Other Apostles of Sri Ramakrishna,* Swami Gahanananda, The Story of Ramakrishna Mission, Advaita Ashrama, Kol., P. 148.
8. *A Man of God,* Swami Vividishananda, Ramakrishna Math, Madras, 1957, P.P. 349 - 350.
9. *Satprasange* — P. 25.
10. *The Gospel of Sri Ramakrishna,* M. trans. by Swami Nikilananda, Sri Ramakrishna Math, Madras, P. 112.
11. *Satprasange* — P. 9.
12. Ibid, V - VI, 8.
13. Ibid, P. 188.
14. Ibid, P.P. 195 - 197.
15. Ibid, P. 180.
16. *Ramakrishna as We Saw Him,* Ed. & Trans. Swami Chetanananda, Vedanta Society, St. Louis, 1990, P.P. 248 - 249.
17. Ibid, P.P. 254 - 255.
18. *Satprasange* — P. 126.
19. Ibid, P.P. 139, 112.
20. Pratyakshadarshir Smritipate Swami Vijnanananda, Comp. & Ed. Suresh Chandra Das and Jyotirmay Basuroy, General Printers and Publishers, Kol., 1977, P.P. 64 - 65.
21. *Gita* — 2 : 55 - 56.
22. *Bhakta Malika,* Swami Gambhirananda, Udbodhan Office, Kol., 1964, II : 116.
23. Bhagavata — 11, 18, 29.
24. *Satprasange* — P. 20.
25. Ibid, P. 16.
26. *Pratyakshadarshir Smritipate Swami Vijnanananda* — P. 67.
27. Divyaprasange, Swami Divyatmananda, Udbodhan Office, Kol., 1972, P.P. 121 - 122.
28. *Satprasange* — P. 123.
29. *Prabuddha Bharata,* 1970, P. 297.

30. *Satprasange* — P.P. 130 - 131.
31. Ibid, P. 22.
32. Ibid, P.P. 92 - 93.
33. Ibid, P. 171.
34. *Divyaprasange* — P. 169.
35. *Pratyakshâdarshir Smritipate Swami Vijnanananda* — P. 106.
36. *Satprasange* — P.P. 14 - 15.
37. *Udbodhan*, 43 : 285 - 286.
38. Ibid, 40 : 547.
39. Ibid, 40 : 606.
40. *Satprasange* — P. 179.
41. Ibid, P.P. 172 - 173.
42. Ibid, P. 173.
43. *Pratyakshadarshir Smritipate* — P. 11.
44. *Udbodhan*, 45 : 223.
45. The Gospel — P. 87.
46. *Pratyakshadarshir Smritipate* — P.P. 86 - 87.
47. *Swami Vijnanananda : His Life and sayings* — P. 27.
48. Ibid, P. 32.
49. *Udbodhan*, 42 : 663.
50. Prabuddha Bharata, 1938, P. 295.
51. *Pratyakshadarshir Smritipate* — P. 67.
52. *Swami Vijnanananda* — P. 107.
53. From Dhireshananda's Diary (Told by Swami Siddheswarananda on 8 Januray 1947; *God lived with them*, Swami Chetanananda, Advaita Ashrama, Kol., P. 617.
54. *Ramakrishna as We Saw Him*, Ed. & Trans by Swami Chetanananda, Vedanta Society, St. Louis, 1990, P.P. 245 - 46.
55. *The Story of Ramakrishna Mission*, The Other Apostles of Sri Ramakrishna by Swami Gahanananda, Advaita Ashrama, Kol., P. 146.
56. *Satprasange* — P. 180.
57. Ramakrishna as We Saw Him — P.P. 248 - 249.
58. *The Story of Ramakrishna Mission* — P. 148.

CHAPTER - 20 'WE ARE ON THE SAME BOAT BROTHER'

1. *The Gospel of Sri Ramakrishna*, M. trans. by Swami Nikilananda, Sri Ramakrishna Math, Madras, P. 46.
2. *Amar Jivan Katha* (Beng.) Swami Abhedananda, Sri Ramakrishna Vedanta Math, Kol.. P. 93.
3. *Sri Ramakrishna the Great Master,* Swami Saradananda, Sri Ramakrishnad Math, Chennai, P.P. 1163 - 1165.
4. *The Life of Swami Vivekananda,* By His Eastern and Western Disciples, Advaita Ashrama, Kol., Vol. II, P. 152.
5. *The Complete Works of Swami Vivekananda,* Advaita Ashrama, Kol., Vol. VI, P.P. 263 - 264.
6. *The Life of Swami Vivekananda,* By His Eastern and Western Disciples, Advaita Ashrama, Kol., Vol. II, P.P. 249 -250.
7. *Swami Premananda,* Swami Ashokananda, Vedanta Society of Northern Colifornia, 1970, P.P. 27 - 28.
8. *The Complete Works of Swami Vivekananda,* Advaita Ashrama, Kol., Vol. V, P. 29.
9. *The Life of Swami Vivekananda,* Vol. I, P. 159.
10. *For Seekers of God,* Advaita Ashrama, Kol., 1975, P. 10.
11. *The Gospel* — P.P. 812 - 813.
12. Swami Vijnanananda, Swami Jagadiswarananda, Ramakrishna Math, Allahabad, 1947, P.P. 5 - 6.
13. *The Gospel of Holy Mother,* Ramakrishna Math, Mylapore, Chennai, 1986, P. 104.
14. *The Gospel* — P. 931.
15. *Complete Works,* Vol. 8, P. 430.
16. *The Life of Swami Vivekananda,* Vol. 2, P. 389.
17. *The Story of Ramakrishna Mission,* Advaita Ashrama, Kol., P. 263.
18. *Complete Works,* Vol. 4, Reply to the Madras Address, P. 352.
19. *The Story.* The Other Apostles of Sri Ramakrishna, Swami Gahanananda, P. 131.
20. *Complete Works,* Vol. 7, P. 168 - 170.
21. Indian Mirror, 28th March, 1875.
22. *The Apostles of Sri Ramakrishna,* Comp. & Ed. Swami Gambhirananda, Advaita Ashrama, Kol., 1967, P. 259.

23. *The Unique Balance Struck by the Math and the Mission*, Amalendu Das Gupta, The Story of Ramakrishna Mission, Advaita Ashrama, Kol., P. 738.
24. *History of Ramakrishna Math and Ramakrishna Mission*, Swami Gambhirananda, Adsvaita Ashrama, Kol., 4th Ed. P.P. 582 - 583.
25. *The Master as I saw him,* Sister Nivedita, Udbodhan Office, Kol., P.P. 70 – 71.
26. *The Life*, Vol. I, P. 182.

GLOSSARY

Advaita : Non-duality; a school of the Vedanta philosophy, declaring the oneness of God soul and universe.

Alasinga Perumal : Prof. of the Pachiyappa's College Madras one of the most staunch disciples of Swami Vivekananda; Swamiji wrote many letters from the West to him; played an important role in publishing *Brahmavadin*.

Arati, Aratrika : The vespers, accompanied by the waving of lights.

Aruni : Aruni of Panchala was a dedicated student of the ancient sage Dhoumya.

Aurobindo, Sri : Aurobindo Ghosh (A.D. 1872 - 1950) successfully competed the ICS examination but did not join the alien Government's service to devote himself to the freedom struggle (1902 - 1910). He retired from politics and went to Pondicherry to lead a saintly life. Amongst his notable writings are *'The Life Divine', 'The Synthesis of Yoga'* and *Savitri*.

Avadhuta : One of a class of anchorites who worship Shiva remarkable for unusual dress and unconventional conduct.

Avidya : Primal ignorance which is responsible for the non-perception of Reality.

Balaram Bose : Came of a Wealthy Vaishnava family. He was one of the most beloved of the householder disciples and one of the rasaddārs (suppliers of stores) of Sir Ramakrishna. The Master slept at his home whenever he spent a night in Kolkata.

Bhairavi Brāhmani : The brahmin woman (Yogeshwari) who taught Sri Ramakrishna the Vaishnava and Tantra disciplines. She proclaimed that Sri Ramakrishna like Sri Chaitanya was an Incarnation of God.

Bhavamukha : An exalted state of spiritual experience, in which the aspirant keeps his mind on the border line between the Absolute and the Relative. From this position he can contemplate the ineffable and attributeless Brahman and also participate in the activities of the relative world, seeing in it the manifestation of God alone.

Bhava Samādhi : Ecstasy in which the devotee retains his ego and enjoys communion with the Personal God.

Bishop : A senior member of the Christian clergy, usually in charge of a diocese and empowered to confer holy orders.

Brahma : The Creator God; the First Person of the Hindu Trinity; the other two being Vishnu and Siva.

Brahmachari : A religious student devoted to the practice of spiritual discipline, a celibate belonging to the first stage of life.

Brahman : The Absolute, the Supreme Reality of the Vedanta philosophy.

Brahmo Samaj ; A theistic organization of India, founded by Raja Rammohan Roy in 1828.

Brahmānanda : The bliss of communion with Brahman.

Buddha : Gautam Buddha, the founder of Buddhism.

Calvinism : The French Protestant and leader of the reformation movement John Calvin (A.D. 1509 – 1564) taught that man, is born a sinner and a few of them may be absolved from sins by the grace of God.

Chaitanya : Spiritual Consciousness, also the name of a prophet Gauranga who was born at Navadvip in A.D. 1485 and emphasized the path of divine love for the realization of God.

Chandala : One belonging to the lowest stratum of the Hindu society.

Chapati : A kind of thin bread or cake of flour.

Dadu : Dadu Dayal (A.D. 1544 – 1663) of Gujarat a religious reformer who spoke against formalism and priestcraft.

Dakshineswar : The village on the bank of the Ganga more than eight kms. north of Kolkata where Sri Ramakrishna lived in a room in the temple premises of Rani Rasmani.

Dana : Ghost.

Darsonas : The six systems of orthodox Hindu philosophy namely, the Samkhya of Kapila, the Yoga of Patanjali, the Vaiśeshika of Kanāda, the Nyāya of Gautama, the Purva Mimāmsā of Jaimini and the Vedanta or Uttara Mimāmsā of Vyasa.

Dayananda Saraswati : The founder of the Arya Samaj.

Devendranath Tagore : The real organizer of the Brāhmo Samāj; was called Maharshi (the 'Great Seer'), father of Rabindranath Tagore and famous for his scholarship, wealth and social position. Sri Ramakrishna found him disappointing for he combined with his saintliness a life of enjoyment.

Disraeli : Benjamin Disraeli (1804 - 1881) British politician who twice served as Prime Minister of the United Kingdom. He played a central role in the creation of the modern Conservative Party.

Einstein Albert : Albert Einstein (1879 - 1955) a German-born theoretical physicist. He like Isaac Newton is the greatest physicist of all time. He developed the theory of relativity, mass-energy equivalence ($E = mc^2$), law of the photoelectric effect etc. He received Nobel Prize in 1921.

Ekalavya : In the Mahabharata, Ekalavya a famous archer was the son of Hiranyadhanus the Chief of the Bhils. He served under King Jarasandha's army as General. He cut off his right thumb as Guru Dakshina as he was asked by Drona to do.

Fawcett : Percy Harrison Fawcett (1867 - 1925) was a British geographer artillery officer, cartographer, archaeologist and explorer of South America.

Florence Nightingale : Florence Nightingale (A.D. 1820 - 1910) was an English social reformer, statistician and the founder of modern nursing. During the Crimean War she organized care for wounded soldiers at Constantinople. She became an icon of Victorian culture, especially in the persona of *'The Lady with the Lamp'* making rounds of wounded soldiers at night.

Fuller Thomas : Thomas Fuller (A.D. 1654 - 1734) was a British physican preacher and intellectual. One of his wise sayings : 'Be you never so high, the law is above you.'

Girish Chandra : Girish Chandra Ghosh (A.D. 1844 - 1912) the father of the modern Bengali stage, a great poet, playwright, actor and director. Sri Ramakrishna said, 'Girish is a devotee of heroic type.'

Goodwin J. J. : Josiah John Goodwin (A.D. 1870 - 1898) was a British Stenographer and a disciple of Swami Vivekananda. He is known for recording Swamiji's speeches. J. J. Goodwin played a vital role in Swami Vivekananda's life.

Hastie William : Principal of the–then General Assembly's Institution (later Scottish Church College). Narendranath heard from him about trance of Ramakrishna Paramahamsa of Dakshineswar.

Hriday : Hridayram Mukhopadhyay was Sri Ramakrishna's nephew, who served as his attendant during the period of his spiritual discipline. He was also called Hridē, and Hridu. He was expelled from the temple garden at Dakshineswar on account of his certain action which displeased the temple authorities.

Hugo, Victor : Victor-Marie Hugo (A.D. 1802 - 1885) was a French poet, novelist and dramatist of the Romantic movement. He wrote abundantly in an exceptional variety of genres, lyrics, satires, epics, philosophical poems, epigrams, novels, history, dramas in verse and prose. His notable works— *Les Miserable, Ruy Blas, The Hunchback of Notre-Dame.*

Hubble-bubble : A water-pipe for smoking.

Iśvarakoti : Divine Messenger. Sri Ramakrishna said, 'An Incarnation of God or one born with some of the characteristics of an Incarnation is called an Iśvarakoti.' The Master earmaked six of his disciples as 'Iśvarakoti' : Narendra, Rakhal, Baburam, Yogin, Niranjan and Purna.

Jatila and Kutila : Two trouble-makers depicted in the Bhagavata, in the episode of Sri Krishna and the gopis of Vrindavan.

Jhandu Bhat Vithalji : A reputed physician (Kaviraj) and a highly spiritual person of Jamnagar in Gujarat. He used to give free medicine to the poor and would even visit them in their homes. He saved the life of Swami Akhandananda whom some notorious persons tried to kill by poisoning his coffee.

Kabir : Kabir Das born in Varanasi was an 15th century Indian mystic poet and saint whose writings influenced Hinduism's Bhakti movement. His early life was in a Muslim family but he was strongly influenced by his teacher the Hindu bhakti leader Ramananda. His verses are found in Sikhism's scripture Guru Grantha Sahib.

Kamalakanta : Kamalakanta Bhattacharya of Burdwan, W.B., a votary, famous for popular devotional songs addressed to Kali, the universal Mother.

Keshab Chandra Sen : The ablest leader of the Brāhmo movement a worthy representative of modern India tried to introduce Christ to the Brāhmo Samaj and ultimately broke with Devendranath Tagore and founded the Brahmo Samaj of India which also broke into two groups — Sādhāran Brahmo Samaj and Navavidhan led by Keshab. Sri Ramakrishna and Keshab held each other in great love and respect. He was entertained by Queen Victoria and was called 'Second Christ from the East' by the English people.

M. : Mahendranath Gupta (1854–1932) one of Sri Ramakrishna's foremost householder disciples and the recorder of *The Gospel of Sri Ramakrishna.*

Madan Mohan Malavya : A great scholar and founder of the Varanasi Hindu University.

Mahendra Lal Sircar : Reputed physician; founder of Indian Association for the cultivation of science (1876); treated Sri Ramakrishna about whom he commented, 'As a man I have the greatest regard for him.'

Mathuranath Biswas : The son-in-law of Rani Rasmani and a great devotee of Sri Ramakrishna whom he provided with all the necessaries of life at the temple garden at Dakshineswar.

Maugham Somerset : William Somerset Maugham (A.D. 1874 - 1965) was an English playwright, novelist and short story writer. He was among the most popular writers of his era. Author of *Liza of Lambeth, of Human Bondage, Rain* etc.

Max Muller : Friedrich Max Muller (1823 - 1900) was a German-born philologist and Orientalist. He was one of the founders of the Western academic disciplines of Indian studies and religious studies. His notable works are - The Sacred Books of the East, Chips from a German Workshop.

Maya : Illusion causing duality; on account of Cosmic Illusion the One appears as many; Maya has two aspects, namely, avidyāmāyā and vidyāmāya. Avidyāmāyā, or the 'mayā of ignorance', consisting of anger, passion and so on, entangles one in worldliness. Vidyāmāyā, or the 'maya of knowledge' consisting of kindness, purity, unselfishness, and so on, leads one to liberation. Both belong to the relative world. Maya denotes attachment also.

Naresh Chandra : A mystic poet of Bengal.

Nirvikalpa sāmadhi : The highest state of samādhi, in which the aspirant realizes his total oneness with Brahman.

Nityānanda : A beloved disciple and companion of Sri Chaitanya.

Nanak : The founder of the Sikh religion and the first of the ten Gurus of the Sikhs. He was born in the Punjab in A.D. 1469 and died in 1538.

Om : The most sacred word of the Vedas; also written as Aum. It is a symbol of God and of Brahman.

Panchatapā : The austerity of five fires. While practising this discipline, the aspirant sits under the blazing sun, with four fires burning around him or her. Seated in the midst of these five fires he or she practises japa and meditation.

Paramahamsa : One belonging to the highest order of sannyāsis.

Patanjala : One of the six systems of orthodox Hindu philosophy.

Pāvhāri Bābā : An ascetic and yogi of great distinction who was a contemporary and admirer of Sri Ramakrishna.

Pratap Chandra Mazumdar : An accomplished Brāhmo preacher in Europe and America, criticized Sri Ramakrishna's use of uncultured language and his austere attitude toward his wife. But he could not avoid the spell of the Master's personality and ideas. In an article in the 'Theistic Quarterly Review' he wrote, "So long as he is spared to us, gladly shall we sit at his feet to learn from him the sublime precepts of purity, unworldliness, spirituality, and inebriation in the love of God."

Pratap Hazra : Leaving his mother, wife and children he had found shelter in the temple garden at Dakshineswar in order to lead a spiritual life. But he was hypercritical of others and cherished a false notion of his own spiritual power. He was wicked and often tried to misguide the Master's young disciples. Sri Ramakrishna compared Hazra to Jatila and Kutila.

Qualified Non-dualism : A school of Vedanta founded by Ramanuja, according to which the soul and nature are the modes of Brahman, and the individual soul is a part of Brahman.

Raja Ramanna : Raja Ramanna (A.D. 1925 - 2004) an Indian physicist best known for his role in India's nuclear programme during its early stages.

Raghuvir : A name of Ramachandra; the Family Deity of Sri Ramakrishna.

Ramprasād : A Bengali mystic and writer of songs about the Divine Mother.

Rajasic : Pertaining to rajas i.e. the principle of activity.

Ramchandra Dutta : A medical practitioner and chemist Ramchandra was sceptical about God and religion. Sri Ramakrishna awakened his spirituality and the latter became one of his foremost lay disciples. Ramchandra introduced his relative Narendranath to Sri Ramakrishna. He wrote the first biography of the Master.

Ramanuja : A famous saint and philosopher (A.D. 1017 – 1137) of southern India, the founder of the school of Qualified Non-dualism.

Rasmani, Rani : A wealthy woman of the sudra caste got married to Rajchandra Das landlord of Janbazar, Kolkata; foundress of the Kali temple at Dakshineswar.

Samaskāra : The tendencies inherited from previous births.

Shivnath Shastri : One of the Brāhmo leaders Shivnath vehemently criticized the Master for his other-worldly attitude toward his wife and described him as an insane. He did not support some saying of the Master about women.

Surendranath Mitra : Suresh Mitra held an important post in an English firm. He was atheist and led a Bohemian life and was addicted to drinking. A victim of mental depression, he was brought to

Sri Ramakrishna by Ramchandra Dutta. By degrees Surendra's entire life was changed. The Master often addressed his beloved disciple as Surendra and designated him as one of those commissioned by the Divine Mother to defray a great part of his expenses.

Shankara : Shankaracharya, one of the chief exponents of the Advaita Vedanta; his commentaries written on the Upanishads, Gita and Vedanta-Sutras are well known.

Subhas Chandra Bose : Popularly known as 'Netaji' (1897 – ????) a great hero and patriot, President of the Indian National Congress (1938), advocated complete independence for India and many times imprisoned. As the chief of the INA (Azad Hind Fauz) he fought against the imperialist British rulers in co-operation with Japan and Germany during the Second World War. Author of *The Indian Struggle (1935), Taruner Swapna.*

Shylock : In the play *The Merchant of Venice* by William Shakespeare Shylock was a rich Jew and heartless money-lender of Venice.

Suka (deva) : The narrator of the *Bhāgavata* and son of Vyāsa, regarded as one of India's ideal monks.

Tesla, Nikola : A reputed electrical inventor deeply impressed by the talk of Swami Vivekananda about the Vedic *prana* (energy), *akasha* and the *Kalpas* (cycles) which he considered the only theories modern science could accept.

Totapuri (Nangta) : Head of a monastery in Ludhiana in the Punjab. Sri Ramakrishna affectionately addressed him as 'Nangtā', the 'Naked one' because of his total renunciation of all earthly objects and attachments including even a piece of wearing cloth. Sri Ramakrishna was initiated into monasticism and Vedanta by Totapuri. As a most orthodox monk Totapuri never stayed at a place more than three days. But he remained at Dakshineswar eleven months and learnt from Sri Ramakrishna significance of Kali, the Great Fact of the relative world and of maya, Her indescribable Power.

Toyenbee, Arnold Joseph : Arnold Joseph Toyenbee (A. D. 1852 – 1883) was a British economic historian also noted for his social commitment and desire to improve the living conditions of the working class. He wrote in twelve volumes '*A Study of History*', a most memorable work.

Trailanga Swami : Premonastic name Shivaram Rao. Born in rich Brahmin family in Andhrapradesh and spent most part of his long spiritual life in Varanasi and was regarded as an incarnation of Lord Shiva. Sri Ramakrishna met him in 1868.

Tulasidas : Goswami Tulasidas (1497–1623) a Vaishnava saint and poet; author of *Ramcharitmanas* in vernacular Awadhi.

Upanishads : The authoritative scriptures of the Hindus forming the philosophical portion of the Vedas and embodying the records of the direct spiritual realizations of the ancient sages; about one hundred and eight in number and forming the main source of the Vedanta philosophy.

Valmiki : A great sage and poet of the ancient India, composed the Ramayana, the oldest epic of the World.

Vedanta : The last part of the Vedas, dealing with meditation and the knowledge of self-Brahman, one of the six systems of orthodox Hindu philosophy, formulated by Vyasa.

Vidya : Knowledge consisting of kindness, purity, unselfishness and so on leads to liberation.

Vidyasagar : Iswar Chandra. A great educator, an architect of Bengali prose and philanthropist of Bengal.

Vijay Krishna Goswami : Though born in a Vaishnava family, he became a member of the Brāhmo Samaj. Later he returned to the worship of the Personal God.

Viraja Homa : A vedic rite preparatory to one's entering the life of a monk, consisting of offering oblations into the sacred fire with the chanting of certain Vedic texts indicative of renunciation.

Vyasa : The compiler of the Vedas and father of Sukadeva; author of the *Brahma Sutras.*

Washington, Booker T. : Booker Taliaferro Washington (A.D. 1856 – 1915) an American educator, author, orator and adviser to multiple Presidents of the United States, He was the dominant leader in the African American Community and became the leading voice of the former slaves and their descendants.

INDEX

B

C

D

E

F

G

H

I

J

K

L

M

W

Y

BOOKS BY DR. BAKSI

Dr. Baksi is a gifted pioneer in introducing a new style of presentation of Bengali essays. His books are rich in originality ideas, profound reflection, variety of subjects, lucidity of language and dexterity of analysis. Dr. Baksi is an author of some repository books highly extolled by the experts and leading dailies and journals. His works include:

1. KANYA KALAMKINI: A full length drama, based on the history of the dawn of Bengali theatre; published in 1971.
2. ANTARANGA PASHIMBANGA: A resourceful book on folk culture of Bengal published by One Touch Publisher in 2005.
3. ARABINDRIK RABINDRANATH: Based on the astonishing anomalies in the activities of and writings of Rabindranath Tagore; published by Punascha in 2007.
4. AMI TOMADERI MADHUSUDAN: An imaginary autobiography of renowned poet and dramatist Madhusudan Dutta; published by Yogmaya Prakashani and Sachetan in 2007.
5. MAHAKABYEY O PURANE PRATIBANDHI CHETANA: A critical approach to the treatment of disability in the epics and mythology of India with reference to the Western counterparts; published by Punascha in 2008.
6. AMI TOMADERI CV RAMAN: An imaginary autobiography of the great scientist; published by Yogmaya Prakashani and Sachetan in 2008.
7. AMI TOMADERI BIDHACHANDRA: An imaginary autobiography of the great physician and statesman; published by Yogmaya Prakashani and Sachetan in 2008.

8. LOKASIKSHAR ALOY SRI RAMAKRISHNA: An analytical study of the teachings of Sri Ramakrishna in comparison with those of the great religious teachers; published by Punascha in 2009.
9. SWAMIJI O SEI BHAYANKAR BHAVISYAD BANI: Life and activities of Swami Vivekananda with special reference to his unfailing prophecies; published by Punascha in 2010.
10. VIRSINGHA: Discovery of new dimensions of Iswarchandra Vidyasagar; published by Praul Prakashani in 2011.
11. MAHAKAVYE MANDODARI, EK MAHIYASI CHARITRA: A critical study on Mandodari of the Ramayana; published by Punascha in 2012.
12. HUM CHU PAMU HAF O RABINDRANATH: A book on Rabindranath Tagore's revolutionary spirit and ignition traits; published by Punascha in 2014.
13. ATMAHATYA SAHITYE – OUCHITYA BICHAR: Consideration of the propriety of the incidence of suicide in literature; published by Punascha in 2015.
14. RABINDRANATH – CHETANAY SAMALOCHANAY: Nature of Tagore's reflection on various objects along with critical assessment of his literary works; published by Punascha in 2016.
15. THE ROARING FIRE – SWAMI VIVEKANANDA: Evaluation of Swamiji as a litterateur; published by Punascha in 2017.
16. BANGLA SAHITYE SERA PANCH BOUTHAN: An analytical study of five outstanding characters of daughter-in-law in Bengali literature; published by Kamalini and distributed by Dey's Publishing in 2019.
17. DVISHATA JANMAVARSEY VIDYASAGAR: An exhaustive study of Pundit Iswar Chandra Vidyasagar's life and activity on the eve of his bicentenary birth anniversary; published by Praul Prakashani in 2019.

Contact details:

Mobile number: + 91 9332422412, + 91 8820544655
Email id: swapneshbakshikolkata@gmail.com
Website: www.pgbaksi.com